Annual Index to POPULAR MUSIC RECORD REVIEWS 1972

by

Andrew D. Armitage

and

Dean Tudor

The Scarecrow Press, Inc.

Metuchen, N.J. 1973

Library of Congress Catalog Card Number: 73-8909

Armitage, Andrew D. and Tudor, Dean
Annual Index to popular music record reviews, 1972.
New Jersey Scarecrow Press

Summer, 1973 5-24-73
ISBN 0-8108-0636-3

TABLE OF CONTENTS

INTRODUCTION

In a Time (February 12, 1973) article on pop records there appeared the following statement: "Last year [i.e., 1972] $2 billion in records and tapes ($3.3 billion world wide) [were spent] making music, for the first measurable time in history, the most popular form of entertainment in America." To produce some of this music, the 53 recording studios in Nashville, Tennessee laid down 15,031 sessions in 1972. The February 1973 issue of the Schwann Catalogue noted the tremendous increase in the number of foreign recordings issued on American labels. It went on to state that 3852 non-classical and non-spoken word records were new listings for 1972. Of these, 1491 artists produced 2203 popular records in the categories of rock, folk, mood, rhythm 'n' blues, and country. The difference--1549 records--was for the remaining fields of jazz, blues, religion, humor, sound tracks, ethnic, and band. We do not know how many records were produced abroad and not released domestically, but we can assume that American independent labels not listed with Schwann produce approximately 10% of the total, or about 400 records. Schwann relates that quantity releases (both new and reissues) were produced by country's George Jones (12 discs), Johnny Cash (6), Roy Clark (4) and Hank Williams, Jr. (4); mood-pop's Rod McKuen (7) and Elvis Presley (5); blues' John Lee Hooker (4) and Jimmy Reed (4); and jazz's John Coltrane (8), Sun Ra (8), Jimmy McGriff (6), Count Basie (5), Miles Davis (5), Charles Mingus (5), and Pharoah Sanders (5).

To add further impetus to the industry, 1972 was the first year that an unambiguous copyright law was passed to protect the contents of records and tapes. This copyright will also apply to future reissues, and this is expected to encourage re-release programs by record manufacturers. The symbol © has been replaced by Ⓟ to indicate "phono record copyright." Another significant development was the refusal of the U. S. Supreme Court to hear the appeal of the Duchess Music Company (California), a tape duplicating concern that was fined for copyright infringement. The stare decisis of the lower court will ensure that few "unauthorized" tape sales will occur in the future.

At the same time, the Ⓟ will discourage outright bootlegging pirates, while there is still some clarification needed about the jazz and blues "unauthorized" reissues of long deleted material (which the major companies will not reissue themselves). This ethical issue resulted in a compromise in 1972 when Columbia leased the rights (but not the masters) of certain older jazz products to Biograph for the purposes of reissuance. Seven albums have thus far resulted. But the problem of royalty payments has not been resolved, and at the same time as the leasing arrangements Columbia, ostensibly to protect the home market, has refused to allow reissues by its own foreign C. B. S. firms unless the masters or the discs are obtainable from outside the U. S. In other words, American Columbia will no longer cooperate with its foreign subsidiaries in the foreign production of reissued material.

Never in any year before has so much been recorded and made available to the general public. All the figures quoted above are staggering, and to some extent they are hurting the specialist and the classical music lover for the bulk of the sales are in only three fields. Records (referred to as "products" by the trade) move from manufacturer to distributor to record store to consumer. Distributors (the rackers and jobbers that stock the friendly neighborhood drug store) will only handle those records which sell well--the big rock, mood, and country albums--and not touch the specialized fields of jazz, blues, folk, and so forth. Thus, for the bulk of purchasers who live far away from the few, large discount record stores (which admit that the rock, mood and country album sales carry their classical and specialist lines) there is no recourse except through the expensive mails or through the libraries. To some extent, then, the library is becoming the preserver of the

American musical tradition, classical, jazz, blues, folk, stage, and so forth. To aid in the selection of records for these collections (presupposing that collections already exist), we have compiled the first in a series of annual publications indexing the record reviews that appear in each calendar year of a magazine's publishing schedule.

We carefully evaluated over 100 magazines that review records and selected 35 for inclusion. Our criteria for the 35 magazines selected included: applicability, availability, signed authorship, critical evaluation of the music, prominence given to reviews and at least some discographic information. Once the magazine was accepted, then all of its pop record reviews were indexed. Some of these magazines would disappear completely if they did not review records, for these reviews are the "meat" that they send to subscribers. As with any list of "essential" items, there is a broad range of "also rans" that could have been included if space and time allowed. They usually failed to meet some of our criteria, such as not being critical (Rock, Words and Music, Fusion, Circus, Blues and Soul, Shout), or being too "puffy," such as the trade publications Billboard, Cashbox, Record World, and Variety. Some were ephemeral publications, not likely to be collected except by the ardent fan, or published on a regional basis only (Bim, Bam, Boom; Who Put The Bomp?; Whiskey, Women, And...). Others ceased publication, such as Blue Flame and Jazz and Pop. Certain foreign publications are generally unavailable, such as Jazz Forum, B.M.G., and Melody Maker. However, with the entrance of the United Kingdom into the European Economic Community, the European Jazz Federation's Jazz Forum should be more accessible (it's written in English), and Melody Maker in late 1972 produced an American edition. Thus, Melody Maker will be added for 1973. We have not indexed foreign language magazines; however, we have accepted a wide range of English language publications from outside the United States. For certain categories of music, these are crucial. Mood music, folk, jazz, blues, and country are widely reviewed in the British press. Records produced in Britain are often available in the United States (and vice versa), thus the inclusion of British reviews is mandatory. Jazz, blues and mood music review indexes would be a skeleton without them. As for Canada, the situation is similar. Much popular music comes from Canada in the form of rock and folk, and that country also has Coda, probably the best jazz magazine in the world.

It should be noted that the better magazines, in terms of coverage, articles and reviews, appear to come from outside the United States. Yet the subject dealt with is mainly American music. This situation has been prevalent for years, with American music being released on foreign labels, articles and books being written by foreign scholars, basic discographic research being compiled and published abroad, and so forth. It is as if the study of American music was clearly exposed to the rest of the world, but hidden to itself. To bring the point closer to home, this index itself was prepared by two Canadian citizens.

We have indexed periodicals from the United States, United Kingdom, and Canada. Librarians in those countries, then, should find this index particularly useful for their native publications. However, we have decided that the primary use of this index would be American, and therefore we have omitted non-American discographic data except where no corresponding record is released in the United States.

To our surprise, the weakest area of library holdings of magazines appear to be in the related fields of bluegrass, old-time, and country music. Libraries in the northeastern United States and Canada do not collect these materials. Part of the fault must lie with the magazines themselves, for they are extremely difficult to deal with, and we do not know why. We sent them money and addresses for subscriptions, but nothing happened for the most part of a year. Followup letters were either lost or ignored. Much time was expended and irretrievably lost. For these reasons, we have not indexed for 1972 the following magazines: Muleskinner News, Bluegrass Unlimited, Kentucky Folklore Record, and Broadside, all of which are leaders in their fields. They will be included for 1973. Even *Sing Out* and Britain's *Old Time Music* were difficult to obtain. We suggest that you order all these periodicals through a sympathetic record store, such as Rounder (see record store addresses list).

Generally, we have been impressed by the care and exactitude of the specialist magazines in their reviews. It is only with the more general magazines that we sometimes must quarrel. In the youth culture magazines, there appears to be too much hype in expressing an opinion about a record. Such non-relative words as "wow" and "far-out," plus the occasional expletive, have their place within the review, but *not* when they comprise the *whole* review, as is often the case when the review is written while the reviewer is stoned (which is often boasted about in the review). Other reviews do not even mention the music under discussion, being a point of departure for the "reviewer" to speak out. We do not mean to put down these reviews; however, we should caution librarians that it is difficult to state when the reviewers are serious and when they are not. Similarly, we are appalled at the utter lack of basic discographic information that often accompanies a youth culture review. And when such information is included, it can easily be incorrect. We really do not know who is being screwed--the readers, the record manufacturers, the artists, the magazines, the reviewers or us--but someone is.

During 1972, several changes occurred in magazine production. *Stereo Review* reversed its record review sections, and now the popular music section precedes the classical section. *Crawdaddy* and *Beetle* changed from a *Rolling Stone*-style newspaper format to a *Time*-style format. New music magazines which appeared included *Country Music*, *Jazz and Blues* (a reorganized *Jazz Monthly*), and *Popular Music and Society*. *Library Journal* spawned *Previews*, while the *Ontario Library Review* opened a record review column, stressing "Canadian Content." *Previews*, along with the *Ontario Library Review*, are the only two library journals evaluating popular music records for library collections.

How effective are reviews? As an aid for purchase, they

can be invaluable, but to generate sales they can not really be considered. A promotion manager of a nameless record company told us:

> The first thing that sells records is air-play. Get it on the radio and you've got it made. Play lists are important, for a top single will sell a whole album. The second most important factor is audience loyalty. This, of course, is for the groups that have already released at least one album in the past or have toured extensively before releasing their first product. It makes no difference what type of review appears in Rolling Stone, or Creem, for letters to those magazines have shown that even if a record is panned then the audience either supports or rejects the review based on already having heard or bought the record. And the same situation occurs when the review praises the album. The third ranking factor are tie-in ads with record stores. For this we give them a bigger discount in return for in-store promotion and newspaper ads. The same goes for our distributors. Reviews are not too effective--even our own ads in the media produce more sales. Impact is what is important in this business--and the only reviews that have impact are those which appear as blurbs in Record World, Cashbox and Billboard, and those which appear in the daily newspapers and in the college student newspapers. Immediate reviews that appear within two weeks of release will sell records. Our market research on campus buying habits prove this; also, our research on immediate purchases after a newspaper review. Other reviews in Rolling Stone or similar fan magazines do generate a certain amount of sales, but their importance is mainly to get the name of the group in print to satisfy egos and managers. A bad review hurts no one, neither does a good review aid anyone. Remember Van Dyke Parks? He got the best reviews possible for "Song Cycle" but it bombed. How about Grand Funk Railroad? They get bad reviews, but they sell. Magazines like Stereo Review come out too late to generate sales. Classical and jazz magazines also review too late, but these are specialized markets where the sales are low anyway and most collectors wait until a majority of favourable reviews are in before purchasing. Here is where reviews can help. At best, for all types of records, reviews serve to sell records to a fringe market--200 to 2000 copies at most--just worth the effort to promote and collect the reviews. We tend to think of it as charity in a way. Without the reviews most of these magazines would fold. Still, it is difficult to justify sending out 50 copies of a disc for review and getting only 200 to 300 sales in return, maybe less if the specialist reviews pan it. We can spend at least $10,000 in promoting a record. We don't know the impact of libraries. They may deprive us of sales, but I really don't think they

> get the records fast enough to be of any assistance one way or the other. Your index may help them purchase uncertain records, but the impact will be lacking. The important thing for us is to get the record on the damn airwaves. Nobody (except loyal fans) is going to buy a record if he does not know what it sounds like.

This book is primarily an index to record reviews. It can be used to find particular reviews and/or be used as a selection tool based on the evaluations given by the reviews themselves. We have not listed certain data, which we think are relatively important to define the field discographically, because of a lack of time and space. Much work needs to be done to describe the following:

(1) the exact tracing of reissues;

(2) the number of tracks, titles, time lags, personnel notes, and total timings;

(3) the release differences that vary from country to country;

(4) an indication of illustrations or portraits that may have accompanied the review;

(5) the inclusion of English or foreign record serial numbers where an American domestic release is available. Such numbers are, however, included where the American release is now deleted.

(6) Library of Congress Catalogue card numbers. In a random sample of 100 domestic records (released before June 1972), only 11 had L. C. numbers by February 1973. Cards may be important for classical music, but because of main entry problems of composer and subsequent retrieval, L. C. cards are of no use for popular music records (except perhaps in the case of anthologies). Entry should be by artist for this musical genre.

(7) an index to record album titles;

(8) an index of record manufacturer's serial numbers;

(9) the inclusion of review columns that dealt with tapes or quadrophonic sound only. These were mainly concerned with reproduction and other technical devices of interest to collectors. While they are invaluable for that type of format, they say little about the musical genre itself. Such columns

are in the technical magazines of Gramophone, High Fidelity, Hi-Fi News and Record Review, Stereo Review, and Audio.

(10) complete tape availability. Often, a tape will only be issued if the disc is successful. Occasionally, it will be released with the disc if the latter is bound to be a sure winner (usually in the fields of "rock" and "country"). The delay in tape issuance may be as much as a year; hence, some "tapeless" records listed here may now have tape configurations. The Harrison Tape Catalogue should be consulted.

(11) the release differences between tapes and records; and

(12) the determination of a "reissue" as:
a straight reissue of a deleted album;
a repackage of existing or deleted albums; or
a first issue of older material onto microgroove (i.e., reissue of 45 and 78 RPM records on 33 1/3 RPM).

The responsibilities for the general preparation, editorial work, and comments have been assigned as follows: Andrew Armitage--rock, folk, country, ethnic, humor; Dean Tudor--jazz, blues, rhythm 'n' blues, mood-pop, band, religion, soundtracks.

Nancy Tudor compiled the list of books, the list of periodical articles, the directory of recording companies, the directory of record stores, the directory of periodicals, and the artist index. Our gracious thanks for her indulgence towards this pet project.

In closing this long introduction, we would like to appeal to librarians to submit to us, c/o the publisher, the titles of any magazines that they would like to see indexed in the future. It is our intention to provide indexes and access to popular music record reviews (as found in selected periodicals) since the advent of the commercial long-playing disc in 1947. These will be published over the next few years.

Andrew D. Armitage
Dean Tudor

March 31, 1973

EXPLANATION OF THE FORMAT

This index to record reviews has 12 form sections. These are: rock, mood-pop, country, folk, ethnic, jazz, blues, rhythm and blues, religion, show and stage, band, and humor. Arrangement within is alphabetical by artist or anthology title. Each record is numbered for easy reference and for retrieval by use of the Artist Index and the Anthology and Concerts Index.

The discographic information is displayed as follows:

Number. Artist. ALBUM TITLE. Label and Serial Number. (Number of discs per set). Price [U. S. releases]. Reel-to-Reel Tape Serial Number and Price. Four Track Cartridge Serial Number and Price. Eight Track Cassette Serial Number and Price. (Country of Origin [if not U. S.]). (Reissued Release).

The review information is displayed as follows:

Periodical Title. Month or number of issue. Page citation. Number of Words in Review [rounded]. Reviewer's evaluation.

Notes

Evaluation: A scale of 0 to 5 has been used to rate the opinions of each record reviewer. This is a simple numerical translation. This should indicate to the user the general evaluation of any single review or group of reviews. Bear in mind the importance of the specialist magazines. "0" means a completely poor production. (In some cases the reviewer so thoroughly rejected an album that the compilers of this Index could have assigned a -5 to several reviews.) "$2\frac{1}{2}$" is either a review that is non-critical and descriptive, or a review where the pros and cons of a release appear to balance out. And "5" is a superb recording--an ultimate release. There were very few of these awarded (except for the overrated reviews in Downbeat). These evaluation numerical translations were based on both the compilers' experiences and the terms of reference under which the reviewer works. By the latter is meant the non-musical concern of the reviewer. For instance, the music may be worthwhile, but a particular album may be downgraded in the eyes of reviewers for any number of reasons: poor pressing, poor recording qualities, derivative stylings, excessive duplication among previous reissues, poor packaging, lack of liner notes, and so forth--all non-musical. It is important to bear in mind that only the reviews are numerically translated, not the record nor the music itself. In certain cases, the compilers have strongly disagreed with the reviewer, but that has not affected their evaluative judgment of the review itself.

Tapes: Tape numbers for Reel-to-Reel, Cartridges, and Cassettes were given only where known or available to Schwann or Harrison. The absence of a tape number does not mean that a tape is not available for a particular release since often record companies issue the tape versions somewhat later than the discs. It is interesting to note that Ampex, which distributes almost all of the Reel-to-Reel tapes in the United States, listed only 200 new entries for 1972 (and this total includes classical music as well). In 1972, W. E. A. discontinued the issuance in a Reel-to-Reel format. The compilers have not listed tape information for foreign records.

Country of Origin: This is not given when there is an American release; also, the comparable initial foreign release is not given as the disc will be available in the United States. The exception has been made for deleted domestic offerings or reissued material. "(E)" stands for a release from the British Isles; all other countries have their names spelled out. Prices in foreign currency are not given for foreign releases because of the changeable international monetary situation and differences in tax and excise applicability (both domestic and foreign).

Stage and Show: The compilers have added two additional pieces of information. Immediately following the entry by title, the user is informed of the composer, the lyricist, and the arranger, where such information is known. After the basic discographical information but before the review citations, each album is notated as to the source of the performance (e.g., Original Film Soundtrack; Original London Cast; and so forth).

More Than One Artist: The compilers have not analyzed each record to pull out the major artists. Besides the evaluative nature of this work (calling for judgment) the sheer numbers cannot be coped with. However, two aspects were noted:

Artist and Artist: This means that the two perform together on the release, and have been given equal billing by the record company.

Artist/Artist: This means that there are two artists who are not performing together. Usually, one side is devoted to one artist, and the flip side is devoted to another.

These secondary artist entries have been indexed in the Artist Index.

THE PERIODICALS INDEXED

The totals of reviews refer to popular music only. In all, 7307 were indexed. Prices quoted are in American dollars, and are the prices for overseas subscriptions in the case of British publications.

AMERICAN RECORD GUIDE. 1935- monthly $6 p.a.
P.O. Box 319, Radio City Station, New York, N.Y. 10019
Record and book reviews are chiefly classical. The popular music reviews are highly personal.
Indexed: Music Index; Readers' Guide to Periodical Literature; Book Review Index; Music Article Guide; Notes.
No. of 1972 Reviews: 70
Average per issue: 7

AUDIO. 1917- monthly $6 p.a.
North American Publishing Co., 134 N. 13th Street, Philadelphia, Pa. 19107
Contains articles on audio equipment. Record reviews emphasize sound dynamics. Lengthy reviews of jazz records.
Indexed: Music Index
No. of 1972 Reviews: 225
Average per issue: 19

BEETLE. 1970- monthly $6 p.a.; $9/2 yrs.
P.O. Box 5696, Postal Station A, Toronto, Canada
Covers the Canadian pop music scene. Extensive record and book reviews. Newspaper format with many photographs.
No. of 1972 reviews: 90
Average per issue: 9

BLUES UNLIMITED. 1963- monthly, except Mar. and Aug. 10 issues--$6.70
38a Sackville Road, Bexhill-on-Sea, Sussex, England.
The leading blues magazine, with exceptional photographs and good record reviews. Includes a column on Cajun, gospel and related blues music.
Indexed: Music Index
No. of 1972 reviews: 288
Average per issue: 29

BLUES WORLD. 1965- quarterly (irregular) $4 p.a.
22 Manor Crescent, Knutsford, Cheshire, England
Includes articles, interviews, blues news, and record reviews. Only two issues were published in 1972.
No. of 1972 reviews: 20
Average per issue: 10

CANADIAN STEREO GUIDE. 1972- 5 no. /yr. $5 p.a.; $8/2yrs.
Independent Publishing Co., Ltd., P.O. Box 527, Postal Station F, Toronto, Canada
Chiefly concerned with stereo equipment. Record reviews of pop and classical music. Only first three issues were published in 1972.
No. of 1972 reviews: 25
Average per issue: 13

CODA. 1958- bimonthly $6 for 12 issues
P.O. Box 87, Postal Station J, Toronto, Canada.
World coverage. Leads the field of jazz magazines with in-depth articles and thorough record reviews.
Indexed: Music Index
No. of 1972 reviews: 271
Average per issue: 45

COUNTRY MUSIC. Oct., 1972- monthly $6 p.a.; $11/2yrs.
P.O. Box 2004, Rock Island, Ill. 61207
A new glossy country magazine with record and book reviews.
No. of 1972 reviews: 41
Average per issue: 13

CRAWDADDY. 1966- monthly $6.75 p.a.; $12/2yrs.; $16/3yrs.
232 Madison Avenue, New York, N.Y. 10016
American rock music and youth culture in "revolutionary rhetoric." Contains record and book reviews. Changed format in October from bi-weekly newspaper format to monthly glossy.
No. of 1972 reviews: 211
Average per issue: 15

CREEM. 1969- monthly $6 p.a.
P.O. Box 202, Walled Lake, Mich. 48088
Calls itself "America's only rock 'n' roll magazine." Format is similar to CRAWDADDY.
No. of 1972 reviews: 419
Average per issue: 35

DOWNBEAT. 1934- biweekly $7 p.a.
Maher Publications, Inc., 222 W. Adams Street, Chicago, Ill. 60606
Contains jazz news, interviews, transcriptions of improvised jazz performances. Self-rated reviews tend to be over-rated.
Indexed: Music Index
No. of 1972 reviews: 310
Average per issue: 15

ENGLISH DANCE AND SONG. 1936- quarterly $3 p.a.
English Folk Dance and Song Society, Cecil Sharp House, 2 Regents Park Road, London NW1 7AY, England
Covers dance, song, folklore and crafts, with thoughtful,

though brief record and book reviews.
Indexed: Music Index
No. of 1972 reviews: 36
Average per issue: 9

ETHNOMUSICOLOGY. 1953- 3 no. /yr. $15 p. a.
Society for Ethnomusicology, c/o William P. Malm, School of Music, University of Michigan, Ann Arbor, Mich. 48104
Scholarly articles and extensive record and book reviews. Each issue has an extensive "Current Bibliography and Discography Section."
Indexed: Music Index
No. of 1972 reviews: 42
Average per issue: 14

GRAMOPHONE. 1923- monthly $8.60 p. a.
General Gramophone Publications, Ltd., 177-179 Kenton Road, Harrow, Middlesex, HA3 OHA, England.
Solid journal on record collecting and audio equipment. Attempts to be comprehensive in coverage of all fields of records.
No. of 1972 reviews: 946
Average per issue: 79

HI-FI NEWS AND RECORD REVIEW. 1956- monthly $9 p. a.
Link House Publications, Ltd., Dingwall Avenue, Croydon, CR9 2TA, England
Articles are chiefly on audio equipment. Numerous popular record reviews give titles information, and relative evaluations for sound and performance are given.
Indexed: British Technology Index.
No. of 1972 reviews: 643
Average per issue: 54

HIGH FIDELITY. 1951- monthly $7.95 p. a.
P. O. Box 14156, Cincinnati, Ohio 45214
Articles on audio equipment. Record reviews are chiefly classical.
Indexed: Readers' Guide to Periodical Literature; Music Index.
No. of 1972 reviews: 377
Average per issue: 32

JAZZ AND BLUES. 1971- monthly $8.40 p. a.
Hanover Books, 61 Berners Street, London W1P 3AE, England
Restyled "Jazz Monthly" (1954-1971). Good coverage of the British scene, and fine discographic essays. Thorough discographic information is furnished with every review.
No. of 1972 reviews: 182
Average number per issue: 15

JAZZ JOURNAL. 1948- monthly $8.40 p. a.
27 Soho Square, London W1V 6BR, England.
Excellent, detailed articles, with thorough discographic information for all reviews.

Indexed: Music Index
No. of 1972 reviews: 463
Average per issue: 39

JAZZ REPORT. 1958- irregular 12 issues for $5
Box 476, Ventura, California 93001
"The record collector's magazine." Informal mimeographed publication. Record reviews, record lists, book reviews. Only American alternative to DOWNBEAT. Only published two issues in 1972.
Indexed: Music Index
No. of 1972 reviews: 47
Average per issue: 24

JOURNAL OF AMERICAN FOLKLORE. 1888- quarterly $12 p.a.
University of Texas Press, Austin, Texas
Scholarly articles and lengthy, comparative record and book reviews. Not limited to music.
Indexed: Music Index
No. of 1972 reviews: 155
Average per issue: 40

LIBRARY JOURNAL. 1876- semi-monthly, except monthly in July and August. $16.20 p.a.
R.R. Bowker Co., Dept. C, Box 1807, Ann Arbor, Mich. 48106
Reliable book reviews. From September, the record reviews were shifted to PREVIEWS.
Indexed: Library Literature; Library and Information Science Abstracts; Readers' Guide to Periodical Literature.
No. of 1972 reviews: 81
Average per issue: 6

LIVING BLUES. 1970- quarterly $2 p.a.
P.O. Box 11303, Chicago, Ill. 60611
Good American coverage of modern blues through news and articles. Record and book reviews tend to be slim.
No. of 1972 reviews: 56
Average per issue: 14

MUSIC JOURNAL. 1943- monthly, except July and Aug $9 p.a.
1776 Broadway, New York, New York 10019
A general interest journal, covering classical and popular music. Most reviews are for jazz or mood-pop items.
Indexed: Music Index
No. of 1972 reviews: 102
Average per issue: 10

NEW YORK TIMES (Sunday edition). Special Section (section D) on Arts and Leisure.
1851- weekly (Sunday edition) $50 p.a.
229 West 43rd Street, New York, N.Y. 10036
Self-indexed. Semi-annual features on High Fidelity products

and records (usually one Sunday in March and in September).
No. of 1972 reviews: 253
Average per issue: 5

OLD TIME MUSIC. 1971- quarterly $3 p. a.
33 Brunswick Gardens, London W8 4AW, England.
Articles, interviews and record reviews on pre-bluegrass American country music. Transcriptions and discographic essays are published.
No. of 1972 reviews: 59
Average per issue: 15

ONTARIO LIBRARY REVIEW. 1916- quarterly $3 for 3 yrs.
Ontario Provincial Library Service, 14th Floor, Mowat Block, Queen's Park, Toronto, M7A 1B9, Canada.
Includes a regular record review column which started in December. Chiefly concerns "Canadian Content." No music book reviews, unless concerned with library work.
Indexed: Canadian Periodical Index; Library Literature; Library and Information Science Abstracts.
No. of 1972 reviews: 28
Average per issue: 28

POPULAR MUSIC AND SOCIETY. 1971- quarterly $5 p. a.
Dept. of Sociology, Bowling Green State University, Bowling Green, Ohio 43403
An interdisciplinary journal "concerned with music in the broadest sense of the term" [editorial policy]. Scholarly articles, books reviewed. Record reviews are <u>not</u> signed.
No. of 1972 reviews: 229
Average per issue: 46

PREVIEWS. 1972- 9 issues a year (monthly Sept. to May) $2.50/yr. for LJ/SLJ subscribers; $7.50 p. a. others
R. R. Bowker Co., Dept. C, Box 1807, Ann Arbor, Mich. 48106
Record reviews (before September, published in LIBRARY JOURNAL). Occasional discographic articles.
Indexed: Multi-Media Review Index
No. of 1972 reviews: 147
Average per issue: 39

RAGTIMER. 1962- bimonthly $6.00 (membership only) p. a.
Ragtime Society, Inc., P. O. Box 520, Weston, Ontario, Canada.
Articles, news, book and record reviews. Reproduction of sheet music. Loose-leaf format. Record reviews tend to go outside ragtime music.
Indexed: Music Index
No. of 1972 reviews: 11
Average per issue: 2

RECORDS AND RECORDINGS. 1957- monthly $8.70 p. a.
Hanson Books, Artillery Mansions, 75 Victoria Street, London SW1, England.

Record news and reviews, chiefly classical. Strong "rock" reviews.
No. of 1972 reviews: 413
Average per issue: 35

ROLLING STONE. 1968- biweekly $10 p.a.
Straight Arrow Publishers, 625 Third Street, San Francisco, Cal. 94107
America's strongest youth culture magazine, now slowly moving away from just music to a description of a life style in general. Very opinionated book and record reviews.
Indexed: Music Index
No. of 1972 reviews: 364
Average per issue: 14

SATURDAY REVIEW (OF THE ARTS). 1972- monthly $12 p.a.
Box 1043, Rock Island, Ill. 61207
Includes record reviews, chiefly classical.
Indexed: Music Index
No. of 1972 reviews: 56
Average per issue: 6

SING OUT. 1950- bimonthly $7.20 p.a.
80 E. 11th Street, New York, N.Y. 10003
News on the folk, blues, and bluegrass scene, plus book and record reviews.
Indexed: Music Index
No. of 1972 reviews: 63
Average per issue: 15

SOUND. 1970- 10 issues/yr. $4 p.a.
62 Shaftesbury Avenue, Toronto M4T 1A4, Canada
Articles on audio equipment and the Canadian music scene.
No. of 1972 reviews: 111
Average per issue: 9

STEREO REVIEW. 1958- monthly $7 p.a.
P.O. Box 2771, Boulder, Colo. 80302
Audio equipment news, articles on performers and composers. Heavier emphasis on popular music in 1972.
Indexed: Music Index
No. of 1972 reviews: 473
Average per issue: 40

RECORD REVIEWS

ROCK

Rock is a form of popular music that is best known for its pronounced, amplified beat. Electric guitars are almost always the main sound and these are often accompanied by one or more vocalists and drums. In these latter days of the genre a piano or electric organ, electric violins, horns, and reeds are not unusual.

Rock emerged in the last years of the fifties. Born out of the largely bland musical styles of the 1940's and 1950's that cross-bred with rhythm and blues and rock and roll, the story of the Beatles and Bob Dylan, Elvis Presley and the Rolling Stones is too familiar to need repeating here.

It will not be difficult to find areas of argument over the inclusion of some artists in this section of the Record Reviews Index _or_ relegating others to FOLK, MOOD-POP, or COUNTRY. However, the rock scene is as fluid as any music may have ever been. Last year's styles and fads are quickly forgotten, musical styles are mixed and re-mixed, everything becomes an influence on the genre and distinct lines tend to blur. One cannot say when listening to a modern rock album that it follows defined lines, and therefore is "this" or "that."

But rock in the sixties did rejuvenate pop music. It helped the counterculture define itself and it has created a major industry. The longplaying album has become the leader in the consumption of entertainment. The major trends of the sixties were folk-rock, acid-rock, country-rock, and, toward the end of the decade, the superbands such as Chicago, Mountain, Grand Funk Railroad and Black Sabbath. Now, in the seventies the music is beginning to fragment as the form begins to decay. The emergence in the last year of "freak" rock, best represented by Alice Cooper, David Bowie, Roxy Music, and Silverhead is one indication. These are groups immensely popular with certain segments of the record-buying audience. Rock-as-theatre which showcases music in an atmosphere of visual gimmickry and cheap dramatics might well lead to another concept of the stage, but can only contribute to the decline and fall of a form of music.

A more important trend in 1972 was the strength shown in the continuation of the James Taylor tradition of vocalizing. The singer-songwriter depending upon a combination of melody and lyrics rather than showmanship or sound ceilings has gained a large following especially among the over-20's and the over-30's. This makes a library of popular albums of this type even more of an imperative.

The reviewing media for this section is wide and varied. The big three publications for the counter-culture are Rolling Stone, Crawdaddy, and Creem. The first two started as musical magazines but have now taken on the role of interpreters of the youth culture. Creem is more related to music, especially "rock and roll." The reviews tend to be highly personal or "in" reviews. The reader is presupposed to have a wide knowledge of groups and subgroups in rock. But, the reviewers often know what they are talking about and often show delightfully critical faculties rather than the blandness that infects so many other record reviewers. The reviews tend to be long and at times quite vulgar. If a reviewer thinks an album is "shit" he will say so.

Not so in the polite world of "straight" reviewing. The best source is probably Stereo Review. This magazine has a greater emphasis on popular culture and not only features excellent reviews but superb articles on rock. The other magazines are lumped together. Most general music magazines review rock. Their approach and evaluations to any single album vary widely: too widely to really pick the best of the year with any confidence that these are the results of a consensus among reviewers. But an estimation of reviewers' choices would be:

David Ackles. American Gothic. Elektra EKS 75032
Eric Anderson. Blue River. Columbia KC 31062
The Band. Rock of Ages (2 discs). Capitol SABB 11045
Captain Beefheart. Spotlight Kid. Reprise MS 2050
Eric Clapton. History of... (2 discs). Atlantic SD 2-803 (Reissue)
Detroit with Mitch Ryder. Paramount PAS 6010
Dr. John. Gumbo. Atco SD 7006
Bob Dylan. Greatest Hits, Vol. 2 (2 discs). Columbia KB 31120 (Reissue)
Family. Fearless. United Artists UAS 5562
Flying Burrito Brothers. Last of the Red Hot Burritos. A & M SP 4343
Dan Hicks and His Hot Licks. Striking It Rich. Blue Thumb BTS 36
Elton John. Honky Chateau. Uni 93135
Janis Joplin. In Concert (2 discs). Columbia C2X 31160
Gordon Lightfoot. Don Quixote. Reprise MS 2056
Van Morrison. St. Dominic's Preview. Warner Bros BS 2633
Randy Newman. Sail Away. Reprise MS 2064
John Prine. Atlantic SD 9296
Rolling Stones. Exile on Main Street (2 discs). Rolling Stones COC 2-2900
Rolling Stones. Hot Rocks 1964-1971 (2 discs). London 2-PS 606/7 (Reissue)

Rod Stewart. Never a Dull Moment. Mercury SRM 1646
Stephen Stills. Manassas (2 discs). Atlantic SD 2-903
Yes. Close to the Edge. Atlantic SD 7244
Neil Young. Harvest. Reprise MS 2032

1 David Ackles. AMERICAN GOTHIC. Elektra EKS 75032 $5.98.
Beetle. October 31. p15-6. 900w. 5
Crawdaddy. August. p20. 700w. 5
Creem. October. p60. 325w. ½
High Fidelity. October. p120. 250w. 3½
Popular Music. Summer. p247. 50w. 4
Records and Recordings. September. p93. 400w. 4
Sound. October. p44. 250w. 4
Stereo Review. October. p87. 275w. 5

2 Alabama State Troopers. ROAD SHOW. Elektra EKS 75022 $5.98. Cart. ET 85022 $6.98. Cass. TC 55022 $6.98.
Crawdaddy. April. p19. 600w. 3
Popular Music. Spring. p185. 75w. 3

3 Alice Cooper. KILLER. Warner Bros. BS 2567 $5.98. Cart. M82567 $6.95. Cass. M52567 $6.95.
Crawdaddy. January 30. p18. 750w. 2
High Fidelity. March. p108. 250w. 2½
Library Journal. March 1. p857. 100w. 2½
Stereo Review. June. p98, 101. 200w. 2½

4 Alice Cooper. SCHOOL'S OUT. Warner Bros. BS 2623 $5.98. Cart. L8 2623 $6.95. Cass. L5 2623 $6.95.
Crawdaddy. September. p17. 400w. 1½
Creem. August. p62-4. 450w. 3
Creem. December. p9. 50w. 4
Hi-Fi News and Record Reviews. September. p1,685. 200w. 2
Popular Music. Summer. p248. 25w. 0
Records and Recordings. September. p94. 325w. 4
Stereo Review. October. p87. 250w. 1½

5 Allman Brothers Band. AT FILLMORE EAST. Capricorn SD 2-802 (2 discs) $6.98. Cart. M82 802 $7.95. Cass. M52 802 $7.95.
Stereo Review. February. p103. 200w. 1½

6 Allman Brothers Band. EAT A PEACH. Capricorn 2CP 0102 (2 discs) $9.95. Cart. J80102 $9.95. Cass. J50102 $9.95
Crawdaddy. May 28. p15. 900w. 4
Creem. June. p64. 1,000w. 2½
Downbeat. July 20. p32. 900w. 5
Stereo Review. October. p87-8. 175w. 1

7 America. Warner Bros. BS 2576 $5.98. Cart. M82576 $6.95. Cass. M52576 $6.95.
Crawdaddy. April 16. p17. 400w. 2½
Creem. April. p71. 25w. 0
Creem. June. p66. 1,675w. 3
High Fidelity. September. p108. 25w. 3
New York Times--Sunday. April 30. pD28. 175w. 2

8 Eric Anderson. BLUE RIVER. Columbia KC 31062 $5.98. Cart. CA 31062 $6.98.
Beetle. October 17. p20-1. 750w. 4
Canadian Stereo Guide. Fall. p29. 75w. 3½
Crawdaddy. November. p83-4. 1,000w. 3½
High Fidelity. December. p121. 150w. 3½
Popular Music. Fall. p92. 50w. 3½
Rolling Stone. August 17. p48. 750w. 5
Stereo Review. December. p91. 225w. 3½

9 Aphrodite's Child. Vertigo-Mercury 500 (2 discs) $9.96. Cart. VCT 8-2-500 $9.95. Cass. VCT 4-2-500 $9.95.
Creem. August. p69. 50w. 1

10 Argent. ALL TOGETHER NOW. Epic KE 31556 $5.98. Cart. EA 31556 $6.98. Cass. ET 31556 $6.98.
Crawdaddy. September. p21. 40w. 1½
New York Times--Sunday. October 22. pD31. 300w. 2
Rolling Stone. July 20. p49. 750w. 3½
Sound. September. p40. 200w. 3

11 Ashton, Gardner and Dyke. RESSURRECTION SHUFFLE. Capitol ST 563 $5.98. Cart. 8XT 563 $6.98. Cass. 4XT 563 $6.98.
Beetle. January 22. p21-2. 450w. 2½

12 Ashton, Gardner and Dyke. WHAT A BLOODY LONG DAY IT'S BEEN. Capitol SMAS 862 $5.98. Cart. 8XT 862 $6.98.
Creem. December. p9. 25w. 3½

13 Assagai. ZIMBAWE. Philips 6308 079 (E).
Records and Recordings. September. p98. 100w. 1

14 Ben Atkins. PATCHOULI. Enterprise ENS 1021 $5.98.
Stereo Review. June. p97. 150w. 1

15 Atomic Rooster. IN HEARING OF... Elektra EKS 74109 $5.98. Cart. 84109 $6.98. Cass. 54109 $6.98.
Creem. April. p71. 50w. 1
Stereo Review. May. p91. 50w. 0

16 Atomic Rooster. MADE IN ENGLAND. Elektra EKS 75039 $5.98. Cart. ET 8039 $6.98. Cass. TC 5039 $6.98.
Records and Recordings. August. p88-9. 250w. 3

17 Audience. THE HOUSE ON THE HILL. Elektra EKS 74100 $5.98. Cart. ET 84100 $6.98. Cass. TC 54100 $6.98.
Stereo Review. February. p103. 75w. 0

18 Audience. LUNCH. Elektra EKS 75026 $5.98. Cart. ET 85026 $6.98. Cass. TC 55026 $6.98.
High Fidelity. September. p108. 25w. 3
New York Times--Sunday. November 19. pD30. 200w. 3
Rolling Stone. July 20. p52. 600w. 2½

19 Brian Auger's Oblivion Express. A BETTER LAND. RCA LSP 4540 $5.98. Cart. P8S 1760 $6.98.
Creem. August. p15. 50w. ½
Stereo Review. May. p91. 50w. 2

20 Brian Auger's Oblivion Express. SECOND WIND. RCA LSP 4703 $5.98. Cart. P8S 1933 $6.98. Cass. PK 1933 $6.98.
Crawdaddy. August. p20. 750w. 3

21 Aura. Mercury SRM 1-620 $5.98.
Audio. May. p95. 25w. 1

22 David Axelrod. MESSIAH. RCA LSP 4636 $5.98. Cart. P8S 1868 $6.98.
Stereo Review. October. p88. 350w. 0

23 Keven Ayers. WHATEVERSHEBRINGSWESING. Harvest SHVL 800 $5.98.
Gramophone. March. p1,619. 75w. 3½

24 Badfinger. STRAIGHT UP. Apple SW 3387 $5.98. R-R. M3387 $6.98. Cass. 8XW 3387 $6.98. Cass. 4XW 3387 $6.98.
Creem. April. p62. 500w. 2
Records and Recordings. March. p118. 250w. 2
Rolling Stone. January 20. p50. 650w. 1
Stereo Review. April. p89. 200w. 3½

25 Ginger Baker. AT HIS BEST. Polydor PD2-3504 2 discs $6.98. Cart. 8F2 3504 $7.95. Cass. CF2 3504 $7.95.
Beetle. November. p30. 1,100w. 3

26 Ginger Baker. STRATAVARIOUS. Atco SD 7013 $5.98. Cart. TP 7013 $6.95. Cass. CS 7013 $6.95.
Records and Recordings. September. p98. 100w. 2½
Rolling Stone. November 9. p64. 750w. 2

27 John Baldry. EVERYTHING STOPS FOR TEA. Warner Bros. BS 2614 $5.98. Cart. M82614 $6.95. Cass. M52614 $6.95.
Canadian Stereo Guide. Summer. p66. 100w. 3
Creem. August. p67. 50w. 2½
High Fidelity. August. p106. 25w. 2½

Records and Recordings. August. p89. 250w. 1
Rolling Stone. March 30. p64. 550w. ½
Stereo Review. August. p71. 250w. 4

28 John Baldry. IT AIN'T EASY. Warner Bros. WS 1921 $5.98. Cart. M81921 $6.95. Cass. U8303 $6.95.
Downbeat. June 22. p21-2. 250w. 3½

29 John Baldry. LONG JOHN'S BLUES. United Artists UAS 5543 $5.98. Cart. U8303 $6.98.
Creem. January. p69. 50w. 0

30 Banana and the Bunch. MID-MOUNTAIN RANCH. Raccoon/Warner Bros. BS 2626 $5.98.
Crawdaddy. December. p81-2. 900w. 2
High Fidelity. November. p118,120. 100w. 2

31 The Band. CAHOOTS. Capitol SMAS 651 $5.98. Cart. 8XW 651 $6.98. Cass. 4XW 651 $6.98.
Beetle. January 22. p14. 1,500w. 5
Creem. January. p62-3. 2,000w. 1
Gramophone. February. p1438,1443. 125w. 4
Popular Music. Fall. p91. 50w. 3½
Sound. February. p18. 200w. 5

32 The Band. ROCK OF AGES. Capitol SABB 11045 (2 discs) $6.98.
Crawdaddy. November. p78-9. 1,250w. 3½
Creem. November. p60-1. 700w. 4
High Fidelity. December. p120. 250w. 4
Popular Music and Society. Fall. p91. 50w. 3½

33 Bang. Capitol ST 11015. $5.98. Cart. 8XT 11015 $6.98. Cass. 4XT 11015 $6.98.
Creem. August. p61-2. 250w. 3

34 The Barbarians. ARE YOU A BOY OR ARE YOU A GIRL? Laurie $4.98.
Creem. September. p57. 75w. 2½

35 Peter Bardens. WRITE MY NAME IN THE DUST. Verve/Forecast FTS 3091 $5.98.
Audio. August. p63. 50w. 0

36 Barefoot Jerry. SOUTHERN DELIGHT. Capitol ST 786 $5.98.
Gramophone. January. p1279. 25w. 0
Library Journal. February 15. p666. 100w. 2½

37 Ronnie Barron. REVEREND ETHER. Decca DL 75303 $5.98.
Stereo Review. March. p101. 50w. 1

38 Batdorf and Rodney. OFF THE SHELF. Atlantic SD 8298 $5.98. Cart. M88298 $6.95. Cass. M58298 $6.95.
Gramaphone. September. p578. 25w. 1
Rolling Stone. March 16. p58. 425w. 2

39 Beach Boys. CARL AND THE PASSIONS/SO TOUGH. Reprise 2 MS 2083 (2 discs) $5.98 (Reissue).
Crawdaddy. August. p16. 1,200w. 2½
Creem. September. p11. 50w. ½
Gramophone. August. p398. 25w. 0
Hi-Fi News and Record Review. August. p1477-8. 75w. 1½
Records and Recordings. August. p89. 300w. 2½
Rolling Stone. June 22. p56. 750w. 2½

40 Beach Boys. PET SOUNDS. Capitol ST 2458 $5.98.
Crawdaddy. April 2. p18. 2,000w. 4

41 Beach Boys. SURFS UP. Reprise S-6453. $5.98. Cart. M86453 $6.95. Cass M56453 $6.95.
Creem. January. p64-5. 600w. ½
Gramophone. January. p1280. 100w. 4

42 Beatles. '65. Capitol ST228 $5.98.
Crawdaddy. May 28. p20. 1,500w. 3

43 Beaver and Krause. ALL GOOD MEN. Warner Bros. BS 2624 $5.98.
Crawdaddy. December. p80. 850w. 3
Gramophone. December. p1225. 75w. 3
High Fidelity. December. p122,124. 150w. 2½
Records and Recordings. December. p94-5. 250w. 4
Popular Music. Fall. p92. 75w. 5

44 Beaver and Krause. GANDHARVA. Warner Bros. BS 1909 $5.98. Cart. M81909 $6.95. Cass. M51909 $6.95.
Records and Recordings. March. p118. 300w. 4

45 Jeff Beck Group. Epic KE 31331 $5.98. Cart. EA 31331 $6.98. Cass. ET 31331 $6.98.
Crawdaddy. August. p18. 700w. 2
Rolling Stone. June 8. p55. 600w. 2

46 Jeff Beck Group. ROUGH AND READY. Epic KE 30973 $5.98. Cart. EA 30973 $6.98.
Beetle. March 29. p16-7. 2,000w. 3
Creem. April. p65. 550w. 0
Downbeat. February 3. p18. 125w. 4

47 David Bedford. NURSES SONG WITH ELEPHANTS. Dandelion Z 310165 (E).
Records and Recordings. April. p111. 100w. 3½

48 Bee Gees. TO WHOM IT MAY CONCERN. Atco SD 7012 $5.98. Cart. TP 7012 $6.95. Cass. CS 7012 $6.95.
Rolling Stone. December 7. p70, 72. 500w. $2\frac{1}{2}$

49 Bee Gees. TRAFALGAR. Atco SD 7003 $5.98. Cart. M87003. $6.95. Cass. M57003. $6.95.
Gramophone. March. p1613. 25w. 0

50 Bell and Arc. Columbia C 31142 $5.98. Cart. CA 31142 $6.98.
Creem. March. p46. 250w. 3

51 Marc Benno. AMBUSH. A & M 4364 $5.98.
Creem. December. p63. 25w. 1

52 Marc Benno. MINNOWS. A & M SP 4303 $5.98.
Crawdaddy. February 20. p16. 300w. $2\frac{1}{2}$
High Fidelity. April. p114. 25w. $2\frac{1}{2}$
Stereo Review. May. p91. 75w. 0

53 Alex Bevan. NO TRUTH TO SELL. Big Tree BTS 2006 $4.98. Cart. 82006 $6.98. Cass. 52006 $6.98.
Stereo Review. April. p90. 125w. $3\frac{1}{2}$

54 Big Bopper. CHANTILLY LACE. Contour 6870 531 (E) (Reissue).
Gramophone. May. p1955. 50w. $2\frac{1}{2}$

55 Big Brother and the Holding Company. Columbia C 30631 $5.98.
Audio. May. p93. 25w. $2\frac{1}{2}$

56 BIG SUR FESTIVAL. Columbia KC 31138 $5.98. Cart. CA 31138 $6.98. Cass. CT 31138 $6.98.
American Record Guide. August. p624-5. 350w. 4
New York Times--Sunday. April 30. pD28. 175w. $3\frac{1}{2}$

57 Birtha. Dunhill DSX 50127 $5.98. Cart. 8023-50127V $6.95. Cass. 8023-M55127. $6.95.
Creem. November. p15. 25w. 0
New York Times--Sunday. October 15. pD30-1. 250w. $2\frac{1}{2}$
Records and Recordings. December. p94. 75w. 1

58 Black Oak, Arkansas. IF AN ANGEL CAME TO SEE YOU, WOULD YOU MAKE HER FEEL AT HOME? Atco SD 7008 $5.98. Cart. TP 7008 $6.95. Cass. CS 7008 $6.95.
Creem. September. p54. 600w. 3
Rolling Stone. July 20. p49-50. 750w. 2

59 Black Oak, Arkansas. KEEP THE FAITH. Atco 33-381 $5.98. Cart. M8381 $6.95. Cass. M5381 $6.95.

Audio. May. p95. 25w. $2\frac{1}{2}$
Creem. May. p64. 900w. $2\frac{1}{2}$
Gramophone. July. p256. 50w. 1
Records and Recordings. July. p92. 200w. 4
Rolling Stone. May 25. p66, 68. 500w. 3

60 Black Sabbath. MASTER OF REALITY. Warner Bros. BS 2562 $5.98. Cart. M82562 $6.95. Cart. M52562 $6.95.
Creem. January. p61. 350w. 3

61 Black Sabbath. VOLUME 4. Warner Bros. BS 2602 $5.98. Cart. M82602 $6.95. Cass. M52602 $6.95.
Beetle. November. p28-9. 1,000w. 2
Rolling Stone. December 7. p63. 450w. 4

62 Ronnie Blakley. Elektra EKS 75027 $5.98. Cart. ET 85027 $6.98. Cass. TC 55027 $6.98.
Creem. August. p11. 25w. $1\frac{1}{2}$

63 Blood, Sweat and Tears. FOUR. Columbia KC 30595 $5.98.
Audio. May. p93. 25w. $2\frac{1}{2}$

64 Blood, Sweat and Tears. GREATEST HITS. Columbia KC 31170 $5.98. Cart. CA 31170 $6.98. Cass. CT 31170 $6.98 (Reissue).
Audio. August. p61. 50w. 4
High Fidelity. June. p110. 25w. $2\frac{1}{2}$
Previews. September. p43. 50w. $2\frac{1}{2}$

65 Blood, Sweat and Tears. NEW BLOOD. Columbia KC 31780 $5.98. Cart. CA 31780 $6.98. Cass. CT 31780 $6.98.
Rolling Stone. December 7. p66. 750w. $2\frac{1}{2}$

66 Blue Mink. A TIME OF CHANGE. Regal Zonophone SRZA 8507 (E).
Gramophone. May. p1952. 25w. 1

67 Blue Oyster Cult. Columbia C 31063 $5.98. Cart. CA 31063 $6.98. Cass. CT 31063 $6.98.
Creem. May. p66. 1,050w. 4
Rolling Stone. March 30. p54, 56. 900w. 4

68 Blues Project. Capitol SMAS 11017 $5.98. Cart. 8XT 11017 $6.98. Cass. 4XT 11017 $6.98.
Crawdaddy. September. p21. 300w. 0
Creem. August. p66. 25w. 0

69 Blues Project. LAZARUS. Capitol ST 782 $5.98.
American Record Guide. February. p285. 275w. 1
Stereo Review. February. p103. 200w. $3\frac{1}{2}$

70 B.B. Blunder. WORKER'S PLAYTIME. Polydor $5.98.
Creem. April. p65. 375w. 3

71 Colin Blunstone. ONE YEAR. Epic E 30974 $5.98.
Audio. August. p62. 50w. 2½
Creem. June. p73-4. 650w. 2
High Fidelity. May. p111-2. 275w. 3½
Popular Music. Spring. p188. 75w. 3

72 Marc Bolan and T. Rex. BOLAN BOOGIE. Fly HI FLY 8 (E). (Reissue.)
Records and Recordings. June. p82. 500w. 1

73 Graham Bond. BOND IN AMERICA. Philips 6382 010 (E).
Gramophone. July. p255. 25w. 0

74 Jack Bonus. Grunt FTR 1005 $5.98. Cart. P8FT 1005 $6.95. Cass. PKFT 1005 $6.95.
Crawdaddy. August. p17. 300w. 3

75 Bonzo Dog Band. BEAST OF THE BONZOS. United Artists UAS 5517 $5.98.
High Fidelity. January. p110. 125w. 3
Popular Music. Fall. p.59. 50w. 3

76 Bonzo Dog Band. LET'S MAKE UP AND BE FRIENDLY. United Artists UAS 5584 $5.98.
Crawdaddy. August. p18. 425w. 3½
Creem. September. p52-3. 900w. 2½

77 Boomerang. RCA LSP 4577 $5.98. Cart. P8S 1823 $6.95.
High Fidelity. March. p116. 25w. 2½

78 David Bowie. HUNKY DORY. RCA LSP 4623 $5.98. Cart. P8S 1850 $6.95. Cass. PK 1850 $6.95.
Crawdaddy. February 20. p15. 700w. 3
Creem. April. p69. 700w. 3
High Fidelity. April. p114. 25w. 3
New York Times--Sunday. February 27. pD32. 150w. 2½

79 David Bowie. THE MAN WHO SOLD THE WORLD. RCA LSP 4816 $5.98. Cart. P8S 2103 $6.98. Cass. PK 2103 $6.98 (Reissue).
American Record Guide. January. p236. 825w. 5

80 David Bowie. THE RISE AND FALL OF ZIGGY STARDUST AND THE SPIDERS FROM MARS. RCA LSP 4702 $5.98. Cart. P8S 1932 $6.98. Cass. PK 1932 $6.98.
Crawdaddy. August. p20. 800w. 2½
Creem. August. p15. 50w. 1½
Creem. September. p51-2. 700w. 3
Gramophone. September. p577. 50w. 2
High Fidelity. September. p104,106. 325w. 2
Rolling Stone. July 20. p54. 1,250w. 4½
Stereo Review. November. p83. 50w. 1

81 Andy Bown. GONE TO MY HEAD. Mercury SRM 1-625 $5.98. Cart. MC8-1-625 $6.95. Cass. MCR-4-1-625. $6.95.
Creem. June. p77. 25w. 1
Hi-Fi News and Record Review. December. p2463. 125w. 2
Previews. September. p43. 150w. 2

82 Andy Bown. LISTEN. Island SW 9308 $5.98.
Stereo Review. March. p101. 50w. 1

83 Brady Bunch. MEET THE... Paramount $4.98.
Creem. August. p66. 25w. 0

84 Bread. BABY I'M-A WANT YOU. Elektra EKS 75015. $5.98. Car. 85015 $6.98. Cass. 55015 $6.98.
High Fidelity. May. p116. 25w. 4
New York Times--Sunday. March 5. pD28. 25w. 2½
Records and Recordings. April. p104. 225w. 1½
Rolling Stone. March 30. p50, 52. 800w. 3
Stereo Review. October. p88. 100w. 2½

85 Bread. BEST OF... Elektra K 42115 (E) (Reissue).
Gramophone. December. p1221. 50w. 3

86 Paul Brett. SCHIZOPHRENIA. Dawn DNLS 3032 (E).
Records and Recordings. April. p104. 225w. 2

87 Brewer and Shipley. SHAKE OFF THE DEMON. Kama Sutra KSBS 2039 $5.98. Cart. M82039 $6.98. Cass. M52039 $6.98.
Crawdaddy. January 30. p18-9. 800w. 2
High Fidelity. March. p116. 25w. 1½
Stereo Review. June. p97-8. 300w. 1½

88 The Bridge. IN BLUE. Buddah. BDS 5107 $5.98. Cart. M85107 $6.95. Cass. M55107 $6.95.
Creem. November. p64. 300w. 2
Stereo Review. December. p91. 225w. 4

89 Brinsley Schwarz. NERVOUS ON THE ROAD. United Artists UAS 5647 $5.98.
Creem. December. p56. 350w. 4

90 Brinsley Schwarz. SILVER PISTOL. United Artists $5.98.
Creem. May. p63. 1,200w. 4
Creem. August. p67. 25w. 2

91 Brown Dust. Family Productions FPS 2701 $4.98. Cart. M82701 $6.95. Cass. M52701 $6.95.
High Fidelity. July. p106. 25w. 2½

92 Jackson Browne. SATURATE BEFORE USING. Asylum 5051 $5.98. Cart. M85051 $6.95. Cass. M55051 $6.95.

Crawdaddy. April 2. p15. 750w. 3
Creem. June. p65. 500w. 2
Hi-Fi News and Record Review. August. p1479. 50w. 2
Records and Recordings. May. p95. 225w. 1½
Rolling Stone. March 2. p58. 900w. 4

93 Jack Bruce. AT HIS BEST. Polydor PD2-3505 (2 discs) $6.98. Cart. 8F2-3505 $7.95. Cass. CF2-3505 $7.95.
Beetle. November. p30. 1,100w. 3

94 Jack Bruce. HARMONY ROW. Atco SD 33-365 $5.98. Cart. M833-365 $6.95. Cass. M533-365 $6.95.
Downbeat. January 20. p19. 175w. 4½

95 Roy Buchanan. Polydor PD 5033 $5.98. Cart. 8F 5033 $6.98. Cass. CF 5033 $6.98.
Audio. December. p96. 500w. 4½
Beetle. November. p30. 1,500w. 3
Crawdaddy. November. p84. 400w. 2
Creem. November. p67. 600w. 2
High Fidelity. December. p120. 100w. 2

96 Buckwheat. MOVIN' ON. London PS 609 $5.98.
Creem. June. p77. 50w. 2½

97 Budgie. Kapp KS 3656 $4.98. Cart. K8 3656 $6.98. Cass. K7 3656 $6.98.
Creem. August. p61-2. 250w. 3
Hi-Fi News and Record Review. December. p2463. 75w. 2½

98 Sandy Bull. DEMOLITION DERBY. Vanguard VSD 6578 $5.98.
Downbeat. October 12. p19. 225w. 4½

99 Bull Angus. Mercury SRM 1-619 $5.98. Cart. MC8-1-619 $6.95. Cass. MCR4-1-619 $6.95.
Creem. May. p68. 400w. 2½

100 Bulldog. Decca $5.98.
Creem. December. p63. 25w. 2½

101 The Bunch. ROCK ON. A & M SP 4354 $5.98.
Crawdaddy. October. p79-80. 900w. 3½
High Fidelity. November. p130. 25w. 1
Hi-Fi News and Record Review. July. p1309. 50w. 3
Records and Recordings. July. p92. 250w. 2½

102 Eric Burdon and Jimmy Witherspoon. GUILTY! MGM S 4791. $5.98.
American Record Guide. September. p673. 100w. 3½
Crawdaddy. April 2. p18. 500w. 0
Jazz Journal. December. p34. 75w. 1
Records and Recordings. January. p96. 25w. 1

103 J. Henry Burnett. UNI 73125 $4.98.
Audio. August. p63. 25w. 0

104 Randy Burns. I'M A LOVER, NOT A FOOL. Poldyor PD 5030 $5.98.
New York Times--Sunday. August 27. pD19. 125w. 3

105 Randy Burns. SONG FOR AN UNCERTAIN LADY. ESP ESP 2007. $5.98.
Stereo Review. March. p101. 50w. 1

106 Paul Butterfield Blues Band. GOLDEN BUTTER. Elektra 7E-2005 (2 discs) $9.98. Cart. ET 82005 $9.98. Cass. TC 52005 $9.98 (Reissue.)
Crawdaddy. August. p18. 750w. 2½
Creem. August. p62-3. 800w. 3
Gramophone. December. p1222. 100w. 3½
New York Times--Sunday. May 21. pD30. 100w. 3
Previews. November. p38. 300w. 3
Records and Recordings. August. p89. 250w. 3½

107 Paul Butterfield Blues Band. SOMETIMES I JUST FEEL LIKE SMILIN'. Elektra 75013 $5.98. Cart. ET 85013 $6.98. Cass. TC 55013 $6.98.
Downbeat. January 20. p19-20. 425w. 3
Popular Music. Fall. p59. 25w. 2

108 The Byrds. FARTHER ALONG. Columbia KC 31050 $5.98. Cart. CA 31050 $6.98. Cass. CT 31050 $6.98.
Crawdaddy. January 30. p16. 875w. 3
Creem. March. p57. 25w. 2½
Gramophone. April. p1779. 75w. 2½
Rolling Stone. March 16. p60. 575w. 2
Stereo Review. June. p98. 250w. 2½

109 The Byrds. THE NOTORIOUS BYRD BROTHERS. Columbia CS 9575 $5.98.
Beetle. January 22. p22. 300w. 3

110 C.C.S. Rak SRAK 503 (E).
Gramophone. May. p1952. 50w. 1
Records and Recordings. May. p95. 275w. 1½

111 Cactus. RESTRICTIONS. Atco SD 33-377 $5.98. Cart. M833-377 $6.95. Cass. M533-377. $6.95.
Records and Recordings. May. p95. 200w. 3
Stereo Review. May. p92. 25w. 0

112 J.J. Cale. NATURALLY. Shelter SW 8908 $5.98. Cart. 8XT 8908 $6.98. Cass. 4XT 8908 $6.98.
American Record Guide. June. p529. 150w. 1
Crawdaddy. February 20. p18. 1,000. 4

Gramophone. September. p580. 75w. 3
Rolling Stone. March 2. p57. 400w. 3

113 John Cale. THE ACADEMY IN PERIL. Reprise. MS 2079 $5.98.
Stereo Review. November. p83. 225w. 1
Gramophone. December. p1225. 25w. 0
Records and Recordings. December. p95. 375w. 0

114 Jimmy Campbell. ALBUM. Philips 6308 100 (E).
Gramophone. July. p255. 25w. 0

115 The Can. TAGO MAGO. United Artists UAS 60009/10 (2 discs) (E).
Records and Recordings. March. p118-20. 500w. 4

116 Canned Heat. HISTORICAL FIGURES AND ANCIENT HEADS. United Artists UAS 5557 $5.98.
Blues Unlimited. July. p23. 50w. 3½
Crawdaddy. June 11. p18. 400w. 1

117 Jim Capaldi. OH, HOW WE DANCED. Island SW 9314 $5.98. Cart. 8XW 9314 $6.95. Cass. 4XW 9314 $6.95.
Crawdaddy. April 30. p15. 900w. 2½
Popular Music. Spring. p184. 75w. 2
Records and Recordings. June. p83. 400w. 5

118 Captain Beefheart. CLEAR SPOT. Warner Bros. MS 2115 $5.98.
Rolling Stone. December 21. p61-2. 1,000w. 4

119 Captain Beefheart. SPOTLIGHT KID. Reprise MS 2050 $5.98. Cart. M82050 $6.98. Cass. M52050 $6.98.
Crawdaddy. April 2. p14. 500w. 4
Creem. April. p56-7. 1,800w. 3
Downbeat. April 13. p22. 175w. 3½
Gramophone. April. p1779. 25w. 2
New York Times--Sunday. March 19. pD30. 425w. 4
Previews. September. p43. 150w. 3
Records and Recordings. March. p120. 150w. 2
Rolling Stone. March 30. p52, 54. 850w. 3½
Stereo Review. June. p97. 175w. 3

120 Captain Beyond. Capricorn 0105 $5.98.
Creem. October. p60-1. 375w. 2½
Records and Recordings. September. p93. 275w. 4

121 Caravan. WATERLOO LILY. London XPS 615 $5.98. Cart. M72195 $6.95. Cass. M57195 $6.95.
Creem. December. p63. 25w. 0
Gramophone. November. p990. 150w. 3
Hi-Fi News and Record Review. December. p2464. 100w. 3

122 Jimmy Castor Bunch. IT'S JUST BEGUN. RCA LSP 4640 $5.98.
Creem. August. p69. 125w. 1

123 Cat Mother. Polydor PD 5017 $5.98.
Crawdaddy. April 16. p15. 700w. 3½
Stereo Review. September. p73. 200w. 4

124 The Chambers Brothers. GREATEST HITS. Columbia C 30871 $5.98. Cart. CA 30871 $6.98. CT 30871 $6.98. (Reissue.)
High Fidelity. February. p120. 25w. 2½

125 Harry Chapin. HEADS AND TALES. Elektra EKS 75023 $5.98. Cart. 85023 $6.98. Cass. TC 75023 $6.98.
Beetle. May 20. p15. 700w. 2
Creem. September. p11. 25w. ½
High Fidelity. August. p96-7. 300w. 1½
New York Times--Sunday. April 30. pD28. 175w. 5
Rolling Stone. May 25. p66. 1,000w. 2½
Stereo Review. June. p98. 125w. 2

126 Harry Chapin. SNIPER AND OTHER LOVE SONGS. Elektra EKS 75042 $5.98. Cart. ET 85042 $6.95. Cass. TC 55042 $6.95.
Rolling Stone. December 7. p63. 400w. 2

127 Michael Chapman. FULLY QUALIFIED SURVIVOR. Harvest SW 816 $4.98.
Popular Music. Fall. p60. 50w. 3

128 Robert Charlebois. Barclay 80123. (French)
Sound. August. p48. 225w. 4

129 Bobby Charles. Bearsville BR 2104 $4.98.
Rolling Stone. November 23. p61. 600w. 4

130 Chase. ENNEA. Epic KE 31097 $5.98. Cart. EA 31097 $6.98. Cass. ET 31097 $6.98.
High Fidelity. July. p98. 150w. 3½

131 Chesapeake Juke Box Band. Greene Bottle Records GBS 1004 $4.98.
Creem. September. p57. 50w. 2½
High Fidelity. July. p100. 150w. 2½

132 Chicago. AT CARNEGIE HALL. Columbia C4X 30865 (4 discs) $12.98. Cart. GA 30863/4 $13.98. Cass. GT 30863/4 $13.98.
Crawdaddy. January 16. p14. 750w. 1
Creem. January. p56-9. 3,000w. 1
Downbeat. April 27. p16-7. 400w. 3½

Library Journal. February 15. p666. 125w. 3
Library Journal. May 1. p1689. 200w. $2\frac{1}{2}$
Stereo Review. March. p74. 350w. 4

133 Chicago. V. Columbia KC 31102. $5.98.
Beetle. October 17. p21. 700w. $1\frac{1}{2}$
Crawdaddy. October. p77-8. 425w. $2\frac{1}{2}$
Creem. August. p64. 300w. 1
Downbeat. December 7. p18. 450w. $1\frac{1}{2}$
New York Times--Sunday. September 10. pD38. 325w. 2
Rolling Stone. December 18. p66. 750w. 1

134 Chicken Shack. IMAGINATION LADY. Deram DES 18063 $4.98.
Records and Recordings. March. p120. 250w. 0

135 The Chi-Lites. A LONELY MAN. Brunswick 74179. Cart. M84179 $6.95. Cass. M54179 $6.95.
Gramophone. September. p580. 75w. 3

136 Chilliwack. A & M S 3508 $5.98.
Creem. June. p77. 50w. $\frac{1}{2}$
Records and Recordings. June. p83. 275w. 4

137 Christian. Can-Base Records 5001. (Canada)
Sound. September. p41. 200w. 3

138 Eric Clapton. AT HIS BEST. Polydor PD2-3503 (2 discs) $6.98. Cart. 8F2-3503 $7.95. Cass. CF2-3503 $7.95. (Reissue)
Beetle. November. p30. 1,100w. 3

139 Eric Clapton. HISTORY OF... Atlantic SD 2-803 (2 discs) $11.96. R-R J803 $11.95. Cart. M8803 $11.95. Cass. M5803 $11.95. (Reissue.)
Audio. August. p61. 25w. 4
Crawdaddy. June 11. p14. 1,200w. $2\frac{1}{2}$
Creem. September. p57. 25w. $2\frac{1}{2}$
Gramophone. October. p782. 300w. 3
Hi-Fi News and Record Review. September. p1683. 150w. $2\frac{1}{2}$
High Fidelity. August. p106. 50w. $3\frac{1}{2}$
New York Times--Sunday. April 30. pD28. 75w. $2\frac{1}{2}$
Popular Music. Summer. p254. 75w. 2
Rolling Stone. June 8. p58. 2,300w. 2
Stereo Review. July. p69-70. 300w. 4

140 Dave Clark. AND FRIENDS. Columbia SCX 6494 (E).
Gramophone. November. p984. 50w. 1

141 Gene Clark. EARLY L.A. SESSIONS. Columbia KC 31123 $5.98. Cart. CA 31123 $6.98.
Crawdaddy. October. p80. 950w. $2\frac{1}{2}$

142 Alan Clarke. MY REAL NAME IS 'AROLD. Epic KE 31757 $5.98. Cart. EA 31757 $6.95. Cass. ET 31757 $6.95.
Gramophone. September. p577. 25w. 1

143 Merry Clayton. Ode SP 77012 $5.98. Cart. 8T 77012 $6.98. Cass. CS 77012 $6.98.
Crawdaddy. March 5. p18. 300w. 2
Gramophone. July. p256. 75w. 1
High Fidelity. March. p117. 25w. 2
New York Times--Sunday. March 12. pHF12. 225w. 2

144 David Clayton-Thomas. Columbia KC 31000 $5.98. Cart. CA 31000 $6.98. Cass. CT 31000 $6.98.
High Fidelity. July. p106. 25w. 1½

145 Clean Living. Vanguard VRS 79318 $5.98.
Stereo Review. November. p84. 150w. 3

146 Climax Blues Band. TIGHTLY KNIT. Sire SI 5903 $4.98.
High Fidelity. May. p112. 150w. 1
Jazz Journal. February. p34. 300w. 4
Stereo Review. September. p73. 200w. 2½

147 Cochise. SO FAR. United Artists UAS 29286 (E).
Gramophone. July. p256-7. 25w. 0

148 Eddie Cochran. CHERISHED MEMORIES. Sunset SLS 50289 (E). (Reissue.)
Records and Recordings. April. p104, 106. 250w. 2

149 Eddie Cochran. LEGENDARY MASTERS SERIES. United Artists UAS 9959 (2 discs) $6.98. (Reissue.)
Audio. May. p94. 25w. 2½
Crawdaddy. May 14. p19. 300w. 3½
Creem. March. p57. 75w. 1½
Popular Music. Spring. p128. 50w. 4
Rolling Stone. March 30. p54. 2,000w. 4

150 Wayne Cochran and the C.C. Riders. COCHRAN. Epic E 30989 $5.98. Cart. EA 30989 $6.98.
Crawdaddy. June 11. p19. 500w. 3
Creem. June. p69. 800w. 2½
Downbeat. September 14. p20. 200w. 5
High Fidelity. June. p102. 125w. ½
Hi-Fi News and Record Review. August. p1479. 50w. 1

151 Bruce Cockburn. True North TN 1 (Canada).
Previews. September. p41. 125w. 3

152 Bruce Cockburn. HIGH WINDS, WHITE SKY. True North TN 3 (Canada).
Previews. September. p41. 125p. 3

153 Bruce Cockburn. SUNWHEEL DANCE. True North TN 7 (Canada).
Beetle. June. p22. 1,000w. 4
Canadian Stereo Guide. Summer. p66. 100w. 3
Previews. September. p41. 125w. 3
Sound. August. p49. 150w. 3

154 Philip Cody. LAUGHING SANDWICH. Kirshner KES 113 $4.98.
Stereo Review. May. p92. 125w. 1

155 Colosseum. LIVE. Warner Bros. WS 1942 $5.98. Cart. M81942 $6.95. Cass. M51942 $6.95.
Creem. January. p69. 25w. 0

156 Chi Coltrane. Columbia KC 31275 $5.98. Cart. CT 31275 $6.98. Cass. CA 31275 $6.98.
High Fidelity. December. p120. 150w. 3

157 Commander Cody and His Lost Planet Airmen. HOT LICKS, COLD STEEL, TRUCKER'S FAVORITES. Paramount PAS 6031 $5.98. Cart. 8091-6031M $6.95. Cass. 5091-6031M. $6.95.
Crawdaddy. November. p82. 950w. 4
Creem. November. p65. 700w. 1½
Creem. December. p9. 25w. 4½
New York Times--Sunday. October 15. pD30. 200w. 1

158 Commander Cody and His Lost Planet Airmen. LOST IN THE OZONE. Paramount PAS 6017 $4.98. Cart. 8091-6017M $6.95. Cass. 5091-6017M $6.95.
Crawdaddy. January 16. p18. 600w. 4
Creem. January. p60. 700w. 4½
High Fidelity. January. p117. 200w. 3
Popular Music. Winter. p122. 50w. 3½

159 Company. Playboy Records 107 $4.98.
Creem. September. p57. 50w. 2½

160 Compost. Columbia KC 31176 $5.98.
Creem. June. p77. 25w. 0
Downbeat. May 11. p21. 225w. 1

161 THE CONCERT FOR BANGLA DESH. Apple STCX 3385 (3 discs) $12.98. Cart. ZAX 31230 $14.98. Cass. ZTX 31230 $14.98.
Audio. April. p66-7. 1,000w. 4
Crawdaddy. March 19. p14. 2,000. 2½
Creem. January. p45-6. 1,750w. 1
Gramophone. March. p1619. 675w. 5
High Fidelity. March. p108. 250w. 4
Library Journal. April 1. p1299. 300w. 1½

New York Times--Sunday. January 9. pD21. 1,600w. 4
Records and Recordings. March. p120. 375w. 1
Stereo Review. May. p66-7. 600w. 4

162 Ry Cooder. BOOMER'S STORY. Reprise MS 2117 $5.98.
Rolling Stone. December 7. p64. 500w. 3

163 Ry Cooder. INTO THE PURPLE VALLEY. Reprise MS 2052 $5.98. Cart. M82052 $6.98. Cass. M52052 $6.98
Crawdaddy. March 19. p15. 850w. 3
Creem. April. p67. 1,175w. 2½
Hi-Fi News and Record Review. July. p1312. 75w. 1
Records and Recordings. April. p106. 225w. 4
Rolling Stone. March 2. p57. 900w. 3½
Stereo Review. July. p91-2. 175w. 2½

164 Roger Cook. MEANWHILE BACK AT THE WORLD. Kama Sutra KSBS 2056 $5.98. Cart. M82056 $6.95. Cass. M52056 $6.95.
Hi-Fi News and Record Review. July. p1312. 50w. 2½
Stereo Review. September. p73-4. 300w. 4

165 Rita Coolidge. NICE FEELIN'. A & M SP 4325 $5.98. Cart. 4325 $6.98. Cass. 4325 $6.98.
High Fidelity. March. p110. 75w. 2½
Rolling Stone. January 20. p54. 550w. 3½
Stereo Review. September. p74. 275w. 2½

166 Ruth Copeland. I AM WHAT I AM. Invictus SMAS 9802 $4.98. Cart. 8XT 9802 $6.98.
New York Times--Sunday. February 27. pD26,32. 150w. 0

167 Ron Cornelius. TIN LUCK. Polydor PD 5011 $4.98.
Audio. May. p95. 25w. 1

168 Coulson, Dean, McGuiness and Flint. LO AND BEHOLD. DJM DJLPS 424 (E).
Hi-Fi News and Record Reviews. December. p2464. 50w. 1½

169 Country. Clean CN 600 $4.98. Cart. M8600 $6.98. Cass. M5600 $6.98.
Stereo Review. May. p92. 125w. 3

170 Country Gazette. A TRAITOR IN OUR MIDST. United Artists UAS 5596 $5.98.
Popular Music and Society. Fall. p1. 75w. 3
Rolling Stone. November 9. p66. 500w. 3½

171 Coven. Sunshine Snake SE 4801 $4.98. Cart. 8130-4801 $6.95. Cass. 5130-4801 $6.95.

American Record Guide. August. p625. 150w. 4
Audio. August. p62. 25w. 2

172 Cowboy. 5'LL GETCHA TEN. Capricorn SD 864 $5.98. Cart. M8864 $6.95. Cass. M5864 $6.95.
Gramophone. August. p398. 25w. 0
High Fidelity. January. p116-7. 125w. 2½

173 Crabby Appleton. ROTTEN TO THE CORE. Elektra EKS 74106 $5.98. Cart. ET 84106 $6.98. Cass. TC 54106 $6.98.
Creem. February. p65-6. 700w. 3½

174 Crazy Horse. LOOSE. Reprise S 2059 $5.98. Cart. M82059 $6.95. Cass. M52059 $6.95.
Beetle. May. p21-2. 1,100w. 3½
Crawdaddy. April 16. p19. 500w. 1½
Creem. August. p60. 675w. 2½
Popular Music. Spring. p186. 50w. 2
Records and Recordings. May. p95-6. 200w. 2
Rolling Stone. March 2. p60, 62. 1,100w. 3

175 [no entry]

176 Papa John Creach. Grunt FTR 1003 $5.98. Cart. P8FT 1003 $6.95. Cass. PKFT 1003 $6.95.
Downbeat. February 17. p18-9. 425w. 1
Library Journal. February 15. p666. 250w. 3
Rolling Stone. March 2. p62. 175w. 3
Stereo Review. May. p92-3. 300w. 3½

177 Cream. HEAVY CREAM. Polydor PD2-3502 $6.98. Cart. 8F2-3502 $7.95. Cass. CF2-3502 $7.95.
Beetle. November. p30. 1,100w. 3

178 Creedence Clearwater Revival. MARDI GRAS. Fantasy 9404 $4.98. Cart. M89404 $6.95. Cass. M59404 $6.95.
Creem. June. p62-3. 2,000w. 5
Creem. August. p11. 50w. 3
High Fidelity. August. p97-8. 175w. 2
Popular Music. Summer. p250. 50w. 3
Rolling Stone. May 25. p63. 850w. 0

179 Jim Croce. YOU DON'T MESS AROUND WITH JIM. ABC X 756 $4.98. Cart. M8756 $6.98. Cass. M5756 $6.98.
Audio. November. p89. 50w. 2½
Crawdaddy. October. p76-7. 750w. 5
Creem. November. p15. 25w. 1½
High Fidelity. September. p126. 25w. 3
New York Times--Sunday. August 27. pD19. 100w. 3½
Popular Music. Summer. p253. 50w. 3
Stereo Review. December. p92. 100w. 1½

180 Crowbar. LARGER THAN LIFE. Daffodil SBBX 16007 (Canada).
Sound. April. p36. 175w. 4

181 CRUISIN' 1955 (anthology). Increase 2001 $5.98. Cart. 8100-100M $6.95. Cass. 5100-2000M $6.95. (Reissue.)
Creem. June. p77. 25w. 2½

182 CRUISIN' 1963 (anthology). Increase 2007 $5.98. Cart. 8100-2008M $6.95. Cass. 5100-2008M $6.95. (Reissue.)
Creem. June. p77. 25w. 3

183 Curved Air. PHANTASMAGORIA. Warner Bros. BS 2628 $5.98.
Records and Recordings. June. p83-4. 250w. 3

184 Curved Air. SECOND ALBUM. Warner Bros. WS 1951 $5.98. Cart. M81951 $6.95. Cass. M51951 $6.95.
Beetle. March 29. p20. 500w. 2

185 Mike D'Abo. DOWN AT RACHEL'S PLACE. A & M 4346 $5.98.
Gramophone. August. p397. 25w. 2
Hi-Fi News and Record Review. July. p1309. 150w. 3
Popular Music. Fall. p87. 50w. 3
Records and Recordings. July. p92. 225w. 3

186 Daddy Cool. DADDY WHO? DADDY COOL! Reprise RS 6471 $5.98. Cart. M86471 $6.95. Cass. M56471 $6.95.
Library Journal. March 15. p997. 100w. 3
Rolling Stone. March 2. p64. 400w. 3½

187 Daddy Cool. TEENAGE HEAVEN. Reprise MS 2088 $5.98.
Creem. September. p57. 25w. 0
Rolling Stone. June 22. p58, 60. 400w. 2

188 Dando Shaft. RCA Neon NE 5 $4.98. Cart. P8NE 1005 $6.95.
Beetle. January 22. p20. 400w. 2½
High Fidelity. January. p120. 50w. 3½

189 Chris Darrow. ARTIST PROOF. Fantasy 9403 $4.98.
Popular Music. Summer. p254. 50w. 3

190 Alun Davies. DAYDO. Columbia KC 31469 $5.98. Cart. CA 31469 $6.98. Cass. CT 31469 $6.98.
New York Times--Sunday. December 17. pD42. 300w. 3
Rolling Stone. November 23. p64. 1,600w. 2

191 Jesse Ed Davis. ULULU. Atco SD 33-382 $5.98. Cart. M8382 $6.95. Cass. M5382 $6.95.

Audio. August. p61. 50w. 3
Crawdaddy. June 11. p18. 350w. 3

192 Spencer Davis. MOUSETRAP. United Artists UAS 5580 $5.98. Cart. U 8413 $6.98. Cass. K0413 $6.98.
Audio. November. p90. 50w. 2½

193 Russell Dean. Metromedia KMD 1046 $4.98.
Crawdaddy. March 5. p20. 250w. 2

194 Deep Purple. FIREBALL. Warner Bros. BS 2564 $5.98. Cart. M82564 $6.95. Cass. M52564 $6.95.
Beetle. January 22. p20. 500w. 1½

195 Deep Purple. MACHINE HEAD. Warner Bros. BS 2607 $5.98. Cart. M82607 $6.95. Cass. M52607 $6.95.
Records and Recordings. July. p92-3. 350w. 2
Rolling Stone. May 25. p63-4. 1,000w. 3½

196 Delaney and Bonnie. D & B TOGETHER. Columbia KC 31377 $5.98. Cart. CA 31377 $6.98. Cass. CT 31377 $6.98.
Crawdaddy. June 11. p14. 450w. 3½
Creem. June. p77. 25w. 0
New York Times--Sunday. April 30. pD28. 100w. 3
Rolling Stone. March 30. p63. 850w. 2
Stereo Review. October. p88. 100w. 4

197 John Denver. AERIE. RCA LSP 4607 $5.98. Cart. P8S 1834 $6.98. Cass. PK 1834 $6.98.
Popular Music. Winter. p125. 100w. 4
Rolling Stone. March 2. p62. 300w. 2
Sound. April. p21. 100w. 3
Stereo Review. April. p71-2. 300w. 4

198 John Denver. POEMS, PRAYERS AND PROMISES. RCA LSP 4499 $5.98. Cart. P8S 1711 $6.95. Cass. PK 1711 $6.95.
Popular Music and Society. Fall. p58-9. 50w. 3½
Sounds. February. p13. 125w. 3

199 John Denver. ROCKY MOUNTAIN HIGH. RCA LSP 4731 $5.98. Cart. P8S 1972 $6.95. Cass. PK 1972 $6.95.
Audio. December. p95. 50w. 4
New York Times--Sunday. October 15. pD31. 600w. 4½
Popular Music. Fall. p91. 25w. 1
Rolling Stone. October 26. p56. 900w. 3½

200 Detroit with Mitch Ryder. DETROIT. Paramount PAS 6010 $4.98. Cart. 8091-6010M $6.95. Cass. 5091-6010M. $6.95.
Beetle. March 29. p21. 400w. 3

Crawdaddy. February 20. p19. 1,000w. 4
Creem. January. p60. 400w. 5
High Fidelity. April. p114. 25w. 3½

201 Dion DiMucci. SANCTUARY. Warner Bros. WS 1945 $5.98. Cart. M81945 $6.95. Cass. M51945 $6.95.
Crawdaddy. February 20. p18. 500w. 3
Gramophone. March. p1613. 75w. 1½
Rolling Stone. March 2. p62, 64. 900w. 3

202 Doctor Hook. DOCTOR HOOK AND THE MEDICINE SHOW. Columbia C30898 $5.98. Cart. CA 30898 $6.98. Cass. CT 30898 $6.98.
Stereo Review. October. P88, 92. 150w. 0

203 Dr. John. GUMBO. Atco SD 7006 $5.98. Cart. M87006 $6.95. Cass. M57006 $6.95.
Crawdaddy. September. p16. 400w. 4
Creem. August. p11. 50w. 3
Downbeat. November 9. p22. 200w. 3
High Fidelity. July. p101-2. 300w. 3½
Rolling Stone. June 8. p54. 1,650w. 5
Stereo Review. November. p79-80. 300w. 4

204 The Doors. FULL CIRCLE. Elektra EKS 75038 $5.98. Cart. ET 85038 $6.98. Cass. TC 55038 $6.98.
Beetle. October 30. p16. 900w. 4
Crawdaddy. November. p79. 800w. 3
Creem. November. p15. 25w. 2
Creem. November. p64-5. 700w. 1
High Fidelity. November. p120, 122. 250w. 3

205 The Doors. OTHER VOICES. Elektra EKS 75017 $5.98. Cart. M85017 $6.98. Cass. M55017 $6.98.
Beetle. March 29. p18. 400w. 2½
Gramophone. March. p1613. 25w. 1
High Fidelity. March. p112-3. 175w. 2½
Popular Music. Winter. p123. 50w. 1
Rolling Stone. January 20. p49. 700w. 2
Stereo Review. March. p102. 200w. 1

206 The Doors. WEIRD SCENES INSIDE THE GOLD MINE. Elektra 8E-6001 (2 discs) $7.98. Cart. T8 6001 $9.98. Cass. C2 6001 $9.98. (Reissue.)
Records and Recordings. April. p106. 300w. 4½

207 Downchild Blues Band. BOOTLEG. Special SS 001 (Canada).
Canadian Stereo Guide. Summer. p67. 100w. 3

208 Nick Drake. PINK MOON. Island SMAS 9318 $5.98
Creem. August. p66. 300w. 2
Records and Recordings. April. p106. 200w. 4

209 Dreams. IMAGINE MY SURPRISE. Columbia C 30960 $5.98. Cart. CA 30960 $6.98.
Downbeat. March 30. p24. 200w. 4

210 Julie Driscoll. Polydor 2383 077 (E).
Gramophone. March. p1613. 50w. 1

211 William Duyn and Maggie McNeal. MOUTH AND McNEAL. Philips PHS 700-000 $4.98.
Previews. December. p46. 200w. 1

212 Bob Dylan. GREATEST HITS, VOLUME 2. Columbia KG 31120 (2 discs) $5.98. Cart. GA 31120 $6.98. Cass. GT 31120 $6.98. (Partial Reissue.)
Crawdaddy. January 16. p10. 1,750w. 3½
High Fidelity. March. p110,112. 275w. 3
Library Journal. March 15. p997. 275w. 3
New York Times--Sunday. May 21. pD32. 75w. 3½
Popular Music. Winter. p123. 50w. 3
Previews. September. p41. 150w. 3½

213 Eagles. Asylum SD 5054 $5.98.
Crawdaddy. September. p17. 300w. 2
Creem. September. p50. 600w. 3
Hi-Fi News and Record Review. November. p2202. 100w. 3
High Fidelity. September. p108. 25w. 2½
Popular Music. Summer. p248. 75w. 4
Rolling Stone. June 22. p54. 850w. 5
Sound. October. p43. 225w. 3

214 Earthquake. WHY DON'T YOU TRY ME. A & M 4337 $5.98.
Creem. December. p63. 50w. 3

215 ECHOES OF A ROCK ERA: THE EARLY YEARS (anthology). Roulette RE 111 (2 discs) $5.98. (Reissue.)
Audio. May. p94. 25w. 2½

216 ECHOES OF A ROCK ERA: THE MIDDLE YEARS (anthology). Roulette RE 112 (2 discs) $5.98. (Reissue.)
Audio. May. p94. 25w. 2½

217 ECHOES OF A ROCK ERA: THE LATER YEARS (anthology). Roulette RE 113 (2 discs) $5.98. (Reissue.)
Audio. May. p94. 25w. 2½

218 Dave Edmonds. ROCKPILE. MAM 3 $5.98.
American Record Guide. August. p624. 175w. 3
Creem. June. p73. 750w. 2½

219 Jonathan Edwards. Capricorn SD 862 $4.98. Cart. M8862 $6.95. Cass. M5862 $6.95.

Gramophone. June. p112. 50w. 2
New York Times--Sunday. March 12. pHF12. 125w. 1½
Records and Recordings. May. p96. 250w. 2½
Sound. March. p21. 75w. 2
Stereo Review. August. p89. 175w. 1½

220 El Avram Group. ANY TIME OF THE YEAR. Monitor MFS 730 $4.98. Cart. M8730 $6.98. Cass. M5730 $6.98.
Stereo Review. May. p91. 100w. 2

221 El Chicano. CELEBRATION. MCA MUPS 456 (E).
Gramophone. November. p990. 225w. 3.

222 El Chicano. REVOLUCION. Kapp KS 3640 $5.98. Cart. 83640 $6.98. Cass. 73640 $6.98.
Hi-Fi News and Record Review. September. p1683. 25w. 2½

223 Electric Light Orchestra. NO ANSWER. United Artists UAS 5573 $5.98.
Crawdaddy. May 28. p16. 750w. 3
Creem. August. p11. 25w. 1½
Creem. August. p66. 50w. 0
Popular Music and Society. Summer. p253. 50w. 5
Rolling Stone. August 17. p54. 1,000w. 3½

224 Elephant's Memory. Apple SMAS 3389 $5.98.
Crawdaddy. December. p77-8. 750w. 3
Creem. August. p62-3. 750w. 4
Rolling Stone. November 9. p61. 600w. 4
Records and Recordings. December. p95-6. 275w. 2

225 Yvonne Elliman. Decca DL 75341 $4.98.
High Fidelity. August. p98. 325w. 1½
Popular Music. Summer. p249. 100w. 3

226 Cass Elliot. RCA LSP 4619 $5.98. Cart. P8S 1846 $6.95 Cass. PK 1846 $6.95.
Gramophone. May. p1951. 50w. 1
Hi-Fi News and Record Review. May. p938. 100w. 2

227 Keith Emerson. WITH THE NICE. Mercury SRM 2-6500 (2 discs) $5.98. Cart. MCT 82 6500 2 cartridges $9.98. (Reissue.)
Audio. May. p95. 50w. 2
New York Times--Sunday. March 12. pHF12. 750w. 2
Stereo Review. September. p74. 200w. 2½

228 Emerson, Lake and Palmer. PICTURES AT AN EXHIBITION. Cotillion ELP 66666 $5.98. Cart. 866666 $6.95. Cass. 566666 $6.95.
American Record Guide. July. p624. 300w. 3

Beetle. May 20. p16. 750w. 3
Creem. May. p67. 350w. 2½
High Fidelity. April. p107-8. 150w. 2
New York Times--Sunday. February 20. pD28, 30. 600w. 2½
Popular Music. Spring. p185. 100w. 4
Rolling Stone. March 2. p57. 950w. 4
Stereo Review. July. p92. 200w. 2½

229 Emerson, Lake and Palmer. TRILOGY. Cotillion 9903 $5.98. Cart. TP 9903 $6.95. Cass. CS 9903 $6.95.
Beetle. October 17. p21-2. 750w. 1½
Hi-Fi News and Record Review. October. p1926. 100w. 3
Popular Music. Fall. p92. 50w. 3
Records and Recordings. October. p126. 150w. 3

230 England Dan and John Ford Coley. FABLES. A & M 4350 $5.98.
High Fidelity. October. p126. 25w. 3

231 English Congregation. SOFTLY WHISPERING I LOVE YOU. Signpost SP 7217 $5.98. Cart. TP 8405 $6.95. Cass. CS 8405 $6.95.
Gramophone. August. p397. 100w. 4
Popular Music. Spring. p185. 75w. 3

232 English Gypsy. Decca DL 75299 $4.98.
Popular Music Winter. p126. 25w. 2½

233 John Entwistle. SMASH YOUR HEAD AGAINST THE WALL. Decca DL 79183 $5.98.
Beetle. January 22. p18. 450w. 1½
Creem. January. p66. 500w. 5
High Fidelity. January. p120. 25w. 2
Stereo Review. April. p90. 100w. 3

234 John Entwistle. WHISTLE RYMES. Decca DL 79190 $5.98.
Rolling Stone. December 21. p61. 550w. 3½

235 The Fabulous Rhinestones. JUST SUNSHINE. Just Sunshine JSS 1 $4.98. Cart. 8156-1M $6.95. Cass. 5156-1M $6.95.
Creem. September. p54-5. 300w. 2½
High Fidelity. August. p106. 25w. 2½

236 Faces. A NOD IS AS GOOD AS A WINK...TO A BLIND HORSE. Warner Bros. BS 2574 $5.98. Cart. M82574 $6.95.
Beetle. March 29. p18-9. 1,000w. 3
Crawdaddy. March 5. p14. 700w. 3
High Fidelity. April. p109. 100w. 2½
New York Times--Sunday. March 5. pD28. 50w. 2½
Sound. April. p21. 100w. 1

237 Georgie Fame. ALL ME OWN WORK. Reprise K 44183 (E).
Gramophone. p984. November. 25w. 1

238 Georgie Fame. SHORTY. Epic $5.98.
Creem. December. p63. 25w. 3

239 Family. BANDSTAND. United Artists UAS 5644 $5.98.
Records and Recordings. November. p105-6. 250w. 1

240 Family. FEARLESS. United Artists UAS 5562 $5.98.
Audio. November. p90. 50w. 3½
Beetle. August. p20. 1,550w. 4
Crawdaddy. April 2. p16. 1,000w. 3
Creem. April. p64. 600w. 3
Gramophone. January. p1280,1283. 50w. 4
High Fidelity. May. p108. 150w. 3
Rolling Stone. March 30. p54. 700w. 3½

241 Family Dogg. THE VIEW FROM RONLAND'S HEAD. Buddah BDS 5100 $5.98. Cart. M85100 $6.95. Cass. M55100 $6.95.
Popular Music. Spring. p184. 75w. 3

242 Fanny. CHARITY BALL. Reprise RS 6456 $5.98. Cart. M86456 $6.98. Cass. M56456 $6.98.
American Record Guide. July. p576. 150w. 5

243 Fanny. FANNY HILL. Reprise MS 2058 $5.98. Cart. M82058 $6.98. Cass. M52058 $6.98.
Popular Music. Spring. p185. 75w. 3
Records and Recordings. July. p92. 200w. 3½
Stereo Review. October. p92. 100w. 2

244 [no entry]

245 Fat City. WELCOME TO... Paramount PAS 6028 $4.98. Cart. 8091-6028M $6.95. Cass. 5091-6028M $6.95.
Audio. August. p62. 50w. 2½
High Fidelity. July. p106. 25w. 2½
New York Times--Sunday. June 11. pD30. 125w. 2

246 FILLMORE--THE LAST DAYS. Fillmore Z3X 31390 <u>or</u> Warner Bros. 3XS 2637 (3 discs) $12.98.
Beetle. October 17. p20. 1,450w. 2½
Canadian Stereo Guide. Fall. p28. 100w. 3
Creem. October. p58. 475w. ½
Gramophone. October. p781-2. 325w. 0
New York Times--Sunday. July 23. pD20. 1,000w. 4
Records and Recordings. October. p126. 150w. 0
Rolling Stone. November 9. p68. 900w. 2
Stereo Review. October. p84. 300w. 5

247 Finnegan & Wood. CRAZED HIPSTERS. Blue Thumb BTS 35. Cart. M835 $6.95. Cass. M535 $6.95.

Creem. August. p66. 200w. ½

248 FIRST GREAT ROCK FESTIVALS OF THE SEVENTIES (anthology). Columbia G3X 30805 (3 discs) $9.98.
Creem. January. p61. 500w. 1
Library Journal. January 1. p55. 150w. 3
Popular Music. Winter. p126. 75w. 2½

249 Five Dollar Shoes. Neighborhood/Famous $5.98.
Crawdaddy. December. p80-1. 1,050w. 3
Creem. December. p61. 325w. 1½

250 Five Man Electrical Band. COMING OF AGE. Lionel LRS 1101 $4.98. Cart. 8143-1101 $6.95. Cass. 5143-1101 $6.95.
American Record Guide. July. p577. 150w. 2

251 Flash. Capitol SMAS 11040 $5.98. Cart. 8XT 11040 $6.98. Cass. 4XT 11040 $6.98.
Beetle. August. p20-1. 300w. 2½
Creem. August. p63. 100w. 3
Gramophone. May. p1952. 25w. 0

252 Fleetwood Mac. BARE TREES. Reprise MS 2080 $5.98. Cart. M82080 $6.98. Cass. M52080 $6.98.
Crawdaddy. August. p21. 500w. 3
Creem. August. p11. 25w. 2½
Records and Recordings. August. p89-90. 250w. 1
Rolling Stone. June 8. p56. 750w. 3

253 Fleetwood Mac. FUTURE GAMES. Reprise RS 6465 $5.98. Cart. M86465 $6.98. Cass. M56465 $6.98.
Creem. January. p69. 50w. ½
Stereo Review. February. p103-4. 275w. 3

254 Flower Traveling Band. SATORI. GRT 9230-1005 (Canada).
Beetle. March 29. p20. 500w. 3

255 Flying Burrito Brothers. A & M SP 4295 $5.98.
High Fidelity. January. p116. 150w. 3½

256 Flying Burrito Brothers. HOT BURRITO. A & M SP 8070 $5.98. (Reissue.)
Audio. May. p93. 25w. 2
High Fidelity. June. p107. 275w. 2
Popular Music. Winter. p122. 25w. 3
Stereo Review. February. p104. 300w. 2½

257 Flying Burrito Brothers. LAST OF THE RED HOT BURRITOS. A & M SP 4343 $5.98. Cart. 8T 4343 $6.95. Cass. CS 4343 $6.95.
Beetle. July. p21. 600w. 3

Crawdaddy. August. p20. 400w. 2½
Creem. September. p11. 25w. 3½
Creem. September. p53. 600w. 2
Gramophone. September. p579. 100w. 3
High Fidelity. August. p106. 25w. 2½
Popular Music. Summer. p251. 75w. 2
Rolling Stone. June 22. p55. 650w. 4

258 Tom Fogerty. Fantasy 9407 $5.98. Cart. M89407 $6.98. Cass. M59407 $6.98.
Creem. August. p11. 25w. ½
Creem. August. p66. 25w. 0
Stereo Review. December. p92, 96. 200w. 3½

259 Foghat. Bearsville BR 2077 $4.98.
Beetle. August. p21. 700w. 2
Creem. August. p65-5. 250w. 2½
Records and Recordings. May. p96. 200w. 3½

260 A Foot in Coldwater. Daffodil SBA 16012 (Canada).
Sound. September. p40. 175w. 2

261 Kim Fowley. I'M BAD. Capitol ST 11075 $5.98. Cart. 8XT 11075 $6.98. Cass. 4XT 11075 $6.98.
Crawdaddy. September. p18. 500w. 2½

262 Peter Frampton. WIND OF CHANGE. A & M 4348 $5.98.
Creem. August. p65. 400w. 4
Hi-Fi News and Record Review. September. p1683. 100w. 3½
Popular Music. Fall. p88. 50w. 3
Records and Recordings. July. p93-4. 250w. 3
Rolling Stone. August 17. p52. 800w. 3

263 Free. AT LAST. A & M 4349 $5.98. Cart. 8T 4349 $6.95. Cass. CS 4349 $6.95.
Records and Recordings. September. p94. 250w. 1

264 Free. LIVE. A & M SP 4306 $5.98. Cart. 8T 4306 $6.95. Cass. CS 4306 $6.95.
Beetle. January 22. p20. 450w. 1
Popular Music. Fall. p61. 25w. 2½

265 Rory Gallagher. DEUCE. Atco S 7004 $5.98. Cart. M87004 $6.95. Cass. M57004 $6.95.
Audio. July. p64. 50w. 2
Creem. June. p77. 25w. ½

266 Rory Gallagher. LIVE IN EUROPE. Polydor PD 5513 $4.98. Cart. 8F 5513 $6.98. Cass. CF 5513 $6.98.
Beetle. November. p27. 750w. 3

267 Gallagher and Lyle. Capitol ST 11016 $5.98. Cart. 8XT 11016 $6.95.
Records and Recordings. May. p96. 225w. 2½

268 Jerry Garcia. GARCIA. Warner Bros. BS 2582 $5.98. Cart. M82582 $6.95. Cass. M52582 $6.95.
Beetle. May 22. 1,000w. 3½
Crawdaddy. April 2. p15. 1,200w. 3½
Records and Recordings. April. p106-7. 250w. 0
Rolling Stone. March 2. p57. 600w. 3

269 Louis Gasca. Blue Thumb $5.98.
Creem. August. p66. 25w. 0

270 Genesis. NURSERY CRYME. Charisma CAS 1052 $5.98.
Rolling Stone. October 26. p62. 550w. 3

271 Gentle Giant. THREE FRIENDS. Columbia KC 31649 $5.98. Cart. CA 31649 $6.95. Cass. CT 31649 $6.95.
Records and Recordings. June. p84. 250w. 3

272 George Gerdes. OBITUARY. United Artists UAS 5549 $5.98.
Crawdaddy. April 30. p18. 800w. 2½
New York Times--Sunday. February 27. pD32. 100w. 2½

273 Geronimo Black. Uni UNLS 127 $5.98.
Creem. September. p57. 25w. 2½
Hi-Fi News and Record Review. November. p2202. 100w. 1

274 Gideon and Power. I GOTTA BE ME. Bell 1104 $5.98. Cart. M81104 $6.95. Cass. M51104 $6.95.
High Fidelity. May. p116. 25w. 2½

275 Glass Harp. SYNERGY. Decca DL 75306 $5.98. Cart. 6-73306 $6.98. Cass. C 735306 $6.98.
Gramophone. August. p398. 25w. 0
New York Times--Sunday. February 27. pD32. 75w. 1

276 Gary Glitter. GLITTER. Bell 1108. $5.98. Cart. M81108 $6.95. Cass. M51108 $6.95.
Gramophone. December. p1221. 25w. 2
Records and Recordings. December. p96. 225w. 5

277 Godfrey Daniel. TAKE A SAD SONG. Atlantic SD 7219 $5.98.
Creem. September. p50. 600w. 3
Popular Music. Summer. p251. 75w. 3

278 Philip Goodhand-Tait. I THINK I'LL WRITE A SONG. DJM 9 102 $5.98.

Creem. May. p70. 825w. 3
High Fidelity. May. p116. 25w. 3
New York Times--Sunday. February 27. pD32, 75w. 2
Stereo Review. August. p89. 125w. 1

279 Steve Goodman. Buddah BDS 5096 $5.98. Cart. M85096 $6.95. Cass. M55096 $6.95.
New York Times--Sunday. December 10. pD37. 25w. 3
Popular Music. Winter. p124. 50w. 4

280 Goose Creek Symphony. WORDS OF EARNEST. Capitol ST 11044 $5.98. Cart. 8XT 11044 $6.98. Cass. 4XT 11044 $6.98.
Creem. September. p55. 375w. 1½

281 Gorgoni, Martin and Taylor. GOT TO GET BACK TO CISCO. Buddah BDS 5089 $5.98. Cart. M85089 $6.95. Cass. M55089 $6.95.
Gramophone. March. p1613. 25w. 0
Hi-Fi News and Record Review. November. p2201. 100w. 2

282 Bobby Gosh. MOTHER MOTOR. Polydor PD 5016 $5.98.
Audio. May. p95. 50w. 2
Creem. April. p71. 25w. 0

283 Gothic Horizon. TOMORROW'S ANOTHER DAY. Argo ZDA 150 (E).
Hi-Fi News and Record Reviews. September. p1685. 125w. 3
Records and Recordings. August. p90. 225w. 1

284 Gracious. THIS IS. Philips 6382 004 (E).
Gramophone. July. p255. 25w. 0

285 Grand Funk Railroad. E PLURIBUS FUNK. Capitol SW 853 $5.98. Cart. 8XW 853 $6.98. Cass. 4XW 853 $6.98.
American Record Guide. April. p381. 300w. 0
Creem. January. p46. 500w. 2½
High Fidelity. June. p104, 106. 500w. 2
Stereo Review. February. p104, 108. 200w. 2

286 Grand Funk Railroad. MARK, DON AND MEL, 1969-1971. Capitol SABB 11042 (2 discs) $8.98. Cart. 8XAB 11042 $13.98. Cass. 4XAB 11042 $13.98. (Reissue.)
Previews. December. p46. 100w. 1
Rolling Stone. June 22. p56. 400w. 0

287 Grand Funk Railroad. PHOENIX. Capitol SMAS 11099 $5.98.
Creem. November. p63. 700w. 3½
New York Times--Sunday. December 24. pD27, 30. 700w. 1½

New York Times--Sunday. December 31. pD27,30. 100w. 1
Rolling Stone. November 9. p62. 650w. 1½

288 Grateful Dead. Warner Bros. 2 WS 1935 (2 discs) $9.96. Cart. M81935 $9.95. Cass. M51935. $9.95.
Beetle. March 29. p19. 1,200w. 3
Beetle. March 29. p20. 500w. 3½
Gramophone. February. p1443. 100w. 3
High Fidelity. January. p111. 300w. 1
Sound. March. p21. 100w. 4

289 Grateful Dead. HISTORIC DEAD. Sunflower SNF 5004 $5.98.
Audio. May. p94. 25w. 2½

290 Grateful Dead. VINTAGE DEAD. Sunflower SNF 5001 $5.98.
Hi-Fi News and Record Review. July. p1312. 50w. 1½

291 Green Bullfrog. Decca. DL 75269 $4.98. Cart. 6 5269 $6.98. Cass. C73 5269 $6.98.
Audio. November. p93. 25w. 0

292 Mick Greenwood. LIVING GAME. Decca DL 75318 $4.98. Cart. 6 5318 $6.98. Cass. C73 5318 $6.98.
Audio. November. p91. 50w. 1
High Fidelity. July. p98. 200w. 2½

293 Larry Groce. THE WHEAT LIES LOW. Daybreak Records DR 2000 $5.98.
Rolling Stone. January 20. p54. 675w. 3

294 Grootna. Columbia C 31033 $5.98. Cart. CA 31033 $6.98.
American Record Guide. March. p332. 225w. 3
Crawdaddy. January 30. p19. 700w. 3
Creem. March. p57. 25w. 3

295 Henry Gross. ABC ABCX 747 $4.98. Cart. M8747 $6.95. Cass. M5749 $6.95.
High Fidelity. June. p110. 25w. 2

296 Gross National Product. P-FLAPS AND LOW BLOWS. Metromedia $4.98.
Creem. August. p66. 50w. 2½

297 Groundhogs. WHO WILL SAVE THE WORLD? United Artists UAS 5570 $5.98. Cart. U 8374 $6.98. Cass. K 0374 $6.98.
Creem. August. p61. 550w. 3
Records and Recordings. April. p107. 250w. 4
Rolling Stone. July 20. p49. 875w. 4

298 Guess Who. BEST. RCA LSP 10004 $5.98. Cart. P8S 1710 $6.95. Cass. PK 1710 $6.95. (Reissue.)
Audio. May. p94. 50w. 3

299 Guess Who. LIVE AT THE PARAMOUNT. RCA LSP 4779 $5.98.
Creem. November. p67-8. 900w. $3\frac{1}{2}$
New York Times--Sunday. December 10. D32, 38. 300w. $2\frac{1}{2}$

300 Guess Who. ROCKIN'. RCA LSP 4602 $5.98. Cart. P8S 1828 $6.95. Cass. PK 1828.
American Record Guide. July. p576. 100w. 0
Sound. March. p34-5. 175w. 1

301 GUITAR BOOGIE (anthology). RCA LSP 4624 $5.98. (Reissue.)
Popular Music. Summer. p253. 50w. 3

302 Guns and Butter. Cotillion SD 9901 $5.98.
High Fidelity. August. p106. 25w. $2\frac{1}{2}$

303 Arlo Guthrie. HOBO'S LULLABY. Warner Bros. MS 2060 $5.98.
Creem. November. p15. 25w. $3\frac{1}{2}$
Gramophone. November. 75w. p989. 3
Hi-Fi News and Record Review. September. p1683. 100w. 2
High Fidelity. September. p108. 25w. 2
New York Times--Sunday. August 27. pD19. 150w. 3
Popular Music. Summer. p250. 100w. 3
Rolling Stone. July 20. p50, 52. 750w. 4
Sing Out. September/October. p38. 75w. 3

304 Gypsy. IN THE GARDEN. Metromedia KM 1044 $5.98. Cart. 8090-1044M $6.95. Cass. 5090-1044M $6.95.
American Record Guide. June. p528. 150w. 2

305 H.P. Lovecraft. THIS IS H.P. LOVECRAFT SAILING ON THE WHITE SHIP. Philips 6336 210 (E). (Reissue.)
Gramophone. September. p577. 50w. 1

306 Bill Haley and the Comets. RAZZLE-DAZZLE. Janus JX2S (2 discs) $9.98.
High Fidelity. March. p117. 25w. $2\frac{1}{2}$

307 Halfnelson. Bearsville BV 2048 $4.98.
New York Times--Sunday. February 27. pD32. 100w. 1

308 Carol Hall. BEADS AND FEATHERS. Elektra EKS 75018 $5.98. Cart. ET 85018 $6.98. Cass. TC 55018 $6.98.
High Fidelity. May. p110. 275w. 2
Records and Recordings. May. p98. 175w. 0

309 Clare Hamill. Island ILPS 9182 (E).
Hi-Fi News and Record Review. June. p1128. 200w. $2\frac{1}{2}$

310 John Paul Hammond. BEST. Vanguard VSD 11/12 (2 discs) $5.98. (Reissue.)
Jazz Journal. November. p38. 100w. 0

311 John Paul Hammond. I'M SATISFIED. Columbia KC 31318 $5.98. Cart. CA 31318 $6.98.
Creem. August. p66. 25w. 0
Previews. September. p40. 150w. 1½
Rolling Stone. June 22. p56. 800w. 3

312 Eddie Hardin. HOME IS WHERE YOU FIND IT. Decca TXS 106 (E).
Hi-Fi News and Record Review. May. p939. 100w. 3

313 Micky Hart. ROLLING THUNDER. Warner Bros. BS 2635 $5.98. Cart. M82635 $6.95. Cass. M52635 $6.95.
Beetle. November. p28. 900w. 3

314 Keef Hartley. OVERDOG. Deram DES 18057 $4.98.
Audio. May. p93. 25w. 3½

315 Richie Havens. THE GREAT BLIND DEGREE. Stormy Forest SFS 6010 $5.98. Cart. 8116-6010 $6.95. Cass. 5116-6010 $6.95.
American Record Guide. July. p576-7. 150w. 0
Crawdaddy. January 30. p18. 700w. 1
Gramophone. July. p256. 50w. 1
High Fidelity. October. p121-2. 200w. 2½

316 Richie Havens. MY BOY. ABC Dunhill DSX 50116 $5.98.
Sound. March. p34. 175w. 3

317 Richie Havens. ON STAGE. Stormy Forest SFS 5012 $5.98. Cart. 8116-6012Z $6.95. Cass. 5116-6012Z $6.95.
Audio. December. p93-4. 300w. 4
Creem. December. p60-1. 350w. 2

318 Richie Havens. SOMETHING ELSE AGAIN. MGM S 4699 $5.98. Cart. 8130-4699M $6.95.
Hi-Fi News and Record Review. May. p939. 100w. 3

319 Ronnie Hawkins. ROCK AND ROLL RESURRECTION. Monument KZ 31330 $4.98. Cart. 8044-31330M $6.95.
Creem. December. p9. 25w. 2

320 Hawkwind. IN SEARCH OF SPACE. United Artists UAS 5567 $5.98.
Creem. June. p72-3. 800w. 2
Rolling Stone. June 22. p58. 900w. 2

321 Heads, Hands, and Feet. Capitol SVBB 680 (2 discs) $6.98. Cart. 8XVV 680 $7.98. Cass. 4XVV 680 $7.98.
American Record Guide. April. p381. 225w. 2

322 Heads, Hands, and Feet. TRACKS. Capitol ST 11051 $5.98. Cart. 8XT 11051 $6.95. Cass. 4XT 11051 $6.95.
Records and Recordings. July. p92. 200w. 2½

323 Dick Heckstall-Smith. DUST IN THE AIR SUSPENDED MARKS THE PLACE WHERE A STORY ENDS. Island ILPS 9196 (E).
Records and Recordings. September. p98-9. 200w. 3

324 Jimi Hendrix. AT HIS BEST, VOLUME 1-3. Sagapan 6313/5 (3 discs) (E). (Reissue.)
Hi-Fi News and Record Review. October. p1926. 75w. 0
Records and Recordings. July. p94. 400w. 2½

325 Jimi Hendrix. HENDRIX IN THE WEST. Reprise MS 2049 $5.98. Cart. M 82049 $6.98. Cass. M 52049 $6.98.
Crawdaddy. May 28. p16. 750w. 4
Creem. May. p65. 750w. 4
High Fidelity. June. p110. 25w. 2½
Previews. September. p43. 75w. 2
Rolling Stone. March 30. p52. 750w. 3½
Stereo Review. July. p92-3. 175w. 2

326 Jimi Hendrix. WAR HEROES. Reprise MS 2103 $5.98.
Gramophone. December. p1225. 50w. 3
Records and Recordings. December. p96. 300w. 4½

327 Dan Hicks and His Hot Licks. STRIKING IT RICH! Blue Thumb BTS 36 $4.98. Cart. M836 $6.95. Cass. M536 $6.95.
Crawdaddy. October. p81. 500w. 3
Creem. October. p57. 1,200w. 5
High Fidelity. August. p98-9. 300w. 3½
New York Times--Sunday. May 21. pD30. 100w. 3½
Popular Music. Summer. p254. 75w. 4
Rolling Stone. March 30. p63. 600w. 3

328 Highway Robbery. FOR LOVE OR MONEY. RCA LSP 4735 $5.98. Cart. P8S 1992 $6.95. Cass. PK 1992 $6.95.
Previews. December. p46. 75w. 1½
Rolling Stone. August 17. p54. 600w. 0

329 Joel Scott Hill, John Barbata, Chris Ethridge. L.A. GETAWAY. Atco SD 33-357 $4.98. Cart. 8357 $6.98. Cass. 5387 $6.98.
Crawdaddy. May 14. p20. 900w. 3
Records and Recordings. May. p98. 175w. 0
Stereo Review. May. p94. 100w. 3

330 The Hollies. Music For Pleasure MFP 5282 (E). (Reissue.)
Gramophone. May. p1952. 52w. 1½

331 The Hollies. DISTANT LIGHT. Epic KE 30958 $5.98. Cart. EA 30958 $6.98.
Crawdaddy. December. p84-5. 450w. 2
Creem. December. p9. 25w. 3
High Fidelity. October 7. p126. 25w. 1
Popular Music and Society. Summer. p251. 50 w. 2

332 The Hollies. GREATEST, VOLUME 2. Parlophone PCS 7148 (E). (Reissue.)
Gramophone. May. p1952. 25w. 2

333 Buddy Holly. A ROCK AND ROLL COLLECTION. Decca DXSE 7 207 (2 discs) $11.96. (Reissue.)
Crawdaddy. November. p82-3. 800w. 1½
High Fidelity. November. p130. 25w. 2½
Popular Music. Fall. p90. 100w. 1½
Previews. October. p47. 150w. 2

334 Jake Holmes. HOW MUCH TIME. Columbia C 30996 $4.98.
Stereo Review. October. p96. 100w. 3

335 Hoodoo Rhythm Devils. BARBECUE OF DEVILLE. Blue Thumb BTS 42 $5.98.
Rolling Stone. November 23. p61. 500w. 3½

336 Mary Hopkin. EARTH SONG, OCEAN SONG. Apple SMAS 3381 $5.98. R-R M3381 $6.95. Cart. 8XW 3381 $6.98. Cass. 4XW 3381 $6.98.
Gramophone. January. p1274. 75w. 3
Rolling Stone. January 20. p54. 400w. 3
Stereo Review. April. p96. 300w. 4

337 Hot Tuna. BURGERS. Grunt FTR 1004 $5.98. Cart. P8FT 1004 $6.98. Cass. PKFT 1004 $6.98.
Crawdaddy. May 14. p14-5. 700w. 3
Gramophone. August. p398-405. 100w. 3
High Fidelity. July. p100. 50w. 2
New York Times--Sunday. April 30. pD28. 125w. 4
Previews. September. p43. 200w. 2½
Records and Recordings. July. p93. 200w. 1½
Rolling Stone. May 25. p68, 70. 600w. 3
Stereo Review. October. p96. 125w. 2½

338 Hotlegs. THINKS SCHOOL STINKS. Capitol ST 587 $5.98. Cart. M5710 $6.95.
American Record Guide. March. p332-3. 150w. 1

339 Lorence Hud. A & M SP 9004 (Canada).
Sound. October. p42. 250w. 4

340 Humble Pie. PERFORMANCE: ROCKIN' THE FILLMORE. A & M SP 3506 (2 discs) $9.98. Cart. 8T 3506 $9.98. Cart. CS 3506 $9.98.

Beetle. March 29. p18. 625w. 3½
Creem. January. p61. 850w. 5

341 Humble Pie. SMOKIN'. A & M SP 4342 $5.98.
Crawdaddy. June 11. p15. 450w. 1
Records and Recordings. May. p98. 325w. 1
Stereo Review. July. p93. 50w. ½

342 Hungry Chuck. Bearsville BR 2071 $5.98. Cart. M82071 $6.95. Cass. M52071 $6.95.
Crawdaddy. August. p20. 250w. 2

343 Hurricane Smith. DON'T LET IT DIE. Columbia SCX 6510 (E).
Gramophone. October. p778. 100w. 3

344 It's A Beautiful Day. IT'S A BIG BAD BEAUTIFUL DAY CHOICE QUALITY STUFF/ANYTIME. Columbia KC 30734 $5.98.
Crawdaddy. April 16. p19. 800w. 3½

345 J. Geils Band. FULL HOUSE. Atlantic SD 7241 $5.98. Cart. TP 7241 $6.95. Cass. CS 7241 $6.95.
Rolling Stone. November 9. p61. 500w. 3½
Stereo Review. December. p87. 300w. 4

346 J. Geils Band. THE MORNING AFTER. Atlantic SD 8297 $5.98. Cart. M88297 $6.95. Cass. M58297 $6.95.
Crawdaddy. June 16. p18. 900w. 2
Records and Recordings. April. p107. 250w. 4

347 Jade Warrior. Vertigo VEL 1007 $5.98.
American Record Guide. March. p333. 200w. 1

348 Jake and the Family Jewels. THE BIG MOOSE CALLS HIS BABY SWEET LORRAINE. Polydor PD 5024 $5.98.
High Fidelity. December. p122. 100w. 2½
New York Times--Sunday. June 11. pD30. 175w. 3
Popular Music. Summer. p253. 25w. 1
Rolling Stone. March 30. p63. 650w. 3½
Stereo Review. September. p74. 100w. 3½

349 Barclay James. EARLY MORNING ONWARDS. Starline SRS 5126 (E).
Records and Recordings. November. p105. 200w. 2

350 Barclay James. HARVEST. Sire SI 5904 $5.98.
Audio. May. p95. 25w. 0

351 John James and Pete Berryman. SKY IN MY PIE. Transatlantic TRA 250 (E).
Hi-Fi News and Record Review. May. p939. 150w. 3

352 James and the Good Brothers. Columbia C 30889 $4.98.
Beetle. January 22. p22. 475w. 3
Creem. January. p69. 50w. 0
Library Journal. January 15. 179p. 150w. 2½

353 The James Gang. PASSIN' THRU. ABC Dunhill ABCX 760 $4.98.
Beetle. November. p29-30. 600w. 2½

354 JAMMING WITH EDWARD! (Nicky Hopkins, Ry Cooder, Mick Jagger, Bill Wyman, and Charley Watts.) Rolling Stone COC 39100 $3.98. Cart. E83910 $6.98. Cass. E53910 $6.98.
Audio. May. p93. 25w. 1
Crawdaddy. March 19. p18. 500w. 3
Creem. April. p65. 400w. 2½
Gramophone. April. p1776. 50w. 2
High Fidelity. May. p110-11. 250w. 1
Downbeat. June 8. p20. 175w. 2
Popular Music. Spring. p185. 75w. 0
Records and Recordings. March. p120-2. 175w. 3
Rolling Stone. March 16. p56. 700w. 2

355 THE JAN AND DEAN ANTHOLOGY ALBUM. Legendary Masters Series United Artists UAS 9961 (2 discs) $5.98. (Reissue.)
Audio. May. p94. 25w. 2½
Crawdaddy. May 14. p18-9. 400w. 3
Popular Music. Spring. p128. 50w. 4
Rolling Stone. March 30. p49. 1,500w. 4

356 Jefferson Airplane. LONG JOHN SILVER. Grunt FTR 1007 $5.98. Cart. P8FTP 1007 $6.95. Cass. FKFTP 1007 $6.95.
Creem. November. p15. 25w. 3½
Creem. November. p66. 700w. 2
Creem. November. p77. 1,000w. 4
Hi-Fi News and Record Review. December. p2464. 100w. 2
High Fidelity. November. p118. 120w. 1
Records and Recordings. November. p106. 200w. 4

357 Jellybread. BACK TO BEGIN AGAIN. Blue Horizon 2931 004 (E).
Hi-Fi News and Record Review. July. p1309. 75w. 3

358 Jennifer. Reprise MS 2065 $5.98. Cart. M82065 $6.95. Cass. M52065 $6.95.
High Fidelity. August. p98. 325w. 3½
Stereo Review. December. p102, 104. 325w. 3

359 Jerusalem. Deram SDL 6 (E).
Gramophone. June. p116. 50w. 3
Hi-Fi News and Record Review. July. p1309. 25w. 0

360 Jethro Tull. THICK AS A BRICK. Warner Bros. BS 2072 $5.98. Cart. M82072 $6.95. Cass. M52072 $6.95.
Beetle. June. p20. 600w. 4
Crawdaddy. August. p17. 650w. 1½
Creem. August. p63. 600w. 1½
High Fidelity. September. p104. 200w. 3½
Rolling Stone. June 22. p54. 1,700w. 3
Stereo Review. September. p71. 350w. 4

361 Jo Jo Gunne. Asylum SD 5053 $5.98. Cart. M85053 $6.95. Cass. M55053 $6.95.
Crawdaddy. May 14. p16. 250w. 3
Records and Recordings. May. p98. 200w. 2½

362 Jo Mama. J IS FOR JUMP. Atlantic S 8288 $5.98. Cart. M88288 $6.95. Cass. M58288 $6.95.
Gramophone. January. p1279. 25w. 0

363 Billy Joel. COLD SPRING HARBOR. Family Productions. FPS 2700 $4.98. Cart. M82700 $6.95. Cass. M52700 $6.95.
Hi-Fi News and Record Review. July. p1311. 50w. 3½
High Fidelity. April. p114. 25w. 3

364 Elton John. EMPTY SKY. DJM DJLPS 403 $4.98.
High Fidelity. April. p114. 25w. 3

365 Elton John. HONKY CHATEAU. Uni 93135 $4.98. Cart. 893135 $6.95. Cass. 293135 $6.95.
Audio. November. p90. 25w. 1
Crawdaddy. October. p78. 400w. 2½
Creem. August. p74. 50w. 3½
Hi-Fi News and Record Review. July. p1311. 200w. 4
High Fidelity. September. p102. 175w. 3½
Popular Music. Summer. p248. 150w. 5
Popular Music. Fall. p88. 75w. 5
Rolling Stone. August 17. p48. 750w. 4
Sound. September. p40. 150w. 3
Stereo Review. October. p96. 75w. 4

366 Elton John. MADMAN ACROSS THE WATER. Uni 93120 $4.98. Cart. 8 93120 $6.98. Cass. 2 93120 $6.98.
Audio. May. p95. 50w. 1
Crawdaddy. March 19. p16. 500w. 3
Rolling Stone. January 20. p49. 750w. 1½
Stereo Review. April. p96. 400w. 0

367 The Johnstons. Mercury SRM 1-640 $5.98.
Crawdaddy. November. p85-6. 1,000w. 3
Creem. November. p15. 25w. 1½
Hi-Fi News and Record Review. May. p936. 100w. 2
Hi-Fi News and Record Review. July. p1311. 200w. 1

Popular Music. Summer. p249. 75w. 4
Records and Recordings. May. p106. 125w. 1

368 Mordicai Jones. Polydor PD 5010 $4.98.
American Record Guide. March. p332. 225w. 1
High Fidelity. April. p107. 50w. 2½
Popular Music. Winter. p124. 50w. 3
Stereo Review. January. p107-8. 300w. 3

369 Paul Jones. CRUCIFIX IN A HORSESHOE. London XPS 605 $5.98.
Rolling Stone. March 30. p54. 650w. 0
Crawdaddy. April 16. p15. 600w. 2½

370 Janis Joplin. IN CONCERT. Columbia C2X 31160 (2 discs) $8.98. Cart. C2A 31160 $9.98. Cass. C2T 31160 $9.98.
Beetle. July. p20-1. 950w. 3
Crawdaddy. August. p16. 900w. 4
Creem. August. p11. 25w. 3½
Creem. August. p61. 775w. 2½
High Fidelity. August. p96. 150w. 2½
Jazz Journal. November. p37. 100w. 1
New York Times--Sunday. May 21. pD30. 400w. 1
Ontario Library Review. December. p242. 25w. 2
Previews. October. p47. 300w. 2
Records and Recordings. October. p126. 200w. 2½
Rolling Stone. June 8. p62. 3,500w. 4

371 Janis Joplin. PEARL. Columbia KC 30322 $5.98. Cart. CA 30322 $6.98. Cass. CT 30322 $6.98.
Audio. May. p93. 75w. 4

372 Joy of Cooking. CASTLES. Capitol ST 11050 $5.98. Cart. 8XT 11050 $6.98. Cass. 4XT 11050 $6.98.
Creem. September. p11. 25w. 3
Creem. October. p56. 350w. 4

373 Joy of Cooking. CLOSER TO THE GROUND. Capitol SMAS 828 $5.98. Cart. 8XT 828 $6.98.
Gramophone. January. p1279. 25w. 1
Stereo Review. January. p108. 50w. 3

374 Joyous Noise. Capitol SMAS 844 $5.98. Cart. 8XT 844 $6.98.
Rolling Stone. March 16. p58. 350w. 2½

375 Juicy Lucy. GET A WHIFFA THIS. Atco SD 33367 $5.98. Cart. M83367 $6.95. Cart. M53367 $6.95.
Popular Music. Winter. p126. 25w. 2½

376 Jukin' Bone. WHISKEY WOMAN. RCA LSP 4621 $5.98. Cart. P8S 1851 $6.95.
American Record Guide. August. p625. 200w. 1

377 Paul Kantner and Grace Slick. SUNFIGHTER. Grunt FTR 1002 $5.98. Cart. P8FT 1002 $6.95. Cass. PKFT 1002 $6.95.
Audio. May. p92. 100w. 2½
Crawdaddy. February 20. p16. 900w. 3
Rolling Stone. March 2. p62. 1,250w. 3

378 John Kay. FORGOTTEN SONGS AND UNSUNG HEROES. ABC Dunhill DSX 50120 $5.98. Cart. M85120 $6.98. Cass. M55120 $6.98.
Beetle. May 21. 450w. p15. 3½
High Fidelity. August. p101-2. 200w. 4
Popular Music. Summer. p251. 75w. 3
Sound. August. p49. 100w. 2
Stereo Review. October. p98. 100w. 1

379 George Kayatta. TIME TO WONDER WHY. RCA LSP 4638 $5.98.
Previews. September. p43. 175w. ½

380 Howard Kaylan and Mark Volman. THE PHLORESCENT LEECH AND EDDIE. Reprise MS 2099 $5.98.
Creem. November. p65-6. 700w. 3
Creem. December. p86. 25w. 3½
Gramophone. November. p990. 100w. 3
High Fidelity. November. p130. 25w. 1½
New York Times--Sunday. September 24. pHF7. 300w. 4
Rolling Stone. November 9. p68. 500w. 3

381 Casey Kelly. Elektra EKS 75040 $5.98. Cart. 85040 $6.98. Cass. 55040 $6.98.
Popular Music. Fall. p91. 25w. 3
Sound. November. p37. 250w. 3

382 Johnny Kidd and the Pirates. SHAKIN' ALL OVER. Regal Starline SRS 5100 (E).
Gramophone. February. p1437. 25w. 3

383 Kindred. NEXT OF KIN. Warner Bros. BS 2640 $5.98.
Stereo Review. December. p96. 125w. 1

384 Carole King. MUSIC. Ode SP 77013 $5.98. Cart. 77013 $6.98. Cass. 77013 $6.98.
Creem. March. p58-9. 1,250w. 4½
High Fidelity. April. p109. 50w. 2
New York Times--Sunday. January 2. pD20. 250w. 3½
Rolling Stone. January 20. p50. 1,250w. 3½
Stereo Review. November. p73-4. 350w. 3

385 Carole King. RHYMES AND REASONS. Ode SP 77016 $5.98.
Popular Music. Fall. p94. 25w. 0

Rolling Stone. December 21. p61. 750w. 4
Sound. December. p41. 275w. 4

386 Jonathan King. TRY SOMETHING DIFFERENT. Decca SKL 5127 (E).
Hi-Fi News and Record Review. July. p1311. 125w. 1

387 Paul King. BEEN IN THE PEN TOO LONG. Dawn DNLS 3035 (E).
Records and Recordings. June. p84. 150w. 1

388 Reg King. United Artists UAS 29157 (E).
Creem. April. p65. 375w. $2\frac{1}{2}$

389 King Biscuit Boy. GOODUNS. Paramount 6023 $4.98. Cart. 8091-6023M $6.95.
Blues Unlimited. February/March. p20. 50w. $3\frac{1}{2}$
High Fidelity. April. p107. 275w. 3
Rolling Stone. March 30. p54. 700w. 4

390 King Crimson. EARTHBOUND. Island HELPS 6 (E).
Hi-Fi News and Record Review. September. p1685. 100w. 0

391 King Crimson. ISLANDS. Atlantic SD 7212 $5.98. Cart. M87212 $6.98. Cass. M57212 $6.98.
Downbeat. April 13. p22. 175w. $3\frac{1}{2}$
Rolling Stone. March 2. p58, 60. 900w. 2
Stereo Review. June. p101. 200w. 0

392 The Kinks. EVERYBODYS IN SHOWBIZ. RCA VPS 6065 $6.98. Cart. P8S 5122 $7.95. Cass. PK 5122 $7.95.
Crawdaddy. December. p76-7. 1,000w. $2\frac{1}{2}$
Creem. November. p61. 750w. $3\frac{1}{2}$
Gramophone. November. p984. 75w. 0
Hi-Fi News and Record Review. November. p2202. 100w. 3
New York Times--Sunday. November 12. pD30. 300w. 1
Records and Recordings. November. p106. 200w. $3\frac{1}{2}$
Rolling Stone. October 26. p54, 56. 1,600w. 4

393 The Kinks. KINK KRONIKLES. Reprise 2XS 6454 (2 discs) $6.98. Cart. M86454 $7.95. Cass. M56454 $7.95. (Reissue.)
Crawdaddy. August. p17. 1,450w. $3\frac{1}{2}$
New York Times--Sunday. April 30. pD28. 100w. 4
Rolling Stone. May 25. p64. 1,500w. $3\frac{1}{2}$

394 The Kinks. MUSWELL HILLBILLIES. RCA LSP 4644 $5.98. Cart. P8S 1878 $6.95. Cass. PK 1878 $6.95.
Crawdaddy. February 20. p14. 2,000w. 5
Creem. January. p63-4. 300w. 1

Library Journal. March 1. p857. 150w. 4
New York Times--Sunday. January 23. pD25. 775w. 4½
Sound. March. p34. 175w. 3
Stereo Review. May. p67-8. 600w. 4

395 Buddy Knox. GREATEST HITS. Liberty LST 7251 $4.98. (Reissue.)
Creem. April. p71. 25w. 0

396 Bonnie Koloc. AFTER ALL THIS TIME. Ovation OVQD (quad) 14-21 $5.98. Cart. (quad) M81421 $6.98. Cass. (quad) M51421 $6.98.
Hi-Fi News and Record Review. August. p1479. 50w. 3½
Stereo Review. March. p102. 300w. 2

397 Bonnie Koloc. HOLD ON TO ME. Ovation OVQD (quad) 14-26. Cart. (quad) M81426 $6.95. Cass. (quad) M51246 $6.95.
Stereo Review. December. p96, 98. 250w. 3

398 John Kongos. KONGOS. Elektra EKS 75019 $5.98. Cart. ET 85019 $6.98. Cass. TC 55019 $6.98.
Crawdaddy. May 14. p21. 400w. 3
New York Times--Sunday. February 20. pD28. 125w. 3½

399 Al Kooper. A POSSIBLE PROJECTION OF THE FUTURE/ CHILDHOOD'S END. Columbia KC 31159 $5.98. Cart. CA 31159 $6.98.
Rolling Stone. June 22. p60. 500w. 2½

400 Alexis Korner. BOOTLEG HIM! Warner Bros. 2WS 1966 (2 Discs) $6.98. Cart. L81966 $7.95. Cass. L51966 $7.95.
Creem. August. p11. 25w. 1
Records and Recordings. October. p119. 225w. 3

401 Koerner, Olson, Willie and the Bumblebees. MUSIC IS JUST A BUNCH OF NOTES. Sweet Jane Ltd. 5872. $5.98.
Rolling Stone. August 17. p52. 1,500w. 3½

402 Leo Kottke. GREENHOUSE. Capitol ST 11000 $5.98. Cart. 8XT 11000 $6.98. Cass. 4XT 11000 $6.98.
Crawdaddy. April 30. p16. 1,000w. 3
Creem. June. p71. 1,600w. 4
Popular Music. Spring. p184. 75w. 3
Stereo Review. July. p94. 175w. 3½

403 Kris Kristofferson. BORDER LORD. Monument KZ 31302 $5.98. Cart 8044-31302 $6.95. Cass. 5044-31302 $6.95.
Audio. August. p61. 50w. 2½
Crawdaddy. May 28. p15. 775w. 2
Creem. June. p70. 850w. 2½

New York Times--Sunday. May 21. pD32. 75w. 1½
Stereo Review. September. p76. 225w. 1½

404 Kris Kristofferson. JESUS WAS A CAPRICORN. Monument KZ 31909 $5.98.
New York Times--Sunday. December 10. pD37. 75w. 3
Popular Music. Fall. p93. 100w. 2

405 Kris Kristofferson. THE SILVER TONGUED DEVIL AND I. Monument KZ 30679 $4.98. Cart. 8044-30679 $6.98. Cass. 5044-30679 $6.98.
Audio. May. p94. 25w. 2½
Sound. March. p21. 125w. 3
Stereo Review. January. p83-4. 250w. 3

406 Richard Landis. NATURAL CAUSES. ABC Dunhill. 50115X $5.98. Cart. M85115 $6.95. Cass. M55115 $6.95.
Audio. August. p62. 50w. 2½

407 Led Zeppelin. FOURTH ALBUM. Atlantic SD 7208 $5.98. R-R M7208 $6.95. Cart. M87208 $6.95. Cass. M57208 $6.95.
Beetle. January 22. p18-9. 375w. 3½
Crawdaddy. January 30. p19. 600w. 3½
Creem. January. p62-3. 1500w. 2½
Downbeat. March 16. p28. 325w. 3
High Fidelity. June. p104,106. 500w. 2½
Stereo Review. March. p102. 250w. 3½

408 Arthur Lee. VINDICATOR. A & M SP 4356 $5.98.
Creem. November. p15,74. 25w. 1½
Creem. November. p66. 700w. 3
High Fidelity. October. p126. 25w. ½
Rolling Stone. August 17. p49. 675w. 0

409 Mylon Le Fevre. MYLON. Columbia C 31085 $4.98.
Stereo Review. April. p96-7. 175w. 0

410 John Lennon and the Plastic Ono Band. IMAGINE. Apple SN 3379 $4.98. Cass. 8XT 3379 $6.98. Cass. 4XT 3379 $6.98. Cart. (quad) Q8W 3379 $7.98.
High Fidelity. January. p77. 475w. 3
Popular Music. Winter. p123. 50w. 2
Stereo Review. January. p108. 400w. 2½

411 John Lennon and Yoko Ono/Plastic Ono Band. SOMETIME IN NEW YORK CITY. Apple SVBB 3392 (2 discs) $6.98. Cart. 8XAB 3392 $8.98. Cass. 4XAB 3392 $8.98.
Crawdaddy. September. p16. 1,500w. 2
Creem. August. p64. 750w. 2½
Records and Recordings. December. p96,98. 850w. 0
Rolling Stone. July 20. p48. 1,500w. 1
Stereo Review. November. p88. 200w. 1

412 Jerry Lee Lewis. THE KILLER ROCKS ON. Mercury SRM 1-637 $4.98. Cart. MC8-1-637 $6.95. Cass. MCR4-1-637 $6.95.
Audio. August. p61-2. 50w. 2½
Gramophone. September. p580. 50w. 0
Popular Music. Summer. p252. 50w. 3
Records and Recordings. August. p90. 200w. 4
Rolling Stone. June 8. p55. 850w. 5

413 Jerry Lee Lewis. MONSTERS. Sun 124 $4.98. (Reissue.)
Audio. August. p65-6. 125w. 1½
Blues Unlimited. February/March. p20. 25w. 4
Gramophone. July. p255. 25w. 3

414 Jerry Lee Lewis. ORIGINAL GOLDEN HITS, VOLUME 3. Sun Records 128 $4.98. Cart. 1074-103M $6.98. (Reissue.)
Creem. April. p71. 50w. 2
Gramophone. July. p255. 25w. 3
Popular Music. Spring. p184. 25w. 3

415 Lori Lieberman. Capitol ST 11081 $5.98.
Stereo Review. December. p98. 175w. 1½

416 Gordon Lightfoot. DON QUIXOTE. Reprise MS 2056 $5.98. Cart. M82056 $6.95. Cass. M52056 $6.95.
Crawdaddy. May 28. p18. 900w. 3½
Gramophone. July. p254. 50w. 3
High Fidelity. June. p110. 25w. 4
Previews. September. p42. 250w. 3½
Records and Recordings. June. p90. 125w. 3
Sound. March. p34. 150w. 1
Stereo Review. August. p89-90. 175w. 3

417 Gordon Lightfoot. OLD DAN'S RECORDS. Reprise MS 2116 $5.98. Cart. M82116 $6.95. Cass. M52116 $6.95.
New York Times--Sunday. December 10. pD38. 300w. 5

418 Lighthouse. LIVE! Evolution 3014 (2 discs) $5.98. Cart. 8117-3014 $6.95. Cass. 5117-3014 $6.95.
Beetle. October 17. p20. 350w. 4

419 Lighthouse. SUNNY DAYS. GRT 9230-1021 (Canada).
Beetle. December 31. p20. 200w. 3½
Sound. December. p40. 200w. 4

420 Lighthouse. THOUGHTS OF MOVIN' ON. Evolution 3010 $4.98. Cart. 8117-3010. $6.95. Cass. 5117-3010 $6.95.
Beetle. March 29. p19. 300w. 3
Stereo Review. June. p101. 100w. 2

421 Buzz Linhart. BUZZY. Kama Sutra KSBS 2053 $5.98. Cart. 82053 $6.95. Cass. M52053 $6.95.
High Fidelity. October. p126. 25w. 2½

422 Little Feat. SAILIN' SHOES. Warner Bros. BS 2600 $5.98. Cart. M82600 $6.95. Cass. M52600 $6.95.
Crawdaddy. April 30. p14-5. 1,000w. 3
Creem. June. p71. 400w. 2½
Rolling Stone. March 30. p54. 750w. 3

423 Nils Lofgren and Grin. 1 + 1. Spindizzy Z 31038 $4.98. Cart. ZA 31038 $6.98.
Crawdaddy. March 19. p17. 375w. 3
Creem. March. p50-1. 2,050w. 4
High Fidelity. July. p98. 250w. 3½
Stereo Review. March. p103. 100w. 3

424 Kenny Loggins and Jim Messina. SITTIN' IN. Columbia C 31044 $5.98. Cart. CA 31044 $6.98. Cass. CT 31044 $6.98.
Crawdaddy. April 30. p16. 900w. 4
Creem. August. p11. 25w. 1
New York Times--Sunday. March 19. pD30. 150w. 3½
Rolling Stone. March 16. p56, 58. 650w. 4

425 Jon Lord. GEMINI SUITE. Capitol SMAS 870 $5.98.
Creem. May. p68-9. 1,250w. 1
Stereo Review. May. p94. 125w. 0

426 Looking Glass. Epic KE 31320 $5.98. Cart. EA 31320 $6.98. Cass. ET 31320 $6.98.
Canadian Stereo Guide. Fall. p29. 75w. 2½
New York Times--Sunday. October 15. pD31. 125w. 1½
Rolling Stone. June 22. p58. p525. 3

427 Lord Sutch and Heavy Friends. HANDS OF JACK THE RIPPER. Cotillion SD 9049 $5.98. Cart. M89049 $6.95. Cass. M59049 $6.95.
Audio. May. p94. 100w. 4
High Fidelity. May. p110-11. 250w. 2½
Records and Recordings. August. p90-1. 200w. ½
Rolling Stone. March 2. 400w. 0

428 Love Unlimited. Uni 73131 $4.98.
Creem. June. p77. 25w. 0
Gramophone. September. p577. 25w. 1

429 Gloria Lynne. HAPPY AND IN LOVE. Canyon 7709 $4.98. Cart. M8359 $6.95. Cass. M5359 $6.95.
Hi-Fi News and Record Review. November. p2202. 75w. 2½

430 The Machine Gun Company. Dawn DNLS 3031 (E).
Records and Recordings. May. p98-9. 225w. 0

431 Lonnie Mack. THE HILLS OF INDIANA. Elektra EKS 74102 $5.98. Cart. M84102 $6.95. Cass. M54102 $6.95.
Creem. January. p69. 50w. 1
High Fidelity. January. p122. 25w. 3
Stereo Review. February. p109. 200w. 1

432 Macondo. Atlantic SD 7234 $5.98. Cart. TP 7234 $6.97. Cass. CS 7234 $6.97.
Previews. December. p46. 100w. 2½

433 Mad River. Capitol $5.98.
Creem. August. p69. 50w. ½

434 Madura. Columbia G 30794 (2 discs) $5.98. Cart. GA 30794 $7.98. Cass. GT 30794 $7.98.
Creem. January. p69. 50w. 0

435 Magic Carpet. Mushroom 200-MR-20 (E).
Hi-Fi News and Record Review. September. p1683. 50w. 1½

436 Magna Carta. IN CONCERT. Vertigo 6360068 (E).
Records and Recordings. July. p93. 200w. 4

437 Mahogany Rush. MAXOOM. Kot'ai KOT 3001 (Canada).
Beetle. December 31. p21. 900w. 4

438 Mainline. CANADA: OUR HOME AND NATIVE LAND. GRT 9230-1011 (Canada).
Beetle. May. p21. 800w. 2½

439 Malo. Warner Bros. BS 2584 $5.98. Cart. M82584 $6.95. Cass. M52584 $6.95.
American Record Guide. August. p624. 225w. 4
Crawdaddy. May 14. p21. 800w. 3
Creem. March. p60-1. 2,000w. 2½
Gramophone. July. p255. 50w. 1
Hi-Fi News and Record Review. July. p1309. 50w. 2½
New York Times--Sunday. February 20. pD28. 75w. 1
Previews. December. p46. 125w. 2½
Records and Recordings. June. p84. 200w. 2

440 Mama Lion. FAMILY. Family Productions FPS 2702 $5.98. Cart. M82702 $6.95. Cass. M52702 $6.95.
High Fidelity. September. p108. 25w. 3
Creem. August. p74. 50w. 1

441 The Mamas and the Papas. PEOPLE LIKE US. ABC Dunhill DSX 50106 $5.98. Cart. M85106 $6.95. Cass. M55106 $6.95.

Crawdaddy. January 16. p14. 300w. 2
Gramophone. February. p1437. 25w. 1
High Fidelity. March. p117. 25w. 1½

442 Mandrill. IS. Polydor PD 5025 $4.98. Cart. 8F 5025 $6.98. Cass. CF 5025 $6.98.
Crawdaddy. August. p21. 650w. 2½

443 Barry Mann. LAY IT ALL OUT. New Design Z 30876 $5.98. Cart. ZA 30876 $6.95.
High Fidelity. March. p116. 25w. 2

444 Manfred Mann. EARTH BAND. Polydor PD 5015 $5.98. Cart. 8F 5015 $6.98. Cass. CF 5015 $6.98.
Audio. October. p89. 50w. 3
Crawdaddy. April 16. p15. 500w. 3
Creem. April. p63-4. 725w. 3
Gramophone. November. p984. 50w. 1
High Fidelity. April. p106-7. 150w. 2½
Records and Recordings. March. p122. 175w. 2
Rolling Stone. March 30. p54. 650w. 1
Stereo Review. July. p94. 200w. 2½

445 Manfred Mann. THE GREATEST... Music for Pleasure MFP 5269 (E). (Reissue.)
Gramophone. August. p397. 75w. 3
Hi-Fi News and Record Review. August. p1479. 50w. 1

446 Manfred Mann. THIS IS... Philips 6382 020 (E). (Reissue.)
Gramophone. February. p1443. 50w. 0

447 THE MANY SIDES OF ROCK 'N' ROLL (anthology). United Artists UAS 60025/6 (2 discs) (E). (Reissue.)
Blues Unlimited. December. p28. 100w. 3

448 The Marmalade. SONGS. Decca SKL 5111 (E).
Gramophone. February. p1443. 125w. 2

449 Mar y Sol. Atco 2SD-705 (2 discs) $7.98.
Beetle. November. p29. 1,000w. 3

450 Mark-Almond. II. Blue Thumb BTS 32 $5.98. Cart. M832 $6.95. Cass. M532 $6.95.
Audio. May. p75. 350w. 3½

451 Dave Mason. HEAD KEEPER. Blue Thumb BTS 34 $5.98. Cart. M834 $6.95. Cass. M534 $6.95.
Crawdaddy. April 30. p15. 600w. 3
New York Times--Sunday. March 12. pHF12. 100w. 2

452 Ray Materick. SIDESTREETS. Kanata KAN 10 (Canada).
Beetle. October 17. p22. 650w. 3½

453 Ian Matthews. TIGERS WILL SURVIVE. Vertigo VEL 1010 $5.95. Cart. VC-8-1010 $6.95. Cass. VCR-4-1010 $6.95
Audio. May. p93. 75w. 3
Creem. August. p11. 50w. 2
Gramophone. June. p116. 100w. 3
Library Journal. May 1. p1689. 150w. 3½
New York Times--Sunday. March 19. pD30. 125w. 3½

454 John Mayall. JAZZ-BLUES FUSION. Polydor PD 5027 $5.98. Cart. 5027 $6.98. Cass. CF 5027 $6.98.
Crawdaddy. August. p18. 700w. 2½
Creem. August. p69. 50w. 2½
Creem. September. p11. 25w. ½
Downbeat. March 9. p23. 200w. 3½
Hi-Fi News and Record Review. June. p1128. 200w. 2½
High Fidelity. August. p96. 75w. 3
Popular Music. Summer. p248. 50w. 2
Sound. September. p41. 200w. 4

455 John Mayall. MEMORIES. Polydor PD 5012 $5.98. Cart. 8T F4072 $6.98. Cass. 4T F4072 $6.98. R-R M5012 $6.98.
Crawdaddy. January 16. p11. 550w. 3
Rolling Stone. January 20. p54. 450w. 2
Stereo Review. March. p103. 225w. 3

456 John Mayall. THRU THE YEARS. London 2PS 600/1 (2 discs) $5.98. Cass. L57188 $6.95.
Crawdaddy. March 19. p16. 600w. 2
Jazz Journal. February. p35. 100w. 2
Rolling Stone. January 20. p54. 450w. 2½

457 Judy Mayhan. Decca DL 75287 $4.98. Cart. 65287 $6.95 Cass. 735287 $6.95.
Stereo Review. March. p103. 100w. 1

458 Bob McBride. BUTTERFLY DAYS. Capitol ST 6384 (Canada).
Beetle. December 31. p20. 200w. 2½

459 Marjorie McCoy. THE OTHER SIDE. Capitol ST 840 $5.98.
Stereo Review. October. p98. 200w. 1

460 Country Joe MacDonald. INCREDIBLE! LIVE! COUNTRY JOE! Vanguard 79316 $5.98. Cart. M89316 $6.95. Cass. M59316 $6.95.
Crawdaddy. April 16. p17. 450w. 3
Creem. June. p66-7. 600w. 1½
Rolling Stone. March 16. p60. 375w. 3

461 Country Joe MacDonald. WAR, WAR, WAR. Vanguard VSD 79315 $5.98.
Gramophone. March. p1614. 50w. 1

462 Michael McGear. WOMAN. Island ILPS 9191 (E).
Hi-Fi News and Record Review. July. p1309. 50w. 3

463 McGuinness Flint. HAPPY BIRTHDAY RUTHY BABY. Capitol ST 794 $5.98.
Library Journal. March 1. p856. 100w. 3

464 Ellen McIlwaine. HONKY TONK ANGEL. Polydor PD 5021 $5.98.
Beetle. August. p21. 600w. 3½
High Fidelity. June. p103. 250w. 3
New York Times--Sunday. June 11. pD28. 175w. 3
Stereo Review. August. p90, 92. 525w. 4

465 McKendree Spring. 3. Decca DL 75332 $4.98.
New York Times--Sunday. June 11. pD28, 30. 125w. 4
Stereo Review. July. p94. 100w. 2

466 Murray McLauchlan. True North TN 9 (Canada).
Sound. December. p40. 200w. 4

467 Murray McLauchlan. SONG FROM THE STREET. Epic E 31166 $5.98.
Library Journal. June 15. p2167. 175w. 3
Sound. April. p21. 100w. 4

468 Don McLean. AMERICAN PIE. United Artists UAS 5535 $5.98. Cart. U 8299 $6.98.
Audio. May. p92-3. 50w. 3
Gramophone. June. p112. 25w. 0
Hi-Fi News and Record Review. May. p938. 150w. 1
High Fidelity. April. p108. 100w. 2
Popular Music. Winter. p125. 100w. 4
Rolling Stone. January 20. p49-50. 1,000w. 4

469 Don McLean. TAPESTRY. United Artists UAS 5522 $5.98. Cart. U8280 $6.98. Cass. K0280 $6.98.
Gramophone. August. p397. 50w. 2
Hi-Fi News and Record Review. August. p1475. 50w. 1

470 Ralph McTell. YOU WELL-MEANING BROUGHT ME HERE. Paramount PAS 6015 $4.98.
Rolling Stone. March 16. p60. 400w. 3

471 Bill Medley. A SONG FOR YOU. A & M 3505 $5.98. Cart. 8T 3505 $6.98. Cass. CS 3505 $6.98.
High Fidelity. January. p110-11. 400w. 5

472 Melanie. THE FOUR SIDES OF MELANIE. Buddah BDS 95005 (2 discs) $6.98. Cart. J89505 DP $7.95. Cass. J59505 DP $7.95. (Reissue.)
New York Times--Sunday. April 30. pD28. 100w. 2½

Records and Recordings. November. p106. 225w. 2½

473 Melanie. GARDEN IN THE CITY. Buddah BDS 5095 $5.98. Cart. M85095 $6.95. Cass. M55095 $6.95.
Gramophone. June. p111. 75w. 1
Hi-Fi News and Record Review. May. p938. 200w. 3

474 Melanie. GATHER ME. Neighborhood NRS 47001 $5.98. Cart. M85003 $6.95. Cass M55003 $6.95.
Crawdaddy. February 20. p14-5. 1,000w. 4
Gramophone. February. p1437. 25w. 2
High Fidelity. April. p111. 100w. 2
Stereo Review. March. p103. 300w. 3

475 Barry Melton. MELTON, LEVY, AND THE DAY BROTHERS. Columbia KC 31279 $5.98. Cart. CA 31279 $6.98.
Creem. December. p86. 25w. 1½

476 Augie Meyer. WESTERN HEAD MUSIC CO. Polydor PD 24 4069 $4.98.
Crawdaddy. January 16. p17. 150w. 3
Popular Music. Fall. p61. 50w. 2½

477 Michaelangelo. ONE VOICE MANY. Columbia C 30686 $5.98.
Popular Music. Winter. p124. 50w. 3

478 Lee Michaels. SPACE AND FIRST TAKES. A & M SP 4336 $5.98.
Crawdaddy. June 11. p18. 375w. 2
Records and Recordings. July. p94. 275w. 4

479 Middle of the Road. ACCELERATION. RCA LSP 4674 $5.98. Cart. P8S 1900 $6.95. Cass. PK 1900 $6.95.
Creem. August. p66. 50w. 0

480 Buddy Miles Express. LIVE. Mercury SRM 2-7500 (2 discs) $9.98. Cart. MCT-8-2-7500 $9.95. Cass. MCT-4-2-7500 $9.95.
Beetle. March 29. p17-8. 600w. 3
Gramophone. May. p1952. 50w. 1
Previews. October. p47. 175w. 2
Records and Recordings. March. p124. 200w. 1

481 Steve Miller Band. RECALL THE BEGINNING...A JOURNEY FROM EDEN. Capitol SMAS 11022 $5.98. Cart. 8XW 11022 $6.95. Cass. 4XW 11022 $6.95.
Popular Music. Summer. p253. 50w. 0
Records and Recordings. August. p90. 250w. 2½

482 Steve Miller Band. ROCK LOVE. Capitol SW 748 $5.98. Cart. 8XW 748 $6.95. Cass. 4XW 748 $6.95.

Beetle. January 22. p17. 450w. $2\frac{1}{2}$
Gramophone. February. p1438. 50w. 1
Records and Recordings. April. p107. 300w. $1\frac{1}{2}$

483 Ronnie Milsap. Warner Bros. WS 1934 $5.98. Cart. M81934 $6.95. Cass. M51934 $6.95.
Creem. January. p69. 50w. $2\frac{1}{2}$

484 Joni Mitchell. BLUE. Reprise MS 2038 $5.98. Cart. M82038 $6.95. Cass. M52038 $6.95.
American Record Guide. February. p284. 375w. 5

485 Joni Mitchell. FOR THE ROSES. Asylum SD 5057 $5.98.
New York Times--Sunday. December 10. pD37. 25w. 3

486 Mixtures. Polydor 2383 083 (E).
Gramophone. March. p1613. 25w. 0

487 Moby Grape. GREAT GRAPE. Columbia C 31098 $5.98. Cart. CA 31098 $6.98. (Reissue.)
Creem. August. p67. 25w. $3\frac{1}{2}$
High Fidelity. May. p116. 25w. 4
New York Times--Sunday. March 12. pHF12. 75w. $2\frac{1}{2}$

488 Moby Grape. 20 GRANITE CREEK. Reprise RS 6460 $5.98. Cart. M86460 $5.95. Cass. M56460 $6.95.
Stereo Review. January. p109. 1,250w. 2

489 Mom's Apple Pie. Brown Bag BB 14200 $5.98.
Rolling Stone. December 21. p68. 750w. 0

490 Moody Blues. SEVENTH SOJOURN. Threshold THS 7 $5.98.
Beetle. December 31. p20. 700w. $2\frac{1}{2}$

491 Moondog. 2. Columbia KC 30897 $5.98.
Crawdaddy. April 16. p18. 600w. 3
Stereo Review. April. p97. 200w. $2\frac{1}{2}$

492 Morning. STRUCK LIKE SILVER. Fantasy 9402 $4.98. Cart. M89402 $6.95. Cass. M59402 $6.95.
Gramophone. August. p398. 25w. 0
Hi-Fi News and Record Review. July. p1309. 50w. 3

493 Ron Paul Morin and Luke P. Williams. PEACEFUL COMPANY. Capitol ST 11052 $5.98.
Popular Music. Summer. p253-4. 50w. 2

494 Van Morrison. ST. DOMINIC'S PREVIEW. Warner Bros. BS 2633 $5.98.
Crawdaddy. November. p77-8. 1,100w. $3\frac{1}{2}$
Creem. October. p54. 400w. 3
Hi-Fi News and Record Review. December. p2463-4. 300w. $3\frac{1}{2}$

High Fidelity. November. p130. 25w. 2½
Popular Music. Summer. p247. 100w. 4
Records and Recordings. November. p106. 250w. 0
Stereo Review. December. p98. 225w. 4

495 Van Morrison. TUPELO HONEY. Warner Bros. WS 1950 $5.98. Cart. M81950 $6.95. Cass. M51950 $6.95.
Beetle. January 22. p17. 550w. 2
Creem. January. p58-9. 1,750w. 5
Gramophone. February. p1438,1443. 125w. 3
High Fidelity. February. p112. 300w. 2½
Library Journal. February 1. p481. 150w. 3½
Sound. March. p21. 125w. 4
Stereo Review. January. p110. 200w. 2

496 Bob Mosley. Reprise MS 2068 $5.98. Cart. M82068 $6.95. Cass. M52068 $6.95.
Creem. September. p50-1. 750w. 4

497 Mother Hen. RCA LSP 4641 $5.98.
Previews. September. p43. 150w. 3

498 The Mothers of Invention. JUST ANOTHER BAND FROM L.A. Bizarre/Reprise MS 2075 $5.98. Cart. M82075 $6.95. Cass. M52075 $6.95.
Beetle. June. p22-3. 750w. 3
Crawdaddy. June 11. p15. 700w. 3
Creem. August. p11. 25w. 1
Creem. August. p69. 50w. 1
Downbeat. September 14. p22. 200w. 5
Gramophone. September. p580. 150w. 3
High Fidelity. July. p100. 200w. 2
Previews. October. p47. 200w. 2
Records and Recordings. August. p90. 200w. 0
Rolling Stone. June 8. p60. 500w. 1
Stereo Review. November. p90-2. 125w. 2

499 Mott the Hoople. ALL THE YOUNG DUDES. Columbia KC 31750 $5.98.
Popular Music. Fall. p93. 50w. 2½
Rolling Stone. December 7. p63. 750w. 3

500 Mott the Hoople. BRAIN CAPERS. Atlantic SD 8304 $5.98. Cart. M88304 $6.95. Cass. M58304 $6.95.
Crawdaddy. April 30. p17. 700w. 3
Creem. April. p62-3. 975w. 3
Rolling Stone. March 2. p60. 350w. 3½

501 Mountain. FLOWERS OF EVIL. Windfall 5501 $4.98. Cart. 8119-5501M $5.95. Cass. 5119-5501M $6.95.
High Fidelity. June. p104,106. 500w. 2
Stereo Review. May. p94. 150w. 3½

502 Mountain. THE ROAD GOES EVER ON. Windfall 5502 $4.98. Cart. 8119-5502M $6.95. Cass. 5119-5520M $6.95.
Rolling Stone. June 22. p58. 550w. 3

503 Martin Mull. Capricorn 0106 $5.98.
Creem. November. p69. 775w. 3
Popular Music. Fall. p90. 25w. 0

504 Mums and Dads. London ZGL 121 (E).
Gramophone. June. p112. 25w. 1

505 J. F. Murphy and Salt. Elektra EKS 75024 $5.98. Cart. 85024 $6.98. Cass. 55024 $6.98.
Creem. June. p77. 25w. 0
New York Times--Sunday. June 11. pD30. 175w. $3\frac{1}{2}$
Stereo Review. July. p69. 375w. 4

506 Michael Murphy. GERONIMO'S CADILLAC. A & M SP 4358 $5.98. Cart. 8T 4358 $6.95. Cass. CS 4358 $6.95.
Sound. October. p42. 275w. 4

507 THE MUSIC PEOPLE (anthology). Columbia C3X 31280 (3 discs) $5.98. Cart. CAX 31280 $7.98. Cass. CTX 31280 $7.98. (Reissue.)
Hi-Fi News and Record Review. July. p1309. 50w. $3\frac{1}{2}$

508 Charlie Musselwhite. TAKIN' MY TIME. Arhoolie 1056 $6.00.
Ethnomusicology. October. p586-7. 600w. 3

509 NRBQ. SCRAPS. Kama Sutra KSBS 2045 $4.98. Cart. M82045 $6.95. Cass. M52045 $6.95.
Creem. June. p77. 50w. $\frac{1}{2}$
High Fidelity. June. p102. 225w. 2
New York Times--Sunday. June 11. pD30. 175w. 3
Rolling Stone. June 8. p56. 550w. 4

510 Narasota. ROOTIN'. ABC ABCX 757 $5.98.
Popular Music. Summer. p248. 50w. 3

511 Graham Nash and David Crosby. Atlantic SD 7220 $5.98.
Beetle. June. p21. 675w. 2
Crawdaddy. August. p16. 350w. 1
Creem. August. p11. 25w. 1
Gramophone. July. p256. 50w. 0
High Fidelity. July. p98. 50w. 1
New York Times--Sunday. August 20. pD22. 250w. 4
Popular Music. Summer. p252. 50w. 3
Records and Recordings. June. p84. 250w. 3
Rolling Stone. May 25. p62-3. 450w. 3
Stereo Review. October. p98. 150w. 5

512 Nanette Natal. THE BEGINNING. Evolution 2023 $4.98.
Audio. October. p89. 50w. 3

513 Ricky Nelson. United Artists UAS 9960 (2 discs) $5.98. (Reissue.)
Audio. May. p94. 25w. 2½
Crawdaddy. May 14. p18. 300w. 3
Popular Music. Spring. p128. 50w. 4
Rolling Stone. March 30. p49-50. 1,500w. 4

514 Ricky Nelson. GARDEN PARTY. Decca $4.98.
Creem. August. p67. 200w. 3

515 Ricky Nelson and the Stone Canyon Band. RUDY THE FIFTH. Decca DL 75297 $4.98. Cart. 6-75297 $6.98. Cass. C-735297 $6.98.
Crawdaddy. February 20. p18. 500w. 2½
Gramophone. April. p1779. 25w. 0
High Fidelity. May. p112. 75w. 2½
Popular Music. Winter. p124. 25w. 1

516 Tracy Nelson and Mother Earth. Reprise MS 2054 $5.98. Cart. M82054 $6.95. Cass. M52054 $6.95.
Crawdaddy. April 2. p16. 800w. 4
New York Times--Sunday. March 19. pD30. 125w. 2½
Rolling Stone. June 8. p58. 350w. 2½
Stereo Review. July. p94. 100w. 2

517 Michael Nesmith. AND THE HITS JUST KEEP ON COMING. RCA LSP 4695 $5.98. Cart. P8S 1926 $6.95. Cass. PK 1926 $6.95.
Creem. October. p56-7. 425w. 2½

518 Michael Nesmith and the Second National Band. TANTAMOUNT TO TREASON, VOLUME 1. RCA SF 8276 (E).
Crawdaddy. April 16. p19. 350w. 2½
Gramophone. November. p910. 225w. 4

519 NEW AGE OF ATLANTIC (anthology). Atlantic K 20024 (E). (Reissue.)
Gramophone. May. p1955. 50w. 3½

520 NEW MAGIC IN A DUSTY WORLD (anthology). Elektra K 22002 (E). (Reissue.)
Gramophone. December. p1222. 25w. 1½

521 New Riders of the Purple Sage. Columbia C 30888 $5.98. Cart. 84088 $6.98. Cass. 54088 $6.98.
Popular Music. Fall. p59-60. 100w. 4½

522 New Riders of the Purple Sage. POWERGLIDE. Columbia KC 31284 $5.98. Cart. CA 31284 $6.98. Cass. CT 31284 $6.98.

Canadian Stereo Guide. Fall. p28. 100w. 3½
Crawdaddy. August. p18. 600w. 3½
Creem. September. p11. 25w. 1

523 New York Rock Ensemble. FREEDOMBURGER. Columbia K 31317 $5.98. Cass. CT 31317 $6.98.
American Record Guide. September. p673. 50w. 1

524 Mickey Newbury. 'FRISCO MABEL JOY. Elektra EKS 74107 $5.98. Cart. ET 84107 $6.98. Cass. TC 54107 $6.98.
Crawdaddy. March 19. p17. 400w. 3
Gramophone. May. p1951. 50w. 2
High Fidelity. February. p112,116. 1,200. 3
New York Times--Sunday. May 21. pD32. 50w. 2½
Stereo Review. March. p104. 75w. ½

525 Mickey Newbury. SINGS HIS OWN. RCA LSP 4675 $5.98. Cart. P8S 1901 $6.95.
Hi-Fi News and Record Review. July. p1312. 25w. 2½
Records and Recordings. September. p101. 100w. 1

526 Randy Newman. LIVE. Reprise RS 6459 $5.98. Cart. M86459 $6.95. Cass. M5659 $6.95.
American Record Guide. June. p529. 275w. 4

527 Randy Newman. SAIL AWAY. Reprise MS 2064 $5.98. Cart. M82064 $6.95. Cass. M52064 $6.95.
Crawdaddy. August. p17. 500w. 4
Creem. September. p11. 50w. 4
Creem. October. p60. 300w. 1½
High Fidelity. September. p102. 300w. 4½
New York Times--Sunday. June 25. pD24. 600w. 5
Popular Music. Fall. p88. 50w. 3
Records and Recordings. September. p94. 200w. 3½
Stereo Review. September. p70-1. 300w. 4

528 Harry Nilsson. NILSSON SCHMILSSON. RCA LSP 4515 $5.98. Cart. P8S 1734 $6.95. Cass. PK 1734 $6.95.
American Record Guide. June. p528. 225w. 4
Crawdaddy. March 5. p20. 500w. 2
Stereo Review. March. p104. 300w. 4

529 Harry Nilsson. SON OF SCHMILSSON. RCA LSP 4717 $5.98.
Creem. August. p74. 50w. 2½
Creem. October. p59-60. 250w. 2
Gramophone. October. p778. 100w. 2
High Fidelity. October. p121. 200w. 3
Popular Music. Fall. p1. 50w. 0
Records and Recordings. November. p106-7. 125w. 1
Rolling Stone. August 17. p49. 1,500w. 2½

530 Nitty Gritty Dirt Band. ALL THE GOOD TIMES. United Artists UAS 5553 $5.98.
Crawdaddy. May 14. p21. 350w. $2\frac{1}{2}$
Creem. May. p71. 475w. 4
Popular Music. Spring. p188. 75w. 3
Records and Recordings. May. p99. 200w. $4\frac{1}{2}$

531 Noah. PEACEMAN'S FARM. Dunhill D 50117 $5.98. Cart. M85117 $6.95. Cass. M55117. $6.95.
Audio. October. p90. 25w. 0

532 Tom Northcott. UPSIDE DOWNSIDE. Uni 73108 $4.98. Cart. 8-73108 $6.95. Cass. 2-73108 $6.95.
Beetle. January 22. p20. 400w. 0
Popular Music. Fall. p62. 50w. 2

533 NUGGETS (anthology). Elektra 7E-2006 (2 discs) $6.98. Cart. T8 2006 $9.98. Cass. C2 2006 $9.98.
Creem. December. p54-6. 1,850w. 5
Popular Music and Society. Fall. p93-4. 75w. 5

534 Laura Nyro and Labelle. GONNA TAKE A MIRACLE. Columbia KC 30987 $5.98. R-R CR 30987 $6.98. Cart. CT 30987 $6.98. Cass. CA 30987 $6.98.
Crawdaddy. February 20. p15. 1,000w. 2
Creem. March. p53-4. 1,150w. $3\frac{1}{2}$
Downbeat. March 2. p20. 250w. $4\frac{1}{2}$
Hi-Fi News and Record Review. July. p1312. 50w. $2\frac{1}{2}$
High Fidelity. April. p109. 50w. 1
Library Journal. February 15. p665. 150w. $1\frac{1}{2}$
Rolling Stone. January 20. p49. 875w. $2\frac{1}{2}$
Stereo Review. April. p97. 350w. 1

535 Yoko Ono and the Plastic Ono Band. FLY. Apple SVBB 3380 $4.98. Cart. 8XFF $6.98. Cass. 4XFF $6.98.
Creem. March. p52-3. 1,775w. 1
High Fidelity. January. p77. 350w. $2\frac{1}{2}$

536 Tony Orlando and Dawn. Bell BELLS 205 (E).
Gramophone. July. p255. 25w. 0

537 Osibisa. HEADS. Decca DL 75368 $5.98.
Beetle. December 31. p19. 600w. 5
Popular Music. Fall. p87. 50w. $3\frac{1}{2}$

538 Osibisa. WAYAYA. Decca DL 75327 $5.98.
Audio. June. p76. 300w. $3\frac{1}{2}$
Downbeat. November 9. p27. 250w. 2
Records and Recordings. March. p122. 150w. 3

539 Donny Osmond. TO YOU WITH LOVE: DONNY. MGM SE 4797 $5.98. Cart. 8130-4797 $6.95. Cass. 5130-4797. $6.95.

American Record Guide. March. p333. 175w. 1

540 The Pack. FUNK OFF. ABKCO AB 4217 $5.98. (Reissue.)
New York Times--Sunday. December 31. pD30. 100w. 2

541 Paladin. CHANGE. Island ILPS 9190 (E).
Records and Recordings. June. p84-5. 200w. 4

542 Panhandle. Decca SKL 5105 (E).
Hi-Fi News and Record Review. July. p1312. 50w. 2½

543 Van Dyke Parks. DISCOVER AMERICA. Warner Bros. BS 2589 $5.98.
Crawdaddy. September. p18. 1,250w. 3½
Creem. October. p61. 350w. 2
High Fidelity. September. p103. 200w. 2½

544 Patto. HOLD YOUR FIRE. Vertigo VER 1008 $5.98.
Creem. April. p71. 50w. 3

545 Patto. ROLL 'EM, SMOKE 'EM, PUT ANOTHER LINE OUT. Island SW 9322 $5.98.
Creem. December. p63. 25w. 3
Rolling Stone. November 23. p70. 400w. 3½

546 Pearls Before Swine. BEAUTIFUL LIES YOU COULD LIVE IN. Reprise RS 6467 $5.98. Cart. M86467 $6.95. Cass. M56467 $6.95.
Stereo Review. October. p98,100. 100w. 2

547 The Peddlers and the London Philharmonic Orchestra. SUITE LONDON. Philips 6308 102 (E).
Hi-Fi News and Record Review. June. p1128. 300w. 3

548 David Peel and the Lower East Side. THE POPE SMOKES DOPE. Apple SW 3391 $5.98. Cart. 8XW 3391 $6.95. Cass. 4XW 3391 $6.98.
Creem. August. p11. 25w. 0
High Fidelity. August. p97. 250w. 2½
Popular Music. Summer. p250. 50w. 1
Previews. November. p46. 175w. 3½
Rolling Stone. June 8. p55-6. 750w. 4

549 People's Victory Orchestra and Chorus. THE SCHOOL. The People's Music Works $3.00.
Crawdaddy. December. p85-6. 300w. 2½

550 People's Victory Orchestra and Chorus. WELTSCHMERZEN. People's Music Works $3.00.
Crawdaddy. December. p85-6. 300w. 3
Stereo Review. December. p98,100. 275w. 0

551 Perth County Conspiracy. ALIVE. Columbia GES 90037 (2 discs) (Canada).
Previews. November. p42. 200w. 2½

552 Shawn Phillips. COLLABORATION. A & M SP 4324 $5.98.
Stereo Review. May. p94-5. 200w. 3

553 Pilot. RCA LSP 4730 $5.98.
Rolling Stone. November 9. p64. 500w. 2½

554 Pink Floyd. MEDDLE. Harvest SMAS 832 $5.98. Cart. 8XW 832 $6.98. Cass. 4XW 832 $6.98.
Gramophone. January. p1283. 50w. 2

555 Pink Floyd. OBSCURED BY CLOUDS. Harvest ST 11078 $4.98. Cart. 8XT 11078 $6.98. Cass. 4XT 11078 $6.98.
Crawdaddy. September. p18. 400w. 3
Popular Music. Fall. p1. 50w. 4

556 Plainsong. IN SEARCH OF AMELIA EARHART. Elektra EKS 75044 $5.98.
Popular Music. Fall. p94. 50w. 2
Records and Recordings. December. p98. 200w. ½

557 Poco. FROM THE INSIDE. Epic KE 30753 $5.98. Cart. EA 30753 $6.98. Cass. ET 30753 $6.98.
High Fidelity. January. p116-7. 150w. 2
Sound. February. p18. 125w. 3

558 Poco. A GOOD FEELIN' TO KNOW. Epic KE 31601 $5.98. Cart. EA 31601 $6.98. Cass. ET 31601 $6.98.
Rolling Stone. December 21. p64. 900w. 4

559 Pamela Polland. Columbia KC 31116 $5.98. Cart. CA 31116 $6.98. Cass. CT 31116 $6.98.
Creem. August. p66. 50w. 0

560 David Pomeranz. TIME TO FLY. Decca DL 75329 $5.98.
Audio. May. p95. 50w. 2½
Crawdaddy. May 14. p15. 675w. 3
Creem. May. p70-1. 375w. 1

561 Jim Post. COLORADO EXILE. Fantasy 9401 $4.98. Cart. M89401 $6.95. Cass. M59401 $6.95.
Crawdaddy. May 28. p20. 400w. 3

562 Jim Post with Jim Schwall. SLOW TO 20. Fantasy 9408 $4.98.
Crawdaddy. December. p81. 950w. 3½

563 Potliquor. LEVEE BLUES. Janus JLS 3033 $5.98.
Crawdaddy. May 14. p16. 375w. 3

564 Risa Potters. TAKE ME AWAY. Buddah BDS 5115 $5.98.
Popular Music. Fall. p91. 50w. 4½

565 Billy Preston. I WROTE A SIMPLE SONG. A & M SP 3507 $5.98. Cart. 8T 3507 $6.95. Cass. CS 8507 $6.95.
Crawdaddy. March 5. p18. 300w. 2½
High Fidelity. March. p112. 250w. 3
Stereo Review. June. p102. 100w. 2

566 Dory Previn. MYTHICAL KINGS AND IGUANAS. Mediarts 41-10 $5.98. Cart. U8282 $6.98. Cass. K0282 $6.98.
Hi-Fi News and Record Review. May. p939. 100w. 3

567 Dory Previn. REFLECTIONS IN A MUD PUDDLE/TAPS, TREMORS AND TIME STEPS. United Artists UAS 5536 $5.98.
American Record Guide. July. p576. 100w. 0
Crawdaddy. March 5. p15. 500w. 2½
Hi-Fi News and Record Review. August. p1479. 25w. 1½
New York Times--Sunday. January 16. pD22. 1000w. 4½

568 Jim Price. SUNDEGO'S TRAVELLING ORCHESTRA. ABC Dunhill DSX 50125 $5.98. Cart. M85125 $6.95. Cass. M55125 $6.95.
Crawdaddy. November. p84-5. 450w. 3
High Fidelity. October. p120. 300w. 2½

569 John Prine. Atlantic SD 8296 $5.98. Cart. M88296 $6.95. Cass. M58296 $6.95.
Audio. August. p63. 50w. 3
Crawdaddy. January 16. p51. 800w. 4
High Fidelity. February. p120. 25w. 2
New York Times--Sunday. May 21. pD32. 150w. 4
Popular Music. Winter. p122. 25w. 3
Records and Recordings. May. p100. 275w. 1

570 John Prine. DIAMONDS IN THE ROUGH. Atlantic SD 7240 $5.98. Cart. TP 7240 $6.97. Cass. CS 7240 $6.97.
Popular Music and Society. Fall. p87. 50w. 3½
Sing Out. September/October. p39. 200w. 3
Sound. November. p36. 325w. 4

571 Procul Harum. THE CONCERT WITH THE EDMONTON SYMPHONY ORCHESTRA. A & M SP 4335 $5.98. Cart. 8T 4335 $6.95. Cass. CA 4335 $6.95.
Beetle. July. p20. 1,500w. 4
Crawdaddy. August. p18. 500w. 2½
Creem. August. p66. 25w. 1
Canadian Stereo Guide. Summer. p66. 100w. 3
Popular Music. Summer. p249-50. 100w. 4

572 Pure Food and Drug Act. CHOICE CUTS. Epic Ke 31401 $5.98. Cart. EA 31401 $6.98. Cass. ET 31401 $6.98.
Popular Music. Fall. p89. 75w. 4½

573 Pure Prairie League. RCA LSP 4650 $5.98. Cart. P8S 1885 $6.98.
Popular Music. Summer. p249. 50w. 2
Sound. September. p41. 200w. 3

574 Pure Prairie League. BUSTIN' OUT. RCA LSP 4769 $5.98.
Popular Music. Fall. p89. 50w. 3

575 Quicksilver Messenger Service. COMIN' THRU. Capitol SMAS 11002 $5.98. Cart. 8XW 11002 $6.98. Cass. 4XW 11002 $6.98.
Rolling Stone. June 8. p58, 60. 300w. 0

576 The Quinaimes Band. Elektra EKS 74096 $5.98. Cart. ET 84096 $6.98. Cass. TC 54096 $6.98.
Stereo Review. January. p113-4. 125w. 3

577 Quintessence. SELF. RCA SF 8273 (E).
Records and Recordings. June. p85. 250w. 4

578 Quiver. GONE IN THE MORNING. Warner Bros. BS 2630 $5.98.
Gramophone. July. p258-7. 25w. 1
Records and Recordings. June. p85. 150w. 2½

579 R.E.O. Speedwagon. Epic KE 31089 $5.98.
American Record Guide. June. p529. 200w. 1
Creem. May. p68. 400w. 3

580 The Raiders. GREATEST HITS, VOLUME 2. Columbia C 30386 $5.98. (Reissue.)
Audio. May. p94. 25w. 2½

581 Rain. THE RAIN ALBUM. Axe 501 (Canada).
Beetle. May. p22. 200w. ½

582 Bonnie Raitt. Warner Bros. WS 1953 $5.98. Cart. M81953 $6.95. Cass. M51953 $6.95.
American Record Guide. July. p576. 400w. 4
Creem. March. p53. 325w. 4
Creem. March. p57. 50w. 3
High Fidelity. March. p108-9. 300w. 3
Stereo Review. March. p104, 108. 300w. 2½

583 Bonnie Raitt. GIVE IT UP. Warner Bros. BS 2643 $5.98.
New York Times--Sunday. December 10. pD32. 350w. 3
Popular Music. Fall. p89. 75w. 4

Rolling Stone. October 26. p60. 600w. 3
Sing Out. September/October. p39. 200w. 2

584 Ramatam. Atlantic SD 7236 $5.98. Cart. TP 7236 $6.95. Cass. CS 7236 $6.95.
Crawdaddy. December. p84. 175w. 2
Creem. December. p86. 25w. 1½
Sound. October. p43. 150w. 4

585 Randy Ramos. HARD KNOCKS AND BAD TIMES. Fantasy 8423 $5.98.
Popular Music. Summer. p247. 50w. 3

586 Elliott Randall. ROCK AND ROLL CITY. Polydor PD 5026 $5.98.
Creem. August. p66. 25w. ½

587 Fela Ransome-Kuti and Africa '70, with Ginger Baker. LIVE! Signpost SP 8401 $5.98. Cart. TP 8401 $6.95. Cass. G8401 $6.95.
Records and Recordings. June. p89. 125w. 2½
Rolling Stone. November 9. p64. 800w. 1½

588 Rare Earth. IN CONCERT. Rare Earth R 5340 (2 discs) $11.96. Cart. R 81534/5 $11.98. Cass. R75534/5 $11.98.
Audio. May. p95. 75w. 3½

589 The Rascals. ISLAND OF REAL. Columbia KC 31103 $5.98. Cart. CA 31103 $6.98. Cass. CT 31103 $6.98.
Crawdaddy. June 11. p16. 850w. 3
Rolling Stone. May 25. p64. 800w. 1

590 Raspberries. Capitol SK 11036 $5.98. Cart. 8XK 11036 $6.98. Cass. 4XK 11036 $6.98.
Beetle. June. p20. 750w. 4
Creem. September. p11. 25w. 0
Stereo Review. December. p100. 100w. 0

591 Rasputin's Stash. Cotillion SD 9046 $5.98. Cart. M89046 $6.95. Cass. M59046 $6.95.
High Fidelity. January. p120. 25w. 3

592 Ratchell. Decca DL 75330 $5.98.
Rolling Stone. June 8. p55. 950w. 1½

593 David Rea. BY THE GRACE OF GOD. Capitol ST 826 $5.98.
Beetle. August. p22. 750w. 3½
Ontario Library Review. December. p242. 25w. 3½
Popular Music. Winter. p126. 25w. 1
Previews. December. p242. 25w. 3½

594 Redbone. MESSAGE FROM A DRUM. Epic KE 30815 $5.98. Cart. EA 30815 $6.98. Cass. ET 30815 $6.98.
Crawdaddy. March 19. p18. 700w. 3½
Creem. April. p71. 50w. ½

595 Helen Reddy. Capitol ST 857 $5.98. Cart. 8XT 857 $6.98. Cass. 4XT 857 $6.98.
Crawdaddy. March 5. p18. 500w. 2½
Gramophone. April. p1775. 100w. 3
New York Times--Sunday. January 2. pD20. 250w. 4
Stereo Review. April. p99. 225w. 1½

596 Redwing. WHAT THE COUNTRY NEEDS... Fantasy 9405 $4.98.
Creem. September. p57. 25w. 2

597 Lou Reed. RCA LSP 4701 $5.98. Cart. P8S 1931 $6.95. Cass. PK 1931 $6.95.
Crawdaddy. September. p20. 300w. 3½
Hi-Fi News and Record Review. September. p1685. 150w. 2½
Popular Music. Summer. p250. 25w. 1
Rolling Stone. May 25. p68. 1,000w. 4

598 Lou Reed. TRANSFORMER. RCA LSP 4807 $5.98.
New York Times--Sunday. December 17. pD34-5. 400w. 1

599 Neil Reid. SMILE. Decca SKL 5136 (E).
Gramophone. September. p578. 25w. 0

600 Renaissance. PROLOGUE. Capitol SMAS 11116 $5.98.
Popular Music. Fall. p93. 25w. 3

601 Reparata and the Delrons. ROCK AND ROLL REVOLUTION. Avco 6467 250 (E).
Gramophone. September. p580. 100w. 1

602 REVELATIONS (anthology). Revelation REV 1A-3F (3 discs) (E).
Hi-Fi News and Record Review. November. p2202. 100w. 0

603 Paul Revere and the Raiders. COUNTRY WINE. Columbia KC 31106 $5.98. Cart. CA 31106 $6.98. Cass. CT 31106 $6.98.
Creem. August. p66. 25w. ½

604 Revival. Kama Sutra KSBS 2047 $5.98. Cart. M82047 $6.95. Cass. M52047 $6.95.
Creem. June. p77. 25w. 0
New York Times--Sunday. March 26. pD28. 125w. 2½

605 Emitt Rhodes. MIRROR. ABC Dunhill DSX 50111 $5.98. Cart. M85111 $6.95. Cass. M55111 $6.95.
Crawdaddy. January 30. p22. 800w. 2½
New York Times--Sunday. February 27. pD32. 150w. 0

606 Charlie Rich. A TIME FOR TEARS. Sun 6467 021 (E). (Reissue.)
Gramophone. September. p580. 200w. 3

607 Road. Kama Sutra KSBS 2012 $5.98. Cart. M82012 $6.95. Cass. M52012 $6.95.
Crawdaddy. December. p84. 175w. 1½
Creem. December. p63. 50w. 2

608 ROCK 'N' ROLL IS HERE TO STAY (anthology). United Artists UAS 29336 (E). (Reissue.)
Blues Unlimited. May. p28. 25w. 2½

609 THE ROCK AND ROLL STARS, VOLUME 4 (anthology). Joy JS 5020 (E). (Reissue.)
Gramophone. December. p1225. 50w. 2½

610 Tommy Roe. BEGINNINGS. ABC S 732 $5.98. Cart. M8732 $6.95. Cass. M5732 $6.95.
Gramophone. May. p1951. 50w. 1½

611 Kenny Rogers and the First Edition. THE BALLAD OF CALICO. Reprise 2XS 6476 (2 discs) $9.98. Cart. L86476 $9.96. Cass. L56476 $9.96.
High Fidelity. June. p103-4. 125w. 2½

612 Rolling Stones. EXILE ON MAIN STREET. Rolling Stones COC 2-2900 (2 discs) $9.95. Cart. TT2 2900 $9.95. Cass. CST 2900 $9.95.
Beetle. July. p22. 2,400w. 2
Crawdaddy. August. p16. 875w. 2½
Creem. August. p58-60. 3,000w. 1
Canadian Stereo Guide. Fall. p29. 75w. 4
Gramophone. August. p398. 150w. 3
High Fidelity. September. p103. 250w. 2½
New York Times--Sunday. June 4. pD24. 800w. 5
Sound. August. p48. 225w. 4
Stereo Review. December. p100. 100w. 1

613 Rolling Stones. HOT ROCKS 1964-1971. London 2PS 606/7 (2 discs) $9.96. Cart. A8T 4201 $9.98. Cass. AC 4201 $9.98. (Reissue.)
Audio. May. p92. 25w. 4
Crawdaddy. March 5. p14. 475w. 4
High Fidelity. April. p106. 100w. 4
New York Times--Sunday. March 5. pD28. 50w. 4½
Sound. April. p36. 250w. 4
Stereo Review. October. p100. 200w. 5

614 Rolling Stones. MILESTONES. Decca SKL 5098 (E). (Reissue.)
Gramophone. May. p1952. 25w. 2½
Hi-Fi News and Record Review. May. p939. 25w. 2

615 Murray Roman. BUSTED. United Artists UAS 5595 $5.98.
Popular Music. Fall. p91-2. 50w. 3

616 Linda Ronstadt. Capitol SMAS 365 $5.98. Cart. 8XT 635 $6.98. Cass. 4XT 635 $6.98.
Crawdaddy. May 14. p16. 875w. 4
Creem. April. p58. 1,150w. 3
Gramophone. July. p256. 75w. 3
Popular Music. Spring. p128. 75w. 4
Stereo Review. May. p68. 700w. 4

617 Tim Rose. Playboy PB 101 $5.98.
Stereo Review. June. p102. 100w. 3

618 Roxy Music. Reprise 2114 $5.98.
Hi-Fi News and Record Review. August. p1479. 150w. 2½
Records and Recordings. September. p95. 700w. 4

619 James Royal. THE LIGHT AND SHADE. Carnaby 6302 011 (E).
Gramophone. April. p1776. 25w. 1½

620 Rumplestiltskin. Bell 6047 $5.98.
Beetle. January 22. p22. 250w. 3

621 Todd Rundgren. SOMETHING/ANYTHING? Bearsville 2BX 2066 (2 discs) $5.98. Cart. L82066 $7.95. Cass. L52066 $7.95.
Beetle. May. p19. 1,000w. 3
Crawdaddy. May 14. p14. 900w. 3
Gramophone. June. p116. 300w. 3
New York Times--Sunday. March 26. pD28. 225w. 4
Records and Recordings. May. p99-100. 250w. 2

622 Tom Rush. MERRIMACK COUNTY. Columbia KC 31306 $5.98. Cart. CA 31306 $6.98. Cass. CT 31306 $6.98.
New York Times--Sunday. September 10. pD38. 225w. 3½
Popular Music. Summer. p252-3. 75w. 1
Stereo Review. November. p92. 100w. 2½

623 Leon Russell and Marc Benno. ASYLUM CHOIR II. Shelter SW 8910 $5.98. Cart. 8XW 8910 $6.98. Cass. 4XW 8910 $6.98.
American Record Guide. March. p380. 150w. 0
Crawdaddy. February 20. p16. 300w. 2
Stereo Review. March. p108. 200w. 2

624 Leon Russell. CARNEY. Shelter SW 8911 $5.98. Cart. 8XW 8911 $6.98. Cass. 4XW 8911 $6.98.
Crawdaddy. October. p76. 500w. 3½
Creem. November. p69. 750w. 3½
Creem. November. p74. 25w. 2½
High Fidelity. November. p130. 25w. 3
Sound. September. p40-1. 225w. 3
Stereo Review. December. p100,102. 150w. 4

625 Leon Russell with Shelter People. Shelter SW 8903 $5.98. Cart. 8XW 8903 $6.98. Cass. 4XW 8903 $6.98.
American Record Guide. April. p380. 150w. 1

626 Saddhu Band. WHOLE EARTH RHYTHM. Uni 73611 $5.98.
American Record Guide. January. p237. 125w. 0

627 Sailcat. MOTORCYCLE MAMA. Elektra EKS 75029 $5.98. Cart. ET 85029 $6.95. Cass. TC 55029 $6.95.
Creem. September. p55. 350w. 1

628 Ed Sanders. BEER CANS ON THE MOON. Reprise MS 2105 $5.98.
Creem. December. p60. 300w. 3
Rolling Stone. October 26. p56. 750w. 2

629 Veronique Sanson. Elektra K 42106 (E).
Records and Recordings. December. p98. 175w. 1

630 Peter Sarstedt. EVERY WORD YOU SAY IS WRITTEN DOWN. United Artists UAS 5558 $5.98.
Gramophone. January. p1283. 150w. 2

631 Santana. CARAVANSERAI. Columbia KC 31610 $5.98. Cart. CA 31610 $6.98. Cass. CT 31610 $6.98.
Rolling Stone. December 7. p62. 1,600w. 3

632 Santana. Columbia KC 30595 $5.98. R-R CR 30595 $6.98. Cart. CA 30595 $6.98. Cass. CT 30595 $6.98.
Creem. March. p60-1. 2,000w. 2½
High Fidelity. January. p110. 100w. 2½
Stereo Review. January. p84. 300w. 3

633 Carlos Santana and Buddy Miles. LIVE! Columbia KC 31308 $5.98. Cart. CA 31308 $6.98. Cass. CT 31308 $6.98.
Crawdaddy. November. p80. 500w. 2½
Creem. October. p56. 500w. 1
High Fidelity. October. p126. 25w. 2½
Popular Music. Fall. p87. 50w. 0
Stereo Review. December. p102. 75w. 0

634 Merle Saunders. HEAVY TURBULENCE. Fantasy 8421 $4.98.
Stereo Review. June. p102. 50w. 1½

635 Savoy Brown. HELLBOUND TRAIN. Parrot XPAS 71052 $5.98. Cart. M78952 $6.95. Cass. M79552 $6.95.
Crawdaddy. June 11. p16. 800w. 0
Creem. June. p68-9. 900w. 3
Hi-Fi News and Record Review. June. p1128. 25w. 1

636 Savoy Brown. STREET CORNER TALKING. Parrot XPAS 71047 $5.98.
High Fidelity. January. p114. 100w. 2

637 Boz Scaggs. Columbia C 30796 $5.98.
Stereo Review. February. p110-11. 225w. 1½

638 Boz Scaggs. MY TIME. Columbia KC 31384 $5.98. Cart. CA 31384 $6.98. Cass. CT 31384 $6.98.
Creem. December. p63. 25w. 0
Rolling Stone. November 9. p61. 650w. 3

639 Lalo Schifrin. ROCK REQUIEM. Verve V6 8801 $5.98.
Stereo Review. February. p111. 175w. 1

640 Gary and Randy Scruggs. THE SCRUGGS BROTHERS. Vanguard VS 6579 $5.98.
Crawdaddy. May 14. p15. 650w. 3
Creem. August. p67. 25w. 2
Journal of American Folklore. October/December. p399. 25w. 1
New York Times--Sunday. August 20. pD22. 200w. 3½

641 Seadog. SEADOG MUCH. CHLP 5002 (Canada).
Beetle. May. p21. 475w. 3

642 Seals and Croft. SUMMER BREEZE. Warner Bros. BS 2629 $5.98.
Records and Recordings. December. p98,100. 175w. 3
Stereo Review. December. p102. 100w. 2

643 Seals and Croft. YEAR OF SUNDAY. Warner Bros. BS 2568 $5.98. Cart. M82568 $6.95. Cass. M52568 $6.95.
Crawdaddy. March 19. p17. 200w. 2½
High Fidelity. May. p112. 150w. 3½
Stereo Review. February. p104. 450w. 4½

644 Seatrain. MARBLEHEAD MESSENGER. Capitol SMAS 829 $5.98. Cart. 8TW 829 $6.98. Cass. 4XW 829 $6.98.
Beetle. January 22. p20. 600w. 2½

645 John Sebastian. THE FOUR OF US. Reprise MS 2041 $5.98. Cart. M82041 $6.95. Cass. M52041 $6.95.
American Record Guide. April. p381. 250w. 3
Stereo Review. January. p114. 300w. 4

646 Seemon and Marijke. SON OF AMERICA. A & M SP 4309 $5.98.
Popular Music. Winter. p125-6. 50w. 4

647 Bob Seger. MONGREL. Capitol SKAO 499 $5.98. Cart. 8XT 499 $6.98. Cass. 4X9 499 $6.98.
Creem. August. p69. 150w. 3

648 Bob Seger. SMOKING O. P'S. Reprise MS 2109 $5.98. Cart. M82109 $6.95. Cass. M52109 $6.95.
Creem. August. p69. 175w. 2

649 Sha Na Na. THE NIGHT IS STILL YOUNG. Kama Sutra KSBS 2050 $4.98. Cart. M82050 $6.95. Cass. M52050 $6.95.
Creem. September. p54. 500w. 4
High Fidelity. September. p108. 25w. 2
Stereo Review. December. p102. 125w. 4

650 Shadows of Knight. GLORIA, OR BACK DOOR MEN. Dunwhich $4.98.
Creem. September. p57. 25w. 3

651 Sidewinders. RCA LSP 4696 $5.98.
Creem. August. p62. 900w. 3½

652 Ben Sidran. FEEL YOUR GROOVE. Capitol ST 825 $5.98.
High Fidelity. February. p120. 25w. 3

653 The Siegal-Schwall Band. Wooden Nickel WNS 1002 $5.98. Cart. P8WN $6.98. Cass. PKWN 1002 $6.98.
American Record Guide. September. p673. 100w. 2
Blues Unlimited. January. p27. 100w. 4
Crawdaddy. April 16. p17. 300w. 2½
Stereo Review. February. p111, 113. 300w. 4

654 Judee Sill. Asylum SD 5050 $5.98. Cart. M85050 $6.95. Cass. M55050 $6.95.
High Fidelity. January. p112, 114. 350w. 4
Stereo Review. June. p102. 250w. 2

655 Silverhead. Signpost SP 8407 $5.98. Cart. TP 8407 $6.95. Cass. CS 8407 $6.95.
Creem. December. p63. 25w. 0

656 Silver-Stevens. DUSTY ROADS. Lion Records LN 1002 $4.98.
Popular Music. Spring. p128, 184. 75w. 3

657 Shel Silverstein. FREAKIN' AT THE FREAKER'S BALL. Columbia KC 31119 $5.98.
New York Times--Sunday. December 17. pD35. 200w. 0

658 Carly Simon. ANTICIPATION. Elektra EKS 75016 $5.98. Cart. M85016 $6.95. Cass. M55016 $6.95.
Gramophone. June. p116. 50w. 2
High Fidelity. April. p106. 100w. 2
New York Times--Sunday. January 2. pD20. 150w. $3\frac{1}{2}$
Records and Recordings. March. p122. 275w. 4

659 Joe Simon. DROWNING IN THE SEA OF LOVE. Spring 5702 $4.98.
Gramophone. October. p782. 150w. 4

660 Paul Simon. Columbia KC 30750 $5.98. R-R CR 30750 $6.98. Cart. CA 30750 $6.98. Cass. CT 30750 $6.98.
Audio. June. p74. 500w. 4
Crawdaddy. April 2. p14. 1,400w. 3
Gramophone. May. p1951. 75w. $3\frac{1}{2}$
High Fidelity. May. p108. 300w. $1\frac{1}{2}$
Library Journal. July. p2369. 100w. 1
New York Times--Sunday. March 5. pD28. 50w. 3
Popular Music. Spring. p188. 100w. 1
Records and Recordings. May. p100. 225w. $2\frac{1}{2}$
Rolling Stone. March 2. p56. 2,500w. $3\frac{1}{2}$
Stereo Review. July. p94. 225w. 2

661 Simon and Garfunkel. GREATEST HITS. Columbia KC 31350 $5.98. Cart. CA 31350 $6.98. Cass. CT 31350 $6.98. (Reissue.)
Audio. September. p119. 50w. 4
High Fidelity. November. p130. 25w. 3
New York Times--Sunday. August 6. pD22. 50w. 4

662 Sir Douglas Quintet. THE RETURN OF DOUG SALDANA. Philips PHS 600-353 $5.98.
Popular Music. Fall. p58. 100w. 4

663 60,000,000 Buffalo. NEVADA JUKE BOX. Atco SD 33-384 $5.98. Cart. M8384 $6.95. Cass. M5384 $6.95.
Audio. October. p90. 50w. 0

664 Skylark. Capitol ST 11048 $5.98.
Popular Music. Fall. p91. 50w. 0

665 Slade. ALIVE! Polydor PD 5508 $5.98. Cart. 8F 5508 $6.95. Cass. CF 5508 $6.95.
Crawdaddy. December. p83. 475w. $1\frac{1}{2}$

666 Slade. PLAY IT LOUD. Cotillion 9035 $5.98. Cart. M89035 $6.95. Cass. M59035 $6.95.
Creem. August. p69. 50w. 3

667 Slim's Blues Gang. THE BLUES AIN'T STRANGE. Sonet SLP 2523 (Sweden).
Blues Unlimited. April. p24. 175w. 1

668 P. F. Sloan. RAISED ON RECORDS. Monument KZ 31260 $5.98. Cart. ZA 31260 $6.98.
Creem. December. p61. 700w. 4
Popular Music. Fall. p87. 50w. 2½

669 Sly and the Family Stone. THERE'S A RIOT GOING ON. Epic KE 30986 $5.98. Cart. EA 30986 $6.98. Cass. ET 30986 $6.98.
Creem. January. p61. 350w. 0
Creem. March. p56. 1,300w. 1
Library Journal. March 1. p857. 125w. 1

670 Small Faces. EARLY FACES. Pride PRD 0001 $5.98. Cart. 8131-001M $6.95. (Reissue.)
Creem. August. p69. 125w. 2½
Popular Music. Summer. p247. 50w. 3

671 Chris Smither. DON'T DRAG IT ON. Poppy PYS 5704 $4.98.
Popular Music. Spring. p186. 100w. 3

672 Sod. FACE THE MUSIC. Decca DL 75353 $5.98.
Audio. November. p90. 25w. 0

673 Soft Machine. 4. Columbia C 30754 $5.98.
Creem. January. p69. 50w. 2

674 Soft Machine. 5. Columbia KC 31604 $5.98. Cart. CA 31604 $6.98. Cass. CT 31604 $6.98.
Creem. December. p63. 25w. ½

675 John David Souther. Asylum SD 5055 $5.98. Cart. TP 5055 $6.95. Cass. CS 5055 $6.95.
Creem. December. p86. 25w. 2½
High Fidelity. December. p121. 200w. 3½
Rolling Stone. January 26. p62. 600w. 3
Rolling Stone. October 26. p62. 500w. 3

676 Southern Comfort. STIR, DON'T SHAKE. Harvest SHSP 4021 (E).
Records and Recordings. December. p100. 150w. ½

677 Sparks. Bearsville. BV 2048 $4.98. Cart. M82048 $6.95. Cass. M52048 $6.95.
Creem. October. p57. 300w. 1½
Sound. October. p43. 200w. 3

678 Chris Spedding. THE ONLY LICK I KNOW. Harvest SHSP 4017 (E).
Hi-Fi News and Record Review. May. p939. 100w. 1

679 Spirit. FEEDBACK. Epic KE 31175 $5.98. Cart. EA 31175 $6.98. Cass. ET 31175 $6.98.
Crawdaddy. May 14. p16. 200w. 3

Creem. August. p67. 25w. 3
Popular Music. Spring. p187. 100w. 3
Rolling Stone. June 8. p56, 58. 250w. 0

680 Spreadeagle. THE PIECE OF PAPER. Charisma CAS 1055 (E).
Hi-Fi News and Record Review. July. p1312. 50w. 2½

681 Spring. United Artists UAS 5571 $5.98.
Creem. August. p65-6. 375w. 3½
Creem. November. p74. 25w. 2½
Rolling Stone. August 17. p54. 800w. 3

682 The Stampeders. CARRYIN' ON. MWC 702 (Canada).
Sound. April. p37. 250w. 2

683 Stark Naked. RCA LSP 4592 $5.98.
Creem. January. p69. 50w. 1

684 Steely Dan. CAN'T BUY A THRILL. ABC ABCX 758 $5.98. Cart. M8758 $6.95. Cass. M5758 $6.95.
Rolling Stone. November 23. p66. 400w. 2

685 Steppenwolf. REST IN PEACE. ABC Dunhill DSX 50124 $5.98. Cart. M85124 $6.95. Cass. M55124 $6.95.
Records and Recordings. November. p107. 200w. 0

686 Cat Stevens. CATCH BULL AT FOUR. A & M SP 4365 $5.98.
New York Times--Sunday. December 10. pD36-7. 50w. 2½
Records and Recordings. December. p100. 150w. 1
Rolling Stone. November 23. p64. 1,600w. 3

687 Cat Stevens. TEASER AND THE FIRECAT. A & M SP 4313 $5.98. Cart. 8T 4313 $6.98. Cass. CS 4313 $6.98.
Creem. January. p63. 725w. 2½
High Fidelity. February. p116. 300w. 3

688 Cat Stevens. VERY YOUNG AND VERY EARLY SONGS. Deram DES 18061 $4.98.
Audio. May. p92. 100w. 3

689 Ray Stevens. TURN YOUR RADIO ON. Barnaby Z 30809 $4.98. Cart. ZA 30809 $6.98. Cass. ZT 30809 $6.98.
Stereo Review. June. p103. 100w. 1½

690 Rod Stewart. NEVER A DULL MOMENT. Mercury SRM 1646 $5.98. Cart. MC8-1-646 $5.95. Cass. MCR4-1-646 $6.95.
Beetle. October 31. p15. 825w. 4½
Crawdaddy. October. p74. 550w. 4
Creem. October. p58-9. 1,100w. 4

Gramophone. October. p782. 150w. 2
High Fidelity. November. p126. 100w. 3
New York Times--Sunday. September 24. pHF7. 300w. 5
New York Times--Sunday. December 10. pD37. 50w. 3
Records and Recordings. October. p126. 150w. 5
Sound. October. p44. 100w. 5

691 Stephen Stills. MANASSAS. Atlantic SD 2-903 (2 discs) $9.96. R-R J 903 $9.95. Cart. J 8903 $9.95. Cass. J5903 $9.95.
Crawdaddy. August. p16. 375w. 3
Creem. August. p67. 25w. 1½
Gramophone. July. p256. 50w. 0
High Fidelity. August. p101. 100w. 3½
New York Times--Sunday. September 10. pD37. 375w. 1
Popular Music. Summer. p252. 50w. 2
Records and Recordings. July. p95. 300w. 4½
Rolling Stone. May 25. p62. 1,600w. 4
Sound. August. p48-9. 275w. 4
Stereo Review. October. p100,102. 100w. 1½

692 Stone the Crows. TEENAGE LICKS. Polydor PD 5020 $5.98.
Crawdaddy. April 30. p17. 475w. 3
High Fidelity. May. p112. 50w. 2½
Stereo Review. June. p103. 100w. 2

693 Stoneground. FAMILY ALBUM. Warner Bros. 2WS 1956 (2 discs) $6.98. Cart. M81956 $6.95. Cass. M51956 $6.95.
Creem. March. p57. 75w. 1
Gramophone. September. p579. 125w. 1

694 Dennis Stoner. Rare Earth R 530L $5.98.
Audio. August. p63. 75w. 3½

695 Paul Stookey. PAUL AND WAR. Warner Bros. WS 1912 $5.98. Cart. M81912 $6.95. Cass. M51912 $6.95.
Beetle. January 22. p19-20. 575w. 4

696 Ronnie Stoots. ASHES TO ASHES. TMI TMS 1002 $5.98.
Music Journal. December. p75. 100w. 3½

697 Stories. Kama Sutra KSBS 2051 $5.98. Cart. M82051 $6.95. Cass. M52051 $6.95.
Creem. August. p67. 25w. 2½

698 Strawbs. GRAVE NEW WORLD. A & M SP 4344 $5.98.
Beetle. August. p20. 400w. 2½
Creem. September. p64. 25w. 0
Records and Recordings. April. p107-8. 475w. 5
Rolling Stone. July 20. p49. 700w. 2

699 Stray. SATURDAY MORNING PICTURES. Mercury SRM 1624 $5.98.
Stereo Review. June. p103. 50w. 0

700 Stray. SUICIDE. Mercury $5.98.
Creem. January. p64. 400w. 3½

701 String Cheese. Wooden Nickel WNS 1001 $5.98. Cart. P8WN 1001 $6.95.
Stereo Review. February. p113. 50w. 0

702 String Driven Thing. Charisma CAS 1062 $5.98.
New York Times--Sunday. December 17. pD35. 400w. 3

703 Styx. Wooden Nickel WNS 1008 $5.98. Cart. P8WN 1008 $6.95. Cass. PKWN 1008 $6.95.
Music Journal. December. p75. 100w. 0

704 Richard Supa. HOMESPUN. Paramount PAS 6027 $4.98.
Creem. November. p74. 25w. 0

705 Supersister. TO THE HIGHEST BIDDER. Dandelion 2310 146 (E).
Records and Recordings. April. p108. 250w. 2

706 The Sutherland Brothers. BROTHERS BAND. Island SW 9315 $5.98.
Popular Music. Summer. p251. 25w. 2
Records and Recordings. April. p108-9. 250w. 2

707 Swampwater. RCA LSP 4572 $5.98. Cart. P8S 1830 $6.98.
Creem. January. p69. 50w. 1
High Fidelity. June. p107. 300w. 2½

708 Sweet. FUNNY HOW CO-CO CAN BE. RCA SF 8238 (E).
Gramophone. March. p1613. 25w. 0

709 Swinging Medallions. DOUBLE SHOT OF MY BABY'S LOVE. Smash $5.98.
Creem. August. p69. 75w. 2

710 Syrinx. LONG LOST RELATIVES. True North TNX5 (Canada).
Library Journal. August. p2557. 100w. 3

711 T. Rex. ELECTRIC WARRIOR. Reprise RS 6466 $5.98.
American Record Guide. January. p237. 150w. 0
Beetle. January 22. p17. 575w. 3
Creem. January. p60-1. 850w. 2½
Library Journal. February 1. p481. 100w. 1½

712 T. Rex. THE SLIDER. Reprise MS 2095 $5.98.
Beetle. October 30. p17. 700w. 3½
Crawdaddy. November. p83. 800w. 2½
Creem. November. p62. 700w. 2
New York Times--Sunday. October 22. pD31. 200w. ½
Records and Recordings. October. p126. 150w. 2½
Sound. October. p43. 200w. 3

713 Tams. THE BEST OF... Capitol ST 567 $5.98. Cart. 8XT 567 $6.98. Cass. 4XT 567 $5.98.
Gramophone. February. p1443. 25w. 1½

714 Taste. LIVE AT THE ISLE OF WIGHT. Polydor 2380-120 (E).
Beetle. November. p27. 750w. 3

715 Taste. LIVE AT MONTREUX. Polydor 2310-082 (E).
Beetle. November. p27. 750w. 3

716 Bernie Taupin. POETRY READING. Elektra EKS 75020 $5.98.
Crawdaddy. March 19. p16. 550w. 1
High Fidelity. June. p103. 500w. 0

717 Alex Taylor. DINNERTIME. Capricorn CP 0101 $4.98. Cart. M80101 $6.95. Cass. M50101 $6.95.
Stereo Review. October. p102. 125w. 2

718 Allan Taylor. SOMETIMES. United Artists UAS 5529 $5.98.
Popular Music. Fall. p58. 50w. 3
Audio. September. p121. 50w. 2½

719 Livingston Taylor. LIV. Capricorn SD 863 $5.98. Cart. M8863 $6.95. Cass. M5863 $6.95.
High Fidelity. March. p116. 25w. 2½
Stereo Review. May. p95. 50w. 2½

720 Ten Years After. ALVIN LEE AND COMPANY. Deram XDES 18064 $5.98. Cart. M77864 $6.95. Cass. M77664 $6.95.
Beetle. May. p20. 500w. 1½
Creem. June. p68-9. 900w. 3

721 Them, featuring Van Morrison. Parrot XPAS 71053/4 (2 discs) $6.98. Cart. L79853 $7.95. Cass. L79653 $7.95. (Reissue.)
Crawdaddy. October. p79. 400w. 3½
Creem. October. p55. 700w. 3½

722 30 Days Out. MIRACLE LICK. Reprise MS 2085 $5.98.
New York Times--Sunday. November 19. pD30. 175w. 3½

723 THIS IS ROCK 'N' ROLL (anthology). Philips 6436 003 (E). (Reissue.)
Blues Unlimited. January. p25. 250w. 2½

724 Peter Thom. United Artist UAS 5587 $5.98.
Crawdaddy. December. p79. 900w. 4

725 B.J. Thomas. BILLY JOE THOMAS. Scepter SPS 5101 $5.98.
Creem. September. p64. 25w. 2
Hi-Fi News and Record Review. October. p1926. 150w. 3
Popular Music. Summer. p252. 75w. 3

726 Vaughan Thomas. JAM JAL 101 (E).
Hi-Fi News and Record Review. August. p1479. 100w. 3

727 Richard Thompson. HENRY THE HUMAN FLY. Island ILPS 9197 (E).
Gramophone. September. p579. 425w. 3

728 Three Dog Night. SEVEN SEPARATE FOOLS. ABC Dunhill DSD 50118 $4.98. Cart. M85118 $6.95. Cass. M55118 $6.95.
Creem. November. p63. 650w. 1
Creem. November. p74. 25w. ½
High Fidelity. December. p124. 100w. 1½

729 Thundermug. STRIKES. Axe AXS 502 (Canada).
Beetle. June. p22. 675w. 4

730 Tin Tin. ASTRAL TAXI. Atco S 33-370 $5.98. Cart. M833-370 $6.95. Cass. M533-370 $6.95.
Hi-Fi News and Record Review. December. p2464. 100w. 3½

731 Tiny Alice. Kama Sutra KSBS 2046 $5.98. Cart. M82046 $6.95. Cass. M52046 $6.95.
High Fidelity. June. p110. 25w. 2
New York Times--Sunday. February 20. pD28. 125w. 3½
Previews. December. p46. 100w. 2½

732 Ken Tobias. DREAM NUMBER TWO. Verve MV 5085 $5.98.
Audio. November. p90. 50w. 3
Beetle. November. p27-8. 800w. 3½

733 TOMMY. Ode SP 99001 (2 discs) $11.96.
New York Times--Sunday. December 17. pD38, 42. 1,000w. 2

734 The Tornados. THE WORLD OF... Decca SPA 253 (E).
Gramophone. November. p984. 50w. 1

735 Tower of Power. BUMP CITY. Warner Bros. BS 2616 $5.98.
Beetle. August. p22. 750w. 3
Creem. November. p64. 700w. 2

736 Peter Townshend. WHO CAME FIRST. Decca DL79189 $5.98.
Popular Music. Fall. p94. 50w. 1
Rolling Stone. December 21. p60-1. 3,000w. 4

737 TRACK ON! THE BEST OF MARK FARNER, TERRY KNIGHT AND DONNIE BREWER. Lucky Eleven 8001 $5.98.
Rolling Stone. June 22. p56,58. 750w. 0

738 Traffic. THE LOW SPARK OF HIGH HEELED BOYS. Island SW 9306 $5.98. Cart. 8XW 9306 $6.98. Cass. 4XW 9306 $6.98.
Crawdaddy. January 30. p17. 900w. 2
High Fidelity. March. p117. 25w. $2\frac{1}{2}$
New York Times--Sunday. March 12. pHF12. 125w. $1\frac{1}{2}$
Rolling Stone. January 20. p48-9. 1,000w. 3

739 Traffic. WELCOME TO THE CANTEEN. United Artists UAS 5550 $5.98. Cart. U8 323 $6.98. Cass. KO 323 $6.98.
Creem. January. p65. 450w. 1
Stereo Review. February. p113. 200w. 3

740 Domonic Troiano. DOM. Mercury SRM 1-639 $5.98. Cart. MC8-1-639 $6.95. Cass. MCR4-1-639 $6.95.
Gramophone. November. p984. 25w. 0

741 TRUTH OF TRUTHS: A CONTEMPORARY ROCK OPERA. Oak Records OR 1001 $9.98.
Library Journal. March 1. p857. 125w. 0

742 Tucky Buzzard. WARM SLASH. Capitol ST 864 $5.98.
Creem. April. p71. 50w. 0
Stereo Review. April. p100. 200w. $1\frac{1}{2}$

743 Tyrannosaurus Rex. A BEGINNING. A & M $5.98. (Reissue.)
Creem. December. p63. 25w. 3

744 Philip Upchurch. DARKNESS, DARKNESS. Blue Thumb BTS 6005 $5.98.
Popular Music. Fall. p87. 50w. 3

745 Uriah Heep. DEMONS AND WIZARDS. Mercury SRM 1-630 $5.98. Cart. MC8-1-630 $6.95. Cass. MCR4-1-630 $6.95.

Beetle. October 17. p22. 700w. $\frac{1}{2}$
Crawdaddy. September. p20. 350w. $\frac{1}{2}$
Creem. September. p52. 550w. $1\frac{1}{2}$
Records and Recordings. August. p91. 275w. 0
Rolling Stone. November 23. p66. 400w. $3\frac{1}{2}$

746 Uriah Heep. LOOK AT YOURSELF. Mercury SRM 1-614 $5.98. Cart. MC8-1-614 $6.95. Cass. MCR4-1-614 $6.95.
Creem. January. p64. 400w. 4

747 Valdy. COUNTRY MAN. Haida 5101 (Canada).
Sound. December. p41. 200w. $3\frac{1}{2}$

748 Van Eaton, Lon and Derrek. BROTHER. Apple SMAS 3990 $5.98.
Rolling Stone. November 23. p62. 450w. 4

749 Dave Van Ronk. VAN RONK. Polydor PD 244052 $4.98.
Popular Music. Fall. p61. 50w. 3
Records and Recordings. April. p108. 200w. 3
Stereo Review. March. p109. 100w. 2

750 Velvet Underground. LIVE AT MAX'S. Atlantic K 30020 (E).
Crawdaddy. September. p20. 250w. 1
Records and Recordings. October. p126. 200w. 1

751 The Ventures. ROCK AND ROLL FOREVER. United Artists UAS 5649 $5.98.
Popular Music. Fall. p93. 50w. $2\frac{1}{2}$

752 Vigrass and Osborne. QUEUES. Uni 73129 $4.98.
Audio. August. p62. 25w. $2\frac{1}{2}$
High Fidelity. December. p124. 125w. $2\frac{1}{2}$

753 Gene Vincent. Starline SRS 5117 (E). (Reissue.)
Gramophone. August. p405. 100w. 2

754 Eric Von Schmidt. 2ND RIGHT, 3RD ROW. Poppy PYS 5705 $4.98. Cart. 11105 $6.95. Cass. 12505 $6.95.
Stereo Review. November. p92. 250w. 4

755 Wackers. WACKERING HEIGHTS. Elektra EKS 74098 $5.98.
American Record Guide. January. p236-7. 300w. 3
Creem. February. p65-6. 700w. $2\frac{1}{2}$

756 Loudon Wainwright III. ALBUM III. Columbia KC 31462 $5.98. Cart. CA 31462 $6.98. Cass. CT 31462 $6.98.
Rolling Stone. October 26. p58. 1,500w. 4

757 Howard Wales and Jerry Garcia. HOOTEROLL? Douglas KZ 30859 $4.98. Cart. ZT 30859 $6.98.
Stereo Review. April. p100. 200w. $2\frac{1}{2}$

758 Clifford T. Ward. SINGER SONGWRITER. Dandelion 2310 216 (E).
Hi-Fi News and Record Review. December. p2463. 100w. 2½

759 Warhorse. RED SEA. Vertigo VT 6360 066 (E).
Hi-Fi News and Record Review. July. p1317. 25w. 1½

760 Warm Dust. PEACE FOR OUR TIME. Uni 73109 $4.98. Cart. 8-73109 $6.95. Cass. 2-73109 $6.95.
Popular Music. Fall. p61. 25w. 2

761 Bob Weir. ACE. Warner Bros. BS 2627 $5.98.
Beetle. August. p21-2. 775w. 3
Crawdaddy. September. p16-7. 800w. 1½
Creem. August. p68. 350w. 2
Creem. September. p64. 50w. 4
Gramophone. October. p782. 200w. 4

762 Wet Willie. Capricorn SD 861 $5.98. Cart. M8861 $6.95. Cass. M5861 $6.95.
Popular Music. Fall. p60. 25w. 2½

763 Wet Willie. II. Capricorn CP 0109 $5.98. Cart. M80109 $6.95. Cass. M50109 $6.95.
Rolling Stone. November 23. p62. 500w. 3½

764 Whiskey Howl. Warner Bros. WSC 9012 (Canada).
Canadian Stereo Guide. Summer. p67. 100w. 3

765 Tony Joe White. Warner Bros. WS 1900 $5.98.
New York Times--Sunday. May 21. pD32. 75w. 3½

766 Tony Joe White. THE TRAIN I'M ON. Warner Bros. BS 2580 $5.98. Cart. M82580 $6.95. Cass. M52580 $6.95.
Crawdaddy. September. p19. 1,000w. 3
Records and Recordings. August. p91. 200w. 4

767 White Cloud. GOOD MEDICINE. Good Music 3500 $5.98.
Crawdaddy. October. p81. 600w. 3
High Fidelity. September. p108. 25w. 2½

768 White Witch. Capricorn CP 0107 $5.98.
Creem. August. p65. 500w. 2

769 Bobby Whitlock. ABC Dunhill DSX 50121 $5.98. Cart. M85121 $6.95. Cass. M55121 $6.95.
Rolling Stone. June 22. p60. 400w. 2½

770 The Who. MEATY, BEATY, BIG AND BOUNCY. Decca DL 79184 $5.98. Cart. 69184 $6.95. Cass. 739184 $6.95. (Reissue.)
American Record Guide. August. p625. 250w. 0

Creem. January. p59-60. 550w. 0
Gramophone. February. p1443. 100w. 3½
High Fidelity. February. p112. 150w. 2
Stereo Review. March. p109. 200w. 4

771 The Who. SELL OUT. Decca DL 74950 $5.98.
Crawdaddy. March 5. p19. 750w. 5

772 The Who. WHO'S NEXT. Decca DL 79182 $5.98. Cart. 6-9182 $6.98. Cass. C73-9182 $6.98.
Popular Music. Fall. p58. 25w. 2½

773 Jack Wild. A BEAUTIFUL WORLD. Buddah BDS 5110 $5.98. Cart. M85110 $6.95. Cass. M55110 $6.95.
High Fidelity. July. p106. 25w. 2½

774 Wilderness Road. Columbia KC 31118 $5.98. Cart. CA 31118 $6.98. Cass. CT 31118 $6.98.
Crawdaddy. October. p82. 1,100w. 4

775 John Buck Wilkin. United Artists UAS 5541 $5.98. Cart. U8311 $6.98. Cass. K0311 $6.98.
Rolling Stone. March 2. p62. 550w. 3

776 Tony Williams. EGO. Polydor PD 24-4065 $4.98.
Downbeat. February 3. p24. 50w. 2½
Downbeat. February 3. p24. 250w. 4

777 Cris Williamson. Ampex A 10134 $4.98. Cart. M80134 $6.95. Cass. M50134 $6.95.
Stereo Review. January. p114. 250w. 3

778 Jesse Winchester. THIRD DOWN, 110 TO GO. Bearsville BR 2101 $5.98. Cart. M82102 $6.95. Cass. M52102 $6.95.
Rolling Stone. December 7. p64. 700w. 4½
Sing Out. September/October. p39. 250w. 4
Sound. November. p36. 300w. 3

779 Wings. WILD LIFE. Apple SW 3386 $4.98. Cart. 8XW 3386 $6.98. Cass. 4XW 3386 $6.98.
American Record Guide. July. p576. 425w. 3
Audio. May. p93. 25w. 1
Crawdaddy. March 5. p15. 700w. 1
Creem. January. p47-8. 1,650w. 3
Gramophone. February. p1443. 25w. 0
High Fidelity. April. p110. 525w. 3
Rolling Stone. January 20. p48. 1,750w. 1

780 Edgar Winter. WHITE TRASH. Epic E 30512 $5.98. Cart. EA 30512 $6.95. Cass. ET 30512 $6.95.
Downbeat. June 22. p26. 300w. 3

781 Edgar Winter Group. THEY ONLY COME OUT AT NIGHT. Columbia KE 31584 $5.98.
New York Times--Sunday. December 17. pD35. 300w. 3

782 Edgar Winter's White Trash. ROADWORK. Epic KEG 31249 (2 discs) $6.98. Cart. EGA 31249 $7.98. Cass. 31249 $7.98.
American Record Guide. August. p625. 225w. 3
Beetle. June. p21-2. 925w. 3½
Creem. June. p64-5. 600w. 1
High Fidelity. June. p102. 175w. 2
Stereo Review. October. p102,104. 200w. 2

783 Wishbone Ash. ARGUS. Decca DL 75347 $4.98.
Gramophone. July. p256-7. 25w. 1
High Fidelity. October. p120. 350w. 2½
Records and Recordings. July. p95. 225w. 3½
Rolling Stone. August 17. p50,52. 1,000w. 2
Sound. August. p48. 100w. 2

784 Bill Withers. JUST AS I AM. Sussex SXBS 7006 $5.98. Cart. M87006 $6.95. Cass. M57006 $6.95.
Crawdaddy. January 16. p15. 800w. 3

785 Bill Withers. STILL BILL. Sussex SXBS 7014 $5.98. Cart. M87014 $6.95. Cass. M57014 $6.95.
Creem. August. p67. 50w. 2½
Creem. December. p86. 25w. 0
Hi-Fi News and Record Review. November. p2202. 100w. 2½
New York Times--Sunday. December 10. pD37. 100w. 3
Rolling Stone. June 8. p60. 600w. 3
Sound. November. p37. 300w. 3
Stereo Review. December. p104. 50w. 1

786 Bobby Womack. UNDERSTANDING. United Artists UAS 5577 $5.98. Cart. K0381 $6.98. Cass. 8381 $6.98.
High Fidelity. December. p120-1. 125w. 3½

787 Gary Wright. FOOTPRINT. A & M SP 4295 $5.98.
Crawdaddy. March 19. p17. 200w. 2

788 Yardbirds. LIVE. Epic EG 30135 (2 discs) $5.98. Cart. EGA 30135 $7.98.
Creem. January. p69. 25w. 0

789 Yes. CLOSE TO THE EDGE. Atlantic SD 7244 $5.98. Cart. TP 7244 $6.95. Cass. CS 7244 $6.95.
Crawdaddy. December. p78-9. 600w. 2½
Creem. December. p56. 500w. 3
Gramophone. December. p1225. 125w. 4

Hi-Fi News and Record Review. December. p2464. 150w. 2½
Records and Recordings. November. p107. 200w. 5
Rolling Stone. November 9. p60. 1,750w. 4
Sound. November. p36-7. 325w. 4

790 Yes. FRAGILE. Atlantic SD 7211 $5.98. Cart. M87211 $6.95. Cass. M57211 $6.95.
Creem. May. p67. 550w. 3½
High Fidelity. May. p116. 25w. 3½
Rolling Stone. March 16. p56. 450w. 3½
Sound. April. p37. 175w. 4

791 Yogi Adonasis. GETTING IT TOGETHER. Universal Awareness 722 $4.98.
Creem. August. p66. 75w. 0
High Fidelity. July. p106. 25w. 1

792 Jesse Colin Young. TOGETHER. Raccoon/Warner Bros. BS 2585 $5.98. Cart. 82588 $6.95. Cass. M52588 $6.95.
Crawdaddy. May 14. p14. 500w. 3
Creem. June. p70-1. 800w. 4
Stereo Review. October. p104. 200w. 1

793 Neil Young. HARVEST. Reprise MS 2032 $5.98. Cart. M82032 $6.95. Cass. M52032 $6.95.
Beetle. May. p19-20. 1,000w. 4
Crawdaddy. April 30. p14. 1,000w. 2½
Gramophone. July. p256. 25w. 2
Popular Music. Spring. p185-6. 75w. 4
Records and Recordings. April. p109. 400w. 4
Rolling Stone. March 30. p52. 1,250w. 1½
Stereo Review. June. p78. 350w. 5

794 Roy Young. MR. FUNKY. Kapp KS 3662 $4.98.
High Fidelity. June. p103. 500w. 2½

795 Youngbloods. GOOD AND DUSTY. Warner Bros. BS 2566 $5.98. Cart. M82566 $6.95. Cass. M52566 $6.95.
American Record Guide. September. p673. 100w. 2½
Crawdaddy. January 30. p17. 1,000w. 1½

796 Youngbloods. RIDE THE WIND. Warner Bros. BS 2563 $5.98. Cart. M82563 $6.95. Cass. M52563 $6.95.
Gramophone. February. p1443. 50w. 2

797 Youngbloods. SUNLIGHT. RCA LSP 4561 $5.98. Cart. P8S 1778 $6.98. Cass. PK 1778 $6.98.
Gramophone. March. p1613. 25w. 0

798 Young-Holt Unlimited. BORN AGAIN. Cotillion 18004 $5.98.
Downbeat. April 13. p30. 100w. 2½

799 ZZ Top. RIO GRANDE MUD. London XPS 612 $5.98. Cart. M72194 $6.95. Cass. M57194 $6.95.
Creem. September. p64. 25w. 1
Rolling Stone. July 20. p52. 600w. 3½

800 Frank Zappa and the Mothers. THE GRAND WAZOO. Bizarre/Reprise MS 2093 $5.98.
New York Times--Sunday. December 17. pD35. 300w. 2½

801 Frank Zappa and the Mothers. WAKA/JAWAKA - HOT RATS. Bizarre/Reprise MS 2094 $5.98.
Crawdaddy. November. p81. 1,000w. 3
Hi-Fi News and Record Review. December. p2464. 150w. 1½
High Fidelity. December. p120. 75w. 4
Records and Recordings. November. p107. 175w. 1

802 Zoo. Barclay 521172 (France).
Jazz Journal. January. p37. 75w. 0

803 Andy Zwerling. SPIDERS IN THE NIGHT. Kama Sutra KSBS 2036 $5.98. Cart. M82036 $6.95. Cass. M52036 $6.95.
Creem. March. p57. 350w. 2½

MOOD-POP

This section comprises what can only be called pure derivative music. For mood, most of it is reinterpretive, second-generation sounds taken from the worlds of the other categories. The nasal twang of country has been dropped, the solo acoustic instrument of folk has been augmented by strings, the beat of rhythm & blues has been modified, the noise and distortion of rock has been softened, the swing of jazz is missing, and the harshness of the blues has been smoothed. All of this music has been given a characteristic full, lush sound, suitable for home stereo consoles or middle-of-the-road (M. O. R.) programming. Included here is dance music, lyrical music, plus other variants that do not jar the nerves, and is suitable for background music just one cut above the level of Muzak. Often this music has been called the Music of Middle America, or of the silent majority. It sells exceptionally well, notably through rackers and jobbers. Standards and ballads are its main repertoire, with borrowings from other fields (especially from the musical stage) for crooners and chanteuses. Usually the format is to create a specific sound for a specific entertainer (for example, Frank Sinatra, Tom Jones, Patti Page) and "bend" the selections chosen to that sound. Under this method, it is possible for each performer to record an album a month, relying on the set arrangements of the studio orchestra. Fortunately, this does not happen because the economics of the market will not sustain the glut. Still, it is not unheard of for an artist to release four or five records a year. In 1972 Schwann listed seven new items by Rod McKuen. The results in mood music is a mixed bag of Latin themes, light cocktail jazz, soft rock, and soft country and western.

For convenience, this section also includes pop music that has been characterized as "bubble gum" or pre-teen variety that appeals mainly to the young set. Such music is based on derivative rock, and is characterized by Top 40 tunes, usually written by someone who is not the singer or performer. These lightweight selections bear common characteristics: they are short; they have sparse instrumentation; they have trite, redundant lyrics; and they leave no lasting impression. This is a singles market for 45 RPM releases, and consequently most albums have one or possibly two hits, followed by nine or so selections to pad the album.

Both mood and pop share several things in common. They both tend to be regarded as background music and not taken seriously; they are listened to with regularity by the automobile driver and his captive passengers; they are listened to by the lonely housewife; they can be soothing and incredibly beautiful if the melody and the arrangements are considered equally in a lush sort of way; and they are the bread-and-butter releases of the major record companies, for these discs make money.

The reviewing media does not take this music very seriously; they have little to say about the music except disparaging comments. The only magazines that give regular coverage are Audio and the two British publications Gramophone and Hi-Fi News and Record Review. The English market, judging from the number of releases, appears to be larger than that in North America, and draws on British, American and Continental sources. Their reissues are more carefully planned, with the original monophonic sound maintained, good liner notes, and packaging design.

According to the reviews, the following were the best in this category:

Mood--New

Laurindo Almeida. BEST OF EVERYTHING. Daybreak DR 2013
BBC Northern Dance Orchestra. BBC Records 133 S (E)
Stan Butcher. THE TED HEATH LEGEND. RCA JET 103 (E)
Les Crane. DESIDERATA. Warner Bros BS 2570
Bing Crosby and Count Basie. BING 'N' BASIE. Daybreak DR 2014
Val Doonican. JUST A SITTIN' AND A-ROCKIN'. Philips 6308 085 (E)
Astrud Gilberto. GILBERTO WITH TURRENTINE. CTI CTI 6008
Jack Jones. BREAD WINNERS. RCA LSP 4692
Peggy Lee. NORMA DELORIS EGSTROM, FROM JAMESTOWN, NORTH DAKOTA. Capitol ST 11077.
Trini Lopez. VIVA. Capitol SK 11009
Vera Lynn. UNFORGETTABLE SONGS. Columbia SCX 6500 (E)
Tony Mercer. SINGS JOHNNY MERCER. Columbia SCX 6503 (E)
Bobby Short. LOVES COLE PORTER (2 discs). Atlantic 2SD-606

Mood--Reissues

Burt Bacharach. HIT MAKER! MCA MUPS 450 (E)
Bing Crosby. I LOVE YOU TRULY. Coral CPS 79 (E)
Bing Crosby. RHYTHM ON THE RANGE. Coral CPS 81 (E)
Bing Crosby. WRAP YOUR TROUBLES IN DREAMS, 1927/31. RCA LPV 584
Bing Crosby and the Andrews Sisters. Coral CPS 80 (E)
Ella Fitzgerald. SINGS GERSHWIN, vol. 2 (2 discs). Metro 2682 023 (E)

Spike Jones. MURDERS THE CLASSICS. RCA LSC 3235
Paul Mauriat. THIS IS. Philips 6444 501 (E)
Matt Monro. LET'S FACE THE MUSIC. Regal Starline SRS 5113 (E)
Edith Piaf. I REGRET NOTHING. Columbia SCX 6477 (E)

Pop--New

Neil Diamond. MOODS. Uni 73136
Kenny Rankin. LIKE A SEED. Little David LD 1003
Neil Sedaka. EMERGENCE. Kirshner KES 111

Pop--Reissues

Four Seasons. THE BIG ONES. Philips 6336 208 (E)
Elvis Presley. ROCK 'N' ROLL. RCA SF 8233 (E)

804 Acceleration. RCA LSP 4679 $5.98.
Audio. October. p89. 25w. 0

805 Addrisi Brothers. WE'VE GOT TO GET IT ON AGAIN. Columbia KC 31296 $5.98. Cart. CA 31296 $6.98. Cass. 31296 $6.98.
Popular Music. Spring. p187-8. 75w. 2

806 Adriano. I LOVE PARIS. Columbia Studio 2 TWO 353 (E).
Gramophone. January. p1279. 25w. 3

807 AFTER THE BALL (anthology). Regal Starline MRSSP 513 (E). (Reissue.)
Gramophone. December. p1222. 25w. 2

808 Air. Ember SD 733 $5.98. Cart. M8733 $6.95. Cass. M5733 $6.95.
Audio. November. p93. 50w. 2½

809 Ronnie Aldrich. INVITATION TO LOVE. London Phase 4 SP 44176 $5.98. Cart. M14176 $6.95. Cass. M84176 $6.95.
Gramophone. September. p377. 25w. 3

810 Ronnie Aldrich. PHASE 4 WORLD OF BURT BACHARACH. Decca SPA 193 (E). (Reissue.)
Gramophone. July. p254. 100w. 3
Hi-Fi News and Record Review. July. p1305. 50w. 2½

811 Augusto Alguero. LAUGH! LAUGH! Polydor 2489 034 (E).
Gramophone. February. p1437. 25w. 1

812 Laurindo Almeida. THE BEST OF EVERYTHING. Daybreak DR 2013 $5.98. Cart. P8DR 2013 $6.98. Cass. PKDR 2013 $6.98.
Gramophone. December. p1222, 1225. 325w. 5
Hi-Fi News and Record Review. November. p2201. 50w. 3

813 Herb Alpert. SOLID BRASS. A & M SP 4341 $5.98. Cart. 8T 4341 $6.95. Cass. CS 4341 $6.95. (Reissue.)
Audio. September. p119. 50w. 4
Gramophone. December. p1221. 25w. 2
Hi-Fi News and Record Review. p1681. 25w. 1

814 Ed Ames. RCA LSP 4634 $5.98. Cart. P8S 1866 $6.95. Cass. PK 1866 $6.95.
Audio. November. p91. 25w. $2\frac{1}{2}$

815 Ed Ames. REMEMBERS JIM REEVES. RCA LSP 4683 $5.98. Cart. P8S 1914 $6.95. Cass. PK 1914 $6.95.
Music Journal. October. p59. 100w. 3

816 Jackie Anderson. HAPPY MUSIC FOR HAPPY PEOPLE. Decca SKL 5123 (E).
Gramophone. August. p397. 25w. 1
Hi-Fi News and Record Review. July. p1305. 25w. $2\frac{1}{2}$

817 Moira Anderson. THIS IS... Philips 6382 033 (E).
Gramophone. February. p1432. 125w. 3

818 Paul Anka. Buddah BDS 5093 $5.98. Cart. M85093 $6.95 Cass. M55093 $6.95.
Gramophone. June. p111. 100w. 3
Stereo Review. April. p89. 275w. 2

819 Antonio. TRUMPETS IN THE SUN. Philips 6308 056 (E).
Gramophone. August. p398. 175w. 3
Hi-Fi News and Record Review. August. p1476. 50w. 3

820 Johnny Arthey. LOVE VIBRATIONS. Polydor 2460 144 (E).
Gramophone. July. p254. 100w. 3
Hi-Fi News and Record Review. July. p1307. 25w. $2\frac{1}{2}$

821 The Association. WATERBEDS IN TRINIDAD. Columbia KC 31348 $5.98. Cart. CA 31348 $6.98. Cass. CT 31348 $6.98.
Hi-Fi News and Record Review. September. p1683. 100w. $2\frac{1}{2}$

822 Winifred Atwell. AROUND THE WORLD IN 80 TUNES. Decca SPA 256 (E).
Gramophone. December. p1222. 25w. 1

823 Josef Augustin und Seine Original Donauschwäbische Blasmusik. ROT BLUHT DER MOHN. Decca SLK 16729 (Germany).
Hi-Fi News and Record Review. July. p1308. 25w. 1

824 THE AWARD WINNERS (anthology). Rediffusion ZS 113 (E).
Hi-Fi News and Record Review. December. p2463. 50w. 2

825 Roy Ayers. HE'S COMING. Polydor PD 5022 $4.98.
Downbeat. July 20. p32. 200w. 4½

826 Roy Ayers. UBIQUITY. Polydor 24-4049 $4.98.
Audio. February. p72. 600w. 3

827 Charles Aznavour. AZNAVOUR SINGS AZNAVOUR, VOLUME 2. Barclay 80418 (France).
Gramophone. January. p1274. 50w. 3

828 BBC NORTHERN DANCE ORCHESTRA. BBC Records REC 133S (E).
Gramophone. July. p254. 225w. 5
Hi-Fi News and Record Review. July. p1307. 50w. 2½

829 BBC PRESENTS DANCE BANDS OF THE AIR, VOLUMES 1 & 2 (anthology). BBC Records 139/140M (2 discs) (E) (Reissue.)
Records and Recordings. December. p101. 150w. 2½

830 BBC Radio Big Band. THE BEST OF BRITISH. BBC Records REC 131S (E).
Gramophone. December. p1221. 25w. 2
Records and Recordings. December. p101. 75w. 2

831 BBC Radio Orchestra. FIFTY YEARS OF POPULAR HITS. BBC Records RBC 136S (E).
Gramophone. December. p1229. 75w. 2½

832 Burt Bacharach. HITMAKER! MCA MUPS 450 (E) (Reissue.)
Gramophone. September. p577. 100w. 4
Hi-Fi News and Record Review. August. p1476. 25w. 1½

833 The Bachelors. UNDER AND OVER. Decca SKL 5107 (E).
Gramophone. January. p1279. 25w. 1

834 The Bachelors and Patricia Cahill. STAGE AND SCREEN SPECTACULAR. Decca SKL 5106 (E).
Gramophone. March. p1613. 25w. 1½

835 Baja Marimba Band. ACUPULCO GOLD. Mayfair AMLB 51031 (E).
Gramophone. June. p115. 50w. 2

836 Elemer Balogh. CYMBALO SOLOS. Qualiton LPX 10124 (E).
Hi-Fi News and Record Review. October. p1923. 25w. $2\frac{1}{2}$

837 La Banda del Mandolino. MANDOLIN MAGIC. Polydor 2489 038 (E).
Gramophone. February. p1437. 25w. 0

838 Charles Barlow. STRICT TEMPO MEMORIES OF BLACKPOOL. Columbia SCX 6486 (E).
Gramophone. May. p1952. 25w. 2
Hi-Fi News and Record Review. May. p937. 25w. $2\frac{1}{2}$

839 George Barnes and Bucky Pizzarelli. GUITARS PURE AND HONEST. A & R ARL 7100 007 $5.98.
Audio. November. p93. 100w. $3\frac{1}{2}$

840 John Barry. REVISITED. Ember SE 8008 (E) (Reissue.)
Gramophone. February. p1437. 25w. $1\frac{1}{2}$

841 Shirley Bassey. COLLECTION. United Artists UAD 60013/4 (2 discs) (E). (Reissue.)
Gramophone. February. p1432. 100w. 2

842 Shirley Bassey. I, CAPRICORN. United Artists UAS 5565 $5.98.
Gramophone. May. p1951. 50w. 1
Hi-Fi News and Record Review. June. p1127. 50w. 2

843 Shirley Bassey. SOMETHING ELSE. United Artists UAS 6797 $5.98. Cart. U8271 $6.98. Cass. K0271 $6.98.
Audio. August. p61. 75w. $3\frac{1}{2}$

844 Shirley Bassey. THIS IS... Philips 6382 028 (E). (Reissue.)
Gramophone. January. p1274. 50w. 2
Gramophone. February. p1432. 100w. 3

845 Shirley Bassey. WHAT NOW, MY LOVE. Music for Pleasure SMFP 5230 (E). (Reissue.)
Gramophone. February. p1432. 100w. 3

846 Mike Batt. PORTRAIT OF SIMON AND GARFUNKEL. DJM Silverline DJSL 020 (E).
Hi-Fi News and Record Review. December. p2461. 25w. 2

847 Bavarian Police Band. 50 DEUTSCHE VOLKSLIEDER. Telefunken Musik Für Alle NT 641 (Germany).
Hi-Fi News and Record Review. July. p1308. 25w. 0

848 Harry Belafonte. CALYPSO CARNIVAL. RCA LSP 4521 $5.98. Cart. P8S 1747 $6.95.

Audio. November. p93. 25w. 1
Stereo Review. April. p89-90. 150w. 3

849 Harry Belafonte. LIVE! RCA VPSX 6077 (2 discs) $7.98. Cart. P8S 5135 $7.95.
Audio. December. p92-3. 625w. 4

850 Harry Belafonte. MIDNIGHT SPECIAL. RCA Camden CSD 1100 (E). (Reissue.)
Hi-Fi News and Record Review. November. p2201. 25w. 3

851 The Bells. LOVE, LUCK 'N' LOLLIPOPS. Polydor PD 5503 $4.98.
Audio. November. p92. 50w. 2½

852 Tony Bennett. ALL-TIME GREATEST HITS. Columbia KG 31494 (2 discs) $6.98. Cart. GA 31494 $7.98. Cass. GT 31494 $7.98. (Reissue.)
Audio. December. p94. 125w. 4

853 Tony Bennett. GET HAPPY WITH THE LONDON PHILHARMONIC ORCHESTRA. Columbia C 30953 $4.98. Cart. CA 30953 $6.98.
Gramophone. April. p1775-6. 225w. 2

854 Stanley Black. FILM SPECTACULAR, VOLUME 4 - "THE EPIC." London SP 44173 $5.98.
Stereo Review. November. p99. 250w. 2½

855 Stanley Black. TROPICAL MOONLIGHT. Decca Eclipse ECS 2098 (E).
Gramophone. March. p1614. 100w. 3

856 Stanley Black. TRIBUTE TO CHARLIE CHAPLIN. London SP 44184 $5.98.
Audio. November. p84. 425w. 3
Gramophone. December. p1221. 50w. 1½
Hi-Fi News and Record Review. December. p2463. 50w. 2

857 Howard Blake. THAT HAMMOND SOUND. Regal Starline SRS 5116 (E).
Gramophone. August. p398. 25w. 1
Hi-Fi News and Record Review. November. p2201. 25w. 2½

858 BLESS' EM ALL (anthology). Philips 6382 031 (E). (Reissue.)
Gramophone. February. p1438. 25w. 1½

859 Blue Mink. LIVE AT THE TALK OF THE TOWN. Regal Zonophone SLRZ 1029 (E).
Gramophone. September. p578. 25w. 2

860 Luiz Bonfá. SANCTUARY. RCA LSP 4376 $5.98.
Gramophone. July. p256. 250w. 4
Hi-Fi News and Record Review. July. p1307. 50w. 3

861 Ray Brooks. LEND ME SOME OF YOUR TIME. Polydor 2310 040 (E).
Gramophone. February. p1437. 25w. 1

862 David Brown. I WANT TO BE WITH YOU. Uni 73128 $4.98.
High Fidelity. June. p103. 500w. 2

863 Friday Brown. Philips 6308 074 (E).
Gramophone. February. p1432. 175w. 3½

864 Les Brown. NEW HORIZONS. Daybreak DR 2007 $4.98. Cart. P8DR 2007 $6.98.
Stereo Review. August. p89. 275w. 0

865 Thomas F. Browne. WEDNESDAY'S CHILD. Vertigo 1011 $5.98.
Audio. August. p62. 25w. 0

866 Darius Brubeck. CHAPLIN'S BACK. Paramount PAS 6026 $4.98. Cart. 8091-6026M $6.95.
Downbeat. March 30. p21-2. 275w. 3½
High Fidelity. May. p114. 250w. 2½

867 Julie Budd. RCA LSP 4622 $5.98. Cart. P8S 1852 $6.98.
Audio. August. p62. 50w. 2½
Stereo Review. July. p91. 275w. 2½

868 Roy Budd. KIDNAPPED. Polydor 2383 102 (E).
Hi-Fi News and Record Review. August. p1476. 25w. 2½

869 Sandy Bull. DEMOLITION DERBY. Vanguard VSD 6578 $4.98.
New York Times--Sunday. August 27. pD19. 100w. 2½

870 The Buoys. Wand WNS 15 $4.98.
Gramophone. May. p1952. 25w. 0

871 James Burton. GUITAR SOUNDS. A & M SP 4293 $5.98.
Gramophone. January. p1279. 25w. 2

872 Stan Butcher. THE TED HEATH LEGEND. RCA JET 103 (E) (2 Discs).
Gramophone. May. p1948. 275w. 4½
Jazz Journal. April. p30. 175w. 2
Records and Recordings. May. p101-2. 125w. 3½

873 Jerry Butler. BEST. Mercury SRM 61281 $4.98. Cart. MC8 61281 $6.95. Cass. MCR4 61281 $6.95. (Reissue.)
Gramophone. July. p256. 50w. 3

874 Jerry Butler. THE SPICE OF LIFE. Mercury SRM 2-7502 (2 discs) $5.98. Cart. MCT 4-2-7502 $9.95. Cass. MCT 8-2-7502 $9.95.
Hi-Fi News and Record Review. December. p2464. 200w. 1½
High Fidelity. December. p121-2. 325w. 2

875 Max Bygraves. GOLDEN HOUR OF... Pye Golden Hour GH 513 (E).
Hi-Fi News and Record Review. December. p2461. 25w. 2

876 Al Caiola. NON-STOP WESTERN THEMES. Sunset SLS 50312 (E). (Reissue.)
Hi-Fi News and Record Review. December. p2461. 50w. 2½

877 Glen Campbell. GREATEST HITS. Capitol SW 752 $5.98. Cart. 8XW 752 $6.98. Cass. 4XW 752 $6.98. (Reissue.)
Gramophone. February. p1437. 25w. 2

878 Jimmie and Vella Cameron. JIMMIE AND VELLA. Atlantic SD 8301 $5.98.
Stereo Review. November. p83. 75w. 3

879 Norman Candler. MAGIC STRINGS, VOLUME 2. Telefunken SLE 14652-P (E).
Gramophone. August. p397. 25w. 2

880 Norman Candler. SUPER STAR SOUND. Telefunken SLE 14614-P (E).
Gramophone. February. p1437. 25w. 1

881 Walter Carlos. SONIC SEASONINGS. Columbia KG 31234 $5.98.
Crawdaddy. August. p21. 1,500w. 3

882 Carpenters. A SONG FOR YOU. A & M SP 3511 $5.98. R-R 3511 $7.98. Cart. 3511 $6.95. Cass. 3511 $6.95.
High Fidelity. October. p126. 25w. 1½
New York Times--Sunday. August 6. pD22. 100w. 3½
Stereo Review. November. p84. 300w. 3½

883 Carpenters. TICKET TO RIDE. A & M SP 4205 $5.98. Cart. 8T 4205 $6.95. Cass. CS 4205 $6.95.
Gramophone. June. p111. 25w. 2
Hi-Fi News and Record Review. May. p937. 50w. 2½

884 Vikki Carr. SUPERSTAR. Columbia C 31040 $4.98. Cart. CA 31040 $6.98. Cass. CT 31040 $6.98.
Hi-Fi News and Record Review. May. p937. 25w. 2½
Stereo Review. May. p92. 100w. 1

885 Vikki Carr. WITH PEN IN HAND. Sunset 5228 $1.89
Gramophone. January. p1274. 25w. 3

886 David Cassidy. CHERISH. Bell 6070 $5.98. Cart. M86070 $6.95. Cass. M56070 $6.95.
Gramophone. August. p397. 25w. 1
High Fidelity. May. p116. 25w. 3
Records and Recordings. July. p92. 300w. 1

887 Frank Chacksfield. NEW YORK. London SP 44141 $5.98. Cart. M14141 $6.95. Cass. M84141 $6.95.
Audio. September. p119. 75w. 2½
Stereo Review. October. p88. 150w. 2

888 Frank Chacksfield. PLAYS EBB TIDE AND OTHER MILLION SELLERS. London BSP 23 (2 discs) $6.98.
Audio. October. p90. 75w. 2½

889 Frank Chacksfield. WORLD OF IMMORTAL CLASSICS. Decca SPA 176 (E).
Hi-Fi News and Record Review. May. p938. 25w. 3

890 Chaquito Big Band. SPIES AND DOLLS. Philips 6308111 (E).
Hi-Fi News and Record Review. October. p1925. 25w. 2

891 Chaquito Big Band. STORY. Philips 6641 015 (2 discs) (E). (Reissue.)
Gramophone. February. p1438. 300w. 2½

892 Cher. Kapp 5549 $5.98. Cart. K8 5549 $6.98. Cass. K7 5549 $6.98.
Gramophone. March. p1613. 100w. 2

893 Maurice Chevalier. MY LOUISE. RCA INTS 1366 (E). (Reissue.)
Hi-Fi News and Record Review. August. p1476. 50w. 3

894 Maurice Chevalier. THIS IS... RCA VPM 6055 (2 discs) $6.98. (Reissue.)
Gramophone. December. p1226. 100w. 2

895 Bobby Christian. VIBE-RATION. Ovation ZG 0116 (E).
Gramophone. May. p1956. 100w. 0
Jazz Journal. May. p28-9. 75w. 0

896 Alice Clark. Mainstream MRL 362 $5.98.
Jazz Journal. October. p39. 100w. 1

897 Gene Clark. A & M SP 4292 $5.98.
Gramophone. January. p1279. 25w. 1

898 Tom Clay. WHAT THE WORLD NEEDS NOW IS LOVE. Mowest MW 103L $5.98.
Popular Music. Fall. p59. 75w. 3½

899 CLIMAX (anthology). Columbia Studio 2 STWO 8 (E). (Reissue.)
Gramophone. December. p1222. 25w. 1½

900 Dennis Coffey. EVOLUTION. Sussex 7004 $5.98. Cart. M87004 $6.95. Cass. M57004 $6.95.
Gramophone. June. p112. 25w. 2

901 Russ Columbo. RCA LSA 3066 $5.98. (Reissue.)
Gramophone. December. p1225. 25w. 2

902 Perry Como. BEST. Readers Digest RDS 6841-6 (6 discs) (E). (Reissue.)
Hi-Fi News and Record Review. December. p2461. 200w. 2

903 Perry Como. NO OTHER LOVE. Camden CAS 941 $2.49. (Reissue.)
Gramophone. January. p1274. 50w. 4

904 Perry Como. SINGS. RCA Camden CDS 1091 (E). (Reissue.)
Hi-Fi News and Record Review. July. p1305. 50w. 2½

905 Ray Conniff Singers. I'D LIKE TO TEACH THE WORLD TO SING. Columbia KC 31220 $5.98. Cart. CA 31220 $6.98. Cass. CT 31220 $6.98.
Music Journal. May. p44. 125w. 2

906 Ray Conniff Singers. IT'S THE TALK OF THE TOWN. DJM Silverline DJSL 020 (E). (Reissue.)
Hi-Fi News and Record Review. July. p1305. 25w. 3

907 Ray Conniff Singers. WITHOUT YOU. CBS 65049 (E). (Reissue.)
Hi-Fi News and Record Review. August. p1476. 25w. 0

908 Chris Connor. SKETCHES. Stanyan SR 10029 $5.98.
Downbeat. February 17. p18. 350w. 2½
Stereo Review. February. p115. 300w. 2½

909 CONSTELLATION (Anthology). Music for Pleasure MFP 5263 (E). (Reissue.)
Hi-Fi News and Record Review. July. p1305. 50w. 3

910 Roger Coulam. HAMMOND STEREO SOUNDS TO SPOIL YOU. Contour 6870 524 (E).
Gramophone. April. p1776. 25w. 1

911 Country. Clean CN 600 $4.98. Cart. M8600 $6.95. Cass. M5600 $6.95.
Audio. December. p98-9. 300w. 3

912 Les Crane. DESIDERATA. Warner Bros. BS 2570 $5.98. Cart. M82570 $6.95. Cass. M52570 $6.95.
American Record Guide. April. p379. 300w. 5
Gramophone. July. p255. 25w. 1

913 Neal Creque. Cobblestone CST 9005 $5.98. Cart. M89005 $6.95. Cass. M59005 $6.95.
Creem. August. p66. 50w. 3

914 Bing Crosby. I LOVE YOU TRULY. Coral CPS 79 (E). (Reissue.)
Gramophone. September. p577. 50w. 4
Hi-Fi News and Record Reviews. September. p1681. 25w. 2½

915 Bing Crosby. RHYTHM ON THE RANGE. Coral CPS 81 (E). (Reissue.)
Gramophone. September. p577. 50w. 4
Hi-Fi News and Record Review. September. p1681. 25w. 2½

916 Bing Crosby. WRAP YOUR TROUBLES IN DREAMS, 1927/1931. RCA LPV 584 $5.98. (Reissue.)
Downbeat. September 14. p20. 275w. 5
Gramophone. December. p1225. 50w. 2
Music Journal. June. p36. 75w. 1

917 Bing Crosby. YOUNG. RCA Camden CD 1084 (E). (Reissue.)
Hi-Fi News and Record Review. June. p1127. 75w. 3

918 Bing Crosby and the Andrews Sisters. VOLUME 1. Coral CPS 80 (E). (Reissue.)
Gramophone. September. p577. 50w. 4
Hi-Fi News and Record Review. September. p1681. 25w. 2

919 Bing Crosby and Louis Armstrong. BING AND SATCHMO. MGM GAS 137 $4.98. (Reissue.)
Audio. November. p96. 450w. 4½

920 Bing Crosby and Count Basie. BING 'N' BASIE. Daybreak DR 2014 $5.98. Cart. P8DR 2014 $6.95. Cass. PKDR 2014 $6.95.
Downbeat. December 7. p19. 300w. 3
Gramophone. November. p984. 225w. 4
Hi-Fi News and Record Review. November. p2199. 75w. 4
Jazz Journal. December. p40. 100w. 0

Records and Recordings. October. p117. 150w. 1
Stereo Review. November. p84. 300w. 3

921 Mike Curb Congregation. HITS FROM THE GLEN CAMPBELL SHOW. MGM SE 4804 $5.98. Cart. 8130-4804M $6.95.
Audio. September. p121. 250w. 0

922 Mike Curb Congregation. SOFTLY WHISPERING I LOVE YOU. MGM SE 4821 $5.98. Cart. 8130-4821M $6.95. Cass. 5130-4821 $6.95.
Audio. September. p121. 50w. 0

923 Ronald Curtis. YOU OUGHT TO BE IN PICTURES. Argo ZRM 1001 (E).
Gramophone. June. p112. 25w. 0
Hi-Fi News and Record Review. June. p1127. 50w. 1½

924 Adge Cutler. DON'T TELL I, TELL 'EE. Regal Starline SRS 5119 (E).
Gramophone. August. p398. 25w. 1

925 Bryan Daley. VELVET GUITAR. Decca Phase 4 PFS 4239 (E).
Gramophone. December. p1221. 25w. 2½
Hi-Fi News and Records Review. June. p1127. 50w. 2½

926 Tony Darrow. A VERY SPECIAL LOVE. Roulette SR 3008 $4.98.
Stereo Review. December. p92. 125w. 2

927 Jack Daugherty and the Class of Nineteen Hundred and Seventy One. A & M SP 3038 $5.98. Cart. 8T 3038 $6.95. Cass. CS 3038 $5.98.
Gramophone. January. p1287. 200w. 4

928 Jim Dawson. YOU'LL NEVER BE LONELY WITH ME. Kama Sutra KSBS 2049 $5.98. Cart. M82049 $6.95. Cass. M52049 $6.95.
Audio. December. p95. 50w. 1

929 Jackie DeShannon. JACKIE. Atlantic SD 7231 $5.98. Cart. TP 7231 $6.95. Cass. CS 7231 $6.95.
Rolling Stone. August 17. p49. 750w. 3
Stereo Review. December. p92. 200w. ½

930 Brian Dexter. STEREO ACCORDIONS. Philips 6414 307 (E).
Gramophone. September. p578. 25w. 1

931 Neil Diamond. MOODS. Uni 73136 $5.98.
Gramophone. September. p577. 50w. 4
High Fidelity. October. p126. 25w. 3
New York Times--Sunday. December 10. pD37. 75w. 2½

Sound. October. p44. 175w. 4
Stereo Review. December. p92. 75w. 0

932 Neal Diamond. STONES. Uni 73106 $5.98. Cart. 8 73106 $6.95. Cass. 2 73106 $6.95.
American Record Guide. March. p333. 150w. 0
Audio. March. p80. 700w. 4
Gramophone. February. p1437. 75w. 1
High Fidelity. March. p117. 25w. 2½
Popular Music. Winter. p124. 50w. 3½
Rolling Stone. January 20. p52, 54. 600w. 1

933 Marlene Dietrich. IN LONDON. Columbia OS 2830 $5.98.
Gramophone. August. p397. 50w. 1

934 Disco Strings. CLOUD 9. Columbia Studio 2 TWO 370 (E).
Gramophone. May. p1952. 25w. 0

935 Sacha Distel. MORE AND MORE. Warner Bros. K 46117 (E).
Gramophone. February. p1437. 50w. 1

936 Reginald Dixon. THIS IS MY SONG. Columbia SCX 6496 (E).
Gramophone. July. p255. 25w. 1

937 Val Doonican. JUST A-SITTIN' AND A-ROCKIN'. Philips 6308 085 (E).
Gramophone. April. p1775. 300w. 4½

938 Val Doonican. THIS IS... Philips 6382 017 (E). (Reissue.)
Gramophone. January. p1274. 25w. 2

939 Val Doonican. THE WORLD OF..., VOLUME 5. Decca SPA 252 (E). (Reissue.)
Gramophone. December. p1221. 25w. 1

940 Nick Drake. PINK MOON. Capitol SMAS 9318 $5.98.
Hi-Fi News and Record Review. May. p939. 100w. 3

941 Dubliners. Music for Pleasure SMFP 5223 (E). (Reissue.)
Gramophone. January. p1279. 25w. 1

942 Archie Duncan. HIGH LEVEL ACCORDION. Beltona SBE 130 (E).
Hi-Fi News and Record Review. August. p1473. 25w. 2½

943 Leslie Duncan. SING CHILDREN SING. Columbia C 30663 $4.98. Cart. CA 30663 $6.98.
Stereo Review. May. p93. 125w. 2

944 Judith Durham. HERE I AM. Mayfair AMLB 51035 (E).
Gramophone. December. p1221. 75w. 3

945 Billy Eckstine. SENIOR SOUL. Enterprise ENS 5004 (2 discs) $9.98.
New York Times--Sunday. July 9. pD28. 50w. 3

946 Kurt Edelhagen. BIG BAND SOUND. Carnival 2941 305 (E).
Jazz and Blues. December. p29. 75w. 1½

947 Shirley Elkhard. Capitol ST 6371 $5.98.
Canadian Stereo Guide. Summer. p67. 100w. 3

948 Ray Ellington. EVERYBODY DANCE. Chapter One CMS 1009 (E).
Gramophone. October. p778. 100w. 4

949 Cass Elliot. RCA LSP 4619 $5.98. Cart. P8S 1846 $6.98. Cass. PK 1846 $6.98.
Audio. May. p95. 50w. 2½
High Fidelity. May. p116. 25w. 2
Stereo Review. June. p100. 1,800w. 3½

950 Cass Elliot. THE ROAD IS NO PLACE FOR A LADY. RCA LSP 4753 $5.98. Cart. P8S 2088 $6.95. Cass. PK 2088 $6.95.
Music Journal. December. p75. 100w. 3

951 Jay Fallen. HEART OF THE COUNTRY. Rediffusion ZS 99 (E).
Hi-Fi News and Record Review. July. p1312. 50w. 2½

952 Georgie Fame. FAME AGAIN! Regal Starline SRS 5107 (E). (Reissue.)
Gramophone. May. p1951. 25w. 2

953 THE FANTASTICS. Bell BELLS 200 (E).
Gramophone. April. p1776. 25w. 1

954 Robert Farnon. PORTRAIT OF FARNON. Eclipse ECS 2107 (E). (Reissue.)
Hi-Fi News and Record Review. July. p1305. 50w. 2

955 Jose Feliciano. MEMPHIS MENU. RCA LSP 4656 $5.98. Cart. P8S 1884 $6.95. Cass. PK 1884 $6.95.
Audio. December. p95. 50w. 1

956 Jose Feliciano. THAT THE SPIRIT NEEDS. RCA LSP 4573 $5.98. Cart. P8S 1786 $6.95. Cass. PK 1786 $6.95.
Audio. November. p91. 50w. 2½
American Record Guide. February. p285. 150w. 2
Gramophone. May. p1951. 50w. 2

Hi-Fi News and Record Review. May. p939. 200w. 2
Stereo Review. April. p90. 75w. 1

957 Ferrante and Teicher. THE TWO PIANOS OF ... PLAY SONGS OF TODAY. United Artists FT 7001/2 (2 discs) (E). (Reissue.)
Gramophone. May. p1613. 50w. $2\frac{1}{2}$

958 Arthur Fiedler and the Boston Pops. ...SUPERSTAR. Polydor PD 5008 $5.98.
Gramophone. September. p578. 50w. 0
Hi-Fi News and Record Review. October. p1925. 100w. $2\frac{1}{2}$
High Fidelity. June. p107. 100w. 3

959 Arthur Fiedler and the Boston Pops. BURT BACHARACH-HAL DAVID SONGBOOK. Polydor PD 5019 $5.98. Cart. CF 5019 $6.98. Cass. 8F 5019 $6.98.
High Fidelity. September. p102. 150w. 1

960 Arthur Fiedler and the Boston Pops. EMBRACEABLE YOU. RCA Camden CDS 1096 (E). (Reissue.)
Gramophone. May. p1948. 50w. $2\frac{1}{2}$
Hi-Fi News and Record Review. May. p937. 50w. 4

961 Arthur Fiedler and the Boston Pops. FORGOTTEN DREAMS. Polydor PD 5007 $5.98. Cart. 8F 5007 $6.98. Cass. CF 5007 $6.98.
High Fidelity. May. p112. 150w. $2\frac{1}{2}$

962 The Fifth Dimension. LIVE! Bell 9000 (2 discs) $11.98. R-R BEL 9000 $9.95. Cart. BEL 89000 $9.95. Cass. BEL 59000 $9.95.
Audio. January. p76. 300w. 4
Gramophone. May. p1951. 100w. 3
Stereo Review. May. p93. 50w. 2

963 The Fifth Dimension. REFLECTIONS. Bell 6065 $4.98. Cart. 86065 $6.95. Cass. 56065 $6.95.
Audio. January. p76. 50w. 3

964 Ella Fitzgerald. ELLA SINGS GERSHWIN, VOLUME 2. Metro 2682 023 (E) (2 discs). (Reissue.)
Gramophone. May. p1951. 100w. 4
Jazz and Blues. April. p26. 250w. $2\frac{1}{2}$
Jazz Journal. March. p32-3. 175w. 4
Records and Recordings. April. p109. 175w. 4

965 Ella Fitzgerald. ELLA SWINGS WITH NELSON. Metro 2682 035 (2 discs) (E). (Reissue.)
Jazz Journal. December. p32. 200w. 3

966 Ella Fitzgerald. WATCH WHAT HAPPENS. BASF 20712 $5.98. Cart. 40712 $6.98. Cass. 30951 $6.98.
Music Journal. November. p40. 25w. 2

967 Jackie Flavelle. ADMISSION FREE. York FYK 408 (E).
Gramophone. December. p1221. 25w. 1

968 Guy Fletcher. WHEN THE MORNING COMES. Philips 6303 037 (E).
Gramophone. September. p577. 25w. 1

969 Tennessee Ernie Ford. I LEFT MY HEART IN SAN FRANCISCO. Music for Pleasure MFP 5251 (E). (Reissue.)
Gramophone. May. p1951. 25w. 2

970 The Fortunes. STORM IN A TEACUP. Capitol ST 11041 $5.98. Cart. 8XT 11041 $6.98. Cass. 4XT 11041 $6.98.
Gramophone. May. p1952. 25w. 1

971 The Four Seasons. THE BIG ONES. Philips 6336 208 (E). (Reissue.)
Gramophone. January. p1274. 25w. 4

972 Connie Francis. GREATEST HITS. MGM GAS 109 $4.98.
Gramophone. February. p1437. 25w. 2

973 Billy Fury. THE WORLD OF... Decca SPA 188 (E). (Reissue.)
Gramophone. May. p1951. 25w. 2

974 Tommy Garrett. THE BEST OF THE FIFTY GUITARS, VOLUME 2/3. Liberty LST 35001 (2 discs) $9.96. Cart. 9118/9 $9.98. Cass. C118/9 $9.98. (Reissue.)
Audio. November. p93. 100w. 0

975 Tommy Garrett. MARIA ELENA. Liberty LST 14007 $5.98. Cart. 8707 $6.98. Cass. 0707 $6.98.
Gramophone. May. p1952. 75w. 2

976 Tommy Garrett. THE WAY OF LOVE. United Artists UAS 5569 $5.98.
Gramophone. November. p984. 100w. 2

977 Gary and Stu. FARE. Carnaby 6302 012 (E).
Gramophone. April. p1776. 25w. 0

978 Gerry and the Ohio. OHIO COUNTRY. Emerald GES 1072 (E).
Hi-Fi News and Record Review. September. p1683. 25w. 2

979 Carroll Gibbons. 1931/48. World Record Club SH 167/8 (2 discs) (E). (Reissue.)

Gramophone. December. p1225. 150w. 4
Records and Recordings. December. p102. 225w. 2½

980 Astrud Gilberto. GILBERTO WITH TURRENTINE. CTI CTI 6008 $5.98. Cart. CT8 6008 $6.95. Cass. CTC 6008 $6.95.
Gramophone. October. p781. 250w. 4
Hi-Fi News and Record Review. September. p1681. 50w. 2
Jazz Journal. August. p31. 150w. 3

981 Alasdair Gillies. HIGHLAND WORLD. Decca SPA 197 (E).
Hi-Fi News and Record Review. August. p1473. 25w. 2½

982 Stuart Gillies. ALL MY LOVE. Philips 6308 118 (E).
Gramophone. November. p984. 50w. 3

983 Stuart Gillies. INTRODUCING. Philips 6308 076 (E).
Gramophone. February. p1437. 25w. 1

984 Willie Glahe. BIRTHDAY SERENADE. Decca SLK 16742 (Germany).
Hi-Fi News and Record Review. July. p1308. 50w. 1½

985 Willie Glahe. O DEUTSCHE HEIMAT. Decca Musik Für Alle ND 678 (Germany).
Hi-Fi News and Record Review. July. p1308. 50w. 3

986 Marty Gold. SOUNDS IMPOSSIBLE. Audio Fidelity AFSD 6248 $4.98.
Music Journal. February. p58. 100w. 3

987 THE GOLDEN AGE OF THE MUSIC HALL (anthology). Rhapsody RHA 6014 (E).
Hi-Fi News and Record Review. October. p1923. 125w. 3

988 GOLDEN HOUR OF THE BEST OF THE BEATLES SONGS (anthology). Golden Hour GH 523 (E).
Gramophone. April. p1776. 25w. 1½

989 GOLDEN HOUR OF ORIGINAL SMASH HITS (anthology). Golden Hour GH 505 (E).
Gramophone. April. p1776. 25w. 2½

990 GOLDEN HOUR PRESENTS A STEREO SHOWCASE (anthology). Golden Hour GH 502 (E).
Gramophone. March. p1613. 50w. 2

991 GOLDEN THEMES OF HOLLYWOOD (anthology). Coral CPS 78 (E). (Reissue.)
Hi-Fi News and Record Review. September. p1682. 50w. 1½

992 Ron Goodwin. SOMEBODY NAMED ... PLAYS SOMEBODY NAMED BURT BACHARACH. Capitol ST 11012 $5.98.
Gramophone. June. p111. 100w. 4
Hi-Fi News and Record Review. July. p1305. 50w. 4
Stereo Review. October. p92, 96. 500w. ½

993 Johnnie Gray. SAX-CESS. Philips 6382 012 (E).
Gramophone. April. p1776. 25w. 1

994 Buddy Greco. IT'S MY LIFE. Pye NSPL 18381 (E).
Gramophone. October. p778. 125w. 4

995 THE GREAT WELSH CHOIRS. Qualiton Daffodil DAF 209 (E).
Hi-Fi News and Record Review. October. p1923. 25w. 2½

996 GRECIAN SUMMER. Rediffusion ZS 100 (E).
Hi-Fi News and Record Review. July. p1305. 50w. 2½

997 Max Gregor. BIG BAND SOUND. Carnival 2941 304 (E).
Hi-Fi News and Record Review. October. p1923. 50w. 3
Jazz Journal. September. p32. 125w. 0
Records and Recordings. October. p118. 75w. 2½

998 John Gregory. THE CASCADING STRINGS PLAY. Philips 6382 035 (E).
Gramophone. May. p1951. 25w. 2

999 John Gregory. GOLDEN MEMORIES. Philips 6308 061 (E).
Gramophone. January. p1279. 50w. 3

1000 DIE GROSSE SCHLAGER-REVUE 6 (anthology). Telefunken TS 3144/1-2 (Germany).
Hi-Fi News and Record Review. July. p1308. 25w. 2½

1001 Jorge Gurascier. SUENO OTONAL. Decca Eclipse ECS 2097 (E).
Gramophone. March. p1614. 50w. 2

1002 Denny Guy. Daybreak DR 2008 $5.98.
Audio. November. p91. 100w. 3½

1003 Lani Hall. SUN DOWN LADY. A & M SP 4359 $5.98. Cart. 8T 4359 $6.95. Cass. CS 4359 $6.95.
High Fidelity. November. p122. 100w. 3
New York Times--Sunday. September 10. pD38. 600w. 4
Popular Music. Fall. p92. 50w. 4

1004 Hamilton, Frank, and Reynolds. HALLWAY SYMPHONY. Dunhill DSX 50113 $5.98. Cart. M850103 $6.95. Cass. M550103 $6.95.
Audio. August. p63. 50w. 2½

1005 John Hanson. THIS IS... Philips 6382 013 (E).
Gramophone. January. p1274. 25w. 3

1006 John Hanson. FILM THEMES. Philips 6308 096 (E).
Hi-Fi News and Record Review. August. p1477. 50w. 3

1007 Richard Harris. MY BOY. Dunhill DSX 50116 $5.98. Cart. M85116 $6.95. Cass. M55116 $6.95.
Gramophone. May. p1951. 50w. 1½

1008 Rolf Harris. ALL TOGETHER NOW. Music for Pleasure MFP 5257 (E). (Reissue.)
Gramophone. July. p254. 25w. 2

1009 Rolf Harris. INSTANT MUSIC. Columbia SCX 6476 (E).
Gramophone. January. p1279. 25w. 3

1010 Cathie Harrop. IRELAND. Emerald Gem GES 1075 (E).
Hi-Fi News and Record Review. October. p1923. 25w. 2½

1011 Tony Hatch. A LATIN HAPPENING. Golden Hour GH 509 (E).
Gramophone. March. p1614. 100w. 2½

1012 Alan Haven. IMAGES. Philips 6382 001 (E).
Gramophone. March. p1623. 125w. 2

1013 Alan Hawkshaw. 27 TOP TV THEMES AND COMMERCIALS. Columbia Studio 2 TWO 391 (E).
Gramophone. December. p1222. 25w. 1

1014 Hawthorn Scottish Dance Band. A TRIBUTE TO JIMMY SHAND. Emerald GEM GES 1073 (E).
Hi-Fi News and Record Review. August. p1473. 25w. 2½

1015 Ted Heath. THOSE WERE THE DAYS. London SP 44164 $5.98.
Jazz Journal. January. p30. 300w. 0
Stereo Review. May. p93-4. 150w. 1

1016 Joe Henderson. ROGERS AND ASTAIRE FAVOURITES. Hallmark/Marble Arch HMA 209 (E). (Reissue.)
Hi-Fi News and Record Review. May. p937. 25w. 2½

1017 Joe Henderson. SECRET LOVE. Columbia Studio 2 TWO 369 (E).
Gramophone. May. p1952. 25w. $1\frac{1}{2}$

1018 Joe Henderson. UNFORGETTABLE HITS OF THE 50's. Columbia Studio 2 TWO 369 (E).
Hi-Fi News and Record Review. May. p937. 25w. 2

1019 Jon Hendricks. TIMES OF LOVE. Philips 6414 302 (E).
Gramophone. May. p1951. 50w. $2\frac{1}{2}$
Jazz Journal. April. p33. 200w. 3

1020 Herd. NOSTALGIA. Bumble GEMP 5001 (E).
Gramophone. December. p1222. 25w. 2

1021 Vince Hill. IN MY THOUGHTS OF YOU. Columbia SCX 6505 (E).
Hi-Fi News and Record Review. October. p1925. 25w. 2

1022 Vince Hill. LOOK AROUND (AND YOU'LL FIND ME THERE). Columbia SCX 6482 (E).
Gramophone. February. p1432. 100w. $2\frac{1}{2}$

1023 Vince Hill. MY BOY BILL. Regal Starline SRS 5115 (E). (Reissue.)
Gramophone. August. p397. 100w. 4

1024 Vince Hill. YOU'RE MY WORLD. Music for Pleasure SMFP 5255 (E). (Reissue.)
Gramophone. April. p1775. 50w. $2\frac{1}{2}$

1025 Hillside Singers. I'D LIKE TO TEACH THE WORLD TO SING. Metromedia KMD 1051 \$5.98. Cart. 8090-1051 \$6.95. Cass. 5090-1051 \$6.95.
Audio. September. p121. 50w. $2\frac{1}{2}$

1026 Rupert Hine and David MacIver. PICK UP A BONE. Capitol SMAS 879 \$4.98.
Sound. April. p37. 150w. 1

1027 Stanley Holloway. Regal Starline. MRS 5104 (E). (Reissue.)
Gramophone. May. p1956. 75w. $3\frac{1}{2}$

1028 Hollyridge Strings. THE BEATLES SONGBOOK. Capitol ST 2116 \$5.98. Cart. 8XT 2116 \$6.98. Cass. 4XT 2116 \$6.98.
Gramophone. August. p398. 25w. 0
Hi-Fi News and Record Review. August. p1476. 25w. $1\frac{1}{2}$

1029 Jake Holmes. HOW MUCH TIME? Columbia C 30996 $5.98.
Hi-Fi News and Record Review. August. p1477. 100w. 4

1030 HOORAY FOR HOLLYWOOD (anthology). RCA LPV 579 $5.98. (Reissue.)
Music Journal. June. p36. 100w. 3

1031 Lena Horne. LENA LIKE LATIN. Ember SE 8005 (E). (Reissue.)
Gramophone. June. p111. 100w. 0

1032 HOT HITS, 10 (anthology). Music for Pleasure MFP 5260 (E).
Hi-Fi News and Record Review. May. p939. 25w. 2½

1033 Englebert Humperdinck. IN TIME. Parrot XPAS 71056 $5.98. Cart. M79856 $6.95. Cass. M79656 $6.95.
Gramophone. November. p984. 100w. 3
Music Journal. November. p57. 100w. 2

1034 Englebert Humperdinck. LIVE AT THE RIVERIA, LAS VEGAS. Parrot XPAS 71051 $5.98.
Audio. October. p90. 50w. 2½
Gramophone. February. p1437. 100w. 2
Stereo Review. October. p96. 300w. 2½

1035 Les Humphries. SUPER STAR SOUND PIANO CONCERTO. Decca SLK 16713 (Germany).
Gramophone. April. p1775. 25w. 2

1036 Les Humphries. TAKE CARE OF ME. Decca SKL 5126 (E).
Gramophone. July. p255. 25w. 1

1037 John Hurley. ...DELIVERS ONE MORE HALLELUJAH. Bell 6075 $5.98. Cart. M86075 $6.95. Cass. M56075 $6.95.
High Fidelity. September. p103. 175w. 3

1038 Brian Hyland. Uni 73097 $4.98. Cart. 8-73097 $6.95. Cass. 2-73097 $6.95.
Gramophone. May. p1951. 25w. 2

1039 Nick Ingman. THE LOVE ALBUM. Polydor 2310 210 (E).
Hi-Fi News and Record Review. November. p2201. 25w. 3

1040 The Inkspots. Rhapsody RHAS 9011 (E). (Reissue.)
Hi-Fi News and Record Review. July. p1307. 50w. 1
Records and Recordings. July. p96. 125w. 0

1041 J.S. BACH IS ALIVE AND WELL AND DOING HIS THING ON THE KOTO. RCA LSC 3227 $5.98.
American Record Guide. January. p237. 150w. 0
Music Journal. February. p58. 125w. 2

1042 Tommy James. CHRISTIAN OF THE WORLD. Roulette SR 3001 $4.98. Cart. 8045-3001M $6.95. Cass. 5045-3001M $6.95.
Audio. August. p61. 25w. 1

1043 Tommy James. MY HEAD, MY BED AND MY RED GUITAR. Roulette SR 3007 $4.98. Cart. 8045-3007M $6.95. Cass. 5045-3007M $6.95.
Audio. November. p92. 25w. 0
Gramophone. September. p578. 25w. 1

1044 Pepe Jaramillo. MEXICAN LOVE. Columbia Studio 2 TWO 366 (E).
Gramophone. April. p1779. 100w. 2½

1045 Pepe Jaramillo. ROMANTICA. Regal Starline SRS 5081 (E). (Reissue.)
Gramophone. January. p1280. 25w. 3

1046 Pepe Jaramillo. SOUTH OF THE BORDER. Music for Pleasure MFP 5242 (E). (Reissue.)
Gramophone. August. p398. 75w. 3
Hi-Fi News and Record Review. December. p2461. 25w. 2½

1047 Antonio Carlos Jobim. STONE FLOWER. CTI CTL 3 (E).
Gramophone. October. p781. 175w. 4
Hi-Fi News and Record Review. October. p1923. 75w. 2½
Jazz Journal. September. p33. 75w. 2½

1048 Jack Jones. BREAD WINNERS. RCA LSP 4692 $5.98. Cart. P8S 1935 $6.95.
High Fidelity. August. p106. 25w. 2½
Gramophone. August. p397. 100w. 4
Music Journal. October. p59. 100w. 3

1049 Jack Jones. IN LOVE. EMI One Up OU 2002 (E). (Reissue.)
Gramophone. December. p1221. 300w. 4½

1050 Jack Jones. SIMPLY. Coral CPS 84 (E). (Reissue.)
Gramophone. September. p577. 50w. 3
Hi-Fi News and Record Review. September. p1681. 50w. 2½

1051 Jack Jones. A SONG FOR YOU. RCA LSP 4613 $5.98. Cart. P8S 1842 $6.95.

Gramophone. June. p111. 150w. 4
Hi-Fi News and Record Review. May. p937. 25w. $2\frac{1}{2}$

1052 Nicky Jones. Philips 6308 069 (E).
Gramophone. January. p1279. 25w. 1

1053 Quincy Jones. SMACKWATER JACK. A & M SP 3037 $5.98. Cart. 8T 3037 $6.95. Cass. CS 3037 $6.95.
Audio. May. p95. 75w. $3\frac{1}{2}$
Hi-Fi News and Record Review. July. p1313. 100w. 1
High Fidelity. January. p112. 300w. $4\frac{1}{2}$

1054 Tom Jones. CLOSE UP. Parrot XPAS 71055 $5.98. Cart. M79855 $6.95. Cass. M79655 $6.95.
Gramophone. August. p397. 25w. 4
Stereo Review. October. p96, 98. 200w. 1

1055 Tom Jones. LIVE AT CAESAR'S PALACE. Parrot XPAS 71049/50 (2 discs) $8.98. Cart. K79850 $9.95. Cass. K79650 $9.95.
Gramophone. February. p1437. 125w. 2

1056 Bert Kaempfert. A TASTE OF KAEMPFERT. World Record Club SM 190-5 (6 discs) (E). (Reissue.)
Hi-Fi News and Record Review. August. p1476. 200w. $3\frac{1}{2}$

1057 Kamahl. ABOUT FALLING IN LOVE. Philips 6308 093 (E).
Gramophone. May. p1951. 50w. 2

1058 Artie Kane. PLAYS ORGAN. RCA LSP 4595 $5.98.
Downbeat. May 11. p21-2. 225w. 2
High Fidelity. May. p109. 300w. $\frac{1}{2}$

1059 Artie Kane. SWINGING SCREEN SCENE. RCA LSP 4693 $5.98.
Music Journal. December. p75. 125w. $2\frac{1}{2}$

1060 George Kayatta. TIME TO WONDER WHY. RCA LSP 4638 $5.98.
Audio. September. p121. 25w. 3

1061 John Keating. KEATING CONDUCTS TV THEMES. Columbia Studio 2 TWO 372 (E).
Hi-Fi News and Record Review. June. p1127. 25w. $2\frac{1}{2}$

1062 Greta Keller and Rod McKuen. AN EVENING IN VIENNA. Stanyan 5040 $5.98.
Stereo Review. September. p74, 76. 700w. 2

1063 Greta Keller. GREAT SONGS OF THE 30'S. Stanyan SR 10042 $5.98.

Stereo Review. September. p74, 76. 700w. 3

1064 Greta Keller. LIVE IS A DAYDREAM AND OTHER SONGS. Monitor MFS 725 $4.98.
Stereo Review. February. p112. 2,000w. 4

1065 Greta Keller. WITH ALL MY LOVE. Decca/Eclipse ECM 2049 (E).
Stereo Review. February. p112. 2000w. 4

1066 Anita Kerr Singers. DAYTIME, NIGHTIME. Philips 6830 093 (E).
Gramophone. July. p254. 75w. 3

1067 Morgana King. CUORE DI MAMA. Mainstream MRL 355 $5.98.
Jazz Journal. September. p38. 50w. 1

1068 Hildegard Knef. FROM HERE ON IN IT GETS ROUGH. London PS 596 $5.98.
Stereo Review. January. p108. 350w. 3

1069 Bonnie Koloc. HOLD ON TO ME. Ovation 1426 $5.98. Cart. M81426 $6.95. Cass. M51426 $6.95.
Gramophone. August. p397. 50w. 1

1070 André Kostelanetz. FOR ALL WE KNOW. Columbia C 30672 $4.98. Cart. CA 30672 $6.98.
Gramophone. February. p1437. 50w. 0

1071 Jackie and Roy Kral. TIME AND LOVE. CTI 6019 $5.98. Cart. CT8 6019 $6.98. Cass. CTC 6019 $6.98.
Stereo Review. December. p88. 350w. 5

1072 Charlie Kunz. THE WORLD OF... VOLUME 3. Decca SPA 194 (E).
Gramophone. May. p1952. 25w. 2

1073 Francis Lai. PLAYS... United Artists UAS 5515 $5.98. Cart. U8275 $6.98. Cass. K0275 $6.98.
Audio. March. p80. 25w. 2

1074 Cleo Laine. FEEL THE WARM. Columbia SCX 6497 (E).
Gramophone. July. p254. 100w. 4
Hi-Fi News and Record Review. July. p1307. 25w. $2\frac{1}{2}$
Jazz and Blues. September. p26-7. 225w. 3
Jazz Journal. July. p30-1. 200w. 1

1075 Cleo Laine. SHAKESPEARE - AND ALL THAT JAZZ. Philips 6382 014 (E).
Gramophone. May. p1958, 61. 175w. $3\frac{1}{2}$
Jazz Journal. April. p34. 175w. 3

1076 Dennis Lambert. BAGS AND THINGS. Dunhill DS 50119 $4.98. Cart. M85119 $6.95. Cass. M55119 $6.95.
Hi-Fi News and Record Review. October. p1926. 125w. 0
High Fidelity. August. p106. 25w. 3½

1077 Richard Landis. NATURAL CAUSES. Dunhill DSX 50115 $5.98. Cart. M85115 $6.95. Cass. M55115 $6.95.
Downbeat. April 13. p28-9. 200w. 4

1078 Orquesta Laronda. AMOR! EMI Doubleup DOU 103 (2 discs) (E).
Gramophone. December. p1225. 100w. 2½

1079 James Last. HAPPY LEHAR. Polydor 2371 169 (E).
Gramophone. January. p1273-4. 175w. 4

1080 James Last. LAST OF OLD ENGLAND. Polydor 2371 164 (E).
Gramophone. January. p1273. 175w. 4

1081 James Last. LOVE MUST BE THE REASON. Polydor PD 5509 $5.98. Cart. 8F 5509 $6.98. Cass. CF 5509 $6.98.
Audio. November. p90. 50w. 1

1082 James Last. NON-STOP DANCING, VOLUME 12. Polydor 2371 141 (E).
Gramophone. January. p1274. 175w. 3

1083 Latin Magic, Volume 1 (Anthology). Carnival 12928 503 (E). (Reissue.)
Gramophone. January. p1280. 150w. 3

1084 Steve Lawrence and Eydie Gorme. THE WORLD OF... MGM SE 4803 $5.98. Cart. 8130-4803M $6.95. Cass. 5130-4803M $6.95. (Reissue.)
Music Journal. November. p59. 100w. 3

1085 Syd Lawrence. THE MUSIC OF GLEN MILLER. Philips 6641 017 (2 discs) (E).
Gramophone. February. p1437. 125w. 2½

1086 Syd Lawrence. SOMETHING OLD, SOMETHING NEW. Philips 6308 909 (E).
Gramophone. May. p1948. 125w. 4

1087 Peggy Lee. NORMA DELORIS EGSTROM FROM JAMESTOWN, NORTH DAKOTA. Capitol ST 11077 $5.98. Cart. 8XT 11077 $6.98.
Stereo Review. October. p94. 1,400w. 5

1088 Peggy Lee. WHERE DID THEY GO? Capitol ST 810 $4.98. Cart. 8XT 810 $6.98.
Library Journal. January 15. p179. 75w. 1½

1089 Phillip John Lee. GUITAR KALEIDOSCOPE. Chapter One LRS 5003 (E).
Gramophone. March. p1613. 25w. 2

1090 Raymond Lefevre. VARIETÉS. Barclay 521146 (France).
Gramophone. April. p1775. 25w. 2

1091 Michel Legrand. BRIAN'S SONG. Bell 6071 $5.98. Cart. M86071 $6.95. Cass. M56071 $6.95.
New York Times--Sunday. August 27. pD20. 75w. 2½
Stereo Review. October. p98. 225w. 2½

1092 The Lettermen. Capitol SW 11010 $5.98. Cart. 8XW 11010 $6.98. Cass. 4XW 11010 $6.98.
Gramophone. September. p577. 25w. 3
Hi-Fi News and Record Review. September. p1685. 150w. 2

1093 The Lettermen. LOVE BOOK. Capitol ST 836 $5.98. Cart. 8XT 836 $6.95. Cass. 4XT 836 $6.95.
American Record Guide. January. p237. 75w. 0

1094 Enoch Light and the Light Brigade. SOUNDS OF THE BIG BANDS, VOLUME 2. Columbia Studio 2 TWO 367 (E).
Gramophone. April. p1775. 50w. 2½

1095 The Linha Singers. VOICES IN RHYTHM. Rediffusion ZS 97 (E).
Records and Recordings. May. p102-3. 150w. 1

1096 Trini Lopez. VIVA. Capitol SK 11009 $5.98.
Gramophone. October. p781. 100w. 4

1097 Lorelei. HOAGY CARMICHAEL'S GREATEST HITS. Columbia SCX 6499 (E).
Gramophone. July. p255. 50w. 1
Hi-Fi News and Record Review. August. p1476. 50w. 1

1098 Joe Loss. DANCES FOR THE WORLD BALLROOM CHAMPIONSHIP. Columbia SCX 6502 (E).
Gramophone. September. p578. 25w. 1

1099 Geoff Love. BIG CONCERTO MOVIE THEMES. Music for Pleasure MFP 5261 (E).
Hi-Fi News and Record Review. July. p1307. 75w. 2½

1100 Geoff Love. LOVE WITH MUSIC. Music for Pleasure MFP 5246 (E). (Reissue.)
Gramophone. May. p1948, 1951. 25w. 2½

1101 Geoff Love. YOUR TOP TV THEMES. Music for Pleasure MFP 5272 (E).

Hi-Fi News and Record Review. June. p1127. 25w. 2½

1102 Lulu. THE MOST OF... Music for Pleasure MFP 5254 (E). (Reissue.)
Gramophone. May. p1951. 50w. 2

1103 Vera Lynn. UNFORGETTABLE SONGS. Columbia SCX 6500 (E).
Gramophone. October. p778. 150w. 4
Hi-Fi News and Record Review. November. p2201. 75w. 3

1104 Vera Lynn. WHEN THE LIGHTS GO ON AGAIN. Stanyan SR 10032 $5.98.
Stereo Review. November. p88. 200w. 3

1105 Vera Lynn. WORLD OF ... VOLUME 4. Decca SPA 255 (E). (Reissue.)
Hi-Fi News and Record Review. November. p2201. 75w. 3½

1106 Gayle McCormick. Dunhill D5 50109 $4.98. Cart. M85109 $6.95. Cass. M55109 $6.95.
Gramophone. March. p1613. 125w. 1½

1107 Los Machucambos. MUSICA LATINA AND LOVE. Decca Phase 4 PES 4238 (E).
Gramophone. April. p1779. 100w. 2

1108 Kenneth McKellar. EVERGREEN WORLD OF... Decca SPA 149 (E). (Reissue.)
Gramophone. February. p1437. 50w. 2

1109 Kenneth McKellar. PEOPLE. London International SW 99538 $5.98.
Audio. November. p90. 50w. 2

1110 Rod McKuen. GRAND TOUR. Warner Bros. 2XS 1947 (2 discs) $6.98. Cart. M81947 $6.95. Cass. M51947 $6.95.
Library Journal. February 1. p481. 100w. 2½

1112 Ray McVay. COME DANCING TO THE HITS OF TODAY. Philips 6414 304 (E).
Gramophone. May. p1952. 25w. 2
Hi-Fi News and Record Review. July. p1305. 25w. 1

1113 Ray McVay. OLE MCVAY. Philips 6308 015 (E).
Gramophone. March. p1614. 75w. 1½

1114 Ray McVay. PLAYS. Philips 6414 750 (E).
Gramophone. September. p578. 25w. 2

1115 Henry Mancini. BIG SCREEN/LITTLE SCREEN. RCA LSP 4630 $5.98. Cart. P8S 1864 $6.95. Cass. PK 1864 $6.95.
Canadian Stereo Guide. Summer. p67. 100w. 3

1116 Henry Mancini and Doc Severinsen. BRASS ON IVORY. RCA LSP 4629 $5.98. Cart. P8S 1862 $6.95. Cass. PK 1862 $6.95.
High Fidelity. July. p106. 25w. ½
Music Journal. October. p59. 100w. 4

1117 Johnny Mann Singers. UP, UP AND AWAY. Sunset SLS 50290 (E). (Reissue.)
Gramophone. May. p1951. 25w. 2
Hi-Fi News and Record Review. May. p938. 25w. 3

1118 Roberto Mann. WORLD OF WALTZES, VOLUME 2. Decca SPA 180 (E). (Reissue.)
Gramophone. February. p1437. 75w. 2½

1119 Bernard Manning. SINGS 16 FAVORITE SONGS. Decca SKL 5130 (E).
Gramophone. September. p578. 25w. 0

1120 Tony Mansell's Coffee Set. EASY TO REMEMBER. DJM Silverline DJSL 021 (E).
Hi-Fi News and Record Review. July. p1305. 25w. 1½

1121 Mantovani. 25TH ANNIVERSARY ALBUM. London XPS 610 $5.98. Cart. M72193 $6.95. Cass. M57193 $6.95.
Music Journal. October. p59-60. 200w. 3

1122 Mantovani. TO LOVERS EVERYWHERE, U.S.A. London X598 $5.98. Cass. M57187 $6.95.
Gramophone. April. p1775. 25w. 2

1123 Manuel and Pepe Jaramillo. MANUEL MEETS... Columbia Studio 2 TWO 359 (E).
Gramophone. January. p1280. 100w. 3

1124 Manuela. SONGS OF LOVE - ... in U.S.A. Telefunken SLE 14632 (Germany).
Hi-Fi News and Record Review. July. p1308. 50w. 3

1125 Marjoe. BAD, BUT NOT EVIL. Chelsea CHE 1005 $5.98.
New York Times--Sunday. December 3. pD26. 250w. 2½

1126 Andreas Markides and his Bouzoukis. MIDNIGHT IN ATHENS. Polydor 2489 039 (E).
Records and Recordings. May. p106. 125w. 1

1127 Brian Marshall. Philips 6303 015 (E).
Gramophone. January. p1279. 25w. 2

1128 Lena Martell. PRESENTING. Pye NSPL 18378 (E).
Hi-Fi News and Record Review. August. p1476. 75w. 2

1129 Lena Martell. THE WORLD OF... Decca SPA 246 (E). (Reissue.)
Gramophone. September. p577. 25w. 3

1130 Dean Martin. CHA CHA DE AMOR. Capitol ST 1702 $5.98.
Gramophone. January. p1280. 50w. 3

1131 Dean Martin. DINO. Reprise MS 2053 $5.98. Cart. M82053 $6.95. Cass. M52053 $6.95.
Gramophone. May. p1951. 25w. 1
Hi-Fi News and Record Review. May. p937. 25w. 2

1132 Ray Martin and Living Brass. TIJUANA SOUNDS. RCA Camden CDS 1104 (E).
Hi-Fi News and Record Review. November. p2201. 25w. 3½

1133 Al Martino. LOVE THEMES FROM "THE GODFATHER." Capitol ST 11071 $5.98. Cart. 8XT 11071 $6.98. Cass. 4XT 11071 $6.98.
Hi-Fi News and Record Review. October. p1925. 25w. 2½

1134 Johnny Mathis. IN PERSON. Columbia KG 30979 $6.98. (2 discs). Cart. GA 30979 $7.98. Cass. GT 30979 $7.98.
Audio. October. p89. 75w. 2½

1135 Paul Mauriat. MAMY BLUE. Philips 6332 016 (E).
Gramophone. July. p255. 25w. 0
Hi-Fi News and Record Review. December. p2,461. 25w. 2

1136 Paul Mauriat. PLAYS WORLD HITS. Philips 6641 036 (2 discs) (E). (Reissue.)
Gramophone. April. p1775. 25w. 2

1137 Paul Mauriat. THIS IS... Philips 6444 501 (E). (Reissue.)
Gramophone. January. p1274. 75w. 4

1138 Billy May. MAD ABOUT MAY. Regal Starline SRS 5108 (E). (Reissue.)
Gramophone. May. p1948. 100w. 3
Hi-Fi News and Record Review. May. p938. 50w. 3
Jazz Journal. December. p41. 125w. 3½

1139 Billy May. SORTA-DIXIE. Creative World ST 1054 $5.50. (Reissue.)
New York Times--Sunday. May 7. pD29. 25w. 2

1140 Billy May. SORTA-MAY. Creative World ST 1051 $5.50. (Reissue.)
Jazz Journal. January. p33. 175w. 2
New York Times--Sunday. May 7. pD29. 25w. 2

1141 Judy Mayhan. Decca DL 75287 $5.98. Cart. 6-5287 $6.98. Cass. C73-5287 $6.98.
Audio. May. p95. 50w. 2½

1142 Los Mayos. THE ROMANTIC GUITAR. Carnival 2928 006 (E).
Gramophone. January. p1274. 50w. 2

1143 Stef Meeder. PROVOCATIVE HAMMOND. Columbia Studio 2 TWO 377 (E).
Gramophone. July. p255. 25w. 1

1144 George Melachrino. THE WORLD OF, VOLUME 2. Decca SPA 247 (E).
Gramophone. December. p1221. 25w. 2½
Hi-Fi News and Record Review. November. p2201. 25w. 3

1145 Sergio Mendes. NIGHT AND DAY. Mayfair AMLB 51032 (E). (Reissue.)
Gramophone. August. p398. 175w. 4
Hi-Fi News and Record Review. August. p1476. 25w. 2½

1146 Sergio Mendes and Brasil 77. PAIS TROPICAL. A & M SP 4315 $5.98. Cart. 4315 $6.98. Cass. CS-4315 $6.98.
Gramophone. February. p1438. 250w. 1
Stereo Review. February. p109-110. 150w. 3

1147 Sergio Mendes and Brasil 77. PRIMAL ROOTS. A & M SP 4353 $5.98. Cart. 8T 4353 $6.95. Cass. CS 4353 $6.95.
Gramophone. November. p989-90. 600w. 4
Hi-Fi News and Record Review. December. p2461. 75w. 2½

1148 Rafael Mendez. TRUMPET EXTRAORDINARY. Coral CPS 82 (E).
Gramophone. August. p397. 25w. 2

1149 Jo Ment's Happy Sound. FILM HITS FOR DANCING. Joy JOY 5238 (E).
Hi-Fi News and Record Review. December. p246. 25w. 1

1150 Tony Mercer. SINGS JOHNNY MERCER. Columbia SCX 6503 (E).
Gramophone. August. p397. 250w. 5
Hi-Fi News and Record Review. October. p1925. 25w. 2

1151 Bette Midler. THE DIVINE MISS M. Atlantic SD 7238 $5.98. Cart. M827238 $6.95. Cass. M57328 $6.95.
New York Times--Sunday. December 3. pD26. 1,000w. 4
Rolling Stone. December 21. p62, 64. 750w. 3

1152 Glenn Miller Orchestra (Members of). GLEN MILLER'S GREATEST HITS. Golden Hour GH 810 (E).
Gramophone. December. p1221. 25w. 1

1153 MILLION SELLER HITS, VOLUME 2 (anthology). Music for Pleasure MFP 5282 (E). (Reissue.)
Gramophone. August. p398. 25w. 1

1154 Mrs. Mills. ANOTHER FLIPPIN' PARTY. Parlophone PCS 7153 (E).
Gramophone. December. p1222. 25w. 1

1155 Mrs. Mills. ANYTIME IS PARTY TIME. Parlophone PCS 7152 (E).
Gramophone. September. p578. 25w. 2

1156 Mrs. Mills. MUSIC HALL PARTY. Parlophone PCS 7143 (E).
Gramophone. March. p1613. 25w. 2

1157 Liza Minnelli. LIVE AT THE OLYMPIA IN PARIS. A & M SP 4345 $5.98.
Gramophone. September. p577. 75w. 4
Hi-Fi News and Record Review. September. p1681-2. 75w. 1
High Fidelity. August. p106. 25w. 3
New York Times--Sunday. May 28. pD21. 325w. 2
Popular Music. Summer. p254. 25w. 3
Stereo Review. November. p88, 90. 325w. 2

1158 Liza Minnelli. NEW FEELIN'. A & M SP 4272 $5.98. Cart. 8T 4272 $6.98. Cass. CS 4272 $6.98.
Gramophone. July. p254. 100w. 3
High Fidelity. July. p1307. 25w. 0

1159 The Modernaires. REMEMBER GLEN MILLER AND TOMMY DORSEY. Sunset SLS 50269 (E). (Reissue.)
Gramophone. January. p1274. 50w. 4
Jazz Journal. January. p33. 125w. 0

1160 Monarchs. ROLL OUT THE BARREL. RCA International INTS 1318 (E).
Gramophone. March. p1613. 25w. 1

1161 Matt Monro. LET'S FACE THE MUSIC. Regal Starline SRS 5113 (E). (Reissue.)
Gramophone. July. p254. 100w. 4

1162 Gerry Monroe. Chapter One CHS 809 (E).
Gramophone. February. p1437. 25w. 1

1163 Dudley Moore Trio. TODAY. Atlantic K 40397 (E).
Gramophone. October. p785. 150w. 2
Hi-Fi News and Record Review. September. p1687. 300w. 1
Jazz and Blues. November. p32. 175w. 1
Jazz Journal. September. p34. 100w. 1

1164 Pete Moore. EVERYBODY'S TALKIN'. Rediffusion ZS 98 (E).
Hi-Fi News and Record Review. May. p937. 50w. 3

1165 Pete Moore. LIVELY AND LATIN. Rediffusion ZS 112 (E).
Hi-Fi News and Record Review. November. p2199. 25w. 3

1166 Alan Moorhouse. BOND STREET BRIGADE. Music for Pleasure SMFP 5268 (E). (Reissue.)
Gramophone. April. p1776. 25w. 1½

1167 Mandy More. BUT THAT IS ME. Philips 6308 109 (E).
Gramophone. September. p577. 25w. 1

1168 Ennio Morricone. BURGLARS. Bell BELL 209 (E).
Hi-Fi News and Record Review. August. p1476. 25w. 2½

1169 Mortier Dance Organ. Regal Starline SRS 5106 (E). (Reissue.)
Gramophone. April. p1776. 25w. 1

1170 Mortier Dance Organ. DANCE PARTY, VOLUME 1/2. Eclipse ECS 2109/2110 (2 discs) (E).
Gramophone. August. p398. 25w. 1
Gramophone. September. p578. 25w. 1

1171 Ernst Mosch and his Original Egerland Musicians. DAAR BIJ DIE MOLEN. Telefunken SLE 14.628 (Germany).
Hi-Fi News and Record Review. July. p1308. 50w. 3

1172 Ernst Mosch and his Original Egerland Musicians. WIEN UND DER WEIN. Telefunken SLE 14.636 (Germany).
Hi-Fi News and Record Review. July. p1308. 25w. 3

1173 Ernst Mosch and his Original Egerland Musicians. ARM IN ARM MIT DIR! Telefunken SLE 14.619 (Germany).
Hi-Fi News and Record Review. July. p1308. 25w. 1½

1174 Nana Mouskouri. BRITISH CONCERT. Fontana 6651003 (2 discs) (E).
Gramophone. September. p577. 125w. 3
Hi-Fi News and Record Review. December. p2461. 25w. 2½

1175 Nana Mouskouri. A PLACE IN MY HEART. Fontana 6312 022 (E).
Gramophone. January. p1274. 25w. 3

1176 Georges Moustaki. HERE'S TO YOU. Polydor 2489 037 (E).
Gramophone. February. p1438. 125w. 3
Hi-Fi News and Record Review. July. p1307-8. 50w. 2

1177 Mouth and MacNeal. HOW DO YOU DO? Philips PHS 700-000 $5.98. Cart. PC8 700000 $6.95. Cass. PCR4 700000 $6.95.
Audio. November. p92. 50w. 0

1178 Werner Müller. SONGS OF JOY. London Phase 4 44166 $5.98.
Gramophone. January. p1274. 75w. 3
Hi-Fi News and Record Review. July. p1308. 50w. 3

1179 Anne Murray. ANNIE. Capitol ST 11024 $5.98. Cart. 8XT 11024 $6.98. Cass. 4XT 11024 $6.98.
Creem. September. p11. 25w. 2½
Rolling Stone. July 20. p52. 600w. 2½
Sound. August. p48. 150w. 2
Stereo Review. August. p93. 125w. 3½

1180 Anne Murray. TALK IT OVER IN THE MORNING. Capitol ST 821 $5.98. Cart. 8XT 821 $6.98. Cass. 4XT 821 $6.98.
Gramophone. June. p111. 100w. 3
Records and Recordings. June. p90. 125w. 0
Stereo Review. January. p110. 250w. 2

1181 Anne Murray and Glen Campbell. Capitol SW 869 $5.98. Cart. 8XW 869 $6.98. Cass. 4XW 869 $6.98.
Gramophone. May. p1951. 25w. 2
Stereo Review. March. p106-7. 2,750w. 2

1182 Mystic Moods Orchestra. COUNTRY LOVIN' FOLK. Philips PHS 600-351 $5.98.
Audio. March. p81. 75w. 2

1183 Nanette Natal. THE BEGINNING. Evolution 2023 $5.98.
Stereo Review. August. p93. 125w. 2

1184 Peter Nero. SHOWTIME. RCA Camden CDS 1097 (E). (Reissue.)
Hi-Fi News and Record Review. December. p2463. 25w. 2

1185 Peter Nero. SUMMER OF '42. Columbia C 31105 $4.98. Cart. CA 31105 $6.98. Cass. CT 31105 $6.98.
Hi-Fi News and Record Review. May. p937. 50w. 3

1186 New Cascading Strings. AMAZING GRACE. Philips 6308 082 (E).
Gramophone. April. p1775. 50w. 1½

1187 New Cascading Strings. CONTRASTS. Philips 6308 107 (E).
Gramophone. September. p577. 50w. 3
Hi-Fi News and Record Review. July. p1307. 25w. 2½

1188 New Seekers. NEVER ENDING SONG OF LOVE. Polydor 2383 126 (E).
Gramophone. September. p577. 25w. 3

1189 New Seekers. NEW COLOURS. Elektra EKS 74108 $5.98. Cart. ET 84108 $6.98. Cass. TC 54108 $6.98.
Gramophone. January. p1279. 25w. 1

1190 New Seekers. WE'D LIKE TO TEACH THE WORLD TO SING. Elektra EKS 74115 $5.98.
Audio. September. p121. 25w. 2½

1191 The New Temperance Seven. IN SWEDEN. Philips 6414 303 (E).
Gramophone. July. p254. 75w. 3

1192 New World. Rak SRAK 502 (E).
Gramophone. February. p1437. 25w. 2

1193 Newbeats. RUN, BABY, RUN. London SHE 8428 (E).
Gramophone. May. p1952. 25w. 1

1194 Norman Newell. ONEDIN LINE AND OTHER WONDERFUL THEMES. Philips 6308 094 (E).
Hi-Fi News and Record Review. July. p1307. 50w. 1½

1195 Anthony Newley. THE LONELY WORLD OF... Decca SPA 185 (E).
Gramophone. June. p111. 25w. 0
Hi-Fi News and Record Review. May. p938. 25w. 2½

1196 Olivia Newton-John. IF NOT FOR YOU. Uni 73117 $4.98. Cart. 8-73117 $6.95. Cass. 2-73117 $6.95.
Gramophone. December. p1221. 25w. ½
Stereo Review. March. p104. 125w. 0

1197 NICE 'N' EASY (anthology). Philips 6641 053 (2 discs) (E). (Reissue.)
Gramophone. December. p1221. 50w. 2½

1198 Lea Nicholson. HORSE MUSIC. Trailer LER 3010 (E).
Gramophone. January. p1279-80. 50w. 2

1199 Nina and Frederik. Music for Pleasure MFP 5249 (E). (Reissue.)
Gramophone. May. p1952. 25w. 1½

1200 Nina and Frederick. MOODS. Regal Starline SRS 5087 (E). (Reissue.)
Gramophone. February. p1437. 25w. 1½

1201 Nite-Lites. INSTRUMENTAL DIRECTIONS. RCA LSP 4580 $5.98. Cart. P8S 1825 $6.95. Cass. PK 1825 $6.95.
Gramophone. September. p578. 25w. 1

1202 NON-STOP LATIN PARTY (anthology). Philips 6382 032 (E).
Gramophone. May. p1952. 100w. 2

1203 Los Nortes Americanos. HAPPY PARTY SOUNDS TIAJUANA STYLE. Golden Hour GH 808 (E).
Gramophone. March. p1613. 25w. 1

1204 Dermot O'Brian. OFF TO DUBLIN IN THE GREEN. Beltone SBE R133 (E).
Hi-Fi News and Record Review. August. p1473. 25w. 2½

1205 Carroll O'Connor. REMEMBERING YOU. A & M SP 4340 $5.98. Cart. 8T 4340 $6.98. Cass. CS 4340 $6.98.
High Fidelity. August. p96. 375w. 3½
New York Times--Sunday. May 28. pD21. 650w. 4
Popular Music. Summer. p254. 25w. 1
Stereo Review. December. p98. 200w. 0

1206 Gilbert O'Sullivan. HIMSELF. MAM 2 $5.98. Cart. M84 $6.95. Cass. M54 $6.95.
High Fidelity. November. p130. 25w. 3
New York Times--Sunday. October 22. pD31. 200w. 1

1207 Esther and Abi O'Farim. CINDERELLA ROCKEFFA. Philips 6436 500 (E).
Gramophone. April. p1776. 50w. 1

1208 OLD TIME MUSIC HALL (anthology). Regal Starline SRS 5118 (E). (Reissue.)
Gramophone. August. p398. 25w. 1

1209 Cyril Ornadel. HITS OF THE OPERETTAS. RCA International INTS 1282 (E).
Gramophone. April. p1776. 25w. 0

1210 Cyril Ornadel. HITS OF THE SEASONS. RCA International INTS 1281 (E).
Gramophone. April. p1776. 25w. 0

1211 Tony Osborne. MOODS FOR ROMANCE. Rediffusion ZS 108 (E).
Hi-Fi News and Record Review. August. p1476. 50w. $2\frac{1}{2}$

1212 The Osmonds. PHASE THREE. MGM ISE 4796 $6.98. Cart. 8130-4796 $6.95. Cass. 5130-4796 $6.95.
Creem. May. p66. 550w. 1

1213 Donny Osmond. PORTRAIT. MGM SE 4820 $5.98. Cart. 8130-4820M $6.95. Cass. 5130-4820M $6.95.
New York Times--Sunday. November 19. pD30. 125w. 1

1214 Donny Osmond. TO YOU WITH LOVE. MGM SE 4797 $5.98. Cart. 8130-4797 $6.95. Cass. 5130-4797 $6.95.
Audio. October. p90. 25w. 0

1215 Marie Ostiz. Vanguard VSD 6575 $4.98.
Stereo Review. April. p97-8. 200w. $1\frac{1}{2}$

1216 Pan Am Steel Band. Chapter One LRS 5007 (E).
Gramophone. September. p579. 100w. 1

1217 Fausto Papetti. INTRODUCING. Philips 6381 002 (E).
Gramophone. May. p1952. 25w. $1\frac{1}{2}$

1218 Fausto Papetti. WE SHALL DANCE. Philips 6381 003 (E).
Gramophone. July. p255. 25w. 1

1219 Paradise Islanders. THROUGH HAWAIIAN EYES. Polydor 2489 040 (E).
Gramophone. June. p112. 25w. 1

1220 Norrie Paramour. THE MAGNIFICENCE OF IVOR NOVELLO. Polydor 2383 142 (E).
Hi-Fi News and Record Review. November. p2201. 25w. 3

1221 Partridge Family. SHOPPING BAG. Bell S-6072 $4.98. Cart. M86072 $6.95. Cass. M56072 $6.95.
Gramophone. July. p255. 25w. 2

1222 Partridge Family. SOUND MAGAZINE. Bell S-6064 $4.98. Cart. M86064 $6.95. Cass. M56064 $6.95.
Gramophone. July. p255. 25w. 2

1223 Jack Payne. SAY IT WITH MUSIC. Decca/Eclipse ECM 2111 (E). (Reissue.)
Gramophone. September. p578. 900w. 4
Hi-Fi News and Record Review. August. p1476, 1481. 50w. 2
Jazz Journal. November. p37. 200w. 1
Records and Recordings. August. p92. 250w. 4

1224 Johnny Pearson. CLASSICAL VIBRATIONS. Polydor 2460 143 (E).
Hi-Fi News and Record Review. July. p1307. 25w. 0

1225 Paco Peña Group. FLAMENCO PURO "LIVE." London SP 44172 $5.98.
Audio. August. p62. 50w. 4
Gramophone. May. p1955. 50w. 3½
Hi-Fi News and Record Review. May. p937. 25w. 2

1226 Jean Jacques Perrey. MOOG INDIGO. Vanguard VSD 6549 $4.98.
Gramophone. November. p984. 50w. 1

1227 Edith Piaf. I REGRET NOTHING. Columbia SCX 6477 (E).
Gramophone. February. p1438. 125w. 4

1228 The Pipkins. WE WANT TO SING. Regal Starline. SRS 5102 (E). (Reissue.)
Gramophone. January. p1279. 25w. 1

1229 Harry Pitch. LONELY HARMONICAS. Columbia Studio 2 TWO 365 (E).
Gramophone. April. p1776. 50w. 1½

1230 Andre Popp. IF YOU GO AWAY. Polydor 2383 142 (E).
Hi-Fi News and Record Review. November. p2201. 25w. 3

1231 The Poppy Family. POPPY SEEDS. London PS 599 $5.98.
Gramophone. May. p1952. 25w. 0

1232 Frank Pourcel. DAY BY DAY. Paramount PAS 6036 $4.98.
Audio. December. p95. 75w. 1

1233 Frank Pourcel. GIRLS (FEMMES). Columbia Stereo 2 TWO 381 (E).
Gramophone. October. p778. 75w. 3

1234 Frank Pourcel. MEETS THE BEATLES. Columbia Studio 2 TWO 371 (E).

Gramophone. May. p1951. 25w. 2
Hi-Fi News and Record Review. May. p938. 25w. 2
Hi-Fi News and Record Review. July. p1307-8. 50w. 2½

1235 Frank Pourcel. THINKING OF YOU. Columbia Studio 2 TWO 355 (E).
Gramophone. January. p1274. 100w. 3

1236 Frank Pourcel. THIS IS... Columbia Studio 2 STWO 7 (E). (Reissue.)
Gramophone. January. p1274. 125w. 3

1237 Lou Preager and his New Band. DANCING CLOSE TOGETHER. Joy JOYS 245 (E).
Gramophone. December. p1222. 25w. 1
Hi-Fi News and Record Review. November. p2201. 50w. 1

1238 Elvis Presley. ELVIS AS RECORDED AT MADISON SQUARE GARDEN. RCA LSP 4776 $5.98. Cart. P8S 2054 $6.95. Cass. PK 2054 $6.95.
Creem. August. p66-7. 1,150w. 1
Gramophone. September. p577. 50w. 1
Hi-Fi News and Record Review. September. p1683. 125w. 1
High Fidelity. November. p74-6. 2,000w. 1
Records and Recordings. September. p95. 250w. 0

1239 Elvis Presley. ELVIS FOR EVERYONE. RCA LSP 3450 $5.98. Cart. P8S 1078 $6.95. Cass. PK 1078 $6.95.
Gramophone. August. p397. 25w. 2
Records and Recordings. July. p94-5. 100w. 2½

1240 Elvis Presley. ELVIS NOW. RCA LSP 4671 $5.98. Cart. P8S 1898 $6.95. Cass. PK 1898 $6.95.
Audio. October. p89. 50w. 2½
Crawdaddy. May 28. p17. 400w. 1
High Fidelity. May. p108. 175w. 2½
High Fidelity. November. p74-6. 2,000w. 1½
New York Times--Sunday. March 12. pHF12. 150w. 2
Records and Recordings. July. p94-5. 100w. 2½

1241 Elvis Presley. I GOT LUCKY. RCA International INT 1322 (E). (Reissue.)
Gramophone. March. p1613. 25w. 2

1242 Elvis Presley. ROCK 'N' ROLL. RCA SF 8233 (E). (Reissue.)
Blues Unlimited. June. p30. 125w. 5
Blues Unlimited. November. p30. 50w. 4
Hi-Fi News and Record Review. July. p1312. 50w. 2½
Records and Recordings. July. p94-5. 100w. 5

1243 Kenny Rankin. LIKE A SEED. Little David 1003 $5.98. Cart. TP 1003 $6.98. Cass. CS 1003 $6.98.
High Fidelity. December. p121. 200w. 4

1244 Ratchell. Decca DL 75330 $5.98.
Audio. October. p88. 25w. 0

1245 Ivan Rebroff. SOMEWHERE, MY LOVE. Columbia C 31023 $4.98.
Stereo Review. March. p108. 300w. 1

1246 Della Reese. BEST. RCA LSP 4651 $5.98. Cart. P8S 1881 $6.95. Cass. PK 1881 $6.95. (Reissue.)
Stereo Review. November. p92. 100w. 2½

1247 Neil Reid. Decca SKL 5122 (E).
Gramophone. May. p1951. 75w. 0

1248 Renaissance Orchestra. CLASSICS '72. Sunset SLS 50284 (E).
Gramophone. January. p1274. 75w. 3

1249 Repairs. ALREADY A HOUSEHOLD WORLD. Rare Earth R 532L $5.98.
Audio. September. p121. 50w. 2

1250 Waldo de Los Rios. IN A ROMANTIC MOOD. Mayfair AMLB 51027 (E). (Reissue.)
Gramophone. June. p111. 50w. 3
Hi-Fi News and Record Review. May. p938. 25w. 1½

1251 Waldo de Los Rios. MOZART IN THE SEVENTIES. A & M AMLS 68066 (E).
Gramophone. January. p1274. 100w. 4

1252 Malcolm Roberts. SOUNDS LIKE MALCOLM ROBERTS. Columbia SCX 6475 (E).
Gramophone. January. p1274. 25w. 3

1253 Harry Roche Constellation. IN ORBIT. Joy JOYS 227 (E). (Reissue.)
Hi-Fi News and Record Review. July. p1307. 25w. 3

1254 The Rock Flowers. NATURALLY. Wheel WLS 1002 $4.98.
Audio. November. p90. 25w. 1

1255 Clodagh Rodgers. IT'S DIFFERENT NOW. RCA SF 8271 (E).
Gramophone. September. p577. 75w. 3

1256 Eric Rogers. A TRIBUTE TO SATCHMO. London Phase 4 SP 44170 $5.98.

Gramophone. April. p1776. 25w. 1
High Fidelity. January. p117. 75w. 0
Jazz Journal. December. p41. 100w. 1

1257 Carlos Romanos. SOUNDS LATIN. Polydor 2344 005 (E).
Gramophone. February. p1438. 75w. 1

1258 Edmondo Ros. IN CONCERT. Decca Phase 4 PFS 4235 (E).
Gramophone. April. p1779. 175w. 3

1259 David Rose. THE STRIPPER. MGM S 4062 $5.98. Cart. M84062 $6.95. Cass. M54062 $6.95.
Gramophone. January. p1274. 25w. 2

1260 Andy Ross. DANCE TO THE HITS FROM THE MOVIE CRAZY YEARS. CBS 67240 (E) (2 discs).
Gramophone. April. p1776. 50w. 1

1261 Andy Ross. THE GODFATHER AND OTHER GREAT SCREEN THEMES. CBS 64910 (E).
Hi-Fi News and Record Review. December. p2463. 50w. 1½

1262 Annie Ross. YOU AND ME BABY. Decca SKL 5099 (E).
Gramophone. March. p1624. 175w. 3

1263 Dennis Roussos. ON THE GREEK SIDE OF MY MIND. MGM SE 4818 $5.98.
Audio. September. p121. 50w. 1

1264 John Rowles. CHERYL MOANA MARIE. Kapp KS 3637 $4.98. Cart. K8-3637 $6.98. Cass. K7-3637 $6.98.
Gramophone. April. p1775. 50w. 2

1265 George Russell. SOFT GUITAR, SILKEN STRINGS. RCA International 1376 (E).
Gramophone. September. p579. 125w. 3
Hi-Fi News and Record Review. September. p1682. 25w. 2
Hi-Fi News and Record Review. December. p246. 50w. 2

1266 Bridge St. John. SONGS FOR THE GENTLEMAN. Elektra/Dandelion EKS 74104 $4.98. Cart. M84104 $6.95. Cass. M54104 $6.95.
Stereo Review. February. p110. 200w. 2½

1267 The Sandpipers. A GIFT OF SONG. A & M SP 4328 $5.98. Cart. 8T 4328 $6.98. Cass. CS 4328 $6.98.
Gramophone. May. p1951. 25w. 2

1268 The Sandpipers. LA BAMBA. Mayfair AMLB 51030 (E). (Reissue.)
Gramophone. June. p111. 50w. 3
Hi-Fi News and Record Review. May. p938. 50w. 2½

1269 Les Sans Nom. LARGELY LATIN. Eclipse ECS 2059 (E).
Gramophone. June. p115. 75w. 0

1270 Telly Savalas. THIS IS... Jam JAL 102 (E).
Hi-Fi News and Record Review. August. p1476. 50w. 2½

1271 Warren Schatz. Columbia C 30685 $4.98.
Stereo Review. January. p114. 75w. 0

1272 Die Schaumburger Märchensänger. WEM GOTT WILL RECHTE GUNST ERWEISEN. Telefunken TS 3157/1-2 (Germany).
Hi-Fi News and Record Review. July. p1308. 50w. 2½

1273 Henry Schifter. OUT OF NOWHERE. Barclay 80446 (France).
Gramophone. August. p397. 25w. 1

1274 Willy Schneider. GOLDENES WUNSCHKONZERT DER ERINNERUNGEN. Telefunken SLE 14603 (Germany).
Hi-Fi News and Record Review. July. p1308. 50w. 2½

1275 Willy Schneider. WUNSCHKONZERT. Telefunken Musik Für Alles NT 677 (Germany).
Hi-Fi News and Record Review. July. p1308. 25w. 2½

1276 John Schroeder. DYLAN VIBRATIONS. Polydor 2460 134 (E).
Gramophone. January. p1279. 25w. 1

1277 John Schroeder. LATIN VIBRATIONS. Polydor 2460 136 (E).
Gramophone. May. p1952. 100w. 2

1278 John Schroeder. PARTY DANCE VIBRATIONS. Polydor 2460 145 (E).
Gramophone. March. p1613. 50w. 2½

1279 John Schroeder. PIANO VIBRATIONS. Polydor 2460 135 (E).
Gramophone. January. p1279. 25w. 2

1280 John Schroeder. TV VIBRATIONS. Polydor 2460 149 (E).
Hi-Fi News and Record Review. June. p1127. 25w. 2½

1281 John Scott. ANTHONY AND CLEOPATRA. Polydor 2383 109 (E).
Hi-Fi News and Record Review. August. p1477. 25w. 2½

1282 Shirley Scott. MYSTICAL LADY. Cadet 50009 $5.98.
Downbeat. March 16. p30. 100w. 3½
Gramophone. January. p1274. 25w. 3
Jazz and Blues. March. p27-8. 250w. 0

1283 Harry Secombe. THE SOUND OF SECOMBE. Philips 6308 092 (E).
Gramophone. April. p1776. 25w. 1½

1284 Harry Secombe and Myrna Rose. THE WORLD'S GREAT LOVE DUETS. Contour 6870 522 (E).
Gramophone. May. p1951. 25w. 2

1285 The Second Generation. Philips 6308 104 (E).
Gramophone. September. p577. 50w. 3

1286 Neil Sedaka. EMERGENCE. Kirshner KES 111 $4.98.
Gramophone. June. p111. 150w. 4
High Fidelity. January. p122. 25w. 2
Stereo Review. February. p111. 225w. 1½

1287 Session Men. SING HITS MADE FAMOUS BY TOM JONES AND ENGLEBERT HUMPERDINCK. Music for Pleasure MFP 5207 (E).
Gramophone. August. p397. 100w. 3

1288 The Settlers. LIGHTNING TREE. York FYK 405 (E).
Gramophone. p577. September. 3

1289 Doc Severinsen. DOC. RCA LSP 4669 $5.98.
Music Journal. December. p75. 125w. 3

1290 Shadows. MUSTANG. Music for Pleasure MFP 5266 (E). (Reissue.)
Gramophone. July. p254. 100w. 3

1291 Jimmy Shand. JIMMY'S FANCY. Emerald GEM GES 1070 (E).
Hi-Fi News and Record Review. August. p1473. 25w. 2½

1292 Brian Sharp. PLAYS MAINLEY HAMMOND. Grosvenor GRS 1012 (E).
Gramophone. September. p578. 25w. 1

1293 Bobby Short. LOVES COLE PORTER. Atlantic SD2-606 (2 discs) $9.96. Cart. M82606 $9.95. Cass. M52606 $9.95.
Downbeat. March 16. p30. 150w. 5
High Fidelity. April. p114. 25w. 3½
Stereo Review. February. p74-5. 600w. 4

1294 Frank Sinatra. GREATEST HITS, VOLUME 2. Reprise FS 1034 $5.98.
Canadian Stereo Guide. Summer. p67. 100w. 3

1295 Frank Sinatra. NICE N' EASY. Music for Pleasure MFP 5258 (E). (Reissue.)
Gramophone. June. p111. 50w. 3
Hi-Fi News and Record Review. May. p938. 50w. 3½

1296 Frank Sinatra. SINGS RODGERS AND HART. Regal Starline SRS 5083 (E). (Reissue.)
Gramophone. January. p1274. 25w. 3

1297 Frank Sinatra. SWINGIN' SINATRA. EMI Double Up DUO 102 (2 discs) (E). (Reissue.)
Gramophone. December. p1221. 100w. 3½

1298 Frank Sinatra. WHERE ARE YOU? Capitol ST 855 $5.98.
Gramophone. September. p577. 50w. 3
Hi-Fi News and Record Review. September. p1682. 25w. 3

1299 Frank Sinatra, Jr. SPICE. Daybreak DR 2003 $5.98. Cart. P8DR 2003 $6.98.
Gramophone. June. p111. 100w. 3
High Fidelity. June. p102. 350w. 1½
Stereo Review. April. p99-100. 300w. 1

1300 Nancy Sinatra and Lee Hazlewood. NANCY AND LEE AGAIN. RCA LSP 4645 $5.98. Cart. P8S 1879 $6.98. Cass. PK 1879 $6.98.
Audio. November. p90. 25w. 1
Gramophone. April. p1775. 25w. 2½
Stereo Review. July. p94. 100w. 2½

1301 Jack Sinclair Television Showband. MY SCOTTISH HOMELAND. Beltona SBE 137 (E).
Gramophone. September. p578. 25w. 1
Hi-Fi News and Record Review. August. p1473. 25w. 2½

1302 SNOWDONIA'S FESTIVAL OF SONG (anthology). Decca SKL 5131 (E).
Hi-Fi News and Record Review. August. p1473. 25w. 1½

1303 SONGS THAT WON THE WAR (anthology). CBS 30026 (E). (Reissue.)
Gramophone. February. p1438. 25w. 1½

1304 Sonny and Cher. ALL I EVER NEED IS YOU. Kapp KS 5560 $4.98. Cart. K8-5560 $6.98. Cass. K7-5560 $6.98

Gramophone. August. p397. 25w. 1
Hi-Fi News and Record Review. July. p1312. 50w. 2½
High Fidelity. June. p110. 25w. 3

1305 Sonny and Cher. LIVE. Kapp KS 5554 $4.98. Cart. K8-5554 $6.98. Cass. K7-5554 $6.98.
Gramophone. March. p1613. 50w. 1½

1306 Sonny and Cher. THE TWO OF US. Atco SD 2-804 (2 discs) $9.96. Cart. TP 2 804 $9.95. Cass. CS2 804 $9.95. (Reissue.)
Creem. November. p68. 700w. 2

1307 Sounds Orchestral. THE EARTH, THE SEA AND THE SKY. Golden Hour GH 511 (E).
Gramophone. March. p1613. 25w. 1

1308 Dusty Springfield. THIS IS... Philips 6382 016 (E). (Reissue.)
Gramophone. January. p1274. 50w. 2

1309 Cyril Stapleton. THE BIG BAND'S BACK. Pye Golden Hour GH 531 (E).
Gramophone. December. p1222. 25w. 1

1310 Cyril Stapleton. GOLDEN HOUR OF STRICT TEMPO. Golden Hour GH 529 (E).
Gramophone. September. p578. 25w. 1

1311 Wont Steenhuis. HAWAIIAN MAGIC. EMI Double Up DUO 101 (E). (Reissue.)
Gramophone. December. p1221. 25w. 2½

1312 Orville Stoeber. SONGS. Uni 73103 $5.98. Cart. 8-73103 $6.95. Cass. 2-73103 $6.95.
Audio. November. p93. 75w. 3

1313 Harry Stoneham. HAMMOND HITS THE HIGHWAY. Columbia Studio 2 TWO 375 (E).
Gramophone. June. p112. 25w. 2
Hi-Fi News and Record Review. June. p1127. 50w. 2½

1314 Harry Stoneham. LATIN LOWREY. Columbia Studio 2 TWO 383 (E).
Gramophone. November. p990. 150w. 2
Hi-Fi News and Record Review. November. p2201. 25w. 2½

1315 Barbra Streisand. BARBRA JOAN STREISAND. Columbia KC 30792 $5.98. Cart. CA 30792 $6.98. Cass. CT 30792 $6.98.
American Record Guide. February. p285. 225w. 1
Audio. October. p90. 25w. 2½

Library Journal. January 15. p179. 100w. 1½

1316 Barbra Streisand. LIVE CONCERT AT THE FORUM. Columbia KC 31760 $5.98. Cart. CA 31760 $6.98. Cass. CT 31760 $6.98.
New York Times--Sunday. December 10. pD37. 75w. 3
Rolling Stone. December 21. p62. 750w. 3

1317 Strings for Pleasure. THE BEST OF HENRY MANCINI. Music for Pleasure MFP 5234 (E).
Gramophone. February. p1437. 25w. 2

1318 STRINGS IN STEREO (anthology). Carnival 2928 507 (E).
Hi-Fi News and Record Review. December. p2461. 25w. 2½

1319 Suisse Romande Orchestra. WORLD OF TV THEMES. Decca SPA 217 (E).
Hi-Fi News and Record Review. June. p1127. 25w. 2½

1320 Maxine Sullivan and Dick Hyman. SULLIVAN, SHAKESPEARE, HYMAN. Monmouth/Evergreen MFS 7038 $5.98.
Downbeat. March 16. p30. 300w. 4

1321 Yma Sumac. MIRACLES. London XPS 608 $5.98. Cart. M72191 $6.95. Cass. M57191 $6.95.
Gramophone. August. p397. 200w. 2
Hi-Fi News and Record Review. September. p1681. 25w. 0

1322 Sunset Dance Orchestra. THE DANCING YEARS. Sunset SLS 50313 (E).
Hi-Fi News and Record Review. December. p2461. 25w. 2½

1323 Surfers. LIVE AND WELL AT LATITUDE 20. Daybreak DR 2001 $5.98.
Gramophone. June. p112. 25w. 0

1324 The Sweet/The Pipkins. Music for Pleasure MFP 5248 (E). (Reissue.)
Gramophone. May. p1952. 25w. 1

1325 Swingle Singers. BACHANALIA. Philips PHS 2-5400 (2 discs) $6.98. (Reissue.)
Audio. December. p97-8. 650w. 4½
Gramophone. June. p122. 150w. 1
Jazz Journal. June. p36. 400w. 0

1326 Norma Tanega. I DON'T THINK IT WILL HURT IF YOU SMILE. RCA SF 8217 (E).
Gramophone. March. p1613. 100w. 2½

1327 The Tattoos. SWINGIN' WITH THE MILLION SELLERS. Telefunken TS 3153/1-2 (2 discs) (E).
Gramophone. August. p397. 25w. 2

1328 Ted Taylor Chorus and Orchestra. BEST OF THE FOOTBALL THEMES. Regal Starline SRS 5122 (E).
Gramophone. September. p578. 25w. 1

1329 Alan Tew. LET'S FLY. CBS 64665 (E).
Gramophone. May. p1951. 25w. 2

1330 THIS IS THE ERA OF MEMORABLE SONG HITS: THE DECADE OF THE THIRTIES (anthology). RCA VPM 6058 (2 discs) $6.98.
Stereo Review. December. p94. 250w. 0

1331 THIS IS THE ERA OF MEMORABLE SONG HITS: THE DECADE OF THE FORTIES (anthology). RCA VPM 6059 (2 discs) $6.98.
Stereo Review. December. p94. 250w. 0

1332 THIS IS THE ERA OF MEMORABLE SONG HITS: THE DECADE OF THE FIFTIES (anthology). RCA VPM 6060 (2 discs) $6.98.
Stereo Review. December. p94. 250w. 0

1333 THIS IS THE ERA OF MEMORABLE SONG HITS: THE DECADE OF THE SIXTIES (anthology). RCA VPM 6061 (2 discs) $6.98.
Stereo Review. December. p94. 250w. 0

1334 Tilsley Orchestra. WORLD OF WALT DISNEY IN STEREO. Philips 6382 015 (E).
Hi-Fi News and Record Review. August. p1477. 25w. $\frac{1}{2}$

1335 TOP OF THE BILL (anthology). Rhapsody RHA 6002 (E).
Hi-Fi News and Record Review. October. p1923. 125w. 3

1336 TRUMPET EXTRAORDINARY (anthology). Coral CPS 82 (E).
Hi-Fi News and Record Review. August. p1473. 25w. 2

1337 Ken Turner. OLD TIME AND MODERN SEQUENCE FESTIVAL REQUESTS. Columbia SCX 6495 (E).
Gramophone. July. p255. 25w. 2

1338 Twiggy. AND THE GIRL FRIENDS. Ember SE 8012 (E).
Gramophone. June. p111. 50w. 0

1339 Two's Company. York BYK 711 (E).
Gramophone. April. p1775. 50w. 2
Hi-Fi News and Record Review. May. p937. 50w. 3
Hi-Fi News and Record Review. June. p1128. 25w. 2

1340 Die Ulmer Spatsen. HOCH AUF DEM GELBEN WAGEN! Telefunken Musik Für Alle NT 681 (Germany).
Hi-Fi News and Record Review. July. p1308. 25w. 2½

1341 Caterina Valente. THE WORLD OF... Decca SPA 192 (E). (Reissue.)
Gramophone. March. p1614. 175w. 4

1342 Caterina Valente and Silvio. LATIN VOICES AND GUITARS. Decca SLK 16705-P (Germany).
Gramophone. June. p115. 300w. 4
Hi-Fi News and Record Review. May. p937. 25w. 2½

1343 Dickie Valentine. VENUS. Hallmark/Marble Arch HMA 220 (E). (Reissue.)
Hi-Fi News and Record Review. May. p938. 50w. 3

1344 Rudy Vallee. RCA International INT 1343 (E). (Reissue.)
Gramophone. December. p1225. 50w. ½

1345 Valverde Orchestra. "IN" CLASSICS. Columbia Stereo 2 TWO 363 (E).
Gramophone. February. p1437. 25w. 0

1346 Frankie Valli and the Four Seasons. CHAMELEON. Mowest MW 108L $5.98. Cart. M8108 $6.95. Cass. M5108 $6.95.
Creem. August. p64. 550w. 1
Popular Music. Summer. p254. 50w. 2

1347 Frankie Vaughan. DOUBLE EXPOSURE. Columbia SCX 6478 (E).
Gramophone. January. p1274-9. 25w. 3

1348 Frankie Vaughan. THIS IS... Philips 6382 021 (E). (Reissue.)
Gramophone. April. p1776. 50w. 1½

1349 Velvet Fire. RCA International INTS 1339 (E). (Reissue.)
Gramophone. April. p1776. 25w. 1

1350 The Ventures. United Artists UAS 29280 (E). (Reissue.)
Gramophone. May. p1952. 25w. 1

1351 The Ventures. PLAY THE CLASSICS. United Artists UAS 29340 (E).
Hi-Fi News and Record Review. July. p1307. 25w. 0

1352 No entry.

1353 Very Original Brasso Band. PLAYS TUNES FROM... Columbia Studio 2 TWO 362 (E).
Gramophone. January. p1279. 25w. 2

1354 Vinegar Joe. Atlantic SD 7007 $5.98. Cart. TP-7007 $6.97. Cass. CS-7007 $6.97.
Audio. November. p90. 25w. 3

1355 Bobby Vinton. EVERY DAY OF MY LIFE. Epic KE 31286 $5.98. Cart. EA 31286 $6.98. Cass. ET 31286 $6.98.
Stereo Review. August. p94. 125w. 0

1356 Waikiki Beach Boys. HAWAIIAN WEDDING SONG. Music for Pleasure MFP 5217 (E).
Gramophone. August. p397-8. 25w. 1

1357 Scott Walker. THIS IS... Philips 6382 007 (E). (Reissue.)
Gramophone. January. p1274. 25w. 3

1358 Gordon Waller. ...AND GORDON. ABC ABCX 749 $5.98. Cart. M8749 $6.95. Cass. M5749 $6.95.
High Fidelity. August. p106. 25w. 2

1359 Kai Warner. PLAY WAGNER. Polydor 2371 195 (E).
Hi-Fi News and Record Review. July. p1305. 50w. 1

1360 Dionne Warwicke. DIONNE. Warner Bros. BS 2585 $5.98. Cart. M82585 $6.95. Cass. M52585 $6.95.
Creem. May. p61-2. 850w. 3½
Gramophone. May. p1951. 50w. 2½
Hi-Fi News and Record Review. July. p1305. 50w. 1½
Library Journal. August. p2557. 100w. 3½
Stereo Review. October. p102. 275w. 2½

1361 Dionne Warwicke. FROM WITHIN, VOLUME 1/2. Sceptre 2-598 (2 discs) $7.98.
Gramophone. September. p577. 50w. 2
Hi-Fi News and Record Review. October. p1926. 150w. 1½

1362 Lovelace Watkins. LOVE IS. Uni UNLS 119 (E).
Gramophone. May. p1951. 50w. 0

1363 Lovelace Watkins. LOVE MAKES THE WORLD GO ROUND. York PYK 404 (E).
Hi-Fi News and Record Review. July. p1311-12. 25w. 2½

1364 Jimmy Webb. LETTERS. Reprise MS 2055 $5.98.
Creem. November. p68-9. 875w. 4
Gramophone. December. p1221. 50w. 1½

Hi-Fi News and Record Review. December. p2464. 125w. 2½
High Fidelity. November. p118. 300w. 2½
New York Times--Sunday. August 6. pD22. 75w. 1
Records and Recordings. November. p107. 175w. 1
Stereo Review. November. p79. 250w. 4

1365 Tim Weisberg. A & M SP 3039 $5.98.
Downbeat. June 22. p24, 26. 100w. 1

1366 Tim Weisberg. ANOTHER TIME. A & M SP 4352 $5.98.
Popular Music and Society. Winter. p123. 50w. 2½

1367 Jack White. MIT ALL DEINER LIEBE... Telefunken Musik Für Alle NT 685 (Germany).
Hi-Fi News and Record Review. July. p1308. 25w. ½

1368 Roger Whittaker. SINGS. Columbia SCX 6483 (E).
Gramophone. February. p1432, 1437. 75w. 2½

1369 Wally Whyton. THE WORLD OF... Decca SPA 250 (E). (Reissue.)
Gramophone. December. p1221. 25w. 1½

1370 Andy Williams. RCA International INTS 1330 (E). (Reissue.)
Gramophone. April. p1775. 75w. 1

1371 Andy Williams. YOU'VE GOT A FRIEND. Columbia KC 30797 $5.98. Cart. CA 30797 $6.98. Cass. CT 30797 $6.98.
Audio. October. p89. 50w. 3

1372 Mason Williams. SHAREPICKERS. Warner Bros. WS 1941 $5.98. Cart. M81941 $6.95. Cass. M51941 $6.95.
Gramophone. March. p1613. 100w. 3½
Stereo Review. February. p114. 200w. 2½
Stereo Review. October. p102. 150w. 1½

1373 Paul Williams. JUST AN OLD FASHIONED LOVE SONG. A & M SP 4327 $5.98. Cart. 8T 4327 $6.98. Cass. CS 4327 $6.98.
Gramophone. May. p1951. 50w. 1
High Fidelity. March. p113-4. 300w. 3
Popular Music. Winter. p122. 50w. 3
Rolling Stone. March 16. p62, 64. 400w. 2
Stereo Review. May. p95. 350w. ½

1374 Alois Wimmer und Seine Bayrische Trachten Kapelle. AUF GEHT'S ZUR WIESEN. Telefunken Musik Für Alle NT 655 (Germany).
Hi-Fi News and Record Review. July. p1308. 25w. 2½

1375 Harold Winkler. GUITAR CONCERTO, VOLUME 2. Telefunken SLF 14664-P (Germany).
Gramophone. December. p1221. 25w. 2½

1376 Pete Winslow. UP, UP AND AWAY. Philips 6414 305 (E).
Gramophone. July. p255. 25w. 0

1377 John Woodhouse. THIS IS... Philips 6440 007 (E). (Reissue.)
Gramophone. July. p255. 25w. 1

1378 Edward Woodward. ALBUM. JAM JAL 103 (E).
Hi-Fi News and Record Review. September. p1682. 25w. 2½

1379 WORLD OF GOLDEN MELODIES (anthology). Decca SPA 207 (E). (Reissue.)
Gramophone. February. p1437. 25w. 2½

1380 THE WORLD OF HITS, VOLUME 6 (anthology). Decca SPA 258 (E). (Reissue.)
Gramophone. December. p1222. 25w. 2

1381 THE WORLD OF THE CINEMA ORGAN (anthology). Decca SPA 195 (E).
Gramophone. April. p1776. 25w. 1

1382 THE WORLD'S FAVOURITE LOVE SONGS (anthology). Sunset SLS 50261 (E).
Hi-Fi News and Record Review. May. p937-8. 50w. 2½

1383 Gary Wright. FOOTPRINT. A & M SP 4296 $5.98.
Gramophone. April. p1776. 25w. 0

1384 Klaus Wunderlich. HAMMOND POPS 7. Telefunken SLE 14639 (Germany).
Hi-Fi News and Record Review. July. p1308. 25w. 2½

1385 Klaus Wunderlich. POLKA POPS. Telefunken SLE 14656-P (Germany).
Gramophone. December. p1222. 25w. 1

1386 Xylos, Inc. PRETTY PERCUSSION. Polydor 2460 141 (E).
Gramophone. February. p1437. 25w. 0

1387 Robert Young. LOVE REMEMBERS. CBS 65095 (E).
Gramophone. December. p1221. 75w. 3

1388 Roy Young. MR. FUNKY. MCA MKPS 2022 (E).
Gramophone. April. p1776. 25w. 2

1389 Die Zwei Peterlesboum Aus Nürnberg. NO. 4. Telefunken Musik Für Alle NT 643 (Germany).
Hi-Fi News and Record Review. July. p1308. 25w. $2\frac{1}{2}$

COUNTRY

This section comprises material known to listeners and collectors variously as "C. & W.," the "Nashville Sound," hillbilly music, old time music, or bluegrass music. The tie that binds this diverse field together and distinguishes it from "folk" is that it is commercial music played for a paying audience and recorded for the industry.

Bill Malone in his excellent study, Country Music, U.S.A. (University of Texas, 1968), offers the uninitiated a handy way to catagorize this genre.

> Before the 1920's: The Southern rural culture, existing outside of the mainstream of American life, had its own music, expressive of the culture and isolation.
>
> The 1920's: The emergence of individual country performers relying upon traditional music are recorded for the growing numbers owning "Victrolas" in rural America. Jimmie Rodgers and the Carter Family begin the "country music industry."
>
> The 1930's: The emergence of individual stars, singing cowboys, advanced recording techniques, and the radio brings change but the songs still reflect the performer's folk origins.
>
> The 1940's: World War II and the move to defense jobs and southern military camps helps make country music nationally popular. This is the boom period of the industry.
>
> The 1950's: Country music enters the urban market and loses many of its distinctive traits. Hank Williams spans the gulf between country and popular music but country-pop and the Nashville sound are replacing tradition.
>
> The 1960's: Country-pop is counterbalanced by the urban folk revival and a renewed interest in traditional country music.

Which is pretty much where the genre stands today. Country has immense popularity in the United States. This music, which is often accused of having no "class," is the daily sound heard by many million Americans. Hundreds of AM radio stations feature it and millions of albums are sold annually. It is the working man's music and the very lyrics tell us much about his concerns; patriotism, automation, unemployment, too rapid social change, unfaithful wives and husbands, alcohol, and the dreariness of the factory and trucking. It is important music for the popular record collection in the library since it has a direct appeal to that segment of the population that traditionally does not use the library much.

There've been a few complaints lately that country music hasn't produced much of interest in the past few years. This may seem true after one listens to the seventeenth Charlie Pride album or the latest releases by Loretta Lynn, Bill Anderson, or even the country music giant, Johnny Cash. There is a sameness about their efforts during the last half decade. The influence of rock is very evident in the not-so-western costumes, amount of electrical instruments, and singing styles seen around the Grand Old Opry in latter days. However, what may be emerging is a hybrid country music that has an appeal not only to the traditional and by now middle-aged listener, but to the younger record buyers as well. A music that does not change to meet new tastes will die.

The significant movement in this field, however, is not the rumored decay of the Nashville Sound, but the re-emergence of older styles that are rapidly capturing a new audience. These older styles center upon "bluegrass" and the old time southern string band. The term "bluegrass" does not refer to a geographic area but comes from the name of Bill Monroe's string band, the Blue Grass Boys. Bluegrass music is recognizable and distinctive: it features a high-pitched strident style of two-three-four part harmony and five instruments, fiddle, guitar, mandolin, string bass, and five-string banjo. Bluegrass has been around for three decades and has never been an overwhelming commercial success.

Today, the primitive non-commercial sound of bluegrass music is stirring up a revival of interest in the more traditional roots of Country music. There is something about this hard driving sound that has captured the imagination not only of rural people but urban youngsters. The growth of summer-time bluegrass festivals has been phenomenal and to attend one is to have an almost déjâ vu feeling of Woodstock. Even more significant is the growth of record companies recording and releasing this style of music. Rounder Records Collective is leading the way with field recordings, re-releases of previously recorded material and acting as a jobber for dozens of small companies. Rounder is attempting to beat the distribution system that fixes prices at their current high levels. For example, Rounder sells its own releases for $3.50 if bought directly by mail. For the pinched library budget Rounder offers considerable savings.

Whether it's Merle Haggard or Donna Fargo or Kenny Baker and Don Stover, country music has a sizeable following. It does not have, however, a distinct and worthwhile reviewing media.

Country Music is the only periodical indexed devoted to the Nashville Sound. Its reviews are "puffs" intended to sell records. The only other journal that attempted to review seriously this genre was Country Sky, now defunct. Some reviews of country releases can be found in nearly every magazine indexed. Often interesting reviews can be found in Rolling Stone, Creem, and Crawdaddy. Traditional and bluegrass is better treated. Old Time Music, Sing Out, and Bluegrass Unlimited offer expert in-depth reviews by followers of old time music. There is a definite need for more and better reviewing in the country music field.

Because of the limited number of reviews an attempt to select the reviewer's picks for 1972 is risky. However, the list might include:

Everly Brothers. Stories We Could Tell. RCA LSP 4620
Merle Haggard. Let Me Tell You About a Song. Capitol ST 882
Waylon Jennings. Ladies Love Outlaws. RCA LSP 4751
Doug Kershaw. Swamp Grass. Warner Bros. BS 2581
George Pegram. Rounder 0001.
Charlie Pride. I'm Just Me. RCA LSP 4560
Jerry Reed. Ko Ko Joe. RCA LSP 4596
Jeannie C. Riley. Jeannie. Plantation 16
Earl Scruggs. His Family and Friends. Columbia C 30584

1390 Roy Acuff. COUNTRY. Hilltop S 6090 $1.89. Cart. P8 245 $6.95. (Reissue.)
Journal of American Folklore. October/December. p396. 25w. 1

1391 Roy Acuff. TIME. Hickory. LPS 156 $4.98. (Reissue.)
Journal of American Folklore. October/December. p396. 50w. 3½

1392 Lynn Anderson. LISTEN TO A COUNTRY SONG. Columbia KC 31647 $4.98. Cart. CA 31647 $6.98. Cass. CT 31647 $6.98.
Country Music. November. p61-2. 200w. 2½

1393 Chet Atkins. PICKS ON THE HITS. RCA LSP 4754 $5.98.
Country Music. November. p62. 250w. 2½
Music Journal. December. p75. 125w. 3

1394 Mike Auldridge. DOBRO. Takoma/Devi D 1033 $5.98.
Rolling Stone. November 23. p62. 450w. 3½

1395 Hoyt Axton. COUNTRY ANTHEM. Capitol SMAS 850 $5.98. Cart. 8XT 850 $6.98.
Popular Music. Winter. p124. 50w. 2

Popular Music. Winter. p126. 50w. 2
Stereo Review. April. p89. 175w. $\frac{1}{2}$

1396 Kenny Baker. A BAKER'S DOZEN: COUNTRY FIDDLE TUNES. Country 730 $4.98.
Old Time Music. Winter 71/72. p29. 150w. 5

1397 Kenny Baker. BILL MONROE'S UNCLE PEN. Decca DL 75348 $5.98.
Sing Out. May/June. p44. 300w. 3

1398 Kenny Baker. COUNTRY. County 736 $5.98.
Sing Out. May/June. p44. 300w. 3

1399 Kenny Baker and Uncle Josh Graves. SOMETHING DIFFERENT. Puritan 5001 $5.98.
Old Time Music. Autumn. p27. 150w. $3\frac{1}{2}$
Sing Out. September/October. p41. 100w. 3

1400 THE BEST OF COUNTRY DUETS (anthology). RCA International INTS 1275 (E). (Reissue.)
Records and Recordings. July. p98. 150w. 3

1401 Norman Blake. HOME IN SULPHER SPRINGS. Rounder 0012 $5.98.
Old Time Music. Summer. p26. 125w. 3

1402 Boondoggle and Balderdash. UNI 73121 $5.98.
Audio. May. p94. 25w. $2\frac{1}{2}$

1403 Tony Booth. THE KEY'S IN THE MAILBOX. Capitol ST 11076 $5.98. Cart. 8XT 11076 $6.98. Cass. 4XT 11076 $6.98.
Country Music. October. p64. 225w. 1

1404 Bottle Hill Boys. BOTTLE HILL, A RUMOR IN THEIR OWN TIME. Biograph BLP RC 6006 $5.98.
Sing Out. May/June. p41-2. 200w. $2\frac{1}{2}$

1405 Don Bowman. THE ALL NEW... Mega M31-1015 $4.98.
Country Music. November. p62-3. 300w. $2\frac{1}{2}$

1406 Brother Oswald. Rounder 0013 $5.95.
Old Time Music. Summer. p26. 125w. $3\frac{1}{2}$
Sing Out. September/October. p41. 50w. $3\frac{1}{2}$

1407 Jim Ed Brown. BROWN IS BLUE. RCA LSP 4755 $5.98. Cart. P8S 2019 $6.95.
Country Music. December. p64. 150w. 2

1408 Jim Ed Brown. SHE'S LEAVIN'. RCA LSP 4614 $5.98. Cart. P8S 1843 $6.98.
Records and Recordings. June. p91. 75w. $2\frac{1}{2}$

1409 Dorsey Burnette. HERE AND NOW. Capitol ST 11094 $5.98. Cart. 8XT 11094 $6.98.
Country Music. December. p61, 64. 200w. 2

1410 Blake Bynum and Roy Harper. ECHOES OF THE PAST. Pine Mountain PMR 208.
Journal of American Folklore. October/December. p399. 50w. $2\frac{1}{2}$

1411 Glen Campbell. TURN AROUND AND LOOK AT ME. Ember NR 5042 (E). (Reissue.)
Gramophone. June. p111. 25w. 0

1412 CAPITOL COUNTRY GREATS, VOLUME 1 (anthology). Capitol ST 21909 (E). (Reissue.)
Gramophone. July. p255. 50w. 2

1413 The Carolina Tar Heels. GHP 1001 $4.98.
Old Time Music. Winter 71/72. p25. 450w. 4

1414 Anita Carter. SO MUCH LOVE. Capitol ST 11085 $5.98. Cart. 8XT 11085 $6.98.
Canadian Stereo Guide. Fall. p28. 75w. 3
Popular Music. Summer. p248. 50w. 4

1415 Carter Family. ALBUM OF OLD FAMILY MELODIES. Country Music History CMH 107 (Germany). (Reissue.)
Old Time Music. Summer. p24. 250w. 4
Sing-Out. March/April. p38. 200w. $2\frac{1}{2}$

1416 Carter Family. LONESOME PINE SPECIAL. Camden CAL 2473 (Canada). (Reissue.)
Journal of American Folklore. October/December. p396. 100w. 4

1417 Johnny Cash. AMERICA. Columbia KC 31645 $5.98. Cart. CA 31645 $6.98. Cass. CT 31645 $6.98.
Country Music. November. p60-61. 150w. $2\frac{1}{2}$

1418 Johnny Cash. GET RHYTHM. Philips 6467 014 (E). (Reissue.)
Gramophone. July. p255. 25w. 1

1419 Johnny Cash. THE MAN, THE WORLD, HIS MUSIC. Philips 6641 008 (2 discs) (E). (Reissue.)
Gramophone. July. p255. 25w. 1

1420 Johnny Cash. ORIGINAL GOLDEN HITS, VOLUME 3. Sun Records 127 $4.98. Cart. T 127 $6.98. Cass. C 127 $6.98. (Reissue.)
Popular Music. Spring. p184. 25w. 3

1421 Johnny Cash. ROCK ISLAND LINE. Hilltop JS 6101 $1.89.
Library Journal. February 15. p666. 125w. 1

1422 Johnny Cash/Jerry Lee Lewis. SING HANK WILLIAMS. Sun 125E $4.98. (Reissue.)
Blues Unlimited. February/March. p20. 25w. 4
Creem. January. p69. 25w. 2½
Gramophone. July. p255. 25w. 0

1423 Roy Clark. COUNTRY! Dot DOS 25997 $4.98. Cart. 8150-2599M $6.98. Cass. 5150-25997M $6.98.
Country Music. December. p64. 150w. 2½

1424 Stompin' Tom Connors. LOVE AND LAUGHTER. Boots BOS 7107 (Canada).
Ontario Library Review. December. p243. 25w. 2½

1425 Stompin' Tom Connors. MY STOMPIN' GROUNDS. Boots BOS 7103 (Canada).
Ontario Library Review. December. p243. 25w. 2½
Previews. November. p42. 275w. 3

1426 COUNTRY AND WESTERN GREATS (anthology). Philips 6336 209 (E). (Reissue.)
Records and Recordings. October. p123. 200w. 2½

1427 Country Cooking. Rounder 0006 $5.95.
Old Time Music. Winter 71/72. p28-9. 200w. 2
Popular Music. Spring. p187. 75w. 3

1428 Floyd Cramer. BEST OF... RCA International INTS 1266 (E). (Reissue.)
Gramophone. January. p1279. 50w. 3
Records and Recordings. February. p103. 75w. 2

1429 Floyd Cramer. DETOURS. RCA LSP 4676 $5.98. Cart. P8S 1903 $6.95. Cass. PK 1903 $6.95.
Previews. November. p42. 75w. 3

1430 Dick Curless. STONIN' AROUND. Capitol ST 11087 $5.98. Cart. 8XT 11087 $6.98.
Country Music. October. p61. 300w. 2½

1431 Dick Curless. TOMBSTONE EVERY MILE. Capitol ST 11011 $5.98. Cart. 8XT 11011 $6.98. Cass. 4XT 11011 $6.98.
Popular Music. Spring. p186. 50w. 4

1432 Charlie Daniels. Capitol ST 790 $5.98.
Popular Music. Fall. p61. 25w. 1½

1433 Tom Darby and Jimmy Tarleton. DARBY AND TARLETON. Old Timey LP 112 $6.00. (Reissue.)
Ethnomusicology. October. p581-3. 750w. 4
Stereo Review. September. p82. 100w. $2\frac{1}{2}$

1434 Dianne Davidson. BACKWOODS WOMAN. Janus 3043 $5.98. Cart. 8098-3043M $6.95.
Crawdaddy. August. p21. 600w. 3
Gramophone. November. p984. 125w. 3
Hi-Fi News and Record Review. September. p1685. 75w. $2\frac{1}{2}$

1435 Danny Davis and the Nashville Brass. NASHVILLE BRASS TURNS TO GOLD. RCA LSP 4627 $5.98. Cart. P8S 1859 $6.95. Cass. PK 1859 $6.95.
Library Journal. July. p2369. 150w. $2\frac{1}{2}$

1436 Mac Davis. BABY DON'T GET HOOKED ON ME. Columbia KC 31770 $5.98. Cart. CA 31770 $6.98. Cass. CT 31770 $6.98.
Country Music. December. p58-9. 150w. $2\frac{1}{2}$
Sound. December. p41. 250w. 4

1437 Skeeter Davis. RCA LSA 3047 (E).
Gramophone. July. p255. 25w. 1

1438 Fred Dixon and the Friday Afternoon. Banff SBS 5408 (Canada).
Sound. April. p37. 175w. 2

1439 Val Doonican. MORNING IN THE COUNTRY. Philips 6326 015 (E).
Gramophone. September. p577. 25w. 1
Hi-Fi News and Record Reviews. December. p2461. 25w. 2

1440 Dave Dudley. WILL THE REAL DAVE DUDLEY PLEASE SING? Mercury 6338 074 (E).
Gramophone. July. p254. 25w. 1

1441 Everly Brothers. ROOTS. Warner Bros. S 1752 $5.98. Cart. M81752 $6.95. Cass. M51752 $6.95.
Gramophone. March. p1613. 75w. 3

1442 Everly Brothers. STORIES WE COULD TELL. RCA LSP 4620 $5.98.
Crawdaddy. June 11. p15. 600w. 3
New York Times--Sunday. August 20. pD22. 225w. 4
Popular Music. Summer. p249. 100w. 4

1443 Raymond Fairchild. HONKY TONKIN' COUNTRY BLUES. Rural Rhythm RR TM 245 $5.00.

Journal of American Folklore. October/December. p400. 25w. $2\frac{1}{2}$

1444 Donna Fargo. THE HAPPIEST GIRL IN THE WHOLE U.S.A. Dot 26000 $4.98. Cart. 8150-26000M $6.98. Cass. 5150-26000M $6.98.
Country Music. October. p62-3. 200w. 2
Gramophone. December. p1221. 25w. 0

1445 Lester Flatt. KENTUCKY RIDGERUNNER. RCA LSP 4633 $5.98. Cart. P8S 1865 $6.98.
Stereo Review. October. p92. 175w. $2\frac{1}{2}$

1446 Lester Flatt. LESTER 'N' MAC. RCA LSP 4547 $5.98. Cart. P8S 1761 $6.95.
Journal of American Folklore. October/December. p399-400. 25w. $2\frac{1}{2}$

1447 Lester Flatt. ON VICTOR. RCA LSP 4495 $5.98. Cart. P8S 1704 $6.95.
Journal of American Folklore. October/December. p399-400. 25w. $2\frac{1}{2}$

1448 Lester Flatt. THE ONE AND ONLY. Nugget NRLP 104 $4.98.
Journal of American Folklore. October/December. p.399. 25w. $2\frac{1}{2}$

1449 Flatt and Scruggs. FINAL FLING: ONE LAST TIME (JUST FOR KICKS). Columbia CS 9945 $5.98.
Journal of American Folklore. October/December. p399. 25w. 1

1450 Flatt and Scruggs. FOGGY MOUNTAIN BREAKDOWN. Hilltop JS 6093 $1.89. Cart. P8 246 $4.95. (Reissue.)
Journal of American Folklore. October/December. p399. 25w. $2\frac{1}{2}$

1451 Tennessee Ernie Ford. IT'S... Capitol ST 11092 $5.98. Cart. 8XT 11092 $6.98. Cass. 4XT 11092 $6.98.
Country Music. December. p59-60. 200w. $2\frac{1}{2}$

1452 Cullen Galyean, Wayburn Johnson and the Foothill Boys. BLUEGRASS IN THE CAROLINA MOUNTAINS. County 731 $5.98.
Old Time Music. Autumn. p28-9. 150w. 4
Sing Out. September/October. p41. 50w. $3\frac{1}{2}$

1453 Tom Ghent. YANKEE'S REBEL SON. Kapp KS 3655 $4.98. Cart. K8 3655 $6.98. Cass. K7 3655 $6.98.
Audio. October. p89. 50w. $2\frac{1}{2}$

1454 Bob Gibson. Capitol ST 742 $5.98.
Popular Music. Fall. p59. 50w. 1

1455 Don Gibson. COUNTRY GREEN. Hickory LPS 160 $4.98. Cart. 8049-160V $6.95.
Sound. April. p36. 150w. 0

1456 Don Gibson. WOMAN (SENSUOUS WOMAN). Hickory LPS 166 $4.98.
Country Music. November. p64. 150w. 2½

1457 GRAND OLD OPRY PAST AND PRESENT (anthology). Hilltop JS 6022 $1.89. (Reissue.)
Journal of American Folklore. October/December. p305. 50w. 2

1458 Jeanie Greene. MARY CALLED JENNIE GREENE. Elektra 74103 $5.98. Cart. ET 84103 $6.98. Cass. TC 54103 $6.98.
Gramophone. April. p1776. 50w. 1

1459 Merle Haggard. THE BEST OF THE BEST. Capitol ST 11082 $5.98. Cart. 8XT 11082 $6.98. Cass. 4XT 11082 $6.98. (Reissue.)
Country Music. December. p58. 150w. 2½

1460 Merle Haggard. LET ME TELL YOU ABOUT A SONG. Capitol ST 882 $5.98. Cart. 8XT 882 $6.98. Cass. 4XT 882 $6.98.
Popular Music. Summer. p253. 50w. 2
Rolling Stone. June 22. p62. 750w. 4½
Stereo Review. November. p84, 88. 300w. 3

1461 Merle Haggard. SAME TRAIN, A DIFFERENT TIME. Capitol SWBB 223 (2 discs) $6.98. Cart. 8XTT 223 $7.98. Cass. 4XTT 223 $7.98.
Creem. December. p58-9. 600w. 2

1462 Merle Haggard. SOMEDAY WE'LL LOOK BACK. Capitol ST 835 $5.98. Cart. 8XT 835 $6.98. Cass. 4XT 835 $6.98.
Gramophone. July. p255. 25w. 2

1463 Merle Haggard and the Strangers. A TRIBUTE TO THE BEST DAMN FIDDLE PLAYER IN THE WORLD (OR, MY SALUTE TO BOB WILLS). Capitol ST 638 $5.98. Cart. 8XT 638 $6.98. Cass. 4XT 638 $6.98.
Rolling Stone. October 26. p60. 750w. 3

1464 Tom T. Hall. IN SEARCH OF A SONG. Mercury SR61350 $4.98. Cart. MC8-61350 $6.95. Cass. MCR4-61350 $6.95.
American Record Guide. January. p285. 175w. 3

New York Times--Sunday. May 21. pD32. 50w. 2½
Sound. March. p21. 75w. 1

1465 Tom T. Hall. THE STORYTELLER. Mercury SR 61368 $4.98. Cart. MC8 61368 $6.95. Cass. MCR4 61368. $6.95.
Country Music. November. p64. 200w. 2½
Rolling Stone. November 23. p68. 2,500w. 3

1466 Tom T. Hall. WE ALL GOT TOGETHER AND... Mercury SR 61362 $4.98. Cart. MC8 61362 $6.95. Cass. MCR4 61362 $6.95.
Gramophone. September. p577. 75w. 2
New York Times--Sunday. May 21. pD32. 50w. 2½

1467 George Hamilton IV. COUNTRY MUSIC IN MY SOUL. RCA LSP 4700 $5.98. Cart. P8S 1930 $6.95.
Canadian Stereo Guide. Summer. p67. 100w. 3

1468 George Hamilton IV. WEST TEXAS HIGHWAY. RCA LSP 4609 $5.98. Cart. P8S 1833 $6.95.
Records and Recordings. June. p91. 100w. 2½

1469 Lee Hazelwood. REQUIEM FOR AN ALMOST LADY. Warner Bros. K44161 (E).
Gramophone. April. p1776. 50w. 1½

1470 James Hendricks. MGM SE 4768 $5.98.
Popular Music. Fall. p60. 50w. 3

1471 High Country. Raccoon/Warner Bros. WS 1937 $5.98. Cart. M81937 $6.95. Cass. M51937 $6.95.
Crawdaddy. August. p20. 250w. 2
Creem. January. p69. 50w. 3
Gramophone. July. p25-6. 25w. 2
Old Time Music. Autumn. p29. 125w. 2½

1472 High Country. DREAMS. Raccoon/Warner Bros. BS 2608 $5.98. Cart. M82608 $6.95. Cass. M52608 $6.95.
Old Time Music. Autumn. p29. 250w. 3½

1473 HOBOES AND BRAKEMEN (anthology). Country Music History CMH 106 (Germany). (Reissue.)
Old Time Music. Summer. p24. 300w. 3
Sing Out. March/April. p38. 200w. 2

1474 Hodges Brothers. WATERMELON HANGIN' ON THE VINE. Arhoolie 5001 $6.00.
Jazz Journal. November. p38. 75w. 1
Old Time Music. Summer. p29. 175w. 3½
Sing Out. March/April. p38. 200w. 2

1475 Thelma Houston. SUNSHOWER. Mowest 102 $5.98.
Gramophone. August. p397. 75w. 1

1476 Jan Howard. ROCK ME BACK TO LITTLE ROCK. Decca 75207 $5.98. Cart. 6-5207 $6.98. Cass. C73-5207 $6.98.
Hi-Fi News and Record Review. July. p1311. 50w. 2½

1477 Tex Isley and the New North Carolina Ramblers. NORTH CAROLINA BOYS. Leader LEA 4040 (E).
Records and Recordings. July. p99. 225w. 4

1478 It's A Crying Time. Red Clay RC 101 (Japan).
Old Time Music. p26-7. 200w. 3

1479 Wanda Jackson. I WOULDN'T WANT YOU ANY OTHER WAY. Capitol ST 11096 $5.98. Cart. 8XT 11096 $6.98.
Country Music. November. p62. 200w. 2½

1480 Sonny James. COUNTRY HITS. Capitol ST 629 $4.98. (Reissue.)
Records and Recordings. July. p99. 100w. 2

1481 Sonny James. TRACES. Capitol ST 11108 $5.98. Cart. 8XT 11108 $6.98. Cass. 4XT 11108 $6.98. (Reissue.)
Popular Music and Society. Fall. p88. 25w. 3½

1482 Sonny James. WHEN THE SNOW IS ON THE ROSES. Columbia KC 31646 $5.98. Cart. CA 31646 $6.98. Cass. CT 31646 $6.98.
Country Music. October. p61-2. 100w. 1

1483 Snuffy Jenkins. CAROLINA BLUE GRASS. Arhoolie 5011 $6.00.
Jazz and Blues. August. p31. 375w. 3
Jazz Journal. December. p41. 750w. 3
Old Time Music. Summer. p29. 175w. 3½
Popular Music. Summer. p251. 25w. 3

1484 Snuffy Jenkins and Pappy Sherrill. 33 YEARS OF PICKIN' AND PLUCKIN'. Rounder 0005 $5.95.
Old Time Music. Winter 71/72. p28-9. 200w. 4

1485 Waylon Jennings. CEDARTOWN GEORGIA. RCA LSP 4567 $5.98. Cart. P8S 1785 $6.95. Cass. PK 1785 $6.95.
Hi-Fi News and Record Review. May. p939. 50w. 2½
Records and Recordings. July. p99. 100w. 3
Sound. March. p21. 100w. 2

1486 Waylon Jennings. GOOD HEARTED WOMAN. RCA LSP 4647 $5.98. Cart. P8S 1886 $6.95. Cass. PK 1886 $6.95.
Popular Music. Spring. p128. 150w. 4

1487 Waylon Jennings. LADIES LOVE OUTLAWS. RCA LSP 4751 $5.98. Cart. P8S 2016 $6.95. Cass. PK 2016 $6.95.
Country Music. December. p59. 200w. 2½
Popular Music and Society. Fall. p1. 50w. 4
Rolling Stone. November 23. p68, 70. 300w. 3

1488 George Jones and Tammy Wynette. ME AND THE FIRST LADY. Epic KE 31554 $5.98. Cart. EA 31554 $6.98. Cass. ET 31554 $6.98.
Country Music. October. p60-1. 125w. 2½

1489 The Jordonaires. WE'D LOVE TO TEACH THE WORLD TO SING. Ember CW 141 (E). (Reissue.)
Gramophone. August. p398. 25w. 1

1490 Christopher Kearney. Capitol ST 11043 $5.98. Cart. 8XT 11043 $6.98. Cass. 4XT 11043 $6.98.
Gramophone. September. p577. 25w. 2

1491 Jerry Kennedy. PLAYS WITH ALL DUE RESPECT TO KRIS KRISTOFFERSON. Mercury SR 61339 $5.98. Cart. MC8 61339 $6.95. Cass. MCR4 61339 $6.95.
Audio. March. p81. 50w. 2

1492 Doug Kershaw. DEVIL'S ELBOW. Warner Bros. BS 2649 $5.98. Cart. M82649 $6.95. Cass. M52649 $6.95.
Sound. November. p37. 250w. 4

1493 Doug Kershaw. SWAMP GRASS. Warner Bros. BS 2581 $5.98. Cart. M82581 $6.95. Cass. M52581 $6.95.
Creem. April. p71. 50w. ½
High Fidelity. May. p109. 200w. 3½
Stereo Review. July. p93-4. 225w. 3½

1494 Jerry Lee Lewis. OLD THYME COUNTRY MUSIC. Sun 6467 020 (E). (Reissue.)
Blues Unlimited. October. p28. 50w. 4

1495 The Lilly Brothers. EARLY RECORDINGS. County 729 $4.98. (Reissue.)
Journal of American Folklore. October/December. p396. 50w. 2½
Old Time Music. Winter 71/72. p28-9. 325w. 5

1496 Hank Locklin. IRISH SONGS, COUNTRY STYLE. RCA LSP 3079 $5.98.
Records and Recordings. October. p123. 75w. 1½

1497 John D. Loudermilk. VOLUME ONE (ELLOREE). Warner Bros. S1922 $5.98. Cart. M81922 $6.95. Cass. M51922 $6.95.
Sound. February. p13. 125w. 3

1498 Louisiana Honeydrippers. BAYOU BLUEGRASS. Arhoolie 5010 $6.00. (Reissue.)
Jazz Journal. December. p41. 50w. $3\frac{1}{2}$
Old Time Music. Summer. p29. 175w. 2
Popular Music and Society. Summer. p252. 75w. 3

1499 Loretta Lynn. HERE I AM AGAIN. Decca DL 75381 $5.98.
Popular Music and Society. Fall. p88. 25w. $3\frac{1}{2}$

1500 Loretta Lynn. ONE'S ON THE WAY. Decca DL 75334 $5.98.
Creem. August. p74. 50w. $2\frac{1}{2}$
Rolling Stone. June 22. p60. 1,200w. 4

1501 Loretta Lynn. YOU'RE LOOKIN' AT COUNTRY. MCA MUPS 447 (E).
Gramophone. July. 25w. p255. 2
Hi-Fi News and Record Review. July. p1311. 25w. $2\frac{1}{2}$

1502 Loretta Lynn and Conway Twitty. LEAD ME ON. Decca DL 75326 $5.98.
Rolling Stone. June 22. p60. 1,200w. 4
Sound. March. p34. 150w. 1

1503 Uncle Dave Macon. THE DIXIE DEWDROPS. Vetco LP 101. (Reissue.)
Journal of American Folklore. October/December. p396. 50w. 4

1504 Uncle Dave Macon. EARLY RECORDINGS. County 521 $4.98. (Reissue.)
Journal of American Folklore. October/December. p396. 25w. 3
Old Time Music. Winter 71/72. p25. 325w. 4

1505 Leo McCaffery. McCAFFERY'S COUNTY. Emerald Gem GES 1064 (E).
Gramophone. August. p397. 25w. 0

1506 Tom McClure. TRIBUTE TO JIM REEVES. Music for Pleasure MFP 5259 (E).
Gramophone. June. p112. 25w. 1

1507 Charlie McCoy. THE REAL McCOY. Monument Z 31329 $5.98. Cart. 8044-31329M $6.95. Cass. 5044-31329M $6.95.
American Record Guide. September. p673. 60w. $3\frac{1}{2}$

1508 Lester McFarland and Robert Gardner. MAC AND BOB. Birch 1944 $5.00. (Reissue.)
Old Time Music. Autumn. p26. 200w. 3

1509 Sam McGee. GRAND DAD OF THE COUNTRY GUITAR PICKERS. Arhoolie 5012 $6.00.
Audio. September. p123. 575w. 5
Ethnomusicology. October. p580-1. 800w. 4

1510 Jody Miller. THERE'S A PARTY GOIN' ON. Epic Ke 31706 $5.98. Cart. EA 31706 $6.98. Cass. ET 31706 $6.98.
Country Music. November. p61. 150w. 2

1511 Roger Miller. RCA International INTS 1319 (E).
Gramophone. January. p1274. 25w. 3
Records and Recordings. February. p103. 100w. 3

1512 Roger Miller. THE BEST OF... Mercury SR 61361 $4.98. Cart. MC-8-61361 $6.95. Cass. MCR-4-61361 $6.95. (Reissue.)
New York Times--Sunday. May 21. pD32. 50w. 2
Previews. November. p42. 175w. 3

1513 Roger Miller. A TRIP TO THE COUNTRY. Mercury SR 61297 $5.98.
New York Times--Sunday. May 21. pD32. 50w. 2

1514 Bill Monroe. BLUEGRASS INSTRUMENTALS. Decca DL 74601 $5.98.
Rolling Stone. March 16. p62. 100w. $2\frac{1}{2}$

1515 Nashville String Band. STRUNG UP. RCA LSP 4553 $5.98. Cart. P8S 1767 $6.95.
American Record Guide. January. p237. 225w. 2

1516 Willie Nelson. THE WILLIE WAY. RCA LSP 4760 $5.98.
Country Music. October. p62. 275w. $2\frac{1}{2}$
Rolling Stone. November 23. p68, 70. 2,500w. 3

1517 North Carolina Ramblers. 1928/1930. Biograph BLP RC 6005 $5.98. (Reissue.)
Old Time Music. Summer. p25. 425w. 4

1518 Roy Orbison. SINGS. MGM 4835 $5.98. Cart. 8130-4835M $6.95. Cass. 5130-4835M $6.95.
Audio. September. p119. 50w. $2\frac{1}{2}$
Gramophone. September. p577. 25w. 2

1519 Osborne Brothers. BLUEGRASS BLUES. Metro Moonshine 2356 056 (E).
Old Time Music. Autumn. p29-30. 225w. $2\frac{1}{2}$
Records and Recordings. October. p123. 125w. 1

1520 Buck Owens. LIVE AT THE NUGGET. Capitol SMAS 11039 $5.98. Cart. 8XT 11039 $6.98. Cass. 4XT 11039 $6.98.

Canadian Stereo Guide. Summer. p67. 100w. $2\frac{1}{2}$

1521 Buck Owens. LIVE AT THE WHITE HOUSE. Capitol SMAS 11105 $5.98. Cart. 8XT 11105 $6.98. Cass. 4XT 11105 $6.98.
Creem. December. p63. 50w. 0

1522 Buck Owens. RUBY. Capitol ST 795 $5.98. Cart. 8XT 795 $6.98. Cass. 4XT 795 $6.98.
Gramophone. July. p255. 50w. 0
Journal of American Folklore. October/December. p400. 25w. 1

1523 Buck Owens. TOO OLD TO CUT THE MUSTARD. Capitol ST 874 $5.98. Cart. 8XT 874 $6.98. Cass. 4XT 874 $6.98.
Sound. March. p35. 100w. 2

1524 Buck Owens and Susan Raye. BEST. Capitol ST 11084 $5.98. Cart. 8XT 11084 $6.98. Cass. 4XT 11084 $6.98.
Country Music. October. p63-4. 400w. 3

1525 Johnny Paycheck. SHE'S ALL I GOT. Epic E 31141 $5.98. Cart. EA 31141 $6.95.
Rolling Stone. July 20. p54, 56. 1,000w. 4

1526 Dolly Parton. TOUCH YOUR WOMAN. RCA LSP 4686 $5.98. Cart. P8S 1915 $6.95. Cass. PK 1915 $6.95.
Canadian Stereo Guide. Summer. p67. 100w. 3

1527 George Pegram. Rounder 0001 $5.95.
Old Time Music. Winter 71/72. p29-9. 200w. 3
Popular Music. Spring. p187. 75w. 3

1528 Sorrells Pickard. Decca DL 75338 $5.98.
Audio. August. p62. 25w. 2

1529 Charlie Poole and the Highlanders. Arbor 201 $5.00. (Reissue.)
Old Time Music. Summer. p25. 425w. 4

1530 Sandy Posey. WHY DON'T WE GO SOMEWHERE AND LOVE. Columbia KC 31594 $5.98.
Country Music. October. p64, 66. 325w. 3

1531 Kenny Price. SUPERSIDEMAN. RCA LSP 4681 $5.98. Cart. P8S 1912 $6.95.
Gramophone. September. p578. 25w. 1

1532 Charley Pride. BEST, VOLUME 2. RCA LSP 4682 $5.98. Cart. P8S 1913 $6.95. Cass. PK 1913 $6.95. (Reissue.)
Sound. April. p37. 150w. 3

1533 Charley Pride. I'M JUST ME. RCA LSP 4560 $5.98. Cart. P8S 1772 $6.95. Cass. PK 1772 $6.95.
Hi-Fi News and Record Review. July. p1312. 50w. 2
Records and Recordings. May. p108. 175w. 2½
Sound. February. p13. 125w. 3
Stereo Review. January. p110,13. 400w. 3

1534 Charley Pride. SINGS HEART SONGS. RCA LSP 4617 $5.98. Cart. P8S 1848 $6.95. Cass. PK 1848 $6.95.
Stereo Review. January. p110,113. 400w. 3

1535 Charley Pride. A SUNSHINY DAY. RCA LSP 4742 $5.98.
Country Music. November. p60. 150w. 2½

1536 Riley Puckett. STORY, 1924/41. Roots RL 701 (Austria).
Journal of American Folklore. October/December. p396. 50w. 3

1537 The Randolph County String Band. OLD TIME MUSIC FROM ALABAMA. Davis Unlimited DU 33003 $5.00.
Journal of American Folklore. October/December. p398. 25w. 3

1538 The Randolph County String Band. UNDER THE WEEPING WILLOW TREE. Davis Unlimited DU 33001 $5.00.
Journal of American Folklore. October/December. p398. 75w. 3½

1539 Blind Alfred Reed. HOW CAN A POOR MAN STAND SUCH TIMES AND LIVE? Rounder 1001 $5.95. (Reissue.)
Old Time Music. Autumn. p25. 400w. 5
Sing Out. September/October. p41. 150w. 4½

1540 Jerry Reed. RCA LSP 4750 $5.98.
Country Music. December. p60. 200w. 2½

1541 Jerry Reed. KO KO JOE. RCA LSP 4596 $5.98. Cart. P8S 1820 $6.95. Cass. PK 1820 $6.95.
American Record Guide. March. p333. 225w. 2
New York Times--Sunday. May 21. pD32. 50w. 2½
Sound. March. p21. 125w. 3

1542 Jerry Reed and Chet Atkins. ME AND CHET. RCA LSP 4707 $5.98. Cart. P8S 1942 $6.95. Cass. PK 1942 $6.95.
American Record Guide. July. p576. 100w. 2

1543 Jerry Reed. NASHVILLE UNDERGROUND. RCA LSA 3056 (E).
Gramophone. July. p255. 25w. 1
Hi-Fi News and Record Review. May. p939. 25w. 2½
Records and Recordings. June. p91. 100w. 4

1544 Jerry Reed. SMELL THE FLOWERS. RCA LSP 4660 $5.98. Cart. P8S 1891 $6.95. Cass. PK 1891 $6.95.
Music Journal. May. p64. 100w. 2
New York Times--Sunday. May 21. pD32. 50w. 3
Sound. March. p35. 175w. 2

1545 Jerry Reed. WHEN YOU'RE HOT, YOU'RE HOT. RCA LSP 4506 $5.98. Cart. P8S 1712 $6.95. Cass. PK 1712 $6.95.
New York Times--Sunday. May 21. pD32. 200w. 3

1546 Jim Reeves. MISSING YOU. RCA LSP 4749 $5.98. (Reissue.)
Country Music. December. p61. 200w. 2

1547 Jim Reeves. 50 ALL TIME WORLD WIDE FAVORITES. RCA LSP 7403 (4 discs). (Reissue.)
Records and Recordings. February. p103. 100w. 3

1548 THE RENFRO VALLEY GATHERIN' (anthology). Renfro Valley Records RVLP 111 and RV 1969 (2 discs).
Journal of American Folklore. October/December. p398-9. 100w. 4

1549 Jeannie C. Riley. JEANNIE. Plantation 16 $4.98. Cart. 8105-16 $6.98. Cass. 5105-16 $6.98.
Audio. May. p95. 25w. 2½
Creem. August. p69. 50w. 3½
Gramophone. September. p931. 25w. 2½

1550 Tex Ritter. Music for Pleasure MFP 5245 (E). (Reissue.)
Gramophone. July. p255. 50w. 3

1551 Marty Robbins. Harmony KH 30316 $1.98. (Reissue.)
Journal of American Folklore. October/December. p397. 25w. 2½

1552 Jimmie Rodgers. RCA DPS 2021 (2 discs) (E). (Reissue.)
Blues Unlimited. July. p23. 25w. 5

1553 Earl Scruggs. HIS FAMILY AND FRIENDS. Columbia C 30584 $4.98. Cart. CA 30584 $6.98.
Creem. April. p66. 400w. 2½
High Fidelity. February. p120. 25w. 3
Popular Music. Winter. p64. 100w. 2½
Sound. April. p21. 75w. 2
Stereo Review. March. p108-9. 300w. 2½

1554 Earl Scruggs. I SAW THE LIGHT WITH SOME HELP FROM MY FRIENDS. Columbia KC 31354 $5.98. Cart. CA 31354 $6.98. Cass. CT 31354 $6.98.
Sing-Out. May/June. p42. 175w. 3

1555 Earl Scruggs. NASHVILLE'S ROCK. Columbia CS 1007 $4.98.
Journal of American Folklore. October/December. p399. 25w. 1

1556 Curley Seckler. SINGS AGAIN. County 732 $4.98.
Journal of American Folklore. October/December. p400. 25w. 2½
Old Time Music. Winter 71/72. p28. 275w. 4

1557 Mike Settle. UNI UNLS 122 (E).
Gramophone. September. p577. 250w. 2

1558 Red Simpson. I'M A TRUCK. Capitol ST 881 $5.98. Cart. 8XT 881 $6.98. Cass. 4XT 881 $6.98.
Creem. June. p77. 50w. ½

1559 Red Simpson. THE VERY REAL... Capitol ST 11093 $5.98. Cart. 8XT 11093 $6.98. Cass 4XT 11093 $6.98.
Country Music. December. p60. 200w. 2½
Creem. December. p63. 50w. 2½

1560 Connie Smith. BEST. RCA LSP 3848 $5.98. Cart. P8S 1314 $6.95. Cass. PK 1314 $6.95. (Reissue.)
Records and Recordings. July. p99. 150w. 2

1561 Connie Smith. IF IT AIN'T LOVE, AND OTHER GREAT DALLAS FRAZIER SONGS. RCA LSP 4748 $5.98. Cart. P8S 2012 $6.95. Cass. PK 2012 $6.95.
Country Music. October. p60. 300w. 3

1562 Connie Smith. WHERE IS MY CASTLE? RCA LSP 4474 $5.98. Cart. P8S 1674 $6.95.
Gramophone. March. p1613. 50w. 2

1563 Hank Snow. THE JIMMIE RODGERS STORY. RCA LSP 4708 $5.98. Cart. P8S 1943 $6.95.
Creem. December. p58-9. 600w. 2½
Stereo Review. November. p92. 200w. 2

1564 Hank Snow. MY NOVA SCOTIA HOME. Camden CAL 2257 $2.49. (Reissue.)
Journal of American Folklore. October/December. p397. 25w. 2

1565 Hank Snow. TRACK AND TRAINS. RCA LSP 4501 $5.98. Cart. P8S 1708 $6.98.
Journal of American Folklore. October/December. p397. 25w. 2½
Gramophone. July. p255. 25w. 3

1566 Hank Snow. THE YODELING RANGER. Country Music History CMH 102 (Germany). (Reissue.)
Old Time Music. Summer. p26. 3

1567 Hank Snow. THE YODELING/SINGING RANGER, v.2. Country Music History CMH 110 (Germany). (Reissue.)
Old Time Music. Autumn. p26. 100w. $3\frac{1}{2}$

1568 Southern Michigan String Band. TRANSPLANTED OLD-TIMEY MUSIC. Pine Tree PTSLP 509 $5.00.
Old Time Music. Autumn. p27. 100w. 3

1569 Spark Gap Wonder Boys. CLUCK OLD HEN. Rounder 0002 $5.95.
Old Time Music. Winter 71/72. p28-9. 3
Popular Music. Spring. p187. 100w. 4

1570 Larry Sparks and the Lonesome Ramblers. BLUEGRASS OLD AND NEW. Old Homestead 90004 $4.00.
Old Time Music. Summer. p27-8. 225w. 5

1571 Ralph Stanley and His Clinch Mountain Boys. MICHIGAN BLUEGRASS. Michigan Bluegrass MB 108 $5.00.
Journal of American Folklore. October/December. p400. 125w. $3\frac{1}{2}$
Old Time Music. Autumn. p29. 75w. 2

1572 The Statler Brothers. COUNTRY MUSIC THEN AND NOW. Mercury SR 61367 $4.98. Cart. MC8 61367 $6.95. Cass. MCR4 61367 $6.95.
Country Music. November. p63. 150w. $2\frac{1}{2}$

1573 Ray Stevens. ...UNREAL! Barnaby Z 30092 $5.98. Cart. ZA 30092 $6.98. Cass. ZT 30092 $6.98.
New York Times--Sunday. May 21. pD32. 200w. $3\frac{1}{2}$

1574 The Stonemans. STONEMAN'S SENSATION. Metro Moonshine 236058 (E). (Reissue.)
Records and Recordings. October. p123-4. 150w. $2\frac{1}{2}$

1575 Earl Taylor and Jim McCall. STONEY MOUNTAIN BOYS. Rural Rhythm RRTM 242/3 (2 discs) $10.00.
Journal of American Folklore. October/December. p400. 100w. 1

1576 Tut Taylor. FRIAR TUT. Rounder 0011 $5.95.
Old Time Music. Summer. p26. 125w. 4

1577 The Tenneva Ramblers. Puritan 3001 $5.00. (Reissue.)
Old Time Music. Autumn. p26. 300w. 4

1578 Mel Tillis. LIVE AT THE SAM HOUSTON COLISEUM, HOUSTON, TEXAS. MGM SE 4788 $5.98. Cart. 8130-4788 $6.95. Cass. 5130-4788 $6.95.
Popular Music. Fall. p59. 100w. 3
Records and Recordings. July. p98-9. 150w. 2

1579 Mel Tillis. VERY BEST. MGM SE 4806 $5.98. Cart. 8130-4806M $6.95. Cass. 5130-4806M $6.95. (Reissue.)
Sound. April. p36. 125w. 2

1580 Tompall and the Glaser Brothers. THE AWARD WINNERS. MGM S 4775 $5.98. Cart. 8130-4775 $6.95.
Records and Recordings. May. p108. 175w. 4

1581 Conway Twitty. HITS. MGM SE 4799 $5.98. Cart. 8130-4799 $6.95. Cass. 5130-4799. $6.95. (Reissue.)
Popular Music. Winter. p126. 25w. 2

1582 Conway Twitty. I CAN'T SEE ME WITHOUT YOU. Decca DL 75335 $5.98.
Rolling Stone. June 22. p60. 1,200w. 3½

1583 Conway Twitty. I CAN'T STOP LOVING YOU. Decca DL 75361 $5.98.
Popular Music and Society. Fall. p90. 50w. 3
Rolling Stone. November 23. p68, 70. 2,500w. 3

1584 Conway Twitty. THE ROCK AND ROLL STORY. Contour 2870151 (E). (Reissue.)
Gramophone. May. p1955. 25w. 1

1585 T. Texas Tyler. HIS GREATEST HITS. Hilltop JS 6042 $1.89. (Reissue.)
Journal of American Folklore. October/December. p397. 25w. 2½

1586 Uncle Jim's Music. Kapp KS 3661 $5.98.
Audio. May. p94-5. 25w. 3

1587 Uncle Jim's Music. THERE'S A SONG IN THIS. Kapp KS 3670 $5.98.
Popular Music and Society. Fall. p93. 50w. 2½

1588 Joe Val and the New England Bluegrass Boys. ONE MORNING IN MAY. Rounder 0003 $5.95.
Old Time Music. Winter 71/72. p28-9. 200w. 3

1589 John Van Horn. OUT BACK MUSIC. Mercury SRM 1-638. $4.98.
Popular Music. Summer. p251. 75w. 3

1590 Porter Wagoner and Dolly Parton. BURNING THE MIDNIGHT OIL. RCA LSP 4628 $5.98. Cart. P8S 1863 $6.95. Cass. PK 1863 $6.95.
Gramophone. September. p580. 125w. 3
Popular Music. Summer. p247. 100w. 3

1591 Porter Wagoner and Dolly Parton. TOGETHER ALWAYS. RCA LSP 4761 $5.98. Cart. P8S 2024 $6.95. Cass. PK 2024 $6.95.
Country Music. December. p59. 200w. 2½

1592 Kitty Wells. A BOUQUET OF COUNTRY HITS. Decca DL 75164 $5.98. Cart. 6-5164 $6.98. Cass. C73-5164 $6.98.
Gramophone. July. p255. 25w. 1

1593 Dottie West. CARELESS HANDS. RCA LSP 4482 $5.98. Cart. P8S 1693 $6.95.
Records and Recordings. February. p103. 50w. 1

1594 Dottie West. HAVE YOU HEARD... RCA LSP 4606 $5.98. Cart. P8S 1934 $6.95.
Gramophone. July. p255. 25w. 1
Records and Recordings. June. p91. 150w. 2½

1595 WESTERN SWING (anthology). Old Timey 105 $6.00. (Reissue.)
Creem. June. p74-5. 300w. 2½

1596 Roger Whittaker. LOOSE AND FIERY. RCA LSP 4652 $5.98.
Audio. August. p63. 50w. 2½

1597 Hank Williams. GREATEST HITS, VOLUME 1. MGM SE 4656 $5.98. (Reissue.)
Gramophone. July. p255. 150w. 5
Music Journal. December. p75. 100w. 2½

1598 Hank Williams. GREATEST HITS, VOLUME 2. MGM SE 4822 $5.98. Cart. 8130-4822M $6.95. Cass. 5130-4822M $6.95. (Reissue.)
Records and Recordings. October. p124. 100w. 4

1599 Hank Williams. 24 GREATEST HITS. MGM SE 4755-2 (2 discs) $6.98.
Music Journal. January. p73. 100w. 4½

1600 Hank Williams, Jr. ELEVEN ROSES. MGM SE 4843 $5.98. Cart. 8130-4843M $6.95. Cass. 5130-4843M $6.95.
Country Music. November. p63. 200w. 2½

1601 Bob Wills. SPECIAL. Harmony HS 11358 $1.98. (Reissue.)
Creem. June. p74-5. 300w. 4

1602 Bob Wills and Tommy Duncan. HALL OF FAME. United Artists Legendary Masters Series. UAS 9962 (2 discs) $6.98. (Reissue.)
Creem. June. p74-5. 300w. 2

1603 THE WORLD OF COUNTRY GIANTS (anthology). Philips 6643 002 (2 discs). (Reissue.)
Records and Recordings. May. p108. 200w. 2½

1604 Rual Yarborough. FIVE STRING BANJO. Tune TRC 1002 $5.00.
Old Time Music. Summer. p30. 50w. 2½

1605 Faron Young. THIS LITTLE GIRL OF MINE. Mercury SR 61364 $4.98. Cart. MC8 61364 $6.95. Cass. MCR4 61364 $6.95.
Country Music. November. p61. 150w. 2

FOLK

It is difficult to arrive at a definition satisfactory to both performers, reviewers, or listeners that explicitly defines the broad spectrum of recordings indexed under FOLK. Even the experts find themselves in basic disagreement. For example, Grove's Dictionary of Music and Musicians [vol. 3, New York: St. Martin's, 1954; p182] describes this genre as "any music which has entered into the heritage of the people, but can be assigned to no composer, school, or as a rule, even period. In general, it may be defined as a type of music which has been submitted for many generations to the process of oral transmission."

Contrary to Grove's learned point of view, Pete Seeger, dean of American folksingers, points out [in The Incompleat Folksinger, New York: Simon & Schuster, 1972; p5] that "folk music" was a term invented by 19th-century scholars and today covers a multitude of sins as to be almost meaningless. For Seeger, it is homemade music played mainly by ear and arising out of older traditions, but with a meaning for today. In fact, he even rejects the term "folksinger," preferring the more awkward appellation "professional singer of amateur music."

The final word on the subject may come from the great Big Bill Broonzy who is credited with the statement, "Folk music just got to be sung by peoples; ain't never heard no horse singing."

In attempting to categorize the records reviewed in 1972 and indexed in this volume, the world of folk music has caused some difficulty. The user of this index will find many familiar names with long connections in performing traditional music. Library folk music collections will already contain representative albums by balladeers such as Woody Guthrie, Peggy, Mike, and Pete Seeger, Ewan MacColl, Doc Watson, Malvina Reynolds, and Happy and Artie Traum. However, in this section of the index will be found many names unfamiliar to folk followers, names such as John Renbourn, Dave Bromberg, Pentangle and Sandy Denny.

Possibly one reason for the confusion that seems to have hold of what was once a well-defined musical genre may be the transitional nature of the current folk scene. Popular acceptance of folk music is, much like the jazz scene, at a near record low. The world of popular music, caught up the rock explosion that began with Elvis Presley and the Beatles, has passed folk music by. The folk revival of the late 1950's is now a part of the historical parade of popular musical tastes and the genre has been relegated to the few still surviving "coffee houses," the scattered folk festivals, and to re-releases of singers and instrumentalists who once commanded a much broader audience.

Folk's future does not look as bleak, however, as does that of jazz. At least two major trends seem to offer a ray of light for followers of the folk field. The first is the emergence of the modern-day singer-songwriter who writes his/her own material. Often the singer-songwriter makes an attempt to find a base in the folk tradition. The sound of the acoustic guitar, though usually accompanied by electrical instruments, is once again being heard. However, because of the tenuous relationship many of these artists have to traditional music, they have been placed in the section of the index reserved for ROCK.

Among this growing genre are such performers as John Prine, Kris Kristofferson, Carole King, Joni Mitchell, Randy Newman, Carly Simon, Murray McLauchlin, and Bruce Cockburn. Listening to their often poetic and always intriguing music indicates that their roots are not "arising from older traditions" but are deep in the popular concerns of the counter-culture. In future years, if this musical movement grows and takes specific form, a separate portion of this index may be devoted to the new Troubadour.

A second trend may be more significant for the immediate presence of folk music. There was a period in the development of modern popular music when every pop vocalist who carried an acoustic guitar was referred to as a "folksinger." Today, when very little real folk music is currently reaching a mass audience, these artists have been absorbed in the pop culture. In England, however, the situation is somewhat different. There are emerging several notable groups and individuals who have won both respect and an audience for their highly personal arrangements of traditional material. They are deeply rooted in traditional music and draw upon the past as well as on popular song styles to arrive at a medium that is both ancient and modern at the same time.

This hybrid form stays close to its folk roots and is attracting a following both in the United States and in England. Examples of this cross pollination of old and new are 1972 releases of Pentangle, Fairport Convention, Steeleye Span, Lindisfarne, Tir Na Nog, Sandy Denny and John Renbourn. Librarians selecting for modern pop music collections should pay some attention to this "new folk music" by selecting representative albums.

Finally, the distance between folk music and country (or country and western) continues to grow. As country and western falls even further under the influence of rock the audience for an older "Grand Old Opry" style becomes smaller. Roy Acuff, Bill Monroe, Earl Scruggs and Merle Travis are losing their mass popular acclaim to the new breed: Merle Haggard, Johnny Paycheck, and Bill Anderson. At the same time country-based music has begun to invade both the rock and folk fields. Listening habits, attendance at folk festivals, and new recordings may indicate an awakening interest in a more rural and traditionally based music.

Like country music, folk enjoys a narrow coverage in the reviewing media. The major periodicals devoting space to this genre are Sing Out, Old Time Music, English Dance and Songe, Ethnomusicology, and the Journal of American Folklore. Four magazines were not indexed in 1972 due to difficulties in obtaining copies from the publishers. These will be included in the 1973 edition of the Index. The four are Broadside, Bluegrass Unlimited, Muleskinner Blues, and Kentucky Folklore Record.

The quality of reviews in these specialty journals is excellent, the reviewers are experts-aficionados in their field, and record selectors can generally rely upon their opinions. However, reviews in these publications often presuppose a prior in-depth knowledge of the folk field.

Nearly all of the other magazines indexed included a small number of folk entries. These are usually the more popular recordings by well known artists such as Buffy Sainte-Marie, Judy Collins, Joan Baez or new releases by any of the English folk-hybrid groups. Only in England do the major review journals devote much space to folk releases. Both Hi-Fi News and Record Review and Gramophone cover what could be called regional releases. Generally, these are recordings of Scottish, Irish, Welsh, and English singers of folk music who continue to attract large numbers of listeners, especially in the pubs and taverns that still feature this type of music.

1972 was not exactly an outstanding year for folk music. Based upon the number of reviews per disc and the general quality of records as seen by the reviewers, the following 15 releases are the pick of the folk field for the year:

Joan Baez. Come From the Shadow. A & M SP4339
David Blue. Stories. Asylum SD 5052
David Bromberg. Columbia C 31104
Judy Collins. Living. Elektra EKS 75014
John Fahey. Of Rivers and Religions. Warner Bros. MS 2089
Fairport Convention. Babbacombe Lee. A & M SP 4333
Woody Guthrie. The Greatest Songs. Vanguard VSD 35/6 (Reissue)
Lindisfarne. Fog on the Tyne. Elektra EKS 75021
Louisiana Cajun Music, Vols. 1, 3. Old Timey LP 108,100 (Reissue)
Pentangle. Reflection. Reprise S 6463
Tom Paxton. Peace Will Come. Reprise MS 2096
Mike Seeger. Music from True Vine. Mercury SRM 1-629
Steeleye Span. Below the Salt. Chrysalis SHR 1008
A Tribute to Woody Guthrie, Vols. 1 & 2. Columbia KC 31171, Warner Bros. BS 2586

Doc Watson. Elementary Doctor Watson! Poppy PYS 5703

1606 Nathan Abshire. PINE GROVE BLUES. Swallow SLP 6014 $5.98.
Blues Unlimited. July. p29. 125w. 4

1607 Sam Agins. SINGIN' SAM'S SADDLEBAG OF SONGS. Haywire ARA 6419 $5.00.
Journal of American Folklore. October/December. p401. 75w. 3

1608 The Albion Country Band. Pegasus 7 (E).
Sing Out. September/October. p37. 25w. 3

1609 Alistair Anderson. PLAYS ENGLISH CONCERTINA. Trailer LER 2074 (E).
Gramophone. November. p989. 50w. 1
Records and Recordings. September. p100. 200w. $3\frac{1}{2}$
Sing Out. September/October. p37. 25w. $2\frac{1}{2}$

1610 Eric Anderson. BEST. Vanguard VSD 7/8 (2 discs) $5.98.
Records and Recordings. May. p108. 200w. 2

1611 Harvey Andrews. WRITER OF SONGS. Hi Fly 10 (E).
Hi-Fi News and Record Review. July. p1304. 100w. 4

1612 Frankie Armstrong. LOVELY ON THE WATER. Topic 12 TS 216 (E).
Hi-Fi News and Record Review. November. p2198. 125w. 5

1613 BACK O' BENACHIE (anthology). Topic 12 T 180 (E).
Journal of American Folklore. July/September. p293. 75w. $3\frac{1}{2}$

1614 Joan Baez. BALLAD BOOK. Vanguard VSD 41/42 $5.98. (Reissue.)
Popular Music. Fall. p88. 25w. 4

1615 Joan Baez. BLESSED ARE... Vanguard VSD 6570/1 (2 discs) $6.98. VSQ (quad) 4001/2 (2 discs).
Audio. January. p76. 550w. 4
Beetle. January 22. p20-1. 900w. $2\frac{1}{2}$
Hi-Fi News and Record Review. July. p1304. 100w. $3\frac{1}{2}$
Popular Music. Winter. p123. 100w. $2\frac{1}{2}$
Stereo Review. November. p83. 225w. $2\frac{1}{2}$

1616 Joan Baez. COME FROM THE SHADOWS. A & M SP 4339 $4.98. R-R 4339 $7.98. Cart. 4339 $6.98. Cass. 4339 $6.98.

Audio. August. p60. 250w. 4
Crawdaddy. August. p21. 400w. 3
Creem. August. p15. 50w. 1½
Creem. August. p65. 750w. 2½
Hi-Fi News and Record Review. September. p1679. 100w. 2½
Popular Music. Summer. p253. 100w. 1
Rolling Stone. June 22. p55. 750w. 3
Stereo Review. September. p73. 250w. 2½

1617 Joan Baez. ONE DAY AT A TIME. Vanguard VSD 79310 $5.98. Cart. M89310 $6.95. Cass. M59310 $6.95.
Hi-Fi News and Record Review. September. p1679. 100w. 2½

1618 Pattie Barklie. DOWN IN THE GLEN. Spindizzy RGS 3035 $4.98.
English Dance and Song. Winter. p158. 50w. 2½

1619 The Bards. DEFINITELY IRISH FOLK. Emerald GES 1069 (E).
Hi-Fi News and Record Review. June. p1125. 25w. 2
Records and Recordings. June. p90. 125w. 1

1620 Peter Bellamy. OAK, ASH AND THORN. Argo ZFB 11 (E).
English Song and Dance. Summer. p74. 375w. 1

1621 Peter Bellamy and Louis Killen. Argo ZD 837 (E).
Sing Out. September/October. p37. 50w. 3

1622 Berkeley Farms. OLD TIME AND COUNTRY STYLE MUSIC OF BERKELEY. Folkways FA 2436 $5.98.
Popular Music. Fall. p94. 50w. 2

1623 Allan Block and Ralph Lee Smith. Meadowlands Records MS - 1.
Sing Out. September/October. p39. 50w. 2½

1624 David Blue. STORIES. Asylum SD 5052 $4.98. Cart. M85052 $6.95. Cass. M55052 $6.95.
Audio. May. p93. 100w. 4
Gramophone. May. p1951. 25w. 2½
High Fidelity. February. p117. 100w. 2
Rolling Stone. March 2. p58. 600w. 3

1625 Gordon Bok. PETER KAGAN AND THE WIND. Folk Legacy FSI 44 $5.98.
Sing Out. March/April. p37. 275w. 4

1626 THE BREEZE FROM ERIN: IRISH FOLK MUSIC ON WIND INSTRUMENTS (anthology). Topic 12 T 184 (E).
Journal of American Folklore. October/December. p408. 750w. 3½

1627 Anne Briggs. THE TIME HAS COME. CBS 64612 (E).
English Dance and Song. Winter. p158. 100w. 5

1628 The Broadside. THE GYPSY'S WEDDING DAY AND OTHER LINCOLNSHIRE FOLK SONGS. Lincolnshire Association LA 4 (E).
English Dance and Song. Summer. 125w. $3\frac{1}{2}$

1629 David Bromberg. Columbia C 31104 $5.98. Cart. CA 31104 $6.98. Cass. CT 31104 $6.98.
Crawdaddy. April 2. p15. 1,000w. 4
High Fidelity. May. p116. 25w. $1\frac{1}{2}$
New York Times--Sunday. March 12. pHF12. 100w. $2\frac{1}{2}$
Previews. September. p41. 165w. 1
Rolling Stone. March 16. p58, 60. 450w. $3\frac{1}{2}$
Sing Out. May/June. p42. 300w. $2\frac{1}{2}$
Stereo Review. July. p91. 450w. 4

1630 David Bromberg. DEMON IN DISGUISE. Columbia KC 31753 $5.98.
Popular Music. Fall. p94. 50w. 3

1631 Tim Buckley. GREETINGS FROM L.A. Warner Bros. BS 2631 $5.98.
Creem. December. p60. 300w. 1
Gramophone. December. p1225. 75w. 3
High Fidelity. December. p122. 75w. $\frac{1}{2}$
Stereo Review. December. p91. 175w. 4

1632 John Burke. THE OLD HAT BAND. Voyager VRLP 307s $5.98.
Sing Out. September/October. p43. 150w. 3

1633 Randy Burns. I'M A LOVER, NOT A FOOL. Polydor PD 5030 $5.98.
High Fidelity. October. p102. 175w. 2

1634 David Bushkin. Epic KE 31233 $5.98.
New York Times--Sunday. August 27. pD19. 175w. 3

1635 Cob. MOYSHE McSTIFF AND THE TARTAN LANCERS OF THE SACRED HEART. Polydor PD 2383 161 (E).
Hi-Fi News and Record Review. December. p2460. 100w. $2\frac{1}{2}$

1636 Patricia Cahill. IRELAND. Rex RPS 104 (E).
Gramophone. June. p111. 50w. 1

1637 THE CAJUNS - SONGS, WALTZES AND TWO-STEPS (anthology). Folkways RBF 21 $5.98.
Blues Unlimited. February/March. p30. 175w. 4

Library Journal. March 1. p856. 100w. 1½
Popular Music. Winter. p123. 50w. 3½
Old Time Music. Winter, 71/72. p27. 325w. 3
Sing Out. September/October. p43. 100w. 2½
Stereo Review. May. p97. 300w. 3

1638 The Callies. ON YOUR SIDE. Rubber RUB 002 (E).
Hi-Fi News and Record Review. August. p1475. 25w. 2

1639 Colin Campbell. LET'S ALL DANCE AND SING. London SW 99504 $5.98.
Journal of American Folklore. July/September. p293. 25w. 2½

1640 David Campbell. SUN WHEEL. Decca SKL 5139 (E).
Gramophone. November. p984. 75w. 2

1641 Ian Campbell Folk Group. THE SUN IS BURNING. Argo ZFB 13 (E).
English Dance and Song. Summer. p75. 100w. 1

1642 Jimmy Campbell. ALBUM. Philips 6308 100 (E).
Records and Recordings. June. p90. 75w. 0

1643 Tony Capstick. HIS ROUND. Rubber RUB 004 (E).
Hi-Fi News and Record Review. August. p1473, 5. 25w. 3
Hi-Fi News and Record Review. October. p1923. 100w. 2½

1644 Sydney Carter. AND NOW IT IS SO EARLY. Galliard GAL 4017 (E).
Records and Recordings. May. p104. 200w. 3

1645 Martin Carthy. THE BONNY BLACK HARE AND OTHER SONGS. Philips 6382 022 (E). (Reissue.)
Hi-Fi News and Record Review. June. p1125. 50w. 2½

1646 Martin Carthy. SHEARWATER. Pegasus PEG 12 (E).
Gramophone. June. p112. 100w. 4
Hi-Fi News and Record Review. May. p936. 100w. 2
Records and Recordings. May. p104. 125w. 3

1647 Martin Carthy. THIS IS... Philips 6382 022 (E).
Gramophone. April. p1779. 50w. 2

1648 The Cheviot Ranters Country Dance Band. SOUND OF THE CHEVIOTS. Topic 12 T 214 (E).
English Dance and Song. Summer. p114. 150w. 3

1649 The Chieftains. VOLUMES 1/3. Claddagh CC 2/7/10 (3 discs) (E).

Hi-Fi News and Record Review. December. p2460. 75w. 3
Records and Recordings. September. p91. 150w. 3

1650 Peg and Bobby Clancy. SONGS FROM IRELAND. Ember 2054 (E).
Journal of American Folklore. July/September. p295. 25w. 2½

1651 Willie Clancy. THE MINSTREL FROM CLARE. Topic 12 T 175 (E).
Journal of American Folklore. October/December. p408. 75w. 4

1652 Gene Clark. A & M SP 4292 $5.98.
Popular Music. Fall. p61. 50w. 3

1653 Bill Clifton. HAPPY DAYS. Golden Guinea GSGL 10476 (E).
Journal of American Folklore. October/December. p399. 75w. 2½

1654 CLUB FOLK, VOLUME 1 (anthology). Pegasus PS 2 (E).
Hi-Fi News and Record Review. November. p2198. 50w. 1½

1655 CLUB FOLK, VOLUME 2 (anthology). Pegasus PS 3 (E).
Hi-Fi News and Record Review. November. p2198. 50w. 1½

1656 Judy Collins. COLORS OF THE DAY. Elektra EKS 75030 $5.98. Cart. M85030 $6.95. Cass. M55030 $6.95.
Hi-Fi News and Record Review. December. p2460. 125w. 2
High Fidelity. November. p118. 150w. 2½
New York Times--Sunday. May 21. pD30. 75w. 3

1657 Judy Collins. LIVING. Elektra EKS 75014 $5.98. R-R M5014 $6.95. Cart. ET 85014 $6.95. Cass. TC 55014 $6.95.
American Record Guide. April. p381. 100w. 0
Audio. May. p93. 50w. 2½
High Fidelity. April. p106. 150w. 3½
New York Times--Sunday. January 2. pD20. 150w. 1
Popular Music. Winter. p125. 100w. 3½
Stereo Review. March. p101-2. 225w. 4

1658 Judy Collins. WHALES AND NIGHTINGALES. Elektra EKS 75010 $5.98. Cart. ET8 75010 $6.95. Cass. TC5 75010 $6.95.
American Record Guide. March. p332. 225w. 2

1659 Shirley Collins. NO ROSES. Pegasus PEG 7 (E).
Gramophone. April. p1776, 1779. 100w. 4

1660 The Common Round. FOUR PENCE A DAY. Galliard GAL 4015 (E).
English Dance and Song. Summer. p76. 50w. 1½

1661 Copper Family. A SONG FOR EVERY SEASON. Leader LEAB 404 (4 discs) (E).
Sing Out. September/October. p37. 25w. 4

1662 COWBOY SONGS (anthology). Arizona Friends of Folklore AFF-33-1 $5.00.
Journal of American Folklore. October/December. p401. 300w. 5

1663 The Critics Group. A MERRY PROGRESS TO LONDON. Argo ZFB 60 (E).
Hi-Fi News and Record Review. May. p936. 25w. 3

1664 The Critics Group. SWEET THAMES FLOW SOFTLY. Argo ZFB 61 (E).
Hi-Fi News and Record Review. p936. 25w. 3

1665 The Crofters. London SW 99535 $5.98.
Audio. October. p90. 75w. 3½

1666 Keith Cross and Peter Ross. BORED CIVILIANS. Decca SKL 5129 (E).
Gramophone. September. p578. 25w. 0

1667 Ludenin Darbone. LOUISIANA CAJUN MUSIC. Arhoolie F 5003 $6.00.
Jazz and Blues. March. p25-6. 350w. 3

1668 Jim Dawson. YOU'LL NEVER BE LONELY WITH ME. Kama Sutra KBS 2049 $5.98. Cart. M82049 $6.95. Cass. M52049 $6.95.
New York Times--Sunday. March 19. pD30. 150w. 2½

1669 Sandy Denny. THE NORTH STAR GRASSMAN AND THE RAVELS. A & M SP 4317 $5.98.
Crawdaddy. January 30. p21. 200w. 1
New York Times--Sunday. February 27. pD26. 125w. 1

1670 Sandy Denny. SANDY. A & M SP 4371 $5.98.
Hi-Fi News and Record Review. November. p2199. 100w. 3½
Rolling Stone. December 21. p64. 750w. 5

1671 Barbara Dickson. FROM THE BEGGARS MANTLE. Decca SKL 5116 (E).
Hi-Fi News and Record Review. July. p1304. 75w. 3

1672 The Dillards. ROOTS AND BRANCHES. Anthem Records ANS 5901 $4.98.
Crawdaddy. September. p21. 400w. 1
Popular Music. Summer. p250. 50w. 2

1673 Bonnie Dobson. Argo ZFB 79 (E).
Hi-Fi News and Record Review. December. p2459. 100w. 2

1674 Eileen Donaghy. THE GREEN GLENS OF ANTRIM. RCA International INTS 1369 (E).
Records and Recordings. September. p100. 150w. 1½

1675 John Doonan. FLUTE FOR THE FEIS. Leader LEA 2043 (E).
Hi-Fi News and Record Review. December. p2460. 75w. 3

1676 Barry Dransfield. Polydor 2383 160 (E).
Hi-Fi News and Record Review. December. p2459. 100w. 4

1677 The Druids. BURNT OFFERING. Argo ZFB 22 (E).
English Dance and Song. Summer. p114. 100w. 5

1678 Teresa Duffy. OFF TO DUBLIN IN THE GREEN. London SW 99511 $5.98.
Journal of American Folklore. July/September. p294. 100w. 1½

1679 EARLY SHAKER SPIRITUALS (anthology). Shaker Society $3.50.
English Dance and Song. Winter. p157. 200w. 4

1680 Derek and Dorothy Elliott. Trailer LER 2023 (E).
Hi-Fi News and Record Review. September. p1679. 225w. 4
Records and Recordings. September. p100. 150w. 2½

1681 Jack Elliott. TALKING WOODY GUTHRIE. Delmark 801 $4.98.
Library Journal. March 1. p856. 100w. 2

1682 ENGLAND BE GLAD! Classics for Pleasure CFP 40015 (E). (Reissue.)
Hi-Fi News and Record Review. September. p1679. 250w. 5

1683 Seamus Ennis. Ember 2054 (E).
Journal of American Folklore. July/September. p295. 25w. 4

1684 John Fahey. AMERICA. Takoma S 1030 $5.98.
Jazz Journal. December. p41. 25w. 2
Popular Music. Summer. p249. 50w. 5

1685 John Fahey. BLIND JOE DEATH. Takoma S 1002 $5.98.
Jazz Journal. December. p41. 75w. 3

1686 John Fahey. DEATH CHANTS, BREAKDOWNS AND MILITARY WALTZES. Takoma S 1003 $5.98.
Jazz Journal. December. p41. 25w. 2

1687 John Fahey. OF RIVERS AND RELIGIONS. Warner Bros. MS 2089 $5.98.
Creem. December. p9. 25w. 5
Popular Music. Fall. p1. 50w. 3
Rolling Stone. November 9. p66. 600w. 3
Stereo Review. December. p92. 175w. 4½

1688 Fairport Convention. ANGEL DELIGHT. A & M SP 4319 $5.98. Cart. 8T 4319 $6.95. Cass. CS 4319 $6.95.
Crawdaddy. January 30. p20-1. 300w. 3
Creem. January. p67-8. 375w. 1
Stereo Review. April. p90. 100w. 1

1689 Fairport Convention. BABBACOMBE LEE. A & M SP 4333 $5.98. Cart. 8T 4333 $6.95. Cass. CS 4333 $6.95.
Crawdaddy. April 16. p16. 1,400w. 4
High Fidelity. June. p103. 500w. 1½
New York Times--Sunday. March 12. pHF12. 250w. 3½
Stereo Review. July. p92. 400w. 4

1690 Joseph Falcon. LOUISIANA CAJUN MUSIC. Arhoolie F 5005 $6.00.
Jazz and Blues. February. p29. 325w. 2½

1691 Mimi and Richard Farina. BEST. Vanguard VSD 21/22 (2 discs) $5.98. (Reissue.)
Gramophone. June. p112. 75w. 3
Ontario Library Review. December. p243. 25w. 2½
Records and Recordings. May. p104-6. 200w. 4

1692 Mimi Farina and Tom Jans. TAKE HEART. A & M SP 4310 $5.98. Cart. 8T 4310 $6.95. Cass. CS 4310 $6.95.
Audio. March. p80-1. 50w. 2½
High Fidelity. January. p122. 50w. 2
Popular Music. Fall. p61. 50w. 3
Stereo Review. January. p107. 100w. 2½

1693 Julie Felix. CLOTHO'S WEB. Rak KZ 31609 $5.98.
Popular Music. Fall. p90. 25w. 2½

1694 Fellowship Singers. COME ALONG; SONGS OF THE EARLY 1800'S. Fellowship Records FR 101.
Music Journal. January. p72. 125w. 3½

1695 FESTIVAL AT BLAIRGOWRIE (anthology). Topic 12 T 181 (E).
Journal of American Folklore. July/September. p293. 150w. 4

1696 Ray Fisher. THE BONNY BIRD. Trailer LER 2038 (E).
Hi-Fi News and Record Review. December. p2459. 4

1697 FOLK BALLADS FROM DONEGAL AND DERRY (anthology). Leader LEA 4055 (E).
Records and Recordings. September. p100-1. 250w. 4

1698 FOLK SONGS OF BRITAIN (anthology). Caedmon 1142/6, 1162/4, 1224/5 (10 discs) (E).
Sing Out. September/October. p37. 100w. 4

1699 FOLK SONGS OF BRITAIN, VOLUME 10: SONGS OF ANIMALS AND OTHER MARVELS (anthology). Topic 12 T 198 (E).
English Dance and Song. Summer. p114. 150w. 5

1700 FOLKSONGS SUNG IN ULSTER (anthology). Mercier Press IRL 11 (E).
English Dance and Song. Summer. p74. 125w. 5

1701 Ritchie Francis. SONG BIRD. Pegasus PEG 11 (E).
Hi-Fi News and Record Review. May. p936. 25w. 2½

1702 Thomas and Richard Frost. Uni 73124 $4.98.
Popular Music. Spring. p186. 50w. 3

1703 Finbar Furey. THE IRISH PIPES OF FINBAR FUREY. Nonesuch H 72048 $2.98.
Sing Out. May/June. p42-3. 50w. 3
Stereo Review. October. p106. 250w. 3

1704 Fuzzy Mountain String Band. Rounder 0010 $5.95.
Sing Out. September/October. p41. 50w. 2½

1705 GARNERS GAY (anthology). English Folk, Dance and Song Society EFDSS LP 1006 (E).
English Dance and Song. Winter. p157. 150w. 3

1706 Dick Gaughan. NO MORE FOREVER. Trailer LER 2072 (E).
Hi-Fi News and Record Review. November. p2198. 100w. 5

1707 Arthur Gee. Tumbleweed Records TWS 101 $5.98.
Library Journal. February 15. p665. 100w. 3

1708 Bob Gibson. Capitol ST 742 $5.98.
High Fidelity. January. p114,116. 200w. 1

1709 Tom Gilfellon. LOVING MAD TOM. Trailer LER 2079 (E).
Sing Out. September/October. p37. 25w. 2½

1710 Alasdair Gillies. HIGHLAND WORLD. Decca SPA 197 (E).
Gramophone. July. p255. 25w. 2
Hi-Fi News and Record Review. June. p1125. 25w. 2½

1711 Girl Guides. FESTIVAL OF SONG. BBC Records REP 1275 (E).
Records and Recordings. October. p125. 225w. 1

1712 Joe Glazer. SINGS GARBAGE. Collector Records 1919.
Popular Music. Spring. p128. 100w. 4

1713 Golden Ring. FIVE DAYS SINGING, VOLUME 1. Folk Legacy FSI 41 $5.98.
Sing Out. March/April. p36-7. 300w. 2

1714 Golden Ring. FIVE DAYS SINGING, VOLUME 2. Folk Legacy FSI 42 $5.98.
Sing Out. March/April. p36-7. 300w. 2½

1715 Dave Goulder and Liz Dyer. JANUARY MAN. Argo ZFB 10 $5.95.
Stereo Review. January. p117. 400w. 2½

1716 GREATEST FOLKSINGERS OF THE SIXTIES (anthology). Vanguard VSD 17/18 (2 discs) $5.98. (Reissue.)
Journal of American Folklore. October/December. p402. 25w. 1
New York Times--Sunday. April 16. pD26. 75w. 2½
Stereo Review. October. p106. 225w. 4

1717 THE GREATEST SONGS OF WOODY GUTHRIE (anthology). Vanguard VSD 35/6 (2 discs) $5.98. (Reissue.)
Journal of American Folklore. October/December. p402. 100w. 3
New York Times--Sunday. April 16. pD26. 75w. 2½
Ontario Library Review. December. p243. 25w. 3
Popular Music. Summer. p247. 50w. 4
Previews. September. p41-2. 175w. 3½
Stereo Review. August. p92. 1000w. 3

1718 Woody Guthrie. POOR BOY. Folkways FTS 31010 $5.98. (Reissue.)
Hi-Fi News and Record Review. October. p1923. 50w. 3
Journal of American Folklore. October/December. p401-2. 25w. 2½

1719 Woody Guthrie. SONGS TO GROW ON. XTRA 1067 (E).
Hi-Fi News and Record Review. October. p1923. 50w. 3

1720 Kenny Hall. Bay TPH 727 $5.00.
Old Time Music. Summer. p30. 425w. 5

1721 Robin Hall and Jimmie MacGregor. ONE OVER THE EIGHT. Contour 6870 523 (E).
Gramophone. May. p1952. 50w. 2½

1722 Tim Hardin. PAINTED HEADS. Columbia KC 31784 $5.98. Cart. CA 31764 $6.98.
Rolling Stone. November 23. p61-2. 700w. 2

1723 Mike Harding. A LANCASHIRE LAD. Trailer LER 2039 (E).
Gramophone. June. p112. 25w. 1
Hi-Fi News and Record Review. June. p1125. 25w. 2½

1724 Rosemary Hardman. FIREBIRD. Trailer LER 2075 (E).
Hi-Fi News and Record Review. December p2460. 100w. 1½

1725 Rosemary Hardman and Bob Axford. SECOND SEASON CAME. Trailer LER 3018 (E).
Gramophone. January. p1279-80. 50w. 3

1726 John Hartford. AEREO-PLAIN. Warner Bros. WS 1916 $5.98. Cart. M81916 $5.95. Cass. M51916 $6.95.
Gramophone. July. p256. 150w. 4
Library Journal. February 1. p481. 100w. 3
Hi-Fi News and Record Review. July. p1311. 100w. 3
New York Times--Sunday. May 21. pD32. 100w. 3½
Sound. February. p18. 100w. 2

1727 James N. Healy. SONGS AND MUSIC OF KERRY. Mercier Press IRL 1 (Ireland).
Journal of American Folklore. July/September. p294. 50w. ½

1728 HEATHER AND GLEN (anthology). Ember 2055 (E).
Journal of American Folklore. July/September. p293. 75w. 5

1729 John Herald and the Greenbriar Boys. BEST. Vanguard VSD 79317 $5.98. (Reissue.)
High Fidelity. October. p126. 25w. 3
Sing Out. September/October. p39. 300w. 4

1730 Carolyn Hester. THURSDAY'S CHILD HAS FAR TO GO. Ember CW 138 (E).
Hi-Fi News and Record Review. November. p2198. 25w. 0

Gramophone. November. p989. 100w. 0

1731 High Level Ranters. HIGH LEVEL. Trailer LFR 2030 (E).
Gramophone. January. p1280. 100w. 4
Records and Recordings. January. p96. 125w. 3

1732 Doc Hopkins. Birch 1945 $5.00.
Old Time Music. Autumn. p27. 175w. 3

1733 Roger Hubbard. BRIGHTON BELLE BLUES. Blue Goose 2005 $5.95.
Blues Unlimited. February/March. p22-3. 300w. 2½

1734 Stan Hugill and the Folk Tradition. MEN AND THE SEA. Bristol City Museum MUS 1 (E).
English Dance and Song. Summer. p74. 75w. 2½

1735 Carol Hull. BEADS AND FEATHERS. Elektra K 42108 (E).
Gramophone. June. p111. 100w. 2

1736 Ian and Sylvia. Columbia C 30736 $5.98. Cart. CA 30736 $5.98. Cass. CT 30736 $6.98.
Audio. August. p61. 25w. 3½
Ontario Library Review. p243. 25w. 2½
Sound. March. p21. 125w. 3
Stereo Review. November. p100. 125w. 1½

1737 Ian and Sylvia. THE GREAT SPECKLED BIRD. Ampex A 10103 $5.98. Cart. M81003 $6.95. Cass. M51003 $6.95.
Ontario Library Review. December. p243. 25w. 2½

1738 Ian and Sylvia. GREATEST HITS, VOLUME 1. Vanguard VSD 5/6 (2 discs) $5.98. (Reissue.)
Ontario Library Review. December. p242-3. 25w. 2½

1739 Ian and Sylvia. GREATEST HITS, VOLUME 2. Vanguard VSD 23/24 (2 discs) $5.98. (Reissue.)
Ontario Library Review. December. p242-3. 25w. 2½

1740 Ian and Sylvia. YOU WERE ON MY MIND. Columbia C 31337 $5.98. Cart. CA 31337 $6.98.
Canadian Stereo Guide. Fall. p28. 100w. 3

1741 Incredible String Band. LIQUID ACROBAT AS REGARDS THE AIR. Elektra EKS 74112 $5.98. Cart. ET 84112 $6.98. Cass. TC 54112 $6.98.
Crawdaddy. April 16. p16. 750w. 3
Creem. May. p65. 675w. 2½

1742 The Irish Country Four. TRADITIONAL MUSIC FROM NORTHERN IRELAND. Topic 12 TS 209 (E).
English Dance and Song. Spring. p34. 125w. 4

1743 AN IRISH JUBILEE (anthology). Mercier Press IRL 10 (Ireland).
Journal of American Folklore. July/September. p294. 100w. 3½

1744 Tex Isley/Gray Graig and the New North Carolina Boys. Leader LEA 4040 (E).
Journal of American Folklore. October/December. p395. 100w. 1

1745 Jacqui and Bridie. NEXT TIME AROUND. Galliard GAL 4019 (E).
Hi-Fi News and Record Review. July. p1304. 75w. 2½

1746 Bert Jansch. ROSEMARY LANE. Reprise S 6455 $5.98. Cart. M86455 $6.95. Cass. M56455 $6.95.
Crawdaddy. January 30. p20. 200w. 2½
Creem. January. p67-8. 350w. 2

1747 Ella Jenkins. MY STREET BEGINS AT MY HOUSE. Folkways FC 7543 $5.98.
Audio. September. p119. 50w. 2½

1748 Lynda Jenkins. LOVE IS ALL AROUND. Decca SKL 5108 (E).
Gramophone. January. p1274. 75w. 3

1749 Wizz Jones. RIGHT NOW. CBS 64809 (E).
Hi-Fi News and Record Review. July. p1304. 125w. 3½

1750 Kathy Kahn. THE WORKING GIRL; WOMEN'S SONGS FROM MOUNTAINS, MINES, AND MILLS. Voyager VRLP 305s $5.00.
Old Time Music. Summer. p28. 325w. 1

1751 Christopher Kearney. Capitol ST 11043 $5.98. Cart. 8XT 11043 $6.98. Cass. 4XT 11043 $6.98.
Beetle. June. p20. 600w. 3
Sound. April. p37. 50w. 1

1752 Graham Kendrick. FOOTSTEPS ON THE SEA. Key KL 011 (E).
Hi-Fi News and Record Review. June. p1125. 50w. 2½

1753 Calum Kennedy. YE HIGHLAND AND YE LOWLANDS. Beltona SBE 135 (E).
Hi-Fi News and Record Review. July. p1304. 50w. 1½
Hi-Fi News and Record Review. August. p1473. 25w. 1½

1754 Moira Kerr. SHADOWS OF MY CHILDHOOD. Beltona SBE 118 (E).

English Dance and Song. Summer. p75. 50w. 1

1755 Clark Kessinger. LEGEND. County 733 $4.98. (Reissue.)
Old Time Music. Autumn. p27. 150w. 5

1756 Clark Kessinger. OLD TIME MUSIC WITH FIDDLE AND GUITAR. Rounder Records $5.95.
Sing Out. March/April. p38. p75. 4

1757 Leadbelly. Ember CW 132 (E). (Reissue.)
Jazz Journal. December. p36. 300w. 1

1758 Leadbelly. SHOUT ON. Folkways FTS 31030 $5.98. (Reissue.)
Blues Unlimited. May. p28. 25w. 4

1759 Leadbelly. TAKE THIS HAMMER. Folkways FTS 31019 $5.98. (Reissue.)
Journal of American Folklore. January/March. p106. 25w. 3½

1760 LET'S ALL GO SCOTTISH COUNTRY DANCING WITH McBAIN'S SCOTTISH COUNTRY DANCE BAND. Rediffusion ZS 86 (E).
English Dance and Song. Spring. p34. 200w. 5

1761 Lindisfarne. FOG ON THE TYNE. Elektra EKS 75021 $5.98. Cart. ET 85021 $6.98. Cass. TC 55021 $6.98.
Crawdaddy. May 28. p17. 800w. 3½
Creem. November. p74. 25w. 1½
High Fidelity. June. p102. 175w. 2½
Rolling Stone. June 8. p60. 800w. 3
Stereo Review. June. p101-2. 200w. 3

1762 Lindisfarne. NICELY OUT OF TUNE. Elektra EKS 74099 $5.98. Cart. ET 84099 $6.98. Cass. TC 54099 $6.98.
Beetle. March 29. p18. 300w. ½
Stereo Review. March. p103. 50w. 0

1763 Gerry Lockran. WUN. Polydor 2383 122 (E).
Hi-Fi News and Record Review. September. p1685. 100w. 3

1764 THE LONG HARVEST (anthology). Argo ZDA 66-75 (10 discs) (E).
Sing Out. September/October. p37-8. 125w. 4

1765 LOUISIANA CAJUN MUSIC, VOLUME 1: THE 1920's (anthology). Old Timey LP 108 $6.00.
Jazz Report. No. 2. 125w. 5

1766 LOUISIANA CAJUN MUSIC, VOLUME 3: THE STRING BANDS OF THE 1930'S (anthology). Old Timey LP 110 $6.00.

Blues Unlimited. June. p25. 450w. 5
Jazz Report. No. 2. 125w. 5
Library Journal. June 1. p2069. 100w. 2½
Old Time Music. Winter 71/72. p27. 325w. 4

1767 LUTE AND GUITAR SONGS OF SCOTLAND AND ENGLAND (anthology). Beltona SBE 111 (E).
English Dance and Song. Winter. p157. 75w. 3

1768 Tim Lyons. THE GREEN LINNET. Trailer LER 3036 (E).
Gramophone. November. p989. 50w. 2
Records and Recordings. September. p101. 200w. 3

1769 J.E. Mainer. LEGENDARY, VOLUME 14/15. Rural Rhythm 240/41 (2 discs) $10.00. (Reissue.)
Journal of American Folklore. October/December. p397. 125w. 2½

1770 Tommy Makem and the Clancy Brothers. IRISH FOLK AIRS. Tradition 2083 $5.98.
Journal of American Folklore. July/September. p295. 25w. 2½

1771 Ian Mannel. THE FROSTY PLOUGHSHARE. Topic 12 TS 220 (E).
English Dance and Song. Winter. p157. 75w. 2½

1772 Margaret MacArthur. ON THE MOUNTAINS HIGH. Living Folk Records F-LFR-100 $5.00.
Journal of American Folklore. July/September. p296. 100w. 4

1773 Ewan MacColl. SOLO FLIGHT. Argo ZFB 12 (E).
Hi-Fi News and Record Review. December. p2459. 125w. 2½

1774 Ewan MacColl and Peggy Seeger. THE AMOROUS MUSE. Argo ZDA 84 (E).
Journal of American Folklore. July/September. p295. 25w. 3

1775 Ewan MacColl and Peggy Seeger. THE ANGRY MUSE. Argo ZDA 83 (E).
Journal of American Folklore. July/September. p295. 125w. 2

1776 Ewan MacColl and Peggy Seeger. BALLAD OF THE TRADES. Argo ZFB 67 (E).
Records and Recordings. August. p87-8. 550w. 5

1777 Ewan MacColl and Peggy Seeger. MANCHESTER ANGEL. Topic 12 T 147 (E).
Journal of American Folklore. July/September. p295. 75w. 2

1778 Ewan MacColl and Peggy Seeger. THE TRAVELLING PEOPLE. Argo DA 113 (E).
Audio. December. p101-2. 450w. 4

1779 Ewan MacColl and Peggy Seeger. THE WANTON MUSE. Argo ZDA 85 (E). (Reissue.)
Hi-Fi News and Record Review. August. p1757. 25w. 3
Journal of American Folklore. July/September. p295. 50w. 3

1780 Matt McGinn. TINNY CAN ON MY TAIL. RCA International INTS 1368 (E).
Records and Recordings. September. p101. 100w. 2

1780a Suni McGrath. THE CALL OF THE MORNING DOVE. Adelphi AD 1014 $5.95.
Sing Out. May/June. p46. 25w. $2\frac{1}{2}$

1781 Mariquita MacGregor. SINGS OF CARDNEY. Rare Recorded Editions SRRE 130 (E).
Records and Recordings. October. p125. 250w. 0

1781a Seumas MacNeill. HIGHLAND BAGPIPES. Tradition 2099 $5.98.
Audio. December. p91. 125w. 3

1782 Tommy Makem. LISTEN FOR THE RAFTERS ARE RINGING. CBS 64481 (E).
Hi-Fi News and Record Review. July. p1304. 50w. $2\frac{1}{2}$

1782a Memphis Jug Band. Roots RL 337 (Austria).
Jazz and Blues. April. p27. 250w. $3\frac{1}{2}$

1783 MEN AT WORK (anthology). Topic TPS 166 (E). (Reissue.)
Journal of American Folklore. July/September. p295-6. 50w. 3

1783a The Men of No Property. THIS IS FREE BELFAST: IRISH REBEL SONGS OF SIX COUNTIES (anthology). Paredon P 1006 $4.00.
Library Journal. March 1. p856-7. 100w. 3

1784 Arthur Miller and all the Little Millers. HANGING OUT AND SETTING DOWN. Columbia C 31090 $5.98.
Downbeat. May 11. p23. 200w. 5

1784a Christy Moore. PROSPEROUS. Trailer LER 3035 (E).
Gramophone. June. p112. 150w. 3
Hi-Fi News and Record Review. May. p936. 25w. 3
Records and Recordings. May. p106. 125w. 4

1785 MORE GRAND AIRS FROM CONNEMARA (anthology). Topic 12 T 202 (E).
English Dance and Song. Summer. p75. 200w. 3½

1785a MORRIS ON (anthology). Island HELP 5 (E).
Hi-Fi News and Record Review. September. p1679. 175w. 4½
Sing Out. May/June. p43. 150w. 2½

1786 Mud Acres. MUSIC AMONG FRIENDS. Rounder 2001 $5.98.
New York Times--Sunday. August 27. pD19. 175w. 4

1786a Mulachy Davis Ceili Band. COTTAGE ON THE OLD DUNGANNON ROAD. RCA International INTS 1362 (E).
Records and Recordings. September. p107. 100w. 1½

1787 Geoff and Maria Muldaur. SWEET POTATOES. Reprise MS 2073 $5.98.
Sing Out. September/October. p38. 100w. 3

1787a Ruby Murray. A LITTLE BIT OF HEAVEN. Talisman STAL 6028 (E).
Gramophone. January. p74. 75w. 3

1788 MUSIC FROM THE FESTIVAL OF AMERICAN FOLK LIFE, VOLUME 1 (anthology). Smithsonian SL 100 $5.50.
Journal of American Folklore. October/December. p401. 100w. 4½

1788a MUSIC FROM THE WESTERN ISLES (anthology). Tangent TNGM 110 (E).
Journal of American Folklore. October/December. p408-9. 100w. 5

1789 The Natural Acoustic Band. LEARNING TO LIVE. RCA SF 8272 (E).
Hi-Fi News and Record Review. December. p2460. 300w. 2

1789a Christopher Neil. WHERE I BELONG. Rak SRAK 6753 (E).
Gramophone. September. p577. 25w. 0

1790 The New Deal String Band. DOWN IN THE WILLOW. Argo ZFB 69 (E).
Gramophone. July. p255. 100w. 2

1791 Lea Nicholson and Stan Ellison. GOD BLESS THE UNEMPLOYED. Transatlantic TRA 254 (E).
Hi-Fi News and Record Review. November. p2198. 50w. 3

1792 Roger Nicholson. NONESUCH FOR DULCIMER. Trailer LER 3034 (E).

Gramophone. June. p112. 25w. 1
Records and Recordings. May. p106. 150w. 3

1793 NORTHUMBRIAN FOLK (anthology). BBC RJC 1185 (E).
English Dance and Song. Summer. p114. 150w. 4½
Hi-Fi News and Record Review. May. p936. 25w. 2½

1794 Notts Alliance. THE CHEERFUL 'ORN. Traditional TSR 011 (E).
English Dance and Song. Summer. p114. 125w. 5

1795 Oak. WELCOME TO OUR FAIR. Topic 12 TS 212 (E).
Gramophone. April. p1779. 50w. 1½

1796 Dermot O'Brien. DUBLIN IN THE GREEN. Beltona SBER 133 (E). (Reissue.)
Hi-Fi News and Record Review. July. p1304. 25w. 2½

1797 Cathal O'Connell and Robin Morton. AN IRISH JUBILEE. Mercier Press IRL 10 (Ireland).
English Dance and Song. Summer. p75. 100w. 3½

1798 The Oldham Tinkers. OLDHAM'S BURNING SANDS. Topic 12 TS 206 (E).
Records and Recordings. January. p96. 100w. 3

1799 OLD TIME BALLADS FROM THE SOUTH, 1927/31 (anthology). County 522 $4.98. (Reissue.)
Journal of American Folklore. October/December. p395. 125w. 5

1800 OLD TIME MOUNTAIN GUITAR; FINGER STYLE GUITAR, 1926/30 (anthology). County 526 $4.98. (Reissue.)
Old Time Music. Summer. p23. 400w. 5
Sing Out. May/June. p44, 46. 50w. 4

1801 Joe Pancerzewski. THE FIDDLING ENGINEER. Voyager VRLP 306s $5.98.
Sing Out. September/October. p43. 50w. 3

1802 THE PAINFUL PLOUGH; SONGS AND BALLADS OF THE AGRICULTURAL LABOUR (anthology). Impact IMP-A 103 (E).
English Dance and Song. Summer. p114. 225w. 2½

1803 Tom Paxton. PEACE WILL COME. Reprise MS 2096 $5.98. R-R C 2096 $7.95.
Hi-Fi News and Record Review. August. p1475. 25w. 2½
Popular Music. Summer. p248. 50w. 4
Stereo Review. November. p80. 300w. 5

1804 Bob and Carole Pegg with Sidney Carter. AND NOW IT IS SO EARLY. Galliard GAL 4017 (E).
Hi-Fi News and Record Review. May. p936. 150w. 2

1805 The Penny Whistlers. A COOL DAY AND CROOKED CORN. Nonesuch Explorer H 72024 $2.98.
Journal of American Folklore. October/December. p407. 75w. 2½

1806 Pentangle. REFLECTION. Reprise S 6463 $5.98. Cart. M86463 $6.95. Cass. M56463 $6.95.
Crawdaddy. January 30. p20. 300w. 3
Creem. January. p67-8. 375w. 2
Jazz Journal. January. p37. 125w. 3

1807 Pentangle. SOLOMON'S SEAL. Reprise MS 2106 $5.98.
Hi-Fi News and Record Review. November. p2199. 50w. 3½
Sing Out. September/October. p37. 50w. 3

1808 Billy Pigg. THE BORDER MINSTREL. Leader LEA 4006 (E).
Gramophone. January. p1280. 75w. 4
Records and Recordings. January. p96. 100w. 3

1809 John Renbourn. FARO ANNIE. Warner Bros. BS 2082 $5.98.
Hi-Fi News and Record Review. June. p1125. 50w. 2½
High Fidelity. November. p130. 25w. 2

1810 Jon Rennard. THE PARTING GLASS. Traditional TSR 010 (E).
English Dance and Song. Spring. p34. 225w. 4

1811 Malvina Reynolds. MALVINA. Cassandra CFS 2807 $5.98.
High Fidelity. November. p120. 200w. 3
New York Times--Sunday. October 15. pD31. 300w. 4

1812 John Roberts and Tony Barrand. SPENCER THE ROVER IS ALIVE AND WELL AND LIVING IN ITHACA. Swallowtail ST 1 $5.00.
Sing Out. April/March. p36. 625w. 1½

1813 Keith Roberts. PIER OF THE REALM. Trailer LER 3031 (E).
Records and Recordings. May. p106. 125w. 3½

1814 Paul Robeson. SONGS OF MY PEOPLE. RCA LM 3292 $5.98. (Reissue.)
Stereo Review. December. p100. 275w. 5

1815 Art Rosenbaum and Al Murphy. Meadowlands MS 2 $5.00
Sing Out. September/October. p39, 41. 150w. 3

1816 Leon Rosselson. THE WORD IS HUGGA MUGGA CHUGGA LUGGA HUMBUGGA BOOM CHIT. Trailer LER 3015 (E).
Gramophone. January. p1279. 150w. 4

1817 Jonathan Round. Westbound $4.98.
Creem. January. p69. 50w. 1

1818 Tom Rush. CLASSIC RUSH. Elektra EKS 74062 $5.98. (Reissue.)
Audio. May. p93-4. 50w. 2½

1819 Betsy Rutherford. TRADITIONAL COUNTRY MUSIC. Biograph RC 6004 $5.98.
Journal of American Folklore. October/December. p397-8. 250w. 5
Stereo Review. October. p106. 250w. 3

1820 Isla St. Clair. TRADITIONAL SCOTTISH SONGS. Tangent TGS 112 (E).
English Dance and Song. Summer. p114. 225w. 3
Hi-Fi News and Record Review. June. p1125. 50w. 4
Records and Recordings. June. p90. 100w. 3

1821 Bridge St. John. SONGS FOR THE GENTLE MAN. Elektra EKS 74104 $5.98. Cart. ET 84104 $6.98. Cass. TC 54104 $6.98.
High Fidelity. February. p120. 25w. 2

1822 Buffy Sainte-Marie. BEST, VOLUME 1. Vanguard VSD 3/4 $5.98. (Reissue.)
Ontario Library Review. December. p243. 25w. 2½

1823 Buffy Sainte-Marie. BEST, VOLUME 2. Vanguard VSD 33/34 $5.98. (Reissue.)
Ontario Library Review. December. p243. 25w. 2½

1824 Buffy Sainte-Marie. ILLUMINATIONS. Vanguard VSD 79300 $5.98.
Records and Recordings. January. p96. 50w. 2

1825 Buffy Sainte-Marie. LITTLE WHEEL SPIN AND SPIN. Vanguard VSD 79211 $5.98.
Gramophone. February. p989. 75w. 2
Hi-Fi News and Record Review. October. p1923. 150w. 2

1826 Buffy Sainte-Marie. MOONSHOT. Vanguard VSD 79312 $5.98. Cart. M89312 $6.95. Cass. M59312 $6.95.
Creem. September. p11, 64. 25w. 2

Gramophone. November. p989. 50w. 1
High Fidelity. November. p118. 250w. 3
Popular Music. Summer. p247. 50w. 3
Rolling Stone. June 22. p55-6. 650w. 2½
Stereo Review. September. p80. 200w. 1

1827 Pete Scott. DON'T PANIC. Rubber RUB 003 (E).
Hi-Fi News and Record Review. August. p1475. 25w. 2

1828 Willis Scott. SHEPHERD'S SONG. Topic 12 T 183 (E).
Journal of American Folklore. July/September. p292. 125w. 3½

1829 SCOTTISH TRADITION, VOLUME 1, BOTHY BALLADS: MUSIC FROM THE NORTH-EAST (anthology). Tangent TNGM 109 (E).
Gramophone. January. p1280. 200w. 4
Journal of American Folklore. July/September. p292. 150w. 4
English Dance and Song. Summer. p75-6. 600w. 5

1830 SCOTTISH TRADITION, VOLUME 2, MUSIC FROM THE WESTERN ISLES. Tangent TNGM 110 (E).
English Dance and Song. Summer. p75-6. 600w. 5
Gramophone. January. p1280. 200w. 4

1831 Mike Seeger. MUSIC FROM TRUE VINE. Mercury SRM 1-627 $5.98.
Audio. November. p96. 400w. 4½
Creem. August. p67. 25w. 2½
Popular Music. Spring. p128. 100w. 4
Previews. November. p43. 200w. 2½
Rolling Stone. July 20. p50. 1,000w. 4
Sing Out. March/April. p34. 200w. 2½

1832 Peggy Seeger. PEGGY ALONE. Argo ZFB 63 (E). (Reissue.)
Gramophone. June. p112. 25w. 3
Hi-Fi News and Record Review. June. p1125. 25w. 2½
Records and Recordings. June. p90. 125w. 4

1833 Peggy and Mike Seeger. PEGGY 'N' MIKE. Argo ZFB 62 (E). (Reissue.)
Gramophone. July. p255. 100w. 3
Hi-Fi News and Record Review. June. p125. 25w. 2½
Old Time Music. Summer. p30. 50w. 3½
Records and Recordings. June. p90. 125w. 4

1834 Pete Seeger. Ember CW 130 (E). (Reissue.)
Hi-Fi News and Record Review. November. p2198. 50w. 3

1835 Pete Seeger. RAINBOW RACE. Columbia C 30739 $5.98.
Audio. August. p62. 50w. 4

1836 THE SELDOM SCENE: ACT 1. Rebel SLP 1511 $4.98. Cart. 8511 $6.95.
Sing Out. May/June. p44. 75w. 3

1837 The Settlers. LIGHTNING TREE. York FYK 405 (E).
Hi-Fi News and Record Review. August. p1475. 50w. 1½

1838 Shenandoah Cut-Ups. BLUEGRASS AUTUMN. Revonah 904.
Sing Out. September/October. p43. 75w. 3

1839 The Ship. A CONTEMPORARY FOLK MUSIC JOURNEY. Elektra EKS 75036 $5.98. Cart. ET 8036 $6.98. Cass. TC 5036 $6.98.
Records and Recordings. December. p101. 275w. 0

1840 Jeffrey Shurtleff. STATE FARM. A & M SP 4332 $5.98.
Audio. August. p61. 50w. 3
High Fidelity. June. p103. 500w. 1
Popular Music. Summer. p252. 75w. 3

1841 The Simmons Family. WANDERING THROUGH THE RACKENSACK. Arkansas Folk Culture Center USR 3053.
Journal of American Folklore. October/December. p399. 150w. 3

1842 Barry Skinner. BED, BATTLE, AND BOOZE. Argo ZFB 34 (E).
Hi-Fi News and Record Review. May. p936. 50w. 1
Records and Recordings. May. p106. 150w. 3

1843 Jon Smith. AMERICAN MOUNTAIN MUSIC. Mulberry Records M 311.
Journal of American Folklore. July/September. p296. 50w. 2½

1844 SONGS AND MUSIC OF THE RED COATS (anthology). Argo ZDA 147 (E).
English Dance and Song. Winter. p158. 100w. 3½

1845 SONGS FROM THE STOCKS: THE BROADSIDE (anthology). Guildhall 5 (E).
Hi-Fi News and Record Review. November. p2198. 100w. 4

1846 SONGS OF THE RAILROAD, 1924-34 (anthology). Vetco LP 103 $5.98. (Reissue.)
Journal of American Folklore. October/December. p395-6. 75w. 4
Sing Out. September/October. p43. 50w. 2½

1847 Rosalie Sorrels. SOMEWHERE BETWEEN. Boise Unitarian Fellowship TAD 3081 $5.98.
Stereo Review. May. p95. 200w. 1

1848 Rosalie Sorrels. TRAVELING LADY. Sire SI 5902 $4.98.
New York Times--Sunday. January 23. pD25. 400w. 2½
Sing Out. May/June. p41. 175w. 2½

1849 SOUNDS LIKE NORTH CORNWALL (anthology).
Hi-Fi News and Record Review. August. p147. 25w. 2

1850 Bruce Spelman. YOU DON'T KNOW WHAT YOU'RE PADDLING IN. Montague MONS 1 (E).
Hi-Fi News and Record Review. May. p936. 25w. 1

1851 Joseph Spence. GOOD MORNING MR. WALKER. Arhoolie 1061 $6.00.
Popular Music. Fall. p91. 50w. 3
Sing Out. September/October. p39. 100w. 3

1852 The Spinners. SHADES OF FOLK. Contour 6870 538 (E).
Hi-Fi News and Record Review. June. p1125. 25w. 2½

1853 The Spinners. STOP, LOOK, LISTEN. Contour 6870 529 (E).
Hi-Fi News and Record Review. June. p1125. 75w. 2½

1854 Steeleye Span. BELOW THE SALT. Chrysalis CHR 1008 $5.98.
Hi-Fi News and Record Review. November. p2198. 50w. 3
New York Times--Sunday. December 10. pD38. 400w. 4
Sing Out. September/October. p37. 50w. 4

1855 Steeleye Span. PLEASE TO SEE THE KING. Big Tree 2004 $4.98. Cart. M82004 $6.95. Cass. M52004 $6.95.
Creem. January. p67-8. 375w. 3

1856 Steeleye Span. TEN MAN MOP, OR MR. RESERVOIR BUTLER RIDES AGAIN. Pegasus PEG 9 (E).
Gramophone. June. p112. 150w. 4

1857 John Stewart. THE LONESOME PICKER RIDES AGAIN. Warner Bros. WS 1948 $5.98. Cart. M81948 $6.95. Cass. M51948 $6.95.
Crawdaddy. January 16. p15. 1,000w. 3
High Fidelity. June. p106-7. 50w. 3

1858 John Stewart. SUNSTORM. Warner Bros. BS 2611 $5.98. Cart. M82611 $6.95. Cass. M52611 $6.95.
High Fidelity. July. p98,100. 200w. 1
High Fidelity. December. p122. 100w. 3½
Stereo Review. October. p100. 250w. 3½

1859 Don Stover. THINGS IN LIFE. Rounder 0014 $5.95.
Sing Out. September/October. p41. 50w. 2½

1860 Strange Creek Singers. Arhoolie 4004 $6.00
Old Time Music. Summer. p30. 75w. 3½
Sing Out. March/April. p34. 200w. 5
Stereo Review. September. p83. 375w. 4

1861 The Stripling Brothers. OLD TIME FIDDLE TUNES, 1928/1936. County 501 $4.98. (Reissue.)
Old Time Music. Autumn. p25-6. 325w. 4

1862 Dave Swarbrick and Martin Carthy. SELECTIONS. Pegasus PEG 6 (E).
Gramophone. January. p1279. 75w. 3

1863 TAKE OFF YOUR HEAD AND LISTEN (anthology). Rubber RUB 001 (E).
Hi-Fi News and Record Review. August. p1473, 5. 25w. 2½

1864 Talisman. PRIMROSE DREAMS. Argo ZFB 33 (E).
Hi-Fi News and Record Review. May. p939. 25w. 2½
Records and Recordings. May. p106. 75w. 1

1865 Cyril Tawney. IN PORT. Argo ZFB 28 (E).
Hi-Fi News and Record Review. December. p2460. 100w. 3

1866 Jeremy Taylor. PIECE OF GROUND. Galliard GAL 4018 (E).
English Dance and Song. Winter. p158. 50w. 2½
Gramophone. April. p1779. 25w. 1
Hi-Fi News and Record Review. June. p1125. 25w. 1½
Records and Recordings. May. p106-8. 100w. 2½

1867 Alan Thomas. A PICTURE. Sire S 15901 $4.98.
Popular Music. Winter. p125. 75w. 2

1868 Steve Tilson. COLLECTION. Transatlantic TRA 252 (E).
Hi-Fi News and Record Review. June. p1125. 50w. 3

1869 Transpennine. Topic 12 TS 215 (E).
English Dance and Song. Summer. p74. 175w. 3½

1870 Happy and Artie Traum. DOUBLE-BACK. Capitol ST 799 $5.98. Cart. 8XT 799 $6.98.
Library Journal. February 15. p665. 50w. 3

1871 Happy and Artie Traum. MUD ACRES. Rounder Records 3001 $5.95.
Sing Out. May/June. p41. 200w. 3

1872 THE TRAVELLING STEWARTS (anthology). Topic 12 T 179 (E).
Journal of American Folklore. July/September. p292-3. 125w. 3½

1873 Mary Travers. MORNING GLORY. Warner Bros. BS 2609 $5.98. Cart. M82609 $6.95. Cass. M52609 $6.95.
Gramophone. December. p1221. 25w. 1½
High Fidelity. July. p98. 225w. 3½
New York Times--Sunday. May 21. pD30. 150w. 1
Stereo Review. August. p93-4. 150w. 2½

1874 A TRIBUTE TO WOODY GUTHRIE, PART 1. Columbia KC 31171 $5.98. Cart. CA 31171 $6.98. Cass. CT 31171 $6.98. PART 2. Warner Bros BS 2586 $5.98.
Crawdaddy. May 28. p14. 1,000w. 4
Gramophone. November. p989. 150w. 3
Hi-Fi News and Record Review. August. p1304. 100w. 2½
Journal of American Folklore. October/December. p402. 25w. 2½
New York Times--Sunday. April 16. pD28. 225w. 3½
Ontario Library Review. December. p243. 50w. 3
Records and Recordings. June. p90-1. 675w. 4
Rolling Stone. July 20. p59. 1,000w. 1
Sing Out. May/June. p41. 400w. 2½
Stereo Review. August. p92. 2,000w. 3

1875 THE TROJAN STORY. Trojan TALL 1 (3 discs) (E).
Gramophone. May. p1952, 55. 400w. 4½

1876 ULSTER'S FLOWERY VALE (anthology). BBC REC 28 (E).
Hi-Fi News and Record Review. May. p936. 25w. 2½

1877 UNTO BRIGG FAIR (anthology). Leader LEA 4050 (E). (Reissue.)
Records and Recordings. June. p90. 225w. 5

1878 Bill Vanaver. Swallowtail ST 2.
Sing Out. March/April. p35-6. 625w. 2½

1879 VIETNAM WILL WIN (anthology). Paredon P 1009 $4.00.
Library Journal. February 15. p665-6. 200w. 3

1880 VIETNAM: SONGS OF LIBERATION (anthology). Paredon P 1008 $4.00.
Library Journal. February 15. p665-6. 200w. 3

1881 Frank Wakefield. Rounder 0007 $5.95.
Old Time Music. Summer. p28. 200w. 2
Sing Out. September/October. p41. 100w. 2½

1882 Cliff Waldron. ONE MORE STEP WITH CLIFF WALDRON AND THE NEW SHADES OF GRASS. Rebel SLP 1510 $4.98. Cart. 8510 $6.95.
Sing Out. May/June. p44. 200w. 2½

1883 Gordon Waller. AND GORDON. Vertigo 749 $5.98. Cart. 8022-749V $6.95.
Gramophone. July. p254-5. 25w. 1

1884 Frank Warner. AMERICAN TRADITIONAL FOLKSONGS. Elektra EKS 7153 $5.98. (Reissue.)
Journal of American Folklore. October/December. p402. 25w. 4

1885 Mike and Lal Waterson. BRIGHT PHOEBUS. Trailer LES 2076 (E).
Sing Out. September/October. p37. 25w. 2½

1886 Doc Watson. ELEMENTARY DOCTOR WATSON! Poppy PYS 5703 $4.98.
Creem. August. p69. 50w. 4
High Fidelity. July. p106. 25w. 2
New York Times--Sunday. August 20. pD22. 225w. 3½
Sing Out. March/April. p34. 425w. 2

1887 Doc Watson. ON STAGE. Vanguard VSD 9/10 (2 discs) $5.98.
Gramophone. July. p255. 75w. 4
Old Time Music. Summer. p27. 200w. 5
Ontario Library Review. December. p242. 25w. 2½
Records and Recordings. May. p108. 200w. 3½

1888 Doc and Merle Watson. BALLADS FROM DEEP GAP. Vanguard VSD 6576 $5.98.
High Fidelity. February. p120. 25w. 2½
Journal of American Folklore. October/December. p399. 50w. 5

1889 Weavers. BEST. Vanguard VSD 15/16 (2 discs) $5.98. (Reissue.)
Ontario Library Review. December. p243. 25w. 2½

1890 Jim Weatherly. RCA LSP 4747 $5.98.
Music Journal. December. p75. 100w. 2½

1891 Hedy West. OLD TIMES AND HARD TIMES. Topic 12 T 117 (E).
Journal of American Folklore. July/September. p296. 100w. 5

1892 David Whiffen. Fantasy 8411 $5.98.
Sound. February. p17. 75w. 2

1893 Roger Whittaker. LOOSE AND FIERY. RCA LSP 4652 $5.98.
Sound. March. p35. 125w. 2

1894 THE WIDE MIDLANDS: SONGS, STORIES AND TUNES FROM THE CENTRAL COUNTIES (anthology). Topic 12 TS 210 (E).
English Dance and Song. Spring. p34. 550w. 1

1895 Jon Wilcox. STAGES OF MY LIFE. Folk Legacy FSI 45 $5.98.
Sing Out. May/June. p42. 175w. 3

1896 Robin Williamson. MYRRH. Island HELP 2 (E).
Hi-Fi News and Record Review. July. p1304. 75w. 2½

1897 Charlie Wills. Trailer LEA 4041 (E).
Gramophone. November. p989. 50w. 2
Hi-Fi News and Record Review. September. p1679. 250w. 5
Records and Recordings. September. p101. 300w. 3½

1898 Tom Winslow. HEY LOOKA YONDER (IT'S THE CLEARWATER). Biograph BLP 12018 $5.98.
Sing Out. September/October. p38. 50w. 3

1899 Da Costa Woltz. SOUTHERN BROADCASTERS 1927. County 524 $4.98.
Sing Out. September/October. p41. 250w. 4

1900 Brenda Wootton and John the Fish. PASTIES AND CREAM. Sentinal Records SENS 1006 (E).
English Dance and Song. Summer. p74. 150w. 3½

1901 THE WORLD OF FOLK (anthology). Argo SPA A132 (E).
English Dance and Song. Winter. p158. 75w. 5

1902 Bernard Wrigley. THE PHENOMENAL... Topic 12 TS 211 (E).
Records and Recordings. January. p96. 75w. 3

1903 Martin Wyndham-Read. Trailer LER 2028 (E).
Gramophone. April. p1779. 50w. 2½

1904 Peter Yarrow. PETER. Warner Bros. BS 2599 $5.98. Cart. M82599 $6.95. Cass. M52599 $6.95.
Gramophone. July. p254. 25w. 1
Hi-Fi News and Record Review. June. p1125. 25w. 3½
High Fidelity. May. p111. 200w. 2
Stereo Review. June. p103-4. 50w. 1½

1905 Kenny Young. CLEVER BOYS CHASE THE SUN. Warner Bros. BS 2579 $5.98. Cart. M82579 $6.95. Cass. M52579 $6.95.
Gramophone. May. p1951. 50w. 2½

ETHNIC

This section contains traditional folk music from around the world performed in any language other than English. Listed in the Schwann Record and Tape Guide No. 2 (Non-Current popular jazz/international pop/folk) under International Folk, a surprisingly large number of recordings in this category are released each year.

Ethnic releases cover a broad spectrum ranging from recordings of drums and chants from Africa to Kurdish folk music from Iran. For inclusion in this section the music must be traditional in nature. Popular music (i.e., commercial) will be found in the MOOD-POP section of the Index.

There are at least two excellent sources of reviews for ethnic recordings. These are Ethnomusicology and the Journal of American Folklore. Reviews in these publications tend to be scholarly in nature. More impressionistic reviews can be found scattered through various periodicals, especially English review sources such as Gramophone and Hi-Fi News and Record Review. Additional reviews are often found in Stereo Review and High Fidelity.

Good bets for library purchase would be selections from the catalogs of Peters International, Folkways, and especially the Nonesuch Explorer series. This latter series is inexpensive and has excellent recording standards. Interest in ethnic music is limited except in urban centers where concentrations of ethnic groups can be found or in universities having strong anthropology or folklore programs.

1906 Mustapha Tettey Addy. MASTER DRUMMER FROM GHANA. Tangent Records TGS 113 (E).
Hi-Fi News and Record Review. November. p2199. 250w. 4

1907 THE AFRICAN MBIRA: MUSIC OF THE SHONA PEOPLE OF RHODESIA (anthology). Nonesuch Explorer H 72043 $2.98.
Audio. February. p66. 200w. 2½

1908 AFRICAN MUSICAL INSTRUMENTS (anthology). Asch Records AH 8460 $5.95.
Journal of American Folklore. October/December. p405. 750w. 1

1909 AFRO-AMERICAN MUSIC: A DEMONSTRATION RECORDING (anthology). Asch AA 702 $5.98.
Journal of American Folklore. January/March. p99. 100w. 3

1910 ALAJERE MUSIC OF OSHOGBO (anthology). Nigerian Institute of African Studies. NCR 6 (Nigeria).
Ethnomusicology. May. p316-8. 325w. 3½

1911 ARAB MUSIC, VOLUME 2 (anthology). Lyrichord LLST 7198 $5.98.
Journal of American Folklore. October/December. p407-8. 25w. 2

1912 ARRIAL NO DOURO: COUNTRY FAIR IN DOURO (anthology). Request SRLP 8089 $4.98.
Journal of American Folklore. October/December. p406-7. 150w. 2

1913 AUTHENTIC MUSIC OF THE AMERICAN INDIAN (anthology). Everest 3450/3 (3 discs) $14.94.
Audio. January. p72. 100w. 3

1914 THE BALALAIKA (anthology). Melodiya/Angel SR 40171 $5.98. Cart. 8XS 40171 $6.98. Cass. 4XS 40171 $6.98.
High Fidelity. January. p114. 150w. 2

1915 BARONG; DRAME MUSICAL BALINAIS (anthology). Vogue LD 763 (French).
Ethnomusicology. October. p563-66. 1,700w. 3

1916 A BELL RINGING IN THE EMPTY SKY (anthology). Nonesuch Explorer $2.98.
New York Times--Sunday. February 13. pD28. 75w. 2½

1917 BEST FOLKSONGS OF JAMAICA (anthology). Request SRLP 8160 $4.98.
Journal of American Folklore. October/December. p407. 25w. 2

1918 THE BLACK CARIBS OF HONDURAS (anthology). Ethnic Folkways Library P 435 $4.98.
Journal of American Folklore. October/December. p405. 25w. 3½

1919 Cleofes Vigil. BUENOS DIAS, PALOMA BLANCA. Taos Recordings TRP 122 $5.00.
Ethnomusicology. January. p162-64. 850w. 5

1920 CORDES ANCIENNES (anthology). Bärenreiter BM 30L 2505 (French).
Ethnomusicology. May. p299-307. 750w. 3½

1921 CORSE ETERNELLE (anthology). Arion 30 U 149 (French).
Records and Recordings. October. p125. 275w. 2

1922 Leonard and Heavy Crow Dog. CROW DOG'S PARADISE--SONG OF THE SIOUX. Elektra EKS 74091 $5.98. Cart. 84091 $6.95. Cass. 54091 $6.95.
New York Times--Sunday. February 13. pD28. 1,400w. 4

1923 El Curro. FLAMENCO. Audiophile APS 106 $5.95.
Augio. August. p66. 200w. 4

1924 DJUNG DJUNG (anthology). Love Records LRLP 12 (Finland) $4.98.
Ethnomusicology. October. p570-572. 1,250w. 3

1925 Don Pedro and Don José. CUMBIA DEL SOL. Decca Eclipse ECS 2096 (E).
Gramophone. June. p115. 150w. 1

1926 EDA (Yoruba Folk Opera). Nigeria Institue of African Studies NCR 5 (Nigeria).
Ethnomusicology. May. p316-8. 325w. 3½

1927 Takis Elenis. DANCE THE GREEK WAY. Monitor MFS 722 $4.98.
Audio. December. p100-1. 200w. 3

1928 L'ENSEMBLE INSTRUMENTAL AU FESTIVAL CULTUREL PAN AFRICAIN D'ALGER (anthology). Bärenreiter BM 30L 2504 (French).
Ethnomusicology. May. p299-307. 750w. 3½

1929 ESKIMO SONGS FROM ALASKA (anthology). Ethnic Folkways Library FE 4069 $5.98.
Journal of American Folklore. October/December. p405. 50w. 3½

1930 FANTA DAMBA; LA TRADITION EPIQUE (anthology). Bärenreiter BM 30L 2506 (French).
Ethnomusicology. May. p299-307. 750w. 3½

1931 FIESTAS OF PERU; MUSIC OF THE HIGH ANDES (anthology). Nonesuch Explorer H 72045 $2.98.
Stereo Review. November. p100. 300w. 5

1932 FOLK FIDDLING FROM SWEDEN: TRADITIONAL FIDDLE TUNES FROM DALARNA (anthology). Nonesuch Explorer H 72033 $2.98.
Journal of American Folklore. October/December. p407. 75w. 4

1933 FOLK MUSIC OF AFGHANISTAN, VOLUME 1/2 (anthology). Lyrichord LLST 7230/31 (2 discs) $9.96.
Journal of American Folklore. October/December. p407-8. 50w. 4

1934 THE FOUR VEDAS. Asch Records AHM 4126 (2 discs) $7.95.
Ethnomusicology. January. p157-8. 525w. 5

1935 A HARVEST, A SHEPHERD AND A BRIDE: VILLAGE MUSIC OF BULGARIA (anthology). Nonesuch Explorer H 72034 $2.98.
Journal of American Folklore. October/December. p407. 125w. 4

1936 HERE COME THE GURKHAS! (anthology). Columbia Studio 2 TWO 342 (E).
English Dance and Song. Winter. p158. 75w. 3

1937 Hiski Saloman. FINNISH-AMERICAN FOLK AND POPULAR MUSIC, 1927/32. Love Records LXLP 505 (Finland).
Ethnomusicology. October. p566-69. 1,850w. 5

1938 HORA DE DESPEDIDA DE BRANCO-LE; MUSIC FROM LIBERATED GUINEA BISSAN (anthology). Eteenpäin ETLP 304 (Finland).
Ethnomusicology. October. p572-4. 1,000w. 3

1939 Los Incas. DANZA DEL INCA.
Gramophone. August. p398. 75w. 2

1940 JAPANESE MUSIC FOR KOTO AND SHAKUHACHI (anthology). Toshiba TH 7003 $5.98.
Library Journal. April 15. p1413. 100w. 3

1941 JAVANESE COURT GAMELAN (anthology). Nonesuch Explorer H 72044 $2.98.
Audio. February. p66. 200w. 2½

1942 JOUJOUKA (anthology). Rolling Stones Records 49100 $5.98. Cart. M849100 $6.95. Cass. M549100 $6.95.
Creem. April. p71. 50w. ½
New York Times--Sunday. February 13. pD28. 125w. 3½

1943 KLANGE FRA DANMARK'S BRONZEALDERLURER (anthology). Nationalmuseet NM 67-001 (Denmark).
Ethnomusicology. October. p575-6. 1,000w. 0

1944 KLASSISCHE TURKISCHE MUSIK (anthology). Klangdokumente zur Musikwissenschaft KM 0002 (Germany).
Ethnomusicology. January. p148-9. 975w. 4

1945 LATIN AMERICAN CHILDREN'S GAME SONGS (anthology). Asch Records AHS 751 $5.95.
Journal of American Folklore. October/December. p405. 125w. 3½

1946 Los Machucambos. MUSICA LATINA. Decca PFS 4238 (E).
Hi-Fi News and Record Review. May. p937. 25w. 2

1947 LE MALI DES SABLES: LES SONGAY (anthology). Bärenreiter BM 30L 2503 (French).
Ethnomusicology. May. p299-307. 750w. 3½

1948 LE MALI DES STEPPES ET DES SAVANES: LES MANDINGUES (anthology). Bärenreiter BM 30L 2501 (French).
Ethnomusicology. May. p299-307. 750w. 3½

1949 LE MALI DU FLEUVE: LE PEULS (anthology). Bärenreiter BM 30L 2502 (French).
Ethnomusicology. May. p299-307. 750w. 3½

1950 MESSE DES I DESHERITES (anthology). Barclay 920 177 (French).
Library Journal. June 15. p2167. 75w. 3

1951 Airto Moreira. SEEDS ON THE GROUND: THE NATIONAL SEEDS OF AIRTO. Buddah $5.98.
Gramophone. January. p1280. 400w. 4

1952 MUSIC FROM BANGLA DESH (anthology). Argo ZFB 74 (E).
Gramophone. April. p1779. 50w. 2½

1953 MUSIC FROM IRAN (anthology). Argo ZFB 51 (E).
Stereo Review. May. p97. 300w. 3½

1954 MUSIC FROM SOUTH NEW GUINEA (anthology). Asch Mankind Series AHM 4216 $5.95.
Journal of American Folklore. October/December. p405-6. 125w. 2½

1955 MUSIC FROM THE SHRINES OF AJMER AND MUNDRA (anthology). Lyrichord LLST 7736 $5.98.
Stereo Review. May. p97-8. 100w. 2½

1956 MUSIC FROM YUGOSLAVIA (anthology). Argo ZFB 53 (E).
Stereo Review. November. p100. 300w. 3½

1957 MUSIC OF AFRICA (anthology). BBC REC 130M (3 discs) (E).
Gramophone. November. p989. 150w. 4
Hi-Fi News and Record Review. August. p1475. 500w. 2

1958 THE MUSIC OF GREECE (anthology). National Geographic Society 2875 $4.95.
Ethnomusicology. October. p577-9. 1,200w. 0

1959 MUSIC OF THE PLAINS APACHE (anthology). Asch Mankind Series AHM 4252 $5.95.
Journal of American Folklore. October/December. p405-6. 50w. 3

1960 MUSIC OF THE TARASCAN INDIANS OF MEXICO (anthology). Asch Mankind Series AHM 4217 $5.95.
Journal of American Folklore. October/December. p405-6. 150w. 5

1961 MUSIC OF TIBET: THE TANTRIC RITUALS (anthology). Anthology AST 4005 $6.98.
Ethnomusicology. January. p153-4. 1,150w. 4

1962 THE MUSIC OF TRINIDAD (anthology). National Geographic Society 3297 $4.95.
Stereo Review. September. p82-3. 450w. 5

1963 THE MUSIC OF VIETNAM, VOLUME 1/2 (anthology). Bärenreiter BM 30L 2022/23 (2 discs) (French).
Ethnomusicology. May. p308-10. 1,250w. 4½

1964 MUSIQUE BONI ET WAYANA DE GUYANE (anthology). Vogue LVLX 290 (French).
Enthnomusicology. January. p159-60. 800w. 4

1965 MUSIQUE BOUDDHIQUE DE COREE (anthology). Vogue LVLX 253 (French).
Enthnomusicology. October. p560-3. 1,600w. 4

1966 MUSIQUE GUERE COTE D'IVOIRE (anthology). Vogue LD 764 (French).
Ethnomusicology. January. p145-7. 750w. 3½

1967 MUSIQUE GOURO DE COTE D'IVOIRE (anthology). OCORA OCR 48 (French).
Ethnomusicology. January. p145-7. 750w. 4

1968 MUSIQUE RITUELLE TIBETAINE (anthology). OCORA OCR 49 (French).
Ethnomusicology. May. p310-13. 1,150w. 3½

1969 LA MUSIQUE POPULAIRE D'EGYPTE (anthology). United Arab Republic, Ministry of Culture EST 52/53 (2 discs) (Egypt).
Ethnomusicology. May. p318. 900w. 5

1970 MUSIQUES BANDA: REPUBLIQUE CENTRAFRICAINE (anthology). Vogue LP 765 (French).
Ethnomusicology. May. p320-22. 1,200w. 4½

1971 MUSIQUES POPULAIRES D'INDONESIE: WEST JAVA (anthology). OCORA OCR 46 (French).
Ethnomusicology. May. p313-16. 1,550w. 4

1972 Na Fili Trio. AN GHAOTH ANIAR: THE WEST WIND. Mercier Press IRE 9 (Ireland).
Journal of American Folklore. July/September. p293-4. 225w. 4½

1973 K.V. Nara Yanswamy. CARNATIC MUSIC OF SOUTH INDIA. World Pacific WPS 21450 $5.98.
Journal of American Folklore. October/December. p408. 125w. 4

1974 New Sound Crusaders Steel Band. Chapter One LRS 5006 (E).
Gramophone. June. p115. 25w. 1

1975 NIGERIAN SONGS (anthology). Afro/Request. SRLP 5028 $4.98.
Journal of American Folklore. October/December. p407. 25w. 2½

1976 THE NONESUCH EXPLORER (anthology). Nonesuch H7-11 (2 discs) $5.98.
Hi-Fi News and Record Review. December. p2460. 150w. 2½
Stereo Review. May. p98. 475w. 3

1977 OBA KO SO (YORUBA FOLK OPERA). Nigeria Institute of African Studies NCR 1/2 (2 discs) (Nigeria).
Ethnomusicology. May. p316-8. 325w. 3½

1978 ORIENTO NO MINZOKU ONGAKU: LIVING HERITAGE OF ASIAN MUSIC--INDIA, PAKISTAN, AFGHANISTAN, IRAN, IRAQ, AND LEBANON (anthology). Columbia EDS 16/19 (4 discs) (Japan).
Ethnomusicology. January. p160-62. 1,300w. 5

1979 Pachacamac. MUSIC OF THE INCAS. Columbia SCX 6489 (E).
Gramophone. May. p1952. 275w. 4

1980 THE PALMNINE DRINKARD (YORUBA FOLK OPERA). Nigeria Institute of African Studies NCR 3/4 (2 discs) (Nigeria).
Ethnomusicology. May. p316-18. 325w. 3½

1981 Pastora Pavón. LA NIÑA DE LOS PEINES (THE GIRL OF THE COMBS). Everest FS 256 $2.98. (Reissue.)
Journal of American Folklore. October/December. 175w. 5

1982 Los Pinguinos Del Norte. TOPICAL SONGS FROM THE RIO GRANDE VALLEY. Arhoolie 3002 $6.00.
Audio. February. p72-3. 600w. 2
Ethnomusicology. January. p154-56. 1,250w. 1

1983 POLYPHONIES MONGO: BATNA, EKONDA (anthology). OCORA OCR 53 (French).
Ethnomusicology. May. p322-3. 700w. 4

1984 Los Reales de Paraguay. Music for Pleasure SMFP 5253 (E).
Gramophone. April. p1779. 100w. 3
Hi-Fi News and Record Review. May. p937. 25w. $2\frac{1}{2}$

1985 RIFI--SOUNDS OF MOROCCO (anthology). Iain Alan, NWB Ltd. 208 Piccadilly, London (E).
English Dance and Song. Winter. p157. 150w. $2\frac{1}{2}$

1986 Saka Acquage. VOICES OF AFRICA. Nonesuch Explorer H 72026 $2.98.
Ethnomusicology. January. p164-5. 625w. $2\frac{1}{2}$

1987 SO THIS IS GHANA (anthology). Folkways FW 8859 $5.98.
Journal of American Folklore. October/December. p405. 25w. 1

1988 SONGS AND DANCES OF NEPAL (anthology). Ethnic Folkways Library FE 4101 $5.98.
Journal of American Folklore. October/December. p405. 25w. $3\frac{1}{2}$

1989 SONGS AND INSTRUMENTS OF NORTHERN INDIA (anthology). Request SRLP 8077 $4.98.
Journal of American Folklore. October/December. p406. 150w. $3\frac{1}{2}$

1990 SONGS FROM CAPE BRETON ISLAND (anthology). Ethnic Folkways Library FE 4450 $5.98.
Journal of American Folklore. October/December. p405. 25w. $3\frac{1}{2}$

1991 SOUNDS OF MOROCCO (anthology). Rifi Discurio (E).
Hi-Fi News and Record Review. July. p1304. 50w. 1

1992 STEEL DRUMS OF BARBADOS (anthology). Request SRLP 10091 $4.98.
Journal of American Folklore. October/December. p407. 25w. 3

1993 THE TEN GRACES PLAYED ON THE VINA; MUSIC OF SOUTH INDIA (anthology). Nonesuch Explorer H 72027 $2.98.
Ethnomusicology. January. p156-7. 625w. 4

1994 TIBETAN FOLK AND MINSTREL MUSIC (anthology). Lyrichord LLST 7196 $5.98.
Journal of American Folklore. October/December. p407-8. 75w. 4

1995 TURKISH MUSIC, II: CLASSICAL AND RELIGIOUS MUSIC (anthology). Bärenreiter BM 30L 2020 (French).
Ethnomusicology. January. p149-52. 1,100w. 2

1996 TWO RAGAS. Sveriges Radios Förlag RELP 1066 (Sweden).
Ethnomusicology. May. p323-25. 800w. 2

1997 Waiata Maori. FESTIVAL OF MAORI SONGS. Oryx EXP 53 (E).
Hi-Fi News and Record Review. August. p1473. 100w. 3½

1998 Zagreb Folklore Festival. VILLAGE FOLK MUSIC OF YUGOSLAVIA (anthology). Nonesuch Explorer H 72042 $2.98.
Audio. February. p66. 200w. 2½

JAZZ

This section contains material from diverse origins: dixieland, ragtime, instrumental blues, swing, avant-garde, and so forth. Music of a light "cocktail jazz" texture usually performed by non-jazz musicians will be found in MOOD-POP. Similarly, the employment of jazz in ROCK will be found in that category. BLUES has its own section, although the 12-bar construction and the "blue" notes are employed extensively in jazz.

Of all the popular music fields, jazz is the best documented. There are sufficient discographies, journals, exchange markets, record store and mail-order outlets to meet the demand, but work continues into the esoteric reaches of descriptive writings and performances. Unfortunately, measured against "classical music" standards, jazz is very far behind in critical and scholarly writing ventures. Articles and books thus far have been of the survey type, employing biographies and personal experiences, histories of ventures, discographic information, and photography, but while there have been lots of words about the subject of jazz, there has been little about the actual jazz music. Everything to say about jazz in the past has probably been said, but nothing much has been cited about the music itself. Many writers and critics do not play any instrument, and some cannot even read nor write music. This is completely opposite from the writers in folk and blues music.

Jazz is an aural music; its written score represents a skeleton of what actually takes place during a performance. Thus, there appears to be no need for the "classical music" approach. Yet it cannot be denied that written transcriptions are valuable for instructional purposes and for structual analysis. Such data are usually not available in published form, and the demand for it at the present time is slight. Educational use is limited to original transcriptions not yet published. Often, critics and reviewers will argue against systematic analysis of jazz, for then the music will not be enjoyable anymore. This visceral reaction, also common to rock music writers, is negated by the continual enjoyment people derive from classical music. What is really meant is that the writers would not be able to understand the musicological terms for they cannot play jazz. Reaction of this kind is missing in folk and blues, for the use of the solo instrument enables detailed study by the listener in order to emulate his favorite performers. One reason advanced for musicological discussions within jazz is that such writings will enhance the level of jazz criticism and make it more acceptable for classical music writers. Yet the other side of the coin is that the performers themselves cannot usually read or write music, playing only by ear and a feel for the subject. Both arguments are specious.

For the moment, then, jazz critics and reviewers are intensely interested in discovering and disseminating all facts that they can locate about the performers and the performances of the music per se. The two British publications Jazz Journal and Jazz and Blues often contain discographical information that consumes more lineage than the review itself, and even within the review there are plenty of informative bits of data that appear to have no relevance to the music at hand. Virtually every jazz record released gets reviewed somewhere, and there are also a proliferation of reissues, and new releases of recently discovered unreleased material never before commercially available. "Bootlegger pirates" have emerged to sell the previously unreleased material, most of it very old and rare. It is not our intention to probe this matter of ethical issues, for that battle is being waged in the media. But "unauthorized" versions -- usually selling 500 copies or less -- serve the purpose of meeting the demand for keeping in print virtually every worthwhile (and some not-so-worthwhile) jazz recording, and this matter of availability is constantly being referred to in the media.

America is thought of as the home of jazz, yet the leading magazines and scholars are European. Europe is now the scene of exciting new jazz and many reissues of earlier material. England has the key reissues, all nicely packaged and often retaining the original monophonic sound. France and Sweden are close behind, and so is Japan. The European Jazz Federation is well organized, and will certainly expand when Great Britain works out the details of its Common Market entry. In the lists of "best" records below, the reader should note that the bulk of the reissues come from England and that much post-Parker material comes initially from Europe. That jazz is neglected at home is evidenced by both the lack of issued product and by the lack of review media devoted to jazz. Downbeat concentrates on American modern jazz labels, while Jazz Report, a mimeographed alternative, concentrates on traditional material. General review publications, such as Stereo Review or Audio have jazz sections, while Rolling Stone will review the occasional jazz record. Canada, on the other hand, has probably the best jazz magazine in the world in Coda, put out by two immigrants from Britain. And Britain itself has the prestigious Jazz Journal and Jazz and Blues, plus excellent sections in the Gramophone and Records and Recordings.

Coda has perhaps the best and longest jazz reviews, and it tends to concentrate on the independent, sometimes obscure labels for all types of jazz and blues, including the significant recordings of various college jazz bands. Downbeat tends to give away "five stars" with abandon, and while we have taken its rating scale intact, it should be noted that the reviews are less demanding and less critical than those of other magazines.

We have noted a tendency for non-jazz magazine reviews to go overboard on the "new black jazz" (e.g., New York Times, Rolling Stone, High Fidelity) with the resulting swings of 0 to 5 on the rating scales when compared with the jazz magazines. This is easily proved with regularity as the jazz review magazines give a wide range of rankings to individual records (from low to high), while the non-jazz publications give a consistently high rating that smacks of appeasement.

The greatest single influence on jazz has been Charlie Parker and his early followers. By changing chord progressions, Parker's innovative style had set jazz free from the printed score and the arranged notes. Some may argue that other musicians were influentual at other times, but such influences only took the shape of imitation plus modest refinement. Parker influenced whole schools of jazz, and brought on bop, cool, time changes, and free jazz. To many fans, there was no jazz before Parker. Accordingly, we have divided the "best" items in the jazz category (based on the reviews themselves) into "Pre-Parker" and "post-Parker" (including Parker himself), further divided into new releases and reissues, as follows:

Pre-Parker--New

Count Basie. HAVE A NICE DAY. Daybreak DR 2005
Don Ewell. A JAZZ PORTRAIT OF THE ARTIST. Chiaroscuro CR 106
Bobby Hackett and Vic Dickenson. LIVE AT THE ROOSEVELT GRILL. Chiaroscuro CR 105
Earl Hines. MY TRIBUTE TO LOUIS. Audiophile APS 111
Earl Hines and Maxine Sullivan. LIVE AT THE OVERSEAS PRESS CLUB. Chiaroscuro CR 107
Carmen McRae. THE GREAT AMERICAN SONGBOOK (2 discs). Atlantic 2SD-904
Max Morath. PLAYS THE BEST OF SCOTT JOPLIN AND OTHER RAG CLASSICS (2 discs). Vanguard VSD 39/40
Joshua Rifkin. PIANO RAGS BY SCOTT JOPLIN. Nonesuch H 71248
Lee Wiley. BACK HOME AGAIN. Monmouth/Evergreen MES 7041

Pre-Parker--Reissues

Louis Armstrong. BEST. Parlophone PMC 7136 (E)
Count Basie. SWINGING AT THE DAISY CHAIN. Coral CP 75 (E)
Buck Clayton. BUCK 'N' THE BLUES. Vanguard VRS 8514 (E)
Vic Dickenson Septet (2 discs). Vanguard VRS 8500/1 (E)
Duke Ellington. AT HIS VERY BEST. RCA LSA 3071 (E)
Woody Herman. AT CARNEGIE HALL. Verve 2317 031 (E)

Billie Holiday. STRANGE FRUIT. Atlantic SD 1614
Art Tatum. AND HIS FRIENDS BENNY CARTER AND LOUIS BELLSON, vol. 1 (2 discs). Metro 2682 024 (E)
Lee Wiley. SINGS GEORGE GERSHWIN AND COLE PORTER. Monmouth/Evergreen MES 7034
Teddy Wilson (2 discs). Columbia GES 90054 (Canada)

Post-Parker--New

Carla Bley and Paul Haines. ESCALATOR OVER THE HILL (3 discs). Jazz Composers' Orchestra Association JCOA 3LP-EOTH
Circle. PARIS CONCERT (2 discs). ECM 1018/19 (Germany)
Ornette Coleman. TWINS. Atlantic SD 1588
Stan Kenton. TODAY (2 discs). London Phase Four BP 4179/80
John McLaughlin. INNER MOUNTING FLAME. Columbia KC 31067
Thelonious Monk. SOMETHING IN BLUE. Black Lion 2460 152 (E)
Gerry Mulligan. AGE OF STEAM. A & M SP 3036
Sonny Stitt. TUNE UP. Cobblestone CST 9013
Cecil Taylor. INNOVATIONS. Freedom 2383 094 (E)
Mike Westbrook. METROPOLIS. RCA Neon NE 10 (E)

Post-Parker--Reissues

Miles Davis (2 discs). United Artists UAS 9952
Stan Getz. DYNASTY (2 discs). Verve 6-8802-2
Dizzy Gillespie. STORY. Ember CJS 837 (E)
Al Haig. JAZZ WILL O' THE WISP. Xtra 1125 (E)
Stan Kenton. ARTISTRY IN JAZZ. Capitol M 11027
Charlie Parker. THE DEFINITIVE, vol. 1-4 (4 discs). Metro 2356 059/082/083/087 (E)
Charlie Parker. ON DIAL (6 discs). Spotlite 101/106 (E)
Sonny Rollins (2 discs). Prestige PR 24004

1999 Richard Abrams. LEVELS AND DEGREES OF LIGHT. Delmark DS 413 $5.98.
Library Journal. February 15. p667. 50w. 3

2000 Richard Abrams. YOUNG AT HEART/WISE IN TIME. Delmark DS 423 $5.98.
Coda. February. p19. 250w. 4

2001 Cannonball Adderley. THE BLACK MESSIAH. Capitol SWBO 846 (2 discs) $6.98. Cart. 8XTB 846 $13.98.
Downbeat. March 30. p21. 325w. 4½

2002 Cannonball Adderley. IN PERSON. Capitol ST 162 $5.98.
Jazz Journal. September. p28. 250w. 3

2003 Cannonball Adderley. THE PRICE YOU GOT TO PAY TO BE FREE. Capitol SWBB 636 (2 discs) $6.98. Cart. 8XWW 636 $7.98.
Jazz Journal. September. p28. 250w. 2

2004 Joe Albany. AT HOME. Spotlite JA 1 (E).
Jazz and Blues. October. p26. 525w. 4½
Jazz Journal. September. p28. 400w. 2
Records and Recordings. October. p117. 250w. 2

2005 Oscar Aleman. LEGENDARY. The Old Masters TOM 31 $6.00.
Jazz Journal. p35. 200w. 1

2006 Harold Alexander. SUNSHINE MAN. Flying Dutchman FD 10145 $5.95.
Downbeat. March 30. p21. 100w. 3½

2007 Monty Alexander. TASTE OF FREEDOM. MGM S 4736 $5.98.
Downbeat. January 20. p19. 150w. 2½

2008 ALL STAR SESSION (anthology). Capitol M 11031 $5.98. (Reissue.)
Coda. December. p15-20. 550w. 3
Downbeat. December 21. p32-3. 200w. 5
Jazz and Blues. August. p22. 350w. 2½
Jazz Journal. May. p36. 350w. 3
Previews. November. p44-5. 115w. 2½
Sound. October. p46. 125w. 3
Stereo Review. September. p78-9. 50w. 2

2009 Mose Allison. Prestige PR 24002 (2 discs) $6.98. (Reissue.) Cart. M8-2402 DP $6.95. Cass. M52402 DP $6.95.
Coda. December. p28. 200w. 4
Downbeat. October 12. p24, 32. 375w. 3½
Gramophone. December. p1231. 125w. 3
Jazz Journal. November. p24. 125w. 3
Music Journal. May. p54. 200w. 3
Previews. November. p43. 200w. 2
Rolling Stone. May 25. p68. 50w. 2½

2010 Mose Allison. WESTERN MAN. Atlantic SD 1584 $5.98. Cart. M 81584 $6.95. Cass. M 51584 $6.95.
Creem. April. p69. 750w. 3
Downbeat. February 17. p18. 200w. 5
Stereo Review. March. p101. 250w. 4

2011 Bert Ambrose. Monmouth/Evergreen. MES 7032 $5.98. (Reissue.)
Coda. April. p27-8. 225w. 4

2012 Gene Ammons. THE BLACK CAT. Prestige 10006 $5.98. Cart. PR 8-10006 $6.95. Cass. PR C 10006 $6.95.
Coda. February. p19. 250w. 4

2013 Gene Ammons/Dodo Marmarosa. JUG AND DODO. Prestige PR 24021 (2 discs) $6.98.
Sound. November. p39. 125w. 3

2014 David Amram. NO MORE WALLS. RCA VCS 7089 (2 discs) $6.98.
Downbeat. May 25. p18. 250w. 3½
Jazz Journal. December. p42. 800w. 4
New York Times--Sunday. March 12. pHF12. 100w. 1½
Rolling Stone. June 22. p62. 700w. 3

2015 Cat Anderson. CAT PLAYS AT 4 A.M. EMI C 048-50665 (France). (Reissue.)
Jazz Journal. May. p28. 175w. 3

2016 ARCHIVE OF JAZZ (anthology). Byg BYG 24 (France) (2 discs). (Reissue.)
Jazz and Blues. March. p22-5. 1000w. 2½
Jazz Journal. January. p29. 225w. 1

2017 Neil Ardley. A SYMPHONY OF AMARANTHS. Regal Zonophone SLRZ 1028 (England).
Gramophone. September. p584. 725w. 5
Jazz Journal. November. p24. 800w. 2
Records and Recordings. September. p98. 325w. 3½

2018 Louis Armstrong. AMBASSADOR SATCH. Hallmark SHM 751 (England). (Reissue.)
Hi-Fi News and Record Review. December. p2461. 25w. 3

2019 Louis Armstrong. BEST. Parlophone PMC 7136 (England). (Reissue.)
Jazz and Blues. February. p26-7. 600w. 5

2020 Louis Armstrong. GENIUS, V.1. (1923/1933). Columbia G 30416 (2 discs) $5.98. (Reissue.)
High Fidelity. January. p118. 180w. 1½
Jazz Journal. February. p34. 300w. 5
Library Journal. February 15. p666. 100w. 3

2021 Louis Armstrong. GREATEST HITS RECORDED LIVE. Brunswick BL 754169 $4.98.
Coda. April. p28. 150w. 2

2022 Louis Armstrong. I REMEMBER LOUIS. Ember CJS 838 (England). (Reissue.)
Jazz Journal. June. p28. 200w. 3

2023 Louis Armstrong. IMMORTAL SESSIONS, V.1. Saga PAN 6901 (England). (Reissue.)
Gramophone. February. p1444. 250w. 3
Jazz and Blues. January. p21. 325w. 2

2024 Louis Armstrong. IMMORTAL SESSIONS, V.2. Saga PAN 6904 (England). (Reissue.)
Gramophone. October. p783. 550w. 4
Jazz Journal. July. p26. 225w. 3
Records and Recordings. July. p95. 275w. $3\frac{1}{2}$

2025 Louis Armstrong. JULY 4, 1900-July 6, 1971. RCA VPM 6044 (2 discs) $6.98. (Reissue.)
Jazz and Blues. June. p29. 700w. $2\frac{1}{2}$
Jazz Journal. October. p24. 550w. 2
Library Journal. February 15. p666. 300w. 2

2026 Louis Armstrong. SATCHMO'S GREATEST, V.1. (1932/33). RCA 730 682 (France). (Reissue.)
Jazz and Blues. April. p22-3. 200w. $2\frac{1}{2}$

2027 Louis Armstrong. SATCHMO'S GREATEST, V.2-5. (1933/56). RCA 731 049/52 (France) (4 discs). (Reissue.)
Jazz and Blues. April. p22-3. 1250w. $3\frac{1}{2}$

2028 Louis Armstrong. WITH LUIS RUSSELL. Swaggie S 1267 (Australia). (Reissue.)
Coda. August. p16. 700w. 4

2029 Louis Armstrong and Sidney Bechet. WITH THE CLARENCE WILLIAMS BLUE FIVE. CBS 63092 (France). (Reissue.)
Downbeat. March 2. p23. 75w. 4

2030 Louis Armstrong and Duke Ellington. THE BEAUTIFUL AMERICANS. Roulette RE 108 (2 discs) $5.98. (Reissue.) Cart. 8045-108M $6.95.
Gramophone. August. p406. 300w. 1
Hi-Fi News and Record Review. September. p1681. 100w. 4
Jazz and Blues. July. p28. 425w. $1\frac{1}{2}$
Jazz Journal. June. p28. 350w. 4
Records and Recordings. June. p86. 225w. 4

2031 Art Ensemble of Chicago. CERTAIN BLACKS. America 30 AM 6098 (France).
Jazz Journal. August. p28. 350w. 1
Records and Recordings. August. p92-3. 200w. 2

2032 Art Ensemble of Chicago. A JACKSON IN YOUR HOUSE. BYG Actuel 2 (France).
Records and Recordings. July. p97-8. 525w. 3

2033 Art Ensemble of Chicago. MESSAGE FOR OUR FOLKS. BYG Actuel 28 (France).
Records and Recordings. July. p97-8. 525w. 2

2034 Art Ensemble of Chicago. PHASE ONE. America 30 AM 6116 (France).
Records and Recordings. August. p92-3. 200w. $2\frac{1}{2}$

2035 Art Ensemble of Chicago. REECE AND THE SMOOTH ONES. Byg Actuel 29 (France).
Records and Recordings. August. p93. 75w. 4

2036 Art Ensemble of Chicago. THE SPIRITUAL. Freedom 2383 098 (England).
Records and Recordings. July. p97-8. 525w. $2\frac{1}{2}$

2037 Art Ensemble of Chicago. "LES STANCES A SOPHIE." Nessa N 4 $5.98.
Stereo Review. June. p105. 100w. 2

2038 Art Ensemble of Chicago. WITH FONTELLA BRASS. America 30 AM 6117 (France).
Records and Recordings. August. p92-3. 200w. 1

2039 Harold Ashby Quartet. BORN TO SWING. Master Jazz Recordings MJR 8112 $5.50.
High Fidelity. November. p126,128. 250w. 3

2040 Donald Ashwander. Jazzology JCE 71 $5.98.
Coda. August. p16. 175w. 2

2041 Lovie Austin. AND HER BLUE SERENADERS. Fountain FJ 105 (England).
Gramophone. November. p994. 600w. 4
Jazz Journal. October. p24-5. 500w. 5

2042 Albert Ayler. THE LAST ALBUM. Impulse AS 9208 $5.98.
Coda. December. p28-9. 500w. 3

2043 Albert Ayler. IN CONCERT. Shandar 10.000/004 (France) (2 discs).
Downbeat. June 22. p18, 21. 700w. 4
Sound. September. p50. 150w. 5

2044 Albert Ayler. WITCHES AND DEVILS. Freedom 2383 081 (England).
Jazz and Blues. May. p20-1. 325w. 3

Jazz Journal. July. p26. 325w. 3
Records and Recordings. May. p100. 325w. 4

2045 THE BBC PRESENTS BRITISH JAZZ, V.1, 1924/41. BBC REC 143M (England). (Reissue.)
Gramophone. December. p1229. 500w. $4\frac{1}{2}$
Jazz Journal. December. p29-30. 200w. $3\frac{1}{2}$
Records and Recordings. December. p101. 175w. 3

2046 THE BBC PRESENTS BRITISH JAZZ, V.2, 1945/1970 (anthology). BBC REC 144 M (England).
Gramophone. December. p1229. 500w. 3
Jazz Journal. December. p29-30. 200w. $3\frac{1}{2}$
Records and Recordings. December. p101. 175w. 3

2047 Derek Baily and Dave Holland. IMPROVISATIONS FOR CELLO AND GUITAR. ECM 1013 ST (Germany).
Jazz Journal. July. p26. 275w. 3
Records and Recordings. p94. 100w. 4

2048 Mildred Bailey. ALL OF ME. Monmouth/Evergreen MES 6814 $5.98. (Reissue.)
Gramophone. October. p783. 325w. 3
Jazz Journal. March. p37. 125w. 2

2049 Kenny Ball and His Jazzmen. GOLDEN HOUR. Pye GH 512 (England).
Gramophone. April. p1780. 75w. 2
Hi-Fi News and Record Review. December. p2461. 25w. 2
Jazz Journal. July. p26. 100w. 2

2050 Kenny Ball and His Jazzmen. KING OF THE SWINGERS. Contour 6870562 (England).
Hi-Fi News and Record Review. August. p1476. 50w. 0

2051 Kenny Ball and His Jazzmen. MY VERY GOOD FRIEND... FATS WALLER. Pye NSPL 18379 (England).
Gramophone. September. p584. 125w. 3
Jazz Journal. July. p26. 100w. 2

2052 Chris Barber. GET ROLLING. Black Lion 2683 001 (England) (2 discs).
Coda. August. p17-8. 550w. 1
Gramophone. February. p1444. 375w. 2

2053 Gato Barbieri. EL PAMPERO. Flying Dutchman FD 10151 $5.95.
Rolling Stone. October 26. p56, 58. 650w. 3

2054 Gato Barbieri. FENIX. Flying Dutchman FD 10144 $5.95.
Downbeat. March 30. p21. 200w. 4½
High Fidelity. February. p119. 150w. 2½
Sound. September. p50. 100w. 4

2055 Charlie Barnet. BIG BAND, 1967. Creative World ST 1056 $5.50. (Reissue.)
Jazz Journal. October. p25. 300w. 3

2056 Bill Barron. MOTIVATION. Savoy 12303 $5.98.
Downbeat. November 23. p18. 225w. 3

2057 Gary Bartz NTU Troop. HARLEM BUSH MUSIC/TAIFA. Milestone MSP 9031 $5.98.
Downbeat. March 2. p18. 450w. 4
Stereo Review. January. p115. 300w. 3½

2058 Gary Bartz NTU Troop. HARLEM BUSH MUSIC/UHURU. Milestone MSP 9032 $5.98.
Stereo Review. July. p98. 75w. 2

2059 Robbie Basho. FALCONER'S ARM. Sonet SNTF 612 (Sweden).
Jazz Journal. December. p41. 25w. 1

2060 Count Basie. V.1, (1947). RCA 731.111 (France). (Reissue.)
Coda. April. p29. 350w. 3

2061 Count Basie. V.3. RCA 741.042 (France). (Reissue.)
Jazz Journal. September. p38. 100w. 4

2062 Count Basie. AFRIQUE. Flying Dutchman FD 10138 $5.95. Cart. M810138 $6.95. Case. M 510138 $6.95.
Coda. April. p28. 150w. 2
Gramophone. August. p406. 150w. 3
Hi-Fi News and Record Review. September. p1682. 75w. 1½
Jazz Journal. September. p28-9. 225w. 0
Records and Recordings. August. p92. 200w. 2

2063 Count Basie. AT THE SAVOY BALL ROOM, 1937. Saga PAN 6903 (England). (Reissue.)
Gramophone. June. p117. 300w. 4
High Fidelity News. May. p940. 300w. 3
Jazz and Blues. April. p24. 400w. 2
Jazz Journal. March. p30-1. 350w. 2
Records and Recordings. January. p95. 150w. 4

2064 Count Basie. BASIE ON THE BEATLES. Happy Tiger HT 1007 $4.98. Cart. M 81007 $6.95. Cass. M 51007 $6.95.
Coda. February. p19-20. 300w. 4

2065 Count Basie. BEST. Roulette RE 118 (2 discs) $5.98. Cass. 8045-118M $6.95.
Jazz Journal. December. p28. 200w. 3

2066 Count Basie. THE BIG BAND SOUND, V.1. Metro 2356 063 (England).
Jazz Journal. December. p28. 100w. $3\frac{1}{2}$

2067 Count Basie. EVERGREENS. Groove Merchant GM 2201 $5.98. Cart. 82201 $6.95. Cass. C 2201 $6.95.
High Fidelity. June. p108-9. 220w. $2\frac{1}{2}$
Saturday Review. August 12. p66. 100w. $2\frac{1}{2}$
Sound. December. p39. 50w. 1

2068 Count Basie. HAVE A NICE DAY. Daybreak DR 2005 $4.98. Cart. P8DR 2005 $6.95.
Coda. December. p29. 275w. 3
Downbeat. April 13. p22. 325w. $3\frac{1}{2}$
Gramophone. May. p1957. 350w. 5
High Fidelity. March. p114-5. 400w. 4
Jazz and Blues. April. p24-5. 375w. $3\frac{1}{2}$
Jazz Journal. April. p30. 300w. 3
Music Journal. May. p14. 200w. 4
New York Times--Sunday. August 13. pD22. 100w. 2
Records and Recordings. April. p109. 250w. 2

2069 Count Basie. HIGH VOLTAGE. BASF 20744 $5.98.
Coda. April. p28. 150w. 4
Gramophone. October. p783-4. 250w. 2
Records and Recordings. October. p117. 300w. 4

2070 Count Basie. THE KID FROM RED BANK. Roulette 2682 030 (England) (2 discs). (Reissue.)
Gramophone. August. p406. 150w. 3
Jazz and Blues. July. p28. 500w. $3\frac{1}{2}$
Jazz Journal. June. p28. 300w. 3
Records and Recordings. June. p86. 300w. 5

2071 Count Basie. SUMMIT MEETING. Roulette 2682 031 (England) (2 discs). (Reissue.)
Gramophone. August. p406. 150w. 3
Jazz and Blues. July. p28-9. 300w. 0
Jazz Journal. June. p28-9. 250w. 3

2072 Count Basie. SUPER CHIEF. Columbia G 31224 (2 discs) $5.98. (Reissue.)
Hi-Fi News and Record Review. October. p1923. 100w. 4
High Fidelity. September. p106-7. 200w. $4\frac{1}{2}$
New York Times--Sunday. July 9. pD18. 100w. 4
New York Times--Sunday. August 13. pD22. 100w. 4
Popular Music. Summer. p250. 100w. 4

Previews. October. p46. 300w. 3½
Saturday Review. August 12. p66. 100w. 2½

2073 Count Basie. SWINGING AT THE DAISY CHAIN. Coral CP 75 (England). (Reissue.)
Gramophone. October. p783-4. 300w. 4
Jazz Journal. August. p28. 300w. 5
Records and Recordings. August. p92. 100w. 4

2074 Count Basie. YOU CAN DEPEND ON BASIE. Coral CP 76 (England). (Reissue.)
Gramophone. October. p783-4. 300w. 4
Jazz Journal. August. p28. 300w. 5
Records and Recordings. August. p92. 100w. 4

2075 Johnny Bastable's Chosen Six. EXACTLY LIKE ... Joy Joys 214 (England).
Jazz and Blues. February. p29. 250w. 1

2076 Johnny Bastable's Chosen Six. SECOND ALBUM. Joy JOYS 234 (E).
Coda. August. p18. 275w. 3
Gramophone. October. p801. 100w. 2
Jazz and Blues. December. p26. 400w. 1
Jazz Journal. August. p28-9. 275w. 3
Jazz Report. No. 2. 75w. 3

2077 Jim Beatty. IN PORTLAND. NWI 2772 $5.50.
Coda. April. p29. 300w. 3

2078 BEBOP SPOKEN HERE (anthology). Capitol M 11061 $5.98. (Reissue.)
Downbeat. December 21. p30-1. 250w. 3½
Jazz Journal. July. p36-7. 500w. 3
Previews. November. p43-4. 125w. 2½

2079 Sidney Bechet. AND FRIENDS. For Discriminate Collectors FDC 1012 (Italy). (Reissue.)
Downbeat. August 17. p26-7. 125w. 5

2080 Sidney Bechet. L'EXPOSITION UNIVERSELLE DE BRUXELLES. Vogue SB 1 (France).
Downbeat. March 2. p23. 50w. 4½

2081 Sidney Bechet. GENIUS. Jazzology J 35 $5.98. (Reissue.)
Downbeat. August 17. p26-7. 125w. 5

2082 Sidney Bechet. IMMORTAL SESSIONS. Saga PAN 6900 (France). (Reissue.)
Gramophone. January. p1284. 300w. 3
Jazz and Blues. January. p21. 400w. 1

2083 Sidney Bechet. SESSIONS. Storyville 671 199 (Denmark). (Reissue.)
Jazz Journal. January. p28. 350w. 2

2084 Sidney Bechet. UNIQUE SIDNEY. CBS 63093 (France). (Reissue.)
Downbeat. March 2. p23. 25w. 3½

2085 Gordon Beck. THE SEVEN AGES OF MAN. Rediffusion ZS 115 (England).
Jazz Journal. November. p37. 50w. 0

2086 Harry Beckett. WARM SMILES. RCA SF 8225 (England).
Gramophone. March. p1620. 300w. 2½
Jazz Journal. June. p29. 625w. 3

2087 Bix Beiderbecke. BIX AND HIS GANG. Swaggie 1271 (Australia). (Reissue.)
Coda. August. p18-9. 100w. 4

2088 Bix Beiderbecke. BIX AND TRAM, 1928. Swaggie 1269 (Australia). (Reissue.)
Coda. August. p18-19. 100w. 4

2089 Bix Beiderbecke. LEGEND, V.3. RCA 731 131 (France). (Reissue.)
Jazz Journal. September. p38. 100w. 3

2090 Graeme Bell. CLASSICS OF AUSTRALIAN JAZZ. Swaggie S 1268 (Australia).
Coda. April. p28. 450w. 4

2091 Han Bennink. SOLO. Instant Composers ICP 011 (Dutch).
Records and Recordings. June. p87. 350w. 5

2092 George Benson. BEYOND THE BLUE HORIZON. CTI CTI 6009 $5.98. Cart. CT 8 6009 $6.95. Cass. CTC 6009 $6.95.
Downbeat. April 13. p22. 150w. 4
Saturday Review. June 17. p80. 100w. 2½

2093 George Benson. WHITE RABBIT. CTI CTI 6015 $5.98. Cart. CT8 6015 $6.95. Cass. CTC 6015 $6.95.
Downbeat. October 26. p16. 300w. 3
Jazz Journal. December. p28. 100w. 1
Saturday Review. June 17. p80. 100w. 2½

2094 Bunny Berigan. HIS TRUMPET AND ORCHESTRA, 1937/39. RCA LPV 581 $5.98. (Reissue.)
Downbeat. August 17. p21. 150w. 5
New York Times--Sunday. May 7. pD29. 25w. 3½

2095 BIG BAND BLAST (anthology). Sunset SLS 50249 (England). (Reissue.)
Records and Recordings. January. p95. 125w. 3

2096 BIG BAND BOUNCE (anthology). Capitol M 11057 $5.98. (Reissue.)
Downbeat. December 21. p32. 200w. 3
Jazz Journal. July. p36. 275w. 3
Previews. November. p43-4. 125w. 2½

2097 THE BIG BANDS, 1933 (anthology). Prestige PR 7645 $5.98.
Coda. August. p26-7. 1000w. 4

2098 BIG BANDS GREATEST HITS, V.1 (anthology). Columbia G 30009 (2 discs) $5.98. (Reissue.)
Jazz Report. No.2. 200w. 2½

2099 Barney Bigard/Albert Nicholas. RCA LPV 566 $5.98. (Reissue.)
Coda. February. p20. 225w. 4

2100 Acker Bilk. ACKER PIE. Pye NSPL 18375 (England).
Gramophone. May. p1957. 150w. 2½
Jazz Journal. September. p38. 150w. 1

2101 Edwin Birdsong. WHAT IT IS. Polydor 24-4071 $4.98.
Downbeat. January 20. p19. 200w. 4

2102 Walter Bishop, Jr. CORAL KEYS. Black Jazz Records BJ 2 $5.98.
Downbeat. February 17. p18. 325w. 3½
Jazz Journal. September. p38. 325w. 4

2103 BLACK & WHITE PIANO RAGTIME, 1921/39 (anthology). Biograph 12047 $5.98. (Reissue.)
High Fidelity. December. p126. 225w. 2½
Jazz Journal. December. p28-9. 425w. 3½
Music Journal. November. p56. 50w. 3

2104 Black Bottom Stompers. VJM LC 735 (England).
Jazz Journal. August. p29. 225w. 0
Records and Recordings. October. p117-8. 175w. 1

2105 Eubie Blake, V.1. Eubie Blake Music EBM 1 $5.95.
High Fidelity. June. p108. 275w. 3
Music Journal. November. p56. 100w. 4
Previews. October. p45. 200w. 3½
Ragtime. M/J. p6-7. 1000w. 5
Stereo Review. June. p105. 225w. 4

2106 Eubie Blake. THE EIGHTY SIX YEARS OF EUBIE BLAKE. Columbia C25 847 $7.98.
Coda. February. p20. 750w. 5

2107 Carla Bley and Paul Haines. ESCALATOR OVER THE HILL. Jazz Composers Orchestra Association JCOA 3 LP-EOTH (3 discs) $14.97.
Downbeat. December 7. p16. 600w. 5
Jazz and Blues. June. p26-7. 1200w. 5
Jazz Journal. June. p29-30. 450w. 4
Records and Recordings. June. p86-7. 650w. 4

2108 Paul Bley. Radio Canada Int. Trans 305 (Canada).
Jazz Journal. December. p42. 150w. 2

2109 Paul Bley. BALLADS. ECM 1010 (Germany).
Downbeat. April 27. p16. 325w. 5
Downbeat. May 11. p26. 250w. 3½

2110 Paul Bley. THE FABULOUS. America 30 AM 6120 (France).
Jazz Journal. October. p25-6. 550w. 4
Records and Recordings. October. p120. 300w. 3

2111 Paul Bley. IMPROVISIE. America 30 AM 6121 (France).
Jazz Journal. October. p26. 575w. 3
Records and Recordings. October. p120. 250w. 3½

2112 Paul Bley. RAMBLIN'. Byg Actuel 529.317 (France).
Downbeat. April 27. p16. 325w. 4½

2113 Paul Bley. SYNTHESIZER SHOW. Milestone MSP 9033 $5.98.
Downbeat. March 16. p22. 450w. 3

2114 Blue Angel Jazz Club. PROCEEDINGS, 1968/69, V.1/2 (anthology). Blue Angel BAJC 505/506 (2 discs) $10.00.
Downbeat. January 20. p27-8. 325w. 3

2115 Blue Angel Jazz Club. PROCEEDINGS, 1970 (anthology). Blue Angel BAJC 507/508 (2 discs) $10.00
Coda. October. p25-6. 350w. 5
Library Journal. August. p2557. 125w. 3½

2116 William Bolcom. HELIOTROPE BOUQUET PIANO RAGS, 1900-1970. Nonesuch H 71257 $2.98.
Coda. August. p19. 225w. 3
Gramophone. June. p122. 225w. 4
High Fidelity. October. p82-3. 500w. 3
Jazz Journal. March. p34-5. 125w. 3
Jazz Report. No.2. 125w. 2½
Ragtimer. M/A. p16-17. 1200w. 4

2117 Boots and His Buddies. RCA 741.043 (France). (Reissue.)
Jazz Journal. September. p38. 175w. 3½

2118 Boots and His Buddies. SAN ANTONIO JAZZ, 1935/36. TAX 8002 $6.00. (Reissue.)
Coda. August. p19. 150w. 3

2119 Boswell Sisters. 1932/34. Biograph BLP C 3 $5.98. (Reissue.)
High Fidelity. October. p124. 450w. 2½
Jazz Journal. September. p29. 325w. 5
Music Journal. December. p15. 100w. 3½

2120 Ruby Braff. HEAR ME TALKIN'. Black Lion 2460 127 (England).
Gramophone. February. p1444. 200w. 1½
Hi-Fi News and Record Reviews. September. p1686. 225w. 2
Jazz and Blues. January. p21-2. 300w. 2½

2121 Dollar Brand. ANATOMY OF A SOUTH AFRICAN VILLAGE. Freedom 2383 099 (England). (Reissue.)
Gramophone. May. p1957. 200w. 3
Jazz and Blues. June. p27. 325w. 3½
Jazz Journal. April. p30. 250w. 4
Records and Recordings. April. p111. 100w. 3½

2122 Anthony Braxton. DONNA LEE. America 30 AM 6122 (France).
Jazz Journal. October. p26. 475w. 4
Records and Recordings. October. p120-1. 200w. 2½

2123 Anthony Braxton. FOR ALTO. Delmark DS 420/421 (2 discs) $5.98.
Audio. December. p96-7. 350w. 4

2124 Anthony Braxton. THIS TIME ... Byg Actuel 47 (France).
Jazz and Blues. March. p25. 500w. 4½
Records and Recordings. August. p93. 350w. 4

2125 Anthony Braxton. THREE COMPOSITIONS OF NEW JAZZ. Delmark DS 415 $5.98.
Library Journal. February 15. p667. 50w. 3

2126 Brewer's Droop. OPENING TIME. RCA SF 8301 (England).
Blues Unlimited. December. p28. 50w. 2

2127 Clifford Brown. BIG BAND IN PARIS. Prestige PR 7840 $4.98. (Reissue.)
Coda. February. p20-1. 350w. 4

2128 Clifford Brown. IN PARIS. Prestige 24020 (2 discs) $6.98. (Reissue.)
Stereo Review. December. p110. 300w. 2

2129 Marion Brown. AFTERNOON OF A GEORGIA FAUN. ECM 1004 ST (Germany).
Coda. April. p15-17. 2700w. 5

2130 Dave Brubeck. ADVENTURES IN TIME. Columbia G 30625 (2 discs) $5.98. (Reissue.)
Creem. January. p66-7. 300w. 4
Downbeat. May 25. p18. 200w. 5
Library Journal. June 1. p2067. 200w. 2½

2131 Dave Brubeck. ON CAMPUS. Columbia KG 31298 (2 discs) $6.98. (Reissue.)
New York Times--Sunday. July 9. pD18. 50w. 2½

2132 Dave Brubeck. SUMMIT SESSION. Columbia C 30522 $4.98. Cart. CA 30522 $6.98.
Audio. December. p99-100. 700w. 3½

2133 Dave Brubeck and Gerry Mulligan. IN CINCINNATI. Decca DL 710181 $5.98. Cart. 610181 $6.98. Cass. C 7310181 $6.98.
Stereo Review. February. p115. 75w. ½

2134 Dave Brubeck. LAST SET AT NEWPORT. Atlantic SD 1607 $5.98.
Downbeat. September 14. p16. 400w. 4
Gramophone. December. p1232-3. 125w. 3
High Fidelity. September. p107. 250w. 2½
Jazz Journal. September. p29. 150w. 2
Stereo Review. November. p94, 96. 200w. 2

2135 Dave Brubeck and Gerry Mulligan. LIVE IN CONCERT AT BERLIN. Columbia GES 90100 (2 discs) $5.98 (Canada).
Ontario Library Review. December. p243. 25w. 3½

2136 Bobby Bryant. SWAHILI STRUT. Cadet 50011 $5.98.
Downbeat. March 30. p22. 200w. 4

2137 Milt Buckner. PLAY CHORDS. BASF 20631 $5.98. Cart. 40631 $6.98. Cass. 30631 $6.98.
Canadian Stereo Guide. Summer. p66. 100w. 3
Music Journal. November. p40. 25w. 4

2138 Dennis Budimir. THE SESSION WITH ALBERT. Revelation S14 $4.98.
Downbeat. June 8. p19. 275w. 3½
Jazz Journal. March. p37. 225w. 3

2139 Papu Bue and His Viking Jazz Band. LIVE IN DRESDEN. Storyville SLP 815/6 (Denmark) (2 discs).
Jazz Journal. November. p25. 500w. 1

2140 Dave Burrell. AFTER LOVE. America 30 AM 6115 (France).
Jazz and Blues. June. p30. 250w. 0

2141 Kenny Burrell. NIGHT SONG. Verve V6-8751 $5.98.
Coda. February. p22. 250w. 2

2142 Gary Burton. ALONE AT LAST. Atlantic SD 1598 $5.98. Cart. M 81598 $6.95. Cass. M 51598 $6.95.
Coda. August. p19-20. 325w. 3
Downbeat. June 8. p19-20. 525w. 4
Gramophone. December. p1231. 175w. 3½
High Fidelity. March. p114. 125w. 2½
Jazz Journal. October. p27-8. 600w. 4
Records and Recordings. October. p117. 150w. 0

2143 Gary Burton and Stephane Grappelly. PARIS ENCOUNTER. Atlantic SD 1597 $5.98.
Crawdaddy. August. p20. 750w. 4
Gramophone. December. p1231. 175w. 3½
High Fidelity. July. p102. 275w. 3
Jazz Journal. November. p30. 250w. 4
New York Times--Sunday. July 9. pD18. 75w. 2½
Saturday Review. May 20. p47. 100w. 2½
Stereo Review. September. p80. 200w. 3

2144 Don Byas. ANTHROPOLOGY. Black Lion 2460 160 (England). (Reissue.)
Gramophone. December. p1231. 275w. 4
Jazz and Blues. November. p24. 350w. 3
Jazz Journal. November. p25. 300w. 2
Records and Recordings. November. p108-9. 175w. 3½

2145 Charlie Byrd. FOR ALL WE KNOW. Columbia G 30622 (2 discs) $5.98.
Audio. March. p81. 50w. 3

2146 Charlie Byrd and Aldemaro Romero. ONDA NUEVA - THE NEW WAVE. Columbia C 31025 $4.98.
Gramophone. September. p579. 325w. 4

2147 Donald Byrd. ETHIOPIAN KNIGHTS. Blue Note BST 84380 $5.98.
Coda. December. p29. 650w. 2
Downbeat. December 7. p16. 400w. 2
Jazz Journal. July. p27. 300w. 0
Previews. November. p45-6. 75w. 1

2148 CALIFORNIA CONCERT (anthology). CTL CTX 2X 2 (2 discs) $11.96.
Coda. August. p20. 500w. 1
Downbeat. April 27. p22. 275w. 3
High Fidelity. May. p115-6. 100w. 2½

2149 Hadley Caliman. IAPETUS. Mainstream MRL 342 $5.98.
Downbeat. April 27. p16. 250w. 4½
Jazz Journal. May. p34. 100w. 0

2150 Rudiger Carl, Inc. KING ALCOHOL. Free Music Production FMP 0060 (Germany).
Records and Recordings. October. p121. 200w. 1

2151 Doug Carn. SPIRIT OF THE NEW LAND. Black Jazz BJ 8 $5.98.
Downbeat. December 7. p18. 225w. 4

2152 Benny Carter. MELANCHOLY BENNY. Tax 8004 $6.00. (Reissue.)
Sound. November. p39. 125w. 5

2153 Benny Carter. 1933. Prestige PR 7643 $4.98. (Reissue.)
Coda. August. p20-1. 575w. 3

2154 Betty Carter. Betcar 1001 $5.00.
Coda. August. p21. 325w. 4

2155 Casa Loma Orchestra. SHALL WE SWING? Creative World ST 1055 $5.50.
Jazz Journal. September. p38. 125w. 0

2156 Serge Chaloff. BLUE SERGE. Capitol M 11032 $5.98. (Reissue.)
Coda. December. p15-20. 550w. 4
Downbeat. December 21. p30. 200w. 5
Jazz and Blues. August. p22. 300w. 4
Jazz Journal. June. p11. 350w. 4
Previews. November. p44-5. 115w. 2½
Sound. October. p37. 125w. 3
Stereo Review. September. p78-9. 50w. 2

2157 Paul Chambers. FIRST BASSMAN. Joy JOYS 208 (England).
Records and Recordings. p103. 100w. 3

2158 Don Cherry. ETERNAL RHYTHM. BASF 20690 $5.98.
Downbeat. November. p18. 475w. 5
Music Journal. November. p40. 25w. 2½

2159 Don Cherry. MU - SECOND PART. BYG 529 331 (France).
Jazz Journal. August. p29. 450w. 4

2160 Bob Chester and His Orchestra. 1939/42. Bandstand BRS 71030 $6.00.
New York Times--Sunday. October 8. pD34. 300w. 3½

2161 CHICAGO JAZZ, 1925/29, V.2 (anthology). Biograph BLP 12043 $5.95. (Reissue.)

Jazz Journal. August. p29-30. 400w. 3
Music Journal. November. p62. 100w. 3

2162 THE CHICAGOANS. Metro 2356.017 (England). (Reissue.)
Jazz Journal. April. p30-1. 300w. 4

2163 Charlie Christian. SOLO FLIGHT. Columbia G 30779 (2 discs) $5.98.
Downbeat. June 8. p18. 900w. 5
Jazz Report. No.1. 250w. 4
Music Journal. June. p37. 50w. 4
New York Times--Sunday. May 7. pD29. 50w. 4
Previews. October. p45. 225w. 2
Saturday Review. September 30. p83. 75w. 2½
Sound. August. p50. 200w. 3

2164 Circle. PARIS CONCERT. ECM 1018/19ST (2 discs) (Germany).
Jazz Journal. July. p27-8. 450w. 5
Records and Recordings. August. p93-4. 300w. 2½
Sound. November. p39. 150w. 5

2165 Clarke-Boland Big Band. ALL BLUES. MPS 15-288 (Germany).
Coda. June. p28. 200w. 4

2166 Clarke-Boland Big Band. ALL SMILES. BASF 29686 $5.98.
Canadian Stereo Guide. Summer. p66. 100w. 2½
High Fidelity. November. p128. 300w. 3½
Music Journal. November. p40. 150w. 4
Records and Recordings. October. p118. 100w. 2
Saturday Review. November 4. p92. 100w. 3

2167 Clarke-Boland Big Band. AT HER MAJESTY'S PLEASURE. Black Lion 2460 131 (England).
Gramophone. January. p1284. 275w. 3
Hi-Fi News and Record Review. May. p940. 200w. 2
Jazz and Blues. February. p26. 300w. 3½
Jazz Journal. January. p29. 350w. 3
Records and Recordings. January. p95. 75w. 1

2168 Clarke-Boland Big Band. MORE SMILES. BASF 29746 $5.98.
Coda. June. p29. 200w. 3
Gramophone. October. p784. 200w. 4

2169 Clarke-Boland Big Band. OFF LIMITS. Polydor 2310.147 (England).
Gramophone. October. p784. 250w. 4
Jazz and Blues. August. p30. 175w. 2½
Jazz Journal. June. p30-1. 450w. 3
Records and Recordings. June. p86. 300w. 1½

2170 Buck Clayton. BUCK 'N' THE BLUES. Vanguard VRS 8514 (England). (Reissue.)
Jazz and Blues. December. p27. 400w. 4
Jazz Journal. November. p26. 300w. 5
Records and Recordings. December. p102. 175w. 5

2171 No Entry.

2172 Larry Clinton. 1938-1941. Swing Era 1006 $5.50. (Reissue.)
Coda. August. p21. 350w. 2

2173 Larry Clinton. A STUDY, 1939/41. Bandstand BRS 7102. (Reissue.)
New York Times--Sunday. October 8. pD34. 200w. 3½

2174 Todd Cochran. WORLDS AROUND THE SUN. United Artists UAS 5596 $5.98.
Rolling Stone. September 11. p66. 500w. 2½

2175 Tony Coe and Brian Lemon. "77" SEU 12/41 (England).
Coda. August. p21-2. 400w. 2
Gramophone. January. p1284. 200w. 3
Records and Recordings. January. p94. 125w. 1

2176 Cohelmec Ensemble. HIPPOTIGRIS ZEBRA ZEBRA. Saravah SH 10024 $5.00.
Jazz and Blues. April. p25. 350w. 3

2177 Nat King Cole. TRIO DAYS. Capitol M 11033 $5.98. (Reissue.)
Coda. December. p15-20. 550w. 3
Downbeat. December 21. p31-2. 150w. 5
Jazz and Blues. August. p22-3. 250w. 3
Jazz Journal. June. p11. 350w. 2
Previews. November. p44-5. 115w. 2½
Saturday Review. September. p78-9. 50w. 3
Sound. October. p37, 46. 75w. 2

2178 Bill Coleman and Ben Webster. SWINGIN' IN LONDON. Black Lion 2460 128 (England).
Gramophone. November. p994. 300w. 2
Jazz and Blues. November. p26. 250w. 2
Jazz Journal. November. p26-7. 250w. 1
Records and Recordings. November. p108. 150w. 4

2179 Ornette Coleman. CRISIS. Impulse AS 9187 $5.98. Cart. M 89187 $6.95. Cass. M 59187 $6.95.
Jazz Journal. November. p27. 375w. 3
Sound. December. p39. 75w. 4

2180 Ornette Coleman. IN EUROPE, V.1/2. Freedom 2383 090/91 (2 discs) (England). (Reissue.)

Jazz and Blues. May. p21. 475w. 4
Jazz Journal. April. p31. 275w. 4
Records and Recordings. p111. 100w. 5

2181 Ornette Coleman. LOVE CALL. Blue Note BST 84356 $5.98. Cart. 9139 $6.98. Cass. C 1139 $6.98.
Coda. February. p22. 175w. 4

2182 Ornette Coleman. SCIENCE FICTION. Columbia KC 31061 $5.98.
Crawdaddy. April 12. p19. 1000w. 4
Creem. May. p69-70. 750w. 3
Downbeat. April 27. p17-8. 625w. 5
Previews. October. p45. 225w. 3
Sound. August. p49. 150w. 3

2183 Ornette Coleman. SKIES OF AMERICA. Columbia KC 31562 $5.98.
New York Times--Sunday. July 9. pD18. 175w. $2\frac{1}{2}$
Rolling Stone. August 17. p52, 54. 750w. 3

2184 Ornette Coleman. TWINS. Atlantic SD 1588 $5.98. Cart. M 81588 $6.98. Cass. M 51588 $6.98.
Creem. January. p66. 400w. 5
Downbeat. May 25. p18, 21. 175w. 5
Jazz and Blues. October. p26. 475w. $4\frac{1}{2}$
Jazz Journal. September. p29-30. 450w. 4
Records and Recordings. July. p98. 200w. 5
Stereo Review. May. p96. 250w. 3

2185 Johnny Coles. KATUMBO DANCE. Mainstream MRL 346 $5.98.
Downbeat. April 27. p18. 200w. $4\frac{1}{2}$
Jazz Journal. May. p34. 100w. 1

2186 Collegiate Neophonic Orchestra. SOUTHERN CALIFORNIA. Neophonic 6-70-1 (2 discs) $6.00.
Coda. February. p27. 150w. 3

2187 Max Collie Rhythm Aces. IN CONCERT. Reality R 105 1 W (England).
Jazz Journal. November. p27. 250w. 0

2188 Graham Collier. DOWN ANOTHER ROAD. Fontana SFJL 922 (England).
Coda. June. p23. 250w. 3

2189 Graham Collier. MOSAICS. Philips 6308.051 (England).
Coda. June. p23. 250w. 3

2190 Alice Coltrane. LORD OF LORDS. Impulse AS 9224 $5.98. Cart. M 89224 $6.95. Cass. M 59224 $6.95.
Popular Music. Fall. p1. 25w. 3

2191 Alice Coltrane. PTAH, THE EL DAOUD. Impulse AS 9196 $5.98. Cart. M 89196 $6.95. Cass. M 59196 $6.95.
Coda. February. p23. 425w. 4

2192 Alice Coltrane. UNIVERSAL CONSCIOUSNESS. Impulse AS 9210 $5.98. Cart. M 89210 $6.95. Cass. M 54210 $6.95.
Coda. August. p22. 175w. 3
Downbeat. February 3. p18. 450w. 5
Jazz Journal. February. p34. 250w. 3

2193 Alice Coltrane. WORLD GALAXY. Impulse AS 9218 $5.98. Cart. M 89218 $6.95. Cass. M 59218 $6.95.
Downbeat. May 25. p21. 275w. 2½

2194 JOHN COLTRANE. Prestige PR 24003 (2 discs) $6.98. Cart. M 82403 DP $9.95. Cass. M 52403 DP $4.95.
Downbeat. October 22. p24-32. 375w. 4½
Jazz and Blues. December. p27-8. 600w. 5
Jazz Journal. November. p27. 400w. 3
Rolling Stone. May 25. p68. 200w. 2½
Records and Recordings. November. p109. 75w. 4

2195 John Coltrane. LIVE IN SEATTLE. Impulse AS 9202-2 (2 discs) $6.98. Cart. M 89202 $6.95. Cass. M 59202 $6.95.
Coda. February. p24. 450w. 4

2196 Ken Colyer. THE EARLY DAYS. Storyville. SLP 144 (Denmark). (Reissue.)
Jazz Journal. October. p28. 275w. 3

2197 Ken Colyer. RAGTIME REVISITED. Joy JOYS 194 (England). (Reissue.)
Jazz Report. No. 2. 75w. 3

2198 Eddie Condon. JAZZ AS IT SHOULD BE PLAYED. Jazzology J 50 $5.98. (Reissue.)
Downbeat. March 16. p22. 550w. 0

2199 Eddie Condon. TOWN HALL CONCERTS. Jazum 4 $6.00. (Reissue.)
Coda. June. p23. 550w. 4
Jazz Journal. April. p37. 150w. 3
Library Journal. May 15. p1793. 50w. 2½

2200 Eddie Condon. THE TOWN HALL CONCERTS, 1944-45, featuring Pee Wee Russell. Chiaroscuro CR 108 $5.98. (Reissue.)
High Fidelity. July. p104. 150w. 2½
Stereo Review. July. p70. 500w. 4½

2201 Eddie Condon. WITH WILD BILL DAVISON AND GEORGE BRUNIES. Fat Cat's Jazz FCJ 114 $5.50.
Jazz Report. No.1. 250w. 4

2202 Contraband. TIME AND SPACE. Epic E 30814 $5.98.
Downbeat. December 7. p19. 300w. 4

2203 Corky Corcoran. PLAYS SOMETHING. RCS Records RCS 2555 $5.50.
High Fidelity. December. p128. 150w. 1
Saturday Review. June 17. p80. 75w. 2½

2204 Chick Corea. A.R.C. ECM 1009 ST (Germany).
Downbeat. May 11. p26. 250w. 4½

2205 Chick Corea. PIANO IMPROVISATIONS, V.1. ECM 1014 ST (Germany).
Downbeat. May 11. p26. 250w. 5
Jazz and Blues. July. p30. 300w. 3½
Jazz Journal. October. p28-9. 150w. 3½

2206 Chick Corea. RETURN TO FOREVER. ECM 1022 ST (Germany).
Jazz Journal. November. p27-8. 350w. 4
Records and Recordings. November. p109. 200w. 2½

2207 Chick Corea. SUNDANCE. Grove Merchant GM 2022 $5.98. Cart. 82202 $6.95. Cass. C 2202 $6.95.
Downbeat. May 25. p21-2. 100w. 2

2208 Larry Coryell. BAREFOOT BOY. Flying Dutchman FD 10139 $5.95. Cart. M 810139 $6.95. Cass. M 510139 $6.95.
Coda. June. p29. 475w. 2
Jazz Journal. September. p30. 175w. 0

2209 Larry Coryell. FAIRYLAND. Flying Dutchman M 51-5000 $5.95.
Downbeat. August 17. p21. 250w. 2½

2210 Larry Coryell. OFFERING. Vanguard VSD 79319 $5.98.
Popular Music. Fall. p90. 50w. 1½
Rolling Stone. October. p58, 60. 650w. 3

2211 Clifford Coulter. DO IT NOW, WORRY ABOUT IT LATER. Impulse AS 9216 $5.98. Cart. M 89216 $6.95. Cass M 59216 $6.95.
Downbeat. April 27. p19. 75w. 2

2212 Stanley Cowell. BRILLIANT CIRCLES. Freedom 2383 092 (England).
Gramophone. May. p1956. 300w. 3½

Jazz and Blues. May. p21. 150w. 1
Jazz Journal. April. p31. 325w. 3

2213 Crawford-Ferguson's Night Owls. SOUNDS OF THE RIVER. Audiophile AP 109 $5.95.
Coda. June. p24. 375w. 3
Downbeat. April 27. p21-2. 250w. 0
Jazz Report. No.1. 200w. 2
Music Journal. March. p64. 50w. 1

2214 BOB CROSBY. Jazum $6.00. (Reissue.)
Coda. June. p25. 375w. 4
Jazz Journal. April. p37. 200w. 3
Library Journal. May 15. p1793. 50w. 2½

2215 CROSSCURRENTS (anthology). Capitol M 11060 $5.98. (Reissue.)
Downbeat. December 21. p27, 29. 450w. 5
Jazz Journal. July. p36. 375w. 3
Previews. November. p43-4. 125w. 2½

2216 Crusaders. CRUSADERS I. Blue Thumb BTS 6001 (2 discs) $6.98.
Downbeat. May 11. p21. 125w. 2½
High Fidelity. June. p110. 25w. 2½

2217 Jim Cullum. THE COLLEGE STREET CAPER. Audiophile AP 114 $5.95.
Coda. August. p22. 150w. 2
Downbeat. March 16. p22-3. 175w. 4
Jazz Journal. September. p38. 175w. 3
Jazz Report. No.1. 250w. 1
Music Journal. March. p57, 64. 100w. 2

2218 Jim Cullum. ELOQUENT CLARINET. Audiophile AP 107 $5.95.
Coda. August. p22. 150w. 2
Downbeat. March 16. p22-3. 175w. 5

2219 Albert Dailey. THE DAY AFTER THE DAWN. Columbia KC 31278 $5.98.
Creem. August. p66. 25w. 0
Downbeat. October 26. p16. 350w. 5

2220 Daly-Wilson Big Band. LIVE! Columbia SCXO 7979 (Australia).
Jazz and Blues. August. p31. 300w. 3

2221 Tadd Dameron. MEMORIAL ALBUM. Prestige PR 7842 $4.98. (Reissue.)
Coda. February. p24. 450w. 3

2222 Wallace Davenport. DARKNESS ON THE DELTA. Fat Cat's Jazz FCJ 122 $5.50.
Downbeat. July 20. p33. 650w. 4

2223 Eddie Davis/Johnny Griffin. TOUGH TENORS AGAIN 'N' AGAIN. MPS 15-283 (Germany).
Coda. June. p25. 300w. 4

2224 Miles Davis. United Artists UAS 9952 (2 discs) $6.98. (Reissue.) Cart. X-04017 $7.98.
Downbeat. June 22. p22. 550w. 5
Jazz Journal. March. p31. 525w. 5
Library Journal. January 1. p55. 150w. 4

2225 Miles Davis. Prestige PR 24001 (2 discs) $6.98. Cart. M 82401 DP $9.98. Cass. M 52401 DP $9.98. (Reissue.)
Downbeat. October 12. p24-32. 375w. 5
Jazz and Blues. November. p24. 600w. 3
Jazz Journal. November. p28. 650w. 5
Records and Recordings. November. p109. 75w. 4
Rolling Stone. May 25. p68. 175w. $2\frac{1}{2}$

2226 Miles Davis. BLUE MOODS. Fantasy 86001 $4.98. (Reissue.)
Jazz Journal. July. p28. 125w. 0

2227 Miles Davis. THE COMPLETE BIRTH OF THE COOL. Capitol M 11026 $5.98. (Reissue.)
Coda. December. p15-20. 550w. 5
Downbeat. December 21. p29. 100w. 5
Jazz and Blues. June. p7. 275w. 5
Jazz Journal. May. p35. 500w. 5
Previews. November. p44-5. 115w. $2\frac{1}{2}$
Sound. October. p37. 150w. 3
Stereo Review. September. p78-9. 50w. 2

2228 Miles Davis. IN A SILENT WAY. Columbia CS 9875 $4.98. Cart. 18-10-0922 $6.98.
Crawdaddy. November. p86. 1500w. 4

2229 Miles Davis. LIVE/EVIL. Columbia G 30954 (2 discs) $5.98. Cart. GA 30954 $6.98. Cass. GT 30954 $6.98.
Coda. August. p22-25. 1200w. 4
Creem. March. p48. 900w. 4
Downbeat. April 13. p22, 25. 1600w. $2\frac{1}{2}$
Jazz Journal. April. p32. 250w. 5
Previews. September. p42. 250w. $2\frac{1}{2}$
Records and Recordings. March. p124-6. 300w. 2
Rolling Stone. January 20. p50, 52. 500w. 3

2230 Miles Davis. OLEO. Prestige PR 7848 $4.98.
Coda. February. p25. 475w. 4

2231 Miles Davis. ON THE CORNER. Columbia KC 31906 $5.98.
Rolling Stone. Dec. 7. p62. 1600w. 3

2232 Nathan Davis. THE SIXTH SENSE IN THE ELEVENTH HOUR. Segue Seg 1002 $6.00.
Downbeat. October 26. p16-7. 500w. 5

2233 Richard Davis. THE PHILOSOPHY OF THE SPIRITUAL. Cobblestone CST 9003 $5.98. Cart. M 89003 $6.95. Cass. M 59003 $6.95.
Downbeat. August 17. p21. 150w. 3½

2234 Dawn of the Century Ragtime Orchestra. Arcane 601 $5.25.
High Fidelity. December. p130. 175w. 2½

2235 Mario Di Marco. UN AUTUNNO A PARIGI. Modern Jazz Record MJC 0087 (Italy).
Coda. August. p25. 300w. 2

2236 VIC DICKENSON SEPTET. Vanguard VRS 8520/21 (England) (2 discs). (Reissue.)
Gramophone. December. p1231. 325w. 4
Jazz and Blues. November. p30. 750w. 5
Jazz Journal. October. p29. 450w. 4

2237 Johnny Dodds and Tommy Ladnier. 1923/28. Biograph BLP 12024 $5.98. (Reissue.)
Jazz Report. No.2. 200w. 4

2238 Bill Dodge. SWING '34, V.1 and 2. Melodeon MLP 7328/29 (2 discs) $11.96. (Reissue.)
Jazz Journal. February. p34-5. 425w. 4

2239 ERIC DOLPHY. Prestige PR 24008 (2 discs) $6.98. (Reissue.) Cart. M82408 DP $9.98. Cass. M52408 DP $9.98.
Creem. August. p67. 25w. 4
Downbeat. October 12. p24-32. 375w. 4½
New York Times--Sunday. May 7. pD29. 25w. 3
Previews. November. 100w. 2½
Rolling Stone. May 25. 125w. 4

2240 Eric Dolphy. IRON MAN. Douglas Z 30873 $4.98.
Creem. January. p66. 400w. 2½

2241 Eric Dolphy. AT THE FIVE SPOT, V.2. Prestige PR 7826 $4.98.
Coda. August. p25. 575w. 4

2242 Lou Donaldson. COSMOS. Blue Note. BST 84370 $5.98. Cart. 9159 $6.98.
Creem. April. p68. 350w. 2

Downbeat. February 17. p19. 150w. $3\frac{1}{2}$

2243 Tommy Dorsey. THIS IS TOMMY DORSEY. RCA VPM 6038 (2 discs) $6.98. (Reissue.)
Coda. April. p26. 125w. 2
Downbeat. February 3. p24-26. 325w. $2\frac{1}{2}$
Library Journal. March 1. p857. 50w. 2

2244 Bob Downes Open Music. DIVERSIONS. Openian BDOM 001 (England).
Jazz Journal. June. p31. 400w. 4
Records and Recordings. August. p94. 375w. 3

2245 Jack Duff and Bobby Breen. IF THE CAP FITS ... WEAR IT. York Records FYK 407 (England).
Gramophone. November. p994. 300w. 2
Jazz Journal. November. p28. 150w. 0

2246 Dutch Swing College Band. DOCTOR JAZZ. Philips 6440. 087 (England).
Gramophone. October. p784. 275w. 1

2247 John Eardley and J.R. Monterose. BODY AND SOUL. Munich 6803 635 M 3 (Germany).
Jazz Journal. August. p30. 325w. 4

2248 Charles Earland. INTENSITY. Prestige 10041 $5.98. Cart. M81041 $6.95. Cass. M 51041 $6.95.
Downbeat. October 26. p17. 200w. 3

2249 EARLY MODERN (anthology). Milestone MSP 9035 $5.98. (Reissue.)
Downbeat. May 25. p25. 200w. 4

2250 ECHOES FROM NEW ORLEANS, V. 2 (anthology). Storyville SLP 212 (Denmark).
Jazz and Blues. December. p28. 475w. 0

2251 Billy Eckstine. TOGETHER. Spotlite 100 (England) (Reissue).
Coda. June. p25. 375w. 4
Jazz Journal. March. p32. 600w. 5
Records and Recordings. May. p102. 250w. 3

2252 Kurt Edelhagen. THE BIG BAND SOUND. Carnival 2941 305 (England).
Jazz Journal. November. p28-9. 275w. 1

2253 Roy Eldridge. THE NIFTY CAT. Master Jazz MJR 8110 $5.50.
Jazz and Blues. October. p25. 200w. 3
Sound. March. p19. 100w. 4

2254 Duke Ellington. AT HIS VERY BEST. RCA LSA 3071 (England). (Reissue.)
Hi-Fi News and Record Reviews. November. p2201. 50w. 3½
Jazz Journal. October. p29. 125w. 5

2255 Duke Ellington. THE BIG BAND SOUND. Carnival 2941 202 (England). (Reissue.)
Gramophone. October. p784-5. 425w. 4
Jazz Journal. September. p30. 225w. 3
Records and Recordings. September. p96. 150w. 4

2256 Duke Ellington. CARNEGIE HALL CONCERT, DECEMBER 11, 1943. Saga PAN 6902 (England). (Reissue.)
Gramophone. May. p1956. 300w. 2
Jazz and Blues. April. p25. 350w. 3
Jazz Journal. March. p32. 225w. 4
Records and Recordings. January. p95. 150w. 4

2257 Duke Ellington. THE FAR EAST SUITE. RCA LSA 3063 (England).
Jazz Journal. October. p29-30. 500w. 2
Records and Recordings. October. p118. 75w. 4

2258 Duke Ellington. IN A MELLOTONE. RCA LSA 3069 (England).
Jazz and Blues. February. p27. 275w. 4
Jazz and Blues. November. p24-5. 200w. 4
Jazz Journal. October. p29. 125w. 4
Records and Recordings. October. p118. 75w. 4

2259 Duke Ellington. INTEGRALE, Volume 1. RCA 731.043 (France). (Reissue.)
Coda. June. p25-6. 300w. 4

2260 Duke Ellington. INTEGRALE, Volume 3. RCA 741.029 (France). (Reissue.)
Coda. June. p25-6. 300w. 4

2261 Duke Ellington. LATIN AMERICAN SUITE. Fantasy 8419 $4.98.
Sound. December. p39. 75w. 1

2262 Duke Ellington. MASTERPIECES, 1928/30. RCA 730.576 (France). (Reissue.)
Jazz and Blues. February. p27-8. 425w. 3

2263 Duke Ellington. MONOLOGUE, 1947/51. CBS 63563 (France). (Reissue.)
Downbeat. March 2. p22. 50w. 4

2264 Duke Ellington. NEW ORLEANS SUITE. Atlantic SD 1580 $5.98. Cart. M 81580 $6.95. Cass. M51580 $6.95.
Coda. February. p25-6. 525w. 4

2265 Duke Ellington. PIANO REFLECTIONS, 1953. Capitol M 11059 $5.98. (Reissue.)
Downbeat. December 21. p31. 250w. 3½
Jazz Journal. July. p36. 450w. 2
Previews. November. 125w. 2½

2266 Duke Ellington. THE POPULAR. RCA LSP 3576 $5.98. Cart. P85-1198 $6.98.
Hi-Fi News and Record Reviews. November. p2201. 50w. 3½
Jazz Journal. November. p29. 250w. 3

2267 Duke Ellington. THIS IS DUKE ELLINGTON. RCA VPM 6042 (2 discs) $6.98. (Reissue.)
Coda. April. p26. 125w. 2
Downbeat. February 2. p24-26. 325w. 2½
Library Journal. March 1. p857. 50w. 2½

2268 Duke Ellington. TOGO BRAVA SUITE. United Artists UXS-92 (2 discs) $5.98.
Saturday Review. November 4. p92. 150w. 3½

2269 Don Ellis. TEARS OF JOY. Columbia G 30927 (2 discs) $5.98.
Coda. June. p26-27. 725w. 3
Coda. June. p27. 400w. 1
Downbeat. March 30. p22, 24. 400w. 4
Library Journal. February 15. p666-7. 300w. 3

2270 ENERGY ESSENTIALS (anthology). Impulse ASD 9228 (3 discs) $9.98. (Reissue.)
Popular Music. Fall. p87. 25w. 2½

2271 Booker Ervin. THAT'S IT! Barnaby Z 30560 $5.98. (Reissue.)
New York Times--Sunday. May 7. pD29. 25w. 3½

2272 JIM EUROPE/ARTHUR PRYOR. Saydisc/Matchbox SDL 221 (E). (Reissue.)
Jazz Journal. March. p32. 225w. 3

2273 Bill Evans. ALBUM. Columbia C 30855 $4.98. Cart. CA 30855 $6.98.
Downbeat. March 16. p23, 26. 400w. 3
Jazz Journal. May. p29. 400w. 3
Library Journal. February 15. p666. 50w. 3
Music Journal. January. p57, 65. 100w. 1
Records and Recordings. April. p111-2. 250w. 2

2274 Bill Evans. MONTREUX II. CTI CTI 6004 $5.98. Cart. CT 86004 $6.95. Cass. CTC 6004 $6.95.
Jazz Journal. December. p31-2. 425w. 3

2275 Bill Evans and George Russell. LIVING TIME. Columbia KC 31490 $5.98. Cart. CA 31490 $6.98. Cass. CT 31490 $6.98.
Stereo Review. December. p106. 2250w. 2

2276 Frank Evans. STRETCHING FORTH. Saydisc SDL 217 (England).
Gramophone. March. p1620, 1623. 300w. 2½
Jazz and Blues. April. p26. 300w. 2½
Jazz Journal. April. p32. 250w. 3
Records and Recordings. March. p126. 450w. 4

2277 AN EVENING WITH SCOTT JOPLIN (anthology). New York Public Library NYPL SJ $10.00
Stereo Review. October. p108. 1400w. 4

2278 Don Ewell. A JAZZ PORTRAIT OF THE ARTIST. Chiaroscuro CR 106 $5.00.
Coda. August. p27. 150w. 5
Downbeat. June 22. p22-3. 250w. 5
High Fidelity. May. p115. 200w. 3
Jazz Report. No. 1. 200w. 5
Music Journal. February. p57-9. 50w. 3
Saturday Review. May 20. p47. 50w. 2½
Stereo Review. April. p101. 100w. 3

2279 Don Ewell. LIVE AT THE 100 CLUB. "77" SEU 12/42 (England).
Coda. August. p27. 150w. 2
Jazz Journal. January. p30. 175w. 1
Records and Recordings. January. p94. 125w. 3

2280 Art Farmer. FROM VIENNA WITH ART. MPS CRM 741 (Germany).
Coda. August. p27. 400w. 3
Downbeat. July 20. p36. 200w. 3½

2281 Art Farmer. GENTLE EYES. Mainstream MRL 371 $5.98. Cart. M 8371 $6.95. Cass. M5371 $6.95.
Downbeat. December 7. p22. 125w. 5

2282 Art Farmer. HOMECOMING. Mainstream MRL 332 $4.98. Cass. M 5332 $6.95.
Downbeat. March 16. p26. 400w. 5
Stereo Review. April. p101. 175w. 4

2283 Maynard Ferguson. ALIVE AND WELL IN LONDON. Columbia C 31117 $4.98. Cart. CA 31117 $6.98.

Coda. August. p27. 325w. 2
Downbeat. April 13. p26. 350w. 5
Gramophone. March. p1623. 425w. 2
High Fidelity. March. p114-5. 400w. 2½
New York Times--Sunday. August 13. pD22. 200w. 3

2284 Maynard Ferguson. SCREAMING THE BLUES. Mainstream MRL 316 $5.98. (Reissue.)
New York Times--Sunday. May 7. pD29. 25w. 3½

2285 Clare Fischer. RECLAMATION ACT OF 1972. Revelation S 15 $4.98.
Downbeat. October 26. p18, 20. 500w. 5
High Fidelity. December. p130. 300w. 2½
Jazz Journal. December. p41. 125w. 3

2286 Frank Foster. THE LOUD MINORITY. Mainstream MRL 349 $5.98.
Downbeat. June 22. p23-4. 425w. 3
Saturday Review. August. p66. 50w. 2

2287 FOUNDATIONS OF MODERN JAZZ (anthology). Everest FS 229 $3.98. (Reissue.)
Coda. August. p29. 100w. 1

2288 Fourmen Only. EWW 2250 (Germany).
Jazz and Blues. December. p29. 400w. 2

2289 Roy Fox and His Band. THIS IS ROY FOX. Halcyon HAL 7 (England). (Reissue.)
Jazz Journal. August. p30-1. 250w. 3
Records and Recordings. October. p118. 150w. 2½

2290 Fredonia College Jazz Workshop. PLAYS FAMOUS ARRANGERS. Mark MES 35858 $5.00.
Coda. February. p26. 650w. 4

2291 Bud Freeman. CHICAGO. Black Lion 2460 126 (England). (Reissue.)
Gramophone. January. p1287. 125w. 0
Hi-Fi News and Record Review. May. p940. 200w. 2
Jazz and Blues. February. p29-30. 350w. 2
Jazz Journal. January. p29-30. 250w. 2

2292 Curtis Fuller. CRANKIN'. Mainstream MRL 333 $5.98.
Downbeat. March 16. p26. 125w. 4

2293 Funk, Inc. Prestige PR 10031 $5.98.
Saturday Review. March 25. p34. 100w. 2½

2294 Hal Galper. THE GUERILLA BAND. Mainstream MRL 337 $5.98.
Downbeat. March 30. p24. 200w. 4

High Fidelity. February. p119. 150w. 2½
New York Times--Sunday. May 7. pD29. 25w. 3½

2295 Hal Galper. WILD BIRD. Mainstream MRL 354 $5.98.
Downbeat. July 20. p36. 200w. 3½
Jazz Journal. July. p35. 75w. 0

2296 Jan Garbarek. AFRIC PEPPERBIRD. ECM 1007 ST (Germany).
Downbeat. January 20. p20, 22. 100w. 5

2297 Jan Garbarek. THE ESOTERIC CIRCLE. Flying Dutchman FD 10125 $5.95.
Downbeat. January 20. p20, 22. 100w. 5
Stereo Review. January. p115-6. 125w. 2½

2298 Red Garland. IT'S A BLUE WORLD. Prestige PR 7838 $4.98.
Coda. February. p28. 275w. 2

2299 ERROLL GARNER. Everest FS 245 $3.98. (Reissue.)
Coda. August. p29. 100w. 3

2300 Erroll Garner. GEMINI. London XPS 617 $5.98.
Downbeat. December 21. p20. 550w. 4

2301 Michael Garrick. COLD MOUNTAIN. Argo ZDA 153 (England).
Hi-Fi News and Record Review. November. p2203. 200w. 3½
Jazz Journal. December. p32. 300w. 3½

2302 Luis Gasca. Blue Thumb BTS 37 $5.98.
High Fidelity. August. p104. 150w. 2½

2303 Geraldo and His Orchestra. HELLO AGAIN. Parlophone PMC 7139 (England). (Reissue.)
Gramophone. June. p115. 150w. 3
Jazz Journal. February. p39. 100w. 3

2304 Stan Getz. CHANGE OF SCENE. Verve 2304.034 (England). (Reissue.)
Jazz Journal. May. p29-30. 200w. 4

2305 Stan Getz. DYNASTY. Verve V 6-8802-2 (2 discs) $11.96. (Reissue.)
Hi-Fi News and Record Review. April. p111-2. 325w. 3½
Jazz and Blues. March. p26. 325w. 4½
Jazz Journal. January. p30. 400w. 5

2306 Stan Getz. FOCUS. Verve V 6-8412 $5.98.
Jazz and Blues. August. p31. 250w. 4½

2307 Stan Getz. GREATEST HITS. Verve 2304 074 (England). (Reissue.)
Gramophone. November. p984. 75w. 4
Jazz and Blues. November. p26. 250w. 3
Jazz Journal. December. p41. 75w. 3½
Records and Recordings. November. p109. 100w. 3

2308 Stan Getz. MARRAKESH EXPRESS. MGM SE-4696 $5.98.
Audio. December. p102. 100w. 3

2309 Stan Getz. PLAYS. Music for Pleasure MFP 5226 (England). (Reissue.)
Gramophone. March. 225w. 3½
Records and Recordings. January. p94. 125w. 3

2310 Stan Getz. PLAYS EDDIE SAUTER'S "FOCUS" AND "MICKEY ONE." Metro 2682.026 (England) (2 discs). (Reissue.)
Hi-Fi News and Record Reviews. May. p938. 50w. 2
Jazz and Blues. July. p30-1. 650w. 2½
Jazz Journal. May. p29-30. 350w. 4

2311 The Giants of Jazz. Atlantic SD2-905 (2 discs) $8.98.
Sound. December. p39. 75w. 4

2312 Mike Gibbs. JUST AHEAD. Polydor 2683 011 (England) (2 discs).
Jazz Journal. December. p32. 500w. 4

2313 Walt Gifford's New Yorkers. Delmark DL 206 $5.98.
Library Journal. February 15. p667. 100w. 3

2314 Dizzy Gillespie. BIG BAND IN CONCERT. London ZGL 119 (England). (Reissue.)
Gramophone. August. p409. 250w. 3
Jazz and Blues. October. p27. 425w. 3
Jazz Journal. July. p28-9. 350w. 3

2315 Dizzy Gillespie. PORTRAIT OF JENNY. Perception PLP 13 $4.95. Cart. M 813 $6.95. Cass. M 513 $6.95.
Downbeat. January 20. p22. 275w. 4
High Fidelity. January. p119. 200w. 3

2316 Dizzy Gillespie. STORY. Ember CJS 837 (England). (Reissue.)
Gramophone. December. p1231-2. 425w. 4
Hi-Fi News and Record Review. November. p2201. 75w. 2½
Jazz Journal. September. p31. 150w. 5

2317 Dizzy Gillespie and the Mitchell-Ruff Duo. IN CONCERT. Mainstream MRL 325 $5.98. Cart. M 8325 $6.95. Cass. M 8325 $6.95.
Downbeat. January 20. p22. 275w. 5
High Fidelity. January. p119. 200w. 2½
New York Times--Sunday. May 7. pD29. 25w. 3½

2318 GOLDEN HOUR OF TRAD JAZZ (anthology). Pye Golden Hour GH 526 (England).
Gramophone. October. p792-801. 300w. 0

2319 Nat Gonella. THE GEORGIA BOY FROM LONDON. Parlophone PMC 7149 (England). (Reissue.)
Gramophone. September. p584. 250w. 4
Hi-Fi News and Record Review. November. p2199. 50w. 3
Jazz Journal. September. p31-2. 250w. 4

2320 PAUL GONSALVES AND HIS ALL STARS. Barclay 521149 (France). (Reissue.)
Records and Recordings. January. p95. 25w. 0

2321 BENNY GOODMAN AND HIS ORCHESTRA. Jazum 7 $6.00. (Reissue.)
Jazz Journal. July. p35. 75w. 3

2322 Benny Goodman, V.4, (1935/39.) RCA 731.092 (France). (Reissue.)
Coda. August. p27-8. 250w. 3

2323 Benny Goodman. GREAT SOLOISTS, 1929/33. Biograph BLP C-1 $5.98. (Reissue.)
High Fidelity. October. p124. 450w. 2½
Jazz Journal. September. p32. 125w. 2
Previews. November. p45. 250w. 2

2324 Benny Goodman. RHYTHM MAKERS ORCHESTRA, June 6, 1935. Sunbeam SB 101/3 $18.00 (3 discs). (Reissue.)
Library Journal. April 15. p1413. 210w. 3½

2325 Benny Goodman. THIS IS BENNY GOODMAN. RCA VPM 6040 (2 discs) $6.98. (Reissue.)
Coda. April. p26. 125w. 2
Downbeat. February 3. p24-26. 325w. 2½
Library Journal. March 1. p857. 50w. 2

2326 Benny Goodman. TODAY. London Phase 4 SPB 21 (2 discs) $9.98. Cass. 5SP 821 $9.98.
Previews. November. p45-6. 200w. 3

2327 BENNY GOODMAN/CHARLIE BARNET. IAJRC 8 $5.00. (Reissue.)
Coda. August. p28. 325w. 3

2328 Dexter Gordon. A DAY IN COPENHAGEN. BASF 20698 $5.98.
Music Journal. November. p40. 25w. 2

2329 Dexter Gordon. DEXTER RIDES AGAIN. BYG 529 116 (France). (Reissue.)
Jazz Journal. August. p31. 300w. 2

2330 Dexter Gordon. THE DIAL SESSIONS. Storyville SLP 814 (Denmark). (Reissue.)
Jazz Journal. November. p30. 300w. 3

2331 Dexter Gordon. THE JUMPIN' BLUES. Prestige PR 10020 $5.98.
Downbeat. June 23. p18. 350w. 4½

2332 Dexter Gordon. THE PANTHER. Prestige PR 7829 $4.98.
Coda. June. p27. 325w. 5
Previews. October. p46. 200w. 2½

2333 Israel Gorman. AT HAPPY LANDING. Center CLP 12 $5.98.
Jazz Report. No. 1. 125w. 1

2334 The Gothic Jazz Band. THERE'LL BE A HOT TIME. Carrot [no serial number] (England).
Jazz Report. No. 2. 75w. 3½

2335 Dusko Goykovich. AS SIMPLE AS IT IS. Session CRF 851 $5.98.
Coda. June. p28-9. 325w. 3

2336 Stephane Grappelly. 1972. Pye NSPL 18374 (England).
Gramophone. July. p260. 175w. 3
Hi-Fi News and Record Review. September. p1687. 200w. 3
Jazz Journal. May. p30. 225w. 3
Records and Recordings. May. p102. 225w. 4

2337 GREAT GUITARS OF JAZZ (anthology). MGM 2315 013 (England). (Reissue.)
Jazz Journal. June. p37. 75w. 0

2338 THE GREAT JAZZ SINGERS (anthology). Music for Pleasure. Mfp 5233 (England).
Gramophone. March. p1624. 225w. 2

2339 THE GREAT TRADITIONALISTS IN EUROPE (anthology). BASF 20696 $5.98.
Gramophone. October. p801. 675w. 5
Jazz Journal. December. p33. 300w. 5
Records and Recordings. October. p120. 350w. 3½

2340 Grant Green. IRON CITY. Cobblestone CST 9002 $5.98. Cart. M 89002 $6.95.
Downbeat. August 17. p21. 200w. 4

2341 Grant Green. SHADES OF GREEN. Blue Note BST 84413 $5.98.
Jazz Journal. August. p31. 175w. 0
Ontario Library Review. December. p242. 25w. 2½

2342 Grant Green. VISIONS. Blue Note BST 84373 $5.98. Cart. 9162 $6.98.
Jazz Journal. August. p31. 175w. 1
Stereo Review. January. p116. 100w. ½

2343 Sonny Greenwich. THE OLD MAN AND THE CHILD/LOVE SONG FOR A VIRGO LADY. Sackville 2002/3 (2 discs) $7.00 (Canada).
Coda. June. p17. 500w. 4

2344 Stan Greig Trio. BOOGIE WOOGIE. Rediffusion ZS 116 (England).
Jazz Journal. October. p30. 125w. 1

2345 Stefan Grossman. THE GRAMERCY PARK SHEIK. Sonet SNTF 627 (Sweden).
Jazz Journal. December. p41. 75w. 3½

2346 Stefan Grossman. HOT DOGS. Transatlantic TRA 257 (England).
Jazz Journal. December. p41. 25w. 0

2347 Stefan Grossman. THE RAGTIME COWBOY JEW. Transatlantic TRA 223 (England) (2 discs).
Blues Unlimited. May. p28. 25w. 2½

2348 Stefan Grossman. THOSE PLEASANT DAYS. Transatlantic TRA 246 (England).
Jazz Journal. February. p37. 100w. 0

2349 THE GUITAR ALBUM (anthology). Columbia KG 31045 (2 discs) $6.98.
Previews. November. p45. 130w. 2½
Saturday Review. September 30. p83. 50w. 2

2350 Friedrich Gulda. AS YOU LIKE IT. BASF 20731 $5.98.
Gramophone. October. p785. 400w. 3
Records and Recordings. October. p118. 50w. 0

2351 Friedrich Gulda. THE LONG ROAD TO FREEDOM. BASF 20872 (2 discs) $9.98.
Gramophone. October. p785. 400w. 3
Jazz Journal. December. p34. 225w. 2½
Records and Recordings. October. p118. 50w. 0

2352 Bobby Hackett and Vic Dickenson. LIVE AT THE ROOSEVELT GRILL. Chiaroscuro CR 105 $5.98.
Coda. October. p15-6. 350w. 5
Downbeat. March 2. p18. 350w. 5
High Fidelity. March. p114. 100w. 3
Jazz Report. No.1. 300w. 5
Stereo Review. May. p96. 300w. 2½

2353 Bobby Hackett and Jack Teagarden. JAZZ ULTIMATE. EMI 052-81005 (Denmark). (Reissue.)
Jazz Journal. May. p34. 225w. 4

2354 Jerry Hahn. Arhoolie 8006 $6.00
Jazz Journal. September. p38. 125w. 0
Popular Music. Summer. p250. 100w. 2

2355 Al Haig. JAZZ WILL O' THE WISP. XTRA 1125 (England). (Reissue.)
Jazz Journal. November. p30. 350w. 5
Records and Recordings. November. p109. 100w. 4

2356 Al Haig. TRIO AND QUINTET. Prestige PR 7841 $4.98.
Coda. February. p28. 300w. 4

2357 Jim Hall. IT'S NICE TO BE WITH YOU. BASF 20708 $5.98.
Music Journal. November. p40. 25w. 2

2358 Jim Hall. WHERE WOULD I BE? Milestone MSP 9037 $5.98.
Downbeat. April 13. p26, 28. 150w. 4½
High Fidelity. July. p104, 106. 175w. 3
New York Times--Sunday. March 19. p30. 300w. 3
Saturday Review. April 22. p51. 100w. 2

2359 Hall Brothers Jazz Band. JAZZ CONCERT. Emporium of Jazz 1 $5.95.
Coda. October. p16. 150w. 4
High Fidelity. May. p114-5. 250w. 2

2360 Hall Brothers Jazz Band. KENTUCKY CONCERT. Minnesota Jazz Sponsors MJS 501.
Coda. June. p28. 250w. 4
Coda. October. p16. 150w. 4

2361 Gunter Hampel. OUT OF NEW YORK. BASF 20900 $5.98.
Jazz and Blues. June. p27-8. 200w. 0

2362 Lionel Hampton. V.1 (STOMPOLOGY). RCA LPV 575 $5.98. (Reissue.)
Downbeat. February 3. p24-26. 325w. 5
High Fidelity. February. p118-9. 300w. 3

Jazz and Blues. July. p14-5. 275w. 4
Music Journal. February. p36. 75w. 3
Rolling Stone. June 22. p62, 64. 200w. $2\frac{1}{2}$

2363 Lionel Hampton. V. 2. RCA 730 641 (France). (Reissue.)
Coda. October. p16. 175w. 4

2364 Lionel Hampton. V. 4. (1940/41). RCA 731 053 (France). (Reissue.)
Coda. October. p16. 250w. 4

2365 Lionel Hampton. AND THE JUST JAZZ ALL STARS. London ZGL 120 (England). (Reissue.)
Gramophone. August. p409. 250w. 3
Hi-Fi News and Record Review. June. p1129. 150w. 3
Jazz and Blues. November. p27. 325w. 3
Jazz Journal. July. p29. 275w. 3

2366 Herbie Hancock. CROSSINGS. Warner Bros. BS 2617 $5.98.
Downbeat. November 23. p18-9. 650w. 2
Jazz Journal. September. p32. 225w. 2
Records and Recordings. October. p121. 325w. $2\frac{1}{2}$

2367 John Hardy. MEMORIAL. La Croix LP 7 (England). (Reissue.)
Jazz Journal. October. p30. 325w. 1

2368 Annette Hanshaw. THE EARLY YEARS, 1926, V. 1. Fountain FV 201 (England). (Reissue.)
Jazz Journal. April. p32-3. 175w. 3
Records and Recordings. April. p110. 200w. $2\frac{1}{2}$

2369 Eddie Harris. LIVE AT NEWPORT. Atlantic SD 1595 $5.98. Cart. M 81595 $6.95. Cass. M 51595 $6.95.
Downbeat. February 3. p18. 125w. $2\frac{1}{2}$

2370 GENE HARRIS AND THE THREE SOUNDS. Blue Note BST 84378 $5.98. Cart. 9169 $6.98. Cass. 1169 $6.98.
Creem. April. p68. 350w. $2\frac{1}{2}$
Stereo Review. May. p96. 150w. 0

2371 Coleman Hawkins. BODY AND SOUL. RCA 730.566 (France). (Reissue.)
Jazz and Blues. January. p22. 300w. 3

2372 Coleman Hawkins. HAWK IN HOLLAND. Ace of Clubs ACL 1247 (England). (Reissue.)
Downbeat. March 2. p22. 75w. 5

2373 Coleman Hawkins. HIS GREATEST HITS, 1939/42. RCA

730 625 (France). (Reissue.)
Downbeat. March 2. p22. 75w. 3½

2374 Coleman Hawkins. HOLLYWOOD STAMPEDE. Capitol M 11030 $5.98. (Reissue.)
Coda. December. p15-20. 550w. 5
Downbeat. December 21. p27. 250w. 5
Jazz and Blues. June. p8. 200w. 3½
Jazz Journal. May. p36. 200w. 4
Previews. November. p44-5. 115w. 2½
Sound. October. p37. 125w. 4
Stereo Review. September. p78-9. 50w. 2

2375 Coleman Hawkins. MEMORIAL. Jazz Society AA 504 $5.50. (Reissue.)
Coda. June. p28. 375w. 4

2376 Coleman Hawkins and Bud Powell. HAWK IN GERMANY. Black Lion 2460 159 (England). (Reissue.)
Gramophone. November. p994. 225w. 4
Jazz and Blues. November. p28. 300w. 4
Jazz Journal. December. p34. 200w. 4
Records and Recordings. November. p108. 150w. 3

2377 Isaac Hayes. BLACK MOSES. Enterprise ENS 5003 (2 discs) $9.96. Cart. EN 8 25003 $9.98. Cass. ENC 25003 $9.98.
Stereo Review. April. p96. 325w. 3½

2378 Tubby Hayes Orchestra. 100% PROOF. Philips 6382 041 (England). (Reissue.)
Gramophone. December. p1232. 250w. 5
Records and Recordings. November. p109. 100w. 2½

2379 Roy Haynes. SENYAH. Mainstream MRL 351 $5.98.
Downbeat. October 26. p20, 27. 125w. 4
Jazz Journal. July. p35. 75w. 2

2380 Jimmy Heath. THE GAP SEALER. Cobblestone CST 9012 $5.98.
Downbeat. November 9. p19, 20. 725w. 5
New York Times--Sunday. June 11. pD30. 75w. 2½

2381 HEAVY AND ALIVE (anthology). Atlantic K 20034 (England). (Reissue.)
Jazz and Blues. September. p26. 375w. 0
Jazz Journal. November. p37. 100w. 0

2382 Fletcher Henderson. THE DIXIE STOMPERS, 1925/6. Swaggie S 1277 (Australia). (Reissue.)
Coda. August. p28. 250w. 3

2383 Fletcher Henderson. 1923/1924. Biograph BLP 12039 $5.98. (Reissue.)
Jazz Journal. October. p30-1. 525w. 1
Previews. November. p45. 175w. 2½
Stereo Review. December. p110,12. 300w. 1½

2384 Fletcher Henderson. 1927/36. RCA 730 584 (France). (Reissue.)
Jazz and Blues. February. p30-1. 450w. 3

2385 Fletcher Henderson. V.1. Collectors' Classics CC 27 (Denmark). (Reissue.)
Jazz Journal. August. p32. 300w. 3

2386 Joe Henderson. IN PURSUIT OF BLACKNESS. Milestone MSP 9034 $5.98.
Downbeat. April 13. p28. 275w. 5

2387 Joe Henderson. POWER TO THE PEOPLE. Milestone MSP 9024 $5.98. Cart. 8-9024 $6.95.
Coda. October. p16. 300w. 2

2388 Woody Herman. AT CARNEGIE HALL. Verve 2317 031 (England). (Reissue.)
Downbeat. July 20. p36,38. 900w. 5
Gramophone. June. p117. 600w. 5
Hi-Fi News and Record Reviews. July. p1307. 75w. 3½
Jazz Journal. June. p31. 175w. 5
Records and Recordings. September. p97. 200w. 4

2389 Woody Herman. EARLY AUTUMN. Capitol M 11034 $5.98. (Reissue.)
Coda. December. p15-20. 550w. 5
Downbeat. December 21. p30. 200w. 5
Jazz and Blues. August. p23. 325w. 4½
Jazz Journal. June. p11. 425w. 3
Previews. November. p44-5. 115w. 2½
Saturday Review. August 12. p66. 100w. 2½
Sound. October. p46. 50w. 4
Stereo Review. September. p78-9. 50w. 1

2390 Woody Herman. BRAND NEW. Fantasy 8414 $4.98.
New York Times--Sunday. August 13. pD22. 150w. 2½

2391 Earl Hines. Everest FS 246 $3.98. (Reissue.)
Coda. August. p29. 100w. 4

2392 Earl Hines. AT HOME. Delmark DS 212 $5.98.
Gramophone. January. p1287. 150w. 3
Stereo Review. January. p116. 300w. 3

2393 Earl Hines. FATHER AND HIS FLOCK ON TOUR. BASF 20749 $5.98.
Coda. October. p19. 250w. 2
Downbeat. October 26. p27. 200w. 2½
High Fidelity. December. p126. 225w. 3
Music Journal. November. p40. 50w. 3

2394 Earl Hines. HINES '65. Master Jazz Recordings MJR 8109 $5.50. (Reissue.)
Downbeat. June 8. p20-1. 200w. 5
High Fidelity. January. p119-120w. 4
Music Journal. January. p65. 100w. 4
Stereo Review. January. p116. 300w. 3

2395 Earl Hines. MY TRIBUTE TO LOUIS. Audiophile APS 111 $5.95.
Audio. November. p98-9. 800w. 4½
Coda. October. p16-18. 300w. 5
Downbeat. June 8. p20-1. 200w. 4
High Fidelity. June. p108. 200w. 2½
Jazz Journal. July. p35. 75w. 5
Jazz Report. No.1. 200w. 5
Library Journal. June 1. p2067. 150w. 3
Music Journal. February. p37. 200w. 5

2396 Earl Hines. ONCE UPON A TIME. Impulse AS 9108 $5.98.
Jazz Journal. November. p30-1. 325w. 4

2397 Earl Hines. PARIS SESSION. EMI C-048-50756 (France). (Reissue.)
Jazz Journal. May. p30. 200w. 4

2398 Earl Hines. PLAYS DUKE ELLINGTON. Master Jazz MJR 8114 $5.50.
Coda. October. p16-18. 300w. 5
Downbeat. December 7. p22. 250w. 3½
High Fidelity. August. p102, 104. 300w. 2½
Music Journal. June. p24. 75w. 4
Sound. September. p50. 100w. 4

2399 Earl Hines. SOLO. Fantasy 3238 $4.98. (Reissue.)
Jazz Journal. June. p31. 300w. 4

2400 Earl Hines & Maxine Sullivan. LIVE AT THE OVERSEAS PRESS CLUB. Chiaroscuro CR 107 $5.98.
Coda. October. p18-9. 750w. 5
Downbeat. December 7. p22. 250w. 4½
High Fidelity. July. p102, 104. 150w. 4
Saturday Review. April 22. p51. 125w. 3
Stereo Review. August. p94. 125w. 4½

2401 Chris Hinze Combination. WHO CAN SEE THE SHADOW OF THE SUN. CBS 64977 (England).
Records and Recordings. September. p99. 150w. 3

2402 Art Hodes. SELECTIONS FROM THE GUTTER. Storyville SLP 215 (Denmark).
Jazz Journal. November. p31. 275w. 2

2403 Billie Holiday. BEST. Verve V 6-8808 $5.98. (Reissue.)
Audio. December. p95. 100w. 4
Downbeat. December 21. p27. 125w. 3½

2404 Billie Holiday. GALLANT LADY. Monmouth/Evergreen MES 7046 $5.98. (Reissue.)
Downbeat. December 21. p26-7. 150w. 3½
High Fidelity. September. p106. 330w. 5

2405 Billie Holiday. GOD BLESS THE CHILD. Columbia G 30782 (2 discs) $5.98. (Reissue.)
Downbeat. December 21. p21, 26. 325w. 4
Jazz Report. No. 1. 175w. 3
Music Journal. June. p37. 75w. 0
New York Times--Sunday. May 7. pD29. 25w. 2½
Previews. October. p46. 150w. 1
Saturday Review. June 17. p80. 50w. 2½
Sound. August. p50. 250w. 3

2406 Billie Holiday. IMMORTAL SESSIONS, V.1. Saga PAN 6905 (England). (Reissue.)
Gramophone. October. p785. 275w. 0
Jazz and Blues. September. p26. 300w. 3
Jazz Journal. July. p29-30. 400w. 3
Records and Recordings. July. p96. 250w. 2½

2407 Billie Holiday. THE LADY LIVES. ESP 3002 $5.00. (Reissue.)
Coda. August. p28. 175w. 0

2408 Billie Holiday. ONE FOR MY BABY. Music for Pleasure MFP 5231 (England). (Reissue.)
Gramophone. May. p1456. 350w. 4

2409 Billie Holiday. STRANGE FRUIT. Atlantic SD 1614 $5.98. (Reissue.)
Downbeat. December 21. p26. 250w. 5
Jazz Journal. August. p32. 225w. 5

2410 Dave Holland and Barre Phillips. MUSIC FOR TWO BASSES. ECM ECM 1011 ST (Germany).
Downbeat. May 11. p26. 250w. 3½
Jazz and Blues. August. p33-4. 300w. 3

2411 Richard "Groove" Holmes. AMERICAN PIE. Groove

Merchant GM 505 $4.98. Cart. 8505 $6.98. Cass. C 505 $6.98.
Downbeat. October 12. p19. 300w. 5

2412 Richard "Groove" Holmes. COMIN' ON HOME. Blue Note BST 84372 $5.98. Cart. M 9161 $6.98.
Creem. April. p68. 350w. 2½
Downbeat. Februrary 17. p19, 21. 75w. 2
Stereo Review. April. p101-2. 150w. 2½

2413 STAN HOPE. Mainstream MRL 327 $5.98. Cart. M 8327 $6.95. Cass. M 5327 $6.95.
Downbeat. May 11. p21. 100w. 2½

2414 Claude Hopkins. SOLILOQUY. Sackville 3004 (Canada) $5.00.
Jazz Journal. December. p42. 100w. 1
Sound. November. p39. 75w. 4

2415 HOT JAZZ ON FILM, V.2 (anthology). Extreme Rarities 1004 $5.25. (Reissue.)
Coda. October. p19. 350w. 3

2416 Noah Howard. THE BLACK ARK. Freedom 2383 093 (England).
Gramophone. August. p409. 275w. 3
Jazz and Blues. June. p28. 325w. 1½
Jazz Journal. April. p33. 250w. 3
Records and Recordings. May. p100-1. 300w. 2½

2417 Noah Howard. SPACE DIMENSION. America 33 AM 6108 (France).
Jazz and Blues. June. p28. 175w. 0

2418 Freddie Hubbard. FIRST LIGHT. CTI CTI 6013 $5.98. Cart. CT8-6013 $6.95. Cass. CTC 6013 $6.95.
Saturday Review. September 30. p83. 75w. 2

2419 Freddie Hubbard. HUB OF BUBBARD. BASF 20726 $5.98.
Music Journal. November. p40. 25w. 2

2420 Freddie Hubbard. SING ME A SONG OF SONGMY. Atlantic SD 1576 $5.98.
Coda. June. p28-9. 625w. 3

2421 Freddie Hubbard. STRAIGHT LIFE. CTI CTI 6007 $5.98. Cart. CT 86007 $6.95. Cass. CTC 6007 $6.95.
Coda. February. p29. 275w. 0
Jazz Journal. December. p34. 200w. 0

2422 Armand Hug. Swaggie S 1281 (Australia). (Reissue.)
Coda. October. p20. 300w. 4

2423 Bobbi Humphrey. FLUTE-IN. Blue Note BST 84379 $5.98.
Downbeat. November 9. p22. 125w. 3
Jazz Journal. July. p30. 200w. 1
Ontario Library Review. December. p242. 25w. 2

2424 Percy Humphrey. AT MANNY'S TAVERN. Center CLP 13 $5.50.
Jazz Report. No. 1. 125w. 3

2425 Bobby Hutcherson. HEAD ON. Blue Note BST 84376 $5.98. Cart. 9167 $6.98.
Coda. August. p19-20. 325w. 2
Downbeat. March 16. p26-7. 275w. 4

2426 Bobby Hutcherson. SAN FRANCISCO. Blue Note 84362 $5.98. Cart. 9163 $6.98. Cass. C 1163 $6.98.
Coda. October. p20. 200w. 3

2427 Jack Hylton. Monmouth/Evergreen MES 7033 $5.98. (Reissue.)
Coda. April. p27-8. 225w. 4

2428 JPJ Quartet. MONTREUX '71. Master Jazz MJR 8111 $5.50.
Downbeat. March 16. p27-8. 350w. 4½
High Fidelity. May. p114. 325w. 3½
Jazz Journal. May. p34. 200w. 4
Music Journal. May. p15, 76. 700w. 5
Saturday Review. April 22. p51. 100w. 3
Stereo Review. July. p98. 175w. 3

2429 Milt Jackson and Ray Brown. MEMPHIS JACKSON. Impulse AS 9193 $5.98.
Coda. October. p20. 150w. 1

2430 Milt Jackson and Sonny Stitt. IN THE BEGINNING. America 30 AM 6072 (France). (Reissue.)
Records and Recordings. April. p110. 250w. 4

2431 Rudolph Jackson. SPRING RAIN. Black Jazz BJ 4 $5.98.
Downbeat. April 13. p28. 150w. 2

2432 Illinois Jacquet. GENIUS AT WORK! Black Lion 2460 146 (England). (Reissue.)
Jazz and Blues. April. p26. 300w. 2½
Jazz Journal. January. p31. 275w. 3
Records and Recordings. February. p103. 250w. 4

2433 Harry James. AN EVENING OF JAZZ. Metro 2682.029 (England) (2 discs). (Reissue.)
Gramophone. October. p785. 275w. 4
Jazz Journal. October. p32-3. 200w. 3

Records and Recordings. May. p102. 175w. 4
Records and Recordings. October. p118. 150w. 3

2434 John James and Pete Berryman. SKY IN MY PIE. Transatlantic TRA 250 (England).
Jazz Journal. April. p34. 200w. 3

2435 Horst Jankowski. JANKOWSKINETIK. BASF 20732 $5.98.
Gramophone. October. p786. 275w. 2

2436 Keith Jarrett. BIRTH. Atlantic SD 1612 $5.98. Cart. TP 1612 $6.97. Cass. Cs 1612 $6.97.
Rolling Stone. December 21. p66. 750w. 3

2437 Keith Jarrett. EXPECTATIONS. Columbia KG 31580 (2 discs) $6.98. Cart. GA 31580 $7.98.
Rolling Stone. December 21. p66. 750w. 3

2438 Keith Jarrett. FACING YOU. ECM 1017 ST (Germany).
Jazz and Blues. July. p30. 300w. 3
Jazz Journal. October. p28-9. 150w. 4
Records and Recordings. October. p121. 175w. 2½
Rolling Stone. December 21. p66. 750w. 4

2439 Keith Jarrett. THE MOURNING OF A STAR. Atlantic SD 1596 $5.98. Cart. M 81596 $6.95. Cass. M 51596 $6.95.
Coda. April. p17. 350w. 1
Crawdaddy. March 5. p17. 900w. 1½
Downbeat. February 3. p22. 250w. 4
Gramophone. November. p1003. 225w. 2
Jazz and Blues. September. p25. 325w. 3
Jazz Journal. September. p32-3. 200w. 1
Records and Recordings. October. p121. 175w. 2½

2440 Joseph Jarman. AS IF IT WERE THE SEASONS. Delmark DS 417 $5.98.
Library Journal. February 15. p667. 50w. 3

2441 David Jasen. FINGER BUSTIN' RAGTIME. Blue Goose 3001 $5.95.
Blues Unlimited. September. p23. 125w. 4
Coda. October. p20. 250w. 3
Downbeat. September 14. p21. 250w. 5
High Fidelity. August. p102. 300w. 3
Jazz Journal. July. p30. 250w. 2
Music Journal. November. p56. 50w. 4
Sing Out. May/June. p46. 75w. 3½

2442 JAZUM 8. Jazum 8 $5.00
Jazz Journal. December. p42. 150w. 2½

2443 The Jazz Giants. Biography BLP 3002 $5.95.
Jazz Report. No. 2. 150w. 5

2444 JAZZ IN BRITAIN - THE THIRTIES (anthology). Parlophone PMC 7095 (England). (Reissue.)
Downbeat. March 2. p22. 50w. 3

2445 JAZZ MASTERS (anthology). Byg BYG 22 (France) (2 discs). (Reissue.)
Hi-Fi News and Record Review. June. p1129. 350w. $2\frac{1}{2}$
Jazz and Blues. January. p23-4. 650w. 1
Jazz Journal. January. p29. 225w. 1

2446 JAZZ SOUNDS OF THE TWENTIES (anthology). Swaggie S 1270 (Australia). (Reissue.)
Coda. October. p20-1. 375w. 3

2447 THE JAZZ WIZARDS, v.1/2 (anthology). Herwin 102/3 (2 discs) $11.90. (Reissue.)
Jazz Journal. October. p33. 550w. 5

2448 JOHN HAMMOND'S SPIRITUALS TO SWING: 30TH ANNIVERSARY CONCERT, 1967. (anthology).
Blues Unlimited. June. p28. 200w. 4
Jazz Report. No.1. 150w. 4
Music Journal. June. p37. 125w. 3
New York Times--Sunday. May 7. pD29. 50w. $3\frac{1}{2}$
Saturday Review. June 17. p80. 150w. $2\frac{1}{2}$

2449 James P. Johnson. 1917/21. Biograph BLP 1003 Q $5.98. (Reissue.)
Journal of American Folklore. January/March. p106. 25w. $2\frac{1}{2}$

2450 Lamont Johnson. SUN, MOON AND STARS. Mainstream MRL 328 $5.98. Cart. M 8328 $6.95. Cass. M 5328 $6.95.
Coda. October. p21. 450w. 0
Downbeat. April 27. p19. 175w. 2

2451 Arthur Jones. SCORPIO. America 30 AM 6112 (France).
Jazz and Blues. June. p28. 200w. $1\frac{1}{2}$

2452 Dill Jones. UP JUMPED YOU WITH LOVE. "77" SEU 12/45 (England).
Jazz Journal. December. p34-5. 225w. 2

2453 Elvin Jones. GENESIS. Blue Note BST 84369 $5.98. Cart. 9158 $6.95.
Downbeat. February 17. p21. 250w. 4

2454 Elvin Jones. MERRY-GO-ROUND. Blue Note BST 84414 $5.98.
Downbeat. November 9. p22-3. 175w. $4\frac{1}{2}$

High Fidelity. October. p124,126. 200w. 3
Jazz and Blues. September. p27. 275w. $1\frac{1}{2}$
Previews. November. p45-6. 75w. 2

2455 Jo Jones. SPECIAL. Vanguard VRS 8503 (England). (Reissue.)
Gramophone. December. p1232. 250w. $3\frac{1}{2}$
Records and Recordings. November. p108. 150w. 5

2456 Jonah Jones. Capitol SMK 1058 $5.98.
Jazz Journal. August. p33. 150w. 0

2457 Philly Joe Jones. TRAILWAYS EXPRESS. Black Lion 2470 142 (England).
Gramophone. May. p1958. 250w. $2\frac{1}{2}$
Jazz and Blues. March. p26. 275w. 3
Jazz Journal. January. p31-2. 250w. 2
Records and Recordings. January. p94. 125w. 1

2458 Quincy Jones. SMACKWATER JACK. A & M SP 3037 $5.98. Cart. 8T 3037 $6.98. Cass. CS 3032 $6.98.
Gramophone. October. p786. 350w. 3

2459 Thad Jones and Mel Lewis. CENTRAL PARK NORTH. Solid State SS 18058 $5.98.
Coda. February. p29. 250w. 1

2460 Scott Joplin. 1916. Biograph 1006 Q $5.98. (Reissue.)
Journal of American Folklore. January/March. p99-100. 25w. 2
Music Journal. April. p52. 200w. 3
Ragtimer. July/August. p6-7. 600w. 4
Stereo Review. May. p94. 125w. $1\frac{1}{2}$

2461 Scott Joplin. RAGTIME, v2. Biograph BLP 1008 Q $5.98. (Reissue.)
Ragtimer. November/December. p4-6. 200w. 4

2462 Duke Jordon. JORDU. Prestige PR 7849 $4.98
Coda. April. p17. 300w. 4

2463 Kent State Lab Band. PLAY FAMOUS ARRANGERS. Mark MES 39091 $5.00.
Coda. February. p27. 150w. 3

2464 Stan Kenton. ARTISTRY IN BOSA NOVA. Creative World ST 1045 $5.50. (Reissue.)
Jazz Journal. November. p32-3. 150w. 3

2465 Stan Kenton. ARTISTRY IN JAZZ. Capitol M 11027 $5.98. (Reissue.)
Coda. August. p15. 150w. 5

Coda. December. p15-20. 550w. 3
Downbeat. December 21. p30. 150w. 4
Jazz and Blues. June. p7-8. 250w. 4
Jazz Journal. May. p35-6. 300w. 5
Previews. November. p44-5. 115w. 3½
Stereo Review. September. p78-9. 50w. 2½

2466 Stan Kenton. ARTISTRY IN RHYTHM. Creative World ST 1043 $5.50. (Reissue.)
Jazz Journal. November. p32-3. 150w. 4

2467 Stan Kenton. BY REQUEST, v.1. Creative World ST 1036 $5.50. (Reissue.)
New York Times--Sunday. May 7. pD29. 25w. 3½

2468 Stan Kenton. BY REQUEST, v.2. Creative World ST 1040 $5.50. (Reissue.)
Jazz Journal. June. p31-2. 300w. 4
New York Times--Sunday. May 7. pD29. 25w. 3½

2469 Stan Kenton. THE CHRISTY YEARS. Creative World ST 1035 $5.50. (Reissue.)
Jazz Journal. January. p32. 350w. 3

2470 Stan Kenton. A CONCERT IN PROGRESSIVE JAZZ. Creative World ST 1037 $5.50. (Reissue.)
New York Times--Sunday. May 7. pD29. 25w. 3½

2471 Stan Kenton. DUET. Creative World ST 1048 $5.50. (Reissue.)
Jazz Journal. December. p35-6. 150w. 0

2472 Stan Kenton. ENCORES. Creative World ST 1034 $5.50. (Reissue.)
Jazz Journal. January. p32. 175w. 2

2473 Stan Kenton. THE KENTON TOUCH. Creative World ST 1033 $5.50. (Reissue.)
Jazz Journal. January. p32. 275w. 0

2474 Stan Kenton. KENTON'S CHRISTMAS. Creative World ST 1001 $5.50. (Reissue.)
Jazz Journal. January. p32. 150w. 2

2475 Stan Kenton. THE LIGHTER SIDE. Creative World ST 1050 $5.50. (Reissue.)
Jazz Journal. December. p36. 175w. 1

2476 Stan Kenton. LIVE AT BRIGHAM YOUNG UNIVERSITY. Creative World ST 1039 (2 discs) $11.00.
Downbeat. March 2. p18-9. 550w. 4½

High Fidelity. March. p114-5. 400w. 2
New York Times--Sunday. August 13. pD22. 650w. 4
Saturday Review. March 25. p34. 150w. 1

2477 Stan Kenton. MILESTONES. Creative World ST 1047 $5.50. (Reissue.)
Jazz Journal. December. p35-6. 150w. 1

2478 Stan Kenton. PORTRAITS ON STANDARDS. Creative World ST 1042 $5.50. (Reissue.)
Jazz Journal. June. p32. 250w. 3

2479 Stan Kenton. SKETCHES ON STANDARDS. Creative World ST 1041 $5.50. (Reissue.)
Jazz Journal. June. p32. 550w. 3

2480 Stan Kenton. THE STAGE DOOR SWINGS. Creative World ST 1044 $5.50. (Reissue.)
Jazz Journal. November. p32-3. 150w. 2

2481 Stan Kenton. STANDARDS IN SILHOUETTE. Creative World ST 1049 $5.50. (Reissue.)
Jazz Journal. November. p32. 300w. 3

2482 Stan Kenton. TODAY. London Phase 4 BP 44179/80 (2 discs) $6.98. Cart. L 14179 $7.95. Cass. L 84179 $7.95.
Gramophone. June. p118. 900w. 4
Hi-Fi News and Record Review. June. p1127. 100w. 2½
Hi-Fi News and Record Review. September. p1686-7. 225w. 2
High Fidelity. October. p124. 250w. 2½
Jazz and Blues. September. p22. 625w. 4
Jazz Journal. May. p31. 925w. 4
Records and Recordings. July. p98. 150w. 1
Sound. September. p50. 150w. 3

2483 Stan Kenton. WITH JEAN TURNER. Creative World ST 1046 $5.50. (Reissue.)
Jazz Journal. November. p32-3. 150w. 2

2484 Robin Kenyatta. GIRL FROM MARTINIQUE. ECM 1008 ST (Germany).
Downbeat. May 11. p26. 250w. 3½

2485 Freddie Keppard. Herwin 101 $5.50. (Reissue.)
High Fidelity. March. p115. 75w. 2½
Jazz Journal. October. p33. 550w. 3½

2486 Knut Kiesewetter. STOP! WATCH! AND LISTEN! MPS 15284 (Germany).
Coda. April. p17. 350w. 2

2487 King Pleasure. CLARENCE BEEKS. Everest FS 262 $3.98.
Stereo Review. November. p94. 150w. 4

2488 Morgana King. CUORE DI MAMA. Mainstream MRL 355 $5.98.
Downbeat. July 20. p38. 125w. 4½

2489 Morgana King. TASTE OF HONEY. Mainstream MRL 321 $5.98. Cart. M 8321 $6.95. Cass. M 5321 $6.95.
New York Times--Sunday. May 7. pD29. 25w. 3½

2490 Andy Kirk. LIVE FROM THE TRIANON BALLROOM. Jazz Society [no serial number]. (Reissue.)
Coda. April. p18. 175w. 3

2491 Roland Kirk. BEST. Atlantic SD 1592 $5.98. (Reissue.) Cart. M 81592 $6.97. Cass. M 51592 $6.97.
Coda. October. p22. 200w. 0
Downbeat. May 25. p18. 25w. 5

2492 Roland Kirk. BLACKNUSS. Atlantic SD 1601 $5.98. Cart. M 81601 $6.97. Cass. M 51601 $6.97.
Coda. October. p21-2. 850w. 2
Crawdaddy. April 16. p18. 675w. 3
Downbeat. April 27. p21. 150w. 3
Gramophone. July. p260. 175w. 2
High Fidelity. May. p115. 275w. 3½
Records and Recordings. June. p89. 125w. 0

2493 Roland Kirk. NATURAL BLACK INVENTIONS: ROOT STRATA. Atlantic SD 1578 $5.98. Cart. M 81578 $6.97. Cass. M 51578 $6.97.
Coda. April. p17-8. 275w. 3

2494 JEAN KITTRELL AND BOLL WEEVIL JAZZ BAND. GHB 51 $5.98.
Coda. October. p22. 300w. 3

2495 John Klemmer. CONSTANT THROB. Impulse AS 9214 $5.98. Cart. M 89214 $6.95. Cass. M 59214 $6.95.
Downbeat. May 25. p22-3. 225w. 4

2496 Eric Kloss. DOORS. Cobblestone CST 9006 $5.98. Cart. M 89006 $6.95. Cass. M59006 $6.95.
Downbeat. November 23. p19. 200w. 3
High Fidelity. September. p106. 180w. 2½

2497 Eric Kloss. IN THE LAND OF THE GIANTS. Prestige PR 7627 $4.98.
Coda. June. p17. 500w. 3

2498 Lee Konitz. SPIRITS. Milestone MSP 9038 $5.98.
Downbeat. October 12. p19-20. 500w. 4½
New York Times--Sunday. pD18. 150w. 4

2499 Leo Kottke. SIX AND TWELVE STRING GUITAR. Sonet SNTF 629 (Sweden).
Jazz Journal. December. p41. 50w. 3

2500 Peter Kowald Quintet. Free Music Production FMP 0070 (Germany).
Jazz Journal. August. p33. 300w. 3
Records and Recordings. October. p121-2. 300w. 3½

2501 Steve Kuhn. Buddah BDS 5098 $5.98.
Downbeat. June 8. p21. 500w. 3

2502 Steve Lacy. MOON. BYG Actuel 21 (France).
Records and Recordings. April. p112. 350w. 2½

2503 Guy La Fitte. BLUES IN SUMMERTIME. RCA 730 106 (France). (Reissue.)
Coda. June. p17. 300w. 3

2504 David Laibman and Eric Schoenberg. THE NEW RAGTIME GUITAR. Transatlantic TRA 253 (England).
Jazz Journal. March. p34-5. 125w. 4

2505 Harold Land. CHOMA (BURN). Mainstream MRL 344 $5.98.
Downbeat. May 11. p22. 450w. 2
Jazz Journal. May. p34. 100w. 1

2506 Steve Lane's Southern Stompers. VJM LC 145 (England).
Jazz Journal. December. p36. 125w. 1

2507 Yusef Lateef. Prestige PR 24007 (2 discs) $6.98. (Reissue.) Cart. M 82407 $9.95. Cass. M 52407 $9.95.
Coda. October. p22. 375w. 3
Downbeat. October 12. p24-32. 375w. 3
Previews. November. p43. 100w. 2
Rolling Stone. May 25. p68. 200w. 4

2508 Yusef Lateef. BEST. Atlantic SD 1591 $5.98. (Reissue.) Cart. M 81591 $6.97. Cass. M 51591 $6.97.
Downbeat. May 25. p18. 25w. 4

2509 Yusef Lateef. THE GENTLE GIANT. Atlantic SD 1602 $5.98. Cart. M 81602 $6.97. Cass. M 51602 $6.97.
Coda. October. p23. 400w. 0
Downbeat. June 8. p20. 125w. 2½
Gramophone. November. p994, 997. 500w. 1

Records and Recordings. September. p99. 250w. 3
Stereo Review. July. p98. 175w. 2½

2510 O'Donel Levy. BLACK VELVET. Groove Merchant GM 501 $4.95. Cart. 8501 $6.95. Cass. C 501 $6.95.
Gramophone. September. p584-5. 275w. 3
Jazz Journal. August. p33. 125w. 1

2511 George Lewis. ON PARADE. Delmark 202 $5.98. (Reissue.)
Library Journal. February 15. p667. 100w. 3

2512 Abby Lincoln. STRAIGHT AHEAD. Barnaby KZ 31037 $5.98. (Reissue.)
Previews. November. p46. 150w. 3
Rolling Stone. May 25. p68. 200w. 3½
Stereo Review. July. p98. 200w. 3

2513 Mike Lipskin and Willie "The Lion" Smith. CALIFORNIA HERE I COME. Flying Dutchman FD 10140 $5.95. Cart. M 810140 $6.95. Cass. M 510140 $6.95.
Coda. October. p24. 350w. 1
Downbeat. February 17. p21. 300w. 2

2514 Charles Lloyd. THE FLOWERING OF THE ORIGINAL QUARTET. Atlantic SD 1586 $5.98. Cart. M 81586 $6.97. Cass. M 51586 $6.97.
Coda. June. p18. 550w. 2
Gramophone. January. p1287. 150w. 2

2515 Charles Lloyd. IN THE SOVIET UNION. Atlantic SD 1571 $5.98. Cart. M 81571 $6.97. Cass. M 51571 $6.97.
Coda. October. p24. 300w. 2

2516 Charles Lloyd. WARM WATERS. Kapp KS 3647 $4.98. Cart. 83647 $6.98. Cass. 73647 $6.98.
Downbeat. January 20. p22, 26. 375w. 0

2517 London Jazz Chamber Group. ADAM'S RIB SUITE. Ember CJS 823 (England).
Gramophone. December. p1232. 150w. 2½

2518 Mike Longo. THE AWAKENING. Mainstream MRL 357 $5.98. Cart. M 8357 $6.95. Cass. M 5357 $6.95.
Downbeat. October 26. p27-8. 150w. 4

2519 Mike Longo. MATRIX. Mainstream MRL 334 $5.98.
Downbeat. April 13. p29. 300w. 4
New York Times--Sunday. May 7. pD29. 25w. 3½

2520 Jimmie Lunceford. TAKIN' OFF WITH JIMMIE. Tax 8003 $6.00. (Reissue.)
Sound. November. p39. 125w. 4

2521 Johnny Lytle. THE SOULFUL REBEL. Milestone MSP 9030 $5.98.
Downbeat. June 8. p21, 26. 125w. 3½

2522 Humphrey Lyttelton. THE BEST OF HUMPH, 1949/1956. Parlophone PMC 7147 (England). (Reissue.)
Gramophone. June. p118-9. 475w. 4
Hi-Fi News and Record Review. July. p1313. 200w. 2
Jazz and Blues. July. p30. 600w. 3
Jazz Journal. June. p32-3. 350w. 3
Records and Recordings. September. p97. 350w. 4

2523 Humphrey Lyttelton. DUKE ELLINGTON CLASSICS. Black Lion 2460 140 (England).
Gramophone. March. p1623. 325w. 3
Jazz Journal. October. p34. 325w. 3

2524 Les McCann. INVITATION TO OPENESS. Atlantic SD 1603 $5.98.
Downbeat. May 11. p22-3. 250w. 4

2525 Jack McDuff. THE HEATIN' SYSTEM. Cadet 2CA 60017 (2 discs) $6.98. Cart. 8035-60017C $7.95.
Downbeat. October 26. p28. 175w. 4½

2526 Jack McDuff. WHO KNOWS WHAT TOMORROW'S GONNA BRING? Blue Note 84358 $5.98. Cart. 9155 $6.98. Cass. C1155 $6.98.
Coda. June. p21. 200w. 1

2527 Chris McGregor's Brotherhood of Breath. BROTHERHOOD. Neon NE 2 (England).
Coda. April. p18-9. 575w. 4
Jazz and Blues. November. p28. 300w. 2
Jazz Journal. July. p31. 250w. 2
Records and Recordings. July. p98. 425w. 5

2528 Jimmy McGriff. GROOVE GREASE. Groove Merchant GM 503 $4.98. Cart. 8503 $6.95. Cass. C 503 $6.95.
Gramophone. October. p786. 175w. 0
Hi-Fi News and Record Review. August. p1477. 50w. 2½
Jazz Journal. August. p34. 125w. 1

2529 Bill McGuffie. AN ALTO AND SOME BRASS. Rediffusion ZS 48 (England).
Gramophone. December. p1221. 75w. 3½
Jazz Journal. January. p33. 225w. 0

2530 Bill McGuffie. IT'S EASY TO REMEMBER. Philips 6382 036 (England).
Gramophone. May. p1961. 300w. 3½

2531 Jim McHarg. Columbia ES 90071 (Canada).
Coda. October. p27. 275w. 0

2532 Hal McIntyre. 1944/45. First Time FTS 1518 $5.50. (Reissue.)
New York Times--Sunday. October 8. pD34. 125w. 4

2533 John McLaughlin. DEVOTION. Douglas KZ 31568 $5.98.
Popular Music. Fall. p93. 25w. 3½

2534 John McLaughlin. INNER MOUNTING FLAME. Columbia KC 31067 $5.98. Cart. CA 31067 $6.98. Cass. CT 31067 $6.98.
Crawdaddy. March 5. p16. 600w. 4
Downbeat. June 22. p24. 300w. 5
Jazz Journal. August. p34. 300w. 2
Records and Recordings. June. p88. 425w. 4
Stereo Review. April. p72. 250w. 4

2535 John McLaughlin. MY GOAL'S BEYOND. Douglas Z 30766 $4.98. Cart. ZA 30766 $6.98. Cass. ZT 30766 $6.98.
Coda. June. p21. 275w. 3
Downbeat. January 20. p26. 400w. 3½
Downbeat. January 20. p26. 700w. 3½

2536 Harold McNair. B & C Records CAS 1045 (England).
Gramophone. May. p1961. 175w. 2½

2537 Marion McPartland. A DELICATE BALANCE. Halcyon 105 $4.98.
Saturday Review. August 12. p66. 75w. 2½
Stereo Review. October. p110. 150w. 3

2538 Joe McPhee. TRINITY. CJR Record Productions CJR 3 $4.00.
Coda. October. p27-8. 350w. 2
Downbeat. October 26. p26. 450w. 4½

2539 Charles McPherson. SIKU YA BIBI (DAY OF THE LADY). Mainstream MRL 365 $5.98. Cart. M 8365 $6.95. Cass. M 5365 $6.95.
Downbeat. December 7. p22-3. 400w. 4
High Fidelity. December. p131. 300w. 2½
Jazz Journal. October. p39. 300w. 5

2540 Carmen McRae. Mainstream MRL 309 $5.98.
Downbeat. February 3. p23-4. 150w. 5

2541 Carmen McRae. CARMEN'S GOLD. Mainstream MRL 338 $5.98.
Downbeat. February 3. p23-4. 150w. 5

2542 Carmen McRae. THE GREAT AMERICAN SONGBOOK. Atlantic SD 2-904 (2 discs) $11.96.
Downbeat. October 26. p28. 350w. 5
Saturday Review. November 4. p92. 75w. 2½
Stereo Review. November. p96, 98. 900w. 4½

2543 Carmen McRae. "IN PERSON." Mainstream MRL 352 $5.98.
Downbeat. July 20. p38. 125w. 4
Jazz Journal. July. p35. 100w. 4
Stereo Review. November. p96, 98. 900w. 2½

2544 Jay McShann. GOING TO KANSAS CITY. Master Jazz Recordings MJR 8113 $5.50.
High Fidelity. December. p128. 120w. 2½
Saturday Review. September 30. p83. 150w. 3
Sound. November. p39. 100w. 2

2545 Jay McShann. JUMPIN' BLUES. Black and Blue 33.039 (France).
Blues Unlimited. December. p27. 150w. 3

2546 Jay McShann. THE MAN FROM MUSKOGEE. Sackville 3005 (Canada).
Sound. December. p39. 100w. 3½

2547 Albert Mangelsdorff. AND HIS FRIENDS. MPS 15210 (Germany).
Coda. June. p19. 400w. 4

2548 Albert Mangelsdorff. NEVER LET IT END. MPS 15274 (Germany).
Coda. June. p19. 400w. 4

2549 Chuck Mangione. Mercury SRM 1-631 $5.98. Cart. MC 8-1-631 $6.98. Cass. MCR 4-1-631 $6.98.
Beetle. August 22. 600w. 2½

2550 Chuck Mangione. "ALIVE." Mercury SRM 1-650 $5.98. Cart. MC 8-1-650 $6.98. Cass. MCR 4-1-650 $6.98.
Beetle. December 31. p20-1. 800w. 4

2551 Chuck Mangione. TOGETHER. Mercury SRM2-7501 $7.98 Cart. MCT-8-2-7501 $9.95. Cass. MCT-4-2-7501 $9.95.
Coda. October. p27. 500w. 0
Downbeat. May 25. p24. 650w. 4

2552 Gap Mangione. DIANA IN THE AUTUMN WIND. GRC 9001 $4.98.
Coda. April. p18. 500w. 4

2553 Herbie Mann. MEMPHIS TWO-STEP. Embryo SD 531 $5.98. Cart. M 8531 $6.95. Cass. M 5531 $6.95.
Downbeat. February 3. p28. 100w. 2½

2554 Herbie Mann. MISSISSIPPI GAMBLER. Atlantic SD 1610 $5.98.
Audio. November. p88. 250w. 4
Downbeat. November 9. p23,27. 150w. 4
Jazz and Blues. September. p25. 100w. 0
Jazz Journal. September. p33-4. 100w. 1
Records and Recordings. September. p99. 150w. 0

2555 Herbie Mann. PUSH PUSH. Embryo SD 532 $5.98. Cart. M8532 $6.95. Cass. M 5532 $6.95.
Downbeat. February 3. p22-3. 250w. 3
Jazz and Blues. April. p27. 125w. 0
Records and Recordings. April. p112,114. 225w. 0

2556 Shelly Manne. ALIVE IN LONDON. Contemporary S 7629 $5.98.
Coda. June. p19. 275w. 2

2557 Guido Manusardi. CBS 64454 (Italy).
Jazz Journal. March. p37. 100w. 3

2558 Charlie Mariano. MIRROR, MIRROR, MIRROR. Atlantic SD 1608 $5.98.
Downbeat. August 17. p21-2. 175w. 4
High Fidelity. July. p102. 275w. $2\frac{1}{2}$
New York Times--Sunday. June 11. pD30. 175w. 5

2559 Pat Martino. THE VISIT! Cobblestone CST 9105 $5.98. Cart. M 89015 $6.95. Cass. M 59015 $6.95.
High Fidelity. December. p128. 150w. 3

2560 Barry Martyn's Band. WHERE HE LEADS ME. Swift 6 (England).
Jazz Journal. December. p36. 325w. $3\frac{1}{2}$

2561 MASTER JAZZ PIANO, V.2 (anthology). Master Jazz Recordings MJR 8108 $5.50.
Stereo Review. March. p110. 300w. 5

2562 MEMPHIS KICK UP (anthology). IAJRC 9 $5.50. (Reissue.)
Jazz Journal. December. p42. 200w. 3

2563 Mezz Mezzrow - Sidney Bechet Quintet. REALLY THE BLUES. Storyville SLP 137 (Denmark). (Reissue.)
Jazz Journal. February. p35. 300w. 4

2564 MIDWAY DANCE ORCHESTRA/TONY PARENTI'S LIBERTY SYNCOPATORS. VJM VLP 34 (England). (Reissue.)
Jazz Journal. March. p34. 275w. 3
Records and Recordings. May. p103. 350w. 4

2565 Barry Miles. WHITE HEAT. Mainstream MRL 353 $5.98.

Downbeat. August 17. p23. 325w. 4
Jazz Journal. July. p35. 100w. 1
New York Times--Sunday. May 7. pD29. 25w. 3½

2566 Eddie Miller. A PORTRAIT OF EDDIE. Blue Angel BAJC 509 $6.00.
Coda. October. p28. 350w. 4
Library Journal. May 15. p1793. 100w. 3

2567 Charles Mingus. BYG 529.105 (France). (Reissue.)
Jazz Journal. February. p35-6. 450w. 1

2568 Charles Mingus. Everest FS 235 $3.98. (Reissue.)
Coda. August. p29. 100w. 3

2569 Charles Mingus. Prestige 24010 (2 discs) $6.98. (Reissue.)
Coda. December. p20. 275w. 1
Creem. August. p68. 150w. 2½
Downbeat. August 17. p28-31. 400w. 4
New York Times--Sunday. May 7. pD29. 25w. 3
Previews. November. p43. 100w. 2
Rolling Stone. May 25. p68. 100w. 3
Saturday Review. April 22. p51. 100w. 2½

2570 Charles Mingus. BETTER GET IT IN YOUR SOUL. Columbia G 30628 (2 discs) $5.98. (Reissue.)
Coda. October. p28-9. 700w. 4
Library Journal. February 15. p667. 200w. 3½
Popular Music. Winter. p64. 50w. 3
Saturday Review. April 22. p51. 100w. 2½

2571 Charles Mingus. BLUEBIRD. America 30 AM 6109 (France).
Records and Recordings. October. p122. 125w. 3½

2572 Charles Mingus. THE CANDID RECORDINGS. Barnaby KZ 31034 $5.98. (Reissue.)
Crawdaddy. April 30. p16-7. 500w. 3
Creem. August. p68. 225w. 3½
New York Times--Sunday. May 7. pD29. 25w. 3
Previews. November. p46. 150w. 2½
Rolling Stone. May 25. p68. 75w. 4
Saturday Review. April 22. p51. 100w. 2½

2573 Charles Mingus. THE GREAT CONCERT. Prestige 34001 (3 discs) $12.98.
New York Times--Sunday. July 9. pD18. 75w. 3
Previews. November. p45. 225w. 3½
Records and Recordings. May. p101. 225w. 5

2574 Charles Mingus. LET MY CHILDREN HEAR MUSIC. Columbia KC 31039 $5.98.

Coda. October. p28-9. 700w. 3
Crawdaddy. April 30. p16-7. 500w. 3
Creem. August. p68. 650w. 3
Downbeat. October 12. p20-1. 650w. 5
Jazz Journal. November. p33. 600w. 4
New York Times--Sunday. July 9. pD18. 125w. 4
Previews. October. p46. 250w. 3½
Records and Recordings. October. p122. 125w. 4½
Stereo Review. August. p94. 125w. 4

2575 Charles Mingus. MINGUS AT MONTEREY. America 30 AM 001/002 (France) (2 discs).
Records and Recordings. October. p122. 125w. 4

2576 Charles Mingus. PITHYCANTHROPUS ERECTUS. America 30 AM 6109 (France).
Jazz Journal. June. p33. 325w. 2
Records and Recordings. October. p122. 125w. 4

2577 Charles Mingus. QUARTET, FEATURING ERIC DOLPHY. Barnaby KZ 30561 $5.98. (Reissue.)
New York Times--Sunday. May 7. pD29. 25w. 2½
Rolling Stone. May 25. p68. 25w. 4

2578 Charles Mingus. TOWN HALL CONCERT. Fantasy 2823 $4.98.
Audio. July. p66. 800w. 4½
Coda. August. p25-6. 575w. 3

2579 Bill Mitchell. RAGTIME RECYCLED. Ethelyn ER 1750 $6.00.
Jazz Report. No. 2. 200w. 4

2580 Blue Mitchell. VITAL BLUE. Mainstream MRL 343 $5.98.
Downbeat. May 11. p23. 325w. 3
Jazz Journal. May. p34. 100w. 3
Stereo Review. May. p96. 100w. 2½

2581 Roscoe Mitchell Sextet. SOUND. Delmark DS 408 $5.98.
Library Journal. February 15. p667. 50w. 3

2582 Mitchell-Ruff Duo. STRAYHORN. Mainstream MRL 335 $5.98.
Downbeat. February 3. p24. 200w. 2½
Stereo Review. February. p115. 200w. 3

2583 Modern Jazz Quartet. Prestige PR 24005 (2 discs) $6.98. (Reissue.) Cart. M 82405 $9.95. Cass. M 52405 $9.95.
Downbeat. August 17. p28-31. 400w. 3½
Jazz and Blues. November. p30-1. 350w. 4
Jazz Journal. November. p33-4. 400w. 4

New York Times--Sunday. May 7. pD29. 25w. 3
Records and Recordings. December. p103. 175w. 3½
Rolling Stone. May 25. p68. 25w. 3

2584 Modern Jazz Quartet. LEGENDARY PROFILE. Atlantic K 40421 (England). (Reissue.)
Records and Recordings. December. p102. 175w. 1

2585 Modern Jazz Quartet. PLASTIC DREAMS. Atlantic SD 1589 $5.98. Cart. M 81589 $6.97. Cass. M 51589 $6.97.
Coda. June. p21. 475w. 2
Gramophone. May. p1961. 350w. 3
Jazz and Blues. May. p22. 325w. 2½
Jazz Journal. April. p34. 250w. 2
Stereo Review. March. p110. 200w. 2½

2586 Thelonious Monk. Prestige PR 24006 (2 discs) $6.98. Cart. M 82406 $9.95. Cass. M 52406 $9.95.
Downbeat. August 17. p28-31. 400w. 5
Jazz Journal. December. p34. 200w. 5
New York Times--Sunday. May 7. pD29. 25w. 3
Previews. November. p43. 100w. 2
Rolling Stone. May 25. p68. 100w. 4

2587 Thelonious Monk. BLUE MONK, V.2. Prestige PR 7848 $4.98.
Coda. April. p19-20. 325w. 4

2588 Thelonious Monk. SOMETHING IN BLUE. Black Lion 2460 152 (England).
Gramophone. November. p997. 525w. 5
Jazz and Blues. September. p28. 300w. 4
Jazz Journal. October. p34-5. 400w. 4

2589 Lazy Ade Monsbourgh. LATE HOUR BOYS. Swaggie 1273 (Australia).
Coda. October. p25. 275w. 2

2590 Wes Montgomery. CALIFORNIA NIGHTS. A & M Mayfair AM LB 4001 (England) (2 discs). (Reissue.)
Gramophone. June. p112. 50w. 1
Records and Recordings. July. p98. 50w. 1

2591 Wes Montgomery. GENIUS. Riverside 109561/63 (3 discs) (England). (Reissue.)
Records and Recordings. December. p104. 300w. 4

2592 Wes Montgomery. JUST WALKIN'. Verve V 6-8804 $5.98. Cart. 8140-8804 $6.95. Cass. 5104-8804 $6.95.
Downbeat. March 30. p24. 150w. 3½
Saturday Review. March 25. p34. 100w. 2½

2593 Wes Montgomery. THE VERY BEST. Verve 2304 025 (Germany). (Reissue.)
Jazz and Blues. June. p28. 100w. 2

2594 James Moody. EVERYTHING YOU'VE ALWAYS WANTED TO KNOW ABOUT SAX (AND FLUTE). Cadet 2CA 60010 (2 discs) $6.98. (Reissue.)
Crawdaddy. April 30. p18. 1250w. 3
Downbeat. March 2. p20. 250w. 4½

2595 Reggie Moore. WISHBONE. Mainstream MRL 341 $5.98.
Downbeat. May 11. p24. 100w. 3½
Jazz Journal. May. p34. 100w. 2

2596 Max Morath. PLAYS THE BEST OF SCOTT JOPLIN AND OTHER RAG CLASSICS. Vanguard VSD 39/40 (2 discs) $5.98.
High Fidelity. October. p82-3. 500w. 3
Jazz Report. No. 2. 500w. 5
Ragtimer. November/December. p4-5. 750w. 5
Stereo Review. November. p90. 300w. 4

2597 Joe Morello. ANOTHER STEP FORWARD. Ovation ZGO 117 (England).
Gramophone. May. p1961. 200w. 1
Jazz Journal. March. p34. 100w. 0

2598 Lee Morgan. THE GENIUS OF LEE MORGAN. Tradition 2079 $5.98. (Reissue.)
Records and Recordings. November. p109. 125w. 1½

2599 Sam Morgan's Jazz Band/The Get Happy Band/The Blue Ribbon Syncopators. VJM VLP 32 (England).
Jazz Journal. August. p34-5. 500w. 3

2600 JELLY ROLL MORTON. BYG 529 056 (France). (Reissue.)
Jazz Journal. March. p34-5. 125w. 4

2601 JELLY ROLL MORTON. BYG 529 080 (France). (Reissue.)
Jazz and Blues. June. p30. 500w. 1

2602 Jelly Roll Morton. V.1, 2, 3. RCA 730 599/730 605/731 059 (France). (Reissue.)
Coda. October. p25. 500w. 3

2603 Jelly Roll Morton. LIBRARY OF CONGRESS RECORDINGS, V.1. Classic Jazz Masters CJM 2. (Reissue.)
Coda. April. p21. 400w. 5

2604 Jelly Roll Morton. THE 1923/24 PIANO SOLOS. Fountain FJ 104 (England). (Reissue.)
Gramophone. November. p997. 525w. 5

Hi-Fi News and Record Review. November. p2203. 225w. $2\frac{1}{2}$
Jazz Journal. October. p35. 250w. 4

2605 Jelly Roll Morton. RARITIES. Rhapsody RHA 6021 (England).
Jazz Journal. December. p39. 500w. 4
Records and Recordings. December. p103. 275w. $4\frac{1}{2}$

2606 Andy Moses. PLAYS AND SINGS DIXIE. Centaur 699 $5.50.
Coda. December. p20. 425w. 3

2607 Bennie Moten. KANSAS CITY ORCHESTRA, 1923/25. Parlophone PMC 7119 (England). (Reissue.)
Coda. August. p28-9. 225w. 4
Downbeat. March 2. p23. 75w. $2\frac{1}{2}$

2608 Idris Muhammad. PEACE AND RHYTHM. Prestige PR 10036 $5.98. Cart. M 81036 $6.95. Cass. M 51036 $5.95.
Downbeat. October 26. p20, 22. 125w. 3

2609 Gerry Mulligan. THE AGE OF STEAM. A & M SP 3036 $5.98. Cart. 8T 3036 $6.98. Cass. CS 3036 $6.98.
Crawdaddy. December. p83-4. 900w. $2\frac{1}{2}$
Downbeat. December 21. p20. 325w. 5
Gramophone. December. p1232. 400w. 5
New York Times--Sunday. June 11. pD30. 150w. 5
Records and Recordings. October. p122. 100w. 0

2610 Gerry Mulligan and Paul Desmond. QUARTET AND QUINTET. Fantasy 8082 $4.98.
Jazz Journal. July. p31. 325w. 2

2611 Gerry Mulligan/Red Norvo/Stan Hasselgard. WALKING SHOES. Capitol M 11029 $5.98. (Reissue.)
Coda. December. p15-20. 550w. 4
Downbeat. December 21. p29-30. 275w. $3\frac{1}{2}$
Jazz and Blues. June. p8. 275w. 3
Jazz Journal. May. p36. 350w. 3
Previews. November. p44-5. 115w. 2
Sound. October. p46. 50w. 3
Stereo Review. September. p78-9. 50w. 2

2612 Turk Murphy. Merry Makers MMRC 105/6 (2 discs) $11.96.
Coda. December. p21. 475w. 4
Jazz Report. No. 2. 150w. 4

2613 Turk Murphy. THE MANY FACES OF RAGTIME. Atlantic SD 1613 $5.98. Cart. TP 1613 $6.97. Cass. CS 1613 $6.97
High Fidelity. December. p126. 300w. 3
Music Journal. November. p56. 50w. 3

2614 Sunny Murray. SUNSHINE. Byg Actuel 48 (France).
Records and Recordings. June. p88-9. 300w. 3½

2615 The Music Improvisation Company. ECM 1005 ST (Germany).
Records and Recordings. August. p94. 425w. 4

2616 A MUSICAL TRIBUTE TO CHARLIE PARKER ON HIS FIFTIETH BIRTHDAY ANNIVERSARY (anthology). Chess 6310 103/4 (England) (2 discs).
Gramophone. January. p1287-8. 575w. 4
Jazz and Blues. January. p24-5. 600w. 3

2617 Ray Nance. BODY AND SOUL. Sold State SS 18062 $5.98.
Coda. February. p29. 175w. 1

2618 Natural Food. Seeds Records [no serial number] $5.00
Stereo Review. September. p81-2. 275w. 3

2619 Oliver Naylor's Seven Aces. COMPLETE 1924/25 RECORDINGS. Fountain FJ 103 (England). (Reissue.)
Jazz Journal. April. p34. 250w. 3
Records and Recordings. April. p110-1. 250w. 2½

2620 Oliver Nelson. BERLIN DIALOGUE FOR ORCHESTRA. Flying Dutchman FD 10734 $5.95. Cart. M 810134 $6.95. Cass. M 510134 $6.95.
Coda. June. p22. 275w. 3

2621 Oliver Nelson. BLACK, BROWN AND BEAUTIFUL. Flying Dutchman FD 10116 $5.95. Cart. M 8411 $6.95. Cass. M 5411 $6.95.
Coda. April. p21. 475w. 3

2622 Oliver Nelson. THE BLUES AND THE ABSTRACT TRUTH. Impulse AS 5 $5.98.
Jazz Journal. December. p39-40. 400w. 3

2623 Oliver Nelson. MORE BLUES AND ABSTRACT TRUTH. Impulse S 75 $5.98. Cart. M 80075 $6.95.
Jazz Journal. December. p40. 150w. 3

2624 New Iberia Stompers. ONE NIGHT WITH THE NEW IBERIA STOMPERS. "77" SEU 12/40 (England).
Coda. December. p20-1. 275w. 1
Gramophone. March. p1623. 175w. 1
Jazz Journal. January. p33. 300w. 2
Records and Recordings. January. p94. 300w. 3

2625 New Orleans Ragtime Orchestra. Pearl PLP 7 $5.00.
High Fidelity. January. p118. 200w. 3

2626 New Orleans Ragtime Orchestra. Volume 2. Pearl PLP 8 $5.00
Ragtimer. September/October. p10-11. 650w. 3

2627 New Orleans Ragtime Orchestra. Arhoolie 1058 $6.00.
High Fidelity. December. p130. 250w. 2½
Jazz Journal. September. p38. 100w. 2
Library Journal. April 15. p1413. 165w. 2
Music Journal. April. p52. 100w. 3
Music Journal. November. p56. 25w. 2
Stereo Review. June. p102. 75w. 3

2628 New Sunshine Jazz Band. PRESENTS EARLY JAZZ NUMBERS. Fat Cat's Jazz FCJ 115 $5.50.
Coda. December. p21. 575w. 0
Jazz Report. No.1. 225w. 3

2629 NEW THING (anthology). Byg BYG 23 (France) (2 discs). (Reissue.)
Jazz and Blues. February. p28-9. 675w. 2
Jazz Journal. January. p29. 225w. 1

2630 The New York Art Quartet. ESP 1004 $5.50.
Records and Recordings. March. p126. 550w. 5

2631 New York Contemporary Five. LIVE AT JAZZHUS MONTMARTRE, V.2. Sonet SLP 51 (Sweden). (Reissue.)
Jazz Journal. July. p31. 275w. 4

2632 Andy Newman. RAINBOW. Track 2406 103 (England).
Jazz and Blues. December. p29-30. 125w. 3½

2633 David Newman. BEST. Atlantic SD 1590 $5.98. (Reissue.) Cart. M 81590 $6.97. Cass. M 51590 $6.97.
Downbeat. May 25. p18. 25w. 4

2634 David Newman. LONELY AVENUE. Atlantic SD 1600 $5.98. Cart. M 81600 $6.97. Cass. M 51600 $6.97.
Downbeat. May 11. p24. 125w. 4

2635 Newport All Stars. TRIBUTE TO DUKE. BASF 20717 $5.98.
Canadian Stereo Guide. Fall. p29. 50w. 3½
Music Journal. November. p40. 25w. 1

2636 Newport All Stars, 1967. Black Lion 2460 138 (England). (Reissue.)
Gramophone. February. p1447. 150w. 2
Hi-Fi News and Record Review. May. p940. 200w. 3
Jazz and Blues. April. p27-8. 350w. 2½
Jazz Journal. February. p36. 375w. 0
Records and Recordings. January. p94. 125w. 1

2637 Albert Nicholas. Delmark 209 $5.98.
Library Journal. February 15. p667. 100w. 3

2638 The Night Blooming Jazzmen. Mainstream MRL 348 $5.98.
Downbeat. September 14. p20. 350w. 3
Jazz Journal. May. p34. 100w. 2

2639 North Texas State University Lab Band. LAB '69. Century 34297 $5.00.
Coda. February. p28. 150w. 4

2640 North Texas State University Lab Band. LAB '71. Precision 3435 $5.00.
Coda. February. p28. 150w. 4

2641 North Texas State University Lab Band. LIVE! Precision 3274 $5.00.
Coda. February. p28. 150w. 4

2642 Now Creative Arts Jazz Ensemble. NOW. Arhoolie 8002 $6.00.
Jazz Report. No. 2. 75w. 3

2643 Anita O'Day. ANITA AND RHYTHM SECTION. Anita O'Day Records AOD 1 $6.00.
Jazz and Blues. October. p25. 300w. 2
Jazz Journal. September. p38. 150w. 3

2644 King Oliver. PAPA JOE. Decca 79246 $5.98. (Reissue.)
Coda. December. p21-2. 450w. 3

2645 The Olympia Brass Band of New Orleans. Audiophile AP 108 $5.98.
Audio. September. p124. 500w. $3\frac{1}{2}$
Downbeat. April 27. p21-2. 250w. 0
Jazz Report. No. 1. 200w. 4
Music Journal. March. p64. 100w. 2

2646 Original Dixieland Jazz Band. RCA 730 703/4 (France) (2 discs). (Reissue.)
Coda. December. p22. 600w. 5

2647 Harold Ousley. THE KID. Cobblestone CST 9017 $5.98. Cart. M 89017 $6.95. Cass. M 59017 $6.95.
Downbeat. November 23. p19. 125w. 4

2648 Tony Oxley. ICHNOS. RCA SF 8215 (England).
Jazz Journal. January. p33-4. 250w. 3
Records and Recordings. January. p95-6. 100w. 2

2649 "HOT LIPS" Page. FEELIN' HIGH AND HAPPY. RCA LPV 576 $5.98. (Reissue.)

Downbeat. February 3. p24-26. 325w. 4
High Fidelity. February. p118-9. 300w. 2
Jazz and Blues. July. p15. 300w. 2
Music Journal. February. p37. 75w. 1
Rolling Stone. June 22. p62, 64. 325w. $2\frac{1}{2}$

2650 CHARLIE PARKER. Prestige PR 24009 (2 discs) $6.98. (Reissue.)
Coda. December. p24. 425w. 4
Downbeat. August 17. p28-31. 400w. 5
Previews. November. p43. 100w. $2\frac{1}{2}$
Rolling Stone. May 25. p68. 200w. 2

2651 Charlie Parker. THE DEFINITIVE, V.1-3. Metro 2356 059/082/083 (England) (3 discs). (Reissue.)
Gramophone. November. p997-8. 975w. 4
Jazz and Blues. September. p28-9. 550w. 4
Jazz and Blues. November. p28, 30. 550w. 3
Jazz Journal. August. p35. 425w. 5
Jazz Journal. September. p34-5. 475w. 4
Records and Recordings. September. p99. 450w. $3\frac{1}{2}$

2652 Charlie Parker. THE DEFINITIVE, V.4. Metro 2356 087 (England). (Reissue.)
Jazz and Blues. December. p30. 325w. 5
Jazz Journal. November. p34. 250w. 3
Records and Recordings. December. p104. 475w. $3\frac{1}{2}$

2653 Charlie Parker. THE DEFINITIVE, V.5. Metro 2356 088 (England). (Reissue.)
Jazz Journal. December. p40. 400w. 4

2654 Charlie Parker. LULLABY IN RHYTHM. Spotlite 107 (England). (Reissue.)
Coda. April. p22. 350w. 3
Jazz Journal. April. p35. 75w. 3
Records and Recordings. May. p103-4. 175w. 3

2655 Charlie Parker. ON DIAL, V.1-6. Spotlite 101/6 (England). (Reissue.)
Jazz and Blues. April. p28-9. 1000w. 5
Jazz Journal. April. p34-5. 1250w. 5
Records and Recordings. May. p103. 550w. 5

2656 Charlie Parker. PENSIVE BIRD. Ember CJS 821 (England). (Reissue.)
Jazz Journal. July. p31-2. 275w. 5

2657 Evan Parker/Derek Bailey/Han Bennink. THE TOPOGRAPHY OF THINGS. Incus 1 (England).
Coda. February. p23. 675w. 4

2658 Cecil Payne. BROOKFIELD ANDANTE. Spotlite CP 2 (England).
Jazz and Blues. November. p33. 400w. 2½
Jazz Journal. September. p35. 400w. 5
Records and Recordings. September. p97. 225w. 2½

2659 Annette Peacock. I'M THE ONE. RCA LSP 4578 $5.98.
Downbeat. April 27. p16. 325w. 4½
Records and Recordings. August. p94-5. 200w. 0

2660 Pearce-Pickering Ragtime Five. JAZZMANIA. Swaggie 1272 (Australia).
Coda. December. p24. 200w. 3

2661 Jim Pepper. PEPPER'S POW WOW. Embryo SD 731 $5.98. Cart. M 8731 $6.98. Cass. M 5731 $6.95.
Beetle. March 29. 500w. 3

2662 Oscar Peterson. EXCLUSIVELY FOR MY FRIENDS, V.1 (Action). BASF 20668 $5.98. (Reissue.)
Gramophone. October. p786. 300w. 5
Records and Recordings. October. p120. 100w. 5

2663 Oscar Peterson. HELLO HERBIE. BASF 20723 $5.98. Cart. 40723 $6.98. Cass. 30723 $6.98.
Canadian Stereo Guide. Summer. p67. 100w. 3
Music Journal. November. p40. 25w. 3

2664 Oscar Peterson. MOTIONS AND EMOTIONS. BASF 20713 $5.98. Cart. 40713 $6.98. Cass. 30713 $6.98.
Music Journal. November. p40. 25w. 3

2665 Oscar Peterson. WALKING THE LINE. MPS CRM 868 (Germany).
Coda. December. p24. 250w. 4

2666 The Pharoahs. AWAKENING, V.1. Scarab 001 A $5.98.
Downbeat. August 17. p23, 26. 150w. 4

2667 Sid Phillips. CHICAGO AND ALL THAT JAZZ. Rediffusion ZS 27 (England).
Jazz Journal. April. p36. 125w. 2

2668 Sid Phillips. PLAYS BARRELHOUSE PIANO. Rediffusion ZS 106 (England).
Hi-Fi News and Record Review. September. p1681. 50w. 2½
Jazz Journal. August. p36. 100w. 1

2669 Sid Phillips. PLAY STOMP, RAGS AND BLUES. Rediffusion ZS 110 (England).
Hi-Fi News and Record Review. September. p1681. 50w. 2½
Jazz and Blues. September. p29-30. 200w. 1
Jazz Journal. September. p35. 125w. 0

2670 PICTURE RAGS (anthology). Trans Atlantic TRA SAM 26 (England). (Reissue.)
Jazz Journal. August. p38. 200w. 3

2671 Bobby Pierce. INTRODUCING. Cobblestone CST 9016 $5.98. Cart. M 89016 $6.95. Cass. M 59016 $6.95.
Downbeat. December 7. p23. 250w. 5

2672 PITCHIN' BOGGIE; A SECOND COLLECTION OF BOOGIE WOOGIE RARITIES (anthology). Milestone MLP 2018 $4.98. (Reissue.)
Stereo Review. December. p112. 100w. 2½

2673 Portena Jazz Band. V.5. Trova XT 80029 (Argentina).
Jazz Report. No.2. 125w. 5

2674 Baden Powell. TRISTEZA ON GUITAR. BASF 29623 $5.98. Cart. 49623 $6.98. Cass. 39623 $6.98.
Coda. April. p28. 250w. 3
Gramophone. October. p783. 400w. 4
Music Journal. November. p40. 75w. 3

2675 Bud Powell. BOUNCING WITH BUD. Delmark 406 $5.98. (Reissue.)
Library Journal. June 1. p2067. 150w. 3½

2676 Bud Powell. THE INVISIBLE CAGE. Polydor 2460 153 (England). (Reissue.)
Gramophone. October. p786, 791. 375w. 4
Jazz and Blues. July. p30-1. 400w. 2
Jazz Journal. July. p32. 200w. 3
Records and Recordings. June. p86-7. 175w. 4

2677 Bud Powell. 1924/66. ESP DISK 1066 $5.98. (Reissue.)
Coda. April. p22. 175w. 2

2678 Andre Previn. AT SUNSET. Black Lion 2460 154 (England). (Reissue.)
Gramophone. October. p791. 375w. 3
Hi-Fi News and Record Review. September. p1682. 50w. 2½
Jazz and Blues. July. p31-2. 375w. 2½
Jazz Journal. June. p33. 350w. 2
Records and Recordings. June. p87. 150w. 4

2679 RAGTIME 1: THE CITY (BANJOS, BRASS BANDS, AND NICKEL PIANOS) (anthology). RBF 17 $5.95. (Reissue.)
Journal of American Folklore. January/March. p100. 25w. $2\frac{1}{2}$
Old Time Music. Winter. p26. 300w. 3

2680 RAGTIME 2: THE COUNTRY (MANDOLINS, FIDDLES, AND GUITARS) (anthology). RBF 18 $5.95. (Reissue.)
Journal of American Folklore. January/March. p100. 25w. $2\frac{1}{2}$
Old Time Music. Winter. p26. 300w. 3

2681 RAGTIME PIANO ROLL CLASSICS (anthology). BYG 529 063 (France). (Reissue.)
Jazz Journal. March. p34-5. 125w. 3

2682 Chuck Rainey Coalition. Cobblestone CST 9008 $5.98. Cart. M 89008 $6.95. Cass. M 59008 $6.95.
Downbeat. September 14. p22. 100w. 3
High Fidelity. September. p102-3. 300w. 3

2683 Freddie Randall. Rediffusion ZS 84 (England).
Jazz Journal. April. p36. 550w. 3

2684 Django Reinhardt. Barclay 920 366 (France). (Reissue.)
Gramophone. November. p998. 325w. 4

2685 Django Reinhardt. DJANGO IN ROME, 1949/50. Parlophone PCS 7146 (England). (Reissue.)
Gramophone. June. p121-2. 250w. 3
Jazz Journal. May. p30. 500w. 3

2686 Django Reinhardt. DJANGOLOGIE, 1938/39, V. 8. EMI C-054 16008 (France). (Reissue.)
Downbeat. March 2. p22. 125w. $4\frac{1}{2}$

2687 Don Rendell. SPACE WALK. Columbia SCX 6491 (England).
Gramophone. October. p791. 425w. 4
Hi-Fi News and Record Review. September. p1687. 225w. $2\frac{1}{2}$
Jazz and Blues. July. p32. 275w. $2\frac{1}{2}$
Jazz Journal. June. p34. 300w. 3
Records and Recordings. September. p99-100. 300w. $3\frac{1}{2}$

2688 Buddy Rich. A DIFFERENT DRUMMER. RCA Victor LSP 4593 $5.98. Cart. PS * 1819 $6.95. Cass. PK 1819 $6.95.
Gramophone. March. p1624. 175w. 3
High Fidelity. March. p114-5. 400w. $3\frac{1}{2}$
Hi-Fi News and Record Review. June. p1129. 200w. 2

Jazz Journal. January. p34. 300w. 3
Saturday Review. May 20. p42. 50w. 2½

2689 Buddy Rich. RICH IN LONDON. RCA LSP 4666 $5.98. Cart. P 8S 1895 $6.98. Cass. PK 1895 $6.98.
Downbeat. July 20. p39. 400w. 4
High Fidelity. November. p128, 130. 200w. 2½
Music Journal. June. p36. 125w. 0
New York Times--Sunday. May 7. pD29. 25w. 2½
Saturday Review. May 20. p47. 50w. 2½
Stereo Review. October. p110. 100w. 0

2690 Buddy Rich and Louis Bellson. ARE YOU READY FOR THIS? Roulette 2432 003 (England). (Reissue.)
Gramophone. March. p1624. 100w. 3½

2691 Buddy Rich, et al. CONVERSATIONS - A DRUMS SPECTACULAR, WITH KENNY CLARKE AND LOUIS BELLSON. Parlophone PCS 7151 (England). (Reissue.)
Jazz Journal. July. p32. 550w. 3
Records and Recordings. July. p95-6. 200w. 0

2692 Johnny Richards. WIDE RANGE. Creative World ST 1052 $5.50.
Jazz Journal. January. p34. 525w. 0

2693 Joshua Rifkin. PIANO RAGS BY SCOTT JOPLIN. Nonesuch H 71248 $2.98.
Gramophone. June. p122. 225w. 4
High Fidelity. October. p82-3. 500w. 3
Jazz Journal. March. p34-5. 125w. 5
Jazz Report. No. 2. 125w. 4

2694 Joshua Rifkin. SCOTT JOPLIN PIANO RAGS, V. 2. Nonesuch H 71264 $2.98.
High Fidelity. October. p82-3. 500w. 3
Hi-Fi News and Records Review. September. p1686. 175w. 5
Sound. September. p50. 75w. 3

2695 Sonny Rollins. Everest FS 220 $3.98. (Reissue.)
Coda. August. p29. 100w. 3

2696 Sonny Rollins. Prestige 24004 (2 discs) $6.98. Cart. M 82404 DP $9.95. Cass. M 52404 DP $9.95. (Reissue.)
Coda. December. p24-5. 575w. 4
Downbeat. August 17. p28-31. 400w. 3½
Gramophone. December. p1233. 600w. 4
Jazz and Blues. December. p27-8. 600w. 5
Jazz Journal. November. p34. 250w. 3
Previews. November. p43. 100w. 2
Records and Recordings. November. p109. 75w. 5
Rolling Stone. May 25. p68. 200w. 4

2697 Sonny Rollins. NEXT ALBUM. Milestone MSP 9042 $5.98.
Downbeat. November 9. p19. 550w. 5
Rolling Stone. July 12. p66. 1200w. 4

2698 Wally Rose. ON PIANO. Blackbird S 12007 $4.98.
High Fidelity. September. p107-8. 200w. 2

2699 Roswell Rudd. America 30 AM 6114 (France). (Reissue.)
Jazz Journal. June. p34-5. 275w. 3
Records and Recordings. April. p112. 500w. 5

2700 RUGGED PIANO CLASSICS, 1927/29 (anthology). Origin. Jazz Library OJL 15 $6.00.
Journal of American Folklore. January/March. p106. 25w. 2½

2701 George Russell. ELECTRONIC SONATA FOR SOULS LOVED BY NATURE. Flying Dutchman FD 10124 $5.95.
Downbeat. March 16. p28, 30. 275w. 2

2702 [no entry.]

2703 Luis Russell. CBS 63721 (France). (Reissue.)
Downbeat. March 2. p23. 75w. 4

2704 Luis Russell. Collector's Classics CC 34 (Denmark). (Reissue.)
Jazz Journal. January. p34-5. 300w. 1

2705 Pee Wee Russell. MAINSTREAM JAZZ. Ember CJS 824 (England). (Reissue.)
Gramophone. October. p791. 275w. 3
Jazz Journal. September. p35. 275w. 3½

2706 Ray Russell. LIVE AT THE ICA. RCA SF 8214 (England).
Jazz Journal. February. p36. 200w. 0
Records and Recordings. January. p96. 100w. 2

2707 Jean Sablon and Django Reinhardt. Parlophone PMC 7134 (England). (Reissue.)
Gramophone. January. p1288. 150w. 3
Jazz Journal. January. p35. 550w. 4

2708 Pharoah Sanders. BLACK UNITY. Impulse AS 9219 $5.98. Cart. M 89219 $6.95. Cass. M 59219 $6.95.
Crawdaddy. May 28. p16. 750w. 4
Downbeat. September 14. p22. 400w. 3½

2709 Pharoah Sanders. DEAF, DUMB, BLIND. Impulse AS 9199 $5.98.
Coda. April. p22. 525w. 3
Jazz and Blues. January. p25. 300w. 2½

2710 Pharoah Sanders. JEWELS OF THOUGHT. Impulse AS 9190 $5.98. Cart. M 89190 $6.95.
Coda. February. p23. 425w. 4

2711 Pharoah Sanders. LIVE AT THE EAST. Impulse AS 9227 $5.98. Cart. M 89227 $6.95. Cass. M 59227 $6.95.
Downbeat. December 21. p20, 22. 150w. 3

2712 Pharoah Sanders. THEMBI. Impulse AS 9206 $5.98. Cart. 8027-9206 V $6.95.
Coda. December. p25-7. 1700w. 4
Downbeat. February 17. p21-2. 500w. 4

2713 Mongo Santamaria. MONGO AT MONTREUX. Atlantic SD 1593 $5.98. Cart. M 81593 $6.97. Cass. M 51593 $6.97.
Downbeat. March 2. p22. 75w. 3½

2714 Sart. ECM 1015 ST (Germany).
Records and Recordings. August. p95. 200w. 2½

2715 Sauter-Finegan Orchestra. RCA DPM 2025 (England) (2 discs). (Reissue.)
Gramophone. November. p998. 525w. 4
Hi-Fi News and Record Review. November. p2201. 75w. 4

2716 Sauter-Finegan Orchestra. Sunset SLS 50253 (England).
Jazz Journal. January. p37. 75w. 1
Records and Recordings. January. p95. 100w. 0

2717 Jan Savitt. 1938/39. First Time FTR 1505 $5.50.
New York Times--Sunday. October 8. pD34. 275w. 4

2718 Seatown Seven. READY FOR THE RIVER. After Hours 1204 ST (Germany).
Coda. June. p22. 350w. 3
Jazz and Blues. January. p24. 325w. 4

2719 Septober Energy. RCA Neon NE 9 (England).
Records and Recordings. January. p95. 100w. 1

2720 SESSION AT MIDNIGHT. Capitol 052-81006 (Denmark). (Reissue.)
Jazz and Blues. October. p24. 275w. 2½
Jazz Journal. May. p34. 250w. 3

2721 SESSION AT RIVERSIDE. Capitol 052 81004 (Denmark). (Reissue.)
Jazz and Blues. October. p24. 275w. 2
Jazz Journal. May. p34. 200w. 4

2722 The Seven Ages of Man. Rediffusion ZS 105 (England).
Jazz and Blues. October. p24-5. 375w. 0

2723 Sonny Shamrock. MONKEY-POCKIE-BOO. Byg Actuel 37 (France).
Records and Recordings. June. p89. 75w. 0

2724 Artie Shaw. FEATURING ROY ELDRIDGE, 1944/45. RCA LPV 582 $5.98.
Downbeat. July 20. p39-40. 600w. 3½
New York Times--Sunday. May 7. pD29. 25w. 3
New York Times--Sunday. June 11. pD28. 550w. 3½
Saturday Review. June 17. p80. 125w. 2½

2725 Artie Shaw. 1937/38, V.1/3. First Time Records 1501/3 (3 discs) $16.50.
New York Times--Sunday. June 11. pD28. 500w. 4

2726 Artie Shaw. THIS IS. RCA VPM 6039 (2 discs) $6.98. (Reissue.). Cart. P85-5096 $6.95. Cass. PU 5096 $6.95.
Coda. April. p26. 125w. 2
Downbeat. February 3. p24-26. 375w. 2½
Library Journal. March 1. p857. 50w. 2½

2727 Artie Shaw. THIS IS, V.2. RCA VPM 6062 (2 discs) $6.98. (Reissue.)
Gramophone. December. p1226. 25w. 2½

2728 Woody Shaw. BLACKSTONE LEGACY. Contemporary S 7627/8 (2 discs) $11.96.
Coda. June. p22. 525w. 3
Downbeat. May 25. p25. 625w. 4

2729 Dave Shepherd. MR. SHEPHERD PLAYS MR. GOODMAN. Rediffusion ZS 30 (England).
Jazz Journal. January. p35. 150w. 1

2730 Dave Shepherd. PLAYS MORE GOODMAN. Rediffusion ZS 31 (England).
Jazz Journal. January. p35. 150w. 1

2731 Archie Shepp. ATTICA BLUES. Impulse AS 9222 $5.98. Cart. M 89222 $6.95. Cass. M 59222 $6.95.
Downbeat. November. p19, 22. 450w. 4
Jazz Journal. November. p35. 550w. 0
New York Times--Sunday. June 11. pD30. 300w. 5
Popular Music. Summer. p247. 25w. 4
Rolling Stone. August 17. p50. 1000w. 5
Saturday Review. August 12. p66. 50w. 2

2732 Archie Shepp. FOR LOSERS. Impulse AS 9188 $5.98. Cart. M 87188 $6.95. Cass. M 59188 $6.95
Jazz Journal. January. p35. 300w. 3

2733 Archie Shepp. IN EUROPE, V.1. Delmark DS 409 $5.98.
Library Journal. June 1. p2069. 175w. 2

2734 Archie Shepp. LIVE AT THE PANAFRICAN FESTIVAL. Byg Actuel 51 (France).
Records and Recordings. August. p95. 350w. 4

2735 Archie Shepp. THINGS HAVE GOT TO CHANGE. Impulse AS 9212 $5.98. Cart. M 89212 $6.95. Cass. M 59212 $6.95.
Jazz Journal. February. p36. 300w. 4

2736 Alan Shorter. PARABOLIC. Verve 2304 060 (England).
Jazz and Blues. July. p32. 350w. $3\frac{1}{2}$
Jazz Journal. June. p35. 300w. 3
Records and Recordings. August. p95. 225w. $2\frac{1}{2}$

2737 Alan Shorter. TES ESAT. America 30 AM 6118 (France).
Records and Recordings. August. p95. 225w. 3

2738 Alan Silva. CELESTIAL COMMUNICATION ORCHESTRA. Byg Actuel 42/44 (France) (3 discs).
Jazz and Blues. March. p28. 475w. 3
Records and Recordings. June. p89. 125w. 0

2739 Horace Silver. THE UNITED STATES OF MIND: PHASE 2 (TOTAL RESPONSE). Blue Note. BST 84380 $5.98.
Downbeat. October 26. p28-9. 275w. $3\frac{1}{2}$
Jazz and Blues. September. p30. 200w. 0
Jazz Journal. July. p27. 225w. 0
Previews. November. p45-6. 75w. 2
Saturday Review. November 4. p92. 50w. 2

2740 Horace Silver. THE UNITED STATES OF MIND: PHASE 3 (ALL). Blue Note BST 84420 $5.98.
Saturday Review. November 4. p92. 50w. 2

2741 Zoot Sims. FIRST RECORDINGS. Prestige PR 7817 $4.98.
Coda. April. p23. 500w. 3

2742 Zutty Singleton and Johnny Wiggs. JAZZ FOR THE SEVENTIES. Fat Cat's Jazz FCT 116 $5.50.
Jazz Report. No.1. 250w. 1

2743 Jabbo Smith. THE TRUMPET ACE OF THE TWENTIES, V.1/2. Melodeon MLP 7326/7 (2 discs) $5.98 each. (Reissue.)
Previews. October. p46. 200w. $2\frac{1}{2}$

2744 Jimmy Smith. BEST, V1. Verve V6-8721 $5.98. Cart. 8140 8721M $6.95. (Reissue.)
Gramophone. March. p1624. 125w. 3

Records and Recordings. January. p96. 75w. 3

2745 Jimmy Smith. BEST, V. 2. Verve 2304 004 (England). (Reissue.)
Jazz and Blues. December. p31. 300w. 2½
Jazz Journal. December. p40. 75w. 0

2746 Jimmy Smith. I'M GOIN' GIT MYSELF TOGETHER. MGM S-4751 $5.98. Cart. 8130-4751M $6.95.
Gramophone. January. p1288. 75w. 2

2747 Jimmy Smith. A WALK ON THE WILD SIDE. Metro 2682 025 (England) (2 discs). (Reissue.)
Jazz Journal. August. p36. 300w. 4
Records and Recordings. May. p104. 200w. 3

2748 Stuff Smith. BLACK VIOLIN. MPS 15147 (Germany).
Coda. February. p29. 175w. 1

2749 Stuff Smith and Stephane Grappelly. STUFF AND STEFF. Everest FS 238 $3.98. (Reissue.)
Gramophone. April. p1780. 175w. 2½
Hi-Fi News and Record Review. September. p1686. 150w. 2½
Jazz and Blues. May. p22-3. 275w. 2
Jazz Journal. March. p35. 250w. 3
Records and Recordings. May. p104. 200w. 2½

2750 Willie Smith. ALTO SAXOPHONIST SUPREME! GNP Crescendo GNP 52055 $4.98. Cart. 8-2055 $6.95. Cass. 5-2055 $6.95.
Gramophone. July. p260. 300w. 3
Jazz and Blues. October. p25-6. 325w. 2½
Jazz Journal. July. p33. 450w. 3

2751 Willie "The Lion" Smith and Don Ewell. GRAND PIANO. Exclusive 501 (Canada).
Jazz and Blues. January. p24. 200w. 4

2752 Willie "The Lion" Smith. MEMOIRS. RCA LSP 6016 (2 discs) $6.98.
Ragtimer. September/October. p10-11. 650w. 3

2753 Willie "The Lion" Smith. PORK AND BEANS. Black Lion 2460 156 (England).
Gramophone. October. p791. 150w. 3
Jazz and Blues. September. p30. 325w. 3½
Jazz Journal. July. p33-4. 325w. 3
Records and Recordings. July. p96-7. 175w. 2½

2754 Martial Solal. SANS TAMBOR NI TROMPETTE. RCA 730 105 (France).
Coda. June. p22-3. 225w. 3

2755 Muggsy Spanier. THIS IS JAZZ. Jazzology J 33 $5.98. (Reissue.)
Downbeat. August 17. p26-7. 125w. 5

2756 SPIRITUALS TO SWING; LEGENDARY CARNEGIE HALL CONCERTS OF 1938/39 (anthology). Vanguard VRS 8523/4 (England) (2 discs). (Reissue.)
Blues Unlimited. December. p28. 50w. 2
Jazz and Blues. December. p31-2. 450w. 3½
Records and Recordings. December. p104. 150w. 5

2757 Spontaneous Music Ensemble. BIRDS OF A FEATHER. BYG 529 023 (England).
Jazz Journal. June. p36. 250w. 3
Records and Recordings. May. p101. 300w. 2½

2758 The Squadronaires. THERE'S SOMETHING IN THE AIR. Decca/Eclipse ECM 2112 (England). (Reissue.)
Gramophone. September. p585. 350w. 3
Hi-Fi News and Record Review. September. p1682. 75w. 3
Jazz Journal. August. p36-7. 500w. 3

2759 Jess Stacy. PIANO SOLOS. Swaggie 1248 (Australia). (Reissue.)
Coda. April. p23. 300w. 4

2760 Jeremy Steig. WAY FARING STRANGER. Blue Note BST 84354 $5.98.
Coda. April. p23-4. 225w. 3

2761 Sonny Stitt. BLACK VIBRATIONS. Prestige 10032 $5.98. Cart. M 81032 $6.95. Cass. M 51032 $6.95.
Downbeat. September 14. p24-5. 225w. 3½

2762 Sonny Stitt. STITT'S BITS, V.2. Prestige PR 7612 $4.98.
Coda. April. p24. 325w. 3

2763 Sonny Stitt. TUNE-UP. Cobblestone CST 9013 $5.98. Cart. M 89013 $6.95. Cass. M 59013 $6.95.
Downbeat. June 22. p18. 350w. 5
New York Times--Sunday. June 11. pD30. 100w. 4
Saturday Review. June 17. p80. 100w. 2½

2764 Sonny Stitt and Gene Ammons. YOU TALK THAT TALK. Prestige PR 10019 $5.98. Cart. M 81019 $6.95. Cass. M 51019 $6.95.
Downbeat. September 14. p24-5. 225w. 3½

2765 STOMPING AT THE SAVOY (anthology). Black Lion 2460 118 (England). (Reissue.)
Hi-Fi News and Record Review. June. p1129. 250w. 3

2766 Frank Strazzeri. THAT'S HIM AND THIS IS NEW. Revelation S10 $4.98.
Coda. April. p22-3. 175w. 3

2767 STRICTLY BEBOP (anthology). Capitol M 11058 $5.98. (Reissue.)
Downbeat. December 21. p32. 175w. 5
Jazz Journal. July. p36. 225w. 4
Previews. November. p43-4. 125w. 3½

2768 Ira Sullivan. Delmark DL 402 $5.98.
Library Journal. February 15. p667. 125w. 2½

2769 Ira Sullivan. NICKY'S TUNE. Delmark DS 422 $5.98.
Audio. April. p70. 750w. 3½
Library Journal. February 15. p667. 100w. 2½

2770 Sun Ra. SOUND OF JOY. Delmark DS 414 $5.98. (Reissue.)
Library Journal. March 1. p856-7. 200w. 2½

2771 Sun Ra. SUN SONG. Delmark DS 411 $5.98. (Reissue.)
Library Journal. March 1. p856-7. 200w. 2½

2772 Sun Ra and His Solar Arkestra. THE SOLAR MYTH APPROACH, V.1/2. Byg 529 340/1 (France) (2 discs).
Jazz and Blues. March. p28. 650w. 4
Jazz Journal. March. p36. 350w. 4
Records and Recordings. April. p114. 450w. 5

2773 The Sunset All Stars. JAMMIN' AT SUNSET, V.1. Polydor 2460 132 (England). (Reissue.)
Gramophone. July. p260. 375w. 4

2774 The Sunset All Stars. JAMMIN' AT SUNSET, V.2. Polydor 2460 137 (England). (Reissue.)
Gramophone. July. p260. 375w. 4
Jazz Journal. January. p35-6. 550w. 3
Records and Recordings. January. p94. 125w. 4

2775 John Surman. CONFLAGRATION. Dawn DNLS 3022 (England).
Coda. June. p16. 525w. 4

2776 John Surman. HOW MANY CLOUDS CAN YOU SEE. Deram SML-R1045 (England).
Coda. June. p15. 1500w. 4

2777 John Surman. LIVE IN ALTENA. JG Records 018 ST (England).
Coda. June. p16. 350w. 3

2778 John Surman. THE TRIO. Dawn DNLS 3006 (England) (2 discs).
Coda. June. p16. 350w. 3

2779 John Surman. WESTERING HOME. Island HELP 10 (England).
Records and Recordings. December. p104. 300w. 3½

2780 John Surman. WHERE FORTUNE SMILES. Dawn DNLS 3006 (England).
Coda. June. p16. 450w. 3

2781 John Surman and John Warren. TALES OF THE ALGONQUIN. Deram SML 1094 (England).
Jazz and Blues. April. p30. 150w. 2
Jazz Journal. January. p36. 175w. 4

2782 Ralph Sutton. AN ADVENTURE IN JAZZ PIANO. Solo S 103 $5.50.
Jazz and Blues. August. p32. 450w. 3½

2783 Ralph Sutton. KNOCKED-OUT NOCTURNE. Project Three PR 5040 $5.98.
Jazz and Blues. August. p32. 450w. 4

2784 SWING, V.1. RCA LPV 578 $5.98. (Reissue.)
Downbeat. February 3. p24-26. 325w. 4
High Fidelity. February. p118-9. 300w. 2
Jazz and Blues. July. p16. 425w. 3
Music Journal. February. p36-7. 250w. 1
Rolling Stone. June 22. p62, 64. 225w. 4
Sound. March. p19. 75w. 3
Stereo Review. February. p115-6. 575w. 2½

2785 THE SWING ERA; THE MUSIC OF 1937-1938. Time Life STL 343 (3 discs).
Hi-Fi News and Record Reviews. August. p1473. 150w. 5

2786 THE SWING ERA; THE MUSIC OF 1938-1939. Time Life STL 343 (3 discs).
Hi-Fi News and Record Reviews. August. p1473. 150w. 5

2787 SWING EXERCISE (anthology). Capitol M 11035 $5.98. (Reissue.)
Coda. December. p15-20. 550w. 3
Downbeat. December 21. p32. 200w. 3½
Jazz and Blues. August. p23-4. 350w. 2½
Jazz Journal. June. p11, 40. 600w. 3
Previews. November. p44-5. 115w. 2½
Saturday Review. August 12. p66. 100w. 2½

Sound. October. p46. 75w. 2
Stereo Review. September. p78-9. 50w. 2½

2788 SWING SESSIONS; V.1/2, 1937/39 (anthology). EMI C-054-16021/2 (France). (Reissue.)
Jazz Journal. April. p36-7. 400w. 3

2789 SWING SESSIONS, V.3, 1938/39 (anthology). EML C-054-16023 (France). (Reissue.)
Jazz Journal. May. p32. 200w. 3

2790 SWING SESSIONS, V.4, 1937/43 (anthology). EMI C-054-16024 (France). (Reissue.)
Jazz Journal. October. p36-7. 750w. 2½

2791 SWING SESSIONS, V.5, 1940/42 (anthology). EMI C-054-16025 (France). (Reissue.)
Jazz Journal. May. p32. 175w. 1

2792 SWING SESSIONS, V.6, 1946 (anthology). EMI C-054-16026 (France). (Reissue.)
Jazz Journal. June. p36. 150w. 1

2793 SWING SESSIONS, V.7, 1946-1949 (anthology). EMI C-054-16027 (France). (Reissue.)
Jazz Journal. June. p36. 150w. 1

2794 SWING SESSIONS, V.8, (anthology). EMI C-054-16038 (France). (Reissue.)
Jazz Journal. May. p31. 175w. 1

2795 SWING SESSIONS, V.9, 1946/50 (anthology). EMI C-054-16029 (France). (Reissue.)
Jazz Journal. September. p35-6. 675w. 3½

2796 SWING SESSIONS, V.10, 1946/50 (anthology). EMI C-054-16030 (France). (Reissue.)
Jazz Journal. September. p36. 400w. 3½

2797 Gabor Szabo. HIGH CONTRAST. Blue Thumb BTS 28 $5.98. Cart. BT 8-28 $6.95. Cass. BT 5-28 $6.95.
Downbeat. February 17. p22-3. 275w. 3½

2798 Buddy Tate. CELEBRITY CLUB ORCHESTRA, V.2. Black and Blue 33 020 (France).
Coda. February. p15. 115w. 3

2799 Buddy Tate. UNBROKEN. BASF 20740 $5.98.
Coda. February. p15. 115w. 4
High Fidelity. November. p128. 150w. 3
Music Journal. November. p40. 75w. 4
Saturday Review. November 4. p92. 100w. 2½

2800 Art Tatum. AND HIS FRIENDS BENNY CARTER AND LOUIS BELLSON. Metro 2682 024 (England) (2 discs). (Reissue.
Jazz Journal. May. p32. 275w. 5
Records and Recordings. May. p100. 225w. 5

2801 Art Tatum. GENIUS. Black Lion 2460 158 (England). (Reissue.)
Gramophone. November. p998-1003 600w. 3
Jazz and Blues. November. p31-2. 400w. 3
Jazz Journal. November. p35-6. 300w. 4
Records and Recordings. December. p103. 250w. 4

2802 Art Tatum. PIANO SOLOS. Jazz Piano JP 5005 (Denmark). (Reissue.)
Jazz Journal. October. p37-8. 400w. 5

2803 Art Tatum. SOLO PIANO. Capitol M 11028 $5.98. (Reissue.)
Coda. December. p15-20. 550w. 4
Downbeat. December 21. p31. 100w. 5
Jazz and Blues. June. p8. 325w. 4
Jazz Journal. May. p36. 275w. 4
Previews. December. p44-5. 115w. 3
Stereo Review. September. p78-9. 50w. $2\frac{1}{2}$

2804 Billy Taylor. O.K., BILLY! Bell S6049 $4.98. Cart. M 6049 $6.95. Cass. M 56049 $6.95.
Coda. April. p24. 350w. 3

2805 Billy Taylor. SLEEPING BEE. MPS 15234 (Germany).
Coda. April. p22. 175w. 2

2806 Cecil Taylor and Archie Shepp. Barnaby Z 30502 $4.98.
New York Times--Sunday. May 7. pD29. 25w. 3

2807 Cecil Taylor. NEW YORK CITY R & B. Barnaby KZ 31035 $5.98.
Creem. August. p62. 200w. $2\frac{1}{2}$
Downbeat. December 21. p22. 250w. $4\frac{1}{2}$
New York Times--Sunday. May 7. pD29. 25w. 3
Previews. November. p46. 150w. $3\frac{1}{2}$
Rolling Stone. May 25. p68. 150w. 3

2808 Cecil Taylor. INNOVATIONS. Freedom 2383 094 (England).
Gramophone. October. p791. 175w. 3
Jazz and Blues. May. p24. 300w. 4
Jazz Journal. April. p37. 350w. 5
Records and Recordings. April. p111. 100w. 5

2809 Jack Teagarden. GREAT SOLOISTS, 1929/36. Biograph BLP C-2 $5.98. (Reissue.)

High Fidelity. October. p124. 450w. $2\frac{1}{2}$
Jazz Journal. September. p36-7. 150w. 3
Music Journal. December. p15. 50w. $2\frac{1}{2}$
Previews. November. p45. 250w. $2\frac{1}{2}$

2810 Jack Teagarden. THE LEGENDARY. Roulette 2682 034 (England) (2 discs). (Reissue.)
Gramophone. September. p585. 200w. 3
Hi-Fi News and Record Review. September. p1681. 75w. $2\frac{1}{2}$
Jazz and Blues. July. p32, 34. 375w. $3\frac{1}{2}$
Jazz Journal. June. p37. 275w. 2
Records and Recordings. June. p87. 125w. 2

2811 Jack Teagarden. TEXAS T. PARTY. RCA 731 088 (France). (Reissue.)
Jazz and Blues. May. p25. 275w. $3\frac{1}{2}$

2812 Jack Teagarden. THE UNFORGETTABLE. Halcyon HAL 4 (England). (Reissue.)
Coda. April. p24-5. 400w. 5

2813 Jack Teagarden/Pee Wee Russell. byg BYG 529 066 (France). (Reissue.)
Downbeat. March 2. p22-3. 75w. 5

2814 Buddy Terry. AWARENESS. Mainstream MRL 336 $5.98.
Downbeat. February 3. p24. 100w. $3\frac{1}{2}$

2815 Buddy Terry. PURE DYNAMITE. Mainstream MRL 356 $5.98. Cart. M 8356 $6.95. Cass. M 5356 $6.95.
Downbeat. November 9. p27. 200w. 4

2816 Clark Terry. ANGYUMALUMA BONGLIDDLEANY NANNY-ANY AWHAN Y. Mainstream MRL 347 $5.98.
Jazz Journal. May. p34. 100w. 3

2817 Clark Terry-Bob Brookmeyer Quintet. Mainstream MRL 320 $5.98.
Downbeat. March 30. p24. 75w. $4\frac{1}{2}$
New York Times--Sunday. May 7. pD29. 25w. 3

2818 THEY ALL PLAYED THE MAPLE LEAF RAG (anthology). Hermin 401 $5.95. (Reissue.)
Coda. April. p27. 350w. 4
High Fidelity. April. p111. 175w. $2\frac{1}{2}$
Jazz Journal. June. p34. 675w. 4
Music Journal. November. p40, 56. 50w. 3
Previews. September. p42. 200w. $2\frac{1}{2}$
Ragtimer. January/February. p8-9. 1400w. 4

2819 THIS IS THE BIG BAND ERA (anthology). RCA VPM 6042 (2 discs) $6.98. (Reissue.)

Downbeat. February 3. p24-26. 325w. 2
Gramophone. November. p1003. 750w. 3
Hi-Fi News and Record Review. July. p1305. 100w. 3
Jazz Journal. July. p27. 400w. 3
Library Journal. March 1. p857. 50w. 2½

2820 Leon Thomas. GOLD SUNRISE ON MAGIC MOUNTAIN. Flying Dutchman 51-5003 $5.95.
Downbeat. November 9. p28. 200w. 4

2821 Butch Thompson and Chet Ely. MR. JELLY ROLLS ON. Jazette 1004 $5.00.
Coda. February. p16. 500w. 3

2822 Butch Thompson. PLAYS JELLY ROLL MORTON, V.2. Center CLP 9 $5.50.
Ragtimer. September/October. p10-11. 650w. 3

2823 Lucky Thompson. GOODBYE, YESTERDAY! Groove Merchant GM 508 $4.98.
High Fidelity. December. p128. 150w. 2
Music Journal. December. p15, 76. 50w. 2½
Saturday Review. September 30. p83. 100w. 2½

2824 Claude Thornhill. THE EARLY COOL. Ember CJS 828 (England). (Reissue.)
Hi-Fi News and Record Review. September. p1681. 150w. 3
Jazz Journal. August. p37. 250w. 3

2825 Clifford Thornton. THE PANTHER AND THE LASH. America 30 AM 6113 (France).
Records and Recordings. June. p89. 175w. 0

2826 Keith Tippett. BLUEPRINT. RCA SF 8290 (England).
Jazz Journal. November. p36. 250w. 0

2827 Cal Tjader. Fantasy 8406 $4.98. Cart. M 88406 $6.95. Cass. M 58406 $6.95.
Audio. August. p64. 500w. 4

2828 Cal Tjader. LIVE AT THE FUNKY QUARTERS. Fantasy 9409 $5.98. Cart. 8160-9409 M $6.95.
Downbeat. November 23. p22. 150w. 2½

2829 Charles Tolliver. AND HIS ALL STARS. Black Lion 2460 139 (England).
Gramophone. September. p585. 375w. 4
Hi-Fi News and Record Review. May. p940. 225w. 2
Jazz and Blues. February. p31. 325w. 3½
Jazz Journal. January. p37. 425w. 2
Records and Recordings. January. p95. 125w. 4

2830 Charles Tolliver and Stanley Cowell. MUSIC, INC. Freedom 2383 138 (England).
Jazz and Blues. November. p32. 300w. 3
Jazz Journal. November. p36. 325w. 4

2831 Stan Tracey. PERSPECTIVES. Columbia SCX 6485 (England).
Gramophone. May. p1962. 375w. 4
Hi-Fi News and Record Review. July. p1312-3. 350w. $3\frac{1}{2}$
Jazz Journal. May. p32-3. 200w. 3

2832 Traditional Jazz Studio. Supraphon SUA 55830 (Hungary).
Jazz Journal. September. p38. 75w. 2

2833 Traditional Jazz Studio. Edice Gramofonoveho Klubu 15-0794 (Czechoslovakia).
Jazz Journal. September. p38. 75w. 2

2834 Joe Turner. STRIDE BY STRIDE. "77" LEU 12/32 (England).
Coda. April. p26. 125w. 1

2835 Stanley Turrentine. ANOTHER STORY. Blue Note BST 84336 $5.98. Cart. 9071 $6.95. Cass. C 1071 $6.98.
Hi-Fi News and Record Review. September. p1686. 125w. 1

2836 Stanley Turrentine. SUGAR. CTI CTI 6005 $5.98. Cart. CTB 6005 $6.95. Cass. CTC 6005 $6.95.
Jazz Journal. September. p37. 250w. 3

2837 Stanley Turrentine and Milt Jackson. CHERRY. CTI CTI 6017 $5.98. Cart. 8-6017 $6.95. Cass. CTC 6017 $6.95.
Downbeat. October 26. p29. 275w. 4

2838 McCoy Tyner. SAHARA. Milestone MSP 9039 $5.98.
Downbeat. October 12. p22, 24. 250w. 5
Stereo Review. December. p112. 200w. $3\frac{1}{2}$

2839 University of Illinois Jazz Band. AND DIXIE BAND. Century 35865 $5.00.
Coda. February. p27. 150w. 2

2840 University of Illinois Jazz Band. IN STOCKHOLM, SWEDEN. Century 33173 $5.00.
Coda. February. p27. 150w. 3

2841 Thomas Valentine. AT KOHLMAN'S TAVERN. New Orleans NOR 7201 $6.00.
Jazz Report. No. 2. 250w. 4

2842 Sarah Vaughan. Everest FS 250 $3.98. (Reissue.)
Coda. August. p29. 100w. 2

2843 Sarah Vaughan. THE INTIMATE. Roulette 2682 032 (England) (2 discs). (Reissue.)
Gramophone. October. p791-2. 350w. 4
Hi-Fi News and Record Review. September. p1681. 100w. 2½
Jazz Journal. August. p38. 250w. 4

2844 Sarah Vaughan. A TIME IN MY LIFE. Mainstream MRL 340 $5.98. Cart. M 8340 $6.95. Cass. 5340 $6.95.
Downbeat. March 30. p24. 350w. 2½
Jazz Journal. March. p36-7. 175w. 4
Saturday Review. March 25. p34. 100w. 1½
Stereo Review. June. p103. 300w. 4

2845 Sarah Vaughan. WITH MICHEL LEGRAND. Mainstream MRL 361 $5.98. Cart. M 8361 $6.95. Cass. M 5361 $6.95.
Downbeat. November 23. p22. 325w. 3
Jazz Journal. September. p38. 125w. 4
New York Times--Sunday. July 9. pD18. 75w. 2

2846 Charlie Ventura. GENE NORMAN PRESENTS A CHARLIE VENTURA CONCERT. Coral CP 74 (England). (Reissue.)
Gramophone. October. p792. 300w. 5
Jazz Journal. August. p38. 250w. 4
Records and Recordings. July. p97. 200w. 2½

2847 Joe Venuti and Eddie Lang. VENUTI-LANG, 1929/30. The Old Masters TOM 7 $5.50. (Reissue.)
Jazz Journal. July. p35. 225w. 3

2848 Tommy Vig. JUST FOR THE RECORD. Just for the Record [no serial number] (England).
Jazz and Blues. August. p34. 250w. 1

2849 Tommy Vig. IN BUDAPEST. Mortney MR 71425 (E).
Jazz and Blues. July. p32. 200w. 2
Jazz Journal. February. p39. 125w. 0

2850 Leroy Vinnegar. JAZZ'S GREAT WALKER. Joy JOYS 209 (England). (Reissue.)
Jazz and Blues. January. p25. 175w. 0

2851 VINTAGE PIANO (anthology). Emphonic ESR 1203 $5.50. (Reissue.)
Journal of American Folklore. January/March. p106. 25w. 2½

2852 The Visitors. NEPTUNE. Cobblestone CST 9010 $5.98. Cart. M 89010 $6.95. Cass. M 59010 $6.95.
Downbeat. August 17. p27. 225w. 5

2853 Waldo's Gutbucket Syncopators, V.1. GHB 55 $5.98.
High Fidelity. December. p131. 250w. 2½

2854 Mal Waldron and Steve Lacy. America 30 AM 6124 (France).
Jazz Journal. November. p37. 450w. 0
Records and Recordings. October. p122-3. 350w. 3½

2855 Fats Waller. CBS 63366 (France). (Reissue.)
Downbeat. March 2. p23. 75w. 3

2856 Fats Waller. V.2, (1924/31). Biograph 1005 Q $5.98. (Reissue.)
Ragtimer. July/August. p6-7. 600w. 4

2857 George Wallington. LIVE! AT CAFE BOHEMIA, 1955. Prestige PR 7820 $4.98.
Coda. February. p16. 650w. 2

2858 Cedar Walton and Hank Mobley. BREAKTHROUGH. Cobblestone CST 9011 $5.98. Cart. M 89011 $6.95. Cass. M 59011 $6.95.
Downbeat. July 20. p41. 375w. 4
New York Times--Sunday. June 11. pD30. 75w. 1

2859 Weather Report. I SING THE BODY ELECTRIC. Columbia KC 31352 $5.98. Cart. CA 31352 $6.98. Cass. CT 31352 $6.98.
Downbeat. October. p30. 500w. 4
High Fidelity. December. p128. 120w. 1½
Previews. October. p46. 200w. 3

2860 Teddy Weatherford. Jazum 9. $5.00.
Jazz Journal. December. p42. 100w. 3

2861 Chick Webb, 1937/39. First Time FTS 1508.
New York Times--Sunday. October 8. pD34. 125w. 4

2862 Ben Webster. BLOW, BEN, BLOW. Catfish 5 C 054 24159 (Holland).
Downbeat. September 14. p29. 275w. 3

2863 Ben Webster. WEBSTER'S DICTIONARY. Phillips 6308101 (England).
Gramophone. October. p792. 175w. 3
Hi-Fi News and Record Review. December. p2461. 75w. 2
Records and Recordings. September. p98. 125w. 2½

2864 Maxine Weldon. CHILLY WINDS. Mainstream MRL 339 $5.98.
Stereo Review. April. p102. 225w. 2½

2865 Maxine Weldon. RIGHT ON. Mainstream MRL 319 $5.98.
American Record Guide. March. p333. 225w. 4

2866 Dick Wellstood. FROM RAGTIME ON. Chiaroscuro CR 109 $5.50.
Audio. November. p97-8. 450w. 5
Saturday Review. August. p66. 25w. 2½
Sound. September. p50. 100w. 3

2867 Alex Welsh. IF I HAD A TALKING PICTURE OF YOU. Black Lion 2460 150 (England).
Jazz and Blues. July. p34. 600w. 1
Jazz Journal. June. p37. 200w. 2

2868 Mike Westbrook Concert Band. METROPOLIS. Neon NE 10 (England).
Gramophone. September. p585. 500w. 4
Hi-Fi News and Record Reviews. September. p1686. 300w. 3
Jazz and Blues. May. p25. 350w. 1
Jazz Journal. April. p37. 325w. 5
Records and Recordings. April. p114. 400w. 4

2869 Randy Weston. AFRICAN COOKBOOK. Atlantic SD 1609 $5.98. (Reissue.)
Downbeat. November 23. p23-4. 350w. 5
Jazz Journal. December. p42. 150w. 5
Stereo Review. August. p94. 125w. 2½

2870 Randy Weston. BLUE MOSES. CTI CTI 6016 $5.98. Cart. 8 6016 $6.95. Cass. CTC 6016 $6.95.
Downbeat. November 23. p23-4. 350w. 5

2871 Michael White. SPIRIT DANCE. Impulse AS 9215 $5.98. Cart. M 89215 $6.95. Cass. M 59215 $6.95.
Downbeat. May 11. p26. 125w. 4

2872 The Whoopee Makers. 1928/29. Connoisseur CR 523. (Reissue.)
Coda. February. p17. 325w. 2

2873 Bob Wilber and Maxine Sullivan. THE MUSIC OF HOAGY CARMICHAEL. Parlophone PCS 7127 (England).
Gramophone. February. p1447. 175w. 2½
Jazz Journal. January. p37. 500w. 5

2874 Lee Wiley. BACK HOME AGAIN. Monmouth/Evergreen MES 7041 $5.98.

Downbeat. March 30. p26. 225w. 5
Jazz Journal. March. p36. 300w. 4
Ontario Library Review. December. p243. 25w. $3\frac{1}{2}$

2875 Lee Wiley. I'VE GOT THE WORLD ON A STRING. Ember CJS 829 (England). (Reissue.)
Hi-Fi News and Record Review. November. p2199. 75w. 3

2876 Lee Wiley. SINGS GEORGE GERSHWIN AND COLE PORTER. Monmouth/Evergreen MES 7034 $5.98. (Reissue.)
Downbeat. March 30. p26. 225w. 5
Jazz Journal. September. p37. 275w. 5
Ontario Library Review. December. p243. 25w. $3\frac{1}{2}$

2877 Lee Wiley. SINGS RODGERS AND HART AND HAROLD ARLEN. Monmouth/Evergreen MES 6807 $5.98. (Reissue.)
Ontario Library Review. December. p243. 25w. $3\frac{1}{2}$

2878 Charles Williams. Mainstream MRL 312 $5.98.
New York Times--Sunday. May 7. pD29. 25w. $2\frac{1}{2}$
Saturday Review. May 20. p47. 50w. 2

2879 Charles Williams. TREES AND GRASS AND THINGS. Mainstream MRL 345 $5.98.
Downbeat. June 8. p26. 150w. 3
Jazz Journal. May. p34. 100w. 2
Saturday Review. May 20. p47. 50w. 2

2880 Clarence Williams. V.1. Natchez NLP 3002 (Argentina). (Reissue.)
Jazz Journal. March. p37. 100w. 3

2881 Clarence Williams. 1927/1928, V.2. Biograph BLP 12038 $5.98. (Reissue.)
High Fidelity. August. p104. 350w. $2\frac{1}{2}$
Jazz Journal. September. p37. 175w. 3
Previews. November. p45. 320w. $2\frac{1}{2}$

2882 Mary Lou Williams. FROM THE HEART. Chiaroscuro CR 103 $5.98.
High Fidelity. April. p100. 200w. $2\frac{1}{2}$
Jazz Report. No.1. 250w. 4
Music Journal. February. p57. 75w. 3
Saturday Review. May 20. p47. 50w. $2\frac{1}{2}$
Stereo Review. March. p110. 325w. 3

2883 Teddy Wilson. Columbia GES 90054 (Canada) (2 discs). (Reissue.)
Coda. February. p18. 600w. 5
Downbeat. March 2. p23. 125w. 5
Ontario Library Review. December. p243. 25w. $3\frac{1}{2}$

2884 Teddy Wilson. STOMPING AT THE SAVOY. Black Lion 2460 118 (England).
Gramophone. February. p1447. 250w. 1½
Jazz Journal. February. p37. 250w. 3
Records and Recordings. January. p94. 100w. 1

2885 Norma Winstone. EDGE OF TIME. Argo ZDA 148 (England).
Gramophone. November. p1003. 400w. 4
Jazz and News. June. p27. 350w. 1½
Jazz Journal. May. p33. 400w. 3
Records and Recordings. June. p89. 200w. 2

2886 Robert Wood. TAROT. Edici ED 0061020 (France).
Jazz Journal. May. p33. 225w. 3

2887 Phil Woods. AT THE FRANKFURT JAZZ FESTIVAL. Embryo SD 530 $5.98. Cart. M 8530 $6.95. Cass. M 5530 $6.95.
Audio. June. p78-9. 1000w. 5
Coda. April. p26. 225w. 4

2888 Phil Woods. AT THE MONTREUX JAZZ FESTIVAL. MGM S-4695 $5.98.
Jazz and Blues. August. p32-3. 400w. 4

2889 Phil Woods. CHROMATIC BANANA. Pierre Cardin 333 (France).
Coda. April. p26. 225w. 3

2890 Phil Woods. RIGHTS OF SWING. Barnaby KZ 31036 $5.98. (Reissue.)
New York Times--Sunday. May 7. pD29. 25w. 3
Previews. November. p46. 150w. 3½

2891 World's Greatest Jazz Band. Parlophone PCS 7138 (England).
Jazz Journal. February. p37. 250w. 4

2892 World's Greatest Jazz Band. CENTURY PLAZA. World Jazz WJLP 5-1 $5.98.
Downbeat. November 23. p24. 275w. 4½
Jazz Journal. December. p41. 200w. 5
Music Journal. December. p15. 125w. 4
Saturday Review. September 30. p83. 125w. 2½
Sound. September. p50. 100w. 4

2893 World's Greatest Jazz Band. HARK THE HERALD ANGELS SWING. World Jazz WJLP 5-2 $5.98.
Downbeat. December 21. p22. 200w. 4½

2894 World's Greatest Jazz Band. WHAT'S NEW. Atlantic SD 1582 $5.98.
Audio. March. p83-4. 1000w. 4½

2895 Pete Yellin. DANCE OF ALLEGRA. Mainstream MRL 363 $5.98. Cart. M 8363 $6.95. Cass. M 5363 $6.95.
Jazz Journal. October. p39. 200w. 2

2896 DAVID YOUNG. Mainstream MRL 323 $5.98. Cart. M 8323 $6.95. Cass. M 5323 $6.95.
Downbeat. February 17. p23. 125w. 3½

2897 Lester Young. THE ALTERNATIVE LESTER. Tax M 8000. (Reissue.)
Coda. February. p15. 850w. 5

2898 Lester Young. GIANT OF JAZZ. Sunset 5181 $1.89. (Reissue.)
Jazz Journal. May. p33. 225w. 3

2899 Lester Young and Nat "King" Cole. THE HISTORICAL SESSION. Musicdisc 30 CV 983 (France). (Reissue.)
Jazz Journal. July. p34. 175w. 0

2900 Lester Young/Coleman Hawkins. CLASSIC TENORS. Flying Dutchman FD 10146 $5.95.
Gramophone. October. p792. 500w. 5
High Fidelity. March. p116. 150w. 3½
Records and Recordings. August. p91-2. 300w. 5
Saturday Review. May 20. p47. 100w. 3

2901 Young-Holt Unlimited. BORN AGAIN. Cotillion SD 18004 $4.98. Cart. M 88004 $6.95. Cass. M 58004 $6.95.
Stereo Review. September. p82. 50w. 3

2902 Joe Zawinul. ZAWINUL. Atlantic SD 1579 $5.98. Cart. M 81579 $6.95. Cass. M 51579 $6.95.
Gramophone. November. p1003. 225w. 4
Jazz and Blues. October. p27. 300w. 3½
Jazz Journal. September. p37-8. 175w. 4
Records and Recordings. October. p123. 75w. 2

BLUES

This section comprises material generally classified by collectors as pre-World War II or post-World War II vocal blues, and based on the two major discographies of Godrich and Dixon, and Leadbitter and Slavens. Blues music is often of two types--country, rural, solo, and acoustic, or electric, amplified, and urban with ensemble playing. The former has been around since before the turn of the century; however, the latter is a more recent development, often called "Chicago blues," and generally attributed to Muddy Waters but also with roots in the string bands and the Mississippi Delta. Heavy white blues bands are in the ROCK category, for they have used the technical aspects of blues as a format, not as a life style. Instrumental blues is more properly JAZZ, although the odd instrumental turns up on an album of vocals.

Scholars and collectors have tried to break blues into manageable forms with partial success. Regional styles, time periods, format of presentation, type of instrumentation, individuals--the blues get worked over as much as the grieving of the performer. This accounts for the vast number of anthologized offerings and the responses of the so-called "bootlegger pirates."

Anyone can _play_ the blues, for it is a simple technical form of music. Thus, _all_ interest in the blues is dependent on the performer. But not everyone can _feel_ the blues, with the message to be conveyed being essentially _one of_ emotion. Real blues singers used the blues therapeutically to escape from their situation. They stood outside, looking in while singing about their problems. It always felt so good to a blues singer when he finished his song, for he "talked it out" as many people in therapy do. Most typical white blues singers cannot feel the blues because they have not experienced it. They _see_ injustices and become disturbed; the typical black blues singer is _the_ actual recipient of those injustices. He not only sees it, but also he _lives_ it. Thus, for all purposes, the typical white singer cannot get _into_ the blues.

Many blues records are reviewed only once or twice in a well-covered field. Besides the British publications _Blues Unlimited_ and _Blues World,_ and the American _Living Blues,_ blues music is proportionately well off in all jazz magazines, some folk, some rock, and some general publications. Foreign language magazines exist in France, Germany, Sweden and other countries. "The blues is everywhere" is a true statement indeed. While _Blues Unlimited_ stands out for its convincing rave reviews, emphemeral publications like Boston's _Whiskey, Women, and..._ present their fair share of "puffs" that only serve notice to collectors that records exist and are now on the market. Many such publications are student-owned, and they exist for a short period of time, ceasing to exist for a multitude of reasons (as Chicago's Blue Flame did in the summer of 1972).

For reissued material, the reviews themselves often only tend to be notices explaining that certain records are now available for purchase; hence, on our rating scale, there is a heavy preponderance of $2\frac{1}{2}$ to $3\frac{1}{2}$ ratings. The collector knows what he wants, and the reviews only interest him for consideration of sound quality, duplicated tracks on existing albums, and additional biographical information not easily obtained elsewhere.

New material seems to be exceedingly difficult to evaluate. Reviewers appear to be on safe ground with reissues, but uncertain with new post-war material. The case has been made, quite successfully, that electric blues has not matured beyond its mid-fifties development. Nothing new is being played, and the hordes of white imitators are prolonging the status quo. The jazz magazines tend to be more realistic about the music: if it is good, then it is ranked as such; if it is bad, then it is shot down. Tainted by white commercialism, certain "Chicago bluesmen" are virtually ignored or condemned by the blues press while given rave send-ups by the rock media. Thus, these groups are regarded by both types of media as having sold out from one side to another. All the media seems to have agreed that original electric blues have over-saturated the market. Groups such as Julio Finn, B.B. King, James Cotton, John Lee Hooker, Buddy Guy and Junior Wells, and even Muddy Waters himself have been battered around lately by the critics who are still waiting for that "definitive, next album." Yet the records sell well, and this is yet another example of there being no correlation between critical acclaim and sales.

According to the reviews, the following are the best items in this category:

Pre-War Reissues

Louis Armstrong. AND THE BLUES SINGERS, 1925/29. Parlophone PMC 7144 (E)
Louis Armstrong. WITH THE BLUES SINGERS. Jazum 6
BLUES FROM THE WESTERN STATES, 1927/49 (anthology). Yazoo L 1032
Son House. LEGENDARY 1941/42 LIBRARY OF CONGRESS RECORDINGS. Roots RSE - 1 (Austria)
Mississippi John Hurt. 1928: HIS FIRST RECORDINGS. Biograph BLP C-4
SIC 'EM DOGS ON ME (anthology). Herwin 201
Bessie Smith. THE EMPRESS (2 discs). Columbia G 30818

Post-War Reissues

BLUES IN CHICAGO, 1948/57 (anthology) (2 discs). Boogie Disease 101/102
BLUES PIANO ORGY (anthology). Delmark 626
Arthur Crudup. FATHER OF ROCK 'N' ROLL. RCA LPV 573
GENESIS (anthology) (4 discs). Chess 6641 047 (E)
John Lee Hooker. COAST TO COAST BLUES BAND. United Artists UAS 5512
Lightnin' Hopkins. EARLY RECORDINGS, Vol. 2. Arhoolie 2010
Blind Willie McTell/Memphis Minnie. LOVE CHANGIN' BLUES. Biograph BLP 12035
Professor Longhair. NEW ORLEANS PIANO. Atlantic SD 7225
Robert Pete Williams. THESE PRISON BLUES. Arhoolie 2015

Post-War--New

Roosevelt Holts. AND HIS FRIENDS. Arhoolie 1057
Mississippi John Hurt. BEST (2 discs). Vanguard VSD 19/20
Memphis Slim. OLD TIMES/NEW TIMES (2 discs). Barclay 920.332/333 (French)
Tom Shaw. BORN IN TEXAS. Advent 2801
Johnny Shines. SITTIN' ON TOP OF THE WORLD. Biograph BLP 12044
Otis Spann. WALKING THE BLUES. Barnaby KZ 31290

2903 AFTER HOURS BLUES (anthology). Biograph BLP 12010 $5.98.
Previews. September. p39. 250w. $2\frac{1}{2}$

2904 ALL STAR BLUES WORLD OF SPIVEY RECORDS (anthology). Spivey LP 1011 $5.00.
Journal of American Folklore. January/March. p105. 200w. 4
Jazz Report. No.1. 350w. 1

2905 Luther Allison. LOVE ME MAMA. Delmark DS 625 $5.98.
Library Journal. February 15. p665. 150w. 3

2906 AMERICAN FOLK BLUES FESTIVAL, 1970 (anthology). Scout 7 (2 discs) (Germany).
Living Blues. Winter. p36. 350w. 0

2907 ANGOLA PRISONERS' BLUES (anthology). Arhoolie 2011 $6.00. (Reissue.)

Coda. October. p26-7. 175w. 5
Jazz and Blues. February. p30. 400w. 4

2908 Louis Armstrong. LOUIS AND THE BLUES SINGERS, 1925/29. Parlophone PMC 7144 (E). (Reissue.)
Gramophone. April. 225w. p24. $2\frac{1}{2}$
Jazz and Blues. April. p24. 650w. 4
Jazz Journal. March. p30. 600w. 5
Records and Recordings. September. p95-6. 350w. 4

2909 Louis Armstrong. WITH THE BLUES SINGERS. Jazum 6 $5.00. (Reissue.)
Coda. August. p16. 275w. 4
Jazz Journal. July. p35. 175w. 5

2910 BALL AND CHAIN (anthology). Arhoolie 1039 $6.00
Living Blues. Summer. p36. 250w. 3
Records and Recordings. January. p96. 50w. 3

2911 BARRELHOUSE BLUES, 1927/1936 (anthology). Yazoo L 1028 $5.95. (Reissue.)
Blues Unlimited. April. p28. 200w. 4
Blues World. Spring. p21. 150w. 2
Jazz Journal. March. p30. 375w. 3
Previews. September. p39. 250w. $2\frac{1}{2}$

2912 BARRELHOUSE BLUES AND STOMPS (anthology). Euphonic ESR 1205 $4.98. (Reissue.)
Jazz Journal. July. p35. 200w. 2
Jazz Report. No.1. 750w. 4
Jazz Report. No.1. 250w. 2
Jazz Report. No.1. 500w. 3
Journal of American Folklore. January/March. p106. 50w. 3

2913 Big Black. AND THE BLUES. Uni 73134 $4.98.
Downbeat. November 9. p19. 100w. 2
Gramophone. December. p1222. 50w. 2
High Fidelity. October. p126. 25w. 3

2914 BLACK CAT TRAIL (anthology). Mamlish S3800 $5.95. (Reissue.)
Coda. April. p27. 300w. 3
Journal of American Folklore. January/March. p104. 100w. $2\frac{1}{2}$

2915 Scrapper Blackwell. 1928/1934. Yazoo L 1019 $5.95. (Reissue.)
Previews. October. p42. 200w. 3

2916 Blind Blake. NO DOUGH BLUES, 1926/29. Biograph BLP 12031 $5.98. (Reissue.)
Blues Unlimited. May. p29. 150w. 4
Blues World. Spring. p19. 100w. 3

Jazz Report. No. 1. 250w. 3
Journal of American Folklore. January/March. p100. 25w. 2½

2917 Blind Blake. ROPE STRETCHIN' BLUES, 1926/31. Biograph BLP 12037 $5.98. (Reissue.)
Jazz Journal. December. p29. 300w. 3½
Previews. November. p38. 150w. 2½

2918 Blind Blake. SEARCH WARRANT BLUES. Biograph BLP 12023 $5.98. (Reissue.)
Coda. August. p19. 325w. 4
Jazz Report. No. 1. 250w. 4

2919 Blind Lush Cripple. THE GENUINE GHETTO BLUES. DMT Records.
Creem. April. p66. 425w. 2½

2920 Little Joe Blue. HAPPY HERE. Space MJJ 4729 (Holland). (Reissue.)
Living Blues. Autumn. p32. 150w. 3

2921 Little Joe Blue. SOUTHERN COUNTRY BOY. Jewel LPS 5008 $4.98. Cart. M85008 $6.95. Cass. M55008 $6.95.
Blues Unlimited. November. p29. 175w. 4
Living Blues. Autumn. p32. 150w. 3

2922 BLUES FOR YOUR POCKETS (anthology). Transatlantic TRA SAM 25 (E). (Reissue.)
Blues Unlimited. September. p24. 50w. 3½
Jazz Journal. August. p37-8. 275w. 4

2923 BLUES FROM "BIG BILL'S" COPA CABANA (anthology). Chess LPS 1533 $5.98.
Journal of American Folklore. January/March. p103. 50w. 4

2924 BLUES FROM THE DELTA (anthology). Matchbox SDM 226 (E). (Reissue.)
Blues Unlimited. December. p28. 100w. 3

2925 BLUES FROM THE WESTERN STATES, 1927/49. Yazoo L 1032 $5.95. (Reissue).
Blues Unlimited. February/March. p28. 100w. 5
Previews. October. p42. 175w. 3½

2926 THE BLUES IN CHICAGO, 1948/57 (anthology). Boogie Disease 101/102 (2 discs) $10.00. (Reissue.)
Blues Unlimited. June. p22. 350w. 5
Coda. October. p26. 400w. 5

2927 BLUES LIVE IN BATON ROUGE AT THE SPEAKEASY (anthology). Excello 8021 $4.98.
Blues Unlimited. July. p24. 100w. 3
Living Blues. Summer. p323. 275w. 0

2928 BLUES OBSCURITIES, VOLUME 1/3 (anthology). Blues Obscurities BOV 1/3 (3 discs) (E). (Reissue.)
Blues Unlimited. January. p29. 175w. 3
Blues Unlimited. February/March. p21. 175w. $2\frac{1}{2}$
Jazz and Blues. May. p19-20. 1,500w. 3
Jazz Journal. January. p28. 600w. 5

2929 BLUES PIANO - CHICAGO PLUS (anthology). Atlantic SD 7227 $5.98. (Reissue.)
Blues Unlimited. December. p27. 175w. 4
Records and Recordings. December. p102. 150w. 3

2930 BLUES PIANO ORGY (anthology). Delmark DS 626 $5.98. (Reissue.)
Blues Unlimited. November. p31. 150w. 4
Jazz and Blues. December. p26. 300w. 4
Music Journal. November. p62. 50w. 4
Previews. September. p39-40. 200w. 4

2931 BLUES RARITIES, VOLUME 1 (anthology). Blues Rarities [lacks serial number] (2 discs) (E). (Reissue.)
Blues Unlimited. April. p29. 200w. 4

2932 BLUES ROOTS (anthology). Poppy PYS 60003 (2 discs) $9.96. (Reissue.)
Journal of American Folklore. January/March. p107. 25w. 4

2933 BLUES SCENE, USA, VOLUME 1 (anthology). Storyville SLP 176 (Denmark). (Reissue.)
Jazz Journal. November. p25. 300w. 0

2934 BLUES SOUNDS OF THE HASTINGS STREET ERA (anthology). Fortune 3012 $4.98. (Reissue.)
Blues Unlimited. November. p26-7. 450w. 3
Living Blues. Summer. p32. 1,600w. 0

2935 BLUESMEN OF THE MUDDY WATERS CHICAGO BLUES BAND, VOLUME 2 (anthology). Spivey Records LP 1010 $5.00
Previews. November. p38. 150w. 3

2936 BOTTLENECK BLUES GUITAR CLASSICS, 1926/37 (anthology). Yazoo L 1026 $5.98. (Reissue.)
Blues Unlimited. January. p23. 200w. 4
Blues World. Spring. p17. 175w. 4
Jazz Journal. May. p28. 475w. 3

Living Blues. Winter. p34. 200w. 4
Previews. October. p43. 300w. 3½

2937 Charles Brown. BLUES 'N' BROWN. Jewel LPS 5006 $4.98.
Blues Unlimited. April. p25. 75w. 2½

2938 Clarence "Gatemouth" Brown. THE BLUES AIN'T NOTHIN'. Black and Blue 33 033 (France).
Blues Unlimited. June. p27. 75w. 3½
Blues Unlimited. September. p28. 50w. 4
Living Blues. Summer. p36. 100w. 5

2939 BULL CITY BLUES (anthology). Flyright LP 106 (E). (Reissue.)
Blues Unlimited. September. p29. 200w. 4½

2940 Eddie "Guitar" Burns. BOTTLE UP AND GO. Action ACMP 100 (E).
Blues Unlimited. December. p26. 250w. 1

2941 George Butler. WILD CHILD. Carnival 2941 006 (E).
Blues Unlimited. December. p29. 300w. 4½
Jazz and Blues. December. p26-7. 200w. 0
Jazz Journal. December. p30. 200w. 1½
Records and Recordings. December. p101-2. 200w. 3½

2942 C.J'S ROOTS OF CHICAGO'S BLUES (anthology). Blue Flame 101 $4.98.
Living Blues. Spring. p35. 200w. 3

2943 CALIFORNIA BLUES (anthology). Kent KST 9003 $4.98. (Reissue.)
Previews. October. p42. 225w. 2½

2944 Leroy Carr. BLUES BEFORE SUNRISE. Columbia C 30496 $4.98. (Reissue.)
Audio. January. p78. 800w. 4

2945 Bo Carter. GREATEST HITS, 1930/40. Yazoo L 1014 $5.95. (Reissue.)
Previews. October. p42. 225w. 2½

2946 Sam Chatman. THE MISSISSIPPI SHEIK. Blue Goose 2006 $5.95.
Blues Unlimited. February/March. p30. 175w. 4
Jazz Journal. October. p28. 300w. 4
Previews. October. p42. 200w. 3
Sing Out. May/June. p46. 50w. 3½

2947 Clifton Chenier. BAYOU BLUES. Specialty SPS 2139 $4.98.
Blues Unlimited. June. p23. 100w. 4

2948 Clifton Chenier. LIVE AT A FRENCH CREOLE DANCE. Arhoolie 1059 $6.00.
Blues Unlimited. December. p28. 125w. 3
Jazz Report. No. 2. 125w. 4
Saturday Review. November 4. p92. 100w. 2½
Sing Out. September/October. p39. 50w. 3

2949 CHICAGO AIN'T NOTHIN' BUT A BLUES BAND (anthology). Delmark DS 624 $5.98. (Reissue.)
Blues Unlimited. July. p26. 250w. 3
Jazz Journal. November. p26. 350w. 4
Living Blues. Summer. p36. 375w. 4
Music Journal. November. p62. 25w. 2
Previews. October. p42. 200w. 2½

2950 Chicago Blues All Stars. LOADED WITH THE BLUES. BASF 20707 $5.98.
Music Journal. November. p40. 25w. 1

2951 CHICAGO BLUES ANTHOLOGY (anthology). Chess 2CH-60012 (2 discs) $6.98. Cart. 8033-60012 $6.95. (Reissue.)
Blues Unlimited. November. p27. 50w. 3
New York Times--Sunday. October 15. pD31. 75w. 5

2952 CHICAGO BLUES FESTIVAL, VOLUME 1 (anthology). Black and Blue 33.034 (France).
Blues Unlimited. June. p27. 100w. 2½

2953 THE CHICAGO STRING BAND (anthology). Testament T 2220 $4.98.
Journal of American Folklore. January/March. p104. 100w. 3

2954 COLLECTION OF LAWRENCE GELLERT NEGRO SONGS OF PROTEST (anthology). Timely TL 112 $6.00.
Journal of American Folklore. January/March. p105-6. 200w. 3

2955 Albert Collins. THERE'S GOTTA BE A CHANGE. Thumbleweed 103 $4.98.
Blues Unlimited. April. p23. 125w. 3
Coda. August. p22. 100w. 0

2956 Albert Collins. TRUCKIN'. Blue Thumb BTS 8808 $5.98.
Living Blues. Spring. p35. 250w. 5

2957 COLOSSAL BLUES, VOLUME 1 (anthology). Bea and Baby 075 927 $5.50.
Blues Unlimited. May. p27. 350w. 3½
Living Blues. Spring. p35. 200w. 3

2958 James Cotton Blues Band. TAKING CARE OF BUSINESS. Capitol ST 814 $5.98.
Library Journal. June 15. p2167. 100w. 1

2959 COUNTRY BLUES OBSCURITIES, VOLUME 2, 1927/36 (anthology). Roots RL 340 $5.50 (Austria). (Reissue.)
Blues Unlimited. May. p28. 225w. 3½
Previews. November. p39. 350w. 2½

2960 Pee Wee Crayton. THINGS I USED TO DO. Vanguard VSD 6566 $4.98.
Blues Unlimited. April. p23. 125w. 4
Coda. August. p19. 175w. 1
Journal of American Folklore. January/March. p105. 25w. 2½

2961 CREAM OF THE CROP (anthology). Roots RL 332 (Austria). (Reissue.)
Living Blues. Winter. p346. 225w. 4

2962 Arthur "Big Boy" Crudup. THE FATHER OF ROCK AND ROLL. RCA LPV 573 $5.98. (Reissue.)
Blues Unlimited. January. p22. 275w. 5
Blues Unlimited. May. p28. 25w. 4
Blues Unlimited. July. p14. 200w. 2½
Crawdaddy. March 19. p20. 500w. 4
Creem. March. p57. 50w. 2
Gramophone. October. p778. 300w. 3
High Fidelity. February. p118-9. 300w. 3
Jazz and Blues. July. p14. 200w. 2½
Jazz Journal. April. p31. 300w. 5
Music Journal. February. p37. 150w. 2
Popular Music. Winter. p125. 75w. 3½
Records and Recordings. May. p101. 150w. 3
Rolling Stone. March 16. p62. 250w. 3

2963 DARK MUDDY BOTTOM BLUES (anthology). Specialty LP 2149 $4.98. (Reissue.)
Blues Unlimited. December. p26. 125w. 2

2964 Rev. Gary Davis. LEGENDARY. Biograph BLP 12030 $5.98.
Journal of American Folklore. January/March. p101. 100w. 3½

2965 DEEP SOUTH COUNTRY BLUES (anthology). Flyright LP 102 (E). (Reissue.)
Blues Unlimited. January. p26. 200w. 5

2966 DELTA BLUES, 1929/1969 (anthology). Roots RL 339 $5.50 (Austria). (Reissue.)
Previews. November. p39. 350w. 2½

2967 DETROIT BLUES (anthology). Kent KST 9006 $4.98. (Reissue.)
Previews. October. p42-3. 275w. 2½

2968 DETROIT BLUES: THE EARLY 1950'S (anthology). Blues Classics BC 12 $6.00. (Reissue.)
Previews. October. p42-3. 275w. 2½

2969 Willie Dixon. I AM THE BLUES. Columbia CS 9987 $4.98.
Living Blues. Autumn. p32. 100w. 1

2970 Willie Dixon. PEACE? Yambo 777-15 $4.98.
Blues Unlimited. December. p29. 350w. 2
Living Blues. Autumn. p32. 225w. 2

2971 Scott Dunbar. FROM LAKE MARY. Ahura Mazda SDS 1 $5.00.
Journal of American Folklore. January/March. p101. 100w. 3½

2972 Champion Jack Dupree. I'M HAPPY TO BE FREE. Vogue SLDP 828 (France).
Blues Unlimited. July. p25. 100w. 3½
Living Blues. Summer. p36. 150w. 3

2973 Champion Jack Dupree. LEGACY OF THE BLUES, VOLUME 3. Sonet SNTF 626 (Sweden).
Blues Unlimited. October. p24. 150w. 4
Jazz Journal. December. p31. 275w. 3

2974 Champion Jack Dupree and Mickey Baker. JACK AND MICKEY IN HEAVY BLUES. Sire SES 97010 $4.98.
Journal of American Folklore. January/March. p106. 25w. 2½

2975 Snooks Eaglin. POSSUM UP A SIMMON TREE. Arhoolie 2014 $6.00. (Reissue.)
Ethnomusicology. October. p583-4. 650w. 4

2976 Snooks Eaglin. LEGACY OF THE BLUES, VOLUME 2. Sonet SNTF 625 (Sweden).
Blues Unlimited. September. p28. 175w. 2½
Jazz Journal. December. p31. 100w. 1

2977 Sleepy John Estes. ELECTRIC SLEEP. Delmark DS 619 $5.98.
Blues Unlimited. September. p28. 75w. 1
Gramophone. October. p781. 100w. 3
Jazz and Blues. July. p29. 275w. 1
Jazz Journal. August. p30. 200w. 1
Records and Recordings. July. p96. 100w. 3½

2978 THE EXCELLO STORY (anthology). Blue Horizon 2683 007 (2 discs) (E). (Reissue.)
Blues Unlimited. September. p24. 125w. 5
Jazz and Blues. November. p25-6. 500w. 2
Records and Recordings. September. p96. 350w. 3

2979 FAVORITE COUNTRY BLUES PIANO-GUITAR DUETS, 1929/1937 (anthology). Yazoo L 1015 $5. 95. (Reissue.)
Previews. October. p43. 300w. $2\frac{1}{2}$

2980 Julio Finn Blues Band. DEAL FOR SERVICE. Barclay 920. 395 (France).
Living Blues. Autumn. p32. 100w. 0

2981 Julio Finn Blues Band. RAINBOWS ALL OVER MY BLUES. Barclay 920. 241 (France).
Blues Unlimited. May. p28. 50w. 2
Living Blues. Summer. p36. 250w. 3

2982 Backwards Sam Firk. THE MEMPHIS BLUES AGAIN. VOLUMES 1/2. Adelphi Records AD 1009S/AD 1010S (2 discs) $10. 00.
Sing Out. March/April. p37-8. 75w. 2

2983 Blind Boy Fuller/Brownie McGhee. CAROLINA BLUES. Flyright LP 105 (E). (Reissue.)
Blues Unlimited. June. p22. 225w. 4

2984 Jesse Fuller. MOVE ON DOWN THE LINE. Topic 12 T 134 (E). (Reissue.)
Journal of American Folklore. January/March. p100. 25w. 3

2985 GENESIS: THE BEGINNINGS OF ROCK (anthology). Chess 6641 047 (4 discs) (E) <u>or</u> Chess 6310 116/119 (4 discs) (E). (Reissue.)
Blues Unlimited. September. p22. 300w. 5
Jazz and Blues. August. p28. 575w. 5
Jazz Journal. September. p30-1. 550w. 5
Records and Recordings. September. p96-7. 375w. 5

2986 Clifford Gibson. BEAT YOU DOING IT. Yazoo L 1027 $5. 95. (Reissue.)
Blues Unlimited. January. p26. 225w. 3
Blues World. Spring. p17. 150w. 4
Jazz Journal. March. p33-4. 325w. 3
Living Blues. Spring. p36. 150w. 2
Previews. November. p43. 100w. 2

2987 Tony "Little Sun" Glover. BLUES HARP: AN INSTRUCTION METHOD. Folkways FM 8358 $5. 98.
Journal of American Folklore. January/March. p99. 125w. $3\frac{1}{2}$

2988 GOIN' AWAY WALKIN' (anthology). Flyright LP 103 (E). (Reissue.)
Blues Unlimited. February/March. p27. 175w. 3½

2989 GOIN' TO CHICAGO (anthology). Testament T 2218 $4.98. (Reissue.)
Journal of American Folklore. January/March. p103. 25w. 2½

2990 THE GREAT BLUESMEN (anthology). Vanguard VSD 25/26 (2 discs) $5.98. (Reissue.)
New York Times--Sunday. April 16. pD26. 125w. 3½
Saturday Review. September 30. p83. 100w. 3

2991 THE GREAT HARMONICA PLAYERS, VOLUMES 1/2 (anthology). Roots RL 320/1 (2 discs) (Austria) $12.00. (Reissue.)
Previews. November. p39. 100w. 2

2992 THE GREAT JUG BANDS, 1926/34 (anthology). Historical HLP 36 $5.98. (Reissue.)
Journal of American Folklore. January/March. p99. 150w. 2½

2993 Lil Green. ROMANCE IN THE DARK. RCA LPV 574 $5.98. (Reissue.)
Blues Unlimited. February/March. p28. 75w. 3
Crawdaddy. March 19. p20. 200w. 2½
High Fidelity. February. p118-19. 300w. 2½
Jazz and Blues. July. p14. 175w. 1½
Music Journal. February. p37. 150w. 1
Rolling Stone. March 16. p62. 100w. 3
Saturday Review. March 25. p34. 100w. 2
Stereo Review. June. p103. 175w. 3½

2994 Guitar Shorty. CAROLINA SLIDE GUITAR. Flyright LP 500 (E). (Reissue.)
Blues Unlimited. September. p23. 200w. 4½
Jazz and Blues. November. p26-7. 350w. 4

2995 Guitar Slim. THE THINGS THAT I USED TO DO. Specialty SPS 2120 $4.98.
Blues World. Spring. p17. 150w. 4

2996 Guitar Slim and Jelly Belly. CAROLINA BLUES. Arhoolie R 2005 $6.00.
Previews. December. p45. 175w. 2½

2997 Arthur Gunter. BLACK AND BLUES. Excello 8017 $4.98.
Blues Unlimited. February/March. p21. 150w. 4
Blues Unlimited. April. p21. 75w. 4
Blues Unlimited. July. p24. 50w. 4

Coda. October. p15. 125w. 1
Gramophone. October. p781. 125w. 1
Records and Recordings. April. p109-110. 200w. 2

2998 Buddy Guy and Junior Wells. PLAY THE BLUES. Atco SD 33-364 $5.98.
Blues Unlimited. November. p26. 75w. 1
Creem. December. p9. 50w. 5
Gramophone. December. p1222. 100w. 2½
Popular Music. Fall. p90. 25w. 1
Previews. December. p43. 150w. 1
Records and Recordings. November. p108. 100w. 2
Sound. September. p41. 225w. 5

2999 HARD LUCK BLUES (anthology). VJM VLP 40 (E). (Reissue.)
Jazz and Blues. November. p27-8. 300w. 0
Jazz Journal. August. p31-2. 75w. 5

3000 Slim Harpo. BEST. Excello 8010 $4.98. (Reissue.) Cart. EX8 8010 $6.95.
Blues Unlimited. February/March. p26. 100w. 3½
Coda. October. p15. 125w. 2
Gramophone. October. p781. 50w. 2

3001 Slim Harpo. KNEW THE BLUES. Excello 8013 $4.98. (Reissue.)
Coda. October. p15. 125w. 2
Journal of American Folklore. January/March. p85. 25w. 2½
Previews. December. p43-4. 175w. 3
Records and Recordings. April. p110. 100w. 2

3002 Shakey Jake Harris. THE DEVIL'S HARMONICA. Polydor PD 5014 $4.98.
Blues Unlimited. November. p29. 50w. 1

3003 Silas Hogan. TROUBLE. Excello 8019 $4.98.
Blues Unlimited. July. p24. 50w. 4
Living Blues. Summer. p32-4. 275w. 4

3004 Smokey Hogg. SING THE BLUES. Ember EMB 3405 (E). (Reissue.)
Blues Unlimited. January. p24. 150w. 4
Jazz Journal. January. p30-1. 350w. 2

3005 Roosevelt Holts. AND HIS FRIENDS. Arhoolie 1057 $6.00.
Blues Unlimited. July. p25. 300w. 5
Coda. October. p19. 200w. 3
Jazz Journal. October. p31-2. 250w. 3
Jazz Report. No. 2. 250w. 4
Music Journal. November. p62. 25w. 2

Previews. November. p39. 175w. 2½
Rolling Stone. November 9. p66. 750w. 4

3006 Roosevelt Holts. PRESENTING THE COUNTRY BLUES. Blue Horizon 7-63201 (E).
Journal of American Folklore. January/March. p101. 100w. 3½

3007 Homesick James. THE COUNTRY BLUES. Blues on Blues BOB 10000 $5.95.
Blues Unlimited. April. p27. 50w. 1½
Downbeat. June 8. p26-7. 150w. 2½

3008 Earl Hooker. FUNK: LAST OF THE GREAT... Blues on Blues BOB 10002 $5.95.
Blues Unlimited. April. p27. 50w. 2
Downbeat. June. p27. 150w. 2
Living Blues. Spring. p35-6. 225w. 2

3009 Earl Hooker. GENIUS. Cuca KS 3400 $4.98.
Journal of American Folklore. January/March. p102. 2

3010 Earl Hooker. HOOKER AND STEVE. Arhoolie 1051 $6.00.
Records and Recordings. January. p96. 100w. 3

3011 John Lee Hooker. ALONE. Specialty S 2125 $4.98.
Blues Unlimited. January. p25. 25w. 3½

3012 John Lee Hooker. BIG BAND BLUES. Buddah BDS 7506 $5.98. (Reissue.)
Journal of American Folklore. January/March. p102. 25w. 2½

3013 John Lee Hooker. COAST TO COAST BLUES BAND. United Artists UAS 5512 $5.98. Cart. U8276 $6.98. Cass. K0276 $6.98. (Reissue.)
Blues Unlimited. January. p25. 25w. 4
Blues World. Summer. p18. 150w. 4
Jazz Journal. January. p31. 350w. 5
Records and Recordings. January. p96. 50w. 3
Popular Music. Fall. p58. 25w. 2½

3014 John Lee Hooker. DETROIT SPECIAL. Atlantic SD 7228 $5.98. (Reissue.)
Records and Recordings. November. p108. 125w. 2½

3015 John Lee Hooker. ENDLESS BOOGIE. ABC ABCS 720 $5.98. Cart. M8720 $6.95. Cass. M5720 $6.95.
Gramophone. January. p1279. 150w. 2

3016 John Lee Hooker. I FEEL GOOD. Jewel LPS 5005 $4.98. (Reissue.)

Blues Unlimited. January. p29. 50w. 2
Journal of American Folklore. January/March. 50w. 3

3017 John Lee Hooker. JOHNNY LEE. Greene Bottle GBS 3130 (2 discs) $4.98. (Reissue.)
Blues Unlimited. October. p27. 175w. 2½

3018 John Lee Hooker. THE KING OF FOLK BLUES. America 30 AM 6074 (France). (Reissue.)
Jazz Journal. August. p32-3. 400w. 0

3019 John Lee Hooker. LIVE AT SOLEDAD PRISON. ABC ABCX 761 $5.98. Cart. M8761 $6.95. Cass. M5761 $6.95.
Blues Unlimited. December. p26. 100w. 1
Popular Music. Fall. p90. 25w. 1

3020 John Lee Hooker. MAD MAN BLUES. Chess 2CH-60011 (2 discs) $6.98. (Reissue.)
Blues Unlimited. December. p26. 50w. 3
Saturday Review. April 22. p51. 50w. 3

3021 John Lee Hooker. NEVER GET OUT OF THESE BLUES ALIVE. ABC Dunhill ABCX 736 $5.98. Cart. M8736 $6.95. Cass. M5736 $6.95. Quad disc available.
Blues Unlimited. May. p24. 150w. 2
Blues Unlimited. November. p30. 50w. 2½
Gramophone. December. p1222. 50w. 2
Jazz and Blues. November. p30. 250w. 2
Jazz Journal. November. p31-2. 475w. 4
Popular Music. Summer. p252. 75w. 2
Records and Recordings. October. p119. 250w. 2½

3022 John Lee Hooker. VERY BEST. Buddah BDS 4002 $5.98. (Reissue.)
Journal of American Folklore. January/March. p102. 25w. 2½

3023 John Lee Hooker/Big Maceo Merriwether. Fortune LP 3002 $4.98. (Reissue.)
Journal of American Folklore. January/March. p102. 25w. 1

3024 Lightnin' Hopkins. Poppy PYS 60,002 (2 discs) $9.96. (Reissue.)
Journal of American Folklore. January/March. p102. 50w. 2½

3025 Lightnin' Hopkins. BLUE LIGHTNIN'. Jewel LPS 5000 $4.98.
Journal of American Folklore. January/March. p102. 50w. 2½

3026 Lightnin' Hopkins. THE BLUES. Mainstream MRL 311 $5.98. (Reissue.)
Blues Unlimited. January. p25. 25w. 3½
New York Times--Sunday. May 7. pD29. 25w. 3½

3027 Lightnin' Hopkins. BLUES IN MY BOTTLE. Vogue SLDP 829 (France). (Reissue.)
Blues Unlimited. July. p28. 100w. 4

3028 Lightnin' Hopkins. EARLY RECORDINGS, VOLUME 2. Arhoolie 2010 $6.00. (Reissue.)
Ethnomusicology. October. p584-5. 650w. 4
Living Blues. Spring. p36. 375w. 4
Music Journal. November. p62. 25w. 4

3029 Lightnin' Hopkins. THE GREAT ELECTRIC SHOW AND DANCE. Jewel LPS 5002.
Journal of American Folklore. January/March. p102. 25w. 1

3030 Lightnin' Hopkins. LIGHTNIN' STRIKES. Tradition 2103 (2 discs) $9.96. (Reissue.)
Blues Unlimited. July. p25. 75w. 2½
Gramophone. October. p778, 789. 75w. 2
Records and Recordings. June. p86. 150w. 3

3031 Lightnin' Hopkins. LONESOME LIGHTNIN'. Carnival 2941 005 (E). (Reissue.)
Blues Unlimited. December. p27. 250w. 3
Jazz and Blues. December. p29. 275w. 3½
Records and Recordings. December. p102. 175w. 3½

3032 Lightnin' Hopkins. ROOTS. Folkways 31011 $5.98.
Blues Unlimited. May. p28. 50w. 4

3033 Lightnin' Hopkins. TALKIN' SOME SENSE. Jewel LPS 5001 $4.98. Cart. M85001 $6.95. Cass. M55001 $6.95.
Journal of American Folklore. January/March. p102. 50w. 2½

3034 Big Walter Horton. Alligator 4702 $5.98.
Blues Unlimited. October. p27. 200w. 1
Living Blues. Autumn. p31. 225w. 3

3035 Big Walter Horton. KING OF THE HARMONICA PLAYERS. Memphis LP 3372 (Sweden). (Reissue.)
Blues Unlimited. July. p28. 175w. 3½

3036 Son House. LEGENDARY 1941/42 RECORDINGS. Roots RSE 1 (Austria). (Reissue.)
Blues Unlimited. April. p26. 125w. 5
Blues World. Spring. p18. 450w. 5
Jazz and Blues. May. p23-4. 700w. 5
Records and Recordings. August. p92. 350w. 5

3037 Son House/Blind Lemon Jefferson. Biograph BLP 12040 $5.98. (Reissue.)
Blues Unlimited. September. p25. 200w. 5
Jazz Journal. October. p32. 300w. 3
Sing Out. April/March. p34-5. 450w. $2\frac{1}{2}$

3038 Howlin' Wolf. Cadet LPS 319 $5.98. Cart. 8037-8319 $6.95.
Journal of American Folklore. January/March. p104. 25w. 0

3039 Howlin' Wolf. CHESTER BURNETT A.K.A. HOWLIN' WOLF. Chess 2CH-60016 (2 discs) $6.98. Cart. 8033-60016M $6.95. (Reissue.)
Rolling Stone. June 22. p60. 650w. 4
Sound. August. p49. 150w. 4

3040 Howlin' Wolf. GOING BACK HOME. Syndicate Chapter SC 003 (E). (Reissue.)
Blues Unlimited. February/March. p23. 175w. 3

3041 Howlin' Wolf. THE LONDON ... SESSIONS. Chess CH 60008 $6.95.
Gramophone. January. p1279. 125w. 2
Library Journal. January 1. p55. 325w. 3

3042 Howlin' Wolf. MESSAGE OF THE YOUNG. Chess CH 50002 $5.98. Cart. 8033-50002M $6.95. Cass. 5033-50002M $6.95.
Blues Unlimited. January. p25. 25w. 0
Gramophone. April. p1776. 25w. 0

3043 Mississippi John Hurt. BEST. Vanguard VSD 19/20 (2 discs) $5.98.
Blues Unlimited. February/March. p26. 200w. 4
Creem. December. p242. 25w. $2\frac{1}{2}$
Gramophone. January. p1279. 125w. 3
Jazz and Blues. January. p22-3. 600w. 4
Journal of American Folklore. January/March. p107. 25w. $2\frac{1}{2}$
Previews. December. p44. 150w. $3\frac{1}{2}$

3044 Mississippi John Hurt. 1928: HIS FIRST RECORDINGS. Biograph BLP C4 $5.98. (Reissue.)
Blues Unlimited. September. p26. 225w. 5

Jazz Journal. December. p30. 300w. 2
Old Time Music. Summer. p23. 225w. 4
Previews. November. p39. 150w. 3½
Sing Out. May/June. p43. 150w. 3½
Sound. December. p39. 100w. 5

3045 John Jackson. VOLUME 2. Arhoolie 1035 $6.00
Previews. December. p44. 200w. 3

3046 John Jackson. BLUES AND COUNTRY DANCE TUNES FROM VIRGINIA. Arhoolie 1025 $6.00.
Jazz Journal. October. p32. 400w. 4
Music Journal. November. p62. 25w. 3
Old Time Music. Autumn. p27-8. 250w. 4
Previews. December. p44. 200w. 3

3047 John Jackson. IN EUROPE. Arhoolie 1047 $6.00.
Previews. December. p44. 200w. 3

3048 Papa Charlie Jackson. FAT MOUTH, 1924/29. Yazoo L 1029 $5.95. (Reissue.)
Blues Unlimited. February/March. p27. 250w. 4
Previews. December. p44. 175w. 3

3049 Papa Charlie Jackson. 1925/28. Biograph BLP 12042 $5.98. (Reissue.)
Blues Unlimited. November. p27. 125w. 3
Jazz Journal. August. p33. 275w. 3

3050 JACKSON BLUES, 1928/1938 (anthology). Yazoo L 1007 $5.95. (Reissue.)
Previews. December. p45. 225w. 3

3051 Elmore James/Eddie Taylor. SOUTHSIDE BLUES. Cobblestone CST 9001 $5.98. Cart. M89001 $6.95. Cass. M59001 $6.95. (Reissue.)
Blues Unlimited. July. p23. 200w. 4
Popular Music. Spring. p186. 50w. 4

3052 Elmore James. HISTORY OF... Trip 8007-2 (2 discs) $5.98. (Reissue.)
Blues Unlimited. February/March. p21. 300w. 1

3053 Skip James. Melodeon MLP 7321 $5.98.
Journal of American Folklore. January/March. p100. 50w. 3½

3054 Skip James. KING OF THE DELTA SINGERS. Biograph BLP 12029 $5.98. (Reissue.)
Blues World. Spring. p19. 100w. 3
Journal of American Folklore. January/March. p100. 50w. 2½

3055 Bobo Jenkins. LIFE OF ... Big Star BB 008-19 $5.00.
Blues Unlimited. April. p25. 150w. 2
Living Blues. Winter. p36. 200w. 5

3056 Larry Johnson. COUNTRY BLUES. Biograph BLP 12028 $5.98.
Coda. February. p26. 275w. 3
Journal of American Folklore. January/March. p102. 25w. $3\frac{1}{2}$
Previews. December. p44. 150w. $2\frac{1}{2}$

3057 Larry Johnson. FAST AND FUNKY. Blue Goose 2001 $5.95.
Coda. February. p26. 275w. 4
Previews. December. p44. 150w. $3\frac{1}{2}$

3058 Larry Johnson. PRESENTING THE COUNTRY BLUES. Blue Horizon 7-63851 (E).
Journal of American Folklore. January/March. p102. 125w. $3\frac{1}{2}$

3059 Lonnie Johnson. Collector's Classics CC 30 (Denmark). (Reissue.)
Jazz Journal. January. p31. 300w. 2

3060 Lonnie Johnson. TOMORROW NIGHT. King KS 1083 $4.98. (Reissue.)
Blues Unlimited. January. p23. 100w. 3

3061 Albert King. LOVEJOY. Stax STS 2040 $5.98. Cart. ST82040 $6.95. Cass. STC 2040 $6.95.
Audio. November. p93. 25w. 3

3062 B.B. King. GUESS WHO. ABC ABCX 759 $5.98. Cart. M8759 $6.95. Cass. M5759 $6.95.
Creem. December. p59. 250w. $2\frac{1}{2}$
Rolling Stone. November. p64, 66. 600w. 2

3063 B.B. King. IN LONDON. ABC ABCX 730 $5.98. Cart. M8730 $6.95. Cass. M5730 $6.95.
Blues Unlimited. January. p24. 100w. 3
Blues Unlimited. February/March. p30. 125w. 1
High Fidelity. January. p120. 25w. $2\frac{1}{2}$
Jazz and Blues. April. p26-7. 250w. 0
Jazz Journal. February. p35. 400w. 2

3064 B.B. King. INCREDIBLE SOUL. Festival FLDX 532 (France). (Reissue.)
Blues Unlimited. July. p23. 25w. 3
Records and Recordings. April. p110. 200w. 4

3065 B.B. King. L.A. MIDNIGHT. ABC ABCX 743 $5.98. Cart. M8743 $6.95. Cass. M5743 $6.95.

Blues Unlimited. May. p24. 100w. 1
Blues Unlimited. July. p23. 50w. 1
Crawdaddy. May 14. p19. 525w. 1
Downbeat. May 25. p22. 425w. 3
Gramophone. June. p111. 25w. 2
Jazz and Blues. July. p30. 400w. 1
Jazz Journal. October. p34. 350w. 2
Saturday Review. June 17. p80. 100w. 3

3066 B.B. King. LIVE AT THE REGAL. ABC ABCS 724 $5.98. Cart. M8724 $6.95. Cass. M5724 $6.95.
Blues Unlimited. October. p28. 25w. 4

3067 B.B. King. LIVE AT COOK COUNTY JAIL. ABC ABCS 723 $5.98. Cart. M8723 $6.95. Cass. M5723 $6.95.
Gramophone. January. p1279. 125w. 2

3068 Freddie King. GETTING READY. Shelter SHE 8905 $5.98.
Library Journal. February 15. p665. 100w. 3

3069 Freddie King. HIS EARLY YEARS. Juke Blues 2343 047 (E). (Reissue.)
Blues Unlimited. July. p27. 150w. 4
Jazz and Blues. August. p34. 300w. 3
Jazz Journal. July. p30. 325w. 3

3070 Freddie King. TEXAS CANNONBALL. Shelter SW 8913 $5.98. Cart. 8XW 8913 $6.98. Cass. 4XW 8913 $6.98.
Blues Unlimited. September. p28. 100w. 2½
Blues Unlimited. November. p30. 50w. 2½
Hi-Fi News and Record Review. November. p2202. 100w. 3
Rolling Stone. July 20. p52. 400w. 3

3071 KINGS AND THE QUEEN, VOLUME 2 (anthology). Spivey 1014 $5.00.
Previews. November. p40. 300w. 3

3072 KINGS OF MEMPHIS TOWN (anthology). Roots RL 333 (Austria). (Reissue.)
Living Blues. Winter. p34-6. 225w. 4

3073 Eddie Lang and Lonnie Johnson. Swaggie 1276 (Australia). (Reissue.)
Coda. August. p18-9. 100w. 4

3074 LEGENDARY SESSIONS - MEMPHIS STYLE (anthology). Roots RSE-2 (Austria). (Reissue.)
Blues Unlimited. May. p26. 200w. 3½
Blues World. Spring. p20-1. 150w. 3

3075 Furry Lewis. BEALE STREET BLUES. Barclay 920.352 (France).
Blues Unlimited. July. p22. 50w. 0

3076 Johnnie Lewis. ALABAMA SLIDE GUITAR. Arhoolie 1055 $6.00.
Ethnomusicology. October. p585-86. 650w. $2\frac{1}{2}$
Music Journal. November. p62. 25w. 3

3077 Lightnin' Slim. HIGH AND LOW DOWN. Excello 8018.
Blues Unlimited. July. p24. 50w. 0
Coda. October. p15. 125w. 2
Living Blues. Summer. p36. 150w. 2

3078 Lightnin' Slim. LONDON GUMBO. Blue Horizon 2931 005 (E).
Blues Unlimited. September. p23. 225w. $3\frac{1}{2}$
Gramophone. December. p1222. 50w. 2
Jazz Journal. September. p33. 125w. 1

3079 Mance Lipscomb. TROUBLE IN MIND. Reprise RS 6404. (Reissue.)
Journal of American Folklore. January/March. p107. 25w. $2\frac{1}{2}$

3080 Little Walter. BOSS BLUES HARMONICA. Chess 2CH-60014 (2 discs) $6.98. (Reissue.)
Blues Unlimited. November. p27. 50w. 3
Living Blues. Autumn. p31. 300w. 4
Rolling Stone. December 7. p72. 1,300w. $4\frac{1}{2}$

3081 Cripple Clarence Lofton/Jimmy Yancey. Gannet 5136 (E). (Reissue.)
Blues Unlimited. September. p28. 75w. 4

3082 Joe Hill Louis. THE ONE MAN BAND. Muskadine M 101 $4.98.
Blues Unlimited. February/March. p22. 125w. 4
Downbeat. September 14. p22. 100w. 4.

3083 LOUISIANA BLUES (anthology). Arhoolie 1054 $6.00
Coda. October. p26-7. 175w. 3

3084 Louisiana Red. THE SEVENTH SUN. Carnival 2941 002 (E). (Reissue.)
Blues Unlimited. September. p25. 150w. 3
Jazz Journal. December. p36-7. 325w. $3\frac{1}{2}$
Records and Recordings. October. p119. 300w. 4

3085 Jerry McCash/Frank Frost/Arthur Crudup. HARPIN' ON IT. Carnival 2941 001 (E). (Reissue.)
Blues Unlimited. October. p24. 300w. 5

Jazz and Blues. September. p27-8. 400w. 3
Jazz Journal. October. p30. 225w. 2
Records and Recordings. October. p119. 200w. $3\frac{1}{2}$

3086 Tommy McClennan. 1939/1941. Roots RL 305 (Austria) $5.95. (Reissue.)
Previews. December. p44. 100w. $2\frac{1}{2}$

3087 George and Ethel McCoy. EARLY IN THE MORNING. Adelphi AD 10045 $5.95.
Journal of American Folklore. January/March. p101. 25w. $2\frac{1}{2}$

3088 Fred McDowell. VOLUME 2. Arhoolie 1027 $6.00.
Previews. November. p39. 225w. 3

3089 Fred McDowell. IN LONDON. Sire SES 97018 $4.98.
Journal of American Folklore. January/March. p101. 25w. $2\frac{1}{2}$

3090 Fred McDowell. LIVE IN NEW YORK. Oblivion OD 1 $5.00.
Blues Unlimited. June. p23. 175w. 5
Living Blues. Summer. p34. 600w. 3

3091 Fred McDowell. MISSISSIPPI DELTA BLUES. Arhoolie 1021 $6.00.
Previews. November. p39. 225w. 3

3092 Fred McDowell. WITH HIS BLUES BOYS. Arhoolie 1046 $6.00.
Previews. November. p39. 225w. 3

3093 Sam McGrath. THE CALL OF THE MORNING DOVE. Adelphi AD 10145 $5.95.
Jazz Journal. February. p39. 100w. 3

3094 Blind Willie McTell. ATLANTA TWELVE STRING. Atlantic SD 7224 $5.98. (Reissue.)
Blues Unlimited. November. p25. 100w. 5
Records and Recordings. December. p102. 275w. 4

3095 Blind Willie McTell. THE EARLY YEARS, 1927/1933. Yazoo L 1005 $5.95. (Reissue.)
Previews. December. p44-5. 200w. 3

3096 Blind Willie McTell/Memphis Minnie. LOVE CHANGIN' BLUES. Biograph BLP 12035 $5.98. (Reissue.)
Blues Unlimited. February/March. p21. 125w. 5
Living Blues. Winter. p36. 500w. 4

3097 Taj Mahal. HAPPY TO BE JUST LIKE I AM. Columbia C 30767 $4.98. Cart. CA 30767 $6.98. Cass. CT 30767 $6.98.

American Record Guide. April. p380. 225w. 3
Crawdaddy. April 2. p17. 1,000w. $3\frac{1}{2}$
Creem. April. p66. 525w. $2\frac{1}{2}$
Downbeat. March 16. p28. 175w. 3
Popular Music. Winter. p122. 100w. $3\frac{1}{2}$

3098 Taj Mahal. RECYCLING THE BLUES AND OTHER RELATED STUFF. Columbia KC 31605 $5.98. Cart. CA 31605 $6.98. Cass. CT 31605 $6.98.
Rolling Stone. November 23. p61. 800w. 4

3099 Martin, Bogan and Armstrong. BARNYARD DANCE. Rounder Records 2003 $5.95.
Blues Unlimited. December. p26. 175w. 3
Old Time Music. Autumn. p28. 300w. 4

3100 MASTERS OF MODERN BLUES, VOLUME 1/4 (anthology). Testament T2212/5 (4 discs) $4.98 each.
Journal of American Folklore. January/March. p103. 300w. $3\frac{1}{2}$

3101 THE MEMPHIS BLUES, 1927/1931 (anthology). Yazoo L 1008 $5.95. (Reissue.)
Previews. October. p43-4. 300w. $2\frac{1}{2}$

3102 THE MEMPHIS BLUES AGAIN, VOLUMES 1/2 (anthology). Adelphi AD 1009/10 (2 discs) $11.90.
Audio. May. p97. 1,100w. $4\frac{1}{2}$
Blues Unlimited. January. p28. 350w. $3\frac{1}{2}$
Blues World. Spring. p19-20. 650w. 4
Rolling Stone. March 2. p60. 400w. 3

3103 MEMPHIS JAMBOREE, 1927/1936 (anthology). Yazoo L 1021 $5.95. (Reissue.)
Previews. October. p43-4. 300w. $2\frac{1}{2}$

3104 Memphis Jug Band, Volume 2. Roots 337 (Austria). (Reissue.)
Blues Unlimited. January. p24. 350w. 4
Blues World. Spring. p17. 50w. 3
Coda. June. p21. 300w. 4

3105 Memphis Jug Band/Cannon's Jug Stompers. VOLUMES 1/2. Natchez NFP 701 and 703 (Argentina). (Reissue.)
Coda. April. p19. 300w. 4

3106 Memphis Slim. BAD LUCK AND TROUBLE. Barclay ZG 31291 (2 discs) $6.98. (Reissue.)
Blues Unlimited. October. p29. 75w. 0
Downbeat. September 14. p22-4. 200w. 2

3107 Memphis Slim. BLUE MEMPHIS. Barclay 920214 (France).
Gramophone. January. p1279. 100w. 0

3108 Memphis Slim. BORN WITH THE BLUES. Jewel LPS 5004 $4.98. (Reissue.)
Blues Unlimited. January. p29. 50w. 1

3109 Memphis Slim. GREAT. America 30 AM 6076 (France).
Blues Unlimited. January. p25. 25w. 2½

3110 Memphis Slim. OLD TIMES/NEW TIMES. Barclay 920 332/3 (2 discs) (France).
Blues Unlimited. May. p28. 75w. 4
Blues Unlimited. October. p28. 50w. 3½
Coda. October. p24. 275w. 5
Gramophone. December. p1222. 100w. 2½
Jazz Journal. September. p34. 350w. 3
Previews. October. p43. 300w. 3
Records and Recordings. October. p119-20. 175w. 4
Sound. August. p49. 150w. 3

3111 Memphis Slim. ROCK ME, BABY. Black Lion 2460 155 (E). (Reissue.)
Blues Unlimited. October. p29. 75w. 1
Hi-Fi News and Record Review. July. p1313. 200w. 2½
Jazz and Blues. August. p34. 275w. 2½
Jazz Journal. August. p34. 200w. 0

3112 Mississippi Sheiks/Beale Street Sheiks. Biograph BLP 12041 $5.98. (Reissue.)
Blues Unlimited. October. p29. 300w. 4
Jazz Journal. August. p34. 200w. 3

3113 MISSISSIPPI BLUES, 1927/1941 (anthology). Yazoo L 1001 $5.95. (Reissue.)
Previews. December. p45. 225w. 3

3114 MISSISSIPPI MOANERS, 1928/1938 (anthology). Yazoo L 1009 $5.95. (Reissue.)
Previews. December. p45. 225w. 3

3115 Little Brother Montgomery. HOME AGAIN. Saydisc/Matchbox SDM 223 (E).
Blues Unlimited. October. p30. 150w. 3½
Jazz Journal. December. p38-9. 250w. 4

3116 Thomas Morris/Perry Bradford. Natchez NLP 3003 (Argentina). (Reissue.)
Jazz Journal. June. p37. 100w. 1

3117 Muddy Waters. GOOD NEWS. Syndicate Chapter SC 002 (E). (Reissue.)
Blues Unlimited. February/March. p30. 150w. 4

3118 Muddy Waters. LIVE AT MISTER KELLY'S. Chess CH 50012 $5.98.
Blues Unlimited. April. p23-4. 100w. 2½
Blues World. Summer. p18. 200w. 3
Downbeat. May 11. p24, 26. 250w. 4
Downbeat. June 8. p26-7. 150w. 4½
High Fidelity. March. p116. 25w. 2
Previews. November. p405. 225w. 2

3119 Muddy Waters. LONDON ... SESSIONS. Chess 60013 $5.98. Cart. 8033-60013M $6.95. Cass. 5033-60013M $6.95.
Blues Unlimited. October. p27-8. 100w. 2
Crawdaddy. September. p19. 500w. 3½
Creem. September. p48-9. 200w. 2½
Creem. September. p64. 50w. 3
Gramophone. October. p781. 150w. 0
Records and Recordings. September. p97-8. 150w. 1

3120 Muddy Waters. McKINLEY MORGANFIELD A.K.A. ... Chess 2CH 60006 (2 discs) $6.98. (Reissue.)
Saturday Review. April 22. p51. 50w. 3

3121 Muddy Waters. THEY CALL ME ... Chess CH 1553 $5.98.
Living Blues. Winter. p34. 250w. 3
Previews. November. p41. 75w. 2½

3122 NEW DEAL BLUES (anthology). Mamlish S 3801 $5.95. (Reissue.)
Journal of American Folklore. January/March. p100. 50w. 3

3123 NEW YORK CITY BLUES (anthology). Flyright LP 4706 (E). (Reissue.)
Blues Unlimited. October. p30. 250w. 3½

3124 NEW YORK COUNTRY BLUES (anthology). Flyright LP 4705 (E). (Reissue.)
Blues Unlimited. July. p22. 200w. 4

3125 OAKLAND BLUES (anthology). Arhoolie 2008 $6.00. (Reissue.)
Coda. October. p26-7. 175w. 4
Jazz and Blues. March. p27. 500w. 3½
Music Journal. November. p62. 50w. 4

3126 ON THE ROAD AGAIN (anthology). Adelphi AD 1007S $5.95.
Journal of American Folklore. January/March. p100. 50w. 3

3127 Jack Owens. IT MUST HAVE BEEN THE DEVIL. Testament T 2222 $4.98.
Living Blues. Summer. p32. 175w. 3
Stereo Review. January. p110. 225w. 3

3128 Junior Parker. I TELL STORIES SAD AND TRUE, I SING THE BLUES AND PLAY HARMONICA TOO, IT IS VERY FUNKY. Groove Merchant GM 513 $4.98. Cart. 8513 $6.95. Cass. 5513 $6.95.
Creem. November. p74. 25w. 2½

3129 Junior Parker. YOU DON'T HAVE TO BE BLACK TO LOVE THE BLUES. Groove Merchant GM 502 $5.98. Cart. 8502 $6.95. Cass. 5502 $6.95.
Blues Unlimited. April. p22. 200w. 5
Blues Unlimited. November. p29. 150w. 4
Gramophone. October. p781. 75w. 2
Jazz Journal. August. p35. 225w. 4
Saturday Review. June 17. p80. 100w. 3

3130 Piano Red. UNDERGROUND ATLANTA. King KS 1117 $4.98.
Living Blues. Autumn. p32. 50w. 0

3131 PIEDMONT BLUES (anthology). Flyright LP 104 (E). (Reissue.)
Blues Unlimited. February/March. p28. 150w. 4

3132 Billie and De De Pierce. NEW ORLEANS MUSIC. Arhoolie 2016 $6.00. (Reissue.)
Blues Unlimited. October. p24. 150w. 2
Jazz and Blues. September. p30. 350w. 3
Jazz Journal. September. p38. 100w. 2
Popular Music. Spring. p188. 100w. 3

3133 Cousin Joe Pleasant. BAD LUCK BLUES. Black and Blue 33.035 (France).
Blues Unlimited. September. p25. 75w. 4

3134 Professor Longhair. NEW ORLEANS PIANO. Atlantic SD 7225 $5.98. (Reissue.)
Blues Unlimited. October. p25. 350w. 5
Creem. December. p86. 25w. 3½
Living Blues. Autumn. p31. 375w. 4

3135 Doug Quattlebaum. SOFTEE MAN BLUES. Vogue CLDP 830 (France). (Reissue.)
Blues Unlimited. December. p27. 125w. 4

3136 THE QUEEN AND HER KNIGHTS (anthology). Spivey 1006 $5.00.
Previews. November. p40. 300w. 3

3137 Ma Rainey. DOWN IN THE BASEMENT. Milestone MLP 2017 $5.98. (Reissue.)
Jazz Report. No.1. 300w. 4

3138 Ma Rainey. 1924/28. Biograph BLP 12001 $5.98. (Reissue.)
Previews. December. p45. 125w. 2½

3139 Ma Rainey. 1924/28, VOLUME 2. Biograph BLP 12011 $5.98. (Reissue.)
Previews. December. p45. 125w. 2½

3140 Ma Rainey. QUEEN OF THE BLUES. Biograph BLP 12032 $5.98. (Reissue.)
Blues Unlimited. June. p28. 125w. 3½
Previews. December. p45. 125w. 2½

3141 REALLY CHICAGO BLUES (anthology). Adelphi AD 1005S (2 discs) $10.00.
Journal of American Folklore. January/March. p103-4. 125w. 3

3142 Jimmy Reed. LET THE BOSSMAN SPEAK. Blues on Blues BOB 10001 $5.95.
Blues Unlimited. April. p27. 75w. 2
Downbeat. June 8. p27. 150w. 1½
Living Blues. Winter. p34. 350w. 2

3143 Jimmy Reed. VERY BEST. Buddah BDS 4003 $5.98. (Reissue.
Journal of American Folklore. January/March. p107. 25w. 2½

3144 RIVERTOWN BLUES (anthology). Hi SHL 32063 $4.98. (Reissue.)
Blues Unlimited. April. p24. 50w. 3½
Coda. June. p18. 225w. 4
Gramophone. April. p1776. 50w. 2½
Living Blues. Winter. p36. 200w. 3
Jazz Journal. March. p35. 225w. 0
Rolling Stone. March 2. p60. 300w. 3½

3145 Fenton Robinson. MONDAY MORNING BOOGIE AND BLUES. Seventy-7 S7 2001 $5.98.
Blues Unlimited. April. p22. 125w. 3½
Living Blues. Spring. p36. 200w. 2

3146 Freddy Robinson. AT THE DRIVE-IN. Enterprise ENS 1025 $5.98.
Living Blues. Autumn. p31. 250w. 3

3147 L.C. Robinson. UPS AND DOWNS. Arhoolie 1062 $6.00.
Blues Unlimited. July. p25. 125w. 4
Jazz Journal. October. p36. 350w. 4
Jazz Report. No. 2. 150w. 4
Music Journal. November. p62. 50w. 4
Previews. November. p40. 200w. 4

3148 ROCK BOTTOM (anthology). Chess CH 9033-60003 (2 discs) $6.98 (Canada). (Reissue.)
Blues Unlimited. May. p26. 100w. 2
Library Journal. February 15. p665. 175w. 2
Ontario Library Review. December. p244. 25w. 2½

3149 Doctor Ross. HIS FIRST RECORDINGS. Arhoolie 1065 $6.00. (Reissue.)
Blues Unlimited. December. p25. 175w. 3½

3150 Doctor Ross. I'D RATHER BE AN OLD WOMAN'S BABY THAN A YOUNG WOMAN'S SLAVE. Fortune FTS 3011 $4.98.
Living Blues. Spring. p35. 300w. 3
Journal of American Folklore. January/March. p104. 75w. 2½

3151 Jimmy Rushing. GOING TO CHICAGO. Vanguard VRS 8518 (E). (Reissue.)
Blues Unlimited. December. p28. 25w. 4
Jazz and Blues. December. p30-1. 300w. 4
Jazz Journal. November. p35. 200w. 4
Records and Recordings. December. p103. 150w. 4½

3152 Jimmy Rushing. THE YOU AND ME THAT USED TO BE. RCA LSP 4566 $5.98. Cart. P8S 1784 $6.95.
Audio. May. p96. 800w. 5
Blues Unlimited. April. p24. 25w. 3½
Coda. December. p25. 350w. 5
Gramophone. May. p1961-2. 200w. 2
Hi-Fi News and Record Review. May. p940. 200w. 2
Jazz and Blues. April. p29-30. 225w. 3
Jazz Journal. March. p35. 125w. 3
Records and Recordings. March. p124. 225w. 4

3153 ST. LOUIS BLUES, 1929/1935 (anthology). Yazoo L 1030 $5.95. (Reissue.)
Blues Unlimited. February/March. p26. 175w. 4
Blues World. Spring. p21. 200w. 3
Jazz Journal. April. p36. 350w. 3

3154 Robert Shaw. TEXAS BARRELHOUSE PIANO. Arhoolie 1010 $6.00.
Previews. November. p40. 225w. 3

3155 Thomas Shaw. BLIND LEMON'S BUDDY. Blue Goose 2008 $5.95.
Sing Out. May/June. p46. 100w. 2½

3156 Thomas Shaw. BORN IN TEXAS. Advent 2801 $5.98.
Blues Unlimited. February/March. p25. 225w. 5
Blues World. Spring. p20. 400w. 4
Downbeat. September 14. p22. 100w. 4
Living Blues. Spring. p35. 175w. 3

3157 Johnny Shines. SITTIN' ON TOP OF THE WORLD. Biograph BLP 12044 $5.98.
Blues Unlimited. November. p26. 200w. 4
Jazz Journal. October. p36. 250w. 3
Previews. November. p40. 200w. 3
Sing Out. May/June. p43-4. 150w. 3

3158 Johnny Shines and Big Walter Horton. Testament T 2217 $4.98.
Journal of American Folklore. January/March. p103. 75w. 4

3159 SHOUTIN', SWINGIN', AND MAKIN' LOVE (anthology). Chess CHV 412 $5.98. (Reissue.)
Coda. February. p28-9. 250w. 2

3160 SIC EM DOGS ON ME (anthology). Herwin 201 $5.95. (Reissue.)
Blues Unlimited. May. p25. 250w. 4½
Coda. December. p27. 700w. 5
Jazz Journal. July. p34. 575w. 3
Living Blues. Autumn. p31. 425w. 4

3161 Frankie Lee Sims. LUCY MAE BLUES. Sonet SNTF 5004 (Sweden). (Reissue.)
Blues Unlimited. January. p25. 25w. 2½

3162 Bessie Smith. THE EMPRESS. Columbia G 30818 (2 discs) $5.98. (Reissue.)
Blues Unlimited. February/March. p29. 225w. 5
Coda. February. p18. 250w. 5
Gramophone. April. p1776. 75w. 5
Jazz Journal. February. p36-7. 375w. 5
Library Journal. February 15. p665. 175w. 4
Records and Recordings. March. p124. 225w. 4

3163 Bessie Smith. EMPTY BED BLUES. Columbia G 30450 (2 discs) $5.98. (Reissue.)
Coda. February. p18. 250w. 5

3164 Bessie Smith. NOBODY'S BLUES BUT MINE. Columbia G 31093 (2 discs) $5.98. (Reissue.)

Popular Music. Fall. p87. 50w. 2½
Sound. December. p39. 50w. 4

3165 Clara Smith. VOLUME 3. VJM VLP 17 (E). (Reissue.)
Blues World. Spring. p18. 125w. 3
Jazz Journal. March. p35-6. 650w. 4
Jazz and Blues. April. p30. 350w. 4

3166 Funny Papa Smith. THE ORIGINAL HOWLIN' WOLF. Yazoo L1031 $5.95. (Reissue.)
Blues Unlimited. April. p24. 250w. 4½
Previews. December. p45. 100w. 2½

3167 George Smith. ARKANSAS TRAP. Deram DES 18059 $4.98.
Stereo Review. March. p109. 300w. 2½

3168 Moses "Whispering" Smith. OVER EASY. Excello 8020 $4.98.
Blues Unlimited. July. p24. 125w. 4
Jazz Journal. August. p36. 200w. 2
Living Blues. Summer. p36. 150w. 3

3169 Trixie Smith. Collector's Classics CC 29 (Denmark). (Reissue.)
Jazz Journal. March. p36. 300w. 2

3170 Smokey Babe. HOT BLUES. Arhoolie 2019 $6.00. (Reissue.)
Blues Unlimited. September. p24. 125w. 4
Jazz Report. No. 2. 125w. 4
Music Journal. November. p62. 25w. 4
Popular Music. Spring. p184. 75w. 4

3171 SOUL IN THE BEGINNING (anthology). Avco-Embassy LP 33006 (E). (Reissue.)
Blues Unlimited. November. p31. 175w. 4

3172 Otis Spann. THE BOTTOM OF THE BLUES. Bluesway BLS 6013 $4.98.
Coda. June. p23. 300w. 5

3173 Otis Spann. THE EVERLASTING BLUES VERSUS ... Spivey LP 1013 $5.00.
Blues Unlimited. November. p27. 200w. 2
Previews. November. p40. 200w. 2½

3174 Otis Spann. WALKING THE BLUES. Barnaby KZ 31290 $5.98.
Blues Unlimited. July. p22. 75w. 4½
Downbeat. September 14. p22-4. 200w. 4
Saturday Review. June 17. p80. 100w. 3

3175 Joseph Spence. BAHAMAN GUITARIST. Arhoolie 1061 $6.00.
Jazz Report. No. 2. 100w. 3½

3176 SPIVEY'S BLUES PARADE (anthology). Spivey LP 1012 $5.00.
Blues Unlimited. April. p26. 125w. 2½
Journal of American Folklore. January/March. p105. 75w. 2½

3177 Arbee Stidham. A TIME FOR BLUES. Mainstream MRL 360 $5.98.
Blues Unlimited. September. p29. 50w. 0
Living Blues. Autumn. p32. 500w. 0

3178 SUPER BLACK BLUES, VOLUME 2 (anthology). Flying Dutchman BTS 9009 $5.95.
Journal of American Folklore. January/March. p105. 100w. 3½

3179 SWAMP BLUES (anthology). Excello EXC 8015/16 (2 discs) $9.96.
Journal of American Folklore. January/March. p104. 100w. 3½

3180 Roosevelt Sykes. THE COUNTRY BLUES PIANO ACE. Yazoo L 1033 $5.95. (Reissue.)
Blues Unlimited. February/March. p29. 150w. 5

3181 Roosevelt Sykes. THE HONEYDRIPPER'S DUKE'S MIXTURE. Barclay 920.294 (France).
Blues Unlimited. May. p25. 100w. 2½
Gramophone. April. p1776. 25w. 2½
Jazz and Blues. May. p24. 250w. 3½
Jazz Journal. January. p36-7. 250w. 2
Records and Recordings. January. p96. 75w. 4

3182 Roosevelt Sykes and Homesick James. Black and Blue 33.034 (France).
Blues Unlimited. September. p28. 25w. 2

3183 Hound Dog Taylor. Alligator 4701 $5.98.
Audio. August. p64. 500w. 2
Downbeat. June 8. p26. 150w. 3½
Jazz Report. No. 2. 125w. 3
Living Blues. Winter. p34. 100w. 3

3184 TEN YEARS IN MEMPHIS, 1927/1937 (anthology). Yazoo L 1002 $5.95. (Reissue.)
Previews. October. p43-4. 300w. 2½

3185 Sonny Terry and Woody Guthrie. Ember CW 136 (E). (Reissue.)

Blues Unlimited. September. p28. 50w. 2½
Jazz Journal. August. p37. 175w. 3

3186 Sonny Terry and Brownie McGhee. AT SUGAR HILL. America 30 AM 6071 (France). (Reissue.)
Blues Unlimited. January. p25. 25w. 2½
Records and Recordings. May. p101. 150w. 4

3187 Sonny Terry and Brownie McGhee. HOME TOWN BLUES. Mainstream MRL 308 $4.98. (Reissue.)
Blues Unlimited. January. p25. 25w. 3

3188 Sonny Terry and Brownie McGhee. PREACHIN' THE BLUES. Folkways FTS 31024 $5.98. (Reissue.)
Journal of American Folklore. January/March. p107. 25w. 2½

3189 TEXAS BLUES, 1927/52 (anthology). Paltram PL 102 (Austria) $6.00. (Reissue.)
Blues Unlimited. January. p22. 225w. 3½
Blues World. Spring. p18. 100w. 3
Coda. December. p27-8. 200w. 3

3190 TEXAS COUNTRY MUSIC, VOLUME 3 (anthology). Roots 327 (Austria) $6.00. (Reissue.)
Coda. April. p25-6. 625w. 4

3191 TEXAS GUITAR - FROM DALLAS TO L.A. (anthology). Atlantic SD 7226 $5.98. (Reissue.)
Blues Unlimited. November. p25. 150w. 3

3192 THINGS HAVE CHANGED: AN ANTHOLOGY OF TODAY'S BLUES FROM ST. LOUIS (anthology). Adelphi AD 1012S $5.95.
Blues Unlimited. January. p27. 350w. 2½
Blues World. Spring. p20. 225w. 3
Living Blues. Spring. p36. 225w. 4
Sing Out. March/April. p38. 50w. 2

3193 THREE KINGS AND THE QUEEN (anthology). Spivey 1004 $5.00.
Previews. November. p40. 300w. 3

3194 Big Joe Turner. Musidisc CV 1010 (France). (Reissue.)
Blues Unlimited. July. p23. 25w. 4

3195 Big Joe Turner. HIS GREATEST RECORDINGS. Atco SD 33-376 $5.98. Cart. M833 376 $6.95. Cass. M533 376 $6.95. (Reissue.)
Blues Unlimited. February/March. p24. 25w. 4
Crawdaddy. February 20. p17. 300w. 2½
Creem. March. p48-9. 25w. 2
Stereo Review. April. p100. 200w. 3½

3196 Big Joe Turner. TEXAS STYLE. Black and Blue 33.028 (France).
Blues Unlimited. October. p30. 100w. 3

3197 Big Joe Turner. TURNS ON THE BLUES. Kent 542 $4.98.
Blues Unlimited. July. p23. 25w. 3

3198 Victoria VareKamp. RATTLESNAKES COMING OUT OF THE BASKET. Space SP 2 (Holland).
Blues Unlimited. May. p25. 100w. 2½

3199 Victoria VareKamp/Mark Jansen. BLUES AND BOOGIE WOOGIE. Space SP 1 (Holland).
Blues Unlimited. April. p26. 100w. 2½

3200 Eddie "Cleanhead" Vinson. YOU CAN'T MAKE LOVE ALONE. Flying Dutchman FD 31 1012 $5.95.
Blues Unlimited. September. p26. 75w. 3
Downbeat. June 8. p26. 175w. 3½
Gramophone. December. p1222. 75w. 3
Jazz Journal. October. p38-9. 200w. 2
New York Times--Sunday. June 11. pD30. 100w. 2

3201 Eddie "Cleanhead" Vinson/Wynonie Harris. JUMP BLUES. Polydor 2343 048 (E). (Reissue.)
Blues Unlimited. July. p27. 300w. 3½
Jazz Journal. November. p36-7. 400w. 3

3202 Johnny "Big Moose" Walker. RAMBLING WOMAN. Bluesway BLS 6036 $4.98.
Blues Unlimited. October. p28. 25w. 4

3203 T-Bone Walker. T-BONE BLUES. Atlantic SD 8256 $5.98. (Reissue.)
Blues Unlimited. January. p26. 75w. 4

3204 Sippie Wallace. SINGS THE BLUES. Storyville SLP 198 (Denmark).
Jazz Journal. November. p37. 250w. 3

3205 Washboard Sam. FEELING LOWDOWN. RCA LPV 577 $5.98. (Reissue.)
Blues Unlimited. January. p22. 300w. 2
Blues Unlimited. November. p30. 50w. 4
Crawdaddy. March 19. p20. 500w. 3
Gramophone. December. p1222. 100w. 1½
High Fidelity. February. p118-9. 300w. 2
Jazz and Blues. July. p15-6. 325w. 3
Music Journal. February. p37. 75w. 2
Rolling Stone. March 16. p62. 200w. 3½

3206 WATER COAST BLUES (anthology). Flyright LP 4704 (E). (Reissue.)
Blues Unlimited. May. p26. 200w. 4

3207 Ethel Waters. JAZZIN' BABIES BLUES, 1921/27, VOLUME 2. Biograph BLP 12026 $5.98. (Reissue.)
Coda. February. p16. 350w. 1
Jazz Report. No.2. 150w. 2½

3208 WE THREE KINGS (anthology). Syndicate Chapter SC 005 (E). (Reissue.)
Blues Unlimited. May. p29. 100w. 3½

3209 Junior Wells. IN MY YOUNGER DAYS. Red Lightnin' LP RL 007 (E). (Reissue.)
Blues Unlimited. October. p24. 100w. 3

3210 Junior Wells. SOUTH SIDE BLUES JAM. Delmark DS 628 $5.98.
Gramophone. January. p1279. 125w. 3

3211 WEST COAST BLUES (anthology). Kent KST 9012 $4.98. (Reissue.)
Previews. October. p42. 225w. 2½

3212 Peetie Wheatstraw. VOLUE 1/2 (DEVIL'S SON-IN-LAW/ HIGH SHERIFF FROM HELL). Saydisc Matchbox 191/2 (E). (Reissue.)
Coda. February. p17. 800w. 4

3213 WHEN GIRLS DO IT (anthology). Red Lightnin' RL 006 (2 discs) (E). (Reissue.)
Blues Unlimited. November. p25. 350w. 3

3214 Bukka White. LEGACY OF THE BLUES, VOLUME 1. Sonet SNTF 809 (Sweden). (Reissue.)
Blues Unlimited. October. p29. 150w. 3½
Jazz Journal. December. p40-1. 350w. 4

3215 Josh White. BEST. Elektra EKS 75008 (2 discs) $5.98. (Reissue.)
Journal of American Folklore. January/March. p107. 25w. 2½

3216 Big Joe Williams. BLUES FROM THE MISSISSIPPI DELTA. Blues on Blues BOB 10003 $5.95.
Blues Unlimited. April. p27. 50w. 2½
Downbeat. June 8. p27. 150w. 2

3217 Big Joe Williams. NINE STRING GUITAR. Delmark 627 $5.98.
Music Journal. November. p62. 25w. 3

3218 Bill Williams. LOW AND LONESOME. Blue Goose 2004 $5.95.
Coda. December. p27. 350w. 3
Previews. November. p41. 175w. 3

3219 Harmonica Williams. WITH LITTLE FREDDIE KING. Ahura Mazda AMS 2003 $5.00.
Blues Unlimited. June. p27. 125w. 2
Living Blues. Winter. p34. 225w. 0

3220 Robert Pete Williams. Ahura Mazda AMS 2002 $5.00.
Journal of American Folklore. January/March. p101. 75w. 3

3221 Robert Pete Williams. SUGAR FARM. Roots SL 512 (Austria).
Blues Unlimited. July. p26. 100w. 4

3222 Robert Pete Williams. THOSE PRISON BLUES. Arhoolie 2015 $6.00. (Reissue.)
Blues Unlimited. June. p28. 150w. 5
Jazz Report. No. 2. 125w. 3½
Music Journal. November. p62. 25w. 3
Popular Music. Spring. 100w. 4
Previews. November. p41. 225w. 3

3223 Ralph Willis. CAROLINA BLUES. Blues Classics BC 22 $6.00. (Reissue.)
Previews. December. p45. 175w. 2½

3224 Ralph Willis/Country Paul/Robert Henry. FADED PICTURE BLUES. Carnival 2941 201 (E). (Reissue.)
Blues Unlimited. October. p27. 250w. 3½
Jazz Journal. December. p30. 300w. 2
Records and Recordings. October. p124. 200w. 4

3225 THE WORLD'S RAREST COUNTRY BLUES RECORDS (anthology). For Specialists Only FSO 001 (Austria). (Reissue.)
Blues Unlimited. April. p29. 150w. 2½
Blues World. Spring. p19. 400w. 3

3226 Mighty Joe Young. BLUES WITH A TOUCH OF SOUL. Delmark DS 629 $5.98.
Blues Unlimited. April. p23. 125w. 4
Blues Unlimited. July. p22. 275w. 3
Gramophone. October. p781. 125w. 4
Living Blues. Spring. p36. 200w. 3
Records and Recordings. July. p96. 200w. 4

RHYTHM & BLUES [and SOUL]

This section covers the basic "rhythm 'n' blues" market--the black alternative to rock music. Included here are soul music and other gospel-inspired and inflected artists or records. Most of this music is vocal. Attempts to pass off rock and jazz records as r & b (to sell the record) have been corrected, and those appropriate sections should be consulted for those records which usually include, in their titles, the words: "funky," "right on," "dues," "soul," "dig it," and other forms of jive talk. This is not to say that this music is not r & b--certainly, it is not pure r & b, and as a hybrid it is best placed from where it originated.

There are few review mechanisms for r & b. Ebony has a few watered down reviews (mostly of the New Jazz). Shout and Blues 'n' Soul, two British magazines, are not all that critical; indeed, they are "puff" reviews that include a lot of blues material more adequately handled elsewhere. No fanzines of rhythm and blues review records. Mention is made of albums, but no serial number or title is given. What are often reviewed (as in Shout, Blues Unlimited, Living Blues, and Blues 'n' Soul) are the 45 RPM singles, and this is where the soul market lies, in the three-minute miniature. Singles are important because they all sound the same, with no extended lengths for improvisation, and the guaranteed formula seems to strike pay dirt each time. Artists rarely play around with success. Many performers go into the studio to cut singles, with few ideas or plans for albums; consequently, the music is mainly a variation on a few hit themes at the same tempo. Such speeds and other technical devices (riffing horns, for example) render a whole album monotonous if one number follows another in the same manner and mode. The best purchases in this category are the anthologies, for a selection of different stylings. All male vocalists may sound like James Brown, but they sure don't sound like the Temptations, Diana Ross or Aretha Franklin, or vice versa.

A blues magazine and a good rock magazine will always review a good r & b disc, but the reviewer may come from a white background. Such periodicals as the British Blues Unlimited and the American Rolling Stone, Living Blues, and Creem appear to be fair, although the records never seem to come in as raves. At the other end of the spectrum, Shout, Blues 'n' Soul, and fanzines seem to give nothing but rave puffs. This is still an independent label's field, but the best of the smaller majors come from the Mowest complex, Atlantic (and Atco), Chess, Excello and Jewel.

According to the reviews, the following were the best in this category:

New

Ray Charles. MESSAGE FROM THE PEOPLE. Tangerine ABCX 755
Roberta Flack and Donny Hathaway. Atlantic SD 7216
Aretha Franklin. YOUNG, GIFTED AND BLACK. Atlantic SD 7213
Lowell Fulson. IN A HEAVY BAG. Jewel LP 5003
Al Green. LET'S STAY TOGETHER. HI SHL 32070
Johnny Otis Show. LIVE AT MONTEREY, 1970 (2 discs). Epic EG 30473
Stevie Wonder. MUSIC OF MY MIND. Tamla T314L

Reissues

Fats Domino. LEGENDARY MASTERS (2 discs). United Artists UAS 9958
KEEP THE FAITH (anthology) (3 discs). Joy JOYS 223/5 (E)
Otis Redding. BEST (2 discs). Atco 2SA-801

3227 La Vern Baker. HER GREATEST RECORDINGS. Atco SD 33-372 $5.98. Cart. M833-372 $6.95. Cass. M533-372 $6.95. (Reissue.)
Blues Unlimited. February/March. p24. 25w. 4
Crawdaddy. February 20. p17. 200w. 1
Creem. March. p48-9. 25w. 2

3228 Brook Benton. STORY TELLER. Cotillion 9050 $5.98. Cart. M8 9050 $6.95. Cass. M5 9050 $6.95.
Gramophone. May. p1951-2. 25w. 1

3229 Chuck Berry. BACK HOME. Chess S 1550 $5.98. Cart. 8033-1550M $6.95.
Blues Unlimited. February/March. p20. 25w. 2
Gramophone. April. p1776. 50w. 1
Living Blues. Winter. p36. 125w. 3

3230 Chuck Berry. GOLDEN DECADE. Chess S1514 (2 discs) $7.98. (Reissue.) Cart. 8033-1514N $8.95. Cass. 5033-1514N $8.95.
Gramophone. July. p257. 25w. 2
Records and Recordings. August. p89. 175w. 5

3231 Chuck Berry. THE LONDON CHUCK BERRY SESSIONS. Chess CH 60020 $5.98. Cart. 8033-600010M $6.95. Cass. 5033-60020M $6.95.

Blues Unlimited. September. p24. 100w. 1
Crawdaddy. September. p19. 400w. 1
Creem. September. p11. 50w. 1
Creem. September. p48-9. 1,000w. 5
Gramophone. September. p579-80. 50w. 3
Hi-Fi News and Record Review. September. p1685. 200w. 2
High Fidelity. September. p103-4. 300w. 2
Records and Recordings. September. p93. 250w. 5

3232 Chuck Berry. SAN FRANCISCO DUES. Chess 50008 $5.98. Cart. 8033-5008M $6.95.
Blues Unlimited. May. p28. 25w. 3½
Hi-Fi News and Record Review. July. p1313. 250w. 2½

3233 Big Black and His Congregation. IF YOU'RE DIGGIN' WHAT YOU'RE DOIN' KEEP ON DOIN' WHAT YOU'RE DIGGIN'. Uni 73114 $4.98.
Stereo Review. April. p90. 100w. 2

3234 BIRTH OF SOUL (anthology). Decca DL 79245 $5.98. (Reissue.)
Coda. December. p28. 100w. 0

3235 Booker T. and Priscilla. A & M SP 3504 (2 discs) $6.98.
Creem. December. p63. 25w. 1

3236 Booker T. and Priscilla. HOME GROWN. Share SP 4351 $5.98.
Creem. November. p74. 25w. 1
High Fidelity. October. p123. 175w. 0

3237 Charles Brown. BLUES 'N' BROWN. Jewel S 5006 $4.98.
Living Blues. Summer. p34. 150w. 2

3238 James Brown. HOT PANTS. Polydor PD 4054 $4.98.
American Record Guide. February. p284-5. 450w. 2
Gramophone. January. p1283. 25w. 3
Stereo Review. January. p107. 225w. 3

3239 James Brown. POPCORN. King KS 1055 $4.98.
Previews. September. p40. 250w. 2½

3240 James Brown. REVOLUTION OF THE MIND. Polydor PD 2-3003 (2 discs) $7.98. R-R J3003 $9.95. Cart. F 3003 $9.98. Cass. CF 3003 $9.98.
Beetle. March 29. p18. 200w. 4
Crawdaddy. March 19. p19. 1,400w. 3
Stereo Review. May. p91-2. 250w. 3

3241 James Brown. SEX MACHINE. King KS 71115 (2 discs) $6.98. Cart. 8032-1115N $8.95. Cass. 5032-1115N $8.95.
Previews. September. p40. 250w. 2½

3242 James Brown. SHO IS FUNKY DOWN HERE. King KS 1110 $4.98. Cart. 8032-1110M $6.95. Cass. 5032-1110M $6.95.
Previews. September. p40. 250w. 3

3243 James Brown. THIS IS... Philips 6336 201 (E). (Reissue.)
Gramophone. May. p1952. 25w. 2

3244 Mel Brown. FIFTH. Impulse AS 9209 $5.98.
Downbeat. April 13. p30. 100w. 4

3245 Solomon Burke. WE'RE ALMOST HOME. MGM SE 4830 $5.98. Cart. 8130-4830M $6.95.
Creem. November. p15. 25w. ½

3246 Ace Cannon. COOL 'N' SAXY. Hi SHL 32060 $4.98.
Audio. March. p80. 75w. 2½

3247 Ray Charles. A MESSAGE FROM THE PEOPLE. Tangerine ABCX 755 $5.98. Cart. M8755 $6.95. Cass. M5755 $6.95.
Creem. August. p66. 75w. ½
Creem. September. p11. 50w. 2
Downbeat. September 12. p19. 300w. 4
Gramophone. November. p984. 75w. 1
Jazz Journal. November. p25-6. 400w. 3
New York Times--Sunday. May 21. pD30. 100w. 2
Popular Music and Society. Summer. p254. 25w. 3
Rolling Stone. June 22. p54-5. 800w. 4
Popular Music. Summer. p254. 25w. 3

3248 Ray Charles. 25TH YEAR IN SHOW BUSINESS SALUTE. ABC ABCSD 731 (2 discs) $5.98. Cart. M8731 $6.95. Cass. M5731 $6.95.
Blues Unlimited. January. p25. 25w. 2½
Blues Unlimited. January. p29. 50w. 3½
Jazz Journal. March. p31. 450w. 3

3249 Ray Charles. WITH ARBEE STIDHAM, LI'L SON JACKSON, AND JAMES WAYNE. Mainstream MRL 310 $5.98. (Reissue.)
American Record Guide. June. p528. 450w. 3

3250 Ray Charles/Memphis Slim. L'INCOMPARABLE. Musidisc 30 CV964 (France). (Reissue.)
Jazz Journal. June. p30. 175w. 0

3251 Chiffons. SWEET TALKIN' GUY. Laurie S 2036 $4.98.
Gramophone. December. p1222. 25w. 1

3252 Chi-Lites. A LONELY MAN. Brunswick BL 754179 $5.98. Cart. M84179 $6.95. Cass. M54179 $6.95.
Crawdaddy. October. p84-5. 400w. 4

3253 The Clovers. THEIR GREATEST RECORDINGS. Atco SD 33-374 $5.98. Cart. M833-374 $6.95. Cass. M833-374 $6.95. (Reissue.)
Crawdaddy. February 20. p17. 300w. $2\frac{1}{2}$
Creem. March. p48-9. 100w. 2
Stereo Review. June. p98. 175w. 3

3254 The Coasters. GREATEST RECORDINGS. Atco SD 33-371 $5.98. Cart. M833-371 $6.95. Cass. M533-371 $6.95. (Reissue.)
Blues Unlimited. February/March. p24. 25w. 4
Crawdaddy. February 20. p17. 400w. 3
Creem. March. p48-9. 300w. 4

3255 Dennis Coffey and the Detroit Guitar Band. EVOLUTION. Sussex 7004 $5.98. Cart. M87004 $6.95. Cass. M57004 $6.95.
Hi-Fi News and Record Review. August. p1479. 25w. 2

3256 The Contours. DO YOU LOVE ME? Gordy $5.98.
Creem. September. p57. 25w. 3

3257 Don Crawford. ANOTHER SHADE OF BLACK. Roulette SR 3005 $4.98.
Audio. November. p92. 25w. 2

3258 CRAZY ROCK (anthology). Contour 6870 527 (E). (Reissue.)
Blues Unlimited. April. p24. 25w. $2\frac{1}{2}$
Gramophone. May. p1953. 100w. $3\frac{1}{2}$

3259 King Curtis. EVERYBODY'S TALKIN'. Atco SD 33-385 $5.98. Cart. M8385 $6.95. Cass. M5385 $6.95.
Downbeat. April 27. p19. 150w. 3

3260 King Curtis. LIVE AT FILLMORE WEST. Atco SD 33-359 $5.98. Cart. M8359 $6.95. Cass. M5385 $6.95.
Downbeat. February 3. p18. 200w. 4
Gramophone. January. p1283. 25w. 2

3261 Greater Davis. SWEET WOMAN'S LOVE. House of Orange LPS 6000 $4.98.
Living Blues. Summer. p36. 150w. 4

3262 Detroit Emeralds. YOU WANT IT, YOU GOT IT. West Bound WE 2013 $4.98. Cart. 8198-2013M $6.95. Cass. 5198-2013M $6.95.
Crawdaddy. October. p85. 250w. 3
Gramophone. July. p256. 25w. 0

3263 Detroit Emeralds. DO ME RIGHT. Westbound WE 2006. Cart. 8098-2006 $6.95. Cass. 5098-2006 $6.95.
Crawdaddy. October. p85. 200w. 3

3264 Bo Diddley. ANOTHER DIMENSION. Chess 50001 $5.98. Cart. 8033-50001M $6.95.
Blues Unlimited. January. p25. 25w. 0
Gramophone. January. p1283. 50w. 0

3265 Bo Diddley. THE BLACK GLADIATOR. Checker 3013 $5.98.
Living Blues. Winter. p36. 125w. 3

3266 Bo Diddley. GOT MY OWN BAG OF TRICKS. Chess 2CH 60005 (2 discs) $6.98. Cart. 60005 $7.95. Cass. 60005 $7.95. (Reissue.)
Blues Unlimited. October. p28. 25w. 2½
Gramophone. November. p984. 25w. 1

3267 Bo Diddley. WHERE IT ALL BEGAN. Chess CH 50016 $5.98. Cart. 8033-50016M $6.95.
Creem. September. p48. 500w. 2½
Creem. November. p15. 25w. 2½

3268 Ernie K. Doe. Janus JLS 3030 $5.98.
Crawdaddy. March 5. p16. 150w. 2½

3269 Fats Domino. FATS. Reprise RS 6439 $5.98.
Blues Unlimited. January. p26. 75w. 0

3270 Fats Domino. United Artists UAS 9958 (2 discs) $7.98. (Reissue.)
Audio. May. p94. 25w. 2½
Blues Unlimited. July. p23. 50w. 4
Crawdaddy. May 14. p18. 300w. 4
Gramophone. April. p1776. 50w. 3
Popular Music. Spring. p128. 50w. 4
Rolling Stone. March 30. p49. 1,500w. 4

3271 Lee Dorsey. YES WE CAN. Polydor PD 24-4042 $5.98.
Crawdaddy. March 5. p16. 300w. 2½

3272 Big Al Downing. AND HIS FRIENDS. Collector CL 1007 (Holland).
Blues Unlimited. October. p25. 50w. 2½

3273 The Dramatics. WHATCA SEE IS WHATCHA GET. Volt VOS 6018 $4.98.
High Fidelity. July. p106. 25w. 3
Hi-Fi News and Record Review. August. p1479. 50w. 2½

3274 The Drifters. THEIR GREATEST RECORDINGS. Atco SD 33-375 $5.98. Cart. M833-375 $6.95. Cass. M533-375 $6.95. (Reissue.)
Crawdaddy. February 20. p17. 300w. 2½
Creem. March. p48. 100w. 2½

3275 Family Vibes. STRANGE FRUIT. United Artists UAS 5560 $5.98.
Blues Unlimited. July. p23. 50w. 3½
Downbeat. April 27. p19. 150w. 1
Gramophone. July. p255. 25w. 2
Hi-Fi News and Record Review. June. p1128. 50w. 2½
Ontario Library Review. December. p242. 25w. 2½

3276 FANTASTIC ROCK (anthology). Contour 6870 528 (E). (Reissue.)
Blues Unlimited. April. p24. 25w. 2½
Gramophone. May. p1955. 100w. 3

3277 Roberta Flack. QUIET FIRE. Atlantic SD 1594 $5.98. Cart. M81594 $6.95. Cass. M51594 $6.95.
New York Times--Sunday. January 2. pD20. 125w. 3
Records and Recordings. May. p96. 175w. 3
Stereo Review. April. p90, 96. 250w. 4

3278 Roberta Flack and Donny Hathaway. Atlantic SD 7216 $5.98. Cart. M87216 $6.95. Cass. M57216 $6.95.
Audio. October. p90. 50w. 3½
Beetle. July. p21-2. 700w. 2
Hi-Fi News and Record Review. September. p1683. 100w. 3
High Fidelity. August. p98. 250w. 4
New York Times--Sunday. May 21. pD30. 100w. 1
Rolling Stone. August 17. p49. 750w. 1
Stereo Review. September. p74. 300w. 4

3279 The Flirtations. THE WORLD OF... Deram SPA 218 (E).
Hi-Fi News and Record Review. July. p1312. 25w. ½

3280 King Floyd. Chimneyville SD 9047 $5.98. Cart. M89047 $6.95. Cass. M59047 $6.95.
Rolling Stone. January 20. p52. 300w. 3

3281 The Fortunes. HERE COMES THAT RAINY DAY FEELING AGAIN. Capitol ST 809 $5.98. Cart. U8276 $6.98. Cass. K0276 $6.98.
Stereo Review. January. p107. 275w. 2½

3282 The Four Tops. GREATEST HITS, VOLUME 2. Tamla MS 740L $5.98. (Reissue.)
Audio. March. p81. 50w. 3½
Creem. January. p69. 25w. 1
Gramophone. February. p1437. 25w. 2½

3283 The Four Tops. KEEPER OF THE CASTLE. ABC Dunhill DSX 50129 $5.98. Cart. 8023-50129V $6.95. Cass. 5023-50129V $6.95.

New York Times--Sunday. December 17. pD35. 400w. 2
Rolling Stone. December 21. p68. 600w. 2

3284 The Four Tops. NATURE PLANNED IT. Tamla MS 748L $5.98. Cart. M8748 $6.95. Cass. M5748 $6.95.
Rolling Stone. December 21. p68. 900w. 4

3285 Aretha Franklin. ARETHA. Columbia CS 8412 $4.98.
Rolling Stone. October 26. p60, 62. 800w. 3

3286 Aretha Franklin. IN THE BEGINNING: THE WORLD OF..., 1960-67. Columbia KG 31355 (2 discs) $6.98. Cart. GA 31355 $7.98. Cass. GT 31355 $7.98. (Reissue.)
Crawdaddy. October. p74-5. 500w. 4
Rolling Stone. October 26. p60, 62. 850w. 3

3287 Aretha Franklin. GREATEST HITS. Atlantic SD 8295 $4.98. Cart. M8295 $6.95. Cass. M58295. (Reissue.)
Audio. May. p93. 25w. 4
High Fidelity. January. p120. 25w. 4

3288 Aretha Franklin. YOUNG, GIFTED, AND BLACK. Atlantic SD 7213 $5.98. Cart. M87213 $6.95. Cass. M57213 $6.95.
Crawdaddy. April 16. p14. 1,250w. 1
Creem. May. p59-60. 2,000w. 5
Gramophone. June. p111. 25w. 1
High Fidelity. May. p108. 350w. 5
New York Times--Sunday. March 5. pD28. 200w. 5
Records and Recordings. May. p96. 225w. 4
Rolling Stone. March 16. p58. 500w. 3
Stereo Review. July. p92. 200w. $3\frac{1}{2}$

3289 Lowell Fulson. Arhoolie R 2003 $6.00. (Reissue.)
Previews. November. p39. 100w. $2\frac{1}{2}$

3290 Lowell Fulson. IN A HEAVY BAG. Jewel LP 5003 $4.98.
Blues Unlimited. July. p27. 325w. 5
Jazz and Blues. August. p33. 350w. $3\frac{1}{2}$
Journal of American Folklore. January/March. p105. 25w. $2\frac{1}{2}$
Jazz Journal. July. p28. 350w. 4

3291 Lowell Fulson. SOUL. Kent KLP 5016 $4.98. (Reissue.)
Previews. November. p39. 100w. $2\frac{1}{2}$

3292 Lowell Fulson. TRAMP. Kent KST 520 $4.98. (Reissue.)
Previews. November. p39. 100w. $2\frac{1}{2}$

3293 Funkadelic. AMERICA EATS ITS YOUNG. West Bound WE 2020 (2 discs) $6.98. Cart. 8198-2020C $7.95. Cass. 5198-2020C $7.95.
Creem. September. p11. 25w. 0

3294 Marvin Gaye. **GREATEST HITS.** Tamla Motown MS 302L $5.98. (Reissue.)
Gramophone. April. p1779. 50w. 1

3295 THE GOLDEN AGE OF RHYTHM 'N' BLUES (anthology). Chess 2CH 50030 (2 discs) $5.98. (Reissue.)
New York Times--Sunday. October 15. pD31. 100w. 4

3296 Al Green. Bell 6076 $4.98. Cart. M86076 $6.95. Cass. M56076 $6.95.
Creem. December. p9. 25w. 3

3297 Al Green. GETS NEXT TO YOU. Hi SHL 32062 $4.98.
American Record Guide. April. p380. 200w. 4

3298 Al Green. I'M STILL IN LOVE WITH YOU. Hi SHL 32074 $4.98. Cart. M92074 $6.95. Cass. M52074 $6.95.
Rolling Stone. November 23. p60. 1,450w. 4

3299 Al Green. LET'S STAY TOGETHER. Hi SHL 32070 $4.98. Cart. M92070 $6.95. Cass. M52070 $6.95.
Audio. November. p91. 50w. 1
Blues Unlimited. July. p23. 25w. 2½
Crawdaddy. April 16. p14. 1,000w. 3
Gramophone. June. p116. 100w. 3
Hi-Fi News and Record Review. May. p939. 125w. 2½
New York Times--Sunday. March 5. pD28. 100w. 1½
Rolling Stone. March 30. p50. 750w. 4

3300 Don "Sugarcane" Harris. FIDDLER ON THE ROCK. BASF 20878 $5.98.
Canadian Stereo Guide. Fall. p29. 50w. 3½

3301 Don "Sugarcane" Harris and Dewey Martin. DON AND DEWEY. Specialty LP 2131 $4.98. (Reissue.)
Blues Unlimited. February/March. p23. 100w. 3

3302 Wilbert Harrison. Buddah BDS 5092 $5.98. Cart. M85092 $6.95. Cass. M55092 $6.95.
Blues Unlimited. April. p25. 75w. 2½
Crawdaddy. March 5. p16. 200w. 1

3303 Donny Hathaway. EVERYTHING IS EVERYTHING. Atco SD 33-332 $5.98. Cart. M8332 $6.95. Cass. M5332 $6.95.
Gramophone. November. p984. 50w. 0

3304 Donny Hathaway. LIVE. Atco SD 33-386 $5.98. Cart. M8386 $6.95. Cass. M5386 $6.95.
Audio. August. p62. 75w. 3
Crawdaddy. May 28. p18. 1,000w. 3

Downbeat. May 11. p21. 250w. 2½
Gramophone. July. p254. 25w. 2
High Fidelity. June. p103. 500w. 3
New York Times--Sunday. March 5. pD28. 200w. 4
Stereo Review. July. p92. 175w. 3

3305 Isaac Hayes. BLACK MOSES. Enterprise ENS 5003 (2 discs) $9.98.
Rolling Stone. January 20. p52. 375w. 0

3306 Isaac Hayes. IN THE BEGINNING. Atlantic SD 1599 $5.98. Cart. M81599 $6.95. Cass. M51599 $6.95.
Downbeat. September 14. p20-1. 175w. 4

3307 HEAVY SOUL (anthology). Atlantic SD 500 $5.98. (Reissue.)
New York Times--Sunday. March 5. pD28. 25w. 2½

3308 Z.Z. Hill. THE BRAND NEW... Mankind LP 201 $4.98.
Blues Unlimited. June. p25. 125w. 3
Blues Unlimited. December. p28. 25w. 2

3309 Honey Cone. SOULFUL TAPESTRY. Hot Wax 713 $5.98. Cart. M8713 $6.95. Cass. M5713 $6.95.
Gramophone. November. p984. 50w. 0
Hi-Fi News and Record Review. November. p2202. 100w. 2

3310 Hookfoot. A & M SP 4316 $4.98.
Stereo Review. January. p116. 300w. 2½

3311 Linda Hopkins. RCA LSP 4756 $5.98.
New York Times--Sunday. September 24. pHF7. 200w. 2

3312 Impressions. TIMES HAVE CHANGED. Curtom CRS 8612 $5.98. Cart. M88012 $6.95. Cass. M58012 $6.95.
Hi-Fi News and Record Review. October. p1926. 50w. 1½
New York Times--Sunday. September 10. pD37-8. 175w. 4

3313 Luther Ingram. IF LOVING YOU IS WRONG I DON'T WANT TO BE RIGHT. Koko KOS 2202 $4.98.
Rolling Stone. December 21. p68. 1,000w. 4

3314 Isley Brothers. Regal Starline SRS 5098 (E). (Reissue.)
Gramophone. May. p1952. 25w. 0

3315 Isley Brothers. BROTHER, BROTHER, BROTHER. T-Neck TNS 3009 $5.98. Cart. M83009 $6.95. Cass. M53009 $6.95.
Creem. November. p15. 25w. 2

Rolling Stone. July 20. p50. 400w. 3½
Stereo Review. October. p83-4. 300w. 5

3316 Isley Brothers. GIVIN' IT BACK. T-Neck TNS 3008 $5.98.
Popular Music. Fall. p62. 25w. 2

3317 IT ALL STARTED HERE (anthology). Atlantic K 20025 (E). (Reissue.)
Gramophone. May. p1955. 50w. 3
Hi-Fi News and Record Review. July. p1311. 50w. 3

3318 The Jackson Five. GREATEST HITS. Tamla Motown MS 741 L $5.98. (Reissue.)
Creem. April. p68. 500w. 3

3319 The Jackson Five. LOOKING THROUGH THE WINDOWS. Tamla Motown MS 750 L $5.98. Cart. M8750 $6.95. Cass. M5750 $6.95.
Rolling Stone. December 7. p68,70. 2,350w. 2

3320 Jermaine Jackson. JERMAINE. Tamla Motown MS 752 L $5.98. Cart. M8752 $6.95. Cass. M5752 $6.95.
Rolling Stone. December 7. p68,70. 2,350w. 3

3321 Michael Jackson. BEN. Tamla Motown MS 755 L $5.98. Cart. M8755 $6.95. Cass. M5755 $6.95.
Rolling Stone. December 7. p68,70. 1,175w. 3

3322 Michael Jackson. GOT TO BE THERE. Tamla Motown MS 747 L $5.98. Cart. M8747 $6.95. Cass. M5747 $6.95.
Creem. June. p75. 800w. 2½
Gramophone. July. p254. 75w. 3
Rolling Stone. December 7. p68,70. 1,175w. 3

3323 Millie Jackson. Spring 5703 $4.98. Cart. 8F 5703 $6.95. Cass. CF 5703 $6.95.
Creem. December. p9,86. 25w. 2½

3324 Etta James. PEACHES. Chess 6671 003 (E) (2 discs). (Reissue.)
Blues Unlimited. January. p25. 25w. 2½

3325 Lou Johnson. WITH YOU IN MIND. Volt VOS 6017 $4.98. Cart. VO 86017 $6.95. Cass. VO C6017 $6.95.
Rolling Stone. January 20. p52. 300w. 3

3326 John Ka Sandra. BEAUTIFUL NEW WORLD. Respect TAS 2603 $4.98.
Audio. January. p77. 175w. 4

3327 KEEP THE FAITH, VOLUME 1-3 (anthology). Joy JOYS 223/5 (3 discs) (E). (Reissue.)

Blues Unlimited. July. p23. 50w. 3
Gramophone. July. p256. 175w. 4

3328 Eddie Kendricks. PEOPLE HOLD ON. Tamla TS 315L $5.98. Cart. M315 $6.95. Cass. M5315 $6.95.
Rolling Stone. November 9. p64. 700w. 1

3329 Gladys Knight and the Pips. STANDING OVATION. Soul S 736L $5.98.
Creem. May. p62. 475w. 4
Gramophone. September. p578. 25w. 1
Hi-Fi News and Record Review. September. p1683. 50w. 3

3330 Jean Knight. MR. BIG STUFF. Stax STS 2045 $5.98. Cart. ST 82045 $6.95. Cass. STC 2045 $6.95.
Rolling Stone. January 20. p52. 300w. 3

3331 Charles Kynard. Mainstream. MRL 331 $5.98.
Downbeat. April 13. p30. 100w. $2\frac{1}{2}$

3331a LaBelle. MOON SHADOW. Warner Bros. BS 2618 $5.98.
New York Times--Sunday. August 6. pD20, 22. 400w. 4

3332 Patti LaBelle and the Bluebells. LA BELLE. Warner Bros. WS 1943 $5.98. Cart. M81943 $6.95. Cass. M51943 $6.95.
American Record Guide. April. p380-1. 225w. 0

3333 Denise La Salle. TRAPPED BY A THING CALLED LOVE. Westbound $5.98.
Creem. May. p60-1. 1,100w. 4
Gramophone. July. p254. 50w. 2

3334 The Last Poets. CHASTISEMENT. Blue Thumb BTS 39 $5.98. Cart. M839 $6.95. Cass. M539 $6.95.
High Fidelity. October. p126. 25w. 3

3335 Laura Lee. WOMEN'S LOVE RIGHTS. Hot Wax SHW 708 $5.98. Cart. M8708 $6.95. Cass. M5708 $6.95.
Creem. March. p53. 500w. 3
Creem. November. p74. 25w. $1\frac{1}{2}$
Gramophone. November. p984. 75w. 0
Hi-Fi News and Record Review. October. p1926. 25w. $2\frac{1}{2}$

3336 Ramsey Lewis. BACK TO THE ROOTS. Chess CH 60001 $6.98. Cart. 8035-60001M $6.95. Cass. 5035-60001M $6.95.
Gramophone. January. p1287. 150w. 3
Jazz and Blues. January. p23. 250w. 1

3337 Ramsey Lewis. INSIDE. Cadet 2CA 60018 (2 discs) $6.98. Cart. 8035-60018M $6.98.
Downbeat. March 2. p19. 100w. 1

3338 Ramsey Lewis. TOBACCO ROAD. Chess 6310 124 (E). (Reissue.)
Gramophone. December. p1222. 25w. 1

3339 Ramsey Lewis. UPENDO NI PAMOJA. Columbia KC 31096 $5.98. Cart. CA 31096 $6.98. Cass. CT 31096 $6.98.
Downbeat. September 14. p21-2. 50w. 2

3340 Little Milton. GREATEST HITS. Chess CH 50013 $5.98. Cart. 8033-50013M $6.95. (Reissue.)
Blues Unlimited. October. p28. 50w. 3
Crawdaddy. June 11. p19. 700w. 4
Gramophone. December. p1222. 100w. $3\frac{1}{2}$

3341 Little Richard. EVERY HOUR. Camden CAS 2430 $2.49. (Reissue.)
American Record Guide. June. p529. 450w. 3

3342 Little Richard. THE INCREDIBLE LITTLE RICHARD SINGS HIS GREATEST HITS RECORDED LIVE. Contour 2870 150 (E). (Reissue.)
Blues Unlimited. April. p24. 25w. $2\frac{1}{2}$
Gramophone. May. p1955. 50w. 2

3343 Little Richard. KING OF ROCK 'N' ROLL. Reprise RS 6462 $5.98. Cart. M86462 $6.95. Cass. M56462 $6.95.
Blues Unlimited. February/March. p20. 25w. 0
Crawdaddy. January 16. p18. 600w. 1
Creem. February. p64-5. 800w. 2
Gramophone. February. p1437. 25w. 2
High Fidelity. February. p120. 25w. $2\frac{1}{2}$

3344 A LITTLE SHOT OF RHYTHM 'N' BLUES (anthology). Rhapsody RHAS 9010 (E). (Reissue.)
Blues Unlimited. February/March. p20. 250w. 1

3345 LIGHTS OUT: SAN FRANCISCO (anthology). Blue Thumb BTS 60004 (2 discs).
Audio. December. p93. 300w. 4

3346 Love, Peace and Happiness. LOVE IS STRONGER. RCA LSP 4535 $5.98.
Audio. March. p80. 50w. 0

3347 Love Sculpture. BLUES HELPING. Rare Earth RS 505L $5.98.
Popular Music. Spring. p188. 75w. 3

3348 Love Unlimited. Uni 73131 $4.98.
Hi-Fi News and Record Review. August. p1479. 50w. $2\frac{1}{2}$

3349 Gloria Lynne. HAPPY AND IN LOVE. Canyon 7709 $4.98. Cart. Ampex M8359 $6.95. Cass. Ampex M5359 $6.95.
Blues Unlimited. October. p30. 25w. 1

3350 Gloria Lynne. A VERY GENTLE SOUND. Mercury SRM 1 633 $5.98. Cart. MC8-1-633 $6.98. Cass. MCR4-1-633 $6.98.
Stereo Review. November. p88. 100w. $3\frac{1}{2}$

3351 Jimmy McCracklin. YESTERDAY IS GONE. Stax STS 2047 $5.98.
Blues Unlimited. May. p24. 100w. $3\frac{1}{2}$

3352 Hugh Masekela. HOME IS WHERE THE MUSIC IS. Chisa/Blue Thumb BTS 6003 $5.98. Cart. L 86003 $7.95. Cass. L56003 $7.95.
Crawdaddy. September. p20. 450w. 3
High Fidelity. October. p120. 350w. $2\frac{1}{2}$

3353 Hugh Masekela. UNION OF SOUTH AFRICA. Chisa CS 808 $5.98.
Gramophone. January. p1279. 25w. 2
Jazz Journal. January. p32-3. 175w. 0

3354 Curtis Mayfield. ROOTS. Curtom 8009 $5.98. Cart. M88009 $6.95. Cass. M58009 $6.95.
Gramophone. March. p1614. 50w. 3

3355 Harold Melvin and the Bluenotes. I MISS YOU. Philadelphia International KZ 31648 $5.98. Cart. ZA 31648 $6.98. Cass. ZT 31648 $6.98.
Rolling Stone. October 26. p62. 800w. $2\frac{1}{2}$

3356 The Moonglows. THE RETURN OF THE... RCA LSP 4722 $5.98. Cart. P8S 1958 $6.95.
Crawdaddy. October. p85. 450w. $3\frac{1}{2}$
Creem. November. p74. 25w. 1
High Fidelity. October. p120. 150w. $2\frac{1}{2}$

3357 MOTOWN MEMORIES (anthology). Tamla Motown STML 11200 (E). (Reissue.)
Gramophone. April. p1779. 75w. 3

3358 MOTOWN STORY (anthology). Tamla Motown MS5-726 (5 discs) $24.95. Cart. M81727/31 $34.75 (5 cart).
Gramophone. May. p1952, 55. 400w. $2\frac{1}{2}$

3359 Johnny Nash. I CAN SEE CLEARLY NOW. Epic KE 31607

$5.98. Cart. EA 31607 $6.98. Cass. ET 31607 $6.98.
Sound. December. p40-1. 200w. 3½

3360 New Generation Singers. FLYING HIGH. Polydor PD 2460 133 (E).
Gramophone. February. p1437. 25w. 1

3361 The O'Jays. BACK STABBERS. Philadelphia International KZ 31712 $5.98. Cart. ZA 31712 $6.95. Cass. ZT 31712 $6.95.
Creem. December. p86. 25w. 2½
Rolling Stone. October 26. p62. 700w. 3

3362 Johnny Otis Show. FORMIDABLE (anthology). Ember SPE 6604 (E). (Reissue.)
Blues Unlimited. October. p28. 50w. 2½
Hi-Fi News and Record Review. October. p1926. 100w. 2

3363 Johnny Otis Show. LIVE AT MONTEREY, 1970. Epic EG 30473 (2 discs) $6.98.
American Record Guide. February. p284. 225w. 0
Coda. April. p21. 275w. 5
Living Blues. Spring. p35. 225w. 5

3364 Johnny Otis Show. ROCK 'N' CLASSICS, VOLUME 7. Capitol 5 CO 52-80 676 (Holland). (Reissue.)
Blues Unlimited. October. p28. 50w. 4

3365 Shuggie Otis. FREEDOM FLIGHT. Epic E 30752 $4.98.
Blues Unlimited. April. p23. 150w. 3½
Living Blues. Spring. p36. 150w. 3
Stereo Review. February. p110. 100w. 2½

3366 Bobby Patterson. IT'S JUST A MATTER OF TIME. Paula LPS 2215 $4.98. Cart. M82215 $6.95.
Blues Unlimited. November. p30. 100w. 2

3367 Ann Peebles. STRAIGHT FROM THE HEART. Hi SHL 32065 $5.98. Cart. M92065 $6.95. Cass. M52065 $6.95.
Blues Unlimited. October. p28. 50w. 3½
Creem. October. p61. 350w. 2½
Hi-Fi News and Record Review. December. p2459. 50w. 3

3368 Paul Pena. Capitol ST 11005 $5.98. Cart. 8XT 11005 $6.98.
Creem. August. p11, 67. 50w. 3½

3369 The Persuasions. SPREAD THE WORD. Capitol ST/1101 $5.98.
Creem. December. p57. 525w. 4½

New York Times--Sunday. December 10. pD38. 300w. 4
Rolling Stone. December 7. p70. 1,000w. 4

3370 The Persuasions. STREET CORNER SYMPHONY. Capitol ST 872 $5.98. Cart. 8XT 872 $6.98. Cass. 4XT 872 $6.98.
Creem. April. p61. 700w. 3
High Fidelity. May. p116. 25w. 2½
Records and Recordings. September. p94-5. 250w. 3
Rolling Stone. March 2. p57-8. 850w. 1½
Stereo Review. June. p102. 100w. 2½

3371 Lucky Peterson. OUR FUTURE. Perception Today LP 1002 $4.98.
Blues Unlimited. June. p27. 125w. 0

3372 Esther Phillips. FROM A WHISPER TO A SCREAM. Kudu KU 02 $5.98.
Hi-Fi News and Record Review. August. p1479. 125w. 4
Jazz Journal. August. p36. 150w. 0

3373 Wilson Pickett. DON'T KNOCK MY LOVE. Atlantic SD 8300 $5.98. Cart. M88300 $6.95. Cass. M58300 $6.95.
American Record Guide. September. p673. 100w. 1
Crawdaddy. March 5. p17. 1,000w. 1½
Gramophone. June. p112. 25w. 1
Records and Recordings. May. p99. 225w. 2

3374 Platters. TWO DECADES OF HITS. Pye PKL 4411 (E).
Blues Unlimited. January. p25. 25w. 1

3375 Billy Preston. I WROTE A SIMPLE SONG. A & M SP 3507 $5.98. Cart. 8T 3507 $6.95. Cass. CS 3507 $6.95.
Downbeat. March 2. p20, 22. 325w. 4½

3376 Lloyd Price. 16 GREATEST HITS. ABC ABCX 763 $5.98. Cart. M8763 $6.95. Cass. M5763 $6.95. (Reissue.)
Rolling Stone. November 23. p66. 400w. 3

3377 Lloyd Price. ORIGINAL HITS. Sonet SNTF 5007 (Sweden). (Reissue.)
Blues Unlimited. September. p22. 50w. 3½

3378 Lloyd Price. TO THE ROOTS AND BACK. GSF 1003 $5.98.
Rolling Stone. November 23. p66. 400w. 3

3379 Lloyd Price Group. WEST INDIES SOUL. Joy JOYS 183 (E).
Gramophone. June. p115. 25w. 2

3380 Pretty Purdie and the Playboys. STAND BY ME (WHATCHA SEE IS WHATCHA GET). Mega M51-5001 $4.98.
Downbeat. June 8. p26. 150w. 5

3381 The Rascals. THE ISLAND OF REAL. Columbia KC 31103 $5.98. Cart. CA 31103 $6.98. Cass. CT 31103 $6.98.
Hi-Fi News and Record Review. October. p1926. 75w. 1½

3382 Lou Rawls. NATURAL MAN. MGM SE 4771 $5.98. Cart. 8130-4771 $6.95. Cass. 5130-4771 $6.95.
Gramophone. February. p1477. 50w. 2
Records and Recordings. January. p96. 25w. 1

3383 Otis Redding. BEST. Atco 2SA-801 (2 discs) $7.98. (Reissue.)
Audio. December. p94. 200w. 4
Creem. December. p57-8. 700w. 4½
Records and Recordings. December. p100. 250w. 5

3384 ROCK 'N' ROLL (anthology). Contour 6870 536 (E). (Reissue.)
Blues Unlimited. April. p24. 25w. 3

3385 ROCK REVIVAL (anthology). Contour 6870 535 (E). (Reissue.)
Blues Unlimited. April. p24. 25w. 3

3386 Diana Ross. DIANA! Tamla Motown MS 711L $5.98. Cart. 81711 $6.95. Cass. 75711 $6.95.
Gramophone. February. p1437. 25w. 3

3387 Diana Ross. GREATEST HITS. Tamla Motown STMA 8006 (E). (Reissue.)
Gramophone. December. p1221. 50w. 1½

3388 Diana Ross. SURRENDER. Tamla Motown MS 723L $5.98.
Audio. November. p93. 50w. 2½

3389 Oliver Sain. MAIN MAN. A-Bet 404 $4.98.
Blues Unlimited. June. p30. 100w. 3½

3390 Gil Scott-Heron. PIECES OF A MAN. Flying Dutchman FD 10143 $5.95.
Creem. April. p71. 50w. 3
Rolling Stone. July 20. p52. 800w. 3

3391 The Shirelles. RCA LSP 4698 $5.98. Cart. P8S 1929 $6.95.
Gramophone. November. p984. 25w. 0

3392 The Shirelles. HAPPY AND IN LOVE. RCA LSP 4581 $5.98. Cart. P8S 1803 $6.95. Cass. PK 1803 $6.95.

Gramophone. June. p112. 25w. 2
Hi-Fi News and Record Review. July. p1312. 75w. 2
High Fidelity. January. p122. 25w. 2½
Stereo Review. February. p111. 150w. 2½

3393 Joe Simon. DROWNING IN THE SEA OF LOVE. Spring 5702 $4.98.
Hi-Fi News and Record Review. August. p1477. 100w. 2

3394 Nina Simone. EMERGENCY WARD! RCA LSP 4757 $5.98. Cart. P8S 2022 $6.95. Cass. PK 2022 $6.95.
Rolling Stone. November 9. p62. 650w. 3

3395 Nina Simone. THIS IS... Philips International 6336 202 (E). (Reissue.)
Jazz Journal. June. p35. 200w. 0

3396 Valarie Simpson. Tamla TS 317L $5.98. Cart. M8317 $6.95. Cass. M5317 $6.95.
Creem. December. p86. 25w. 1½

3397 Valarie Simpson. EXPOSED. Tamla S 311L $5.98. Cart. T81311 $6.95. Cass. T75311 $6.95.
Gramophone. June. p116. 200w. 3

3398 Sly and the Family Stone. THERE'S A RIOT GOING ON. Epic KE 30986 $5.98. R-R ER 30986 $6.98. Cart. EA 30986 $6.98. Cass. ET 30986 $6.98.
High Fidelity. February. p112. 100w. 1

3399 The Soul Children. GENESIS. Stax STS 3003 $5.98.
Hi-Fi News and Record Review. October. p1926. 50w. 2

3400 Edwin Starr. HITS. Tamla Motown STML 11209 (E). (Reissue.)
Gramophone. November. p984. 50w. 2

3401 Billy Stewart. GOLDEN DECADE. Chess 6310 125 (E). (Reissue.)
Blues Unlimited. December. p28. 25w. 3
Hi-Fi News and Record Review. December. p2464. 50w. 3

3402 The Stylistics. Avco Embassy AV 33023 $4.98.
Crawdaddy. October. p84. 200w. 4
Creem. September. p64. 25w. 0
Gramophone. September. p578. 25w. 1
Hi-Fi News and Record Review. September. p1685. 125w. 2½

3403 The Supremes. FLOY JOY. Tamla Motown M 751L $5.98. Cart. M8751 $6.95. Cass. M5751 $6.95.
Creem. September. p64. 25w. 2½
Gramophone. November. p984. 50w. 1
Popular Music. Summer. p254. 25w. 2

3404 The Supremes. GREATEST HITS. Tamla Motown MS 2-663 (2 discs) $9.96. (Reissue.)
Ontario Library Review. December. p242. 25w. 2½

3405 The Supremes. TOUCH. Tamla Motown MS 737L $5.98. Cart. M8 1737 $6.95. Cass. M75 737 $6.95.
Audio. November. p93. 25w. 2½

3406 The Supremes and the Four Tops. THE RETURN OF THE MAGNIFICANT SEVEN. Tamla Motown MS 717L $5.98. Cart. M8717 $6.95. Cass. M5717 $6.95.
Audio. November. p93. 25w. 2½
Gramophone. February. p1437. 50w. 2½

3407 Swamp Dogg. TOTAL DESTRUCTION TO YOUR MIND. Canyon 7706 $4.98. Cart. Ampex M8302 $6.95. Cass. Ampex M5302 $6.95.
Blues Unlimited. October. p30. 25w. 0

3408 SWAMPLAND SOUL FROM THE BAYOUS OF LOUISIANA (anthology). Goldband LP 7754 $4.98.
Blues Unlimited. May. p26. 75w. 3

3409 Howard Tate. Atlantic SD 8303 $5.98. Cart. M88303 $6.95. Cass. M58303 $6.95.
High Fidelity. June. p103. 500w. 2½

3410 Little Johnny Taylor. EVERYBODY KNOWS ABOUT MY GOOD THING. Ronn LPS 7530 $4.98. Cart. M87530 $6.95. Cass. M57530 $6.95.
Blues Unlimited. June. p27. 100w. 4
Blues Unlimited. October. p28. 25w. 2½
Living Blues. Summer. p34. 150w. 1

3411 Koko Taylor. BASIC SOUL. Chess 50018 $5.98.
Blues Unlimited. December. p28. 75w. 2
Creem. March. p55. 475w. 4

3412 Ted Taylor. SHADES OF BLUE. Ronn LPS 7528 $4.98.
Blues Unlimited. June. p23. 100w. 3

3413 Ted Taylor. YOU CAN DIG IT. Ronn LPS 7529 $4.98.
Blues Unlimited. June. p23. 100w. 3
Living Blues. Summer. p34. 150w. 4

3414 The Temptations. ALL DIRECTIONS. Gordy G 962L $5.98. Cart. M8962 $6.95. Cass. M5962 $6.95.
Rolling Stone. December 21. p64. 750w. 0

3415 The Temptations. SOLID ROCK. Gordy G 961L $5.98. Cart. M8961 $6.95. Cass. M5961 $6.95. (Reissue.)
Creem. April. p71. 25w. 0

3416 TEN LONG FINGERS (anthology). Collector CL 1005 (Holland). (Reissue.)
Blues Unlimited. October. p25. 50w. 2½

3417 Dewey Terry. CHIEF. Tumbleweed TWS 104 $4.98.
Blues Unlimited. November. p29. 50w. 0

3418 Joe Tex. I GOTCHA. Dial DL 6002 $5.98. Cart. DC8 6002 $6.95. Cass. DCR4 6002 $6.95.
Rolling Stone. June 8. p60. 600w. 4

3419 THIS IS HOW IT ALL BEGAN, VOLUME 1-2 (anthology). Specialty S 2117/8 (2 discs) $9.96. (Reissue.)
Blues Unlimited. January. p25. 50w. 3½

3420 Carla Thomas. LOVE MEANS... Stax STS 2044 $4.98. Cart. ST 82044 $6.95. Cass. STC 2044 $6.95.
Audio. November. p93. 50w. 2
Hi-Fi News and Record Review. July. p1309. 25w. 2½
Stereo Review. February. p113. 200w. 3

3421 Rufus Thomas. FUNKY CHICKEN. Stax STS 2028 $4.98. Cart. ST 82028 $6.95. Cass. STC 2028 $6.95.
Blues Unlimited. December. p28. 25w. 1
Hi-Fi News and Record Review. December. p2463. 50w. ½

3422 Israel Tolbert. POPPER STOPPER. Warren 2038 $4.98.
Blues Unlimited. July. p25. 50w. 0

3423 Allen Toussaint. Sceptre SPS 24003.
Crawdaddy. March 5. p16. 300w. 2½
Rolling Stone. January 20. p52. 350w. 3

3424 Allen Toussaint. Tiffany 0014 $4.98.
Blues Unlimited. May. p28. 25w. 0
Gramophone. April. p1779. 25w. 3½

3425 Ike Turner. BLUES ROOTS. United Artists UAS 5576 $5.98. Cart. U 8380 $6.98.
Blues Unlimited. September. p26. 100w. 2½
Creem. December. p86. 25w. 3
Living Blues. Summer. p36. 225w. 4
Previews. October. p47. 200w. 2½

3426 Ike and Tina Turner. FEEL GOOD. United Artists UAS 5598 $5.98.
Crawdaddy. November. p80-1. 1,000w. 3
Creem. December. p9. 25w. 2½
High Fidelity. November. p126. 300w. 1
Sound. October. p42-3. 250w. 4
Stereo Review. December. p100. 150w. 2

3427 Ike and Tina Turner. 'NUFF SAID. United Artists UAS 5530 $5.98. Cart. U 8296 $6.95. Cass. K 0296 $6.95.
Crawdaddy. January 30. p16. 800w. 3
Creem. February. p66. 200w. 1
High Fidelity. March. p117. 25w. 2½

3428 The Undisputed Truth. Gordy S 955L $5.98.
Gramophone. April. p1779. 75w. 1

3429 The Undisputed Truth. FACE TO FACE WITH THE TRUTH. Gordy G 959L $5.98.
Audio. May. p75-6. 325w. 3½

3430 Melvin Van Peebles. BRER SOUL. A & M SP 4161 $5.98.
Popular Music. Fall. p60. 25w. 2½

3431 Vinegar Joe. Atco SD 7007 $5.98. Cart. TP 7007 $6.95. Cass. CS 7007 $6.95.
Records and Recordings. June. p85. 200w. 3½

3432 Jr. Walker and the All Stars. MOODY, JR. Soul S 733L $5.98.
Ontario Library Review. December. p242. 25w. 2½

3433 Jr. Walker and the All Stars. RAINBOW FUNK. Soul S 732L $5.98. Cart. 81732 $6.95. Cass. 75732 $6.95.
Gramophone. April. p1779. 25w. 2½

3434 U.S. Warren. FOR A FEW FUNKY DUES MORE. Chytowns 2001 $5.95.
Blues Unlimited. May. p24. 175w. 1½

3435 Grover Washington, Jr. INNER CITY BLUES. Kudu KU 03 $5.98. Cart. KU 8 03 $6.95. Cass. KUC 03 $6.95.
Downbeat. April 13. p30. 300w. 4
Jazz Journal. August. p38. 125w. 0

3436 Ernie Watts. THE WONDER BAG. Vault S 9011 $5.98.
Downbeat. February 17. p23. 125w. 2

3437 Larry Williams. ORIGINAL HITS. Sonet SNTF 5008 (Sweden). (Reissue.)
Blues Unlimited. September. p22. 50w. 3½

3438 Chuck Willis. GREATEST HITS. Atco SD 33-373 $5.98.

Cart. M833-373 $6.95. Cass. 533-373 $6.95. (Reissue.)
Blues Unlimited. February/March. p24. 25w. 4
Crawdaddy. February 20. p17. 300w. 2½
Creem. March. p48-9. 50w. 0

3439 Bobby Womack. COMMUNICATION. United Artists UAS 5539 $5.98. Cart. U8302 $6.95.
Downbeat. April 13. p30. 100w. 3

3440 Bobby Womack. UNDERSTANDING. United Artists UAS 5577 $5.98. Cart. U 8381 $6.95. Cass. K 0381 $6.95.
New York Times--Sunday. October 22. pD31. 200w. 3

3441 Stevie Wonder. GREATEST HITS, VOLUME 2. Tamla S 298L $5.98. Cart. T8 7298 $6.95. Cass. T7 5298 $6.95. (Reissue.)
Crawdaddy. April 2. p17. 1,000w. 3
Gramophone. April. p1779. 50w. 3½

3442 Stevie Wonder. MUSIC OF MY MIND. Tamla T 314L $5.98.
Creem. June. p67-8. 50w. 2½
Creem. August. p74. 50w. 3
Gramophone. July. p256. 125w. 4
Hi-Fi News and Record Review. July. p1309. 250w. 5
High Fidelity. July. p100-1. 375w. 4
New York Times--Sunday. July 30. pD20. 600w. 4½

3443 Betty Wright. I LOVE THE WAY YOU LOVE. Alston S 33 388 $4.98. Cart. M8388 $6.95. Cass. M5388 $6.95.
Creem. May. p62. 300w. 3

3444 Gary Wright. FOOTPRINT. A & M SP 4296 $5.98.
Rolling Stone. March 2. p58. 700w. 2½

3445 Syreeta Wright. SYREETA. Mowest MW 113L $5.98. Cart. M8113 $6.95. Cass. M5113 $6.95.
Rolling Stone. November 23. p66. 400w. 1
Sound. October. p42. 250w. 3

POPULAR RELIGIOUS MUSIC

Without regard to format, this section comprises all religious items except for classically based Church music such as cantatas, masses, "authorized" hymns, and soundtracks. Here will be found those items expressed in another genre: the country and western hymn, the old timey call, the spiritual and gospel elements, the jazz masses, the "Jesus Rock," and so forth. In other words, "secular" or "vulgar" religious music.

There is no one review mechanism for this music as there is for classical Church music that is reviewed under "Classical" sections in magazines. Secular items are reviewed when they appear in a genre format. Jazz Journal seems to be the best for jazz, and both Blues Unlimited and Jazz Journal are the best for gospel. The latter, plus country and western hymns, are still underdeveloped areas in the recording field. Most blues and country albums have a smattering of religious music, but seldom are the tracks ever compiled into one specific disc. This is still a big singles market. Gospel production may be increased, however, because of the critical success of the four-disc Columbia release (The Gospel Sound, volumes one and two) and the popular resurgence of rhythm and blues, in itself gospel inspired (look up Aretha Franklin, for example). There are, though, two distinct markets of appeal, based on the dichotomy between the styles of the happy black gospel and the solemn white country hymn.

Significant reissue programs for gospel have included the British label Joy (Argo Singers, Staple Singers), the Austrian label Truth, and the American labels Biograph (the Rev. Gary Davis), Herwin (Blind Joe Taggart, Bessie Johnson) and Folkways. In jazz, there were four significant productions: Bonnemere's "Mass," Brubeck's "Truth is Fallen," Ellington's "Second Sacred Concert," and Garrick's "Apocalypse."

According to the reviews, the following were the best in this category:

Eddie Bonnemere. MISSA LAETARE. Fortress CSS 795
Rev. Gary Davis. CHILDREN OF ZION. Transatlantic TRA 249 (E)
Aretha Franklin. AMAZING GRACE (2 discs). Atlantic 2SD-906
Michael Garrick. MR. SMITH'S APOCALYPSE. Argo ZAGF 1 (E)
GOSPEL SOUND, vols 1 and 2 (2 discs each). Columbia G 31086 and KG 31595

Mahalia Jackson. GREAT (2 discs). Columbia KG 31379
Bessie Johnson. Herwin 202
Staple Singers. UNCLOUDY DAY. Joy JS 5019 (E)

3446 Argo Singers. SOUL OF... Joy JS 5012 (E). (Reissue.)
Blues Unlimited. May. p28. 25w. 2
Jazz and Blues. May. p20. 275w. $2\frac{1}{2}$
Jazz Journal. April. p32. 175w. 2

3447 Beers Family. THE SEASONS OF PEACE. Biograph BLP 12033 $5.98.
Jazz Journal. January. p37. 100w. 0

3448 Eddie Bonnemere. MISSA LAETARE. Fortress CSS 795 $5.98.
Downbeat. January 20. p18. 250w. 5

3449 Brotherhood of Man. WE'RE THE... Deram SML 1089 (E).
Gramophone. June. p112. 25w. 1
Hi-Fi News and Record Review. June. p1128. 50w. 1

3450 Dave Brubeck. TRUTH IS FALLEN. Atlantic SD 1606 $5.98.
Downbeat. November 9. p19. 250w. $3\frac{1}{2}$
Gramophone. December. p1232-3. 75w. $2\frac{1}{2}$
Hi-Fi News and Record Review. November. p2203. 150w. $1\frac{1}{2}$
Jazz Journal. October. p26-7. 625w. 0
Records and Recordings. September. p86. 525w. 1
Stereo Review. December. p110. 200w. 2

3451 Bill Carpenter. MEETING IN THE AIR. Michigan Bluegrass MB 105 $5.00.
Old Time Music. Summer. p27. 75w. 0

3452 The Colmanaires of Washington, D.C. Cotillion 059 $5.98.
Creem. January. p65-6. 1,200w. 5

3453 Cornelius Brothers and Sister Rose. United Artists UAS 5568 $5.98.
Creem. November. p66-7. 700w. 3

3454 COUNTRY GOSPEL SONG (anthology). Folkways RBF 19 $5.95. (Reissue.)
Blues Unlimited. April. p25. 200w. 2
Library Journal. January 15. p179. 150w. 2
Old Time Music. Winter. p26-7. 500w. 3
Popular Music. Winter. p126. 50w. $3\frac{1}{2}$

3455 Tommy Crank. SINGS REVIVAL SONGS. Old Homestead 90007 $5.00.
Old Time Music. Autumn. p30. 75w. $3\frac{1}{2}$

3456 Rev. Gary Davis. CHILDREN OF ZION. Transatlantic TRA 249 (E).
Blues Unlimited. April. p27. 150w. 5
Jazz Journal. April. p31-2. 300w. 3

3457 Rev. Gary Davis. LORD, I WISH I COULD SEE. Biograph BLP 12034 $5.98.
Blues Unlimited. May. p27. 125w. 4
Jazz and Blues. May. p21-2. 250w. $2\frac{1}{2}$

3458 Rev. Gary Davis. NEW BLUES AND GOSPEL. Biograph BLP 12030 $5.98.
Blues Unlimited. May. p27. 125w. 4
Jazz Report. No. 1. 250w. 4

3459 Duke Ellington. SECOND SACRED CONCERT. Fantasy 8407/8 (2 discs) $5.98.
Gramophone. May. p1958. 300w. $2\frac{1}{2}$
Hi-Fi News and Record Review. July. p1313. 150w. $2\frac{1}{2}$
Jazz and Blues. February. p28. 725w. $3\frac{1}{2}$

3460 Aretha Franklin. AMAZING GRACE. Atlantic SD 2-906 (2 discs) $9.96.
Crawdaddy. October. p74-6. 1,000w. 5
New York Times--Sunday. June 25. p24. 225w. 5
Records and Recordings. November. p106. 150w. 4
Saturday Review. August 12. p66. 75w. $2\frac{1}{2}$
Stereo Review. December. p96. 75w. 4

3461 Aretha Franklin. THE GOSPEL SOUL... Checker 1009 $5.98. Cart. 8034-10009M $6.95. Cass. 5034-10009M $6.95.
Crawdaddy. October. p74-6. 500w. 4

3462 Michael Garrick. MR. SMITH'S APOCALYPSE. Argo ZAGF 1 (E).
Jazz Journal. March. p33. 625w. 5

3463 GOD GIVE ME LIGHT, 1926/31 (SANCTIFIED, VOLUME 2) (anthology). Herwin 203 $5.95. (Reissue.)
Blues Unlimited. October. p28. 200w. 5

3464 God Squad. JESUS CHRIST'S GREATEST HITS. Rare Earth R 531L $5.98.
Popular Music. Spring. p186. 50w. 4

3465 THE GOSPEL SOUND, VOLUME 1 (anthology). Columbia G 31086 (2 discs) $5.98. (Reissue.)
Blues Unlimited. April. p29. 250w. 5
Jazz Report. No. 1. 400w. 5
Music Journal. April. p54. 325w. 3

Music Journal. May. p44. 200w. 3
New York Times--Sunday. March 12. pHF2. 300w. 4
Previews. November. p43. 300w. 3
Rolling Stone. March 16. p58. 450w. 4
Saturday Review. May 20. p47. 75w. $2\frac{1}{2}$
Stereo Review. June. p104. 425w. 5

3466 THE GOSPEL SOUND, VOLUME 2 (anthology). Columbia KG 31595 (2 discs) $6.98. (Reissue.)
Jazz Report. No. 2. 200w. $3\frac{1}{2}$
New York Times--Sunday. October 15. pD31. 100w. 5
Rolling Stone. November 23. p70. 750w. $2\frac{1}{2}$

3467 Gospel-Ayres. Philips 6414 312 (E).
Gramophone. December. p1222. 25w. 0

3468 GUITAR EVANGELISTS, VOLUME 2 (anthology). Truth TLP 1003 (Austria). (Reissue.)
Blues Unlimited. February/March. p28. 150w. 4
Blues World. Spring. p17-8. 100w. 4

3469 Jeanie Greene. MARY CALLED... Elektra EKS 74103 $4.98.
Stereo Review. March. p102. 75w. 1

3470 HEAVENLY STARS (anthology). Cotillion 052 $5.98. (Reissue.)
Gramophone. March. p1613-4. 25w. 2

3471 The Institutional Church of God in Christ. GRACE. Cotillion 055 $5.98.
Creem. January. p65-6. 1,200w. 5

3472 Mahalia Jackson. GREAT. Columbia KG 31379 (2 discs) $6.98. (Reissue.)
New York Times--Sunday. August 6. pD22. 100w. 4

3473 Bessie Johnson. SANCTIFIED, 1928/29, VOLUME 1. Herwin 202 $5.95. (Reissue.)
Blues Unlimited. September. p26. 300w. 5

3474 KEY TO THE KINGDOM (anthology). Motown M 743L $5.98.
Popular Music. Winter. p122. 25w. 2

3475 Danny Lee and the Children of Truth. ONE WAY. RCA LSP 4611 $5.98.
Stereo Review. April. p96. 200w. 1

3476 A LONG TIME (anthology). Asch AHS 850 $5.95. (Reissue.)
Audio. November. p90. 50w. 4

3477 Lucifer. BLACK MASS. Uni 73111 $5.98. Cart. 8-73111 $6.95. Cass. 2-73111 $6.95.
Popular Music. Fall. p62. 25w. 1

3478 Reverend F.W. McGhee. Roots RL 338 (Austria). (Reissue.)
Blues Unlimited. February/March. p27. 175w. 4
Blues World. Spring. p17. 75w. 3

3479 Medical Mission Sisters. IN LOVE. Avant-Garde AVS 132 $4.98.
Hi-Fi News and Record Review. August. p1475. 50w. 2½

3480 The Miller Brothers. TEENAGE ANGEL IN HEAVEN. Michigan Bluegrass MB 117 $5.00.
Old Time Music. Summer. p27. 100w. 3½

3481 New Freedom Singers. OH, HAPPY DAY. Music for Pleasure MFP 5445 (E). (Reissue.)
Gramophone. April. p1776. 25w. 2

3482 Larry Norman. UPON THIS ROCK. Capitol ST 446 $5.98.
Hi-Fi News and Record Review. June. p1128. 50w. 3

3483 The Original Blind Boys of Alabama. TRUE CONVICTIONS. Joy JS 5016 (E). (Reissue.)
Blues Unlimited. September. p28. 25w. 4
Jazz Journal. July. p29. 425w. 3
Records and Recordings. July. p96. 125w. 4

3484 The Pleasant Valley Boys. HE'S CALLING ME. Old Homestead 90003 $5.00.
Old Time Music. Autumn. p30. 50w. 3

3485 Elvis Presley. HE TOUCHED ME. RCA LSP 4690 $5.98. Cart. P8S 1923 $6.95. Cass. PK 1923 $6.95.
Audio. August. p63. 25w. 2½
Crawdaddy. May 28. p17. 400w. 3
High Fidelity. November. p74-6. 750w. 2

3486 Elvis Presley. SINGS THE WONDERFUL WORLD OF CHRISTMAS. RCA LSP 4579 $5.98. Cart. P8S 1809 $6.95. Cass. PK 1809 $6.95.
Creem. January. p68. 500w. 0
High Fidelity. November. p74-6. 750w. 1

3487 Paul Robeson. SONGS OF MY PEOPLE. RCA LM 3292 $5.98. (Reissue.)
Audio. September. p118. 625w. 5

3488 Dan Smith. GOD IS NOT DEAD. Biograph BLP 12036 $5.98.
Blues Unlimited. June. p23. 175w. 3
Jazz and Blues. May. p22. 375w. 2½
Sing Out. April/March. p35. 75w. 3

3489 SONGS OF PRAISE (anthology). BBC REC 1415 (E).
Gramophone. December. p1229. 50w. $3\frac{1}{2}$

3490 Dorothy Squires. THE ESSENTIAL... Starline SRS 5114 (E). (Reissue.)
Gramophone. July. p254. 100w. 2

3491 Dorothy Squires. THIS IS MY LIFE. Joy JOYS 230 (E). (Reissue.)
Gramophone. September. p577. 50w. 2

3492 The Staple Singers. BE-ALTITUDE: RESPECT YOURSELF. STAX STS 3002 $5.98. R-R X3002 $6.95. Cart. ST 8 3002 $6.98. Cass. STC 3002 $6.98.
Audio. October. p89. 75w. 3
New York Times--Sunday. September 10. pD38. 150w. $4\frac{1}{2}$
Rolling Stone. June 22. p62. 575w. 1
Stereo Review. October. p100. 100w. 0

3493 The Staple Singers. SWING LOW. Joy JS 5014 (E). (Reissue.)
Blues Unlimited. May. p28. 50w. $3\frac{1}{2}$
Jazz and Blues. May. p24. 325w. $3\frac{1}{2}$
Jazz Journal. April. p32. 175w. 3

3494 The Staple Singers. UNCLOUDY DAY. Joy JS 5019 (E). (Reissue.)
Blues Unlimited. September. p28. 25w. 4
Gramophone. August. p398. 150w. 4
Jazz Journal. July. p29. 425w. 4

3495 Stars of Faith. IN EUROPE. BASF 20718 $5.98.
Music Journal. November. p40. 25w. 3

3496 Blind Joe Taggert. Herwin 204 $5.95. (Reissue.)
Blues Unlimited. September. p29. 125w. 5
Jazz Journal. October. p37. 400w. 3

3497 THIS OLD WORLD'S IN A HELL OF A FIX (anthology). Biograph BLP 12027 $5.98. (Reissue.)
Jazz Report. No.1. 300w. 4

3498 Rev. Jasper Williams. I'M BLACK AND I'M PROUD. Jewel LPS 0024 $3.98.
Blues Unlimited. December. p29. 100w. 3

3499 Rev. Jasper Williams. IF WALLS COULD TALK. Jewel LPS 0038 $3.98.
Blues Unlimited. December. p29. 100w. 3

3500 WONDERFUL MEMORIES FROM THE FAMILY PRAYER BOOK (anthology). Joy JS 5013 (E). (Reissue.)
Blues Unlimited. May. p28. 50w. 4

STAGE AND SHOW

Included here are soundtracks from films, radio and television; original cast stage productions; studio recordings of the original item; and reissues of original soundtracks. For convenience, we have grouped the original cast stage productions here, although they are not properly "soundtracks." The chief criterion is music, and those soundtracks which have little or no music will be found elsewhere in this book as (spoken) HUMOR (if such is the case), or indexed in other books as "Spoken Word."

There is no proper review mechanism for soundtracks. Reviews are scattered, often depending on content for inclusion among regular records, as for example, Baez's _Carry It On_ under "folk," Hendrix' _Rainbow Bridge_ under "rock," and Davis' _Jack Johnson_ under "jazz." Consistently good, well-thought out reviews appear in the _Gramophone_, with _Stereo Review_ and _High Fidelity_ not far behind. Stage shows are reviewed most often, followed by film soundtracks. Television and radio music is virtually non-existent. Reviews of any kind are usually harsh, and the lack of an audience usually precludes tape release. At best, most sound tracks serve as mementoes, except for the outstanding stage musicals and classically-derived film sound tracks.

The format for entries has been changed slightly to take into account the authorship and the source of the recording. According to the reviews, the following were the best in this category:

Film

CABARET. ABC ABCD 752
FIDDLER ON THE ROOF (2 discs). United Artists UAS 10900
GREAT MOVIE STARS OF THE THIRTIES (anthology). Parlophone PMC 7141 (E)
HENRY VIII AND HIS SIX WIVES. Angel SFO 36895

Stage

AIN'T SUPPOSED TO DIE A NATURAL DEATH (2 discs). A & M SP 3510
COMPANY. Columbia OS 3550
THE GRASS HARP. Painted Smiles PS 1354
ON THE TOWN. Columbia S 31005
REVUE, 1912/1918. Parlophone PMC 7145 (E)
REVUE, 1919/1929. Parlophone PMC 7150 (E)

3501 AIN'T SUPPOSED TO DIE A NATURAL DEATH (Van Peebles). A & M SP 3510 (2 discs) $9.98. Original Broadway Cast.
High Fidelity. June. p109. 650w. 4
Popular Music. Fall. p60. 25w. $2\frac{1}{2}$
Stereo Review. June. p106. 400w. $2\frac{1}{2}$

3502 THE AMBASSADORS (Hackardy; Gohman). RCA SER 5618 (E). Original London Cast.
Gramophone. March. p1619. 125w. 1

3503 APPLAUSE (Strouse; Adams). ABC OCS 11 $6.98. Cart. L811 $7.95. Cass. L511 $7.95. Original Broadway Cast.
Gramophone. November. p993. 300w. 2

3504 ANTHONY AND CLEOPATRA (Scott). Polydor 2383 109 (E). Cass. 3170 056 (E). Music from the Original Film Soundtrack.
Gramophone. June. p117. 100w. 3

3505 THE BLACK AND WHITE MINSTRELS SPECTACULAR. World Record Club SM 196-201 (6 discs) (E). Studio Recording of the Original TV and Theatre Production.
Gramophone. September. p583. 350w. 3

3506 BLESS THE BEASTS AND THE CHILDREN (De Vorzon and Botkan). A & M SP 4322 $5.98. Cart. 8T 4322 $6.95. Cass. CS 4322 $6.95. Music from the Original Film Soundtrack.
Audio. November. p93. 50w. 2
Gramophone. March. p1619. 125w. 3
High Fidelity. April. p113-14. 250w. 2

3507 BLOOMFIELD (Harris). Pye NSPL 18376 (E). Music from the Original Film Soundtrack.
Gramophone. April. p1780. 75w. 1

3508 BORN FREE/LIVING FREE (Barry). MGM S 4368 $5.98. Cart. 8130-4368M $6.95. Original Film Soundtrack Recording.
Hi-Fi News and Record Review. August. p1477. 25w. $2\frac{1}{2}$

3509 THE BOY FRIEND (Wilson). MGM 1SE-32ST $6.98. Cart. 8130-32C $6.98. Original Film Soundtrack Recording.
Gramophone. April. p1780. 175w. 0
Stereo Review. March. p111. 250w. 0

3510 THE BOY FRIEND (Wilson). Contour 2870 157 (E). Studio Selections from the Original Stage Show.
Hi-Fi News and Record Review. June. p1127. 25w. 1

3511 BROADWAY RHYTHMS (anthology). Biograph BLP 1007Q $5.98. (Reissue.) Recordings from Original Piano Rolls.
Ragtimer. November/December. p4-6. 200w. 3

3512 THE BURGLARS (Morricone). Bell 1103 $5.98. Music from the Original Film Soundtrack.
New York Times--Sunday. August 27. pD20. 50w. 3

3513 CABARET (Kander; Ebb). ABC ABCD 752 $6.98. Cart. 8022-752 $6.98. Cass. 5022-752 $6.98. Music from the Original Film Soundtrack.
Gramophone. July. p259. 475w. 2
Hi-Fi News and Record Review. August. p1477. 75w. 2½
High Fidelity. May. p73-5. 750w. 5
Stereo Review. October. p110. 175w. 1½

3514 CARRY IT ON (Baez). Vanguard VSD 79313 $5.98. Music from the Original Film Soundtrack.
Audio. May. p94. 50w. 3½
Hi-Fi News and Record Review. September. p1679. 100w. 2½
New York Times--Sunday. April 16. pD26. 300w. 4
Stereo Review. June. p97. 200w. 1½

3515 A CLOCKWORK ORANGE (Carlos, Elgen). Warner Bros. BS 2573 $5.98. Cart. M82573 $6.95. Cass. M52573 $6.95. Music from the Original Film Soundtrack.
Gramophone. March. p1620. 150w. 0
High Fidelity. May. p76-7. 750w. 3
Library Journal. May 15. p1793. 125w. 2½
New York Times--Sunday. August 27. pD20. 350w. 4

3516 A CLOCKWORK ORANGE. Columbia KC 31480 $5.98. Studio Music Based on the Soundtrack.
New York Times--Sunday. August 27. pD20. 350w. 4

3517 A CLOCKWORK ORANGE: GREAT CLASSICAL THEMES. Angel S 36855 $5.98. Cart. 8XS 36855 $7.98. Cass. 4XS 36855 $7.98. Selections by Various Orchestras, Conductors and Soloists.
High Fidelity. May. p76-7. 750w. 2

3518 A CLOCKWORK ORANGE: GREATEST HITS. RCA LSC 3268 $5.98. Cart. R8S 1261 $6.95. Cass. RK 1261 $6.95. Selections by Various Orchestras, Conductors, and Soloists.
Gramophone. May. p1955-6. 325w. 2
High Fidelity. May. p76-7. 750w. 2

3519 COMPANY (Sondheim). Columbia OS 3550 $5.98. Cart. 18-12-0052 $6.98. Cass. 16-12-0052 $6.98. Original New York Cast.
Gramophone. August. p405. 375w. 4

3520 DE SYLVA, BROWN AND HENDERSON REVISITED. Painted Smiles PS 1351 $4.98.

High Fidelity. October. p122-3. 300w. 3
Stereo Review. August. p96. 1,000w. $1\frac{1}{2}$

3521 DIAMONDS ARE FOREVER (Barry). United Artists UAS 5220 $6.98. Music from the Original Film Soundtrack.
Gramophone. March. p1619. 75w. 1

3522 DUCK YOU SUCKER (Morricone). United Artists UAS 5221 $6.98. Music from the Original Film Soundtrack.
High Fidelity. December. p124. 125w. $2\frac{1}{2}$
New York Times--Sunday. August 27. pD20. 150w. 3

3523 Deanna Durbin. ORIGINAL VOICE TRACKS. Decca DL 75289 $4.98. Cart. 6-5289 $6.98. Cass. C73-5289 $6.98. (Reissue.)
Stereo Review. November. p86. 2,500w. 4

3524 FIDDLER ON THE ROOF (Stein; Bock, Harwick). RCA LSO 1093 $6.98. Cart. 08S 1005 $7.95. Cass. OK 1005 $7.95. Original Broadway Cast.
High Fidelity. February. p114. 225w. 3

3525 FIDDLER ON THE ROOF (Stein; Bock, Harwick). Columbia SX 30742 $6.98. Cart. SA 30742 $6.98. Cass. ST 30742 $6.98. Original London Cast.
High Fidelity. February. p114. 225w. $2\frac{1}{2}$
Stereo Review. March. p111. 50w. $2\frac{1}{2}$

3526 FIDDLER ON THE ROOF (Stein; Bock, Harwick). London SW 99470 $4.98. Original German Cast.
High Fidelity. February. p114. 225w. 3

3527 FIDDLER ON THE ROOF (Stein; Bock, Harwick). [Yiddish]. Columbia OS 3050 $5.98. Original Israeli Cast.
High Fidelity. February. p114. 225w. 3

3528 FIDDLER ON THE ROOF (Stein; Bock, Harwick). United Artists UAS 10900 (2 discs) $9.98. R-R P 10900 $9.98. Cart. U 5013 $9.98. Cass. K 5013 $9.98. Music from the Original Film Soundtrack.
Audio. January. p76. 300w. 4
Gramophone. February. p1443. 175w. $2\frac{1}{2}$
High Fidelity. February. p114. 225w. $2\frac{1}{2}$
Stereo Review. March. p111. 400w. 5

3529 FIDDLER ON THE ROOF (Stein; Bock, Harwick). London SP 44121 $5.98. Studio Recording.
High Fidelity. February. p114. 225w. 2

3530 FIDDLER ON THE ROOF (Stein; Bock, Harwick). Harmony KH 30757 $1.89. Studio Songs by Hershel Bernardi.
High Fidelity. February. p114. 225w. 2

3531 Gracie Fields. STAGE AND SCREEN. World Record Club SH 170 (E). (Reissue.)
Gramophone. December. p1229-30. 275w. 3½

3532 FUNNY FACE (Gershwin). Monmouth-Evergreen MES 7037 $5.98. Original 1928 Broadway Cast. (Reissue.)
New York Times--Sunday. February 6. pD28. 175w. 4½
Stereo Review. June. p106. 150w. 0

3533 THE GARDEN OF THE FINZI-CONTINIS (Manual De Sica). RCA LSP 4712 $5.98. Cart. P8S 1945 $6.98. Music from the Original Film Soundtrack.
Gramophone. October. p782. 600w. 3
New York Times--Sunday. August 27. pD20. 50w. 2½
Stereo Review. August. p96-7. 200w. 3

3534 IRA GERSHWIN REVISITED. Painted Smiles PS 1353 $4.98.
High Fidelity. October. p122-3. 300w. 3
Stereo Review. August. p96. 1,000w. 1½

3535 THE GODFATHER (Rota). Paramount PAS 1003 $4.98. Cart. 8091-1003C $7.95. Cass. 5091-1003C $7.95. Music from the Original Film Soundtrack.
Audio. November. p92. 50w. 1
Gramophone. December. p1230. 675w. 3½
Hi-Fi News and Record Review. October. p1925. 25w. 1
High Fidelity. August. p106. 275w. 3
New York Times--Sunday. August 27. pD27. 75w. 2

3536 GODSPELL (Schwartz). Bell 1102 $5.98. Cart. M81102 $6.95. Cass. M51102 $6.95. Original London Cast.
Gramophone. April. p1779-80. 75w. 3
Library Journal. March 15. p997. 100w. 1

3537 GODSPELL (Schwartz). Music for Pleasure MFP 5271 (E). Studio Cast Recording.
Gramophone. May. p1956. 50w. 1
Hi-Fi News and Record Review. June. p1128. 25w. 2½

3538 GODSPELL (Schwartz). Saga Pan 6312 (E). Studio Cast Recording.
Gramophone. April. p1779-80. 75w. 0

3539 GONE WITH THE WIND (Rome). Columbia SCXA 9262 (E). Original London Cast.
Gramophone. November. p990-93. 550w. 2
Hi-Fi News and Record Review. December. p2463. 50w. 2

3540 THE GRASS HARP (Richardson; Elmslie). Painted Smiles PS 1354 $4.98. Original New York Cast.
Stereo Review. June. p77-8. 375w. 4½

3541 GREAT MGM FILM THEMES (anthology). MGM 2353 060 (E). (Reissue.)
Hi-Fi News and Record Review. December. p2463. 25w. 2

3542 GREAT MOVIE STARS OF THE TWENTIES (anthology). Parlophone PMC 7141 (E). (Reissue.) English Recordings.
Gramophone. January. p1283-4. 350w. 5

3543 GREASE. MGM 1SE-340C $6.98. Cart. C813034 $7.95. Cass. C513034 $7.95. Original New York Cast.
Audio. October. p88. 25w. 1
Stereo Review. October. p110. 200w. 1

3544 H.M.S. PINAFORE (Gilbert; Sullivan). London SPCA 12001 (2 discs) $11.96.
Stereo Review. April. p102-3. 900w. 3

3545 HAIR (McDermot). RCA LSO 1170 $5.98. Original Japanese Cast.
Audio. May. p94. 25w. 3½

3546 HAIR: MASS IN F (McDermot; arr. Rado and Ragni). RCA LSP 4632 $5.98. Cart. P8S 1860 $6.95. Cass. PK 1860 $6.95.
High Fidelity. February. p112. 175w. 1½

3547 HENRY VIII AND HIS SIX WIVES. Angel SFO 36895 $5.98. Cart. 8XS 36895 $6.98. Cass. 4XS 36895 $6.98. Music from the Original Film Soundtrack.
Stereo Review. December. p112. 300w. 4

3548 HIS MONKEY WIFE (Wilson). President PTLS 1051 (E). Original Hampstead Theatre Club Cast.
Gramophone. July. p259. 325w. 5

3549 HOT ROCK (Quincy Jones). Prophecy 6055 $5.98. Cart. M86055 $6.95. Cass. M56055 $6.95. Music from the Original Film Soundtrack.
Gramophone. August. p405. 200w. 3

3550 INNER CITY: A STREET CANTATA (Miller; Merriam). RCA LSO 1171 $5.98. Cart. 08S 1047 $7.95. Cass. OK 1047 $7.95. Original Broadway Cast.
High Fidelity. June. p109. 650w. 3
Music Journal. May. p45. 100w. 1
Stereo Review. October. p110. 300w. 1

3551 JACK JOHNSON (Davis). Columbia KC 30455 $5.98. Music from the Original Film Soundtrack.
Audio. March. p82-3. 850w. $4\frac{1}{2}$
Coda. February. p25. 300w. 4

3552 JESUS CHRIST SUPERSTAR (Webber; Rice; arr. O'Horgan). Decca DL 71503 (2 discs) $6.98. Cart. 6-1503 $7.98. Cass. C73-1503 $7.98. 1971 Broadway Cast.
New York Times--Sunday. February 6. pD28. 250w. 1

3553 JESUS CHRIST SUPERSTAR (Webber; Rice). Regal Starline SR 5125 (E). Studio Selections from the Original.
Hi-Fi News and Record Review. December. p2463. 25w. 1

3554 JOURNEY THROUGH THE PAST (Young). Reprise 2XS 6480 (2 discs). Original Film Soundtrack.
New York Times--Sunday. December 10. pD37. 25w. 3

3555 KISMET (Borodin; arr. Wright; Forrest). Metro 2353 057 (E). (Reissue.) Music from the Original Film Soundtrack.
Gramophone. September. p583. 125w. 1
Hi-Fi News and Record Review. August. p1477. 75w. 1

3556 KISMET (Borodin; arr. Wright; Forrest). Regal Starline SRS 5054 (E). Studio Cast Recording.
Gramophone. January. p1283. 100w. 0

3557 LADY BE GOOD (Gershwin). Monmouth-Evergreen MES 7036 $5.98. (Reissue.) Original 1926 Broadway Cast.
New York Times--Sunday. February 6. pD28. 175w. $4\frac{1}{2}$
Stereo Review. June. p106. 150w. 0

3558 THE LAST PICTURE SHOW (Various). Columbia S 31143 $5.98. Cart. SA 31143 $6.98. Music from the Original Film Soundtrack.
Hi-Fi News and Record Review. September. p1682. 25w. 2

3559 THE LAST PICTURE SHOW. MGM 1SE-33ST $6.98. Cart. 8130-33C $7.95. Cass. 5130-33C $7.95. Music from the Original Film Soundtrack by Hank Williams.
Gramophone. June. p116. 100w. 3
Hi-Fi News and Record Review. August. p1477. 25w. $2\frac{1}{2}$

3560 THE LAST RUN (Goldsmith). MGM 1SE 30ST $6.98. Music from the Original Film Soundtrack.
New York Times--Sunday. August. p27. pD20. 50w. $2\frac{1}{2}$

3561 LIVING FREE (Kaplan). RCA LSO 1172 $6.98. Cart. 08S 1048 $7.95. Music from the Original Film Soundtrack.
Gramophone. July. p259. 125w. 3

3562 LUCKY LUKE. United Artists UAS 29290 (E). Music from the Original Film Soundtrack.
Hi-Fi News and Record Review. October. p1925. 25w. 2½

3563 MACBETH (Third Ear Band). Harvest SHSP 4019 (E). Music from the Original Film Soundtrack.
Gramophone. May. p1956. 150w. 2

3564 MAID OF THE MOUNTAINS (Graham, Harris, Valentine; Fraser-Simpson and Tate). World Record Club SH 169 (E). (Reissue.) Original 1917 London Cast.
Gramophone. December. p1230. 275w. 2½

3565 MAID OF THE MOUNTAINS (Graham, Harris, Valentine; Fraser-Simpson and Tate). Columbia SCX 6504 (E). Current London Cast (1972).
Gramophone. September. p583. 200w. 2½

3566 A MAN IN THE WILDERNESS (Harris). Warner Bros. Music from the Original Film Soundtrack.
Gramophone. April. p1780. 75w. 1

3567 MAN OF LA MANCHA (Leigh; Darion). Columbia S 31237 $5.98. Cart. SA 31237 $6.98. Cass. ST 31237 $6.98. Studio Recording.
Stereo Review. December. p112. 600w. 2

3568 MARY, QUEEN OF SCOTS (Barry). Decca DL 79186 $5.98. Music from the Original Film Soundtrack.
Gramophone. April. p1780. 75w. 1

3569 MURMUR OF THE HEART (Parker, Gillespie, et al.) Roulette SR 3006 $4.98. Music from the Original Film Soundtrack.
Saturday Review. April 22. p51. 75w. 2

3570 NICHOLAS AND ALEXANDRA (Bennett). Bell 1103 $5.98. Cart. M81103 $6.95. Cass. M51103 $6.95. Music from the Original Film Soundtrack.
New York Times--Sunday. August 27. pD20. 100w. 2½

3571 NO, NO NANETTE/SUNNY (Youmans; Mandel and Barbach). Stanyan SR 10035 $5.98. Original Cast Recording.
Stereo Review. February. p114. 375w. 2½

3572 ON THE TOWN (Bernstein). Columbia S 31005 $6.98. (Reissue.) Original Cast Recording.

High Fidelity. February. p78-9. 1,500w. 4
Stereo Review. April. p98. 1,950w. 5

3573 ONCE UPON A TIME IN THE WEST (Morricone). RCA LSP 4736 $5.98. Music from the Original Film Soundtrack.
New York Times--Sunday. August 27. pD20. 50w. 1

3574 OUTLAW RIDERS (various). MGM 1SE 26ST $6.98. Music from the Original Film Soundtrack.
Popular Music. Fall. p60. 50w. 1

3575 PLAY IT AGAIN SAM. Paramount PAS 1004 $5.98. Cart. 8091-1004C $7.95. Music and Dialogue from the Original Film Soundtrack.
High Fidelity. November. p130. 25w. 2½

3576 Elvis Presley. SINGS HITS FROM HIS MOVIES, VOLUME 1. RCA Camden CAS 2567 $2.49. (Reissue.)
High Fidelity. November. p74-6. 2,000w. 0

3577 RAINBOW BRIDGE (Hendrix). Reprise MS 2040 $5.98. Cart. M82040 $6.95. Cass. M52040 $6.95. Music from the Original Film Soundtrack, with Jimi Hendrix.
Gramophone. February. p1438. 125w. 3
High Fidelity. January. p117. 450w. 3
Library Journal. August. p2557. 150w. 3

3578 REVUE, 1912/1918 (anthology). Parlophone PMC 7145 (E). (Reissue.)
Gramophone. June. p115. 600w. 5
Gramophone. July. p259. 375w. 5

3579 REVUE, 1919/1929 (anthology). Parlophone PMC 7150 (E). (Reissue.)
Gramophone. August. p405. 850w. 5

3580 SACCO AND VANZETTI (Morricone). RCA LSP 4612 $5.98. Cart. P8S 1837 $6.95. Music from the Original Film Soundtrack.
High Fidelity. April. p112. 250w. 3½

3581 SAIL AWAY (Coward). Stanyan Records SR 10027 $5.98. Original London Cast.
Stereo Review. July. p99. 525w. 3

3582 SHAFT (Hayes). Enterprise ENS 2-5002 (2 discs) $9.98. Music from the Original Film Soundtrack.
Gramophone. January. p1283. 100w. 0
Stereo Review. April. p103. 125w. 2

3583 SHOWBOAT (Hammerstein and Wodehouse; Kern). Stanyan SR 10036 $5.98. 1971 London Cast Recording.

Gramophone. January. p1283. 400w. 4
Stereo Review. July. p96-7. 1,000w. $2\frac{1}{2}$

3584 SHOWBOAT (Hammerstein and Wodehouse; Kern). Stanyan 2 SR 10048 (2 discs) $8.95. 1972 London Cast Revival on Broadway.
Stereo Review. July. p96-7. 2,000w. 3

3585 SHOWBOAT (Hammerstein and Wodehouse; Kern). Contour 2870 145 (E). Studio Selections from the Original Stage Show.
Hi-Fi News and Record Reviews. June. p1127. 25w. 1

3586 SILENT RUNNING (Schickele). Decca DL 79188 $5.98. Music from the Original Film Soundtrack.
New York Times--Sunday. August 27. pD20. 50w. 2
Stereo Review. August. p97. 200w. $1\frac{1}{2}$

3587 SMILIN' THROUGH (Hanson). Philips 6308 095 (E). Original Touring Cast.
Gramophone. May. p1956. 150w. 0

3588 SONG OF NORWAY (Grieg; arr. Wright and Forrest). Music for Pleasure SMFP 5239 (E). Studio Cast Recording.
Gramophone. January. p1284. 75w. 3

3589 SOUL TO SOUL. Atlantic SD 7207 $5.98. Music from the Original Film Soundtrack.
Audio. May. p93. 100w. 4
Popular Music. Fall. p62. 50w. 2

3590 STARS OF THE SILVER SCREEN, 1929/1930 (anthology). RCA LSA 3074 $5.98. (Reissue.)
Gramophone. December. p1225-6. 100w. 2

3591 STUDENT PRINCE/VAGABOND KING (Romberg). Hallmark/ Marble Arch HMA 208 (E). Studio Selections from the Original Stage Shows.
Hi-Fi News and Record Review. June. p1127. 50w. 2

3592 SUGAR (Styne; Merrill). United Artists UAS 9905 $6.98. Cart. U 3066 $6.98. Cass. K 9066 $6.98. Original New York Cast.
Stereo Review. November. p98-9. 300w. $2\frac{1}{2}$

3593 SUPER FLY (Mayfield). Curtom CRS 8014-ST $5.98. Cart. M88014 $6.95. Cass. M58014 $6.95. Music from the Original Film Soundtrack.
Rolling Stone. November 9. p61. 600w. 3

3594 'S WONDERFUL, 'S MARVELOUS, 'S GERSHWIN (Gershwin). Daybreak DR 2009 $5.98. Cart. P8DR 2009 $6.95. Music from the Original TV Show.

Audio. October. p89. 50w. 1
Hi-Fi News and Record Review. July. p1307. 100w. 1
Music Journal. May. p45. 150w. 3

3595 TCHAIKOVSKY (arr. Tiomkin). Philips 6641 048 (E) (2 discs). Music from the Original Soundtrack of the Russian Film.
Gramophone. September. p580. 500w. 4

3596 Shirley Temple. GREATEST HITS. Regal Starline MRS 4086 (E). (Reissue.)
Gramophone. February. p1437. 50w. 2½

3597 THE TEN COMMANDMENTS (Bernstein). Sunset SLS 50315 (E). (Reissue.) Music Featured in the Film.
Gramophone. September. p583. 125w. 4
Hi-Fi News and Record Review. September. p1682. 25w. 2

3598 THEATRELAND SHOW STOPPERS, 1943/1968 (anthology). Columbia SCX-SP 652 (3 discs). (Reissue.) Original London Casts.
Gramophone. November. p993. 1,300w. 3

3599 "THEMES" LIKE OLD TIMES: RECORDINGS FROM THE ARCHIVES OF RADIO YESTERYEAR. Viva/Warner Bros. 2VV 2572 (2 discs) $6.98.
Library Journal. June 1. p2069. 100w. 2½

3600 THE THREEPENNY OPERA (Brecht, trans. Blitzstein; Weill). Metro 2356 025 (E). (Reissue.) Original Off Broadway Cast.
Gramophone. May. p1956. 175w. 5

3601 TO LIVE ANOTHER SUMMER, TO PASS ANOTHER WINTER (Seltzer; add. lyrics by Shemer). Buddah BDS 95004 (2 discs) $6.98. Original Broadway Cast.
Audio. November. p91. 50w. 3
High Fidelity. April. p112-3. 300w. 2½
New York Times--Sunday. February 6. pD28. 75w. 3

3602 TOM BROWN'S SCHOOLDAYS (Maitland; Andrews). Decca SKL 5137 (E). Original London Cast.
Gramophone. August. p406. 100w. 1
Hi-Fi News and Record Recording. September. p1682. 25w. 0

3603 TRELAWNY. Decca SKL 5144 (E). Original London Cast.
Gramophone. November. p993. 225w. 4

3604 TWO GENTLEMEN OF VERONA (Guare and MacDermot). ABC 1001 $9.96 (2 discs). Cart. J 81001 DP $9.95. Cass. J 51001 DP $9.95. Original Broadway Cast.

New York Times--Sunday. February 6. pD28. 475w. 4

3605 200 MOTELS (Zappa; Mothers of Invention). United Artists UAS 9956 (2 discs) $9.98. Cart. XO 4020 $9.98. Cass. XC 4020 $9.98. Music from the Original Film Soundtrack and from the Studio.
Creem. February. p60. 675w. 0
Downbeat. January 20. p28. 200w. 3
High Fidelity. February. p117-8. 175w. 2
Library Journal. January 1. p55. 300w. 2

3606 LA VALLIE (Pink Floyd). Harvest SHSP 4020 (E). Music from the Original Film Soundtrack.
Gramophone. August. p405. 75w. 1

3607 THE WILD ROVERS (Goldsmith). MGM 1SE 31ST $6.98. Music from the Original Film Soundtrack.
Gramophone. June. p117. 100w. 4

3608 WILLY WONKA AND THE CHOCOLATE FACTORY (Bricusse, Newley). Paramount SPFL 274 (E). Music from the Original Film Soundtrack.
Gramophone. February. p1443. 125w. 0

3609 VINCENT YOUMANS REVISITED. Painted Smiles PS 1352 $4.98.
High Fidelity. October. p122-3. 300w. 3
Stereo Review. August. p96. 1,000w. 1½

3610 YOUNG WINSTON (Ralston). Angel SFO 36901 $5.98. Cart. 8XS 36901 $7.98. Cass. 4XS 36901 $7.98. Music from the Original Film Soundtrack.
Gramophone. September. p580-3. 500w. 2
Hi-Fi News and Record Review. September. p1682. 25w. 2½

BAND

This section covers marching bands, military bands, pipers, college and school bands, plus any other type of music that comprises marches. Excluded, of course, are those jazz variants of dixieland marches and ragtime.

There is no review mechanism for recorded music of this type, although there is the scholarly Journal of Band Research which, unfortunately, does not review records. Schwann 2 lists extensive amounts of band music, but unless the listener knows what he wants, there is no competent guide for adequate selection. Band music has had a solid tradition and following in the British Isles; hence, the Gramophone provides some reviews. Although bands, marching music and tattooes draw on a limited repertoire, this music is still very popular and prevalent among school and college activities in North America, the land of John Philip Sousa. Perhaps the recent release of the Amazing Grace album will stimulate interest in other aspects of military music.

3611 Band of the Irish Army. Columbia Studio 2 TWO 376 (E).
Gramophone. July. p253. 100w. 3

3612 Bilston Glen Pipe Band. THE PIPERS' WELCOME. Talisman STAL 5027 (E).
Gramophone. August. p396. 50w. 3

3613 The Black Watch. HIGHLAND PAGENTRY. Beltona SBE 131 (E).
Hi-Fi News and Record Review. August. p1473. 25w. 2

3614 BRASS BAND CLASSICS (anthology). Regal Starline SRS 5105 (E).
Hi-Fi News and Record Review. August. p1473. 25w. 2½

3615 Coldstream Guards. IN LONDON. Decca Eclipse ECS 2101 (E).
Gramophone. May. p1948. 50w. 2½

3616 Czechoslovak Brass Orchestra. AMERICAN MARCHES. Supraphon 1 140586 (Czech).
Hi-Fi News and Record Review. October. p1923. 25w. 2

3617 Edinburgh Corporation Transport Band. THE PIPES OF EDINBURGH. Beltona SBE 132 (E).
Hi-Fi News and Record Review. August. p1473. 25w. 3

3618 The Fairey Band. Decca SB 301 (E).
Hi-Fi News and Record Review. October. p1923. 25w. 3

3619 GOLDEN MARCH FAVORITES (anthology). Coral CPS 83 (E). (Reissue.)
Gramophone. August. p392. 250w. 4

3620 GRANADA FESTIVAL '71. Granada Television GTVSP 101 (E) (2 discs).
Gramophone. August. p395. 175w. 2

3621 H.M. Lifeguards Band. Decca Eclipse ECS 2103 (E).
Gramophone. June. p109-10. 75w. 2

3622 Martin-Coulter Marching Band. Philips 6382 034 (E).
Gramophone. May. p1952. 25w. 2

3623 MASSED PIPES AND DRUMS OF THE SCOTTISH REGIMENTS (anthology). Music for Pleasure MFP 5240 (E). (Reissue.)
Gramophone. May. p1948. 50w. 2

3624 Men O'Brass. SOUSA. Columbia Studio 2 TWO 385 (E).
Gramophone. December. p1218. 100w. 3½

3625 Military Band of the Gordon Highlanders. THE GAY AND GALLANT. Waverly SZLP 2130 (E).
Gramophone. June. p109. 100w. 3

3626 MILITARY MUSICAL PAGEANT, 1971 (anthology). Philips 6308 078 (E).
Gramophone. March. p1607. 175w. 1½

3627 OLD AUSTRIAN MILITARY MARCHES (anthology). Supraphon 1141 020 (Czech).
Gramophone. May. p1947. 75w. 1

3628 Royal Highland Regiment (Black Watch). HIGHLAND PAGENTRY. Beltona SBE 131 (E).
Gramophone. August. p396. 50w. 3

3629 Royal Scots Dragoon Guards. AMAZING GRACE. RCA LSP 4744 $5.98. Cart. P8S 2008 $6.98. Cass. PK 2008 $6.98.
High Fidelity. September. p102. 300w. 3
Stereo Review. September. p76, 80. 300w. 2½

3630 Yorkshire Imperial Metals Band. Decca SB 302 (E).
Hi-Fi News and Record Review. October. p1923. 25w. 3

HUMOR

This section includes recordings of comedy groups, stand-up comedians, excerpts from radio and television comedies, humorous monologues and skits. Theatrical comedies are not included and can be found in other reference works on the "Spoken Word."

There is no single review mechanism for humor records. Reviews of popular releases turn up in just about every magazine. The approach of the reviewer may well be related to the periodical for which he reviews. This is particularly true in 1972 when a number of "hip" humor recordings were released with skits on abortion, "grass," VD, and dirty words. The counter-culture publications such as Rolling Stone, Creem, and Crawdaddy tended to give favorable ratings to these "far-out" creations while High Fidelity and Stereo Review led the chorus of "boring," "juvenile," and "irreverent."

Humor records enjoyed a peak of popularity at the end of the 1950's. During the golden age of Lenny Bruce, Mort Sahl, Vaughn Meader, and Bob Newhart, recordings of this type sold hundreds of thousands of albums. Humor records of the sixties were limited in number with occasional interest in one artist or the other. Dick Gregory and Bill Cosby saw momentary bursts of popularity. However, these seem to be isolated occurrences in recording history.

By the end of the decade there was some indication that a new age of comedy records was about to begin. One interpretation of this new interest may lie in the serious sixties when war, social change, and protest captured the audience for this form of comedy. By 1972 Americans may have been ready for a few laughs no matter how outlandish and irreverent the material might be. Closely related is the emergence of a counter-culture that has adopted a habit of listening to records while "stoned." Indeed, many of the new humor records, particularly the work of the Firesign Theatre, can only be comprehended when under the influence of one of the many hallucinogens popularly available.

The big news in 1972 was the release of albums by the Mexican-Chinese comedy team Cheech and Chong. Their first albums have gained great popularity among young people and mirror the language, attitudes, and behavior of their audiences. Pro-dope and anti-establishment, they pose problems for libraries whose users may be sensitive to the repeated use of "fuck" or "shit." More sophisticated is George Carlin's Class Clown. Carlin, a standup comedian with extensive TV exposure has gone through a number of "changes" and his humor also reflects the current shock value phenomena of releases of this genre. "Seven words you can never say on TV" is one of his routines that has earned Carlin short jail sentences in mid-American cities.

Other closely related releases that have drawn attention are the last recordings of the psychedelic group, The Firesign Theatre (their last since they have, like many rock groups, split up) and the National Lampoon's Radio Dinner. The Lampoon crowd presently have a smash off-Broadway hit, Lemmings which is due to be released on vinyl in 1973.

Whatever the individual listener or reviewer may think of this new breed of humor recording, the trend does indicate a loosening of self-imposed censorship on the part of recording companies. Can libraries be far behind?

Keeping in mind the prejudices of reviewers the following humor recordings are the significant releases for 1972:

George Carlin. FM AND AM. Little David 7214
Cheech and Chong. BIG BAMBU. Ode 77014
Firesign Theatre. DEAR FRIENDS (2 discs). Columbia KG 31099
Don Imus. 1,200 HAMBURGERS TO GO. RCA LSP 4699
Vaughn Meader. THE SECOND COMING. Kama Sutra KSBS 2038
National Lampoon. RADIO DINNER. Blue Thumb BTS 38
Mike Nichols and Elaine May. RETROSPECT (2 discs). Mercury SRM 2-628. (Reissue.)

3631 Spiro Agnew. THE GREAT COMEDY RECORD. Flying Dutchman FDS 10137 $5.95. Cart. M810137 $6.95. Cass. M510137 $6.95.
New York Times--Sunday. March 12. pHF12. 100w. 0

3632 ALL IN THE FAMILY. Atlantic SD 7210 $5.98. Cart. M87210 $6.95. Cass. M57210 $6.95.
American Record Guide. June. p526. 300w. 0
Audio. February. p78. 100w. $2\frac{1}{2}$
Stereo Review. May. p98-9. 300w. 3

3633 The Amazing Spiderman. FROM BEYOND THE GRAVE. Buddah BDS 5119 $5.98.
New York Times--Sunday. November 19. pD30. 175w. 2

3634 Sandy Baron. GOD SAVE THE QUEENS. A & M 4355 $5.98.
High Fidelity. November. p122, 26. 200w. 1

3635 Lenny Bruce. AT THE CURRAN THEATER. Fantasy 34201 (3 discs) $4.98 each. (Reissue.)
Audio. July. p64. 50w. 2

3636 Lenny Bruce. INTERVIEWS OF OUR TIMES. Fantasy $4.98.
Records and Recordings. January. p96. 100w. 4

3637 Lenny Bruce. MIDNIGHT CONCERT. United Artists UAS 6794 $4.98.
American Record Guide. January. p235. 375w. 3

3638 Lenny Bruce. WHAT I WAS ARRESTED FOR. Douglas KZ 30872 $5.98.
High Fidelity. January. p110. 200w. $4\frac{1}{2}$

3639 George Carlin. FM AND AM. Little David LD 7214 $4.98. Cart. M87214 $6.95. Cass. M57214 $6.95.
American Record Guide. September. p670. 150w. 4
Audio. July. p64. 125w. $3\frac{1}{2}$
Creem. August. p67. 50w. 3
High Fidelity. June. p110. 25w. $3\frac{1}{2}$
Popular Music. Spring. p185. 75w. 4

3640 Cheech and Chong. Ode SP 77010 $5.98. Cart. 8T 77010 $6.98. Cass. CS 77010 $6.98.
Blues Unlimited. May. p28. 25w. 0
New York Times--Sunday. March 12. pHF12. 100w. 0
Stereo Review. March. p112. 150w. $2\frac{1}{2}$

3641 Cheech and Chong. BIG BAMBU. Ode SP 77014 $5.98.
Creem. December. p59. 400w. $\frac{1}{2}$
High Fidelity. November. p130. 25w. $2\frac{1}{2}$
Popular Music and Society. Fall. p89. 50w. 3

3642 A CHILD'S GARDEN OF GRASS. Elektra EKS 75012 $5.98. Cart. ET8 15012 $6.98. Cass. TC5 51012 $6.98.
American Record Guide. February. p283. 375w. 4
New York Times--Sunday. March 12. pHF12. 50w. $2\frac{1}{2}$

3643 The Conception Corporation. CONCEPTIONLAND, AND OTHER STATES OF MIND. Cotillion SD 9051 $5.98. Cart. M89051 $6.95. Cass. M59051 $6.95.
Audio. July. p65. 75w. 1

3644 Congress of Wonders. REVOLTING. Fantasy 7016 $4.98.
American Record Guide. July. p575. 225w. 1
New York Times--Sunday. March 12. pHF12. 50w. 0

3645 Bill Cosby. FOR ADULTS ONLY. Uni 73112 $4.98. Cart. 8-73112 $6.95. Cass. 2-73112 $6.95.
American Record Guide. June. p527. 225w. 3

3646 Credibility Gap. PRESENTS "WOODSCHTICK." Capitol ST681 $4.98.
American Record Guide. March. p330. 25w. 0

3647 Firesign Theatre. DEAR FRIENDS. Columbia KG 31099 (2 discs) $6.98. Cart. GA 31099 $7.98. Cass. GT 31099 $7.98.
Canadian Stereo Guide. Fall. p28. 125w. 2½
Popular Music. Spring. p188. 75w. 3
Rolling Stone. March 30. p50. 850w. 3½

3648 Firesign Theatre. I THINK WE'RE ALL BOZOS ON THIS BUS. Columbia C 30737 $5.98. Cart. CA 30737 $6.98. Cass. CT 30737 $6.98.
New York Times--Sunday. March 12. pHF12. 50w. 1

3649 FIFTY YEARS OF RADIO COMEDY (anthology). BBC REC 138 M (E).
Gramophone. December. p1,226. 75w. 3

3650 Fannie Flagg. "MY HUSBAND DOESN'T KNOW I'M MAKING THIS PHONE CALL." Sunflower SNF 5008 $5.98.
New York Times--Sunday. March 12. pHF12. 50w. 0

3651 Flanagan and Allen. BEST. Starline SRS 5730 (E). (Reissue.)
Gramophone. December. p1,225. 50w. 3

3652 David Frost. REPORT ON BRITAIN. Regal Starline MRS 5084 (E). (Reissue.)
Gramophone. February. p1437-8. 25w. 2

3653 David Frye. RICHARD NIXON SUPERSTAR. Buddah 5097 $5.98. Cart. M85097 $6.95. Cass. M55097 $6.95.
Audio. July. p64. 75w. 1
High Fidelity. April. p106. 100w. 3
New York Times--Sunday. March 12. pHF12. 400w. 4

3654 THE GOLDEN AGE OF COMEDY (anthology). RCA LPV 580 $5.98. (Reissue.)
Audio. July. p64. 75w. 2½
Gramophone. December. p1,225. 50w. 1
Stereo Review. October. p112. 300w. 2

3655 GOLDEN HOUR OF COMEDY (anthology). Pye Golden Hour GH 530 (E). (Reissue.)
Gramophone. October. p778. 125w. 5

3656 Benny Hill. WORDS AND MUSIC. Columbia SCX 6479 (E).
Gramophone. February. p38. 25w. 2

3657 Don Imus. 1,200 HAMBURGERS TO GO/IMUS IN THE MORNING. RCA LSP 4699 $5.98.

Creem. August. p67. 75w. 4
High Fidelity. August. p106. 25w. 1½
Popular Music. Summer. p251. 100w. 5
Popular Music and Society. Fall. p88. 75w. 5

3658 JEWISH AMERICAN PRINCESS. Bell S-6063 $5.98. Cart. M86063 $6.95. Cass. M56063 $6.95.
Audio. August. p61. 50w. 2

3659 Spike Jones. IS MURDERING THE CLASSICS. RCA LSC 3235 $5.98. Cart. R8S 1207 $6.95. (Reissue.)
Audio. March. p78. 75w. 4
High Fidelity. January. p110. 120w. 3
Stereo Review. January. p108. 375w. 4

3660 THE LAST GOON SHOW OF ALL. BBC RFB 142S (E).
Gramophone. December. p1,226. 50w. 0

3661 Rich Little. POLITICS AND POPCORN. Mercury SRM 1-617 $4.98. Cart. MC 8-1-617 $6.95.
Audio. July. p64-5. 75w. 1

3662 Moms Mabley. LIVE AT THE GREEK THEATER. Mercury SR 61360 $4.98. Cart. MC 8-61360 $6.95. Cass. MCR 4-61360 $6.95.
American Record Guide. April. p379. 150w. 2

3663 Bill Martin. CONCERTO FOR HEAD PHONES AND CONTRA-BUFFOON IN ASIA MINOR. Warner Bros. $5.98.
Creem. September. p57. 25w. 4

3664 Vaughn Meader. THE SECOND COMING. Kama Sutra KSBS 2038 $5.98.
Audio. July. p64. 125w. 2½
Popular Music. Winter. p123. 50w. 2

3664a Spike Milligan. A RECORD LOAD OF RUBBISH. BBC Records RED 98M (E).
Records and Recordings. January. p93. 125w. 4

3665 Morecambe and Wise. GET OUT OF THAT! Philips 6382 005 (E).
Gramophone. February. p1,437. 25w. 2

3666 Morecambe and Wise. IT'S MORECAMBE AND WISE. BBC Records RED 128M (E).
Gramophone. February. p1438. 25w. 2

3667 Rudy Ray Moore. EAT OUT MORE OFTEN. Comedian COM S 1104 $4.98.
Journal of American Folklore. January/March. p106. 100w. 3½

3668 Rudy Ray Moore. THIS PUSSY BELONGS TO ME. Comedian COM S 1105 $4.98.
Journal of American Folklore. January/March. p106. 150w. 3

3669 National Lampoon. RADIO DINNER/ASSORTED BRILLIANT SICKOIDS. Banana/Blue Thumb BTS 38 $4.98.
Audio. November. p90. 75w. 4½
Creem. November. p62. 700w. 4
Popular Music and Society. Fall. p1. 50w. 3

3670 Mike Nichols and Elaine May. RETROSPECT. Mercury SRM 2-628 (2 discs) $5.98. Cart. MCT 8 2-628 $9.98. (Reissue.)
Audio. July. p65. 50w. 4
Creem. August. p67. 25w. 5
Popular Music. Spring. p186. 75w. 5
Stereo Review. September. p84. 350w. 5

3671 Ken Nordine. HOW ARE THINGS IN YOUR TOWN? Blue Thumb BTS 33 $5.98.
Audio. December. p94-5. 325w. 4½

3672 Jean Shepherd. DECLASSIFIED. Mercury SRM 1-615 $5.98.
American Record Guide. April. p378. 200w. 0
Audio. July. p65. 50w. 2

3673 Steptoe. GOLDEN HOUR. Pye Golden Hour GH 527 (E).
Gramophone. July. p254. 100w. 3

3674 Lee Sutton. DRAG FOR CAMP FOLLOWERS. Columbia SCX 6481 (E).
Gramophone. March. p1,613. 25w. 3

3675 Lily Tomlin. AND THAT'S THE TRUTH. Polydor PD 5023 $4.98. Cart. 8F 5023 $6.98. Cass. CF 5023 $6.98.
Audio. July. p64. 100w. 2
Creem. August. p67. 25w. 0
High Fidelity. June. p103. 250w. 1½
Stereo Review. November. p101. 350w. 2½

3676 Uncle Dirty. THE UNCLE DIRTY PRIMER. Elektra EKS 74097 $4.98.
High Fidelity. February. p116-7. 75w. 2½

3677 Gore Vidal. AN EVENING WITH RICHARD NIXON. Ode 0598 $5.98.
Popular Music and Society. Fall. p91. 25w. 3

3678 Flip Wilson. GERALDINE/DON'T FIGHT THE FEELING. Little David LD 1001 $5.98. Cart. M81001 $6.95. Cass. M51001 $6.95.
Stereo Review. September. p88. 400w. 4

3679 Justin Wilson. HUNTING. Paula LPS 2214 $4.98. Cart. M82214 $6.95.
Blues Unlimited. September. p24. 75w. 3½

SELECTED BOOKS

The following books were given significant or favorable reviews in the periodicals indexed. No subject categories were made because many of the titles fall into two or more categories. Explanatory annotations are given where needed.

Allen, Walter C., ed. Studies in Jazz Discography I. New Brunswick, N.J.: Institute of Jazz Studies, Rutgers University, 1971. 112p. $3.25.
Edited proceedings of the 1968 and 1969 Conference on Discographical Research. Valuable for discographers and collectors.

Arma, Paul, comp. The Gambit Book of French Folk Songs. New York: Gambit, 1972. 152p. illus. $9.50 (dist. by Houghton). LC: 79-160414.
Arranged and translated by Elizabeth Poston. Fifty-seven songs from the Middle Ages to the 19th century, including some French-Canadian versions. Bilingual lyrics, piano and guitar arrangements.

Bailey, Pearl. Talking to Myself. New York: Harcourt Brace Jovanovich, 1971. 233p. $5.95. LC: 78-153679.

Balliet, Whitney. Ecstasy at the Onion: Thirty-One Pieces on Jazz. Indianapolis: Bobbs-Merril, 1971. 284p. $6.95. LC: 76-161239.

Bart, Teddy. Inside Music City, U.S.A. Nashville: Aurora, 1970. 164p. illus. $4.95. LC: 76-108291.
How to succeed in Nashville, illuminated by personal histories.

Belz, Carl. The Story of Rock. 2d ed. New York: Oxford University Press, 1972. 286p. illus. bibliog. discog. $7.50. LC: 77-183870.

Berteault, Simone. Piaf: A Biography. New York: Harper & Row, 1972. 488p. $10. LC: 75-138706.

Blesh, Rudi. Combo: U.S.A.; Eight Lives in Jazz. Philadelphia: Chilton, 1971. 240p. illus. $6.95 (pap. $3.95). LC: 78-145802.

Descriptive biographies of Louis Armstrong, Billie Holiday, Gene Krupa, Jack Teagarden, Sidney Bechet, Eubie Blake, Charlie Christian, and Lester Young.

Bluestein, Gene. The Voice of the Folk: Folklore and American Literary Theory. Amherst: University of Massachusetts Press, 1972. 170p. bibliog. $9.00 (pap. $2.95). LC: 70-16443

Only half is devoted to folk music, but it does include a study of blues as a literary tradition, the black influence, and rock as poetry.

Boeckman, Charles. And the Beat Goes On: A Survey of Pop Music in America. Washington, D.C.: R.B. Luce, 1972. 224p. illus. $5.95 (dist. by: McKay). LC: 77-178880.

Bogaert, Karel. Blues Lexicon: Blues, Cajun, Boogie Woogie, and Gospel. Antwerp: Standard Uitg., 1972. 480p. 465 B. fr.

In English.

Bronson, Bertrand Harris. The Traditional Tunes of the Child Ballads; With Their Texts According to Extant Records of Great Britain and America, v.4. Princeton, N.J.: Princeton University Press, 1971. 576p. $40. LC: 57-5468.

Brown, Len and Gary Friedrich. Encyclopedia of Rock and Roll. New York: Tower Publications, 1970. 217p. illus. bibliog. pap. $1.25. LC: 72-21353.

Chasins, Abram. Music at the Crossroads. New York: Macmillan, 1972. 240p. $5.95. LC: 78-169232.

An appraisal of the current state of instrumental music, both classical and popular, with consideration of the effects of jazz-rock-folk on "serious" music.

Chilton, John. Who's Who of Jazz: Storyville to Swing Street. Philadelphia: Chilton, 1972. 419p. illus. bibliog. $7.50. LC: 72-188159.

Information on over 1000 American jazz musicians born before 1920.

Chipman, Bruce L., ed. Hardening Rock: An Organic Anthology of the Adolescence of Rock 'N' Roll. New York: Little, 1972. 176p. illus. $8.95 (pap. $3.95). LC: 75-186964.

Lyrics to 72 songs from the 1950's.

Cole, Maria. Nat King Cole: An Intimate Biography. New York: Morrow, 1971. 184p. illus. discog. $5.95. LC: 75-151921.

Cone, James H. The Spirituals and the Blues: An Interpretation. New York: Seabury, 1972. 152p. bibliog. $4.95 (pap. $2.95). LC: 73-186165.

Cook, Bruce. The Beat Generation. New York: Scribners, 1971. 248p. illus. $6.95 (pap. $2.95). LC: 73-143950.
The influence of jazz on the beatniks, with the conclusion that they misinterpreted it.

Country Music Who's Who: 1972. New York: Record World Publications, 1971. 420p. illus. $19.95. LC: 60-1664 rev.
Features list of 2000 hit songs of last 50 years (with comprehensive index), and capsule biographies of 300 prominent persons in the business.

Cyporyn, Dennis. The Bluegrass Songbook. New York: Macmillan, 1972. 154p. illus. $7.95 (pap. $3.95). LC: 79-187071.
88 traditional and modern songs, with bibliographical data.

Dalton, David. Janis. New York: Simon & Schuster, 1971. 212p. illus. pap. $4.95. LC: 72-159128.
Includes 56 pages of songs, plus an 8 minute, one-sided 33 1/3 rpm disc. The definitive biography of Janis Joplin, with in-depth interviews.

Dalton, David, ed. Rolling Stones. New York: Amsco Music Publishing Company, 1972. 351p. illus. discog. $9.95. LC: 72-75161.
Songs, record reviews, chronology, and an interview with Mick Jagger.

Dance, Stanley. The World of Duke Ellington. New York: Scribners, 1970. 311p. illus. discog. $8.95 (pap. $2.95). LC: 79-123844.

Deans, Mickey. Weep No More, My Lady: An Intimate Biography of Judy Garland. Boston: G.K. Hall, 1972. 238p. illus. $9.95. LC: 72-4462.

Denisoff, R. Serge, comp. American Protest Songs of War and Peace: A Selected Bibliography and Discography. Los Angeles: Center for the Study of Armament and Disarmament at California State College, 1970. 15p. $1.95. LC: 73-24735.
Mostly from left-wing sources, but includes 23 citations containing attacks on leftist songs.

Denisoff, R. Serge. Great Day Coming: Folk Music and the American Left. Urbana: University of Illinois Press, 1971. 219 p. illus. bibliog. $12.50. LC: 74-155498.
Attempts to prove that music cannot change society by tracing history of some leading folk singers.

Denisoff, R. Serge, comp. The Sounds of Social Change: Studies in Popular Culture. Chicago: Rand McNally, 1972. 332p. pap. $3.95. LC: 75-188638.

Dilello, Richard. The Longest Cocktail Party: A Personal History of Apple. Chicago: Playboy, 1972. 336p. discog. $8.95 (dist. by Simon & Schuster). LC: 72-85965.

An inside view of Apple, the business venture of the Beatles.

Dixon, Robert M. W. and John Godrich. Recording the Blues. New York: Stein and Day, 1970. 112p. illus. bibliog. discog. $4.95 (pap. $1.95). LC: 76-120111.

Traces blues records from the beginning in 1902 to 1945.

Emrich, Duncan. Folklore of the American Land. Boston: Little, Brown, 1972. 707p. illus. bibliog. $15.00. LC: 72-161865.

Includes unaccompanied melodies for over 70 folksongs and ballads.

Evans, David. Tommy Johnson. London: Studio Vista, 1971. 112p. illus. bibliog. discog. pap $1.95. LC: 76-868967.

Feather, Leonard. From Satchmo to Miles. New York: Stein and Day, 1972. 258p. $7.95. LC: 70-187311.

Thirteen biographical essays, most published before.

Ferris, William R. Blues from the Delta. London: Studio Vista, 1970. 111p. bibliog. discog. pap. $1.95. LC: 78-590331.

An overview of the blues tradition in Mississippi with emphasis on the people and the social context of their performances. Interesting comparison of black and white blues songs. Some texts.

Ferris, William R. Mississippi Black Folklore: A Research Bibliography and Discography. Hattiesburg: University and College Press of Mississippi, 1971. 61p. LC: 70-158331.

Lacks annotations and index.

Fife, Austin, comp. Cowboy and Western Songs: A Comprehensive Anthology. New York: C.N. Potter, 1969. 372p. illus. music. $12.50. LC: 69-13400.

200 songs, including variations in words and music.

Flower, John. Moonlight Serenade: A Bio-Discography of the Glenn Miller Civilian Band. New Rochelle, N.Y.: Arlington House, 1972. 554p. illus. $10. LC: 74-179717.

A day-by-day account of the performances and recordings of the band. Index to song titles and personnel.

Foster, Pops. Pops Foster: The Autobiography of a New Orleans Jazzman, As Told to Tom Stoddard. Berkeley: University of California Press, 1971. 208p. illus. bibliog. discog. $8.95. LC: 75-132414.

Fox, Charles. The Jazz Scene. New York: Hamlyn, 1972. 128p. Chiefly illus.
Contains 130 color photos by Valerie Wilmer.

Fuld, James F., ed. The Book of World-Famous Music: Classical, Popular and Folk. Rev. and enl. ed. New York: Crown, 1971. 688p. illus. bibliog. $15. LC: 70-147348.
Traces 1000 famous melodies back to their original printed sources.

Garcia, Jerry. Garcia: the Rolling Stone Interview. San Francisco: Straight Arrow Press, 1972. 254p. illus. $7 (pap. $3.50). LC: 72-79027.
Part of this was previously published in Rolling Stone.

Garon, Paul. The Devil's Son-In-Law: The Story of Peetie Wheatstraw and His Songs. London: Studio Vista, 1971. 111p. illus. bibliog. discog. pap. $1.95. LC: 72-176214.

Garvin, Richard and Edmond G. Addeo. The Midnight Special: The Legend of Leadbelly. New York: B. Geis Associates, 1971. 312p. $6.95. LC: 70-134214.
A novel of Leadbelly's life with "imagined scenes and reconstructed events."

Giannaris, George. Mikis Theodorakis: Music and Social Change. New York: Praeger, 1972. 322p. illus. bibliog. $8.95. LC: 72-165835.

Gillett, Charlie. The Sound of the City: The Rise of Rock 'N' Roll. New York: Dell, 1972. 343p. bibliog. discog. pap. $0.95.

Govoni, Albert. A Boy Named Cash. New York: Lancer Books, 1970. 190p. illus. discog. pap. $0.75. LC: 79-14343.
Based on second-hand sources.

Green, Archie. Only a Miner: Studies in Recorded Coal-Mining Songs. Urbana: University of Illinois Press, 1972. 504p. illus. bibliog. $12.50. LC: 78-155499.

Grissim, John. Country Music: White Man's Blues. New York: Paperback Library, 1970. 299p. illus. pap. $1.25. LC: 76-20202.
The mechanics and the personalities of the contemporary country and western music industry, well-researched.

Grissim, John. We Have Come for Your Daughters: What Went Down on the Medicine Caravan. New York: Morrow, 1972. 254p. illus. $6.95. LC: 78-158080.
The narrative of a month-long tour by 150 West Coast freaks to make a film of their rock concerts and hippie life (i.e., Medicine Ball Caravan).

Groom, Bob. The Blues Revival. London: Studio Vista, 1971. 112p. illus. bibliog. pap. $1.95. LC: 74-855082.
A summary of renewed interest in blues music by the editor of Blues World.

Guralnick, Peter. Feel Like Goin' Home: Portraits in Blues and Rock 'N' Roll. New York: Outerbridge and Dienstfrey, 1971. 224p. illus. bibliog. $6.95. LC: 70-174733.

Haglund, Urban and Lillie Ohlsson. A Listing of Bluegrass LPs. Vasteras, Sweden: Kountry Korral Productions, 197-? 72p. pap. $3 (distributed by County Sales).
A nearly complete list of albums issued in the United States and abroad.

Handy, W.C., ed. Blues: An Anthology. New York: Macmillan, 1972. 224p. $7.95. LC: 74-160086.
These 53 songs, with words and music, were originally published in 1926 and republished in 1949 as Treasury of the Blues.

Haufrecht, Herbert, comp. Folksongs in Settings by Master Composers. New York: Funk and Wagnalls, 1970. 236p. bibliog. discog. $12.50. LC: 68-21721.
A compilation of 44 English language songs with brief notes and piano accompaniment.

Heilbut, Tony. The Gospel Sound: Good News and Bad Times. New York: Simon & Schuster, 1971. 350p. illus. discog. $7.95. LC: 76-156151.

Herman, Gary. The Who. New York: Macmillan, 1972. 159p. illus. $5.95 (pap. $1.95). LC: 70-186439.

Hodeir, André. The Worlds of Jazz. New York: Grove Press, 1972. 288p. illus. $8.95 (pap. $2.95). LC: 74-155132.
Covers the problems of jazz performances, composing and evaluation.

Hoover, Cynthia. Music Machines--American Style: A Catalog of an Exhibition. Washington, D.C.: Smithsonian Institution Press; for sale by the U.S. Govt. Print. Off., 1971. 139p. illus. bibliog. $2.75. LC: 70-614474.
The exhibition portrayed the development of music machines from cylinders and player pianos to Moog synthesizers, and the effect of technology on performers and audiences.

Hopkins, Jerry. Elvis. New York: Simon & Schuster, 1971. 448p. illus. discog. $7.95. LC: 77-156154.
Official biography.

Ives, Edward D. Lawrence Doyle: The Farmer Poet of Prince Edward Island; A Study in Local Songmaking. Orono: University of Maine Press, 1971. 269p. illus. $7.95. LC: 71-30045.

Jackson, Bruce, ed. Wake Up Dead Man: Afro-American worksongs from Texas prisons. Cambridge, Mass.: Harvard University Press, 1972. 326p. illus. bibliog. discog. $14.95. LC: 70-169857.
65 worksongs, both funny and sad, with excellent commentary.

Jasper, Tony. Understand Pop. London: S.C.M. Press, 1972. 192p. illus. bibliog. $5. LC: 75-185408.

Jones, Bessie and Bess Lomax Hawes. Step It Down: Games, Plays, Songs, and Stories from the Afro-American Heritage. New York: Harper & Row, 1972. 233p. bibliog. discog. $10. LC: 71-83598.
Folk material recollected by Bessie Jones, with annotations, instructions, and musical themes.

Jones, Max and John Chilton. Louis: The Louis Armstrong Story, 1900-1971. New York: Little, 1971. 256p. illus. $9.50. LC: 76-175031.

Joplin, Scott. The Collected Works of Scott Joplin. Edited by Vera Brodsky Lawrence. New York: New York Public Library, 1971. 2 vols. illus. discog. $50 set. LC: 78-164697.
Perfectly playable facsimiles of the piano music, songs, and the opera "Treemonisha" by this ragtime great. Comprehensive index and good long introduction.

Joyner, Charles W. Folk Song in South Carolina. Columbia: University of South Carolina Press for the South Carolina Tricentennial Commission, 1971. 112p. bibliog. LC: 70-164707.
A collection of 45 songs with discussion of the black and white tradition.

Karpeles, Maud, ed. Folk Songs from Newfoundland. Hamden, Conn.: Archon Books, 1970. 340p. bibliog. $20. LC: 74-22358.
The results of ballad collecting trips in 1929 and 1930. Valuable, but unfortunately very little explication. Unaccompanied melodies.

Karshner, Roger. The Music Machine. Los Angeles: Nash, 1971. 196p. $7.95. LC: 79-167529.
An opinionated and not-documented exposé of dishonesty in the pop music field.

Kimball, Robert, ed. Cole. New York: Holt, 1971. 283p. illus. discog. $25. LC: 76-155521.

A beautiful, elegant book of pictures, memorabilia, texts of many songs, and a chronology.

Klymasz, Robert Bogdan. An Introduction to the Ukrainian-Canadian Immigrant Folksong Cycle. Ottawa: National Museums of Canada; dist. by Information Canada, 1970. 106p. illus. discog. pap. $4.25. LC: 79-294176.

28 songs reflecting the Canadian experience of immigrants, with commentary. Unaccompanied melodies with Ukrainian and English words. There is a phonodisc attached.

Klymasz, Robert Bogdan. The Ukrainian Winter Folksong Cycle in Canada. Ottawa: National Museums of Canada; dist. by Information Canada, 1970. 156p. illus. bibliog. discog. pap. $4.25. LC: 75-295175.

Unaccompanied melodies with English and Ukrainian words. There is a phonodisc attached.

Kodaly, Zoltan. Folk Music of Hungary. Rev. and enl. by Lajos Vangyas. New York: Praeger, 1971 [i.e., 1972]. 195p. illus. bibliog. $6.50. LC: 75-125391.

Kurath, Gertrude Prokosch and Antonio Garcia. Music and Dance of the Tewa Pueblos. Santa Fe: Museum of New Mexico Press, 1970. 309p. illus. paper. LC: 76-113265.

An extensive study based on 10 years' field research.

Laing, Dave. Buddy Holly. New York: Macmillan, 1972. 144p. illus. $5.95 (pap. $1.95). LC: 79-186441.

Landau, Jon. It's Too Late to Stop Now: A Rock and Roll Journal. San Francisco: Straight Arrow Books, 1972. 227p. $7.95 (pap. $3.95). LC: 74-181713.

A well-organized collection of the author's articles from Crawdaddy, Rolling Stone, and Phoenix.

Larson, Bob. Rock & Roll: The Devil's Diverson. McCook, Neb.: The Author, 1970. 176p. illus. $2. LC: 70-16729.

A fundamentalist view of rock and roll as a satanic plot.

Laufe, Abe. Broadway's Greatest Musicals. New York: Funk & Wagnalls, 1970. 481p. illus. bibliog. $10. LC: 77-124148.

The emphasis is on economic success (500 or more performances). The shows are arranged chronologically with an index to performers and song titles.

Leadbitter, Mike, ed. Nothing but the Blues. London: Hanover Books, 1971. 261p. illus. $10. LC: 70-147845.

Articles reprinted from Blues Unlimited.

Lee, Edward. Jazz: An Introduction. London: Kahn and Averill, 1972. 188p. illus. bibliog. discog. $7.50. LC: 72-196976.

Lee, George W. Beale Street: Where the Blues Began. Washington, D.C.: McGrath Publishing Company, 1969. 298p. illus. $12.

Introduction by W.C. Handy. Reprint of 1934 edition.

Lennon, John. John Lennon Remembers. San Francisco: Straight Arrow Press, 1971. 189p. illus. $4.95. LC: 79-158521.

Based on the 1970 Rolling Stone interview.

Levy, Lester S. Flashes of Merriment: A Century of Humorous Songs in America, 1805-1905. Norman: University of Oklahoma Press, 1971. 370p. illus. bibliog. $12.50. LC: 74-108805.

Anecdotes, more than 100 songs, and sheet music covers.

Lonstein, Albert and Vito Marino. The Complete Sinatra. Ellenville, N.Y.: Cameron Publications, 1970. 383p. illus. bibliog. $28. LC: 77-170787.

A Sinatra discography and filmography, plus lists of appearances on radio, television and the stage.

Lovell, John. Black Song: The Forge and the Flame; The Story of How the Afro-American Spiritual Was Hammered Out. New York: Macmillan, 1972. 588p. illus. bibliog. $12.95. LC: 71-150067.

Lydon, Michael. Rock Folk: Portraits from the Rock 'n' Roll Pantheon. New York: Dial Press, 1971. 200p. illus. $6.95. LC: 71-131179.

Interviews, mostly from the New York Times magazine, with Janis Joplin, B. B. King, Chuck Berry, the Grateful Dead, the Rolling Stones, and others.

McCabe, Peter and Robert D. Schonfeld. Apple to the Core: The Unmaking of the Beatles. New York: Pocket Books, 1972. 200p. illus. pap. $1.25.

McCarthy, Albert. The Dance Band Era: The Dancing Decades from Ragtime to Swing, 1910-1950. Philadelphia: Chilton, 1972. 176p. illus. bibliog. discog. $10. LC: 73-171968.

Covers England, the United States, and Europe.

McCutcheon, Lynn. Rhythm and Blues. Arlington, Va.: Beatty, 1971. 305p. illus. discog. $2.95. LC: 74-167856.

A discriptive list of records from 1948 to the Soul era, which the author thought should have been successes, but were not because of the fickle taste of the masses.

McGregor, Craig, comp. Bob Dylan: A Retrospective. New York: Morrow, 1972. 408p. bibliog. $10 (pap. $2.95). LC: 77-182455.
Anthology of writings from the media, liner notes, reviews, etc.

Meeker, David. Jazz in the Movies: A Tentative Index to the Work of Jazz Musicians in the Cinema. London: British Film Institute, 1972. 89p. illus. $2. LC: 72-190097.
709 film entries (American and European), cross-indexed for 270 jazz artists.

Millar, Bill. The Drifters: The Rise and Fall of the Black Vocal Group. New York: Macmillan, 1972. 180p. illus. $5.95 (pap. $1.95). LC: 72-186442.

Mingus, Charles. Beneath the Underdog: His World as Composed by Mingus. Edited by Nel King. New York: Knopf, 1971. 365p. $6.95. LC: 72-111243.

Mitchell, George. Blow My Blues Away. Baton Rouge: Louisiana State University Press, 1971. 208p. illus. $10. LC: 79-119111.
A series of self-portraits and descriptions of Mississippi Delta life to document the music and the people. Texts to some songs.

Moore, Thurston, ed. Hank Williams: The Legend. Denver: Heather Enterprises, 1972. 63p. illus. bibliog. discog. LC: 78-185425.

Morath, Max, comp. Giants of Ragtime. New York: Edward B. Marks Music Corp., 1971. 64p. illus. $3.50. LC: 72-212589.
13 piano solos by Scott Joplin, Eubie Blake and others, plus background text.

Morse, David. Grandfather Rock: The New Poetry and the Old. New York: Delacorte Press, 1972. 142p. $4.95. LC: 76-156048.
Pairs rock lyrics and their counterparts in classical poetry to show that both express similar emotions.

Morse, David. Motown and the Arrival of Black Music. New York: Macmillan, 1972. 144p. illus. $5.95 (pap. $1.95). LC: 76-186443.

The Motown Era. New York: Grosset and Dunlap, 1972. 319p. illus. discog. pap. $4.95.
112 songs, with piano or guitar accompaniment, plus introductory text and many photographs.

The Music Yearbook: A Survey and Directory with Statistics and

Reference Articles for 1972-73. London: Macmillan, 1972. 750p. $17.50. LC: 70-185857.

Although primarily British, it includes about 100 pages for the rest of the world. This is its first year of publication.

The Musicians' Guide: The Directory of the World of Music. 1972 ed. New York: Music Information Service, 1972. 1013p. LC: 54-14954.

Includes information on a wide variety of written sources, including discographies and important addresses. Published every four years.

Mussulman, Joseph A. Music in the Cultured Generation: A Social History of Music in America, 1870-1900. Evanston, Ill.: Northwestern University Press, 1971. 298p. illus. bibliog. $9.75. LC: 77-149920.

Draws on magazines of the day to illustrate the place of music in American life.

Nanry, Charles, ed. American Music: From Storyville to Woodstock. New Brunswick, N.J.: Transaction Books, 1972. 290p. $7.50 (pap. $2.95). (dist. by Dutton). LC: 71-164978.

Interesting articles on jazz, but poor on other areas of popular music.

National Portrait Gallery, Washington, D.C. "A Glimmer of Their Own Beauty: Black Sounds of the Twenties." Washington, D.C.: for sale by the U.S. Govt. Print. Off., 1971. 32p. chiefly illus. bibliog. LC: 78-614200.

A catalog of an exhibition of pictures of Negro musicians.

Nicholas, A.X., ed. The Poetry of Soul. New York: Bantam, 1971. 103p. pap. $1.

The texts of 43 recently recorded songs.

No One Waved Goodbye: A Casualty Report on Rock and Roll. Edited by Robert Somna. New York: Outerbridge and Dienstfrey, 1971. 121p. illus. $4.95. LC: 70-150526.

A collection of writings on Janis Joplin, Jimi Hendrix, and others who had died tragically.

Noebel, David A. The Beatles: A Study in Drugs, Sex, and Revolution. Tulsa, Okla.: Christian Crusade Publications, 1969. 64p. pap. $1.

The author charges the Beatles with immorality and political subversion.

Oliver, Paul. Savannah Syncopators: African Retentions in the Blues. New York: Stein and Day, 1970. 172p. illus. bibliog. $4.95 (pap. $1.95). LC: 74-120108.

An attempt to relate American blues to West African inland music.

Ortega, Ruben, comp. The Jesus People Speak Out. New York: Pyramid Books, 1972. 128p. pap. $0.95. LC: 71-187727.

Panassie, Hughes and Madelaine Gautier. Le Dictionnaire du Jazz. Paris: Editions A. Michel, 1971. 363p. illus. 39F. LC: 72-322636.
A newly expanded edition of this reference work. Good biographies of traditional jazz musicians.

Passman, Arnold. The Deejays. New York: Macmillan, 1971. 320p. illus. $7.95. LC: 71-119127.
The evolution of the disc jockey and the make-or-break power he wields today.

Riddle, Almeda. Almeda Riddle: A Singer and Her Songs. Baton Rouge: Louisiana University Press, 1970. 191p. illus. $8.50. LC: 77-122352.
The relationships of the Ozark ballads to her life, plus 51 songs.

Roberts, John Storm. Black Music of Two Worlds. New York: Praeger, 1972. 296p. illus. bibliog. discog. $10. LC: 77-184031.
A detailed survey of black music in Africa and America.

The Rolling Stone Record Review. New York: Pocket Books, 1971. 566p. pap. $1.95. LC: 70-28421.
Record reviews and excerpts from other items from Rolling Stone, 1967-1970.

Rooney, James. Bossmen: Bill Monroe and Muddy Waters. New York: Dial, 1971. 159p. illus. $5.95. LC: 70-131181.

Russell, Ross. Jazz Style in Kansas City and the Southwest. Berkeley: University of California Press, 1971. 324p. illus. bibliog. $12.50. LC: 72-138507.

Russell, Tony. Blacks, Whites and Blues. New York: Stein and Day, 1970. 112p. illus. bibliog. discog. $4.95 (pap. $1.95). LC: 78-120109.
Examines the relations of black blues musicians and white musicians, emphasizing their traditions and differences.

Rust, Brian. The Dance Bands. Shepperton, Middlesex, Eng.: Ian Allen Ltd., 1972. 160p. illus. £3.75.

Sanford, Herb. Tommy and Jimmy: The Dorsey Years. New Rochelle, N.Y.: Arlington House, 1972. 256p. illus. $8.95. LC: 72-78483.

Scaduto, Anthony. Bob Dylan. New York: Grosset and Dunlap, 1972. 280p. illus. discog. $7.95. LC: 72-144064.

Scheips, Paul J. Hold the Fort! The Story of a Song from the Sawdust Trail to the Picket Line. Washington, D.C.: Smithsonian Institution Press; for sale by U.S. Govt. Print. Off., 1971. 57p. illus. pap. $1.25. LC: 79-614246.
The history of one song in its different versions since the Civil War.

Scoppa, Bud. The Byrds. New York: Scholastic Book Services, 1971. 175p. illus. pap. $0.75.

Shaw, Arnold. The Street That Never Slept: New York's Fabled 52nd St. New York: Coward, 1971. 378p. illus. discog. $10. LC: 76-154776.

Shaw, Arnold. The World of Soul: Black America's Contribution to the Pop Music Scene. New York: Cowles, 1970. 306p. illus. discog. $6.95. LC: 73-90064.

Short, Bobby. Black and White Baby. New York: Dodd, Mead, 1971. 304p. illus. $7.95. LC: 70-150167.
Reminiscences of his childhood and introduction to show business.

Silber, Irwin, comp. Songs America Voted By. Harrisburg, Pa.: Stackpole Books, 1971. 320p. bibliog. $12.95. LC: 79-162451.
A compendium of Presidential campaign songs, with good documentation; weakest on post-war songs.

Simon, George T. The Big Bands. 2d ed. New York: Macmillan, 1971. 584p. illus. $10. LC: 71-175594.
A complete survey of the big bands and the big names. The first edition had a set of three records to accompany it.

Simon, George T. Simon Says: The Sights and Sounds of the Swing Era, 1935-1955. New Rochelle, N.Y.: Arlington House, 1971. 491p. illus. $19.95. LC: 73-154420.
His articles from Metronome (now ceased).

Sinclair, John and Robert Levin. Music and Politics. New York: World Pub. Co., 1971. 133p. illus. $6.95. LC: 72-149584.
Their articles from Jazz and Pop (now ceased).

Southern, Eileen, comp. and ed. Readings in Black American Music. New York: Norton, 1972. 288p. illus. $12 (pap. $3.95). LC: 70-98892.
An anthology from the 17th century to the present day.

Stambler, Irwin and Grelun Landon. Golden Guitars: The Story of Country Music. New York: Four Winds Press, 1971. 186p. illus. bibliog. $5.95. LC: 77-161022.

Stewart, Rex. Jazz Masters of the 30s. New York: Collier-Macmillan, 1972. 223p. $6.95. LC: 73-169239.
Previously published essays on Louis Armstrong, Duke Ellington, Count Basie, Fletcher Henderson and others.

Stewart-Baxter, Derrick. Ma Rainey and the Classic Blues Singers. New York: Stein and Day, 1970. 112p. illus. bibliog. discog. $4.95 (pap. $1.95). LC: 72-120110.
Includes Bessie Smith, Victoria Spivey, and other "classic" female blues singers.

Stillman, Norton, comp. Trust Me with Your Heart Again: A Fireside Treasury of Turn-of-the-Century Sheet Music. New York: Simon & Schuster, 1971. 251p. $9.95. LC: 70-159138.
A potpouri of reproduced sheet music (56 in all) from 1891-1916.

Taylor, John Russell. The Hollywood Musical. New York: McGraw-Hill, 1971. 278p. illus. $12.95. LC: 70-888628.
275 major films and brief details on 1443 others. Features a biographical index and an index to 2750 songs. Cross-referenced and profusely illustrated.

Tomlinson, Roger. Elvis Presley. New York: Macmillan, 1972. 224p. illus. filmography. $5.95 (pap. $1.95). LC: 72-86038.

Vian, Boris. Chroniques de Jazz. Paris: Union Général d'Editions, 1971. 512p. LC: 67-113858/mn.
Extracts from Jazz Hot and Combat.

Vreede, Max E. Paramount 12000/13000 Series. London: Storyville Publications, 1971. 260p. illus. $13.75.
Numerical listing of the Paramount race record series of 1922/1933, with artist and title indexes. Illustrated with reproductions of labels.

Walley, David. No Commercial Potential: The Saga of Frank Zappa and the Mothers of Invention. New York: Outerbridge and Lazard, 1972. 184p. discog. $6.95 (pap. $2.95). (dist. by Dutton). LC: 73-190639.

Weiner, Andrew. The Byrds. New York: Macmillan, 1972. 160p. illus. $5.95 (pap. $1.95). LC: 72-86039.

Welk, Lawrence. Wunnerful, Wunnerful! Englewood Cliffs, N.J.: Prentice-Hall, 1971. 294p. illus. $7.95. LC: 70-155983.

Wells, Dicky. The Night People. Boston: Crescendo Pub. Co., 1971. 118p. illus. $6. LC: 72-143284.
Entertaining and vivid stories about the jazz scene, as told to Stanley Dance.

Wilder, Alec. *American Popular Song: The Great Innovators, 1900-1950.* New York: Oxford University Press, 1972. 536p. illus. $15. LC: 70-159643.
A study of important songs, grouped by their composers.

Williams, Richard. *Out of His Head: The Sound of Phil Spector.* New York: Outerbridge and Lazard, 1972. 206p. illus. $5.95. (dist. by Dutton). LC: 71-190491.
Includes history of recent record business and an introduction to the Los Angeles pop music scene.

Wilson, Burton. *Burton's Book of the Blues.* Austin, Tex.: Speleo Press, 1971. [77p]. chiefly illus. pap. $5. LC: 75-181387.
A collection of his photographs of the Austin, Texas rock scene, 1966-1972.

Wren, Christopher S. *Winners Got Scars Too: The Life and Legends of Johnny Cash.* New York: Dial, 1971. 229p. $6.95. LC: 75-150399.

Zur Heide, Karl Gert. *Deep South Piano: The Story of Little Brother Montgomery.* London: Studio Vista, 1970. 112p. illus. discog. £1.50. LC: 76-587813.
Includes a who's who of jazz and blues personalities that Little Brother Montgomery came in contact with.

SIGNIFICANT ARTICLES

and

PRE-SELECTED RECORD GUIDES

Omitted material usually included the following, which comprises the bulk of the articles: biographical studies, interviews, reprints, and longer, thorough record reviews (the latter may be found through the index proper).

GENERAL

"The New Federal Copyright Law" [unsigned editorial] High Fidelity, December, p54-5.

ROCK

Breschard, Jack. "Rock, Film, Pan-Media Consciousness and the Whole Earth," Crawdaddy, April 16, p44-5.

Coppage, Noel. "Troubadettes, Troubadoras, and Troubadines" [female singer composers], Stereo Review, September, p58-61.

Glover, Tony. "Bound to Rock; Rock Book Roundup," Creem, January, p51-6.

"Inside the Music Business--Cheap Thrills on a Two-Year Option," Crawdaddy, August, p25-46 [discusses the record company, the manager, the attorney, the promoter, the booking agent, the artist, the media, publicity, and do-it-yourself recording].

Reitman, David. "The Great Trane Robbery," Crawdaddy, March 19, p40-42 [jazz influences in rock].

Sander, Ellen. "Rock 'n' Roll Woman," Crawdaddy, April 2, p25-31.

Vance, Joel. "The Fragmentation of Rock," Stereo Review, February, p62-7.

Yurdin, Larry. "Waves Upon the Ether," Crawdaddy, April 30, p30-5 [part one] May 14, p30-5 [part two] [free-form radio].

MOOD-POP

Lee, Owen. "America's Changing Tastes in Popular Music," High Fidelity, October, p62-5, 68-71.

Lohof, Bruce A. "The Bacharach Phenomenon: A Study in Popular Heroism," Popular Music and Society, Winter, p73-82.

Warren, Tony. "Fancy Forgetting," Records and Recordings, December, p24-7.

COUNTRY

Cohen, John. "NCLR Reflections; the Bread Cast on the Waters Returns," Old Time Music, Autumn, p4-6 [old time music revival].

Coppage, Noel. "Whatever Happened to Nashville?" Stereo Review, January, p60-6.

Smith, William R. "Hell Among the Yearlings: Some Notes on Cowboy Songs, Fiddle Tunes, and Fiddlers," Old Time Music, Summer, p16-9.

JAZZ

Allen, Daniel. "78 RPM Phonorecords in the Jazz Archive," I. P. L. O. Quarterly, January, p119-161. Responses by Dean Tudor (April, p175-181) and Roger Misiewicz (April, p181-4) [catalogue manual].

Buck, George. "Witness for the Prosecution," Coda, December, p6-7 [pirate "bootlegger" record manufacturers].

Burns, Jim. "Alto Bop," Jazz and Blues, December, p9-12.

________. "Bopping Bones," Jazz and Blues, October, p15-9.

________. "The Forgotten Boppers: The History of the Clarinet in Bop/Cool Jazz," Jazz and Blues, June, p4-6.

Coda. Histories of Record Companies. No. 1: Instant Composers' Pool (June, p11-14); No. 2: Canadian Broadcasting Corporation (August, p8-9); No. 3: Jazz Composers' Orchestra Association (October, p11-14).

Keating, Liam. "On Record: Coleman Hawkins, 1939-1949:" Jazz and Blues, May, p5-6 [part one] June, p12-13 [part two] July, p25-6 [part three] August, p25-6 [part four] September, p23-4 [part five] October, p23 [part six] November, p34-5 [part seven] December, p33-4 [part eight]. To be continued through 1973.

Kendall, Ian. "Surprise! The Tradition of Jazz," Jazz and Blues, June, p9-11 [part one] August, p20-1 [part two] October, p14-5 [part three].

Lambert, Eddie. "King Jazz," Jazz and Blues, August, p12-5 [part one] September, p20-2 [part two] October, p28-30 [part three] November, p14-5 [part four] [record label history].

Love, William C. "Witness for the Defense," Coda, December, p2-4 [pirate "bootlegger" record manufacturers].

Lutsky, Irv. "Should the Jazz Collector Buy Bootleg or Pirate Records?" Coda, December, p8-9.

MacDonald, J. Frederick. " 'Hot Jazz,' The Jitterbug, and Misunderstanding: The Generation Gap in Swing, 1935-1945," Popular Music and Society, Fall, p43-55.

Norris, John. "The Listening Dog Barks Back," Coda, April, p6-8 [lack of integrity among reissues].

Peterson, Owen. "The Consummate Artistry of Dodo Marmarosa," Jazz and Blues, April, p4-8 [part one] May, p7-10 [part two].

Tudor, Dean. "Play That Ol' Ragtime Revival," Previews, December, p5-17.

BLUES

Jahn, Mike. "The Royalty Cheaters," High Fidelity, December, p56-8.

Oliver, Paul. "African Influence and the Blues," Living Blues, Spring, p13-7.

________. "Arhoolie and Mister Chris," Jazz and Blues, February, p4-6.

O'Neal, Jim. "Atomic Blues," Living Blues, Summer, p8-15 [Atomic-H label].

Stolper, Darryl. "It was Very Rewarding: Trumpet Records History," Blues Unlimited, January, p4-6.

Tracy, Steve. "King of the Blues: The Story of a Record Label," Blues Unlimited, January, p7-10 [part one] February, p8-10 [part two] [King record label].

Tudor, Dean. "The Real Blues: A Discography," Library Journal, February 15, p633-49.

Welding, Pete. "The Testament Story," Blues World, Spring, p3-4 [part one] Summer, p3-4 [part two].

Wolfe, Charles K. "Where the Blues Is At: A Survey of Recent Research," Popular Music and Society, Summer, p152-166.

RHYTHM & BLUES

Burns, Jim. "Let the Good Times Roll," Jazz and Blues, February, p16-24.

Peterson, Owen. "Why Bother About Soul Music?" Jazz and Blues, November, p4-7 [part one] December, p4-7 [part two].

Trick, Bob. "Second Line Jump; R 'n' B in New Orleans," Jazz and Blues, September, p10-13 [part one] October, p8-10, 12-14 [part two].

RELIGIOUS

Bethel, Tom. "Good News, Bad Times: Reflections on Gospel Music and Black Culture," Jazz Journal, May, p4-5.

"Gospel Records," New York Times (Sunday edition), March 12, pHIFI 2.

Pearson, W.D. "Going Down to the Crossroads: The Bluesmen and Religion," Jazz and Blues, April, p13-5.

SOUNDTRACKS

Bernstein, Elmer. "Whatever Happened to Great Movie Music?" High Fidelity, July, p55-8.

Bolcom, William. "The Words and Music of Noble Sissle and Eubie Blake," Stereo Review, November, p57-64.

Kreuger, Miles. "The Birth of the American Film Musical," High Fidelity, July, p42-48.

________. "Dubbers to the Stars; or, Whose Was that Voice I Heard You Singing With?" High Fidelity, July, p49-54.

Margolis, Garry. "Why Soundtrack Albums Don't Sound Better," High Fidelity, July, p59-61.

"Musical Comedies," New York Times (Sunday edition), September 24, pHIHI 6.

"Screen Records," New York Times (Sunday edition), August 20, pD20.

Simon, Alfred. "Jerome Kern: The Franz Schubert of American Musical Theatre." Stereo Review, July, p47-55.

Sutak, Ken. "The Investment Market in Movie Music Albums," High Fidelity, July, p62-66.

DIRECTORY OF RECORD LABELS

This directory is divided by three countries--the United States, England, and Canada. The section on the United States contains the addresses of record manufacturers. "See" references will direct the searcher to the appropriate distributor for a manufacturer that does not distribute for itself. Each distributer listing also contains the names of the labels that it distributes. Certain names which are not labels but series lines (such as "Explorer") were added to these lists for purposes of clarification; the "See" references will direct the searcher to the manufacturer (in this case, for example, "Elektra" which distributes "Nonesuch," the producer of the "Explorer" series). Ownership of the labels has not been determined. The name of the manufacturer has not been repeated in the listing address.

These lists are complete, in terms of the following restrictions: (a) only record labels which were indexed in 1972 are included; (b) only English and Canadian labels and records which were not released in the United States are listed; and (c) no addresses are provided for labels manufactured outside the three countries. It is suggested that a record store or record importer could deal with the foreign pressings, perhaps better than a library or an individual could.

United States

A & M 1416 North LaBrea Avenue, Hollywood, Cal. 90028 Distributes: Ode, Share

A & R see Mercury

ABC/DUNHILL 8255 Beverly Blvd., Los Angeles, Cal. 90048 Distributes: Bluesway, Dunhill, Impulse, Tangerine

ABET see Nashboro

ADELPHI P.O. Box 288, Silver Spring, Md. 20907

ADVENT P.O. Box 635, Manhattan Beach, Cal. 90266 Distributes: Muskadine

AFRO REQUEST see Request

AHURA MAZDA Box 15582, New Orleans, La. 70115

ALLIGATOR P.O. Box 11741, Fort Dearborn Station, Chicago, Ill. 60611

ALSTON see Atlantic

AMBASSADOR 145 Konora Street, Newark, N.J. 07105 Distributes: Sunshine

AMPEX 555 Madison Avenue, New York, N.Y. 10022

ANGEL see Capitol

ANITA O'DAY Box 442, Hesperia, Cal. 92345

ANTHOLOGY Anthology Records and Tape Corporation, 135 West 41st Street, New York, N.Y. 10036

APPLE see Capitol

ARBOR 7319 N. Bell Avenue, Chicago, Ill. 60645

ARCANE Maple Leaf Club, 5560 W. 62nd Street, Los Angeles, Cal. 90056

ARHOOLIE Box 9195, Berkeley, Cal. 94719 Distributes: Blues Classics, Old Timey

ARIZONA FRIENDS OF FOLKLORE Box 4064, Northern Arizona University, Flagstaff, Ariz.

ARKANSAS FOLK CULTURE CENTRE Mountain View, Ark.

ASCH see Folkways

ASYLUM see Atlantic

ATCO see Atlantic

ATLANTIC 1841 Broadway, New York, N.Y. 10023 Distributes: Alston, Asylum, Atco, Chimneyville, Clean, Cotillion, Embryo, Little David, Rolling Stone, Signpost.

AUDIOFIDELITY 221 West 57th Street, New York, N.Y. 10019

AUDIOPHILE P.O. Box 66, San Antonio, Tex. 78291

AVCO EMBASSY 1301 Avenue of the Americas, New York, N.Y. 10019

BASF Crosby Drive, Bedford, Mass. 01730

BANANA see Blue Thumb

BANDSTAND P.O. Box 740, Artesia, Cal.

BARNABY see Columbia

BATTERY 1860 Broadway, New York, N.Y. 10023 Distributes: Painted Smiles

BEA & BABY 4405 S. State Street, Chicago, Ill. 60609

BEARSVILLE see Warner Brothers

BELL 1776 Broadway, New York, N.Y. 10019 Distributes: Windfall

BETCAR 333 North Drive, North Plainfield, N.J.

BIG STAR Bobo Jenkins, 4228 Joy Road, Detroit, Michigan 48204

BIG TREE 555 Madison Avenue, New York, N.Y. 10022

BIOGRAPH P.O. Box 109, Canaan, New York 12029 Distributes: Historical, Melodeon

BIRCH Box 92, Wilmette, Ill. 60091

BIZARRE see Warner Brothers

BLACK JAZZ see Ovation

BLACKBIRD Lakko Record Co., 607 W. Deming, Chicago, Ill. 60614

BLUE ANGEL Pine Crest Drive, Altadena, Cal. 91001

BLUE FLAME 4827 Prairie Avenue, Chicago, Ill. 60615

BLUE GOOSE see Yazoo

BLUE NOTE see United Artists

BLUE THUMB 427 N. Canyon Drive, Beverly Hills, Cal. 90210 Distributes: Banana, Chisa

BLUES CLASSICS see Arhoolie

BLUES ON BLUES 2131 S. Michigan Avenue, Chicago, Ill. 60613

BLUESWAY see ABC/Dunhill

BOISE UNITARIAN FELLOWSHIP 6116 Edgewater Drive, Boise, Ida. 83705

BOOGIE DISEASE Box 10925, St. Louis, Mo. 63135

BROTHER see Warner Brothers

BRUNSWICK 888 Seventh Avenue, New York, N.Y. 10019

BUDDAH/KAMA SUTRA 810 Seventh Avenue, New York, N.Y. 10019 Distributes: Charisma, Cobblestone, Hot Wax, Kama Sutra, Sussex, T-Neck

CJR see New Music Distribution Service

CTI Creed Taylor, Inc., 1 Rockefeller Plaza, New York, N.Y. 10020 Distributes: Kudu

CADET see Chess/Janus

CAEDMON 505 Eighth Avenue, New York, N.Y. 10018

CAMDEN see RCA

CANYON 4143 N. 16th Street, Phoenix, Arizona 85016

CAPITOL Hollywood and Vine, Hollywood, Cal. 90028 Distributes: Angel, Apple, Invictus, Island, Melodiya/Angel, Purple, Shelter

CAPRICORN see Warner Brothers

CENTAUR 82 Aldine Street, Rochester, N.Y. 14619

CENTER Route 3, Box 754, Salisbury, N.C. 28144

CENTURY School of Music, University of Illinois, Urbana, Ill. 60801

CHARISMA see Buddah/Kama Sutra

CHECKER see Chess/Janus

CHESS/JANUS 1301 Avenue of the Americas, New York, N.Y. 10014 Distributes: Cadet, Checker, Chess, Increase, Janus, Westbound

CHIAROSCURO 15 Charles Street, New York, N.Y. 10014

CHIMNEYVILLE see Atlantic

CHISA see Blue Thumb

CHRYSALIS see Warner Brothers

CHYTOWNS 1410 E. 72nd Street, Chicago, Ill. 60619

CIRCA 123 Water Street, Sauk City, Wis. 53283

CLEAN see Atlantic

COBBLESTONE see Buddah/Kama Sutra

COLLECTOR 8422 Georgia Avenue, # 209, Silver Springs, Md. 20910

COLUMBIA 51 West 52nd Street, New York, N.Y. 10019 Distributes: Barnaby, Douglas, Enterprise, Epic, Fillmore, Harmony, Ko-Ko, Monument, Mums, New Design, Philadelphia International, Respect, Spindizzy, Stax, Vault, Volt

COMEDIAN 1066 E. 42nd Street, Los Angeles, Cal. 90011

CONNOISSEUR 470 West End Avenue, New York, N.Y. 10024

CONTEMPORARY 8481 Melrose Place, Los Angeles, Cal. 90069

COTILLION see Atlantic

COUNTY 309 E. 37th Street, New York, N.Y. 10016

CREATIVE WORLD Box 35216, Los Angeles, Cal. 90035 Distributes: Daybreak, Neophonic

CURTOM 6212 North Lincoln Ave., Chicago, Ill. 60645

DANDELION see Elektra

DANIELS P.O. Box 266, River Forest, Ill. 60305 Distributes: Session One

DAVIS UNLIMITED Route 11, 16 Bond Street, Clarkesville, Tenn. 37040

DAYBREAK see Creative World

DECCA see MCA

DELMARK 4243 N. Lincoln, Chicago, Ill. 60618

DERAM see London

DEVI see Takoma

DIAL P.O. Box 1273, Nashville, Tenn. 37202

DOT see Famous

DOUGLAS see Columbia

DUNHILL see ABC/Dunhill

EBM Eubie Blake Music, 284-A Stuyvesant Avenue, Brooklyn, N.Y. 11221

ESP 5 Riverside Drive, New York, N.Y. 10023

ELEKTRA 15 Columbus Circle, New York, N.Y. 10023 Distributes: Dandelion, Nonesuch

EMBASSY see Avco Embassy

EMBRYO see Atlantic

EMPORIUM OF JAZZ Box 712, Mendota, Minn. 55436

ENTERPRISE see Columbia

EPIC see Columbia

ETHELYN 13240 Fidler Avenue, Downey, Cal. 90242

ETHNIC FOLKWAYS LIBRARY see Folkways

EUPHONIC P.O. Box 476, Ventura, Cal. 93001

EVEREST 10920 Wiltshire Blvd. West, Los Angeles, Cal. 90024 Distributes: Tradition

EVOLUTION see Stereo Dimension

EXCELLO see Nashboro

EXPLORER (NONESUCH) see Elektra

EXTREME RARITIES Ken Crawford, 215 Steuben Avenue, Pittsburgh, Pa. 15205 Distributes: International Association of Jazz Record Collectors

FAMILY PRODUCTIONS see Famous

FAMOUS 1 Gulf and Western Plaza, New York, N.Y. 10023 Distributes: Dot, Family Productions, Just Sunshine, Neighborhood

FANTASY 10th and Parker Streets, Berkeley, Cal. 94710 Distributes: JWS, Milestone, Prestige

FAT CAT'S JAZZ Box 458, Manassas, Virginia 22110

FILLMORE see Columbia

FIRST TIME P.O. Box 03202 - R, Portland, Ore. 97203

FLYING DUTCHMAN 1841 Broadway, New York, N.Y. 10023

FOLK LEGACY Sharon Mt. Road, Sharon, Conn. 06069

FOLKWAYS Pioneer Record Sales Corp., 701 Seventh Ave., New York, N.Y. 10036 Distributes: Asch, Ethnic Folkways Library, Mankind (Asch), RBF

FORECAST see MGM

FORTRESS 2900 Queen Lane, Philadelphia, Pa. 19129

FORTUNE 3942 Third Avenue, Detroit, Michigan 48201

GHB see Jazzology

GHP see Genesis

GNP CRESCENDO 9165 Sunset Blvd., Hollywood, Cal. 90069

GRC Greater Recording Co., 901 Times Square Building, Rochester, N.Y. 14614

GSF 888 Seventh Avenue, New York, N.Y. 10019

GENESIS 302 Garfield, Bay City, Mich. 48706 Distributes: GHP

GOLDBAND P.O. Box 1485, Lake Charles, La. 70601 Distributes: Seventy-7, Swallow

GORDY see Motown

GREAT HOUSE 24 N. Wabash Avenue, Chicago, Ill. 60602 Distributes: Scarab

GREENE BOTTLE 7033 Sunset Blvd., Hollywood, Cal. 90028

GROOVE MERCHANT 1 Gulf and Western Plaza, New York, N.Y. 10023

GRUNT see RCA

HAPPY TIGER 6565 Sunset Blvd., Hollywood, Cal. 90028

HARMONY see Columbia

HAYWIRE P.O. Box 3197, W. Sodona, Ariz. 96340

HERWIN P.O. Box 306, Glen Cove, N.Y. 11542

HI see London

HICKORY 2510 Franklin Road, Nashville, Tenn 37204

HILLTOP see Pickwick International

HISTORICAL see Biograph

HOMESTEAD see Old Homestead

HOT WAX see Buddah/Kama Sutra

I.A.J.R.C. see Extreme Rarities

IMPULSE see ABC/Dunhill

INCREASE see Chess/Janus

INTERNATIONAL ASSOCIATION OF JAZZ RECORD COLLECTORS see Extreme Rarities

INVICTUS see Capitol

ISLAND see Capitol

JWS see Fantasy

JANUS see Chess/Janus

JAZUM 5808 Northumberland Street, Pittsburgh, Pa. 15217

JAZZ COMPOSERS' ORCHESTRA ASSOCIATION see New Music Distribution Service

JAZZETTE 796 Reddoch Street, Memphis, Tenn. 38117

JAZZOLOGY 2001 Suttle Avenue, Charlotte, N.C. 28208 Distributes: GHB

JESSUP 3150 Francis Street, Jackson, Mich. 49203 Distributes: Michigan Bluegrass

JEWEL 728 Texas Street, Shreveport, La. 71163 Distributes: Paula, Ronn

JUST SUNSHINE see Famous

KAMA SUTRA see Buddah/Kama Sutra

KAPP see MCA

KENT 5810 S. Normandie Ave., Los Angeles, Cal. 90044

KING see Starday King

KIRSHNER see RCA

KO-KO see Columbia

KUDU see CTI

LIBERTY see United Artists

LION see MGM

LIONEL see MGM

LITTLE DAVID see Atlantic

LIVING FOLK 65 Mt. Auburn Street, Cambridge, Mass.

LONDON 539 West 25th Street, New York, N.Y. 10001 Distributes: Deram, Hi, MAM, Parrot, Threshold

LYRICHORD 141 Perry Street, New York, N.Y. 10014

MAM see London

MCA 445 Park Avenue, New York, N.Y. 10022 Distributes: Decca, Kapp, Uni

MGM 7165 Sunset Blvd., Hollywood, Cal. 90046 Distributes: Forecast, Lion, Lionel, Pride, Stormy Forest, Sunflower, Verve

MAINSTREAM 1700 Broadway, New York, N.Y. 10019

MAMLISH Cathedral Station, Box 417, New York, N.Y. 10025

MANKIND (ASCH) see Folkways

MARK 4249 Cameron Drive, Buffalo, N.Y. 14221

MASTER JAZZ RECORDINGS Box 579, Lenox Hill Station, New York, N.Y. 10024

MEADOWLAND 2301 Loring Place, Bronx, N.Y. 10468

MEGA 911 17th Ave. S., Nashville, Tenn. 37212

MELODIYA/ANGEL see Capitol

MELODEON see Biograph

MERCURY 35 East Wacker Drive, Chicago, Ill. 60601 Distributes: A & R, Smash, Vertigo

METROMEDIA 1700 Broadway, New York, N.Y. 10019

MICHIGAN BLUEGRASS see Jessup

MILESTONE see Fantasy

MINNESOTA JAZZ SPONSORS 5704 Schaifer Road, Minneapolis, Minn. 55436

MONITOR 156 Fifth Avenue, New York, N.Y. 10010

MONMOUTH/EVERGREEN 1697 Broadway, N.Y., N.Y. 10019

MONUMENT see Columbia

MORTNEY Suite 303, 14400 Addison St., Sherman Oaks, Cal. 91403

MOTOWN 6464 Sunset Blvd., Hollywood, Cal. 90028 Distributes: Gordy, Mowest, Rare Earth, Soul, Tamla

MOWEST see Motown

MULBERRY 299 West Street, White Plains, N.Y.

MUMS see Columbia

MUSKADINE see Advent

NWI Jim Beatty, 16666 S.W. Roosevelt Drive, Lake Oswego, Ore. 97034

NASHBORO 1011 Woodland Street, Nashville, Tenn. 37206 Distributes: Abet, Excello

NATIONAL GEOGRAPHIC SOCIETY Dept. 100, Wash., D.C. 20036

NEIGHBORHOOD see Famous

NEON see RCA

NEOPHONIC see Creative World

NESSA see New Music Distribution Service

NEW DESIGN see Columbia

NEW MUSIC DISTRIBUTION SERVICE 6 W. 95th St., N.Y., N.Y. 10024 Distributes: CJR, Jazz Composers' Orchestra Assn., Nessa, Peoples' Music Works, Seeds

NEW YORK PUBLIC LIBRARY Fifth Ave. and 42nd St., New York, N.Y. 10018

NONESUCH see Elektra

NUGGET see PIP

OAK RECORDS 6430 Sunset Blvd., Hollywood, Cal. 90028

OBLIVION P.O. Box "X," Roslyn Heights, N.Y. 11577

ODE see A & M

OLD HOMESTEAD 6241 Three Lakes Drive, Brighton, Mich. 48116

OLD MASTERS Max Abrams, Box 76082, Los Angeles, Cal. 90076

OLD TIMEY see Arhoolie

ORIGIN JAZZ LIBRARY Box 863, Berkeley, Cal. 94701

OVATION 1249 Waukegan, Glenview, Ill. 60025 Distributes: Black Jazz

P.I.P. 1370 Avenue of the Americas, New York, N.Y. 10019 Distributes: Nugget

PAINTED SMILES see Battery

PARAMOUNT 6430 Sunset Blvd., Hollywood, Cal. 90028

PARROT see London

PAULA see Jewel

PEARL Sonny Faggart, P.O. Box 1411, Salisbury, N.C. 28144

PEOPLES' MUSIC WORKS see New Music Distribution Service

PERCEPTION TODAY see Yambo

PHILADELPHIA INTERNATIONAL see Columbia

PICKWICK INTERNATIONAL 135 Crossways Park Drive, Woodbury, Long Island, N.Y. 11797 Distributes: Hilltop

PINE MOUNTAIN Box 584, Barbourville, Ky

PINE TREE Melody Records, 1912 St. Clair St., Hamilton, O. 45011

PLANTATION see Shelby Singleton Corporation

PLAYBOY Playboy Music Inc., 8560 Sunset Blvd., Hollywood, Cal. 90069

POLYDOR 1700 Broadway, New York, N.Y. 10019 Distributes: Sire, Spring

POPPY see United Artists

PRECISION North Texas Lab Band, Box 5038, North Texas Station, Denton, Texas 76203

PRESTIGE see Fantasy

PRIDE see MGM

PRODUCTIONS 127 Phoenix Village, Fort Smith, Arkansas 72901 Distributes: Testament

PROJECT THREE 1270 Avenue of the Americas, New York, N.Y. 10020

PURITAN P.O. Box 946, Evanston, Ill. 60204

PURPLE see Capitol

RBF see Folkways

RCA 1133 Avenue of the Americas, New York, N.Y. 10036 Distributes: Camden, Grunt, Kirshner, Neon TMI, Wheel, Wooden Nickel

RCS P.O. Box 362, Tacoma, Washington 98409

RACCOON see Warner Brothers

RARE EARTH see Motown

REBEL P.O. Box 246, Mount Rainier, Md. 20822

REPRISE see Warner Brothers

REQUEST 66 Memorial Highway, New Rochelle, N.Y. 10801 Distributes: Afro Request

RESPECT see Columbia

REVELATION 148 Armadale Ave., Los Angeles, Cal. 90042

REVONAH Box 217, Ferndale, N.Y. 12734

ROLLING STONES see Atlantic

RONN see Jewel

ROULETTE 17 West 60th Street, New York, N.Y. 10023

ROUNDER 65 Park Street, Somerville, Mass. 02143

RURAL RHYTHM Box A, Arcadia, Cal. 91006

SAVOY 56 Ferry Street, Newark, N.J. 17105

SCARAB see Great House

SCEPTER 254 W. 54th Street, New York, N.Y. 10019 Distributes: Wand

SEEDS see New Music Distribution Service

SEGUE P.O. Box 7126, Pittsburgh, Pa. 15213

SESSION ONE see Daniels

SEVENTY-7 see Goldband

SHAKER SOCIETY Sabbathday Lane, Poland Spring, Maine 04274

SHARE see A & M

SHELBY SINGELTON CORPORATION 3106 Belmont Blvd., Nashville, Tenn. 37212 Distributes: Plantation, Sun

SHELTER see Capitol

SIGNPOST see Atlantic

SIRE see Polydor

SMASH see Mercury

SMITHSONIAN Division of Performing Arts, Washington, D.C.

SOLID STATE see United Artists

SOLO Kirkwood Lane, Camden, S.C.

SOUL see Motown

SPECIALTY 8300 Santa Monica Blvd., Hollywood, Cal. 90069

SPINDIZZY see Columbia

SPINN Box 100 N, RFD 3, Stuart, Va. 24171

SPIVEY 65 Grand Avenue, Brooklyn, N.Y. 11205

SPRING see Polydor

SPRINGBOARD 1135 W. Elizabeth Avenue, Linden, N.J. 07036
Distributes: Trip

STANYAN P.O. Box 2783, Hollywood, Cal. 90028

STARDAY KING P.O. Box 8188, Nashville, Tenn. 37207

STAX see Columbia

STEREO DIMENSION 888 Seventh Avenue, New York, N.Y. 10019
Distributes: Evolution

STORMY FOREST see MGM

SUN RECORDS see Shelby Singleton Corporation

SUNBEAM Box 4748, San Jose, Cal. 95126

SUNFLOWER see MGM

SUNSHINE see Ambassador

SUSSEX see Buddah/Kama Sutra

SWALLOW see Goldband

SWALLOWTAIL Phil Shapiro, 304 College Avenue, Ithaca, N.Y. 14850

TMI see RCA

T-NECK see Buddah/Kama Sutra

T.O.M. see Old Masters

TAKOMA P.O. Box 5403, Santa Monica, Cal. 90405 Distributes: Devi

TAMLA see Motown

TANGERINE see ABC/Dunhill

TAOS Box 276, Taos, N.M. 87571

TESTAMENT see Productions

THE OLD MASTERS see Old Masters

THRESHOLD see London

TRADITION see Everest

TUMBLEWEED 1368 Gilpin Street, Denver, Col. 80218

TRIP see Springboard

TUNE Rual's Music Service, 2211 Woodward Avenue, Muscle Shoals, Ala. 35660

UNI see MCA

UNITED ARTISTS 6920 Sunset Boulevard, Hollywood, Cal. 90028 Distributes: Blue Note, Liberty, Poppy, Solid State, World Pacific

UNIVERSAL AWARENESS 1650 Broadway, New York, N.Y. 10019

VANGUARD 71 W. 23rd Street, New York, N.Y. 10010

VAULT see Columbia

VERTIGO see Mercury

VERVE see MGM

VETCO 5825 Vine Street, Cincinnati, Ohio

VOLT see Columbia

VOYAGER 2312 N.E. 85th Street, Seattle, Wash. 98115

WAND see Scepter

WARNER BROTHERS 4000 Warner Blvd., Burbank, Cal. 91505 Distributes: Bearsville, Bizarre, Brother, Capricorn, Chrysalis, Raccoon, Reprise,

WARREN 3126 E Street, S.E., No. 4, Washington, D.C. 20019

WESTBOUND see Chess/Janus

WHEEL see RCA

WINDFALL see Bell

WOODEN NICKEL see RCA

WORLD JAZZ 4350 East Camelback Road, Phoenix, Ariz. 85108

WORLD PACIFIC see United Artists

YAMBO Sine Productions, 7111 S. Racine, Chicago, Ill. 60620 Distributes: Perception Today

YAZOO 54 King Street, New York, N.Y. 10014 Distributed: Blue Goose

England

A & M 1-2 St. George Street, London W9 Distributes: Mayfair

ACE OF CLUBS see Decca

ACTION see B & C

ALAN, Iain c/o NWB Ltd., 208 Piccadilly, London

ARGO see Decca

ASYLUM see EMI

ATLANTIC see WEA

AVCO-EMBASSY see Phonogram

B & C RECORDS 37 Soho Square, London W1V 5DG Distributes: Action, Charisma

BBC RECORDS BBC Radio Enterprises, 156 Great Portland Street, London W1N 6AJ

BEACON Beacon Industries, Ltd., 98 Seymour Place, London W1R 9FE Distributes: Montague

BELL 49 Conduit Street, London W1R 9FE

BELTONA see Decca

BLACK JAZZ see Decca

BLACK LION see Polydor

BLUE HORIZON, 2000 series see Polydor

BLUE HORIZON, 7-60,000 series see CBS

CBS 28-30 Theobalds Road, London WC1X 8PB Distributes: Blue Horizon, 7-60,000 series

CFP see Music for Pleasure

CAMDEN see Pickwick International

CAPITOL see EMI

CARNABY see Phonogram

CARNIVAL see Polydor

CARROT 103 Tuam Road, Plumstead, London SE 18

CHAPTER ONE see Decca

CHARISMA see B & C

CHESS see Phonogram

CHRYSALIS see Island

CLADDAGH see EMI

COLUMBIA see EMI

COLUMBIA STUDIO 2 see EMI

CONTOUR 16 St. George St., London W1R 9DE

CORAL see Decca

CUBE RECORDS AND TAPES Noel House, 19-20 Poland Street, London W1V 3DD Distributes: Fly, Hi Fly

DJM see Pye

DJM SILVERLINE see Pye

DAFFODIL see Decca

DAWN see Pye

DAYBREAK see Polydor

DECCA 9 Albert Embankment, London SE1 7SW Distributes: Ace of Clubs, Argo, Beltona, Black Jazz, Chapter One, Coral, Daffodil, Deram, Eclipse, Emerald, London, MCA, Ovation, Qualiton, Rex, Telefunken, Uni

DERAM see Decca

DOUBLE UP see EMI

EMI 20 Manchester Square, London W1A 1ES Distributes: Asylum, Capitol, Claddagh, Columbia, Columbia Studio 2, Double Up, HMV, Harvest, One Up, Parlophone, Probe, Rare Recorded Editions, Regal Starline, Regal Zonophone, Signpost, Talisman, Waverley

ECLIPSE see Decca

EMBASSY see Phonogram

EMBER see Pye

EMERALD see Decca

ENGLISH FOLK, DANCE, AND SONG SOCIETY 2 Regent's Park Road, London NW1 7AY

FLY see Cube Records and Tapes

FLYRIGHT 47 Grange Street, New Haw, Weybridge, Surrey

FONTANA see Phonogram

FOUNTAIN Fountain Press, 46-7 Chancery Lane, London WC2

FREEDOM see Polydor

GALLIARD Queen Anne's Road, Great Yarmouth, Norfolk

GOLDEN GUINEA see Pye

GOLDEN HOUR see Pye

GRANADA TELEVISION 36 Golden Square, London W1

GROSVENOR 16 Grosvenor Road, Handsworth Wood, Birmingham B20 3NP

HMV see EMI

HALCYON see Vintage Jazz Music Society

HALLMARK see Pickwick International

HARVEST see EMI

HELP see Island

HI FLY see Cube Records and Tapes

IMPACT see Topic

INCUS 22b Edward Road, Bromley, Kent

ISLAND 8-11 Basing Street, London W10 Distributes: Chyrsalis, Help

JANUS see Phonogram

JOY see President

JUKE BLUES see Polydor

KEY 10 Seaforth Avenue, New Malden, Surrey

LEADER Leader Sound, Ltd., 5 North Villas, London NW1 Distributes: Pegasus, Trailer

LIBERTY see United Artists

LONDON see Decca

MCA see Decca

MGM see Polydor

MARBLE ARCH see Pickwick International

MATCHBOX see Saydisc Matchbox

MAYFAIR see A & M

MERCURY see Phonogram

METRO see Polydor

MONTAGUE see Beacon

MOONSHINE see Polydor

MUSHROOM 1a Belmont St., London NW1

MUSIC FOR PLEASURE 42 The Centre, Feltham, Middlesex Distributes: Classics for Pleasure, Cfp.

ONE UP see EMI

OPENIAN Garden Flats, 15 Randolph Crescent, London W9

ORYX 167 Burwood Road, Walton-on-Thames, Surrey

OVATION see Decca

PAN see Saga

PARLOPHONE see EMI

PEGASUS see Leader

PHILIPS see Phonogram

PHONOGRAM Stanhope House, Stanhope Place, London W2 2HH Distributes: Avco-Embassy, Carnaby, Chess, Embassy, Fontana, Janus, Mercury, Philips, Sun, Vertigo

PICKWICK INTERNATIONAL Victoria Works, Edgeware Road, London NW 2 Distributes: Hallmark, Marble Arch

POLYDOR 17-19 Stratford Place, London W1N OBl Distributes: Black Lion, Blue Horizon 2000 series, Carnival, Daybreak, Freedom, Juke Blues, MGM, Metro, Moonshine, Roulette, Select, Track, Verve

PRESIDENT RECORDS Kassner House, 1 Westbourne Gardens, Porchester Road, London W2 5NR Distributes: Joy, Rhapsody

PROBE see EMI

PYE 17 Great Cumberland Place, London W1H 8AA Distributes: DJM, DJM Silverline, Dawn, Ember, Golden Guinea, Golden Hour

QUALITON see Decca

RAK 155-157 Oxford Street, London W1

RCA 50-52 Curzon Street, London W1Y 8EU Distributes: RCA International, Vanguard

RCA INTERNATIONAL see RCA

RARE RECORDED EDITIONS see EMI

RED LIGHTNIN' 35 Cantley Gardens, Gants Hill, Ilford, Essex

REDIFFUSION Rediffusion International Music, 2-16 Goodge St., London W1P LFF

REGAL STARLINE see EMI

REGAL ZONOPHONE see EMI

REPRISE see WEA

REX see Decca

RHAPSODY see President

RIFI DISCURO 9 Shepherd Street, Mayfair, London

ROULETTE see Polydor

SAGA 326 Kensal Road, London W10

SAYDISC MATCHBOX Saydisc Specialized Recordings, The Barton, Inglestone Common, Badminton, Gloucestershire, GL9 1BX

SELECT see Polydor

77 77 Charing Cross Road, London WC2 Distributes: Swift

SIGNPOST see EMI

SPOTLITE Tony Williams, 300 Brocklesmead, Harlow, Essex

STARLINE see EMI

SUN see Phonogram

SUNSET see United Artists

SWIFT see 77

TALISMAN see EMI

TANGENT 52 Shaftsbury Ave., London W1V 7DE

TELEFUNKEN see Decca

TOPIC 27 Nassington Road, London NW3 2TX Distributes: Impact

TRACK see Polydor

TRAILER see Leader

TRANSATLANTIC 86 Marylebone High Street, London W1M 4AY Distributes: Xtra

TROJAN 12 Neasden Lane, London NW10

UNI see Decca

UNITED ARTISTS 37-41 Mortimer Street, London W1 Distributes: Liberty, Sunset

VJM see Vintage Jazz Music Society

VANGUARD see RCA

VERTIGO see Phonogram

VERVE see Polydor

VINTAGE JAZZ MUSIC SOCIETY 12 Slough Lane, London NW 9 Distributes: Halcyon, VJM

WEA 69 New Oxford, London WC1 Distributes: Atlantic, Reprise, Warner Brothers

WARNER BROTHERS see WEA

WAVERLEY see EMI

WORLD RECORD CLUB P.O. Box 13, Richmond, Surrey

XTRA see Transatlantic

YORK 106 Kinkstall Road, Leeds LS5 1JS

ZONOPHONE see EMI

Canada

A & M 255 Yorkland Blvd., Willowdale, Ontario Distributes: Haida

AXE see London

BANFF see London

BOOTS see London

CBC see Radio Canada International Transcription

CAMDEN see RCA

CAPITOL 3109 American Drive, Malton, Ontario Distributes: Daffodil

CHESS see GRT

CODA Box 87, Station J, Toronto, Ontario Distributes: Exclusive, Sackville

COLUMBIA 1121 Leslie Street, Don Mills, Ontario Distributes: True North

DAFFODIL see Capitol

EXCLUSIVE see Coda

GRT 150 Consumers Road, Willowdale, Ontario M2J 1P9 Distributes: Chess

HAIDA see A & M

KANATA see London

KOT'AI see London

LONDON 1630 Midland Avenue, Scarborough, Ontario Distributes: Axe, Banff, Boots, Kanata, Kot'ai

RCA 101 Duncan Mills Road, Don Mills, Ontario Distributes: Camden

RADIO CANADA INTERNATIONAL TRANSCRIPTION C.B.C. International Service, Box 6000, Montreal, Quebec Distributes: CBC

SACKVILLE see Coda

TRUE NORTH see Columbia

SPECIALTY RECORD STORES

The following record stores handle specialized orders for rare or difficult material to acquire (mainly in the fields of jazz, blues, folk, country, and ethnic). With many labels, record stores are the only source of distribution. Superior service for the smaller, independent labels makes the following stores highly recommended. Write for catalogues.

UNITED STATES

J & F Southern Record Sales
4501 Risinghill Road
Altadena, Cal. 91001

Rare Record Distributing Company
415 East Broadway
Glendale, Cal. 91205

Rounder Records
65 Park Street
Somerville, Mass. 02143

ENGLAND

Colletts Record Centre
70 New Oxford Street
London WC 1

Dobell's Record Shop
77 Charing Cross Road
London WC 2

Peter Russell Record Store
24 Market Avenue
Plymouth PL1 1PJ

Chris Wellard Records
6 Lewisham Way, New Cross
London SE14 6NN

CANADA

Coda Jazz and Blues Record Centre
893 Yonge Street
Toronto M4W 2H2

ARTIST INDEX

An alphabetical arrangement of primary artists and groups, as discribed by the entries. No attempt was made to analyze each record for assisting major artist, nor to break down anthologies. However, major artists from STAGE AND SHOW are included because the entry under that section is by title of the production, and entries are also made for those records which feature two or three artists recorded independently, so long as these are the total number of major artists on those particular records.

ANTHOLOGY AND CONCERTS INDEX

An alphabetical arrangement by title of those albums entered under title by reason of their being anthologized collections or concert performances. STAGE AND SHOW were already entered by title, and the ETHNIC section is too slim to warrant a subject or geographical breakdown (the items can be skimmed). Thus, the indexes to these two sections have been restricted.